CW01507216

بسم الله الرحمن الرحيم

"The house of al-Arqam is the house of Islām"

Al-Ḥākim (d. 405 h.) in *al-Mustadrak 'ala al-Ṣaḥiḥayn* (6185)

A Commentary on *Ash-Shamā'il al-Muḥammadiyyah*

Primarily taken from the commentaries of Ibn Ḥajar al-Haytamī (974/1566), ʿAlī al-Qārī (1014/1605), Ibrāhīm al-Bājūrī (1276/1860) and ʿAbd al-Razzāq al-Badr

Al-Imām Abū ʿĪsā al-Tirmidhī (279/892)

DAR AL-ARQAM

ISBN: 978 1 7392940 3 8

British Library Cataloguing in Publishing Data
A catalogue record for this book is available from the British Library

© Copyright 2023 Dar al-Arqam Publishing

All rights reserved worldwide. No part of this publication may be reproduced in any language, stored in a retrieval system or transmitted in any form or by any means, electronic, mechanical, photocopying, recording or otherwise without the express permission of the publisher.

Original edition: 2014 (formerly *A Commentary on the Depiction of the Prophet*), revised edition: 2023

Prepared and published by Dar al-Arqam Publishing
Birmingham, United Kingdom

www.daral-arqam.co.uk
Email: daralarqam@hotmail.co.uk

Original edition translated by Ayman b. Khalid
Edited by Adnan Karim

If you would like to support our work, donations can be made via:

- www.daral-arqam.co.uk/product/donate
- www.patreon.com/daralarqam
- www.paypal.me/daralarqam

Printed in Turkey by Mega | export@mega.com.tr

A COMMENTARY ON

ASH-SHAMĀ'IL AL-MUḤAMMADIYYAH

Primarily taken from the commentaries of Ibn Ḥajar al-Haytamī (974/1566), 'Alī al-Qārī (1014/1605), Ibrāhīm al-Bājūrī (1276/1860) and 'Abd al-Razzāq al-Badr

The ḥadīth master and imām,

Abū 'Īsā al-Tirmidhī (279/892)

DAR AL-ARQAM

الفهرس

Contents

Publisher's Foreword

All praise to Allāh, after this book was originally published in 2015, it was a success and received a wide readership globally. As we ran out of copies in 2022, we decided to revamp the design to our current style and revise the content. Commentary was added into places deemed fit, wordings were edited where needed and commentary taken from outside of the main four sources has been referenced. We also decided to change the title to make it clearer that it is a commentary on al-Imām al-Tirmidhī's blessed book.

May Allāh make it spread and be a benefit like the original edition.

We thank and ask Allāh to reward the translator, editors, the author, the commentators and everyone who played a role in this project.

Dar al-Arqam Publishing
Birmingham, UK
20th August 2023

Author's Biography

His Name and Birth

He is the *imām*, the *ḥāfiẓ*, the great *muḥaddith*: Abū 'Īsa, Muḥammad b. 'Īsa b. Sawrah b. Mūsā b. al-Ḍaḥḥāk al-Sulamī al-Tirmidhī, better known as al-Imām al-Tirmidhī. There are different views regarding the year in which he was born, but the general consensus is that he was born around 210 AH[1] in the city of Tirmidh.

His Life

Historical works regarding the scholars of ḥadīth (such as the works of al-Khaṭīb al-Baghdādī) serve as witnesses that the area of Khurasan was a centre of the study of ḥadīth during the time of the early generations. From this area arose the *imāms* of ḥadīth: Muḥammad b. Ismā'īl al-Bukhārī, Muslim b. al-Ḥajjāj, Abū Dāwūd al-Sijistānī, Muḥammad b. Mājah, Aḥmad b. Shu'ayb al-Nasā'ī and lastly, Abū 'Īsa al-Tirmidhī. Al-Imām al-Tirmidhī was considered by the scholars to be a student of al-Imām al-Bukhari and he also heard ḥadīth from al-Imām Muslim and Abū Dāwūd. Though he resided in such a hub of knowledge, he followed the Sunnah of the ḥadīth masters by travelling to the other centres of knowledge such as Iraq and the Hejaz to sit and learn from the scholars. Thus, he travelled to hear from giants such as Abū Muṣ'ab al-Zuhrī from Madīnah, Muḥammad b. Ma'mar from Basrah and Isma'īl al-Fazarī from Kufah.

Al-Imām al-Tirmidhī was considered to be from al-Imām al-Bukhārī's most exceptional students and he rose to such a high level that he had the privilege of his teacher hearing ḥadīths from him. Furthermore, it is narrated that al-Imām al-Bukhārī said to his student, "I have benefited from you more than you have benefited from me."[2]

---

1 As stated by al-Dhahabī in his *Siyar A'lām al-Nubalā*

2 *Al-Tadhīb*

His Works

Al-Imām al-Tirmidhī is most famously known for his vast and highly praised collection of ḥadīth entitled *al-Jāmiʿ*. Two of the most famous explanations of this are *ʿĀriḍat al-Aḥwadhī* of Abū Bakr b. al-ʿArabī and *Tuḥfat al-Aḥwadhī* of ʿAbd al-Raḥmān al-Mubārakfūrī. In Ibn al-ʿArabī's explanation, he states regarding the *Jāmiʿ*, "There is no book that matches the rank of Abū ʿĪsa's with respect to the sweetness of its passages, its excellence and its charm." In ʿAbd al-Raḥmān al-Mubārakfūrī's explanation, he lists his other works as *al-ʿIlal al-Kabīr*, a work on *tafsīr*, *al-Tārikh*, *al-Zuhd* and *al-Asmā' wa al-Kuna*. Furthermore, he states, "**There is also *al-Shamā'il al-Muḥammadiyyah*. It is the best of the books written concerning this subject and full of blessings.**"

In al-Bājūrī's explanation of *al-Shamā'il al-Muḥammadiyyah*, he states, "His *Jāmiʿ* is sufficient for you in terms of benefits regarding *fiqh* and ḥadīth and also regarding the knowledge of the way of the *salaf* and the *khalaf*. Thus, it is sufficient for the *mujtahids* and likewise for the laypeople." In *Dhayl Ṭabaqāt al-Ḥanābilah*, it is reported that Abū Ismāʿīl al-Anṣārī said, "In my opinion, the book of al-Tirmidhi is superior in terms of its benefit than the books of al-Bukhārī and Muslim." When he was asked for the reason regarding this, he replied, "Because only those who are well versed in knowledge will benefit from them. As for this book, he has explained the ḥadīths therein and thus everyone can benefit from it: the *faqīh*, the ḥadīth master and others."

His Personal Qualities and Praise from Scholars for Him

He possessed a great mind, possessing both excellent memory and a high degree of intelligence. His memory is displayed by the following famous narration. Al-Imām al-Dhahabī reports in his *Siyar Aʿlām al-Nubalā'* that al-Tirmidhī said, "Whilst on the route to Makkah I wrote two chapters of ḥadīth from a *shaykh*. We met and I requested him to narrate them to me whilst thinking that I had the notes that I previously wrote in my possession. He agreed and began to read whilst I realised that the papers I had were blank. The *shaykh* realised my papers were devoid of writing and said, 'Have you no shame with me?' I explained to him my circumstances and assured him that I had it all committed to memory. So he asked me to repeat them and I did. However the *shaykh* was not convinced and he thought that I had reviewed them before our meeting. I asked him to read to me something else and thus he read forty ḥadīths, then he asked me to repeat them. I did so without error, not even in a single letter."

The praise of the scholars for this great ḥadīth master is vast. What follows are a few examples. In *Ṭabaqāt al-Ḥuffaẓ*, al-Idrīsī said, "He was one of the *imāms* and from the role models in the science of ḥadīth... He is mentioned as an example of great memory." In *al-Thiqāt*, Ibn Ḥibban said, "He is of those who collected, wrote, took to memory and studied." In *Siyar Aʿlām al-Nubalā*, it is reported that Ḥākim said, "I heard ʿUmar b. ʿAlak state, 'Upon al-Bukhāri's passing, he did not leave behind any individual in Khurasan of the same calibre of Abū ʿĪsa in regards to knowledge, memory, piety or ascetism."

His Death

He died in Tirmidh in the year 279 AH on the 13th of Rajab according to al-Dhahabī. It is reported that in the latter part of his life, he lost his sight and became blind. May Allāh have mercy upon him.

Compiler's Foreword

All praise is due to Allāh with Whose grace all good deeds are realised and the *ṣalāt* and *salām* of Allāh be upon His Messenger, his family, his companions and all of his loyal followers.

The methodology followed in this book is intended to make the book more appealing to all people and so an in-depth research was made to present to the readers selective gems from a wide array of books and references. The diversity of quotes and texts researched and included herein are intended to enrich the content and allow non-Arabic speakers access to classical books and references that are not yet translated. The commentaries used are taken from the works of early and contemporary scholars from the main four schools of thought (i.e. Ḥanafī, Shāfiʿī, Mālikī and Ḥanbalī). This diversity of scholars is hoped to bring people closer and make them more accepting and respectful to the scholars without whom we could not have access to this knowledge. It is also hoped that this work will unite the hearts of people from different backgrounds and it is from Allāh's favours upon us that He united us upon the love of His Prophet ﷺ. To this effect, the selection criteria of commentaries used in this book is based on the added value and benefit that will be brought forth. To make the book more interesting, the quotes were researched based on the subject matter of the ḥadīth and this required researching tens of classical books and references that covered a wide array of areas such as history, *fiqh*, commentaries, creed, *tazkiyyah* etc. Emphasis was placed upon providing new gems of knowledge (to the English reader) and to present a book with rich content that covers different topics related to *fiqh*, creed, spirituality and ḥadīth so as to make it more interesting and to suit all tastes.

The references of the ḥadīths of the *Shamā'il* were taken from the book of al-Shaykh ʿAbd al-Razzāq but as some ḥadīths were not referenced in his book, I researched the references and gave the reference based on the text and not the chain of narrators, and in the case where the exact words were not found in other sources, I would use the reference of a similar ḥadīth that has the exact same meaning but may have additions or different wording.

Though many books were referenced, the commentary is based around the books of four main scholars, two of whom are from the contemporary scholars and the other two from the early scholars: (i) ʿAbd al-Razzāq b. ʿAbd al-Muḥsin al-Badr, (ii) Ibrāhīm b. Muḥammad al-Bājūrī al-Shāfiʿī, (iii) Ibn Ḥajar al-Haytamī, (iv) al-Mullah ʿAlī b. Sulṭān Muḥammad al-Qārī. Below is a list of the main books from which commentaries were selected and translated:

- *Sharḥ Shamā'il al-Nabī* ﷺ, ʿAbd al-Razzāq al-Badr (the book consists of the explanation of this book that the *shaykh* gave over forty five lessons in the Prophet's ﷺ Masjid).
- *Al-Mawāhib al-Laduniyyah ʿAla al-Shamā'il al-Muḥammadiyyah*, Ibrāhīm b. Muḥammad al-Bājūrī al-Shāfiʿī (1198 H.–1277 H.), 2nd Edition (2007), Dar al-Minhaj, Jeddah.
- *Ashraf al-Wasā'il Ilā Fahm al-Shamā'il*, Shihāb al-Dīn Aḥmad b. Ḥajar al-Haytamī (974 H.), 1st Edition (1998), Dār al-Kutub al-ʿIlmiyyah, Beirut.
- *Jamʿ al-Wasā'il Fī Sharḥ al-Shamā'il*, ʿAlī b. Ṣultān Muḥammad, Abū al-Ḥasan, Nūr al-Dīn al-Mullāh al-Qārī (1014 H.), al-Matb'āh al-Sharafiyyah (1901), Egypt.
- *Fatḥ al-Bārī Sharḥ Ṣaḥīḥ al-Bukhārī*, al-Ḥāfiẓ Aḥmad b. ʿAlī b. Ḥajar, Abū al-Faḍl al-ʿAsqalānī (852 H.), Dār al-Salam, al-Riyadh and Dār al-Fayhaa, Damascus, 3rd Edition (2000).
- *Al-Minhāj Bi Sharḥ Ṣaḥīḥ Muslim b. al-Hajjāj*, Muhī al-Dīn b. Yaḥyā b. Sharaf al-Nawawī (676 H.), Dār Ibn Hazm, Beirut, 1st Edition (2002).
- *Tuḥfat al-Aḥwadhī bi Sharḥ Jāmiʿ al-Tirmidhī*, Abū al-ʿŪla Muḥammad ʿAbd al-Raḥmān b. ʿAbd al-Raḥīm al-Mubārakfūrī (1353 H.), Dār al-Hadīth, Cairo, 1st Edition (2001).
- *Al-Istidhkār al-Jāmiʿ Li Madhāhib Fuqahā' al-Amsār wa ʿUlamā' al-Aqtār*, Yūsuf b. Abdullāh b. Muḥammed b. ʿAbd al-Barr, Abu Umar al-Namari al-Andalusi al-Qurtubi al-Maliki (463 H.), Dār Qutaybah, Damascus, 1st Edition (1993).
- *Zād al-Maʿād fī Hadī Khayr al-ʿIbād*, Muḥammad b. Abī Bakr b. Ayyūb b. Saʿd Shams al-Dīn, Ibn Qayyim al-Jawziyyah (751 H.),

Mu'assasatu al-Risalah, Beirut, 27th Edition (1994).

- *Zahrat al-Khamā'il ʿAlā al-Shamā'il*, ʿAbd al-Raḥmān b. Abī Bakr, Jalāl al-Dīn al-Suyūṭī (911 H.), Maktabatu al-Quran, Cairo, (1988).
- *Sharḥ Riyāḍ al-Ṣāliḥīn*, Muḥammad b. Ṣaliḥ b. Muḥammad al-ʿUthaymīn (1421 H.), Dār al-Watan, al-Riyadh (1426 H.).
- *Sharḥ Musnad Abī Ḥanīfah*, ʿAlī b. Sulṭān Muḥammad, Abū al-Ḥasan, Nūr al-Dīn al-Mullāh al-Qārī (1014 H.), Dār al-Kutub al-ʿIlmiyyah, Beirut, 1st Edition (1985).
- *Subul al-Salām Sharḥ Bulūgh al-Marām*, Muḥammad b. Ismāʿīl b. Ṣalah al-Amīr al-Kaḥlānī al-Ṣanʿānī (1182 H.), Dār al-Hadīth, Cairo.
- *Sharḥ Ṣaḥīḥ al-Bukhārī*, Abū al-Ḥasan ʿAlī b. Khalaf b. ʿAbd al-Malik, Ibn Baṭṭāl, (449 H.), Maktabtu al-Rushd, Riyadh, 2nd Edition (2003).
- *Kifāyatu al-Ḥājah fī Sharḥ Sunan Ibn Mājah*, Muḥammad b. ʿAbd al-Hādī al-Tatawī, Abū al-Ḥasan Nūr al-Dīn al-Sindī (1138 H.), Dār al-Jīl, Beirut.
- *Fayḍ al-Qadīr Sharḥ al-Jāmiʿ al-Ṣaghīr*, Zayn al-Dīn Muḥammad, ʿAbd al-Raʿūf b. Tāj al-ʿĀrifīn b. ʿAlī b. Zayn al-ʿĀbidīn al-Munāwī (1031 H.), al-Maktabah al-Tijāryyah al-Kubra, Egypt, 1st Edition (1356 H.).
- *Libāb al-Taʾwīl Fī Maʿānī al-Tanzīl*, ʿAlā al-Dīn ʿAlī b. Muḥammad b. Ibrāhīm b. ʿUmar, Abū al-Ḥasan, also known as al-Khāzin (741 H.), Dār al-Kutub al-ʿIlmiyyah, Beirut, 1st Edition (1415 H.).
- *Muntahā al-Su'l ʿAlā Wasā'il al-Wuṣūl Ilā Shamā'il al-Rasūl*, ʿAbdullāh b. Saʿīd b. Muḥammad al-Ḥaḍramī al-Makkī (1410 H.), Dār al-Minhāj, Jeddah, 3rd Edition (2005).
- *Aḍwā al-Bayān Fī Īḍāḥ al-Qur'ān bi al-Qur'ān*, Muḥammad al-Amīn b. Muḥammad al-Mukhṭār al-Shanqīṭī (1393 H.), Dār al-Fikr, Beirut (1995).
- *Bahjat al-Maḥāfil wa Bughyat al-Amāthil Fi Talkhīṣ al-Muʿjizāt wa al-Siyar wa al-Shamā'il*, Yaḥyā b. Abī Bakr b. Muḥammad b. Yaḥyā al-ʿĀmirī (893 H.), Dār Sādir, Beirut.
- *Laṭā'if al-Maʿārif fīmā li Mawāsim al-ʿĀm min al-Waẓā'if*,

Zayn al-Ḍīn 'Abd al-Raḥmān b. Aḥmad b. Rajab al-Ḥanbalī (795 H.), Dār Ibn Hazm, 1st Edition (2004).

- *Nayl al-Awṭār*, Muḥammad b. 'Alī b. Muḥammad b. 'Abdullah al-Shawkānī (1250 H.), Dār al-Hadīth, Egypt, 1st Edition (1993).
- *Iḥyā' 'Ulūm al-Dīn*, Abū Ḥāmid, Muḥammad b. Muḥammad al-Ghazālī (505 H.), Dār al-Ma'rifah, Beirut.
- *Madārij al-Sālikīn Bayna Manāzil Iyyaka Na'budu wa Iyyāka Nasta'īn*, Muḥammad b. Abī Bakr b. Ayyūb b. Sa'd Shams al-Dīn, Ibn Qayyim al-Jawziyyah (751 H.), Dar al-Kitāb al-Arabi, Beirut, 3rd Edition (1996).
- *'Uyūn al-Athar Fī Funūn al-Maghāzī wa al-Shamā'il wa al-Siyar*, Muḥammad b. Muḥammad, Ibn Sayyid al-Nās (734 H.), Dār al-Qalam, Beirut, 2nd Edition (1993).
- *Mukhtaṣar al-Shamā'il al-Muḥammadiyyah*, Nasir al-Dīn al-Albānī, Maktabat al-Marif, Riyadh.

Foreword of al-Shaykh ʿAbd al-Muḥsin al-ʿAbbād

The praise is for Allah. May Allah send salutations, peace, and blessings upon our Prophet Muḥammad, upon his family, his Companions and whoever was a supporter of his, held to his Sunnah, and was guided by his guidance, until the Day of Reward.

The scholars of ḥadīth define the Sunnah of the Prophet ﷺ to be all that which is attributed to the Prophet ﷺ in the form of statements, actions, approvals, physical attributes, manners or conduct. This makes the authentic statements of the companions رضي الله عنهم regarding his beautiful physical attributes and noble character included in this definition.

These superb character traits and beautiful features are either found scattered in ḥadīth collections or compiled into dedicated works, the most important of which is *"al-Shamāʾil"* by al-Imām al-Tirmidhī, the author of the famous book *"al-Jāmiʿ"*, which is known as *Sunan al-Tirmidhī*. It is indeed a reference of a great importance.

The benefit of learning the physical features of the Prophet ﷺ is that it helps us to distinguish the truthful dream from the false dream in which he appears and the benefit of knowing his character is to follow his example, which Allah has praised: **{There has certainly been for you in the Messenger of Allah an excellent pattern for anyone whose hope is in Allah and the Last Day and [who] remembers Allah often.}**[3]

---

3 Qurʾān 33:21

Introduction of al-Shaykh 'Abd al-Razzāq al-Badr

In the name of Allāh, the most benevolent to mankind, the most Merciful to all believers. All praise is for Allah, Lord of the worlds. Peace and prayers be upon Muḥammad, his family, his Companions and all those who follow in their footsteps until the last day.

This book contains a description of the physical features and character of the best of mankind and the most beloved and favoured by Allāh the Most High. A description of the one who knows his Lord the most and the most capable of mankind at fulfilling the rights of servitude. He was the one chosen to be the link between Allāh and His slaves and chosen to be the messenger who calls towards the good and guidance. Al-Ḥāfiẓ b. Kathīr commented on the verse: **{There has certainly been for you in the Messenger of Allah an excellent pattern for anyone whose hope is in Allah and the Last Day and [who] remembers Allah often.}** by saying, "This verse is a fundamental principle towards following the example of the Messenger of Allāh ﷺ in his statements, actions and conditions."[4]

The following of his example necessitates learning about his guidance in life, character and physical features. It is for this reason, each Muslim ought to give priority to learning about the life of the Prophet ﷺ before learning anything about anyone else.

The benefits of learning the Prophet's ﷺ character and physical features are many, some of which are:

- It is from the pillars of *īmān* to believe in the Messenger ﷺ and this cannot happen without acquiring the knowledge about him. That being said, the more a person knows about the Prophet ﷺ, the stronger his belief in him becomes.

- The love of the Prophet ﷺ is an obligation that Allah ﷻ has dictated upon His slaves and He made his love take precedence over one's love for his parents, children and all of mankind including one's own self. The more a person remembers his beloved and knows

4 *Tafsīr Ibn Kathīr* (6/391)

about his beautiful character, the more a person longs to meet him and feels love for him.

- Allah ﷻ has set the Prophet ﷺ as the role model that we need to follow. To be able to do this we need to learn about his life and character.

- The Prophet ﷺ is more worthy of the believers than their own selves. This is because his mercy and efforts to advise and call people to the truth made him more merciful to them than people are merciful to themselves. Also, his favour upon people is incomparable for every good deed that we carry out happens due to his efforts in calling humanity to Islām. Thus, each person should know his great status and this can be achieved through learning about his character and features.

- Allāh ﷻ has made an oath in the Qur'ān in which He testifies to the perfect character of the Prophet ﷺ. The verse says: **{And indeed, you are of a great moral character.}**[5] His sense of morality was based on the guidance of the Qur'ān, thus his character was described by 'Ā'ishah ﵂ as a manifestation of the Qur'ān[6], meaning that he followed all that which is encouraged and made obligatory in the Qur'ān and refrained from all that which is admonished and made forbidden in the Qur'ān.

- Allāh has ordered us in the Qur'ān to pray to Him to confer His Peace and Blessings upon the Prophet ﷺ and the more we are acquainted with his character and life the more we will be encouraged to do so more often. This is why the people who know the Prophet ﷺ more reflect upon matters differently than those who lack this knowledge, whose prayers are nothing but a sound uttered by their tongues.

- The description of the characteristics of the Prophet ﷺ provides a lifestyle that should be followed by all Muslims desiring to live the best life in this world and the Hereafter. It is a lifestyle that should be taught to the younger generation so that their upbringing can be sound and to keep them away from deviation, instead of letting their generation aspire to the lifestyles of the low-life ones.

---

5 Qur'ān 68:4
6 *Ṣaḥīḥ Muslim* (746)

For these reasons, there is only one person whose life should be looked into if one desires to find the perfect manners and best conduct, that is the life of the Prophet ﷺ and this is why it is needed to study and learn more about his manners, conduct and lifestyle. Sufyān b. ʿUyaynah said, "The Messenger of Allah ﷺ is the great balance; whatever complies with his conduct, character and guidance is the truth, otherwise it is falsehood."[7]

This blessed book is from the best and most beneficial books written about the character and depiction of the Prophet ﷺ and its author made it such an excellent work through his structuring of it and the ḥadīths he included therein. This is the reason why many scholars praise the book and consider it from the best books authored about this topic.

7 *Al-Jāmiʿ Li Akhlāq al-Rāwī wa al-Sāmiʿ* (1/9)

باب ما جاء في خلق رسول الله صلى الله عليه وسلم

[1] On the Appearance of Allāh's Messenger ﷺ

ʿAbd al-Razzaq al-Badr said,

> With no doubt, Allāh lavished our Prophet ﷺ with a perfect appearance and endowed him with the most beautiful physical attributes and characteristics. Shaykh al-Islām Ibn Taymiyyah said, "He [the Prophet] ﷺ enjoyed the best stature and appearance, indicating his perfection."[8]

Ibn Ḥajar al-Haytamī said,

> You should know that in order to perfect one's faith in him ﷺ, one must believe that there is no human in possession of as good an appearance as the Prophet ﷺ; this is because the outward beauty and handsomeness of the Prophet ﷺ indicates the inward beauty and noble manners he possessed, and no person could ever equal or exceed his status neither in respect to physical appearance nor manners.

ʿAlī al-Qārī said,

> The Arabic word *bāb* (which translates to chapter in English) means the door through which a person can enter a place and eloquent scholars have understood it to refer to that which leads to one's purpose. In the context [of its use by al-Tirmidhī], it alludes to: the means by which to become acquainted with the ḥadīths describing the physical appearance of the Prophet ﷺ.

١ - حَدَّثَنَا أَبُو رَجَاءٍ قُتَيْبَةُ بْنُ سَعِيدٍ، عَنْ مَالِكِ بْنِ أَنَسٍ، عَنْ رَبِيعَةَ بْنِ أَبِي عَبْدِ الرَّحْمَنِ، عَنْ أَنَسِ بْنِ مَالِكٍ، أَنَّهُ سَمِعَهُ يَقُولُ: كَانَ رَسُولُ اللهِ ﷺ لَيْسَ بِالطَّوِيلِ الْبَائِنِ، وَلاَ بِالْقَصِيرِ ، وَلاَ بِالأَبْيَضِ الأَمْهَقِ، وَلاَ بِالآدَمِ، وَلاَ بِالْجَعْدِ الْقَطَطِ، وَلاَ بِالسَّبْطِ، بَعَثَهُ اللهُ تَعَالَى عَلَى رَأْسِ أَرْبَعِينَ سَنَةً، فَأَقَامَ بِمَكَّةَ عَشْرَ سِنِينَ، وَبِالْمَدِينَةِ

8 Taken from *al-Jawāb al-Ṣaḥīḥ* (5/438)

عَشْرَ سِنِينَ، وَتَوَفَّاهُ اللهُ تَعَالَىٰ عَلَىٰ رَأْسِ سِتِّينَ سَنَةً، وَلَيْسَ فِي رَأْسِهِ وَلِحْيَتِهِ عِشْرُونَ شَعَرَةً بَيْضَاءَ١.

1. Narrated by Rabī'ah b. Abī 'Abd al-Raḥmān ※: "I heard Anas b. Mālik describing the Prophet ※ saying, 'He was neither too tall nor short; neither absolutely white nor brown; his hair was neither very curly nor completely straight. The divine revelation was revealed to him when he was forty years old. He stayed ten years in Makkah, and stayed in Madīnah for ten more years. When he died, he was sixty years old and did not have twenty grey hairs in his head and beard."

'Abd al-Razzāq al-Badr said,

> **"He was neither too tall nor short"**: The Prophet ※ was more apt to be described as tall than short, as it has been explicitly stated in other [authentic] ḥadīths.[10] This is noted in the choice of words that Anas b. Mālik ※ used to describe the height of the Prophet ※ i.e. he did not use the equivalent antonym of "short" when he negated both attributes; rather, he used the ascription "too tall" to explain that he ※ was tall but not to the point where his height exceeded normal or proper limits.
>
> **"He stayed ten years in Makkah"**: This is to specify the length of the period he stayed after receiving the revelation. However, some other ḥadīths stated that he stayed in Makkah for thirteen years. To reconcile between the two statements, it can be asserted that the mention of ten years refers to the period after the public proclamation of his Message, and the other three years refer to the period he kept this news hidden from others. A clearer reconciliation to present is that the ten years refer to the period he stayed in Makkah from the day that Sūrah al-Muddathir was revealed to him wherein he was commanded to warn people, and the other three years refer to the years preceding the aforesaid command. It can even be argued that the narrator counted the age by tens and so he rounded the cardinal number; hence he also omitted the numbers above sixty from the age of the Prophet ※ [as Arabs customarily do].
>
> **"When he died, he was sixty years old"**: As it is established in

---

9 *Ṣaḥīḥ al-Bukhārī* (5900) and *Ṣaḥīḥ Muslim* (2347)
10 As in the report of Abū Hurayrah found in *al-Adab al-Mufrad* (1155) and *Musnad al-Bazzār* (7789)

authentic ḥadīths that the Prophet ﷺ passed away at the age of sixty three, it becomes clear that the narrators chose to count by tens and hence omitted the three years from the earlier part.

ʿAlī al-Qārī said,

> The scholars who explained this ḥadīth stated that the part, **"... When he was forty years old"** is structured in the Arabic language to mean he had completed the age of forty.
>
> **"And did not have twenty grey hairs in his head and beard":** The wisdom behind the Prophet ﷺ having few grey hairs (though there are many ḥadīths stating the honour and virtue of grey hair) was so that the affability and love between him and his wives was maintained in a perfect manner [by Allāh], since women are apt to dislike grey hair on men. Further to the point, the statement of Ibn Ḥajar (see page 27), wherein he mentioned that disliking anything about the Prophet ﷺ is considered a matter of disbelief, cannot be true in all cases because the type of dislike that is naturally implanted in mankind is irrelevant to that which has been dictated.

٢- حَدَّثَنَا حُمَيْدُ بْنُ مَسْعَدَةَ الْبَصْرِيُّ، قَالَ: حَدَّثَنَا عَبْدُ الْوَهَّابِ الثَّقَفِيُّ، عَنْ حُمَيْدٍ، عَنْ أَنَسِ بْنِ مَالِكٍ، قَالَ : كَانَ رَسُولُ اللهِ صلىٰ الله عليه وسلم رَبْعَةً، لَيْسَ بِالطَّوِيلِ وَلا بِالْقَصِيرِ، حَسَنَ الْجِسْمِ، وَكَانَ شَعَرُهُ لَيْسَ بِجَعْدٍ وَلا سَبْطٍ، أَسْمَرَ اللَّوْنِ، إِذَا مَشَىٰ يَتَكَفَّأُ.[١١]

2. Anas b. Mālik ؓ related: "The Prophet ﷺ was of medium height; he was neither [too] tall nor short. He had a good physical build, and his hair was neither curly nor completely straight. He had a tanned complexion, and when he walked, he leaned forward slightly."

ʿAbd al-Razzāq al-Badr said,

> It is noted that in the previous ḥadīth, Anas b. Mālik ؓ stated that the skin tone of the Prophet ﷺ was not brown. This caused some scholars to believe that this part (**"He had a tanned complexion"**) is not authentic because it was only reported from one person, while the rest of the narrators who reported this from Anas stated that, "He had a

---

11 *Sunan al-Tirmidhī* (1754)

rosy complexion."

'Alī al-Qārī said,

> The part where it says, **"He had a good physical build"** refers to his height, skin tone and weight.
>
> The part stating that, **"He had a tanned complexion"** is intended to negate that he had a skin tone that was absolutely white. It does not negate his statement "nor brown" in the previous ḥadīth as the word *"al-ādam"* in the previous ḥadīth means extremely brown. Al-ʿIrāqī critiqued the authenticity of this part. He mentioned that the number of companions who described the skin tone of the Prophet ﷺ was fifteen, and all of them reported that he had a rosy skin tone; furthermore, this description is only reported by one narrator from Anas.
>
> The part where it says, **"When he walked, he leaned forward slightly"** indicates that he walked with wide steps, because walking with small steps is the way that arrogant people walk.

Ibn Ḥajar al-Haytamī said,

> Arabs sometimes call the one with a white skin tone that is mixed with some redness a person with a tanned or deep-brown skin colour. This explains the reason why Anas ؓ stated in this ḥadīth that the Prophet ﷺ had a tanned complexion. Overall, the ḥadīths corroborate this understanding regarding the context of the use of the word tanned.
>
> If one argues that, since the skin colour of the Prophet ﷺ is the most noble and honourable of all colours, and so is the skin colour of the dwellers of Paradise, then why is the skin colour of the latter white with some yellowness as stated by the majority of exegetes? I say: the basis of the skin colour of both is the same and the wisdom behind the aforementioned variation is (and Allah knows best): the red tone mixed with the white is due to the blood and its characteristics, which flows moderately in the veins and it is produced from the worldly nutrition. Whereas the yellow colour that makes the whiteness [of the skin] polished and purified only appears in Paradise as it can only be produced by the nutrition of that world.
>
> From this part, we can understand the statement of some of the Shāfiʿī

scholars who said it is better for a woman not to wear white or silver clothes, because these can cause a resemblance of men in their clothing, and the reason she is encouraged to change the white coloured garment by dying it with saffron is so that the colour becomes closer to gold, as that befits her gender.

٣- حَدَّثَنَا مُحَمَّدُ بْنُ بَشَّارٍ - يَعْنِي العَبْدِيَّ -، قَالَ : حَدَّثَنَا مُحَمَّدُ بْنُ جَعْفَرٍ قَالَ: حَدَّثَنَا شُعْبَةُ، عَنْ أَبِي إِسْحَاقَ قَالَ: سَمِعْتُ الْبَرَاءَ بْنَ عَازِبٍ يَقُولُ : «كَانَ رَسُولُ اللهِ صلىٰ الله عليه وسلم رَجُلًا مَرْبُوعًا، بَعِيدَ مَا بَيْنَ الْمَنْكِبَيْنِ، عَظِيمَ الْجُمَّةِ إِلَىٰ شَحْمَةِ أُذُنَيْهِ، عَلَيْهِ حُلَّةٌ حَمْرَاءُ، مَا رَأَيْتُ شَيْئًا قَطُّ أَحْسَنَ مِنْهُ».[١٢]

3. Al-Barāʾ b. ʿĀzib ﷺ related: "The Prophet ﷺ was a man of medium build; he had broad shoulders; he had dense hair which reached his earlobes. [I saw him wearing] a *ḥullah* (red garment) and I never saw anything more beautiful than him."

ʿAbd al-Razzāq al-Badr said,

The description given concerning his height is intended to be approximate and not to offer the exact measurement. This is deduced from the fact that other ḥadīths stated that he ﷺ was closer to tall than short.

The Arabic word *ḥullah* is used only when the clothing is comprised of two pieces.

To reconcile between the fact that the Prophet ﷺ wore a red garment and his statement wherein he admonished wearing red clothes, it can be said that the order not to wear red clothing refers to clothes comprised completely of red; hence if the garment has other colours such as white or black besides the red, then it does not fall under the category of the forbidden clothing.

The use of the word "anything" rather than "anybody" in the part, **"... Anything more beautiful than him"** makes the comparison refer to both the animate and inanimate creations.

ʿAlī al-Qārī said,

The use of the word "man" is an addition from one of the narrators

12 *Ṣaḥīḥ al-Bukhārī* (3551) and *Ṣaḥīḥ Muslim* (2337)

and not from the words of the companions. However, as all the narrators are trustworthy and credible we accept this addition, and we understand it to be an adjective that is intended to state that he had all the praised qualities of a man. Alternatively, the use of the word can be understood in the context that it is often used as an introduction to what will come afterwards.

The quality of having broad shoulders is deemed by the Arabs as a sign of one's generosity, profound respect and tolerance.

There are numerous ḥadīths about the length of the Prophet's ﷺ hair, some of which indicated that it was between his ears and shoulders, some that it was up to his ears, some that it reached to the middle of his ears, some that it touched his shoulders and some that it reached his shoulder blades. Al-Qāḍī 'Iyāḍ explained that the variance of reports regarding this matter is due to the fact that each narrator reported what he saw at a specific time and thus the length of his hair differed.

Al-Nawawī explained that, "The Arab linguists state that *ḥullah* refers to clothing that is comprised of two pieces and it often refers to the *izār* (a lower garment wrapped around the waist)." To understand the Prophet's ﷺ wearing of a red garment in light of the knowledge that there are other ḥadīths wherein he discouraged people from wearing red clothes, we say either the garment he wore had colours other than red in it (but as red was more prominent, it was identified as a red garment), or it could be that the incident reported was before the admonishment he issued (if the garment was purely red), or that wearing these garments [that are completely red] is one of the exclusive characteristics of the Prophet ﷺ that others are not allowed to do.

Ibn Ḥajar al-Haytamī said,

> There are different ḥadīths that provide different descriptions of the length of his ﷺ hair and this is because each narrator described what he saw [at that specific time], and because when the Prophet ﷺ would leave his hair uncut, he would leave it until it reached his shoulders and when he shortened it, he would let it reach the level of his earlobes; sometimes to the middle of his ears and sometimes to the level of his ear lobes.

> **"A *ḥullah*":** This ḥadīth is authentic and it was used by al-Imām al-Shāfiʿī as evidence that it is permissible to wear red clothing.

٤ - حَدَّثَنَا مَحْمُودُ بْنُ غَيْلانَ، قَالَ: حَدَّثَنَا وَكِيعٌ، قَالَ: حَدَّثَنَا سُفْيَانُ، عَنْ أَبِي إِسْحَاقَ، عَنِ الْبَرَاءِ بْنِ عَازِبٍ، قَالَ: «مَا رَأَيْتُ مِنْ ذِي لِمَّةٍ فِي حُلَّةٍ حَمْرَاءَ أَحْسَنَ مِنْ رَسُولِ اللهِ، لَهُ شَعَرٌ يَضْرِبُ مَنْكِبَيْهِ، بَعِيدُ مَا بَيْنَ الْمَنْكِبَيْنِ، لَمْ يَكُنْ بِالْقَصِيرِ وَلا بِالطَّوِيلِ».[١٣]

4. Al-Barāʾ b. ʿĀzib ﵁ related: "I have never seen someone with a *limmah* wearing a red garment more handsome than the Prophet. He had long hair that reached his shoulders. The distance between his two shoulders was wide. He was neither tall nor short."

ʿAbd al-Razzāq al-Badr said,

> The word "*limmah*" refers to a hairstyle where the length of the hair extends to below the earlobes, whether it reaches the shoulders or not. What follows in this narration comes to state that al-Barāʾ ﵁ considered the Prophet ﷺ to be the most handsome person he ever saw with such a description.

Al-Bājūrī said,

> **"He was neither tall nor short":** I.e. excessively. This does not negate that he leaned towards being tall, as mentioned previously.

٥ - حَدَّثَنَا مُحَمَّدُ بْنُ إِسْمَاعِيلَ، قَالَ: حَدَّثَنَا أَبُو نُعَيْمٍ، قَالَ: حَدَّثَنَا الْمَسْعُودِيُّ، عَنْ عُثْمَانَ بْنِ مُسْلِمِ بْنِ هُرْمُزَ، عَنْ نَافِعِ بْنِ جُبَيْرِ بْنِ مُطْعِمٍ، عَنْ عَلِيِّ بْنِ أَبِي طَالِبٍ، قَالَ: «لَمْ يَكُنِ النَّبِيُّ صلى الله عليه وسلم بِالطَّوِيلِ وَلا بِالْقَصِيرِ، شَثْنُ الْكَفَّيْنِ وَالْقَدَمَيْنِ، ضَخْمُ الرَّأْسِ، ضَخْمُ الْكَرَادِيسِ، طَوِيلُ الْمَسْرُبَةِ، إِذَا مَشَى تَكَفَّأَ تَكَفُّؤًا كَأَنَّمَا يَنْحَطُّ مِنْ صَبَبٍ، لَمْ أَرَ قَبْلَهُ، وَلا بَعْدَهُ مِثْلَهُ، صلى الله عليه وسلم».[١٤]

5. ʿAlī b. Abī Ṭālib ﵁ narrated: "The Prophet ﷺ was neither extreme-

---

13 *Ṣaḥīḥ al-Bukhārī* (3549) and *Ṣaḥīḥ Muslim* (2337)

14 *Sunan al-Tirmidhī* (3637)

ly tall nor short. He had sturdy hands and feet and a large head. The joints of his bones were large and he had a line of hair extending from his chest to the navel. When he walked, it appeared as if he was descending from a high place. I have never seen anyone who was comparable to him."

'Abd al-Razzāq al-Badr said,

> The common attribute that all the narrators who described the Prophet ﷺ mentioned was that he was neither tall nor short.
>
> Having sturdy hands does not entail the attribution of rough skin because Anas ﷺ, as shall be mentioned later, stated that the touch of his hand was softer than silk.

Ibn Ḥajar al-Haytamī said,

> The fact that he had sturdy hands and at the same time soft skin (as narrated by Anas b. Mālik ﷺ in other authentic ḥadīths) shows that he combined strength with fine-spun skin.

'Alī al-Qārī said,

> The last statement of 'Alī b. Abī Tālib ﷺ is a statement that is used (in Arabic) to negate the existence of anything that is similar to the described. It is to show that if there is none like him, then evidently there will be no one who is better than him.

٦- حَدَّثَنَا سُفْيَانُ بْنُ وَكِيعٍ، قَالَ: حَدَّثَنَا أَبِي، عَنِ الْمَسْعُودِيِّ، بِهَذَا الإِسْنَادِ نَحْوَهُ بِمَعْنَاهُ.

6. Sufyān b. Wakī' narrated to us that his father narrated from al-Mas'ūdī through the same chain a similar ḥadīth with the same meaning.

Ibn Ḥajar al-Haytamī said,

> **"A similar ḥadīth with the same meaning":** This denotes emphasis, as the word *naḥwahu* is a term only used when [narrations] accord in meaning only. The term used when [narrations] accord in meaning and wording is *mithluhu* (مثله).

٧– حَدَّثَنَا أَحْمَدُ بْنُ عَبْدَةَ الضَّبِّيُّ الْبَصْرِيُّ، وَعَلِيُّ بْنُ حُجْرٍ، وَأَبُو جَعْفَرٍ مُحَمَّدُ بْنُ الْحُسَيْنِ – وَهُوَ ابْنُ أَبِي حَلِيمَةَ –، وَالْمَعْنَىٰ وَاحِدٌ، قَالُوا: حَدَّثَنَا عِيسَىٰ بْنُ يُونُسَ، عَنْ عُمَرَ بْنِ عَبْدِ اللهِ مَوْلَىٰ غُفْرَةَ، قَالَ: حَدَّثَنِي إِبْرَاهِيمُ بْنُ مُحَمَّدٍ مِنْ وَلَدِ عَلِيِّ بْنِ أَبِي طَالِبٍ قَالَ: كَانَ عَلِيٌّ إِذَا وَصَفَ رَسُولَ اللهِ صلىٰ الله عليه وسلم، قَالَ: «لَمْ يَكُنْ رَسُولُ اللهِ صلىٰ الله عليه وسلم بِالطَّوِيلِ الْمُمَّغِطِ، وَلا بِالْقَصِيرِ الْمُتَرَدِّدِ، وَكَانَ رَبْعَةً مِنَ الْقَوْمِ، لَمْ يَكُنْ بِالْجَعْدِ الْقَطَطِ، وَلا بِالسَّبْطِ، كَانَ جَعْدًا رَجِلا، وَلَمْ يَكُنْ بِالْمُطَهَّمِ، وَلا بِالْمُكَلْثَمِ، وَكَانَ فِي وَجْهِهِ تَدْوِيرٌ، أَبْيَضُ مُشْرَبٌ، أَدْعَجُ الْعَيْنَيْنِ، أَهْدَبُ الأَشْفَارِ، جَلِيلُ الْمُشَاشِ وَالْكَتَدِ، أَجْرَدُ، ذُو مَسْرُبَةٍ، شَثْنُ الْكَفَّيْنِ وَالْقَدَمَيْنِ، إِذَا مَشَىٰ تَقَلَّعَ كَأَنَّمَا يَنْحَطُّ فِي صَبَبٍ، وَإِذَا الْتَفَتَ الْتَفَتَ مَعًا، بَيْنَ كَتِفَيْهِ خَاتَمُ النُّبُوَّةِ، وَهُوَ خَاتَمُ النَّبِيِّينَ، أَجْوَدُ النَّاسِ صَدْرًا، وَأَصْدَقُ النَّاسِ لَهْجَةً، وَأَلْيَنُهُمْ عَرِيكَةً، وَأَكْرَمُهُمْ عِشْرَةً، مَنْ رَآهُ بَدِيهَةً هَابَهُ، وَمَنْ خَالَطَهُ مَعْرِفَةً أَحَبَّهُ، يَقُولُ نَاعِتُهُ: لَمْ أَرَ قَبْلَهُ وَلا بَعْدَهُ مِثْلَهُ.[١٥]

7. Ibrāhīm b. Muḥammad ﷺ (who is from the grandchildren of ʿAlī b. Abī Ṭālib) reported that whenever ʿAlī ﷺ used to describe the Prophet ﷺ, he would say: "The Messenger of Allāh was neither very tall nor very short, but of a medium stature amongst the people. His hair was neither very curly nor completely straight; rather it was in between these two descriptions.

He did not have a fleshy body or a [fully] round face, his face was slightly round. His skin colour was white with some redness. He had extremely black eyes with long eyelashes. He had large joints and broad shoulders. There was no hair [more than normal] on his body and he had a thin line of hair running from the chest to the navel. He had sturdy hands and feet. When he walked, he lifted his legs with vigour and his steps were firm and strong as if he was descending down a slope. When he wished to look behind, he would turn his whole body [and not just the face]. The seal of prophethood was situated between his shoulders. He was the seal of the Prophets, and he had the most generous of hearts and the most truthful tongue. He was the most kind-natured and tolerant person ever. Anyone who

15 *Sunan al-Tirmidhī* (3638)

came across him unexpectedly would become awestruck; and whoever came in close contact with him would love him. One who describes him can only state, 'I have never seen anyone comparable to him.'"

قَالَ أَبُو عِيسَىٰ: سَمِعْتُ أَبَا جَعْفَرٍ مُحَمَّدَ بْنَ الْحُسَيْنِ يَقُولُ: سَمِعْتُ الأَصْمَعِيَّ يَقُولُ فِي تَفْسِيرِ صِفَةِ النَّبِيِّ صلىٰ الله عليه وسلم: الْمُمَّغِطُ: الذَّاهِبُ طُولا، وَقَالَ: سَمِعْتُ أَعْرَابِيًّا يَقُولُ فِي كَلامِهِ: تَمَغَّطَ فِي نَشَّابَتِهِ أَيْ: مَدَّهَا مَدًّا شَدِيدًا وَالْمُتَرَدِّدُ: الدَّاخِلُ بَعْضُهُ فِي بَعْضٍ قِصَرًا، وَأَمَّا الْقَطَطُ: فَالشَّدِيدُ الْجُعُودَةِ، وَالرَّجِلُ: الَّذِي فِي شَعَرِهِ حُجُونَةٌ: أَيْ تَثَنٍّ قَلِيلٌ.

Abū 'Īsā said: I heard Abū Ja'far Muḥammad b. al-Ḥusayn say: I heard al-Aṣma'ī say in explanation of the Prophetic traits, "*Al-mummaghiṭ* means excessively tall." He said, "I heard a Bedouin Arab say in the midst of his speech, '*Tamaghghat fī nashshābatihi*', i.e. he drew his arrows forcefully. *Al-mutaraddid* means some of [the body parts] enter into others due to shortness. *Al-qaṭaṭ* means extreme curliness. *Al-rajil* refers to hair with a little curliness.

وَأَمَّا الْمُطَهَّمُ: فَالْبَادِنُ الْكَثِيرُ اللَّحْمِ. وَالْمُكَلْثَمُ: الْمُدَوَّرُ الْوَجْهِ وَالْمُشْرَبُ: الَّذِي فِي بَيَاضِهِ حُمْرَةٌ. وَالأَدْعَجُ: الشَّدِيدُ سَوَادِ الْعَيْنِ. وَالأَهْدَبُ: الطَّوِيلُ الأَشْفَارِ. وَالْكَتَدُ: مُجْتَمِعُ الْكَتِفَيْنِ وَهُوَ الْكَاهِلُ. وَالْمَسْرُبَةُ: هُوَ الشَّعْرُ الدَّقِيقُ الَّذِي كَأَنَّهُ قَضِيبٌ مِنَ الصَّدْرِ إِلَىٰ السُّرَّةِ. وَالشَّثْنُ: الْغَلِيظُ الأَصَابِعِ مِنَ الْكَفَّيْنِ وَالْقَدَمَيْنِ، وَالتَّقَلُّعُ: أَنْ يَمْشِيَ بِقُوَّةٍ، وَالصَّبَبُ: الْحُدُورُ، يقالُ: انْحَدَرْنَا فِي صَبُوبٍ وَصَبَبٍ.

Al-muṭahham means a very fleshy body. _Al-mukaltham_ means a round face. _Al-musharab_ is one whose whiteness contains redness. _Al-ad'aj_ means deep blackness of the eyes. _Al-ahdab_ means long eyelashes. _Al-katad_ is the meeting place of the shoulder blades, i.e. the upper back. _Al-masrubah_ is a thin line from the chest to the navel. _Al-shathn_ means thick fingers and toes. _Al-taqallu'_ is to walk powerfully. _Al-ṣabab_ is a slope, and it is said: we descended from a _ṣabūb_ and a _ṣabab_.

وَقَوْلُهُ: جَلِيلُ الْمُشَاشِ يُرِيدُ رُءُوسَ الْمَنَاكِبِ، وَالْعِشْرَةُ: الصُّحْبَةُ، وَالْعَشِيرُ:

الصَّاحِبُ، وَالْبَدِيهَةُ: الْمُفَاجَأَةُ، يُقَالُ: بَدَهْتُهُ بِأَمْرٍ أَيْ فَجَأْتُهُ.

His statement *"Jalīl al-mushāsh"* means the head of the shoulder. *Al-ʿishrah* means companionship and *al-ʿashīr* means a companion. *Al-badīhah* means astonishment, as in the sentence, "*Badahtuhu* (I was surprised) with an issue."

ʿAbd al-Razzāq al-Badr said,

> The part, **"He did not have a fleshy body"** indicates that he ﷺ was not fat.
>
> The seal of prophethood refers to an area of raised skin between his shoulders.

Ibn Ḥajar al-Haytamī said,

> The mention of him not turning the neck only is to show that he did not glance secretly or act as the reckless people do whenever they want to look at something.
>
> As Muḥammad ﷺ is the last Prophet, when Īsa عليه السلام descends during the end times, he will rule by and abide to the laws of Islām; he will spread justice, pray towards Makkah and take his judgements from the Qurʾān and Sunnah.
>
> The parts that describe his kind-natured and merciful nature as well as his excellent qualities conform to the event when Jibrīl عليه السلام split his chest and removed the share of the devil from his heart and then washed it with the water of Zamzam.
>
> The part, **"... the most truthful tongue"** means that he used to utter the letters perfectly, beautifully and eloquently.

ʿAlī al-Qārī said,

> In another version of this ḥadīth, the part, **"He was the most kind-hearted and tolerant person ever"** was narrated as, "He is from the most noble tribe" and both versions truly describe him ﷺ.

ʿAbd al-Razzāq al-Badr said,

> Al-Imām al-Tirmidhi then reports al-Aṣmaʿī's explanation of difficult words found in this ḥadīth, though most of them are clear.

Al-Bājūrī said,

> **"Abū 'Īsā said":** This was stated by the author. He referred to himself via his *kunyah* due to him being well-known with it. It is possible that this was stated by one of the narrators from him, but the former (i.e. that it was stated by the author) is more likely. Al-Bukhārī had a similar habit, wherein he would state "Abū 'Abd Allāh said" while referring to himself.

٨- حَدَّثَنَا سُفْيَانُ بْنُ وَكِيعٍ قَالَ: حَدَّثَنَا جُمَيْعُ بْنُ عُمَيرَ بْنِ عَبْدِ الرَّحْمَنِ الْعِجْلِيُّ - إِمْلاءً عَلَيْنَا مِنْ كِتَابِهِ - قَالَ: أَخْبَرَنِي رَجُلٌ مِنْ بَنِي تَمِيمٍ مِنْ وَلَدِ أَبِي هَالَةَ زَوْجِ خَدِيجَةَ، يُكَنَىٰ أَبَا عَبْدِ اللهِ، عَنِ ابْنٍ لأَبِي هَالَةَ، عَنِ الْحَسَنِ بْنِ عَلِيٍّ قَالَ: سَأَلْتُ خَالِي هِنْدَ بْنَ أَبِي هَالَةَ - وَكَانَ وَصَّافًا - عَنْ حِلْيَةِ رَسُولِ اللهِ صلىٰ الله عليه وسلم، وَأَنَا أَشْتَهِي أَنْ يَصِفَ لِي مِنْهَا شَيْئًا أَتَعَلَّقُ بِهِ، فَقَالَ: «كَانَ رَسُولُ اللهِ صلىٰ الله عليه وسلم فَخْمًا مُفَخَّمًا، يَتَلأْلأُ وَجْهُهُ تَلأْلُؤَ الْقَمَرِ لَيْلَةَ الْبَدْرِ، أَطْوَلُ مِنَ الْمَرْبُوعِ، وَأَقْصَرُ مِنَ الْمُشَذَّبِ، عَظِيمُ الْهَامَةِ، رَجِلَ الشَّعْرِ، إِنِ انْفَرَقَتْ عَقِيقَتُهُ فَرَقَهَا وَإِلَّا فَلا يُجَاوِزُ شَعَرُهُ شَحْمَةَ أُذُنَيْهِ إِذَا هُوَ وَفَّرَهُ، أَزْهَرُ اللَّوْنِ، وَاسِعُ الْجَبِينِ، أَزَجُّ الْحَوَاجِبِ، سَوَابِغَ فِي غَيْرِ قَرَنٍ، بَيْنَهُمَا عِرْقٌ يُدِرُّهُ الْغَضَبُ، أَقْنَىٰ الْعِرْنَيْنِ، لَهُ نُورٌ يَعْلُوهُ، يَحْسَبُهُ مَنْ لَمْ يَتَأَمَّلْهُ أَشَمَّ، كَثُّ اللِّحْيَةِ، سَهْلَ الْخَدَّيْنِ، ضَلِيعَ الْفَمِ، مُفْلَجَ الأَسْنَانِ، دَقِيقَ الْمَسْرُبَةِ، كَأَنَّ عُنُقَهُ جِيدُ دُمْيَةٍ فِي صَفَاءِ الْفِضَّةِ، مُعْتَدِلَ الْخَلْقِ، بَادِنٌ مُتَمَاسِكٌ، سَوَاءُ الْبَطْنِ وَالصَّدْرُ، عَرِيضُ الصَّدْرِ، بَعِيدَ مَا بَيْنَ الْمَنْكِبَيْنِ، ضَخْمُ الْكَرَادِيسِ، أَنْوَرُ الْمُتَجَرَّدِ، مَوْصُولُ مَا بَيْنَ اللَّبَّةِ وَالسُّرَّةِ بِشَعَرٍ يَجْرِي كَالْخَطِّ، عَارِي الثَّدْيَيْنِ وَالْبَطْنِ مِمَّا سِوَىٰ ذَلِكَ، أَشْعَرُ الذِّرَاعَيْنِ وَالْمَنْكِبَيْنِ وَأَعَالِي الصَّدْرِ، طَوِيلُ الزَّنْدَيْنِ، رَحْبُ الرَّاحَةِ، شَثْنُ الْكَفَّيْنِ وَالْقَدَمَيْنِ، سَائِلُ الأَطْرَافِ - أَوْ قَالَ: شَائِلُ الأَطْرَافِ - خُمْصَانُ الأَخْمَصَيْنِ، مَسِيحُ الْقَدَمَيْنِ، يَنْبُو عَنْهُمَا الْمَاءُ، إِذَا زَالَ زَالَ قَلَعًا، يَخْطُو تَكَفِّيًا، وَيَمْشِي هَوْنًا، ذَرِيعُ الْمِشْيَةِ، إِذَا مَشَىٰ كَأَنَّمَا يَنْحَطُّ مِنْ صَبَبٍ، وَإِذَا الْتَفَتَ الْتَفَتَ جَمِيعًا، خَافِضُ الطَّرْفِ، نَظَرُهُ إِلَىٰ الأَرْضِ أَطْوَلُ مِنْ نَظَرِهِ إِلَىٰ السَّمَاءِ، جُلُّ نَظَرِهِ الْمُلاحَظَةُ، يَسُوقُ أَصْحَابَهُ، وَيَبْدُرُ مَنْ لَقِيَ

بِالسَّلامِ. ١٦

8. Al-Ḥasan b. ʿAlī ﷺ reported: "I inquired from my maternal uncle, Hind b. Abī Hālah about the awe-inspiring characteristics and features of the Prophet ﷺ as he was known for doing so, as I desired to become well acquainted with and memorise his description."

The uncle described the Prophet ﷺ by saying: "His qualities and attributes were the acme of beauty, and his companions and whoever saw him held him in high esteem. His face used to shine like the full moon. He was of a medium height but closer to tall than average and shorter than a lanky person. His head was [moderately] large and his hair was slightly waved. If his hair could [naturally] be parted, he would have it so; otherwise he would make no efforts to part it and his hair would not go beyond his ear lobes. He had a skin tone that was white with a tinge of red and a wide forehead with perfect and complete eyebrows, consisting of hair that reached to the end of the line of his eyes. His eyebrows were separate and did not meet each other in the middle. There was a vein between them that used to expand due to anger. His nose was prominent and was wrapped with a light that shines out. If one did not look at him closely, it would seem as if he had a large nasal bridge. His beard was full and dense and his cheek bones were not high. His mouth was [moderately] wide and he had a space between his front teeth.

He had a thin line of hair from the chest to the navel and his neck was as beautiful as the neck of a doll made of ivory. All the parts of his body were of moderate size and fully fleshed. His body was proportionately jointed. His chest and stomach were in line, but his chest was broad and wide. The space between his shoulders was wide and the bones of his joints were strong and large. His body parts had a brightness that shined whenever he removed his clothing. Between the upper point of the chest and navel he had a thin line of hair while the rest of the area had no hair on it. He had hair on his arms, shoulders and upper chest. His forearms were long and his palms were wide. The fingers and toes were moderately thick, and both his hands and legs were moderately long.

The soles of his feet were somewhat high from the ground. His feet were smooth [i.e. had no holes or cracks], such that water would

16 *Tahdhīb al-Kamāl* (1/214)

not remain there and flow away quickly. When he walked, he lifted his legs with strength as if he was uprooting a plant; he leaned slightly forward and placed his feet softly on the ground. He walked at a moderate pace and naturally walked with long steps. When he walked it seemed as if he was descending to a lower place. When he wanted to look at something behind him, he would turn his whole body towards it. His gaze would often face down towards the earth; he looked more to the ground than towards the sky, [it was his habit not to stare] and most of his prolonged glances were thoughtful and intended for contemplating. He would let his companions walk in front whilst he himself walked behind, and he always hastened to greet whomsoever he met."

'Abd al-Razzāq al-Badr said,

> The maternal uncle of al-Ḥasan b. 'Alī ﷺ was Hind b. Abī Hālah ﷺ, the son of the mother of believers, Khadījah bint Khuwaylid ﷺ who was raised by the Prophet ﷺ; hence being the maternal stepbrother of Fāṭimah ﷺ.
>
> The reason why al-Ḥasan requested to learn the detailed description of the Prophet ﷺ despite the fact that he had the honour to see him in person was because he was very young at that time [when the Prophet ﷺ was alive]. The request of al-Ḥasan shows that learning the description of the Prophet ﷺ is a knowledge that should be given priority.

Ibn Ḥajar al-Haytamī said,

> **"His face used to shine like the full moon":** Not only did he possess the most handsome face, but also the best character as reported in the two *Ṣaḥīḥ* books.
>
> The narrator preferred to use the term "full moon" instead of "the sun" when describing the brightness of the Prophet's ﷺ face. This is because, contrary to the sun, the moon can be looked at without causing the eye any harm.
>
> It is reported in *Ṣaḥīḥ Muslim* that the Prophet ﷺ used to let his hair hang down while the idolaters used to part their hair, and the People of the Book used to let their hair hang down. He liked to be in harmony with the People of the Book in matters of which he had not received any command. Then later in his life he would part his hair.

Though both practices are permissible, parting the hair is preferable since it was the practice that the Prophet ﷺ settled with.

The part of this ḥadīth that describes the manner in which he would look is intended to mean that he would not glance sneakily when wanting to look at something. "He looked more to the ground than towards the sky," due to his mindfulness of Allāh, his humility and shyness of Him.

'Alī al-Qārī said,

The way the Prophet ﷺ walked (i.e. walking with wide steps) is the praised walk for men as walking with short steps is a characteristic of women.

He used to look down to the earth when his glance was not focused on anything because he used to spend the time contemplating and pondering, and it was also his habit due to the humbleness he possessed. Likewise, he used to ask his companions to walk in front of him out of humbleness and also out of his consideration for the weak and wanting to look after them, as they are normally the ones who fall to the back of the group. Furthermore, it was proven in an authentic ḥadīth that he told his companions, "The angels guard my back, so leave it for them."

The wisdom behind why he used to hasten to greet others (give *salām*) is because this is the nature of the humble and also when one initiates the greeting, his initiation becomes a cause for the one being greeted to reciprocate and attain a reward.

٩ – حَدَّثَنَا أَبُو مُوسَىٰ مُحَمَّدُ بْنُ الْمُثَنَّىٰ، حَدَّثَنَا مُحَمَّدُ بْنُ جَعْفَرٍ، حَدَّثَنَا شُعْبَةُ، عَنْ سِمَاكِ بْنِ حَرْبٍ، قَالَ: سَمِعْتُ جَابِرَ بْنَ سَمُرَةَ، يَقُولُ: «كَانَ رَسُولُ اللهِ صلىٰ الله عليه وسلم ضَلِيعَ الْفَمِ، أَشْكَلَ الْعَيْنِ، مَنْهُوسَ الْعَقِبِ».

9. Jābir b. Samurah ؓ narrated: "The mouth of the Messenger of Allāh ﷺ was wide and there was some redness in the whites of his eyes, and he had only a small amount of flesh on his heels."[17]

---

17 Note: The translation of the part concerning the eyes in this ḥadīth is based on the explanation of al-Qāḍī 'Iyāḍ and the scholars who interpreted the words of this ḥadīth.

قَالَ شُعْبَةُ: قُلْتُ لِسِمَاكٍ: مَا ضَلِيعُ الْفَمِ؟ قَالَ: عَظِيمُ الْفَمِ، قُلْتُ: مَا أَشْكَلُ الْعَيْنِ؟ قَالَ: طَوِيلُ شِقِّ الْعَيْنِ، قُلْتُ: مَا مَنْهُوسُ الْعَقِبِ؟ قَالَ: قَلِيلُ لَحْمِ الْعَقِبِ. [18]

Al-Shu'bah said: I asked Simāk, "What does *ḍalī'u 'l-fam* mean?" He replied, "A large mouth." I asked, "What does *ashkalu 'l-'ayn* mean?" He replied, "Long eye slits." I asked, "What does *manhūsu 'l-'aqib* mean?" He replied, "Lean heels."

'Abd al-Razzāq al-Badr said,

> The quality of having white eyes with a hint of redness is a praised physical appearance amongst the Arabs.

'Alī al-Qārī said,

> Some scholars interpreted the part "wide mouth" to refer to his teeth but the majority understood this part as referring to the mouth.

Al-Bājūrī said,

> **"I asked, 'What does *ashkalu 'l-'ayn* mean?' He replied, 'Long eye slits.'":** This definition is not found in the common dictionaries. From this angle, al-Qāḍī 'Iyāḍ deemed it a mistake from Simāk. The correct view – upon which there is concordance amongst the scholars and those who authored works on difficult words – is that *al-shuklah* is redness in the whites of the eye.

١٠ – حَدَّثَنَا هَنَّادُ بْنُ السَّرِيِّ، قَالَ: حَدَّثَنَا عَبْثَرُ بْنُ الْقَاسِمِ، عَنْ أَشْعَثَ – يَعْنِي ابْنَ سَوَّارٍ –، عَنْ أَبِي إِسْحَاقَ، عَنْ جَابِرِ بْنِ سَمُرَةَ، قَالَ: «رَأَيْتُ رَسُولَ اللهِ صلى الله عليه وسلم فِي لَيْلَةٍ إِضْحِيَانٍ، وَعَلَيْهِ حُلَّةٌ حَمْرَاءُ، فَجَعَلْتُ أَنْظُرُ إِلَيْهِ وَإِلَى الْقَمَرِ، فَلَهُوَ عِنْدِي أَحْسَنُ مِنَ الْقَمَرِ». [19]

10. Jābir b. Samurah ﷺ said: "I saw Allāh's Messenger ﷺ during a night where the moon was full. On that night, he wore a red garment and when I looked at the moon and compared it with him, by Allāh, he was in my eyes better and more beautiful than the moon."

Ibn Ḥajar al-Haytamī said,

18 *Ṣaḥīḥ Muslim* (2339)
19 *Sunan al-Tirmidhī* (2811)

The mention of a "full moon" was intended to show that it was a clear night that was neither dark nor cloudy, having a clear moon from its beginning to its end.

The part of the ḥadīth, "... in my eyes" is to indicate the state he experienced personally and it is not intended to state that it could be otherwise in the eyes of another person.

ʿAbd al-Razzāq al-Badr said,

There are a number of ḥadīths wherein the face of the Prophet ﷺ was likened to the moon, and this is only to explain his beauty because Allāh, the Most High, lavished him with a beauty that is far beyond the beauty of the moon.

ʿAlī al-Qārī said,

The part mentioning the red garment indicates that it made his beauty increase, thereby attracting one's eyes and attention.

The part where the narrator mentioned that he found him more beautiful than the moon in his eyes is not intended to state that others may not have considered such, rather the intention was to show his happiness at what he saw as every believing person would see him ﷺ as such.

١١ - حَدَّثَنَا سُفْيَانُ بْنُ وَكِيعٍ، حَدَّثَنَا حُمَيْدُ بْنُ عَبْدِ الرَّحْمَنِ الرُّؤَاسِيُّ، عَنْ زُهَيْرٍ، عَنْ أَبِي إِسْحَاقَ، قَالَ: سَأَلَ رَجُلٌ الْبَرَاءَ بْنَ عَازِبٍ: «أَكَانَ وَجْهُ رَسُولِ اللهِ صلى الله عليه وسلم مِثْلَ السَّيْفِ؟ قَالَ: لا، بَلْ مِثْلَ الْقَمَرِ».[٢٠]

11. Abū Isḥāq related: "A person asked al-Barāʾ b. ʿĀzib ؓ, 'Was the face of Allāh's Messenger ﷺ like a sword?' He replied, 'No, it was like the moon.'"

ʿAbd al-Razzāq al-Badr said,

Al-Ḥāfiẓ Ibn Ḥajar commented on this ḥadīth in *Fatḥ al-Bārī* saying, "It appears as if the questioner intended to ask if his face was long like how a sword is; hence the answer gave the example of the moon to show that his face was more rounded, and it is possible that he intend-

20 *Ṣaḥīḥ al-Bukhārī* (3549) and *Sunan al-Tirmidhī* (3636)

ed to ask if his face was as bright and refined as a sword, so the answer was the moon to show that the brightness of his face surpassed that of the sword and so selecting the moon was to combine both qualities."

١٢ - حَدَّثَنَا أَبُو دَاوُدَ الْمَصَاحِفِيُّ سُلَيْمَانُ بْنُ سَلْمٍ، قَالَ: حَدَّثَنَا النَّضْرُ بْنُ شُمَيْلٍ، عَنْ صَالِحِ بْنِ أَبِي الأَخْضَرِ، عَنِ ابْنِ شِهَابٍ، عَنْ أَبِي سَلَمَةَ، عَنْ أَبِي هُرَيْرَةَ، قَالَ: «كَانَ رَسُولُ اللهِ صلى الله عليه وسلم أَبْيَضَ كَأَنَّمَا صِيغَ مِنْ فِضَّةٍ، رَجِلَ الشَّعْرِ».[٢١]

12. Abū Hurayrah ﷺ narrated: "The skin tone of the Messenger of Allāh ﷺ was white to a degree that it seemed as if he was moulded from silver, and his hair was slightly curled."

Ibn Ḥajar al-Haytamī said,

> The expression of "... moulded in silver" refers to the brightness and light shining from his skin. It will come under the chapter of the recitation of the Prophet ﷺ that he said, "Allāh has not sent a Prophet except that he has a beautiful face and a beautiful voice, and your Prophet (i.e. Muḥammad) has the most beautiful face and most beautiful voice among them." This indicates that he was more handsome than Prophet Yūsuf ﷺ.

١٣ - حَدَّثَنَا قُتَيْبَةُ بْنُ سَعِيدٍ، قَالَ: أَخْبَرَنِي اللَّيْثُ بْنُ سَعْدٍ، عَنْ أَبِي الزُّبَيْرِ، عَنْ جَابِرِ بْنِ عَبْدِ اللهِ، أَنَّ رَسُولَ اللهِ صلى الله عليه وسلم، قَالَ: «عُرِضَ عَلَيَّ الأَنْبِيَاءُ، فَإِذَا مُوسَى عَلَيْهِ السَّلامُ ضَرْبٌ مِنَ الرِّجَالِ، كَأَنَّهُ مِنْ رِجَالِ شَنُوءَةَ، وَرَأَيْتُ عِيسَى بْنَ مَرْيَمَ عَلَيْهِ السَّلامُ، فَإِذَا أَقْرَبُ مَنْ رَأَيْتُ بِهِ شَبَهًا عُرْوَةُ بْنُ مَسْعُودٍ، وَرَأَيْتُ إِبْرَاهِيمَ عَلَيْهِ السَّلامُ، فَإِذَا أَقْرَبُ مَنْ رَأَيْتُ بِهِ شَبَهًا صَاحِبُكُمْ - يَعْنِي نَفْسَهُ -، وَرَأَيْتُ جِبْرِيلَ عَلَيْهِ السَّلامُ، فَإِذَا أَقْرَبُ مَنْ رَأَيْتُ بِهِ شَبَهًا دِحْيَةُ».[٢٢]

13. Jābir b. ʿAbd Allāh ﷺ narrated that the Messenger of Allāh ﷺ said: "The Prophets were shown to me. I saw Mūsa ﷺ and his build and height were medium as if he was from the tribe of Shanu'ah. I saw ʿĪsā ﷺ and from among all those whom I have seen, ʿUrwah b. Masʿūd resembled him the most. I saw Ibrāhīm ﷺ and from among

21 *Al-Jāmīʿ al-Ṣaghīr* (6471)
22 *Ṣaḥīḥ Muslim* (167)

all those that I have seen, I resembled him the most. I saw Angel Jibrīl عليه السلام and from among all those I have seen, Diḥyyah resembled him the most."

ʿAbd al-Razzāq al-Badr said,

> It is possible that they were shown to him in a dream or when he ascended to the heavens. The tribe of Shanu'ah is from Yemen and were known for having strong bodies and good physical stature.

Ibn Ḥajar al-Haytamī said,

> Diḥyyah رضي الله عنه was one of the companions and he was considered to be from amongst the most handsome and good looking men. It happened in many cases that Jibrīl عليه السلام used to appear in the form of this companion.

ʿAlī al-Qārī said,

> Mīrak stated that this event took place during the night the Prophet ﷺ ascended to the sky as explained in many other authentic ḥadīths, but some reports state that this event happened in different places. However, the most correct view, as it appears to be, is that he ﷺ met them in the heavens after he ascended and then when he descended he gathered with them in Bayt al-Maqdis where he led them in prayers.
>
> Perhaps, the reason why the names of only these three prophets were mentioned is because Ibrāhīm عليه السلام is the forefather of the Arabs and he is accepted by all faiths, while Mūsā عليه السلام and ʿĪsa عليه السلام are Prophets of the People of the Book.

١٤- حَدَّثَنَا سُفْيَانُ بْنُ وَكِيعٍ، وَمُحَمَّدُ بْنُ بَشَّارٍ - الْمَعْنَىٰ وَاحِدٌ - قَالَا: أَخْبَرَنَا يَزِيدُ بْنُ هَارُونَ، عَنْ سَعِيدٍ الْجُرَيْرِيِّ قَالَ: سَمِعْتُ أَبَا الطُّفَيْلِ يَقُولُ: «رَأَيْتُ النَّبِيَّ صلى الله عليه وسلم وَمَا بَقِيَ عَلَىٰ وَجْهِ الْأَرْضِ أَحَدٌ رَآهُ غَيْرِي»، قُلْتُ: صِفْهُ لِي، قَالَ: «كَانَ أَبْيَضَ مَلِيحًا مُقَصَّدًا».[٢٣]

14. Saʿīd al-Jurayrī narrated: "I heard Abū al-Ṭufayl رضي الله عنه say, 'I saw the Prophet ﷺ, and no one who saw him remains on the earth besides me.' I asked him to describe him to me and so he said, 'He ﷺ was a

---

23 *Ṣaḥīḥ Muslim* (2339)

handsome man with a white complexion and his body was moderate.'"

'Alī al-Qārī said,

> Abū al-Ṭufayl ﷺ was the last surviving companion of the Prophet ﷺ. He passed away in 110 after Hijrah.

Ibn Ḥajar al-Haytamī said,

> Abū al-Ṭufayl is 'Āmir b. Wāthilah al-Laythī and he saw the Prophet ﷺ during the last eight years of his life.

Al-Bājūrī said,

> **"I saw the Prophet ﷺ, and no one who saw him remains on the earth besides me":** I.e. from mankind, which omits the angels and jinn. His statement **"on the earth besides me"** omits 'Īsā, as he is not on the face of the earth.

'Abd al-Razzāq al-Badr said,

> **"His body was moderate"** means that he was moderate in all physical aspects, whether in terms of height, skin tone, build and hair type etc.

١٥ – حَدَّثَنَا عَبْدُ اللهِ بْنُ عَبْدِ الرَّحْمَنِ، قَالَ: حَدَّثَنَا إِبْرَاهِيمُ بْنُ الْمُنْذِرِ الْحِزَامِيُّ، قَالَ : حَدَّثَنَا عَبْدُ الْعَزِيزِ بْنُ أَبِي ثَابِتٍ الزُّهْرِيُّ، قَالَ: حَدَّثَنِي إِسْمَاعِيلُ بْنُ إِبْرَاهِيمَ ابْنُ أَخِي مُوسَىٰ بْنِ عُقْبَةَ، عَنْ مُوسَىٰ بْنِ عُقْبَةَ ، عَنْ كُرَيْبٍ، عَنِ ابْنِ عَبَّاسٍ، قَالَ: «كَانَ رَسُولُ اللهِ صلىٰ الله عليه وسلم أَفْلَجَ الثَّنِيَّتَيْنِ، إِذَا تَكَلَّمَ رُئِيَ كَالنُّورِ يَخْرُجُ مِنْ بَيْنِ ثَنَايَاهُ». [٢٤]

15. 'Abdullāh b. 'Abbās ﷺ narrated: "There was a space between the front teeth of the Messenger of Allāh ﷺ. Whenever he talked, it was as if light could be seen emitting from his mouth."

'Alī al-Qārī said,

> **"[It was as if] light could be seen emitting from his mouth":** The letter *kāf* [in the Arabic] is a noun which means "like". It has

24 *Mu'jam al-Ṭabarānī al-Kabīr* (12181)

also been said to be an additional *kāf* for *tafkhīm* (aggrandisement), as stated by Ibn Ḥajar al-Haytamī [who stated that it could mean an actual emitting of light].

ʿAbd al-Razzāq al-Badr said,

There are many ḥadīths describing the Prophet ﷺ having light emitting from between his teeth and that his face was as bright as the moon and so forth. This has caused some authors on the Prophetic description to err as they have understood this literally, as in actual light that shines and enlightens all that surrounds him. In fact, some went to such extremes that they claimed that he did not possess a shadow due to this light. This understanding is obviously fallacious and there are many ḥadīths that prove it to be untenable, one of which is the report of ʿĀʾishah ◉, which is documented in *Ṣaḥīḥ Muslim*, wherein she narrated that she woke up in the night and did not find the Prophet ﷺ in bed, so she began to search for him in the dark using her hands until they landed on his feet while he was saying, "*O Allāh! I seek refuge in Your pleasure from Your anger, and in Your forgiveness from Your punishment. I seek refuge with You from You. I cannot count Your praises. You are as You have praised Yourself.*"[25] If the light referred to in these ḥadīths was an actual light, she would not have needed to search for him in the dark using her hands.

---

25 Reported by Muslim (486).

باب ما جاء في خاتم النبوة

[2] On the Seal of Prophethood

ʿAbd al-Razzāq al-Badr said,

> This is a sub-chapter of the previous one as it is still detailing the physical appearance of the Prophet ﷺ. The scholars are in agreement that it is a sign of his prophethood, but they differ upon whether it was present at his birth or if it arose later. The view which is supported by narrations and evidence is that it arose during the event wherein Jibrīl split open his chest and washed his heart. It was sealed at that event.

ʿAlī al-Qārī said,

> The title of this chapter entails that it will describe the colour, shape, location of the seal and that it is from the signs known to the People of the Book.

Ibn Ḥajar al-Haytamī said,

> The reason it was called a seal was to indicate the authenticity of his prophethood just like how a seal is used to certify the authenticity of documents. It could also be to signify that he is the last prophet as the term "seal" is often used in reference to the end of something.

١٦ – حَدَّثَنَا أَبُو رَجَاءٍ قُتَيْبَةُ بْنُ سَعِيدٍ، قَالَ: حَدَّثَنَا حَاتِمُ بْنُ إِسْمَاعِيلَ، عَنِ الْجَعْدِ بْنِ عَبْدِ الرَّحْمَنِ، قَالَ: سَمِعْتُ السَّائِبَ بْنَ يَزِيدَ، يَقُولُ: «ذَهَبَتْ بِي خَالَتِي إِلَىٰ النَّبِيِّ صلىٰ الله عليه وسلم، فَقَالَتْ: يَا رَسُولَ اللهِ! إِنَّ ابْنَ أُخْتِي وَجِعٌ، فَمَسَحَ رَأْسِي وَدَعَا لِي بِالْبَرَكَةِ، وَتَوَضَّأَ، فَشَرِبْتُ مِنْ وَضُوئِهِ، وَقُمْتُ خَلْفَ ظَهْرِهِ، فَنَظَرْتُ إِلَىٰ الْخَاتَمِ بَيْنَ كَتِفَيْهِ، فَإِذَا هُوَ مِثْلُ زِرِّ الْحَجَلَةِ».[٢٦]

16. Al-Sāʾib b. Yazīd ؓ narrated: "My maternal aunt took me to the Prophet ﷺ and said to him, 'O Messenger of Allāh, this nephew of

---

26 *Ṣaḥīḥ al-Bukhārī* (190) and *Ṣaḥīḥ Muslim* (2345)

mine is ill.' The Prophet ﷺ then wiped his hand over my head and supplicated to Allāh to bless me. Then he ﷺ performed ablution and I drank from the water of his ablution. I stood to his back and saw the seal of prophethood between his shoulders; it was similar to the egg of a partridge."

'Abd al-Razzāq al-Badr said,

> **"This nephew of mine is ill"**: In other ḥadīths, it was mentioned that she said to the Prophet ﷺ that her nephew fell down. This made scholars conclude that the injury was to his foot, and this is what al-Ḥāfiẓ Ibn Ḥajar affirmed after he acknowledged the other ḥadīths.
>
> **"Wiped his hand over my head":** The Prophet ﷺ rubbed the head instead of the injured area as this is a more kind and sympathetic gesture and through it he could examine the boy's heartbeat and body temperature.
>
> **"I drank from the water of his ablution":** The use of the remnants of water that the Prophet ﷺ made ablution with for remedy and treatment was practiced by his companions. However, this attribute is exclusive to him and thus no one should seek remedy or blessing through anyone else's spit, hair, sweat or leftovers etc., regardless of their high status and virtue.
>
> **"Between his shoulders":** This is a rough estimate as the seal's location was not perfectly central, rather it was closer to the left shoulder blade. Some scholars said that the wisdom of the seal being placed closer to the left side was because that location is closer to the heart.

'Alī al-Qārī said,

> Al-Bayhaqī and others reported that the touch of the Prophet ﷺ on the hair of al-Sā'ib ؓ caused his hair to stay black until he died, though grey hairs appeared on his other body parts. The supplication of the Prophet ﷺ was answered in regards to al-Sā'ib. In *Ṣaḥīḥ al-Bukhārī*, a narration of al-Ja'd states that he saw al-Sā'ib b. Yazīd when he was ninety-four years old and he had a strong, upright posture. He said, "I know that I do not enjoy my hearing and sight except via the blessing of the Prophet's ﷺ supplication."

Ibn Ḥajar al-Haytamī said,

"This nephew of mine is ill": The boy had pain in his feet and the reason why the Prophet ﷺ wiped his head instead, was either because the boy felt pain in his head as well or because wiping the head is more noble than wiping the feet.

١٧ - حَدَّثَنَا سَعِيدُ بْنُ يَعْقُوبَ الطَّالْقَانِيُّ قَالَ: حَدَّثَنَا أَيُّوبُ بْنُ جَابِرٍ، عَنْ سِمَاكِ بْنِ حَرْبٍ، عَنْ جَابِرِ بْنِ سَمُرَةَ، قَالَ: ﴿رَأَيْتُ الْخَاتَمَ بَيْنَ كَتِفَيْ رَسُولِ اللهِ صلى الله عليه وسلم غُدَّةً حَمْرَاءَ مِثْلَ بَيْضَةِ الْحَمَامَةِ﴾. ٢٧

17. Jābir b. Samurah ؓ related: "I saw the seal of the prophethood of Allāh's Messenger ﷺ between his two shoulders. It was red raised flesh that appeared like a pigeon's egg."

'Abd al-Razzāq al-Badr said,

"Between his two shoulders": This gives the approximate location only and it is not intended to identify the exact location of the seal. This is because the seal was positioned closer to the left shoulder.

The colour of the seal has been established to be red, just like the colour of the rest of his body.

'Alī al-Qārī said,

"Like a pigeon's egg": This shows the similarity between the size, colour and shape of the pigeon's egg and the seal. Though this comparison entails that the colour of the seal is white, it does not contradict the fact that the skin tone of the Prophet ﷺ was white with some redness. Also, it is possible that the [comparison with something of] white colour was intended to indicate pureness.

Ibn Ḥajar al-Haytamī said,

"It was red raised flesh": This indicates that its colour was the same as his skin.

١٨ - حَدَّثَنَا أَبُو مُصْعَبٍ الْمَدِينِيُّ قَالَ: حَدَّثَنَا يُوسُفُ بْنُ الْمَاجِشُونِ، عَنْ أَبِيهِ، عَنْ عَاصِمِ بْنِ عُمَرَ بْنِ قَتَادَةَ، عَنْ جَدَّتِهِ رُمَيْثَةَ، قَالَتْ: سَمِعْتُ رَسُولَ اللهِ صلى الله

---

27 *Sunan al-Tirmidhī* (3643)

عليه وسلم - وَلَوْ أَشَاءُ أَنْ أُقَبِّلَ الْخَاتَمَ الَّذِي بَيْنَ كَتِفَيْهِ مِنْ قُرْبِهِ لَفَعَلْتُ - يَقُولُ لِسَعْدِ بْنِ مُعَاذٍ يَوْمَ مَاتَ: «اهْتَزَّ لَهُ عَرْشُ الرَّحْمَنِ». [28]

18. Rumaythah رضي الله عنها said: "I heard the Messenger of Allāh ﷺ – and at that time the distance between us was very small, such that if I wanted to, I could have kissed the seal of prophethood between his shoulders – saying after the death of Sā'd b. Mu'ādh رضي الله عنه, 'The Throne of Allāh shook for him.'"

'Abd al-Razzāq al-Badr said,

> **"The distance between us was very small":** This is to affirm that she heard him.
>
> **"The Throne of Allāh shook for him":** The largest creation of Allāh shaking for him shows the great virtue and status of the companion Sā'd b. Mu'ādh رضي الله عنه.

Al-Bājūrī said,

> **"I saw the Prophet ﷺ, and no one who saw him remains on the earth besides me":** Ṣa'd b. Mu'ādh is from the eminent companions. He witnessed Badr and stood firm with the Prophet ﷺ on the day of Uhud.

'Alī al-Qārī said,

> **"The death of Sā'd b. Mu'ādh":** He was the master of the tribe of the Anṣār and he died at the age of thirty seven due to an injury he sustained during the Battle of the Trench.
>
> When the hypocrites joked that his coffin was light, the Prophet ﷺ said that he was carried by seventy thousand angels.

Ibn Ḥajar al-Haytamī said,

> **"The Throne of Allāh shook for him":** It shook literally because it was happy that his soul had ascended above and also to make the angels aware of his virtues and his death. In another interpretation, it was argued that the word "shook" was used metaphorically to mean rejoicing at his arrival.

---

28 *Musnad Aḥmad* (26793)

١٩ - حَدَّثَنَا أَحْمَدُ بْنُ عَبْدَةَ الضَّبِّيُّ، وَعَلِيُّ بْنُ حُجْرٍ، وَغَيْرُ وَاحِدٍ، قَالُوا: حَدَّثَنَا عِيسَىٰ بْنُ يُونُسَ، عَنْ عُمَرَ بْنِ عَبْدِ اللهِ مَوْلَىٰ غُفْرَةَ، قَالَ: حَدَّثَنِي إِبْرَاهِيمُ بْنُ مُحَمَّدٍ - مِنْ وَلَدِ عَلِيِّ بْنِ أَبِي طَالِبٍ - قَالَ: كَانَ عَلِيٌّ إِذَا وَصَفَ رَسُولَ اللهِ صلى الله عليه وسلم - فَذَكَرَ الْحَدِيثَ بِطُولِهِ - وَقَالَ: «بَيْنَ كَتِفَيْهِ خَاتَمُ النُّبُوَّةِ، وَهُوَ خَاتَمُ النَّبِيِّينَ».٢٩

19. Ibrāhīm b. Muḥammad, from the offspring of ʿAlī b. Abī Ṭālib, said: "Whenever ʿAlī ؓ used to describe the Prophet ﷺ, he would narrate the complete ḥadīth and then add, 'The seal of prophethood was between his shoulders, and he was the seal of all Prophets.[30]'"

ʿAlī al-Qārī said,

> This report was mentioned earlier in the first chapter. The purpose of repeating it in this chapter is the statement, **"The seal of prophethood was between his shoulders"**. This affirms the presence of the seal, and specifies its position on the Prophet's ﷺ body.

٢٠ - حَدَّثَنَا مُحَمَّدُ بْنُ بَشَّارٍ، قَالَ: حَدَّثَنَا أَبُو عَاصِمٍ، قَالَ: حَدَّثَنَا عَزْرَةُ بْنُ ثَابِتٍ، قَالَ: حَدَّثَنِي عِلْبَاءُ بْنُ أَحْمَرَ الْيَشْكُرِيُّ، قَالَ: حَدَّثَنِي أَبُو زَيْدٍ عَمْرُو بْنُ أَخْطَبَ الْأَنْصَارِيُّ، قَالَ: قَالَ لِي رَسُولُ اللهِ صلى الله عليه وسلم: «يَا أَبَا زَيْدٍ، ادْنُ مِنِّي فَامْسَحْ ظَهْرِي»، فَمَسَحْتُ ظَهْرَهُ، فَوَقَعَتْ أَصَابِعِي عَلَى الْخَاتَمِ، قُلْتُ: وَمَا الْخَاتَمُ؟ قَالَ: شَعَرَاتٌ مُجْتَمِعَاتٌ.٣١

20. Ilbāʾ b. Aḥmar al-Yashkurī narrated that Abū Zayd ʿAmr b. Akhṭab al-Anṣārī ؓ said: "The Messenger of Allāh ﷺ said to me, 'O Abū Zayd, come closer to me and rub my back.' I began rubbing his back and I felt the seal of prophethood." Ilbāʾ asked ʿAmr ؓ, "What is the seal of prophethood?" He replied, "It was a collection of a few hairs."

Ibn Ḥajar al-Haytamī said,

---

29 See footnote 7

30 It refers to ḥadīth six in this book wherein ʿAlī b. Abī Ṭālib ؓ described the Prophet ﷺ in detail. This ḥadīth is included here because of the addition related to the seal of prophethood.

31 *Musnad Aḥmad* (20732)

"Rub my back": This indicates that it is permissible for one person to touch the body of another person provided that both are from the same gender and the area touched is not from the *'awrah*.

'Abd al-Razzāq al-Badr said,

"O Abū Zayd": This shows the kindness and politeness of the Prophet ﷺ when dealing with his companions i.e. he called his companion using his *kunyah* and not his actual name.

"It was a collection of a few hairs": He stated this based on what his hand touched. However, the seal was not just a collection of hairs. It was a piece of flesh roughly the size of an egg and it was surrounded by a few hairs. His hand touched the hairs. Thus, there is no contradiction between this and the previous accounts.

In a different version of this ḥadīth documented in the *Musnad* of al-Imām Aḥmad, the Prophet ﷺ wiped his hand over his beard and hair and said, "O Allāh, beautify him and make his beauty last." The supplication was answered and Abū Zayd lived over one hundred years, having hardly any grey hairs and skin without wrinkles.

We can also benefit from the supplication of the Prophet ﷺ if we look after his Sunnah and blessed narrations, in memorisation, understanding, action and propagating to them. This is because he said, "May Allāh enlighten the face of a person who hears my words, preserves them and delivers them to others as he heard from me."[32] This is why Sufyān b. 'Uyaynah said, "No one seeks the knowledge of ḥadīth except that his face has brightness."

'Alī al-Qārī said,

'Amr b. Akhṭab al-Ansārī was one of the four companions [from the Ansār] who gathered the entire Qur'ān during the Prophet's ﷺ life.

"Rub my back": He was asked to do so either because the Prophet ﷺ needed to scratch his back, or to check if there was something harmful on his garment, or to receive the honour of touching his noble body.

٢١- حَدَّثَنَا أَبُو عَمَّارٍ الْحُسَيْنُ بْنُ حُرَيْثٍ الْخُزَاعِيُّ، قَالَ: حَدَّثَنَا عَلِيُّ بْنُ حُسَيْنٍ

32 *Sunan al-Tirmidhī* (2658) and *Sunan Ibn Mājah* (230)

بْنِ وَاقِدٍ، قَالَ حَدَّثَنِي أَبِي، قَالَ: حَدَّثَنِي عَبْدُ اللهِ بْنُ بُرَيْدَةَ، قَالَ: سَمِعْتُ أَبِي بُرَيْدَةَ، يَقُولُ: جَاءَ سَلْمَانُ الْفَارِسِيُّ إِلَىٰ رَسُولِ اللهِ صلىٰ الله عليه وسلم حِينَ قَدِمَ الْمَدِينَةَ بِمَائِدَةٍ عَلَيْهَا رُطَبٌ، فَوَضَعَهَا بَيْنَ يَدَيْ رَسُولِ اللهِ صلىٰ الله عليه وسلم، فَقَالَ: «يَا سَلْمَانُ مَا هَذَا؟» فَقَالَ: صَدَقَةٌ عَلَيْكَ وَعَلَىٰ أَصْحَابِكَ، فَقَالَ: «ارْفَعْهَا؛ فَإِنَّا لا نَأْكُلُ الصَّدَقَةَ»، قَالَ: فَرَفَعَهَا، فَجَاءَ الْغَدَ بِمِثْلِهِ، فَوَضَعَهُ بَيْنَ يَدَيْ رَسُولِ اللهِ صلىٰ الله عليه وسلم، فَقَالَ: «مَا هَذَا يَا سَلْمَانُ؟» فَقَالَ: هَدِيَّةٌ لَكَ، فَقَالَ رَسُولُ اللهِ صلىٰ الله عليه وسلم لأَصْحَابِهِ: «ابْسُطُوا»، ثُمَّ نَظَرَ إِلَىٰ الْخَاتَمِ عَلَىٰ ظَهْرِ رَسُولِ اللهِ صلىٰ الله عليه وسلم فَآمَنَ بِهِ، وَكَانَ لِلْيَهُودِ؛ فَاشْتَرَاهُ رَسُولُ اللهِ صلىٰ الله عليه وسلم بِكَذَا وَكَذَا دِرْهَمًا عَلَىٰ أَنْ يَغْرِسَ لَهُمْ نَخْلا، فَيَعْمَلَ سَلْمَانُ فِيهِ حَتَّىٰ تُطْعِمَ، فَغَرَسَ رَسُولُ اللهِ صلىٰ الله عليه وسلم النَّخلَ إِلا نَخْلَةً وَاحِدَةً غَرَسَهَا عُمَرُ، فَحَمَلَتِ النَّخْلُ مِنْ عَامِهَا وَلَمْ تَحْمِلْ نَخْلَةٌ، فَقَالَ رَسُولُ اللهِ صلىٰ الله عليه وسلم: «مَا شَأْنُ هَذِهِ النَّخْلَةِ؟» فَقَالَ عُمَرُ: يَا رَسُولَ اللهِ، أَنَا غَرَسْتُهَا، فَنَزَعَهَا رَسُولُ اللهِ صلىٰ الله عليه وسلم، فَغَرَسَهَا فَحَمَلَتْ مِنْ عَامِهَا.[٣٣]

21. Buraydah ﷺ narrated: "When Salmān al-Fārisī ﷺ came to Madīnah, he visited the Prophet ﷺ and brought a tray on which there were some dates that he placed before the Prophet ﷺ. The Prophet ﷺ asked, 'What are these?' He replied, 'This is an almsgiving to you and your companions.' Allāh's Messenger ﷺ replied, 'We do not eat from charity; take it away from me.' And so Salmān complied and removed them. On the next day he brought some dates and placed them in front of the Prophet ﷺ who asked him, 'O Salmān, what are these?' To which he replied, 'O Messenger of Allāh, it is a present for you.' The Prophet ﷺ invited his companions to eat from these dates. He then saw the seal of prophethood on the back of Allāh's Messenger ﷺ and embraced Islām.

At that time, he was a slave to a Jew so the Prophet ﷺ made an agreement with his master to grant Salmān his freedom in return of a sum of money and after the planting of [a particular number of] date palms for the Jew that Salmān would tend to until they produced dates. The Messenger of Allāh ﷺ planted all the date palms except one

33 *Musnad Aḥmad* (22997)

that 'Umar ⁓ planted. On the same year, all the date palms produced dates except one. So the Prophet ⁓ inquired about it and 'Umar replied that he planted that palm tree. The Prophet ⁓ then uprooted it and planted it again. Thereafter the palm tree produced dates in the same year."

'Abd al-Razzāq al-Badr said,

> The reason why Salmān ⁓ presented the dates to the Prophet ⁓ as a charity on the first occasion and as a gift on the second was because he sought to find the last prophet. He was aware that from the signs of this prophet was that he does not eat from charity but he accepts that which is gifted to him. The other sign that he looked for was the seal which he saw on his back.

> **"All the date palms produced dates except one":** The wisdom behind this was so that the miracle of the Prophet ⁓ could be displayed to the people.

Ibn Ḥajar al-Haytamī said,

> **"We do not eat from charity":** This includes both the obligatory and voluntary charity as well as all that which is deemed obligatory in religion such as compensation and vows.

> **"The Prophet ⁓ agreed with his master to free him... In return of":** It can be concluded from this that it is recommended to help slaves free themselves.

'Alī al-Qārī said,

> **"This is an almsgiving to you and your companions":** One of the commentators said that charity is something that the superior gives to the inferior, seeking the reward in the Hereafter and it entails that the receiver is pitiable. In contrast, a gift is a means to seek closeness to the recipient and it does not entail any sense of pity towards the recipient.

> **"We do not eat from charity":** The pronoun refers to the Prophet as well as his relatives from the tribe of Banū Hāshim and al-Muṭṭalib. It does not include the Companions.

> **"O Salmān, what are these?":** The Prophet ⁓ addressed him on the first occasion without mentioning his name but on the second occa-

sion he mentioned his name to show more kindness as he felt he was about to embrace Islām.

٢٢ - حَدَّثَنَا مُحَمَّدُ بْنُ بَشَّارٍ، قَالَ : حَدَّثَنَا بِشْرُ بْنُ الْوَضَّاحِ، قَالَ: حَدَّثَنَا أَبُو عَقِيلٍ الدَّوْرَقِيُّ، عَنْ أَبِي نَضْرَةَ الْعَوَقِيِّ، قَالَ: سَأَلْتُ أَبَا سَعِيدٍ الْخُدْرِيَّ، عَنْ خَاتَمِ رَسُولِ اللهِ صلىٰ الله عليه وسلم - يَعْنِي خَاتَمَ النُّبُوَّةِ - فَقَالَ : كَانَ فِي ظَهْرِهِ بَضْعَةٌ نَاشِزَةٌ.[٣٤]

22. Abū Naḍrah al-ʿAwaqī related: "I asked Abū Saʿīd al-Khudrī ﵁ about the seal of prophethood of Allāh's Messenger ﷺ. He said, 'It was a raised piece of flesh on his back.'"

ʿAbd al-Razzāq al-Badr said,

> **"... On his back":** As other ḥadīths show, the seal was located on his back between the two shoulders and it was closer to the left one.

٢٣ - حَدَّثَنَا أَحْمَدُ بْنُ الْمِقْدَامِ أَبُو الأَشْعَثِ الْعِجْلِيُّ الْبَصْرِيُّ، قَالَ: أَخْبَرَنَا حَمَّادُ بْنُ زَيْدٍ، عَنْ عَاصِمٍ الأَحْوَلِ، عَنْ عَبْدِ اللهِ بْنِ سَرْجِسَ، قَالَ: أَتَيْتُ رَسُولَ اللهِ صلىٰ الله عليه وسلم وَهُوَ فِي نَاسٍ مِنْ أَصْحَابِهِ، فَدُرْتُ هَكَذَا مِنْ خَلْفِهِ، فَعَرَفَ الَّذِي أُرِيدُ، فَأَلْقَىٰ الرِّدَاءَ عَنْ ظَهْرِهِ، فَرَأَيْتُ مَوْضِعَ الْخَاتَمِ عَلَىٰ كَتِفَيْهِ مِثْلَ الْجُمْعِ حَوْلَهَا خِيلَانٌ كَأَنَّهَا ثَآلِيلُ، فَرَجَعْتُ حَتَّىٰ اسْتَقْبَلْتُهُ، فَقُلْتُ: غَفَرَ اللهُ لَكَ يَا رَسُولَ اللهِ، فَقَالَ: «وَلَكَ» فَقَالَ الْقَوْمُ: أَسْتَغْفَرَ لَكَ رَسُولُ اللهِ صلىٰ الله عليه وسلم؟ فَقَالَ: نَعَمْ، وَلَكُمْ، ثُمَّ تَلَا هَذِهِ الآيَةَ ﴿وَٱسْتَغْفِرْ لِذَنۢبِكَ وَلِلْمُؤْمِنِينَ وَٱلْمُؤْمِنَٰتِ﴾ [مُحَمَّد: ١٩].[٣٥]

23. ʿAbdullāh b. Sarjis ﵁ narrated: "I came to Allāh's Messenger ﷺ while he was sitting with some of his companions. I went to stand behind him – like this – and so the Prophet ﷺ understood my purpose. So, he dropped the cloak he was wearing on his back and then I saw the place of the seal of prophethood on his shoulders. It was like a clenched fist surrounded by spots, which were akin to warts.

34 *Al-Jāmiʿ al-Saghīr* (6484)
35 *Ṣaḥīḥ Muslim* (2346)

I then returned and stood in front of him and said, 'O Messenger of Allāh, may Allāh forgive you.' To that he replied, 'May Allāh forgive you too.' The people said to me, 'Allāh's Messenger ﷺ has asked Allāh to forgive you?' I replied, 'Yes, and he asked Him to forgive you too.' Then, he recited, {[O Muḥammad] seek forgiveness for yourself and the believing males and females.}"

Ibn Ḥajar al-Haytamī said,

"**Understood my purpose**": He understood that the companion wanted to see the seal.

"**O Messenger of Allāh, may Allāh forgive you**": He said it to show his gratitude for allowing him to see the seal.

'Abd al-Razzāq al-Badr said,

"**It was like a clenched fist**": All the ḥadīths describing the size of the seal are similar though each narrator used different examples i.e. one used the size of a partridge's egg, one used the size of an egg, one used the example of a piece of flesh, and the last one used a clenched fist.

"**Allāh's Messenger ﷺ has asked Allāh to forgive you**": This was a statement they said to express the greatness of the supplication of the Prophet ﷺ. Some people err and misunderstand the statement of Allāh, the Exalted, wherein He said, {**And if, when they wronged themselves, they had come to you, [O Muḥammad], and asked forgiveness of Allāh and the Messenger had asked forgiveness for them, they would have found Allāh Accepting of repentance and Merciful.**}[36], thinking that he ﷺ would still ask Allāh to forgive people even after his death. The correct view is that he could ask Allāh to forgive people only during his lifetime as proven in the authentic ḥadīth in *Ṣaḥīḥ al-Bukhārī* when 'Ā'ishah ؓ said, "O my head!" Allāh's Messenger ﷺ said, "If that (your death) should happen while I am still alive, I would ask Allāh to forgive you and would invoke Allāh for you."[37]

The inquiry and surprise of the people who asked whether the Prophet ﷺ asked Allāh to forgive the narrator is another proof because if he

---

36 Qur'ān: 4:64
37 *Ṣaḥīḥ al-Bukhārī* (7217)

could do so after his death they would have not showed such surprise and wishful thinking. They knew that this opportunity only existed during the Prophet's lifetime.

ʿAlī al-Qārī said,

> It is a matter of fact that the Prophet ﷺ was infallible; hence the issue of him seeking Allāh's forgiveness is understood to mean either to forgive him for any thought that crossed his mind unwillingly (as it is the nature of mankind), or to mean that he asked Allāh to maintain his infallibility (though the fact that he was granted it shows his ultimate submission to Allāh), or it can mean that he asked Allāh to forgive his use of lawful matters and his inability to worship Allāh enough to fulfil His ﷻ due rights.

باب ما جاء في شعر رسول الله صلى الله عليه وسلم

[3] On the Hair of Allāh's Messenger ﷺ

ʿAbd al-Razzāq al-Badr said,

> This title is given to show that the subsequent section will include ḥadīths describing the hair of the Prophet ﷺ; its length, style, and how he used to look after it.

Al-Bājūrī said,

> Ibn al-ʿArabī said, "Hair on the head is an adornment. Keeping it is a Sunnah, and shaving it is an innovation." It states in *Sharḥ al-Maṣābīḥ*, "The Prophet ﷺ never shaved his head during the post-Hijrah times except in the year in which the treaty of Ḥudaybiyah took place, the ʿUmrah al-Qaḍāʾ (i.e. the ʿUmrah he performed in order to make up for the one he missed during the year of Ḥudaybiyah), and the farewell Ḥajj. And he only cut his hair short once, as reported in *Ṣaḥīḥ al-Bukhārī* and *Ṣaḥīḥ Muslim*.

٢٤- حَدَّثَنَا عَلِيُّ بْنُ حُجْرٍ، قَالَ: أَخْبَرَنَا إِسْمَاعِيلُ بْنُ إِبْرَاهِيمَ، عَنْ حُمَيْدٍ، عَنْ أَنَسِ بْنِ مَالِكٍ، قَالَ: «كَانَ شَعَرُ رَسُولِ اللهِ صلى الله عليه وسلم إِلَىٰ نِصْفِ أُذُنَيْهِ».[٣٨]

24. Anas b. Mālik ﷺ narrated: "The hair of Allāh's Messenger ﷺ reached to the mid-portion of his ears."

ʿAbd al-Razzāq al-Badr said,

> In other ḥadīths, the narrators stated that the length of the hair of the Prophet ﷺ reached to his shoulders; hence some scholars explained that this is because the length of his hair differed from one time to another and so each narrator described what he saw.

---

38 *Saḥīḥ Muslim* (2338)

Al-Suyūṭī said,

> Al-Ḥāfiẓ al-ʿIrāqī said, "The ḥadīths have provided three different descriptions of the hair of the Prophet ﷺ, namely:
>
> 1. *Wafrah*: It refers to having hair that reaches the earlobe.
> 2. *Lummah*: It refers to having hair that reaches below the earlobe
> 3. *Jummah*: It refers to shoulder length hair."

ʿAlī al-Qārī said,

> There are eights ḥadīths that describe the length of the hair of the Prophet ﷺ.

٢٥- حَدَّثَنَا هَنَّادُ بْنُ السَّرِيِّ، قَالَ: أَخْبَرَنَا عَبْدُ الرَّحْمَنِ بْنُ أَبِي الزِّنَادِ، عَنْ هِشَامِ بْنِ عُرْوَةَ، عَنْ أَبِيهِ، عَنْ عَائِشَةَ، قَالَتْ: «كُنْتُ أَغْتَسِلُ أَنَا وَرَسُولُ اللهِ صلى الله عليه وسلم مِنْ إِنَاءٍ وَاحِدٍ، وَكَانَ لَهُ شَعَرٌ فَوْقَ الْجُمَّةِ، وَدُونَ الْوَفْرَةِ».[٣٩]

25. ʿĀ'ishah ﵂ narrated: "I used to bathe with the Prophet ﷺ in one utensil, and his hair was below his earlobes but above his shoulders."

ʿAbd al-Razzāq al-Badr said,

> **"I used to bathe with the Prophet ﷺ in one utensil":** This displays the permissibility of spouses bathing from a single vessel.

Ibn Ḥajar al-Haytamī said,

> This ḥadīth is evidence that the water remaining from the bath of women is ritually pure.

٢٦- حَدَّثَنَا أَحْمَدُ بْنُ مَنِيعٍ، قَالَ: حَدَّثَنَا أَبُو قَطَنٍ، قَالَ: حَدَّثَنَا شُعْبَةُ، عَنْ أَبِي إِسْحَاقَ، عَنِ الْبَرَاءِ بْنِ عَازِبٍ، قَالَ: «كَانَ رَسُولُ اللهِ صلى الله عليه وسلم مَرْبُوعًا، بَعِيدَ مَا بَيْنَ الْمِنْكَبَيْنِ، وَكَانَتْ جُمَّتُهُ تَضْرِبُ شَحْمَةَ أُذُنَيْهِ».[٤٠]

26. Al-Barā' b. ʿĀzib ﵁ narrated: "The Messenger of Allāh ﷺ was of average height, and the distance between his two shoulders was wide.

39 *Sunan al-Tirmidhī* (1755)
40 See footnote of ḥadīth 4

His hair would fall to his ear lobes."

Al-Bājūrī said,

> This narration was commented upon in the first chapter. The point of its being cited here is the part, **"His hair would fall to his ear lobes"**, meaning most of it would reach the ear lobes.

٢٧ - حَدَّثَنَا مُحَمَّدُ بْنُ بَشَّارٍ، قَالَ: حَدَّثَنَا وَهْبُ بْنُ جَرِيرِ بْنِ حَازِمٍ، قَالَ: حَدَّثَنِي أَبِي، عَنْ قَتَادَةَ، قَالَ: قُلْتُ لأَنَسٍ: «كَيْفَ كَانَ شَعَرُ رَسُولِ اللهِ صلى الله عليه وسلم؟ قَالَ: لَمْ يَكُنْ بِالْجَعْدِ وَلا بِالسَّبْطِ، كَانَ يَبْلُغُ شَعَرُهُ شَحْمَةَ أُذُنَيْهِ». [٤١]

27. Qatādah narrated: "I asked Anas b. Mālik ﵁, 'How was the hair of Allāh's Messenger ﷺ?' He replied, 'It was neither very curly nor very straight; it reached his earlobes.'"

ʿAbd al-Razzāq al-Badr said,

> The point of utilising this report here is the part, **"It reached his earlobes"**, which is a description of the Prophet's ﷺ hair during some occasions.

٢٨ - حَدَّثَنَا مُحَمَّدُ بْنُ يَحْيَى بْنِ أَبِي عُمَرَ الْمَكِّيُّ، قَالَ: حَدَّثَنَا سُفْيَانُ بْنُ عُيَيْنَةَ، عَنِ ابْنِ أَبِي نَجِيحٍ، عَنْ مُجَاهِدٍ، عَنْ أُمِّ هَانِئٍ بِنْتِ أَبِي طَالِبٍ، قَالَتْ: «قَدِمَ رَسُولُ اللهِ صلى الله عليه وسلم مَكَّةَ قَدْمَةً، وَلَهُ أَرْبَعُ غَدَائِرَ». [٤٢]

28. Umm Hāniʾ bint Abī Ṭālib ﵂ said: "Allāh's Messenger ﷺ entered Makkah and he had four plaits."

ʿAbd al-Razzāq al-Badr said,

> Umm Hāniʾ is the sister of ʿAlī b. Abī Ṭālib ﵁.

Ibn Ḥajar al-Haytamī said,

> It appears that she saw him on the day of the conquest of Makkah because he prayed the *Ḍuḥā* prayer in her house.

ʿAlī al-Qārī said,

---

41 *Ṣaḥīḥ al-Bukhārī* (5908) and *Ṣaḥīḥ Muslim* (2338)
42 *Sunan al-Tirmidhī* (1781)

The Prophet ﷺ entered Makkah four times [after the Hijrah]: (i) 'Umrah al-Qaḍā', (ii) the conquest of Makkah, (iii) 'Umrah al-Ji'rānah, (iv) the farewell Ḥajj.

٢٩- حَدَّثَنَا سُوَيْدُ بْنُ نَصْرٍ، قَالَ: حَدَّثَنَا عَبْدُ اللهِ بْنُ الْمُبَارَكِ، عَنْ مَعْمَرٍ، عَنْ ثَابِتٍ الْبُنَانِيِّ، عَنْ أَنَسٍ «أَنَّ شَعْرَ رَسُولِ اللهِ صلى الله عليه وسلم كَانَ إِلَى أَنْصَافِ أُذُنَيْهِ».[٤٣]

29. Thābit al-Bunānī reported that Anas b. Mālik ﵁ said: "The hair of Allāh's Messenger ﷺ reached the mid-portion of his ears."

Al-Bājūrī said,

> **"Reached the mid-portion of his ears":** [In the Arabic wording,] the plural form (أَنْصَافِ) is compounded to a dual word (أُذُنَيْهِ), as in the verse: **{If both of you [wives] repent to God––for your hearts have deviated:}**[44] The plural here means more than one.

٣٠- حَدَّثَنَا سُوَيْدُ بْنُ نَصْرٍ، حَدَّثَنَا عَبْدُ اللهِ بْنُ الْمُبَارَكِ، عَنْ يُونُسَ بْنِ يَزِيدَ، عَنِ الزُّهْرِيِّ قَالَ: حَدَّثَنَا عُبَيْدُ اللهِ بْنُ عَبْدِ اللهِ بْنِ عُتْبَةَ، عَنِ ابْنِ عَبَّاسٍ: «أَنَّ رَسُولَ اللهِ صلى الله عليه وسلم كَانَ يُسْدِلُ شَعْرَهُ، وَكَانَ الْمُشْرِكُونَ يَفْرِقُونَ رُؤُوسَهُمْ، وَكَانَ أَهْلُ الْكِتَابِ يُسْدِلُونَ رُؤُوسَهُمْ، وَكَانَ يُحِبُّ مُوَافَقَةَ أَهْلِ الْكِتَابِ فِيمَا لَمْ يُؤْمَرْ فِيهِ بِشَيْءٍ، ثُمَّ فَرَقَ رَسُولُ اللهِ صلى الله عليه وسلم رَأْسَهُ».[٤٥]

30. 'Abdullāh b. 'Abbās ﵁ narrated: "The hairstyle of the Messenger of Allāh ﷺ was *sadl* and the polytheists used to part their hair while the hairstyle of the People of the Book was *sadl*. He preferred not to oppose the People of the Book unless he was ordered otherwise. Then he would part his hair."

The meaning of *sadl* is disputed over among scholars, some of them (such as al-Bājūrī) stated that it means he let his hair hang down freely around the head, and some (such as al-Nawawī, al-Ṣuyūtī and 'Alī al-Qārī) were of the view that it means he let his hair fall on his forehead.

43 See footnote of ḥadīth 27

44 Al-Taḥrīm: 4

45 *Ṣaḥīḥ al-Bukhārī* (3588) and *Ṣaḥīḥ Muslim* (2336)

ʿAbd al-Razzāq al-Badr said,

> Ibn Ḥajar said that the last practice of the Prophet ﷺ was to part his hair.[46]

ʿAlī al-Qārī said,

> The Prophet ﷺ used to keep a hairstyle similar to that of the People of the Book because he preferred their way over the way of the polytheists, unless he was ordered to oppose them. This is because either they (Christians and Jews) have celestial religions, divine books and prophets, or because they are closer to the truth than the polytheists, since they followed some of the original teachings of their religion during that time (as the scholar Mīrak Shāh explained); hence they deserved better treatment than the polytheists.

Al-Bājūrī said,

> **"He preferred not to oppose the People of the Book unless he was ordered otherwise":** He liked to do so in matters where he was not ordered, regardless whether the divine order entailed an obligation or recommendation. Al-Qurṭubī said, "This was only at the beginning when he arrived at Madīnah, during the time he used to pray towards their *qiblah*. The reason behind this was that he wanted to soften their hearts towards Islām but when this approach did not show any benefit and their hearts remained hard, he ordered the Muslims to oppose them in many affairs.

٣١- حَدَّثَنَا مُحَمَّدُ بْنُ بَشَّارٍ، قَالَ: حَدَّثَنَا عَبْدُ الرَّحْمَنِ بْنُ مَهْدِيٍّ، عَنْ إِبْرَاهِيمَ بْنِ نَافِعٍ الْمَكِّيِّ، عَنِ ابْنِ أَبِي نَجِيحٍ، عَنْ مُجَاهِدٍ، عَنْ أُمِّ هَانِئٍ، قَالَتْ: «رَأَيْتُ رَسُولَ اللهِ صلىٰ الله عليه وسلم ذَا ضَفَائِرَ أَرْبَعٍ».[٤٧]

31. Umm Hānī' bint Abī Ṭālib رضي الله عنها said: "I saw Allāh's Messenger ﷺ having four plaits."

ʿAbd al-Razzāq al-Badr said,

> Al-Shaykh Muḥammad b. Ṣāliḥ al-ʿUthaymīn was asked, "Is it from the Sunnah to prolong the hair?" To which he replied, "No, it is not

46 *Fatḥ al-Bārī* (10/362)
47 See footnote of ḥadīth 28

> from the Sunnah because the Prophet ﷺ did so in a time in which that was the custom of people. This is why he ordered the young boy who shaved part of his head, 'Shave it all or leave it all.' If the hair is supposed to be left to grow long he would have ordered the boy to leave it all only... With that being said, if you live in a place where the custom of the people is to grow their hair long, then do so. Otherwise, do what is the custom of the people. A similar example is clothing. If it is not a forbidden type, the Sunnah is to follow the customs of the people. This is because the Prophet ﷺ followed the customs of the people.
>
> Thus, we say that the custom of the people today is that they do not grow the hair long. Furthermore, our major scholars – the foremost being our teacher, 'Abd al-Raḥmān b. al-Saʿdī, our teacher 'Abd al-ʿAzīz b. Bāz and others, such as al-Shaykh Muḥammad b. Ibrāhīm – did not grow their hair long, as they did not view this to be the Sunnah. We know that if they saw otherwise, they would be the most enthusiastic in following the Sunnah. Therefore, the correct opinion is that the Sunnah follows the custom of the people. If one is in a place where they keep the hair long, then one should do so, and if not then one should not."
>
> It is also worthy to mention that one must not imitate women or disbelievers. This is important to mention as we see some youth prolonging their hair and having their hair fashioned in the style of women, to the point they may use the accessories of women to hold their hair, and even worse, their faces are also clean shaved. He may look very similar to his sister due to this. Likewise some may simulate the disbelievers in their hairstyles or hair dyes, and some of them may argue that prolonging the hair is Sunnah when all the while they do not even commit to praying the obligatory prayers.[48]

Al-Bājūrī said,

> This shows that it is permissible for men to plait their hair and that it is not limited to women, even if it is often the practice of women to plait their hair in this era.

48 *Laqā'āt al-Bāb al-Maftūḥ* (p. 22).

باب ما جاء في ترجل رسول الله صلى الله عليه وسلم

[4] On the Hair Care of Allāh's Messenger ﷺ

ʿAbd al-Razzāq al-Badr said,

> The author dedicated this chapter to listing the ḥadīths that describe the combing and the hair care of the Prophet ﷺ.
>
> The Prophet ﷺ was moderate and balanced about his hair (as he was in all things); neither was he obsessed about his hair or negligent regarding it.

Al-Bājūrī said,

> Hair care is part of the cleanliness and personal hygiene that the legislator encouraged and recommended. The Prophet ﷺ said, "Cleanliness is from *īmān*"[49] and, "Whoever has hair should honour it."[50] There are five ḥadīths in this chapter.

٣٢- حدثنا إسحاق بن موسىٰ الأنصاري، قَالَ: حدثنا مَعْن بن عيسىٰ، قَالَ: حدثنا مالك بن أنس، عَنْ هِشَامِ بْنِ عُرْوَةَ، عَنْ أَبِيهِ، عَنْ عَائِشَةَ، قَالَتْ: «كُنْتُ أُرَجِّلُ رَأْسَ رَسُولِ اللهِ صلىٰ الله عليه وسلم وَأَنَا حَائِضٌ».[٥١]

32. ʿĀ'ishah ﵂ related: "I used to comb the hair of Allāh's Messenger ﷺ even whilst I was in the state of menstruation."

ʿAbd al-Razzāq al-Badr said,

> This is evidence that it is permissible for the wife to comb the hair of her husband and touch him while she is menstruating, and that the body of a menstruating woman is not deemed ritually impure.

Ibn Ḥajar al-Haytamī said,

---

49 This statement is not from the words of the Prophet ﷺ but the meaning is indicated and supported in other ḥadīths.

50 *Sunan Abī Dāwūd* (4163)

51 *Ṣaḥīḥ al-Bukhārī* (295) and *Ṣaḥīḥ Muslim* (297)

> This is evidence that it is only the menstrual blood of the woman that is ritually impure while the rest of her body is pure. There is consensus on this issue. Furthermore, it is not detested to mix with her, utilise her cooking, things such as lying with her, and drinking from something she has drank from. It also shows that the wife should look after her husband in all cases, and that she can still spend time with her husband during menses as avoiding the wife during her menses is the way of the Jews.

Al-Bājūrī said,

> This ḥadīth shows that it is recommended to comb the hair, and to comb the beard as well, based on analogy.

٣٣- حَدَّثَنَا يُوسُفُ بْنُ عِيسَىٰ، قَالَ: حَدَّثَنَا وَكِيعٌ، قَالَ: حَدَّثَنَا الرَّبِيعُ بْنُ صَبِيحٍ، عَنْ يَزِيدَ بْنِ أَبَانَ - هُوَ الرَّقَاشِيُّ -، عَنْ أَنَسِ بْنِ مَالِكٍ، قَالَ: «كَانَ رَسُولُ اللهِ صلىٰ الله عليه وسلم يُكْثِرُ دَهْنَ رَأْسِهِ، وَتَسْرِيحَ لِحْيَتِهِ، وَيُكْثِرُ الْقِنَاعَ حَتَّىٰ كَأَنَّ ثَوْبَهُ ثَوْبُ زَيَّاتٍ».[٥٢]

33. Anas b. Mālik ﵁ narrated: "The Messenger of Allāh ﷺ used to frequently oil his hair and comb his beard. He would often wear a cloth around his head, which would eventually appear to look like the cloth of an oilman."

'Abd al-Razzāq al-Badr said,

> **"Used to frequently oil his hair":** It means that he would often use oil whenever he combed his hair.

Al-Bājūrī said,

> **"Would wear a cloth":** This is a cloth that is put over the head to protect the turban from the stains of oil.

'Alī al-Qārī said,

> **"And comb his beard":** This indicates that he used to oil his beard when combing it.

52 *Hidayatu al-Ruwāt Ilā Takhrīj Aḥādīth al-Maṣābīḥ wa al-Mishkāt* (4/237)

> **"Which would eventually appear to look like the cloth of an oilman":** This refers only to the hair-cover. This meaning is the most suitable and it befits the state of the Prophet ﷺ whose clothes were evidently always clean, not to mention the many ḥadīths wherein he encouraged people to keep their clothes clean. This meaning is also proven from other ḥadīths that explicitly clarified that it refers to the hair-cover.

Al-Suyūṭī said,

> **"He would often wear a cloth around his head":** He ﷺ also used to cover his head during intercourse often and this was done due to his shyness.

٣٤- حَدَّثَنَا هَنَّادُ بْنُ السَّرِيِّ، قَالَ: حَدَّثَنَا أَبُو الأَحْوَصِ، عَنِ الأَشْعَثِ بْنِ أَبِي الشَّعْثَاءِ، عَنْ أَبِيهِ، عَنْ مَسْرُوقٍ، عَنْ عَائِشَةَ، قَالَتْ: «إِنْ كَانَ رَسُولُ اللهِ صلى الله عليه وسلم لَيُحِبُّ التَّيَمُّنَ فِي طُهُورِهِ إِذَا تَطَهَّرَ، وَفِي تَرَجُّلِهِ إِذَا تَرَجَّلَ، وَفِي انْتِعَالِهِ إِذَا انْتَعَلَ». ٥٣

34. ʿĀ'ishah ﵂ narrated: "Allāh's Messenger ﷺ used to like to start with the right side when engaging in his ritual purification, haircare, and putting on his sandals."

ʿAbd al-Razzāq al-Badr said,

> It is recommended to start with the right side in all that which is deemed good such as entering the *masjid*, eating, drinking, shaking the hands, exchanging money or items between people and wearing clothes etc. The opposite should be observed – that is to say – to start with the left side in opposite activities such as entering the toilet, leaving the *masjid*, [taking off shoes and socks] etc.

Al-Bājūrī said,

> **"Used to like to start with the right side":** In his *Ṣaḥīḥ*, al-Imām al-Bukhārī documented the addition, "as long as he was able to", which indicates that one should observe this behaviour unless there is something that prevents us from that. The reason why the Prophet ﷺ liked to start with the right side is because the dwellers of Paradise are

53 *Ṣaḥīḥ Muslim* (268)

the people of the right.

Ibn Ḥajar al-Haytamī said,

> **"Engaging in his ritual purification":** He liked to start with the right side in ablution when washing the hands and the feet, but did not follow the same manner when washing the cheeks and ears.

'Alī al-Qārī said,

> **"Engaging in his ritual purification":** The purification mentioned in this ḥadīth includes *wuḍū*, *ghusl* and *tayammum* but it does not relate to purifying tangible impurity (*najāsah*) on the body and elsewhere.

Al-Nawawī said,

> All scholars are in agreement that starting with the right side in ablution is a Sunnah and whoever opposes it misses its reward but their ablution is valid.

٣٥- حَدَّثَنَا مُحَمَّدُ بْنُ بَشَّارٍ قَالَ: حَدَّثَنَا يَحْيَىٰ بْنُ سَعِيدٍ، عَنْ هِشَامِ بْنِ حَسَّانَ، عَنِ الْحَسَنِ، عَنْ عَبْدِ اللهِ بْنِ مُغَفَّلٍ، قَالَ: «نَهَىٰ رَسُولُ اللهِ صلىٰ الله عليه وسلم عنِ التَّرَجُّلِ إِلا غِبًّا».٥٤

35. 'Abdullāh b. Mughaffal ﵁ narrated: "Allāh's Messenger ﷺ prohibited haircare unless it is done occasionally."

'Abd al-Razzāq al-Badr said,

> This means that one must not let his haircare occupy all of his time and so one should be neither negligent nor excessive.

Al-Bājūrī said,

> The reason behind the prohibition is because overdoing this practice gives the impression that one is excessively indulging in luxury and adornment, which is the habit of women. It is due to this that Abū Bakr b. al-'Arabī said, "Taking care of the hair constantly is pretentiousness, neglecting it is foulness and looking after it occasionally is the Sunnah.

54 *Sunan al-Tirmidhī* (1756)

Ibn Ḥajar al-Haytamī said,

> This prohibition applies to oiling the hair too.

ʿAlī al-Qārī said,

> ʿAbdullāh b. Mughaffal ﷺ was one of the companions who witnessed the Pledge of the Tree.

٣٦- حَدَّثَنَا الْحَسَنُ بْنُ عَرَفَةَ قَالَ: حَدَّثَنَا عَبْدُ السَّلامِ بْنُ حَرْبٍ، عَنْ يَزِيدَ بْنِ أَبِي خَالِدٍ، عَنْ أَبِي الْعَلاءِ الأَوْدِيِّ، عَنْ حُمَيْدِ بْنِ عَبْدِ الرَّحْمَنِ، عَنْ رَجُلٍ مِنْ أَصْحَابِ النَّبِيِّ صلىٰ الله عليه وسلم: «أَنَّ النَّبِيَّ صلىٰ الله عليه وسلم كَانَ يَتَرَجَّلُ غِبًّا». ٥٥

36. Ḥumayd b. ʿAbd al-Raḥmān ﷺ narrated from one of the companions that it was the habit of the Prophet ﷺ to groom his hair occasionally.

Al-Bājūrī said,

> **"From one of the companions":** It is not an issue if a companion is unidentified, as all of them are trustworthy. The identity of this specific companion has been differed over, with three individuals being mentioned: al-Ḥakam b. ʿAmr, ʿAbdullāh b. Sarjis and ʿAbdullāh b. Mughaffal.

55 *Al-Mughnī ʿAn Ḥaml al-Asfār Fi Takhrīj Mā Fī al-Iḥyā min Akhbār* (1/187)

باب ما جاء في شيب رسول الله صلى الله عليه وسلم

[5] On the White Hairs of Allāh's Messenger ﷺ

Al-Bājūrī said,

> The author dedicated this chapter to listing the reports wherein the white hairs of the Prophet ﷺ are mentioned. This chapter was placed after the chapter of the haircare of the Prophet because the latter includes actions (combing, oiling and styling the hair) that we can take as examples to follow. Both of the aforementioned chapters were preceded by the chapter of the hair, as they are contingent on hair.

ʿAbd al-Razzāq al-Badr said,

> This chapter will clarify whether the Prophet ﷺ had any white hairs or not on his head or beard, and how many there were.

٣٧- حَدَّثَنَا مُحَمَّدُ بْنُ بَشَّارٍ، قَالَ: أَخْبَرَنَا أَبُو دَاوُدَ، قَالَ: أَخْبَرَنَا هَمَّامٌ، عَنْ قَتَادَةَ، قَالَ: قُلْتُ لأَنَسِ بْنِ مَالِكٍ: هَلْ خَضَبَ رَسُولُ اللهِ صلى الله عليه وسلم؟ قَالَ: «لَمْ يَبْلُغْ ذَلِكَ، إِنَّمَا كَانَ شَيْبًا فِي صُدْغَيْهِ وَلَكِنْ أَبُو بَكْرٍ خَضَبَ بِالْحِنَّاءِ وَالْكَتَمِ».[٥٦]

37. Qatādah ؓ related: "I asked Anas b. Mālik ؓ, 'Did the Messenger of Allāh ﷺ dye his hair?' He replied, 'He did not need to for all he had were a few white hairs on his temples. However, Abū Bakr ؓ dyed his hair with henna and *katam*.'"

Al-Bājūrī said,

> **"Did the Messenger of Allāh ﷺ dye his hair?":** Meaning, did he change the colour of the white hairs in his head and beard using henna or anything else.

Ibn Ḥajar al-Haytamī said,

> **"He did not need to for all he had were a few white hairs on his**

56 *Ṣaḥīḥ al-Bukhārī* (3550) and *Ṣaḥīḥ Muslim* (2341)

temples": This indicates that he dyed the few white hairs he had on his temples. The Prophet ﷺ dyed his hair, as will be explained in the following chapter.

Abū Bakr dyed his hair using both henna and *katam* at the same time because using *katam* alone would make the hair colour completely black and this is condemned. This is supported by the explicit ḥadīth found in *Ṣaḥīḥ Muslim*.

ʿAlī al-Qārī said,

Henna is a reddish brown dye used especially on hair. *Katam* is a plant that makes the hair black. Al-ʿAsqalānī said, "Pure *katam* produces a black colour which leans slightly to red, whereas henna produces redness. Utilising both produces a colour between black and red."

ʿAbd al-Razzāq al-Badr said,

In this report, Anas negates the Prophet ﷺ having dyed his head or beard. The difference between the companions on this issue will be displayed shortly.

٣٨– حَدَّثَنَا إِسْحَاقُ بْنُ مَنْصُورٍ، وَيَحْيَىٰ بْنُ مُوسَىٰ، قَالَا: حَدَّثَنَا عَبْدُ الرَّزَّاقِ، عَنْ مَعْمَرٍ، عَنْ ثَابِتٍ، عَنْ أَنَسٍ، قَالَ: «مَا عَدَدْتُ فِي رَأْسِ رَسُولِ اللهِ صلى الله عليه وسلم وَلِحْيَتِهِ إِلَّا أَرْبَعَ عَشْرَةَ شَعَرَةً بَيْضَاءَ».[57]

38. Anas b. Mālik ؓ related: "I did not count more than fourteen white hairs on the head and beard of the Messenger of Allāh ﷺ."

ʿAbd al-Razzāq al-Badr said,

The small number of white hairs that Anas ؓ counted in the hair and beard of the Prophet ﷺ explains why he stated that he did not need to dye his hair in the previous report.

Ibn Ḥajar al-Haytamī said,

"Fourteen white hairs": Anas ؓ stated in another ḥadīth that there were seventeen or eighteen white hairs[58] and that could be because he

---

57 *Musnad Aḥmad* (12690)
58 *Ṣaḥīḥ Muslim* (2341), *Musnad Aḥmad* (3/254), *al-Ṭabaqāt* by Ibn Saʿd (1/431, 432), *al-Dalāʾil* by al-Bayhaqī (1/231, 232) and *Ṣaḥīḥ Ibn Ḥibbān* (6292).

counted them on two different occasions.

ʿAlī al-Qārī said,

> Al-ʿAsqalānī said, "In *Ṣaḥīḥ al-Bukhārī*, ʿAbdullāh b. Busr said that the white hairs of the Prophet did not exceed ten. This could be said in reference to the white hairs he had under his lower lip."

٣٩- حَدَّثَنَا مُحَمَّدُ بْنُ الْمُثَنَّى، قَالَ: أَخْبَرَنَا أَبُو دَاوُد، قَالَ: حَدَّثَنَا شُعْبَةُ، عَنْ سِمَاكِ بْنِ حَرْبٍ، قَالَ: سَمِعْتُ جَابِرَ بْنَ سَمُرَةَ، وَقَدْ سُئِلَ عَنْ شَيْبِ رَسُولِ اللهِ صَلَّى اللهُ عَلَيْهِ وَسَلَّمَ، فَقَالَ: «كَانَ إِذَا دَهَنَ رَأْسَهُ لَمْ يُرَ مِنْهُ شَيْبٌ، وَإِذَا لَمْ يَدْهَنْ رُئِيَ مِنْهُ». [٥٩]

39. Jābir b. Samurah ﵁ was asked about the white hair of Allāh's Messenger ﷺ, and so he replied: "Whenever he oiled his hair, it (white hair) did not show. However when he did not oil it, it showed."

ʿAbd al-Razzāq al-Badr said,

> This corroborates the statement of Anas ﵁ that the Prophet ﷺ only had a few white hairs.

Al-Bājūrī said,

> **"Whenever he oiled his hair, it (white hair) did not show":** This is because the white hair became mixed with the glittering of the hair after it was oiled.

٤٠- حَدَّثَنَا مُحَمَّدُ بْنُ عَمْرِو بْنِ الْوَلِيدِ الْكِنْدِيُّ الْكُوفِيُّ، قَالَ: حَدَّثَنَا يَحْيَى بْنُ آدَمَ، عَنْ شَرِيكٍ، عَنْ عُبَيْدِ اللهِ بْنِ عُمَرَ، عَنْ نَافِعٍ، عَنْ عَبْدِ اللهِ بْنِ عُمَرَ، قَالَ: «إِنَّمَا كَانَ شَيْبُ رَسُولِ اللهِ صلى الله عليه وسلم نَحْوًا مِنْ عِشْرِينَ شَعْرَةً بَيْضَاءَ». [٦٠]

40. ʿAbdullāh b. ʿUmar ﵁ narrated: "The Messenger of Allāh ﷺ had around twenty white hairs."

ʿAbd al-Razzāq al-Badr said,

> This conforms to the reports of Jābir and Anas since Ibn ʿUmar gave an approximate number.

---

59 *Ṣaḥīḥ Muslim* (2344)
60 *Musnad Aḥmad* (8/27)

Ibn Ḥajar al-Haytamī said,

> This ḥadīth does not contradict the previous ḥadīth of Anas who stated that he had fourteen white hairs. This is because the number fourteen is more than half of twenty and so it can be used to refer to the higher number [i.e. it is to give an approximate number].

٤١ - حَدَّثَنَا أَبُو كُرَيْبٍ مُحَمَّدُ بْنُ الْعَلاءِ، قَالَ: حَدَّثَنَا مُعَاوِيَةُ بْنُ هِشَامٍ، عَنْ شَيْبَانَ، عَنْ أَبِي إِسْحَاقَ، عَنْ عِكْرِمَةَ، عَنِ ابْنِ عَبَّاسٍ، قَالَ: قَالَ أَبُو بَكْرٍ: يَا رَسُولَ اللهِ، قَدْ شِبْتَ، قَالَ: «شَيَّبَتْنِي هُودٌ، وَالْوَاقِعَةُ، وَالْمُرْسَلاتُ، وَعَمَّ يَتَسَاءَلُونَ، وَإِذَا الشَّمْسُ كُوِّرَتْ».[٦١]

41. 'Abdullāh b. 'Abbās ﵁ narrated: "Abū Bakr ﵁ exclaimed, 'O Messenger of Allāh, you have white hairs!' The Messenger of Allāh ﷺ replied, 'Sūrahs Hūd, al-Wāqi'ah, al-Mursalāt, *'Amma Yatasā'alūn* (al-Nabā) and *Idhā-sh-Shamsu Kuwwirat* (al-Takwīr) have turned my hair white."'

Ibn Ḥajar al-Haytamī said,

> The question of Abū Bakr was because he was surprised to see white hairs on the Prophet ﷺ due to the fact that his nature was balanced and his mood was neutral, and white hairs are less likely to show on one with such characteristics.

'Abd al-Razzāq al-Badr said,

> The reason why these *sūrahs* made his hair turn white is because they talk about the terror of the Day of Judgment. This proves that the white hairs he had were not because of experiencing or worrying about worldly issues (which is a common reason for white hairs) but rather due to his concern and thoughtfulness about the Hereafter.

Al-Bājūrī said,

> The reason why the Prophet ﷺ mentioned Sūrah al-Hūd before the other *sūrahs* is because it includes the order to hold-fast to the straight path that only those whom Allāh has engulfed with the garment of His safety can perfect.

---

61 *Sunan al-Tirmidhī* (3297)

٤٢ - حَدَّثَنَا سُفْيَانُ بْنُ وَكِيعٍ، قَالَ: حَدَّثَنَا مُحَمَّدُ بْنُ بِشْرٍ، عَنْ عَلِيِّ بْنِ صَالِحٍ، عَنْ أَبِي إِسْحَاقَ، عَنْ أَبِي جُحَيْفَةَ، قَالَ: قَالُوا: يَا رَسُولَ اللهِ، نَرَاكَ قَدْ شِبْتَ، قَالَ: «قَدْ شَيَّبَتْنِي هُودٌ وَأَخَوَاتُهَا»[٦٢]

42. Abū Juḥayfah ﷺ narrated: "Some people said to the Prophet ﷺ, 'O Messenger of Allāh! Your hair has turned white!' He replied, 'Sūrah Hūd and its sisters have turned my hair white.'"

Al-Bājūrī said,

> **"... Its sisters":** This refers to all the *sūrahs* that are similar to Sūrah Hūd – that is to say, all the *sūrahs* that talk about the terror of the Day of Judgment.

ʿAbd al-Razzāq al-Badr said,

> The answer of the Prophet ﷺ was an indirect way of stating that he had white hair because of his concern for the Hereafter. It shows the great effect of the Qur'ān and the immense benefits that can be procured when a person contemplates it and understands its meanings and signs. Whoever ponders upon the Qur'ān in the way it should be, they will be focused on the Hereafter without neglecting the necessary affairs in this worldly life. This is why the Prophet ﷺ said, "O Allāh, do not let this worldly life be our biggest concern,"[63] which entails that it is fine for us to look after our worldly affairs but it should not preoccupy us and distract us from the purpose for which we were created – that is: worshipping Allāh alone, preparing to meet Him, and gathering provisions for the hereafter.

٤٣ - حَدَّثَنَا عَلِيُّ بْنُ حُجْرٍ، قَالَ: أَنْبَأَنَا شُعَيْبُ بْنُ صَفْوَانَ، عَنْ عَبْدِ الْمَلِكِ بْنِ عُمَيْرٍ، عَنِ إِيَادِ بْنِ لَقِيطٍ الْعِجْلِيِّ، عَنْ أَبِي رِمْثَةَ التَّيْمِيِّ، تَيْم الرَّبَابِ، قَالَ: «أَتَيْتُ النَّبِيَّ صلىٰ الله عليه وسلم، وَمَعِي ابْنٌ لِي، قَالَ: فَأُرِيتُهُ، فَقُلْتُ لَمَّا رَأَيْتُهُ: هَذَا نَبِيُّ اللهِ صلىٰ الله عليه وسلم وَعَلَيْهِ ثَوْبَانِ أَخْضَرَانِ، وَلَهُ شَعَرٌ قَدْ عَلَاهُ الشَّيْبُ، وَشَيْبُهُ أَحْمَرُ».[٦٤]

62 *Musnad al-Bazzār*
63 *Sunan al-Tirmidhī* (3502)
64 *Musnad Aḥmad* (12/68)

43. Abū Rimthah al-Taymī (the Taym tribe of al-Ribāb) ﵁ related: "I went with my son to see the Prophet ﷺ. When they showed him to me, I said immediately, 'This is the Prophet of Allāh!' He was wearing two pieces of green clothing, and there were some whites in his hair, which were dyed red in colour."

ʿAbd al-Razzāq al-Badr said,

> **"When they showed him to me":** It appears as if this was his first time seeing the Prophet ﷺ as someone pointed him out to him.

Al-Bājūrī said,

> **"This is the Prophet of Allāh!":** He said it to affirm to the one who led him to see the Prophet ﷺ that he believed that the one whom he was shown was truly the Prophet i.e. it is like saying, "I believe you, O you who showed me the Prophet because I am now confident that he is the Prophet of Allāh after seeing the light of his prophethood and aura of his high-esteem." It is also possible that he said that to his son i.e. "[O son,] this is the Prophet of Allāh!"

Ibn Ḥajar al-Haytamī said,

> **"Which were red in colour":** This conforms to the ḥadīth of Ibn ʿUmar who said that the colour of the edges of his white hair was red; they were dyed.

٤٤ – حَدَّثَنَا أَحْمَدُ بْنُ مَنِيعٍ، قَالَ: حَدَّثَنَا سُرَيْجُ بْنُ النُّعْمَانِ، قَالَ: حَدَّثَنَا حَمَّادُ بْنُ سَلَمَةَ، عَنْ سِمَاكِ بْنِ حَرْبٍ، قَالَ: قِيلَ لِجَابِرِ بْنِ سَمُرَةَ: «أَكَانَ فِي رَأْسِ رَسُولِ اللهِ صلىٰ الله عليه وسلم شَيْبٌ؟ قَالَ: لَمْ يَكُنْ فِي رَأْسِ رَسُولِ اللهِ صلىٰ الله عليه وسلم شَيْبٌ إِلا شَعَرَاتٌ فِي مَفْرِقِ رَأْسِهِ، إِذَا ادَّهَنَ وَارَاهُنَّ الدُّهْنُ».[65]

44. Jābir b. Samurah ﵁ was asked: "Were there any white hairs on the head of Allāh's Messenger ﷺ?" He replied, "He only had a few on the middle parting, but whenever he applied oil to his hair, they did not show."

ʿAbd al-Razzāq al-Badr said,

This description of the companions regarding the white hair of the

65 See ḥadīth 39

Prophet ﷺ shows that he used to uncover his head sometimes.

Al-Bājūrī said,

> It is disliked to pluck the white hair according to the majority of scholars based on the ḥadīth, "Do not pluck out white-hairs, for they are the light of the Muslim."[66]

ʿAlī al-Qārī said,

> As the white hairs did not show when he ﷺ oiled his hair, this indicates that they were few.

66 *Musnad Aḥmad* (11/160)

باب ما جاء في خضاب رسول الله صلى الله عليه وسلم

[6] On the Usage of Dye by Allāh's Messenger ﷺ

ʿAbd al-Razzāq al-Badr said,

> The author included this chapter in his book to show whether the Prophet ﷺ dyed his hair or not. In summary, the companions differed in opinion about it as mentioned by Ibn al-Qayyim in *Zād al-Maʿād*.[67] Anas b. Mālik denied that the Prophet ever dyed his hair and Abū Hurayrah affirmed that the Prophet dyed his hair. Some other companions said that he used to perfume his hair abundantly, which made his hair appear reddish and that made people think his hair was dyed when it was not. This is a summary of the issue.

Al-Bājūrī said,

> Dye refers to colouring the hair with henna or any other dyestuff. According to us – the Shāfiʿīs, it is the Sunnah to dye the hair with any colour except black and it is forbidden to dye the hair with black.

٤٥ – حَدَّثَنَا أَحْمَدُ بْنُ مَنِيعٍ، قَالَ: حَدَّثَنَا هُشَيْمٌ، قَالَ: حَدَّثَنَا عَبْدُ الْمَلِكِ بْنُ عُمَيْرٍ، عَنْ إِيَادِ بْنِ لَقِيطٍ، قَالَ: أَخْبَرَنِي أَبُو رِمْثَةَ، قَالَ: أَتَيْتُ رَسُولَ اللهِ صلى الله عليه وسلم مَعَ ابْنٍ لِي، فَقَالَ: «ابْنُكَ هَذَا؟» فَقُلْتُ: نَعَمْ أَشْهَدُ بِهِ، قَالَ: «لَا يَجْنِي عَلَيْكَ، وَلَا تَجْنِي عَلَيْهِ» قَالَ: وَرَأَيْتُ الشَّيْبَ أَحْمَرَ.[٦٨]

45. Abū Rimthah related: "I went with my son to visit the Prophet ﷺ. [When he saw me], he asked, 'Is this your son?' I replied, 'Yes, this is my son. I testify to that.' Then he said, 'You are not held accountable for his crimes, nor is he held accountable for your crimes.'" Abū Rimthah then remarked, "I noticed that the white hairs of the Prophet ﷺ had been dyed red."

---

67 1/176.

68 Additions of ʿAbdullāh b. Aḥmad b. Ḥanbal to *Musnad Aḥmad* (7113)

قَالَ أَبُو عِيسَىٰ: هَذَا أَحْسَنُ شَيْءٍ رُوِيَ فِي هَذَا الْبَابِ، وَأَفْسَرُ؛ لِأَنَّ الرِّوَايَاتِ الصَّحِيحَةَ أَنَّ النَّبِيَّ صَلَّىٰ اللهُ عَلَيْهِ وَسَلَّمَ لَمْ يَبْلُغِ الشَّيْبَ. وَأَبُو رِمْثَةَ اسْمُهُ: رِفَاعَةُ بْنُ يَثْرِبِيٍّ التَّيْمِيُّ.

Abū ʿĪsā commented: "This ḥadīth is the most correct and explanatory report on the subject of using a dye. This is because the authentic ḥadīths state that he did not have many white hairs. The name of Abū Rimthah is Rifāʿah b. Yathrabī al-Taymī"

ʿAbd al-Razzāq al-Badr said,

> This ḥadīth shows that if it is possible for parents to take their children to the gatherings of good such as lectures and visiting scholars etc., then they should do so. This will cause the children to grow up loving the people of knowledge and the circles of knowledge. This should be more emphasised in the current era, as the fruits of deviation and misguidance are everywhere and desires and whims are playing with the Muslim youth. Thus, parents should take their children to the places of knowledge with encouragement and kindness so that the love of these places is instilled into them.
>
> **"I noticed that the white hairs of the Prophet ﷺ had been dyed red":** This could have been because of dye being applied or due to the effect of the oil that he used to use. The people of knowledge differed on this; some of them such as Umm Salamah ﵂ said it was because of dye, and some said it was because of oil and that he never used dye, as affirmed by Anas b. Mālik ؓ.

Al-Bājūrī said,

> **"I testify to that":** [The Arabic words used for this part] could also mean, "[O Prophet of Allāh] be a witness that he is my son" and so the statement is an affirmation of his answer, "Yes, he is my son." It could also mean, "I testify to that [i.e. I testify and acknowledge that he is my son]" to advise the Prophet ﷺ that he will take the consequences of the actions of his son, as this was the norm during the times of *jahiliyyah*.
>
> **"Abū ʿĪsā commented":** This is the author referring to himself. An individual referring to himself with his *kunyah* is not disliked, due to

its more frequent usage over the *laqab* (al-Tirmidhī). His teacher, al-Bukhārī frequently referred to himself as Abū ʿAbdillāh in his *Ṣaḥīḥ* and other works.

"This ḥadīth is the most correct and explanatory report": This statement does not necessitate that the ḥadīth is authentic because scholars use it even if the ḥadīth is weak i.e. they intend to mean with that statement that it is the strongest ḥadīth on the subject or the least weak.

Ibn Ḥajar al-Haytamī said,

"You are not held accountable for his crime": This response was to show Abū Rimthah that he will not be held accountable or take the burden of his son's sins and mistakes, and that his son will not be held accountable for his father's mistakes and sins. From this, our renowned [Shāfiʿī] masters concluded that the father and the children of the killer are not liable to contribute in the blood-money.

٤٦ – حَدَّثَنَا سُفْيَانُ بْنُ وَكِيعٍ، قَالَ: حَدَّثَنَا أَبِي، عَنْ شَرِيكٍ، عَنْ عُثْمَانَ بْنِ مَوْهَبٍ، قَالَ: سُئِلَ أَبُو هُرَيْرَةَ: «هَلْ خَضَبَ رَسُولُ اللهِ صلى الله عليه وسلم؟ قَالَ : نَعَمْ».

46. Abū Hurayrah ⬥ was asked: "Did the Messenger of Allāh ⬥ dye his hair?" He replied, "Yes."

قَالَ أَبُو عِيسَى: وَرَوَى أَبُو عَوَانَةَ هَذَا الْحَدِيثَ عَنْ عُثْمَانَ بْنِ عَبْدِ اللهِ بْنِ مَوْهَبٍ، فَقَالَ: عَنْ أُمِّ سَلَمَةَ. ⁶⁹

Abū ʿĪsā said: ʿAwānah reported this narration via ʿUthmān b. ʿAbdillāh b. Mawhab, who said: "On the authority of Umm Salamah."

Ibn Ḥajar al-Haytamī said,

This conforms to the statement of Ibn ʿUmar ⬥ which is documented in *Ṣaḥīḥ al-Bukhārī* and *Ṣaḥīḥ Muslim* i.e. he narrated that he saw the Prophet ⬥ use a yellow dye.[70] This is our *madhhab's* evidence that

---

69 *Ṣaḥīḥ al-Bukhārī* (5896)
70 *Ṣaḥīḥ al-Bukhārī* (5851) and *Muslim* (1187)

using a dye colour other than black [i.e. it is not allowed to use black dye] is an act of Sunnah. Another ḥadīth documented by Abū Dāwūd also supports this.[71] Al-Nawawī said, "The view that we adopt in our *madhhab* is that it is recommended for both men and women to use reddish-brown or yellow dye, and that it is forbidden for them to dye the hair black except in the case where men do this for the purpose of *jihad*.

Al-Bājūrī said,

This ḥadīth concords with the other ḥadīths that the Prophet ﷺ did dye his hair. To reconcile between these ḥadīths and those ḥadīths that negate his use of dye, we say that he used to dye his hair at one point, then he stopped doing that most of the time or did it very infrequently; hence each narrator reported what they saw.

"Abū 'Īsā said": His intention here is to mention a different route of the narration.

٤٧ – حَدَّثَنَا إِبْرَاهِيمُ بْنُ هَارُونَ، قَالَ: أَنْبَأَنَا النَّضْرُ بْنُ زُرَارَةَ، عَنْ أَبِي جَنَابٍ، عَنْ إِيَادِ بْنِ لَقِيطٍ، عَنِ الْجَهْدَمَةِ، امْرَأَةِ بَشِيرِ ابْنِ الْخَصَاصِيَّةِ، قَالَتْ: «أَنَا رَأَيْتُ رَسُولَ اللهِ صلىٰ الله عليه وسلم يَخْرُجُ مِنْ بَيْتِهِ يَنْفُضُ رَأْسَهُ، وَقَدِ اغْتَسَلَ، وَبِرَأْسِهِ رَدْعٌ مِنْ حِنَّاءٍ، أَوْ قَالَ: رَدْعٌ شَكَّ فِي هَذَا الشَّيْخُ».[٧٢]

47. Al-Jahdamah ﵂ (the wife of Bashir b. al-Khaṣāṣiyah ﵁) related: "I saw the Messenger of Allāh ﷺ coming out of his house; after taking a bath, shaking [water from] his hair. I saw on his head the remnants of saffron or henna (my teacher had doubt in this)."

'Abd al-Razzāq al-Badr said,

"I saw on his head the remnants of saffron or henna": Some ḥadīth commentators stated that this part does not necessitate that he did so to dye his white hairs. Rather, it is possible that he used the henna for medical purposes or to reduce heat from his head (cool down) or for any other similar purposes.

Al-Bājūrī said,

71 *Sunan Abī Dāwūd* (4210).

72 *Mukhtaṣar al-Shamā'il* of al-Albānī (39)

"My teacher had doubt in this": I.e. his teacher mentioned at the beginning of the narration's chain, Ibrāhīm b. Hārūn.

٤٨ - حَدَّثَنَا عَبْدُ اللهِ بْنُ عَبْدِ الرَّحْمَنِ، قَالَ: حَدَّثَنَا عَمْرُو بْنُ عَاصِمٍ، قَالَ: حَدَّثَنَا حَمَّادُ بْنُ سَلَمَةَ، قَالَ: حَدَّثَنَا حُمَيْدٌ، عَنْ أَنَسٍ، قَالَ: «رَأَيْتُ شَعَرَ رَسُولِ اللهِ صلى الله عليه وسلم مَخْضُوبًا». ٧٣

48. Anas b. Mālik ؓ narrated: "I saw the hair of Allāh's Messenger ﷺ dyed."

قَالَ حَمَّادٌ: وَأَخْبَرَنَا عَبْدُ اللهِ بْنُ مُحَمَّدِ بْنِ عَقِيلٍ، قَالَ: رَأَيْتُ شَعْرَ رَسُولِ اللهِ صلى الله عَلَيْهِ وَسَلَم عِنْدَ أَنَسِ بْنِ مَالِكٍ مَخْضُوْبًا.

Ḥammād said, "ʿAbdullāh b. Muḥammad b. ʿAqīl said, 'I saw a hair of Allāh's Messenger ﷺ with Anas b. Mālik and it was dyed.'"

ʿAlī al-Qārī said,

> It has been stated in other authentic ḥadīths that Anas b. Mālik ؓ denied that the Prophet ﷺ dyed his hair. With that said, it is possible that he intended to say that he did not use dye most of the time, and that he used dye infrequently.

Mīrak Shāh said,

> You should know that it is proven in ḥadīths documented in the two *Ṣaḥīḥ* books and other collections of ḥadīth that Anas ؓ held the view that the Prophet ﷺ did not dye his hair and that he did not possess enough white hairs to warrant the use of dye on them. This ḥadīth, however, is the only report from him that states otherwise; hence either this ḥadīth is classified as odd or it refers to when he saw him after his death. This is because it was reported by al-Dāraquṭnī that Abū Hurayrah ؓ said, "After the death of the Prophet ﷺ, those who had some of the hairs of the Prophet ﷺ dyed them in order to preserve them." Hence it is possible that Anas saw his dyed hair in the possession of one of his companions.

ʿAbd al-Razzāq al-Badr said,

---

73 Translator Note: This ḥadīth could not be located from other sources with the exact same text but the meaning is correct and supported by many other authentic ḥadīths.

The conclusion is that all the authentic ḥadīths indicate that the Prophet ﷺ had few white hairs, so he had no need to dye them as reported by Anas b. Mālik ؓ and others. As for the reddish colour that was noticed in his hair, which was thought to be because of dye, it was most probably due to the use of oil or perfume.

باب ما جاء في كُحل رسول اللّٰه صلى اللّٰه عليه وسلم
[7] On the Kohl of Allāh's Messenger ﷺ

'Abd al-Razzāq al-Badr said,

Kohl is a well known stone that is easy to disintegrate and it is used to darken the edges of the eyelids. To produce it [for cosmetic use], it is crushed until it becomes smooth and then it is applied to the eyelids. It comes in two colours, black and red.

Al-Bājūrī said,

The author listed the chapter of kohl right after the chapter of dye due to the similarity between the two since both are means of adornment.

Al-'Asqalānī said, "Applying the kohl to the eyelid is a Sunnah according to all Shāfi'ī scholars, based on the ḥadīths that mention it."

Abū Bakr b. al-'Arabī said, "There are two benefits of the application of kohl: (i) adornment, which religion did not put a restriction on; thus it is used as needed, (ii) medicine, because it improves the sight and helps eyelashes grow, and it has been religiously prescribed to be done every night so that this benefit can be attained."

There are six narrations in this chapter when taking into consideration the varying routes, and they equal four in actuality.

٤٩ - حَدَّثَنَا مُحَمَّدُ بْنُ حُمَيْدٍ الرَّازِيُّ، قَالَ: حَدَّثَنَا أَبُو دَاوُدَ الطَّيَالِسِيُّ، عَنْ عَبَّادِ بْنِ مَنْصُورٍ، عَنْ عِكْرِمَةَ، عَنِ ابْنِ عَبَّاسٍ، أَنَّ النَّبِيَّ صلى الله عليه وسلم قَالَ: «اكْتَحِلُوا بِالإِثْمِدِ، فَإِنَّهُ يَجْلُو الْبَصَرَ، وَيُنْبِتُ الشَّعْرَ». وَزَعَمَ أَنَّ النَّبِيَّ صلى الله عليه وسلم كَانَتْ لَهُ مُكْحُلَةٌ يَكْتَحِلُ مِنْهَا كُلَّ لَيْلَةٍ ثَلَاثَةً فِي هَذِهِ، وَثَلَاثَةً فِي هَذِهِ.٧٤

49. 'Abdullāh b. Abbās ؓ **narrated that the Prophet ﷺ said: "Apply**

---

74 *Sunan al-Tirmidhī* (1757) and *Sunan Ibn Mājah* (3499)

the *ithmid* (kohl) on the eyes; it strengthens the eyesight, and facilitates the growth of the eyelashes." He also asserted that the Prophet ﷺ had a small container for keeping kohl, from which he applied it on each eyelid three times every night.

'Alī al-Qārī said,

> **"Apply the *ithmid*":** It is intended to mean use it frequently.
>
> **"...Every night":** Meaning he did it every night before sleeping.

'Abd al-Razzāq al-Badr said,

> **"Facilitates the growth of the eyelashes":** Not only do long eyelashes protect the eyes from dust, but they also increase the eyes in beauty.
>
> **"On each eyelid three times":** Applying it in an odd number is encouraged because he ﷺ said in another ḥadīth, "When anyone of you applies kohl on their eyes, do it in an odd number."[75] There are two methods that scholars have mentioned based on the different ḥadīths about this topic: (1) Apply kohl on the right eyelid three times, then apply it on the left eyelid three times. (2) Apply kohl on the right eyelid one time then apply it on the left eyelid one time, then apply it on the right eyelid and then on the left eyelid, and then apply it on the right eyelid. This way, the total number is odd and the right eyelid is preferred over the left eyelid with three things: (i) it was the first to start with, (ii) it was the last to end with, (iii) the kohl is applied on it more than the left eyelid.

Ibn Ḥajar al-Haytamī said,

> **"Three times every night":** He preferred three times because it is an odd number, and it is moderate, neither excessive nor little. The best of things are those which are moderate.

Al-Bājūrī said,

> **"Apply the *ithmid*":** Those being addressed regarding this issue are those whose eyes are healthy, because if the eye has a problem then

---

75 *Musnad Aḥmad* (8612)

ithmid may aggravate it.

Ibn al-Qayyim said,

> Applying the kohl on the eyes maintains their healthiness, improves and clears the eyesight, removes the bad elements and it is an adornment in the case of some types of kohl. It is even more beneficial when the *ithmid* is used before sleeping.[76]

٥٠- حَدَّثَنَا عَبْدُ اللهِ بْنُ الصَّبَّاحِ الْهَاشِمِيُّ الْبَصْرِيُّ، أَخْبَرَنَا عُبَيْدُ اللهِ بْنُ مُوسَىٰ، أَخْبَرَنَا إِسْرَائِيلُ بْنُ يُونُسَ، عَنْ عَبَّادِ بْنِ مَنْصُورٍ.

(ح) وَحَدَّثَنَا عَلِيُّ بْنُ حُجْرٍ، حَدَّثَنَا يَزِيدُ بْنُ هَارُونَ، حَدَّثَنَا عَبَّادُ بْنُ مَنْصُورٍ، عَنْ عِكْرِمَةَ، عَنِ ابْنِ عَبَّاسٍ، قَالَ: «كَانَ النَّبِيُّ صلىٰ الله عليه وسلم يَكْتَحِلُ قَبْلَ أَنْ يَنَامَ بِالإِثْمِدِ ثَلاثًا فِي كُلِّ عَيْنٍ».

وَقَالَ يَزِيدُ بْنُ هَارُونَ فِي حَدِيثِهِ: «إِنَّ النَّبِيَّ صلىٰ الله عليه وسلم كَانَتْ لَهُ مُكْحُلَةٌ يَكْتَحِلُ مِنْهَا عِنْدَ النَّوْمِ ثَلاثًا فِي كُلِّ عَيْنٍ».[٧٧]

50. ʿAbdullāh b. ʿAbbās ﵄ narrated that the Prophet ﷺ would apply *ithmid* to his eyes before sleeping, thrice on each eye. Yazīd b. Hārūn said in his report, "The Prophet ﷺ had a small kohl container from which he would apply kohl to his eyes thrice on each night."

Al-Bājūrī said,

> **"ح":** This is a symbol that denotes *taḥwīl* (shifting) from one chain of narration to another. It is a short-form technique utilised by the ḥadīth masters when combining two or more chains of narration. It is found in the later books more than in the earlier ones, and it was used more in *Ṣaḥīḥ Muslim* than in *Ṣaḥīḥ al-Bukhārī*. A question may arise, does one read the symbol itself and then continue reading, or does one read the word that it abbreviates (e.g. *taḥwīl* or *ḥadīth*), or not read anything at all? The great ḥadīth master Ibn al-Ṣalāḥ determined that one reads the symbol as is. He said, "This was the view of the majority of the *salaf*, though some differed and said that one

---

76 *Zād al-Maʿād* (4/281)

77 *Musnad Ibn ʿAbbād* (1/471)

reads a word such as *ḥadīth* and some said that nothing is read."

"Yazīd b. Hārūn said in his report": This is with the second chain of narration, i.e. from ʿAbbād, from ʿIkrimah, from Ibn ʿAbbās. It is not a *muʿallaq* (chainless) or *mursal* (companion omitted) report, as some have mistakenly thought. The purpose of the author was to highlight the difference in wording in the texts of both chains of narration (the first chain being that of Isrāʾīl and the second being that of Yazīd).

٥١ – حَدَّثَنَا أَحْمَدُ بْنُ مَنِيعٍ، قَالَ: حَدَّثَنَا مُحَمَّدُ بْنُ يَزِيدَ، عَنْ مُحَمَّدِ بْنِ إِسْحَاقَ، عَنْ مُحَمَّدِ بْنِ الْمُنْكَدِرِ، عَنْ جَابِرٍ – هُوَ ابْنُ عَبْدِ اللهِ –، قَالَ: قَالَ رَسُولُ اللهِ صلى الله عليه وسلم: «عَلَيْكُمْ بِالإِثْمِدِ عِنْدَ النَّوْمِ، فَإِنَّهُ يَجْلُو الْبَصَرَ، وَيُنْبِتُ الشَّعْرَ». ٧٨

51. Jābir b. ʿAbdullāh ؓ narrated: "The Messenger of Allāh ﷺ said, 'You should use *ithmid*. It gives strength to the eyesight and increases the growth of the eyelashes.'"

ʿAlī al-Qārī said,

> Ibn Ḥajar said that the command in this ḥadīth is understood to mean that it is recommended, as agreed upon by all scholars.
>
> **"It gives strength to the eyesight and increases the growth of the eyelashes":** Mentioning the worldly benefits of kohl does not negate the fact that it is an act of Sunnah since he ﷺ practiced it and encouraged it. In fact, these worldly benefits are means towards learning the religious acts, such as how to perform purification, assessing the direction of the *qiblah* and other matters that require the use of the eyes. The importance of the eyesight is such that some gave it superiority over hearing, may Allāh bless us with both.
>
> Based on the Prophet's ﷺ utilisation of these two benefits as reasons for the use of kohl, we can derive a deeper implication: If a person wants to get the reward of following the Sunnah in this matter, they should establish the intention that it is intended for use as a medicine and not just for adornment. This is why al-Imām Mālik stated that it is disliked for men to apply kohl unless it is for treatment purposes only.

---

78 *Sunan Ibn Mājah* (3496)

٥٢ – حَدَّثَنَا قُتَيْبَةُ بْنُ سَعِيدٍ، قَالَ: حَدَّثَنَا بِشْرُ بْنُ الْمُفَضَّلِ، عَنْ عَبْدِ اللهِ بْنِ عُثْمَانَ
بْنِ خُثَيْمٍ، عَنْ سَعِيدِ بْنِ جُبَيْرٍ، عَنِ ابْنِ عَبَّاسٍ، قَالَ: قَالَ رَسُولُ اللهِ صلىٰ الله عليه
وسلم: "إِنَّ خَيْرَ أَكْحَالِكُمُ الْإِثْمِدُ، يَجْلُو الْبَصَرَ، وَيُنْبِتُ الشَّعْرَ". ٧٩

52. 'Abdullāh b. 'Abbās ﷺ reported: "The Messenger of Allāh ﷺ said,
'The best from among all the kohl used by you is *ithmid*. It strengthens the eyesight and facilitates the growth of the eyelashes.'"

'Abd al-Razzāq al-Badr said,

> **"The best from among all the kohl used by you is *ithmid*"**: This indicates that there are many materials that can be used for kohl, the best of which is *ithmid*.

'Alī al-Qārī said,

> **"The best from among all the kohl used by you is *ithmid*"**: This indicates that *ithmid* is a special type of kohl. It is said that the meaning is that *ithmid* is the best kohl for protecting the eye when it is healthy as kohl is harmful in the case of ophthalmia (inflamed eyes).

٥٣ – حَدَّثَنَا إِبْرَاهِيمُ بْنُ الْمُسْتَمِرِّ الْبَصْرِيُّ، قَالَ: حَدَّثَنَا أَبُو عَاصِمٍ، عَنْ عُثْمَانَ بْنِ
عَبْدِ الْمَلِكِ، عَنْ سَالِمٍ، عَنِ ابْنِ عُمَرَ، قَالَ: قَالَ رَسُولُ اللهِ صلىٰ الله عليه وسلم:
«عَلَيْكُمْ بِالْإِثْمِدِ، فَإِنَّهُ يَجْلُو الْبَصَرَ، وَيُنْبِتُ الشَّعْرَ». ٨٠

53. 'Abdullāh b. 'Umar ﷺ reported: "The Messenger of Allāh ﷺ said,
'Apply *ithmid*, for verily it strengthens the eyesight and facilitates the growth of the eyelashes.'"

'Alī al-Qārī said,

> The purpose of repeating this ḥadīth with different chains is to emphasise its content and to strengthen its classification.

Al-Bājūrī said,

> The Prophet ﷺ had a set that included: a mirror that was called "*al-madalla*", a comb made of ivory, a kohl container, a clipper and a *miswāk*.

---

79 *Sunan Abī Dāwūd* (3878) and *Sunan Ibn Mājah* (3497)
80 *Sunan Ibn Mājah* (3495)

باب ما جاء في لباس رسول الله صلى الله عليه وسلم

[8] On the Clothing of Allāh's Messenger ﷺ

ʿAbd al-Razzāq al-Badr said,

> It should be noted that the general rule is that all types of clothing are lawful except that which is forbidden in religion. Al-Bukhārī documented two ḥadīths establishing this general rule, the first of which is that the Prophet ﷺ said, "Eat, drink, wear clothes and give charity without showing off and being extravagant."[81] The other one is that in which Ibn ʿAbbās ؓ said, "Eat all that you wish and wear all that you like, so long as you are neither showing off nor being extravagant."[82]
>
> The Prophet ﷺ pointed out a number of issues to be avoided in clothing, some of which are:
>
> 1. *Isbāl*: It is letting the garment come below the ankles and according to some scholars it is considered from the major sins.
> 2. Men wearing clothes made of silk.
> 3. Wearing something that makes the person distinguished from others. It is for this reason that one should wear the clothes that are the norm in the society where they live, provided that such clothes are lawful.
> 4. Wearing clothes that are known to be worn only by disbelievers and by which a disbeliever is recognised.

Al-Bājūrī said,

> This followed up the previous chapters (e.g. on haircare, dying, kohl etc) due to their concordance in being forms of adornment.
>
> Clothes are subject to the five rulings: (i) Obligatory, e.g. clothing

81 *Ṣaḥīḥ al-Bukhārī* (51/77)
82 Ibid

that covers the *'awrah* from being shown in the presence of others, (ii) recommended, e.g. to wear one's best clothes on Eid and white clothes on Friday, (iii) forbidden, e.g. for men to wear silk clothes, (iv) disliked, e.g. for the rich to wear ragged clothes constantly and (v) permissible (*mubāḥ*), which is to wear anything else.

There are sixteen ḥadīths in this chapter.

٥٤- حَدَّثَنَا مُحَمَّدُ بْنُ حُمَيْدٍ الرَّازِيُّ، قَالَ: حَدَّثنَا الْفَضْلُ بْنُ مُوسَىٰ، وَأَبُو تُمَيْلَةَ، وَزَيْدُ بْنُ حُبَابٍ، عَنْ عَبْدِ الْمُؤْمِنِ بْنِ خَالِدٍ، عَنْ عَبْدِ اللهِ بْنِ بُرَيْدَةَ، عَنْ أُمِّ سَلَمَةَ، قَالَتْ: «كَانَ أَحَبَّ الثِّيَابِ إِلَىٰ رَسُولِ اللهِ صلىٰ الله عليه وسلم الْقَمِيصُ». [٨٣]

54. Umm Salamah ﵂ said: "In regards to clothing, the Messenger of Allāh ﷺ liked wearing the *qamīṣ* the most."

'Abd al-Razzāq al-Badr said,

> *Qamīṣ* refers to the well known robe with sleeves. It has been said that the Prophet's ﷺ liking of this garment was due to it being easy to put on and remove, and due it being comfortable to move in.

Ibn Ḥajar al-Haytamī said,

> It was his preference as this kind of garment is more concealing than the *izār* (lower wrap) and *ridā'* (upper garment). Al-Ḥāfiẓ al-Dumyātī narrated a ḥadīth stating that the *qamīṣ* of the Prophet ﷺ was made of cotton, short in length and had short sleeves. This ḥadīth indicates that he preferred the one made of cotton because the one made of wool harms the body, makes one sweat and it has a smell that harms others.

'Alī al-Qārī said,

> It was said that the Prophet ﷺ liked wearing the *qamīṣ* because it is lighter than other types of clothing, it conceals more of the body than other clothes and thus the one who wears it is displaying humility.

٥٥- حَدَّثَنَا عَلِيُّ بْنُ حُجْرٍ، قَالَ: حَدَّثَنَا الْفَضْلُ بْنُ مُوسَىٰ، عَنْ عَبْدِ الْمُؤْمِنِ بْنِ خَالِدٍ، عَنْ عَبْدِ اللهِ بْنِ بُرَيْدَةَ، عَنْ أُمِّ سَلَمَةَ، قَالَتْ: «كَانَ أَحَبَّ الثِّيَابِ إِلَىٰ رَسُولِ

83 *Sunan al-Tirmidhī* (1762)

اللهِ صلىٰ الله عليه وسلم الْقَمِيصُ».

55. The same report from Umm Salamah ﵂ through a different chain of narrators.

٥٦- حَدَّثَنَا زِيَادُ بْنُ أَيُّوبَ الْبَغْدَادِيُّ، قَالَ: حَدَّثَنَا أَبُو تُمَيْلَةَ، عَنْ عَبْدِ الْمُؤْمِنِ بْنِ خَالِدٍ، عَنْ عَبْدِ اللهِ بْنِ بُرَيْدَةَ، عَنْ أُمِّهِ، عَنْ أُمِّ سَلَمَةَ، قَالَتْ: «كَانَ أَحَبُّ الثِّيَابِ إِلَىٰ رَسُولِ اللهِ صلىٰ الله عليه وسلم يَلْبَسُهُ الْقَمِيصُ».

قَالَ: هَكَذَا قَالَ زِيَادُ بْنُ أَيُّوبَ، فِي حَدِيثِهِ: عَنْ عَبْدِ اللهِ بْنِ بُرَيْدَةَ، عَنْ أُمِّهِ، عَنْ أُمِّ سَلَمَةَ، وَهَكَذَا رَوَىٰ غَيْرُ وَاحِدٍ عَنْ أَبِي تُمَيْلَةَ مِثْلَ رِوَايَةِ زِيَادِ بْنِ أَيُّوبَ، وَأَبُو تُمَيْلَةَ يَزِيدُ فِي هَذَا الْحَدِيثِ: «عَنْ أُمِّهِ» وَهُوَ أَصَحُّ.

56. The same report from Umm Salamah ﵂ through a different chain of narrators.

ʿAbd al-Razzāq al-Badr said,

> The same ḥadīth from Umm Salamah ﵂ has been reported three times but the last of them has the chain of narrators that al-Tirmidhī believes to be the most authentic. This is why he mentioned the three different routes for the same text.

٥٧- حَدَّثَنَا عَبْدُ اللهِ بْنُ مُحَمَّدِ بْنِ الْحَجَّاجِ، قَالَ: حَدَّثَنَا مُعَاذُ بْنُ هِشَامٍ، قَالَ: حَدَّثَنِي أَبِي، عَنْ بُدَيْلٍ - يَعْنِي ابْنَ مَيْسَرَةَ الْعُقَيْلِيَّ -، عَنْ شَهْرِ بْنِ حَوْشَبٍ، عَنْ أَسْمَاءَ بِنْتِ يَزِيدَ، قَالَتْ: «كَانَ كُمُّ قَمِيصِ رَسُولِ اللهِ صلىٰ الله عليه وسلم إِلَىٰ الرُّسْغِ».[٨٤]

57. Asmāʾ bint Yazīd ﵂ narrated: "The sleeves of the *qamīṣ* of the Messenger of Allāh ﷺ would reach his wrists."

ʿAbd al-Razzāq al-Badr said,

> This shows that his sleeves did not exceed his wrists.

Al-Bājūrī said,

---

84 *Sunan al-Tirmidhī* (1765) and *Sunan Abī Dāwūd* (4026)

The reason behind the sleeves not exceeding the wrists is because if they do exceed them, they hinder the movement of the hands, and if they are too short, they expose the arms to heat and coldness. Therefore, the Prophet ﷺ preferred to be moderate in the length of his sleeves, and moderation is indeed the best of all things.

It has also been reported that the Prophet ﷺ wore a *qamīṣ* which was above his ankles and its sleeves were up to his fingers. Some scholars argued that this could be combined with the ḥadīth in this chapter by saying that he wore this whilst a resident and that when on a journey ([t] and they gave other reasons e.g. that he had different garments, the variances were caused by wetness etc). Saʿīd b. Manṣūr and al-Bayhaqī reported from ʿAlī that he would put on a *qamīṣ* and when the sleeve reached the fingers he would cut what went over. He would say, "The sleeve does not hang beyond the fingers."

ʿAlī al-Qārī said,

> Al-Jazarī said, "This ḥadīth is evidence that the Sunnah is that the sleeves of the *qamīṣ* do not exceed the wrists. As for other clothes, they (the scholars) said that the Sunnah is that the sleeves should not exceed the tips of the fingers."

٥٨- حَدَّثَنَا أَبُو عَمَّارٍ الْحُسَيْنُ بْنُ حُرَيْثٍ، قَالَ: حَدَّثنَا أَبُو نُعَيْم، قَالَ: حَدَّثَنَا زُهَيْرٌ، عَنْ عُرْوَةَ بْنِ عَبْدِ اللهِ بْنِ قُشَيْرٍ، عَنْ مُعَاوِيَةَ بْنِ قُرَّةَ، عَنْ أَبِيهِ، قَالَ: «أَتَيْتُ رَسُولَ اللهِ صلىٰ الله عليه وسلم فِي رَهْطٍ مِنْ مُزَيْنَةَ لِنُبَايِعَهُ، وَإِنَّ قَمِيصَهُ لَمُطْلَقٌ، - أَوْ قَالَ: زِرُّ قَمِيصِهِ مُطْلَقٌ -، قَالَ: فَأَدْخَلْتُ يَدِي فِي جَيْبِ قَمِيصِهِ فَمَسَسْتُ الْخَاتَمَ». [٨٥]

58. Qurrah b. Iyyās ؓ related: "I came with a group from the tribe of Muzaynah to give the pledge to the Messenger of Allāh ﷺ. As I noticed his *qamīṣ*/the button of his *qamīṣ* was open, I inserted my hand into the collar of his *qamīṣ* and I touched the seal."

ʿAbd al-Razzāq al-Badr said,

> The general rule is that one should keep the buttons of the collar fastened unless there is a need to unbutton them. That being said, one should not think that unbuttoning the *qamīṣ* is a Sunnah because

85 *Sunan Abī Dāwūd* (4082) and *Sunan Ibn Mājah* (3578)

this ḥadīth does not indicate so in any form. This is because the reason why his ﷺ collar was open was not specified and so it could have been for any reason such as attempting to cool down due to excessive heat. In fact, it is most likely that this is not an act of Sunnah. If the Sunnah was to keep the buttons of the collar unbuttoned, there would have been no use for having them.

Al-Bājūrī said,

The following can be derived from this ḥadīth:

- It is lawful to wear the *qamīṣ*.
- It is lawful to have buttons on it.
- It is lawful to unbutton them.
- It is lawful to have a wide collar that is enough for the hand to be inserted into it.
- The Prophet ﷺ allowed others to enter their hands through his collar and touch his skin to seek *barakah*.
- It indicates the humbleness of the Prophet ﷺ.

٥٩ - حَدَّثَنَا عَبْدُ بْنُ حُمَيْدٍ، قَالَ: حَدَّثَنَا مُحَمَّدُ بْنُ الْفَضْلِ، قَالَ: حَدَّثَنَا حَمَّادُ بْنُ سَلَمَةَ، عَنْ حَبِيبِ بْنِ الشَّهِيدِ، عَنِ الْحَسَنِ، عَنْ أَنَسِ بْنِ مَالِكٍ، أَنَّ النَّبِيَّ صلىٰ الله عليه وسلم خَرَجَ وَهُوَ يَتَّكِئُ عَلَىٰ أُسَامَةَ بْنِ زَيْدٍ، عَلَيْهِ ثَوْبٌ قِطْرِيٌّ قَدْ تَوَشَّحَ بِهِ، فَصَلَّىٰ بِهِمْ.[٨٦]

وَقَالَ عَبْدُ بْنُ حُمَيْدٍ، قَالَ مُحَمَّدُ بْنُ الْفَضْلِ: سَأَلَنِي يَحْيَىٰ بْنُ مَعِينٍ عَنْ هَذَا الْحَدِيثِ أَوَّلَ مَا جَلَسَ إِلَيَّ، فَقُلْتُ: حَدَّثَنَا حَمَّادُ بْنُ سَلَمَةَ، فَقَالَ: لَوْ كَانَ مِنْ كِتَابِكَ، فَقُمْتُ لأُخْرِجَ كِتَابِي فَقَبَضَ عَلَىٰ ثَوْبِي ثُمَّ قَالَ: أَمْلِهِ عَلَيَّ فَإِنِّي أَخَافُ أَنْ لا أَلْقَاكَ، قَالَ: فَأَمْلَيْتُهُ عَلَيْهِ، ثُمَّ أَخْرَجْتُ كِتَابِي فَقَرَأْتُ عَلَيْهِ.

59. Anas b. Mālik ؓ reported: "Allāh's Messenger ﷺ came out of his house reclining on Usāmah b. Zayd ؓ. He was wearing a *qitrī* wrap and proceeded to lead the prayer."

86 *Musnad Aḥmad* (13763)

'Abd b. Ḥumayd said that Muḥammad b. al-Faḍl said, "Yaḥyā b. Ma'īn asked me about this ḥadīth the first time he sat with me. I said, 'It was reported to us by Ḥammād b. Salamah.' He said, 'I would like it from your written records.' Then I stood to take out my record but he took a hold of my robe and said, 'Recite it, for I fear that we may not meet again.' So, I recited it to him, then I brought my record and I read it to him."

'Abd al-Razzāq al-Badr said,

> **"He was wearing a *qitrī* wrap":** It was placed on his shoulders.

Al-Bājūrī said,

> **"Allāh's Messenger ﷺ came out of his house reclining on Usāmah b. Zayd ؓ"** He left his house doing so because of illness. This occurred during his final illness.
>
> The *qitrī* wrap is a Yemenī sheet with printed columns, made of cotton and it has some redness in its colour.
>
> **"'Abd b. Ḥumayd said that Muḥammad b. al-Faḍl said...":** The author mentioned this incident despite its irrelevance to the chapter so as to display the strength of its chain of narration.
>
> **'Recite it, for I fear that we may not meet again':** I.e. as life is not guaranteed; time is like a sharp blade and a flash of lightning. This displays a total engrossment in attaining knowledge and avoidance of idle expectation, especially in matters that will lead to good.

٦٠ – حَدَّثَنَا سُوَيْدُ بْنُ نَصْرٍ، قَالَ: حَدَّثَنَا عَبْدُ اللهِ بْنُ الْمُبَارَكِ، عَنْ سَعِيدِ بْنِ إِيَاسٍ الْجُرَيْرِيِّ، عَنْ أَبِي نَضْرَةَ، عَنْ أَبِي سَعِيدٍ الْخُدْرِيِّ، قَالَ: كَانَ رَسُولُ اللهِ صلى الله عليه وسلم إِذَا اسْتَجَدَّ ثَوْبًا سَمَّاهُ باسْمِهِ، عِمَامَةً أَوْ قَمِيصًا أَوْ رِدَاءً، ثُمَّ يَقُولُ: «اللَّهُمَّ لَكَ الْحَمْدُ كَمَا كَسَوْتَنِيهِ ، أَسْأَلُكَ خَيْرَهُ وَخَيْرَ مَا صُنِعَ لَهُ، وَأَعُوذُ بِكَ مِنْ شَرِّهِ وَشَرِّ مَا صُنِعَ لَهُ».[٨٧]

60. Abū Sa'īd al-Khudrī ؓ narrated: "When the Messenger of Allāh ﷺ would put on a new garment, he would recite the following supplication whilst also identifying the garment (be it a turban, a sheet or a

87 *Sunan al-Tirmidhī* (1767) and *Sunan Abī Dāwūd* (4020)

wrap etc.), '*O Allāh, all praise be due to You as you clothed me with this [garment]. I ask You for the good of it and the good of what it was made for, and I ask Your protection from the evil of it and the evil of what it was made for.*'"

'Abd al-Razzāq al-Badr said,

> This supplication reminds us that it is Allāh who blessed us with a new garment, and that we did not come to possess it due to our own efforts and power. In other words, it is to direct us to remember the grace of Allāh as was stated in the divine ḥadīth wherein Allāh says, "O My slaves! All of you are naked except those who I clothe. Ask me to clothe you and I will clothe you."[88]

Al-Bājūrī said,

> The purpose of mentioning the name of the garment is to show the praise to Allāh for the particular grace that He has bestowed.

> The supplication is recited after saying *bismillāh* because saying it is an act of Sunnah before wearing the clothes.

Ibn Ḥajar al-Haytamī said,

> This is to say: "O Allāh you clothed us because of our poverty and need to You and not because You are in need of clothing us; therefore we praise You not because of what You have blessed us with but rather because You deserve it."

٦١ - حَدَّثَنَا هِشَامُ بْنُ يُونُسَ الْكُوفِيُّ، قَالَ: حَدَّثَنَا الْقَاسِمُ بْنُ مَالِكٍ الْمُزَنِيُّ، عَنِ الْجُرَيْرِيِّ، عَنْ أَبِي نَضْرَةَ، عَنْ أَبِي سَعِيدٍ الْخُدْرِيِّ، عَنِ النَّبِيِّ صلى الله عليه وسلم نَحْوَهُ.

61. A similar report was narrated via a different route from Abū Sa'īd al-Khudrī ⬧.

'Alī al-Qārī said,

> *"Naḥwuh":* I.e. with the same meaning. If he had said *"mithluh"* it would have meant: with the same wording.

---

88 *Ṣaḥīḥ Muslim* (2577)

٦٢ - حَدَّثَنَا مُحَمَّدُ بْنُ بَشَّارٍ، قَالَ: حَدَّثَنَا مُعَاذُ بْنُ هِشَامٍ، قَالَ: حَدَّثَنِي أَبِي، عَنْ قَتَادَةَ، عَنْ أَنَسِ بْنِ مَالِكٍ، قَالَ: «كَانَ أَحَبَّ الثِّيَابِ إِلَىٰ رَسُولِ اللهِ صلىٰ الله عليه وسلم ، يَلْبَسُهُ الْحِبَرَةُ».[٨٩]

62. Anas b. Mālik ﵁ narrated: "The most beloved garment to the Prophet ﷺ that he would wear was the *hibarah*."

ʿAbd al-Razzāq al-Badr said,

> A *hibarah* is a kind of cloth made of cotton or linen with patterns to make it more beautiful.

Al-Bājūrī said,

> **"That he would wear":** This omits cloths he used for laying down etc.
>
> It seems that he liked this type of clothing due to its softness and nice design. Also, the fabric complimented his body as he possessed very soft skin and due to the softness of the fabric, it suited him perfectly.

Ibn Ḥajar al-Haytamī said,

> It has printed patterns on it and although it is disliked to wear a garment in the prayer with patterns printed on it, the fact that he ﷺ wore it shows that it is permissible to wear them.

٦٣ - حَدَّثَنَا مَحْمُودُ بْنُ غَيْلَانَ، قَالَ: حَدَّثَنَا عَبْدُ الرَّزَّاقِ، قَالَ: حَدَّثَنَا سُفْيَانُ، عَنْ عَوْنِ بْنِ أَبِي جُحَيْفَةَ، عَنْ أَبِيهِ، قَالَ: «رَأَيْتُ النَّبِيَّ صلىٰ الله عليه وسلم وَعَلَيْهِ حُلَّةٌ حَمْرَاءُ، كَأَنِّي أَنْظُرُ إِلَىٰ بَرِيقِ سَاقَيْهِ»، قَالَ سُفْيَانُ: أُرَاهَا حِبَرَةً.[٩٠]

63. Abū Juḥayfah ﵁ related: "I saw Allāh's Messenger ﷺ wearing a red *ḥullah*. I can see the radiance of his shins as if they are still before me." Sufyān said, "I think it (his garment) was a *ḥibarah*."

ʿAbd al-Razzāq al-Badr said,

> **"I can see the radiance of his shins as if they are still before me":** This indicates that when Abū Juḥayfah saw him, the lower wrap of

89 *Ṣaḥīḥ al-Bukhārī* (5813) and *Ṣaḥīḥ Muslim* (2079)
90 *Sunan al-Tirmidhī* (197), *Ṣaḥīḥ al-Bukhārī* (376) and *Ṣaḥīḥ Muslim* (503)

the Prophet ﷺ was to the half point of his shins.

Al-Bājūrī said,

> **"I saw Allāh's Messenger ﷺ":** This was during the farewell Ḥajj, as stated in the ḥadīth documented in *Ṣaḥīḥ al-Bukhārī*.

> **"I can see the radiance of his shins as if they are still before me":** This indicates that it is permissible for a man to look at another man's legs. There is a scholarly consensus on this, wherein there is no temptation present. It indicates that it is recommended to shorten the robe or the *izār* to the mid-point of the shin, though it is permissible to keep its length to the ankles. What extends beyond the ankles is forbidden if it is done pridefully, and if it is not done so, then it is detested *(makrūh)*.

> **"Sufyān said, 'I think it [his garment] was a *hibarah*":** As Sufyān (who is the one narrating this ḥadīth from the companion) held the view that completely red garments are forbidden, he made the remark that he believes it was a *hibarah* as this would mean it had a pattern with another colour.

Ibn Ḥajar al-Haytamī said,

> **"I can see the radiance of his shins as if they are still before me":** While it is recommended for the man to shorten his garment to reach the mid-point of his shin, and it is permissible to make its length reach the ankle, it is recommended for the woman to wear that which covers her and it is allowed to make it long to the point it is dragged on the floor. However, if what she intends with that is showing off then she will be sinful just like if they (men) drag their garments to show off.

٦٤ – حَدَّثَنَا عَلِيُّ بْنُ خَشْرَمٍ، قَالَ: حَدَّثَنَا عِيسَىٰ بْنُ يُونُسَ، عَنْ إِسْرَائِيلَ، عَنْ أَبِي إِسْحَاقَ، عَنِ الْبَرَاءِ بْنِ عَازِبٍ، قَالَ: «مَا رَأَيْتُ أَحَدًا مِنَ النَّاسِ أَحْسَنَ فِي حُلَّةٍ حَمْرَاءَ مِنْ رَسُولِ اللهِ صلىٰ الله عليه وسلم، إِنْ كَانَتْ جُمَّتُهُ لَتَضْرِبُ قَرِيبًا مِنْ مَنْكِبَيْهِ». ٩١

64. Al-Barāʾ b. ʿĀzib ؓ **narrated:** "I have never seen anybody appear more handsome in red clothing than the Messenger of Allāh ﷺ. At

---

91 See ḥadīth 4

that time, his hair reached his shoulders."

Mīrak Shāh al-Ḥanafī said (as quoted by ʿAlī al-Qārī),

> Scholars differed on the permissibility of wearing fully red clothes; some scholars allowed it in all cases, some scholars forbade it in all cases. Some scholars disliked the wearing of clothes which have red prevailing over the other colours, and some scholars said it is disliked in all cases if it is worn for the purpose of adornment and to be known, but it is allowed to be worn inside the house and while working. Some scholars said it is not allowed if it is dyed with red after it was woven, and some scholars said only that which is dyed with safflower is forbidden. Some scholars said only that which is dyed red completely is forbidden, and so any garment with additional colours besides red is permissible.

Ibn al-Qayyim said (as quoted by ʿAlī al-Qārī),

> Some scholars wear clothes dyed in red, assuming that this equates to following the Sunnah. This is a mistake, for the red *ḥullah* is a Yemeni *burūd* garment which is not dyed purely with red.

٦٥- حَدَّثَنَا مُحَمَّدُ بْنُ بَشَّارٍ، قَالَ: حَدَّثَنَا عَبْدُ الرَّحْمَنِ بْنُ مَهْدِيٍّ، قَالَ: حَدَّثَنَا عُبَيْدُ اللهِ بْنُ إِيَادٍ، عَنْ أَبِيهِ، عَنْ أَبِي رِمْثَةَ، قَالَ: «رَأَيْتُ النَّبِيَّ صلىٰ الله عليه وسلم وَعَلَيْهِ بُرْدَانِ أَخْضَرَانِ».[٩٢]

65. Abū Rimthah Taymī ﵁ said, "I saw the Messenger of Allāh ﷺ and he was dressed in two green coloured *burdahs*."

ʿAbd al-Razzāq al-Badr said,

> The colour of the garment was not plain green because a *burdah* has multiple colours in its pattern design.

٦٦- حَدَّثَنَا عَبْدُ بْنُ حُمَيْدٍ ، قَالَ: حَدَّثَنَا عَفَّانُ بْنُ مُسْلِمٍ، قَالَ: حَدَّثَنَا عَبْدُ اللهِ بْنُ حَسَّانَ الْعَنْبَرِيُّ، عَنْ جَدَّتَيْهِ دُحَيْبَةَ، وَعُلَيْبَةَ، عَنْ قَيْلَةَ بِنْتِ مَخْرَمَةَ، قَالَتْ: «رَأَيْتُ النَّبِيَّ صلىٰ الله عليه وسلم وَعَلَيْهِ أَسْمَالُ مُلَيَّتَيْنِ كَانَتَا بِزَعْفَرَانٍ، وَقَدْ نَفَضَتْهُ». وَفِي

---

92 *Sunan al-Tirmidhī* (2812) and *Sunan Abī Dāwūd* (4065)

الْحَدِيثِ قِصَّةٌ طَوِيلَةٌ.^{٩٣}

66. Qaylah bint Makhramah ☙ narrated: "I saw the Messenger of Allāh ﷺ wearing two well worn wraps that had been dyed with saffron yet there was no trace of saffron left upon them."

This ḥadīth contains a lengthy story.

Al-Bājūrī said,

> The fact that the Prophet ﷺ wore something dyed with saffron does not contradict his order not to wear such garments. This is because his prohibition is related to the case where the colour of saffron is evident and it prevails over other colours. It does not relate to where the saffron has faded out and only a small trace remains.

ʿAlī al-Qārī said,

> It is established that the Prophet ﷺ wore nice clothes but he preferred to wear that which manifested his humility and humbleness before his Lord. The *salaf* and the majority of the ascetics followed his way in the type of clothes to wear i.e. wearing clothing that manifests humbleness. This is because they saw people showing off with their fancy garments and adornments; therefore they wanted to remind them of the triviality of what they were proud of. However, later on the heedless started wearing very old clothes as a means to receive worldly pleasures and to make the people like them; thus the Sunnah became to oppose them by wearing nice clothes. It was reported that a man who was wearing old clothes criticized Abū al-Ḥasan al-Shadhilī for wearing nice garments. To that Abū al-Ḥasan replied, "The clothes I wear reflect my state praising Allāh, whereas your clothes reflect your state asking people to give you some of their worldly pleasures." In all cases, one must rectify their intention and avoid showing off whilst not refraining from wearing nice clothes due to stinginess, for indeed the beauty lies in the heart but still the body should reflect the beauty of the heart.

Ibn Ḥajar al-Haytamī said,

> **"This ḥadīth contains a lengthy story":** This was reported by al-Ṭabarānī and its chain of narration has no issues.⁹⁴ It was not men-

93 *Sunan al-Tirmidhī* (2814)
94 *Al-Muʿjam al-Kabīr* (18/183)

tioned by the author due to the lack of relevance here.

٦٧ – حَدَّثَنَا قُتَيْبَةُ بْنُ سَعِيدٍ، قَالَ: حَدَّثَنَا بِشْرُ بْنُ الْمُفَضَّلِ، عَنْ عَبْدِ اللهِ بْنِ عُثْمَانَ
بْنِ خُثَيْمٍ، عَنْ سَعِيدِ بْنِ جُبَيْرٍ، عَنِ ابْنِ عَبَّاسٍ، قَالَ: قَالَ رَسُولُ اللهِ صلى الله عليه
وسلم: «عَلَيْكُمْ بِالْبَيَاضِ مِنَ الثِّيَابِ، لِيَلْبِسْهَا أَحْيَاؤُكُمْ، وَكَفِّنُوا فِيهَا مَوْتَاكُمْ،
فَإِنَّهَا مِنْ خِيَارِ ثِيَابِكُمْ». ⁹⁵

**67. 'Abdullāh b. 'Abbās ؓ related: "The Prophet ﷺ said, 'Wear gar-
ments of white colours. Let the living among you wear them and enshroud the dead therewith, for it is amongst the best of your clothes.'"**

Al-Bājūrī said,

This is to encourage wearing white clothes, as it is recommended to
wear them in gatherings e.g. when attending the Friday prayer, attending the *masjid*, events and sittings that the angels witness such as
gatherings to recite the Qur'ān or to remember Allāh. As for Eid, it is
recommended to wear the best and pricey clothes, even if the colour
is not white, because the day is intended to manifest adornment and
display Allāh's grace upon us.

The best coloured clothings are in the following order: The white, the
green and then the yellow.

Ibn Ḥajar al-Haytamī said,

It is the preferred colour for the shroud because the dead is about to
meet the angels. This is why it is recommended, it is also why we are
directed to perfume the dead.

'Alī al-Qārī said,

In order for the garment to deserve being called the best of clothes in
its absolute form, it has to be (besides being white in colour) pure,
neat and not accompanied by pride, showing off etc.

٦٨ – حَدَّثَنَا مُحَمَّدُ بْنُ بَشَّارٍ، قَالَ: حَدَّثَنَا عَبْدُ الرَّحْمَنِ بْنُ مَهْدِيٍّ، قَالَ: حَدَّثَنَا
سُفْيَانُ، عَنْ حَبِيبِ بْنِ أَبِي ثَابِتٍ، عَنْ مَيْمُونِ بْنِ أَبِي شَبِيبٍ، عَنْ سَمُرَةَ بْنِ جُنْدُبٍ

---

95 See ḥadīth 52

قَالَ: قَالَ رَسُولُ اللهِ صلىٰ الله عليه وسلم: «الْبَسُوا الْبَيَاضَ، فَإِنَّهَا أَطْهَرُ وَأَطْيَبُ، وَكَفِّنُوا فِيهَا مَوْتَاكُمْ».[٩٦]

68. Samurah b. Jundub ﷺ narrated: "The Messenger of Allāh ﷺ said, 'Wear white clothing for it is the purest and most beautiful [of your clothing], and also enshroud your dead with it.'"

ʿAbd al-Razzāq al-Badr said,

> **"It is the purest":** It is described as such because dirt or impurity can easily be identified [when wearing a white garment] unlike other colours that may have unseen dirt or impurity. This is why the Prophet ﷺ used to supplicate, "O Allāh, purify me from my sins just like how a white garment is purified from dirt."

ʿAlī al-Qārī said,

> **"Most beautiful":** It is described as such because white clothing indicates the humility of the one wearing it and negates the qualities of pride and showing off.

٦٩- حَدَّثَنَا أَحْمَدُ بْنُ مَنِيعٍ، قَالَ حَدَّثَنَا يَحْيَىٰ بْنُ زَكَرِيَّا بْنِ أَبِي زَائِدَةَ، قَالَ: حَدَّثَنَا أَبِي، عَنْ مُصْعَبِ بْنِ شَيْبَةَ، عَنْ صَفِيَّةَ بِنْتِ شَيْبَةَ، عَنْ عَائِشَةَ، قَالَتْ: «خَرَجَ رَسُولُ اللهِ صلىٰ الله عليه وسلم ذَاتَ غَدَاةٍ وَعَلَيْهِ مِرْطٌ مِنْ شَعَرٍ أَسْوَدَ».[٩٧]

69. ʿĀ'ishah ﷺ narrated: "One day, the Messenger of Allāh ﷺ left the house early in the morning, wearing a long black wrap made of hair."

Ibn Ḥajar al-Haytamī said,

> The way of the Prophet ﷺ was that he did not prefer wearing a particular type of clothing nor did he have an interest in wearing fancy and expensive clothing. This is because showing off with fancy clothes is from the qualities of women. However, the quality that is praised in men is to ensure that their clothes are clean, modest and decent; therefore he ﷺ preferred wearing the type of clothing that he needed and encouraged others to wear the other types.

---

96 *Sunan al-Tirmidhī* (2810)
97 *Ṣaḥīḥ Muslim* (2082) and *Sunan al-Tirmidhī* (2813)

٧٠- حَدَّثَنَا يُوسُفُ بْنُ عِيسَىٰ، قَالَ: حَدَّثَنَا وَكِيعٌ، قَالَ: حَدَّثَنَا يُونُسُ بْنُ أَبِي

إِسْحَاقَ، عَنْ أَبِيهِ، عَنِ الشَّعْبِيِّ، عَنْ عُرْوَةَ بْنِ الْمُغِيرَةِ بْنِ شُعْبَةَ، عَنْ أَبِيهِ، أَنَّ النَّبِيَّ

صلى الله عليه وسلم لَبِسَ جُبَّةً رُومِيَّةً ضَيِّقَةَ الْكُمَّيْنِ ٩٨

70. Al-Mughīrah b. Shuʿbah ☀ **narrated: "The Prophet** ☀ **wore a Romanic *jubbah* which had tight sleeves."**

ʿAbd al-Razzāq al-Badr said,

> The *jubbah* is an outer garment that is worn over the *qamīṣ*.

> The ḥadīths that the author included in this chapter show the variety of clothes that the Prophet ☀ wore, which indicates that clothing is not a restricted avenue, but rather all garments are lawful except that which is forbidden by evidence.

Al-Bājūrī said,

> He wore it whilst travelling and it is reported that this was in the battle of Tabūk.

> The fact that the garment was made by the Romans shows that the general rule is that all clothes are pure, even those made by disbelievers.

> **"Tight sleeves"**: This means that when he wanted to pull his arms out of the sleeves it was difficult. Some scholars said that it is recommended to wear narrow sleeved garments whilst travelling only. The sleeves of the companions were wide.

> The beautification of appearance in terms of clothing is praised if it is done to help one in the worship of Allāh, such as how the Prophet ☀ took care of his appearance and clothes when welcoming the delegates and it is dispraised when it is done for worldly benefits or to show off.

---

98 *Ṣaḥīḥ Muslim* (274)

باب ما جاء في عيش رسول الله صلى الله عليه وسلم

[9] On the Living Conditions of Allāh's Messenger ﷺ

ʿAlī al-Qārī said,

> There is another chapter towards the end of this book that talks about the food and drink of the Prophet ﷺ. However, it seems that this short chapter is intended to highlight the poverty faced by the Prophet and some of his companions while the other long chapter highlights the poverty faced by the Prophet and his family. The other possible explanation is that this short chapter is dedicated to detailing the hardship he experienced at the beginning [of his prophethood] and the long chapter highlights that which he experienced at the end of his life.

Ibn Ḥajar al-Haytamī said,

> It appears as if this chapter is repeated at the end of the book but this chapter is intended to indicate the poverty of the Prophet ﷺ while the other one is to indicate the type of food and drink he used to consume.

٧١- حَدَّثَنَا قُتَيْبَةُ بْنُ سَعِيدٍ، حَدَّثَنَا حماد بن زيد، عن أيوب، عن محمد بن سيرين، قال: كُنَّا عِنْدَ أَبِي هُرَيْرَةَ، وَعَلَيْهِ ثَوْبَانِ مُمَشَّقَانِ مِنْ كَتَّان فَتَمَخَّطَ فِي أَحَدِهِمَا، فَقَالَ: «بَخْ بَخْ يَتَمَخَّطُ أَبُو هُرَيْرَةَ فِي الْكَتَّانِ، لَقَدْ رَأَيْتُنِي وَإِنِّي لأَخِرُّ فِيمَا بَيْنَ مِنبَرِ رَسُولِ اللهِ صلى الله عليه وسلم وحُجْرَةِ عَائِشَةَ مَغْشِيًّا عَلَيَّ، فَيَجِيءُ الْجَائِي فَيَضَعُ رِجْلَهُ عَلَىٰ عُنُقِي يَرَىٰ أَنَّ بِي جُنُونًا، وَمَا بِي جُنُونٌ، ومَا هو إِلَّا الْجُوعُ».[٩٩]

71. Muḥammad b. Sīrīn narrated: "We were with Abū Hurayrah while he was wearing two linen garments dyed with red clay. He blew his nose with one of them, upon which he said, 'Well done! Well

99 *Ṣaḥīḥ al-Bukhārī* (7324)

done! Abū Hurayrah is cleaning his nose with linen! There came a time when I would fall unconscious between the pulpit of Allāh's Messenger ﷺ and 'Ā'ishah's dwelling whereupon a passer-by would come and put his foot on my neck, thinking I suffer from epilepsy, while in fact, I suffered nothing but hunger.'"

Al-Bājūrī said,

> **"Well done! Well done!":** This is often said to express one's pleasure and joy but it could be used in the context of condemnation in the case of this ḥadīth.

'Abd al-Razzāq al-Badr said,

> **"Abū Hurayrah is cleaning his nose with linen":** This is an expression of the change he experienced in terms of wealth as he was very poor and then later, he was cleaning his nose with a linen garment.

'Alī al-Qārī said,

> **"A passer-by would come and put his foot on my neck":** The habit of people when seeing a person suffering an epileptic seizure was to keep their feet on the neck to hold the person still until the seizure ended.

This ḥadīth was included in this chapter as it indicates the poverty of the Prophet ﷺ at that time. This is because if he had any food he would have shared it with his companions, particularly due to the fact that he used to look after them and treated them as his guests.

٧٢- حَدَّثَنَا قُتَيْبَةُ، قَالَ: حَدَّثَنَا جَعْفَرُ بْنُ سُلَيْمَانَ الضُّبَعِيُّ، عَنْ مَالِكِ بْنِ دِينَارٍ قَالَ: «مَا شَبِعَ رَسُولُ اللهِ صلى الله عليه وسلم مِنْ خُبْزٍ قَطُّ وَلَا لَحْمٍ، إِلَّا عَلَى ضَفَفٍ». قَالَ مَالِكٌ: «سَأَلْتُ رَجُلًا مِنْ أَهْلِ الْبَادِيَةِ: مَا الضَّفَفُ؟ قَالَ: أَنْ يَتَنَاوَلَ مَعَ النَّاسِ». ١٠٠

72. Mālik b. Dīnār ؓ narrated: "The Messenger of Allāh ﷺ never reached the state of being satisfactorily full, neither from bread nor meat, except when he used to eat with people." Mālik said, "I asked

---

100 *Ṣaḥīḥ Ibn Ḥibbān* (6359)

one of the desert folk about the meaning of *al-ḍaffaf*. He stated that it means to eat with the people."

Al-Bājūrī said,

> **"Except when he used to eat with people":** This refers to filling two thirds of his stomach, as in feasts he would stay to show courtesy to the people and to show them that he loves the food. With that said, it is an obvious error on the part of those who claimed that he ﷺ used to reach the state of satiety [or overeat] in feasts. This is because it does not befit his noble status and it would be insulting even if it was said regarding one of us!

ʿAbd al-Razzāq al-Badr said,

> Al-Imām Aḥmad said, "Four qualities in food will make it perfect: if the name of Allāh is mentioned on it in the beginning, Allāh is praised for it at the end, many hands are eating from it, and it is lawful."[101]

Ibn Ḥajar al-Haytamī said,

> **"Neither from bread nor meat":** This indicates that he ﷺ never ate bread and meat together except with people. The state of fullness referred to here is interpreted to mean that he would eat until two thirds of his stomach were full or that he would not be full from meat and bread together, or from either of them.

---

101 *Al-Zād* (4/213).

باب ما جاء في خف رسول الله صلى الله عليه وسلم

[10] On the *Khuff* of Allāh's Messenger ﷺ

ʿAbd al-Razzāq al-Badr said,

> *Khuff* is a well known type of socks. It is made of leather and it covers the entire foot.

Al-Bājūrī said,

> There are two ḥadīths in the chapter.

٧٣- حَدَّثَنَا هَنَّادُ بْنُ السَّرِيِّ، قَالَ: حَدَّثَنَا وَكِيعٌ، عَنْ دَلْهَمِ بْنِ صَالِحٍ، عَنْ حُجَيْرِ بْنِ عَبْدِ اللهِ، عَنِ ابْنِ بُرَيْدَةَ، عَنْ أَبِيهِ، أَنَّ النَّجَاشِيَّ أَهْدَىٰ لِلنَّبِيِّ صلى الله عليه وسلم خُفَّيْنِ أَسْوَدَيْنِ سَاذَجَيْنِ، «فَلَبِسَهُمَا ثُمَّ تَوَضَّأَ وَمَسَحَ عَلَيْهِمَا».[١٠٢]

73. Buraydah ؓ narrated: "Al-Najāshī sent two plain black coloured *khuffs* as a gift to the Messenger of Allāh ﷺ. As soon as he received them, he tried them on, performed ablution and then wiped over them."

ʿAbd al-Razzāq al-Badr said,

> **"Al-Najāshī"** was the title given to the kings of Ethiopia and the name of this particular king was Aṣḥamah; he embraced Islām and died upon it. When he died, the Prophet ﷺ prayed the absentee funeral prayer on him.

Al-Bājūrī said,

> **"As soon as he received them, he tried them on":** This indicates that when a person receives a gift from someone, using it immediately shows one's acceptance of the gift and it also indicates the continuous signals of love between the one receiving the gift and its sender. This ḥadīth also indicates that one should accept gifts even if they come

102 *Sunan al-Tirmidhī* (2820) and *Sunan Abī Dāwūd* (155)

from the People of the Book because at that time al-Najāshī was still a disbeliever, as stated by Abū Bakr b. al-Arabī.

Ibn Ḥajar al-Haytamī said,

> **"Performed ablution and then wiped over them":** This indicates that when an object's purity cannot be ascertained, it is deemed to be pure. It also indicates towards the permissibility of wiping over the *khuff*, which is a consensus amongst the scholars who are given regard. Reports from scholastic luminaries contrary to this are merely interpretations, in the face of which we have reports from eighty companions that they can be wiped over. On this basis, some major scholars said, "The aḥādīth on it are *mutawātir* (mass-transmitted), so repudiating it is feared to be disbelief."

٧٤- حَدَّثَنَا قُتَيْبَةُ بْنُ سَعِيدٍ، قَالَ: حَدَّثَنَا يَحْيَىٰ بْنُ زَكَرِيَّا بْنِ أَبِي زَائِدَةَ، عَنِ الْحَسَنِ بْنِ عَيَّاشٍ، عَنْ أَبِي إِسْحَاقَ، عَنِ الشَّعْبِيِّ، قَالَ: قَالَ الْمُغِيرَةُ بْنُ شُعْبَةَ: «أَهْدَىٰ دِحْيَةُ لِلنَّبِيِّ صلى الله عليه وسلم خُفَّيْنِ، فَلَبِسَهُمَا - وَقَالَ إِسْرَائِيلُ: عَنْ جَابِرٍ، عَنْ عَامِرٍ، وَجُبَّةً فَلَبِسَهُمَا - حَتَّىٰ تَخَرَّقَا لا يَدْرِي النَّبِيُّ صلى الله عليه وسلم أَذَكِيٌّ هُمَا أَمْ لا. قَالَ أَبُو عِيسَىٰ: وَأَبُو إِسْحَاقَ هَذَا هُوَ أَبُو إِسْحَاقَ الشَّيْبَانِيُّ، وَاسْمُهُ سُلَيْمَانُ.[١٠٣]

74. Al-Mughīrah b. Shu'bah ؓ narrated: "Diḥyyah gifted the Prophet ﷺ with a pair of *khuffs* that he wore right away and he kept wearing them until they became torn. The Prophet ﷺ did not know whether the skin of the *khuffs* was from an animal that was slaughtered properly or not."

From another route, it adds, "He was also gifted a robe and he wore them..."

Abū 'Īsā said, "The Abū Isḥāq mentioned in the chain of narration is Abū Isḥāq al-Shaybānī, whose name is Sulaymān."

'Abd al-Razzāq al-Badr said,

> **"That he wore right away":** This teaches us to hasten in accepting the gift and to use it right away so as to make the one who gave the gift

103 *Sunan al-Tirmidhī* (1769)

happy and pleased.

ʿAlī al-Qārī said,

"The Prophet ﷺ did not know whether the skin of the khuffs was from an animal that was slaughtered properly or not": [The companion reported this] because either he ﷺ stated it, or the companion determined this because the Prophet ﷺ did not inquire about it.

Al-Bājūrī said,

"Until they became torn": This indicates that the Prophet ﷺ used to keep wearing the clothes he had until they became worn out, as this is from humility.

باب ما جاء في نعل رسول الله صلى الله عليه وسلم

[11] On the Sandals of Allāh's Messenger ﷺ

ʿAbd al-Razzāq al-Badr said,

> This chapter is dedicated to describing the shoes of the Prophet ﷺ and his guidance in this regard. However, it is noteworthy to mention that it is permissible to wear anything we want, so long as what we wear is not forbidden in the religion. This is because the shoes that people wear in each era and in each culture are different. The general rule regarding clothes is that everything is permissible until there is evidence to prove it is forbidden.

Al-Bājūrī said,

> *Naʿl* refers to footwear that keeps the feet away from the floor and when the term is used it does not normally include the *khuff*, which is why it was given a separate chapter.
>
> The Prophet ﷺ had three different types of footwear, as Ibn Saʿd narrated in his work *al-Ṭabaqāt*:
>
> 1. Footwear that was narrow in the middle.
> 2. Footwear with a leather piece in the back to support the ankle.
> 3. Footwear with a long front part, that took the shape of a tongue. It was designed this way to fit his second toe, which was the tallest of his toes.
>
> He ﷺ used to walk barefoot sometimes out of humility, especially when he would go to visit an ill person.
>
> There are eleven ḥadīths in this chapter.

٧٥- حَدَّثَنَا مُحَمَّدُ بْنُ بَشَّارٍ، قَالَ: حَدَّثَنَا أَبُو دَاوُدَ الطَّيَالِسِيُّ، قَالَ: حَدَّثَنَا هَمَّامٌ، عَنْ قَتَادَةَ، قَالَ: قُلْتُ لأَنَسِ بْنِ مَالِكٍ: «كَيْفَ كَانَ نَعْلُ رَسُولِ اللهِ صلى الله عليه

وسلم؟ قَالَ: لَهُمَا قِبَالانِ». ١٠٤

75. Qatādah narrated: "I asked Anas b. Mālik ﷺ to describe the sandals of Allāh's Messenger ﷺ. He replied, 'Each sandal had two *qibālān*.'"

Ibn Ḥajar al-Haytamī said,

> *Qibālān* are two ribbons fastened to the sole of the sandal. The joining point of the ribbons separates the middle toes from the next one. It has also been said that one ribbon separates the foot's thumb and the next toe, and the other ribbon separates the middle toe and the next one.

٧٦- حَدَّثَنَا أَبُو كُرَيْبٍ مُحَمَّدُ بْنُ الْعَلاءِ، قَالَ: حَدَّثَنَا وَكِيعٌ، عَنْ سُفْيَانَ، عَنْ خَالِدٍ الْحَذَّاءِ، عَنْ عَبْدِ اللهِ بْنِ الْحَارِثِ، عَنِ ابْنِ عَبَّاسٍ، قَالَ: «كَانَ لِنَعْلِ رَسُولِ اللهِ صلى الله عليه وسلم قِبَالانِ مَثْنِيٌّ شِرَاكُهُمَا». ١٠٥

76. ʿAbdullāh b. ʿAbbās ﷺ related: "The sandal of the Messenger of Allāh ﷺ had two ribbons and two upper straps."

ʿAbd al-Muḥsin al-ʿAbbād said,

> The ribbon refers to that which separates the toes, whereas the upper straps are that which secure the sandal to the upper part of the feet.

ʿAbd al-Razzāq al-Badr said,

> This means that each sandal had two ribbons and two straps were connected with each ribbon.

٧٧- حَدَّثَنَا أَحْمَدُ بْنُ مَنِيعٍ، قَالَ: حَدَّثَنَا أَبُو أَحْمَدَ الزُّبَيْرِيُّ، قَالَ: حَدَّثَنَا عِيسَى بْنُ طَهْمَانَ، قَالَ: أَخْرَجَ إِلَيْنَا أَنَسُ بْنُ مَالِكٍ نَعْلَيْنِ جَرْدَاوَيْنِ، لَهُمَا قِبَالانِ.

قَالَ: فَحَدَّثَنِي ثَابِتٌ بَعْدُ عَنْ أَنَسٍ أَنَّهُمَا كَانَتَا نَعْلَيِ النَّبِيِّ صلى الله عليه وسلم. ١٠٦

77. ʿĪsā b. Ṭahmān narrated: "Anas b. Mālik ﷺ showed us a pair of sandals that had two straps and were hairless. Later on, Thābit told me on the authority of Anas that these were the sandals of the Proph-

---

104 *Ṣaḥīḥ al-Bukhārī* (5857
105 *Sunan Ibn Mājah* (3614)
106 *Ṣaḥīḥ al-Bukhārī* (5858)

et ﷺ."

ʿAbd al-Razzāq al-Badr said,

> This indicates that Anas kept these sandals of the Prophet ﷺ in his house. Seeking blessing from the relics of the Prophet ﷺ – be they separated from his body e.g. his hair, or worn by him e.g. his sandals – will be mentioned later.

٧٨- حَدَّثَنَا إِسْحَاقُ بْنُ مُوسَىٰ الأَنْصَارِيُّ قَالَ: حَدَّثَنَا مَعْنٌ ، قَالَ: حَدَّثَنَا مَالِكٌ، قَالَ: حَدَّثَنَا سَعِيدُ بْنُ أَبِي سَعِيدٍ الْمَقْبُرِيُّ، عَنْ عُبَيْدِ بْنِ جُرَيْجٍ، أَنَّهُ قَالَ لابْنِ عُمَرَ: رَأَيْتُكَ تَلْبَسُ النِّعَالَ السِّبْتِيَّةَ، قَالَ: «إِنِّي رَأَيْتُ رَسُولَ اللهِ صلىٰ الله عليه وسلم يَلْبَسُ النِّعَالَ الَّتِي لَيْسَ فِيهَا شَعَرٌ، وَيَتَوَضَّأُ فِيهَا، فَأَنَا أُحِبُّ أَنْ أَلْبَسَهَا».[١٠٧]

78. ʿUbayd b. Jurayj asked Ibn ʿUmar ؓ: "Why do you [prefer] wearing the *sibti* type of sandals?" He replied, "I saw the Messenger of Allāh ﷺ wearing sandals that did not have hair on them, performing ablution while he had them on. This is why I like wearing them."

Al-Bājūrī and ʿAbd al-Razzāq al-Badr said,

> *Sibti* sandals refer to the sandals made of tanned cow leather and they are called *sibti* because the hair falls off when the leather is dyed.

ʿAlī al-Qārī said,

> The answer of Ibn ʿUmar ؓ was to show that he preferred wearing this type of sandal to follow the guidance of the Prophet ﷺ and not because of personal preference.

٧٩- حَدَّثَنَا إِسْحَاقُ بْنُ مَنْصُورٍ، قَالَ: حَدَّثَنَا عَبْدُ الرَّزَّاقِ، عَنْ مَعْمَرٍ، عَنِ ابْنِ أَبِي ذِئْبٍ، عَنْ صَالِحٍ مَوْلَىٰ التَّوْءَمَةِ، عَنْ أَبِي هُرَيْرَةَ، قَالَ: «كَانَ لِنَعْلِ رَسُولِ اللهِ صلىٰ الله عليه وسلم قِبَالانِ».[١٠٨]

79. Abū Hurayrah ؓ related: "The sandals of Allāh's Messenger ﷺ had two upper straps."

---

107 *Ṣaḥīḥ al-Bukhārī* (5851) and *Ṣaḥīḥ Muslim* (1187)
108 *Al-ʿIlal al-Kabīr* of al-Bukhārī (291)

Al-Bājūrī said,

> In the report of Abū al-Shaykh from Abū Dharr, it states that they were made from cow leather, and it has been said that they were yellow. ʿAlī b. Abī Ṭālib ﷺ and Ibn ʿAbbās ﷺ reportedly encouraged wearing yellow sandals, because yellow is from the colours that indicate happiness.

٨٠- حَدَّثَنَا أَحْمَدُ بْنُ مَنِيعٍ، قَالَ: حَدَّثنا أَبُو أَحْمَدَ، قَالَ: حَدَّثنا سُفْيَانُ، عَنِ السُّدِّيِّ، قَالَ: حَدَّثَنِي مَنْ سَمِعَ عَمْرَو بْنَ حُرَيْثٍ يَقُولُ: «رَأَيْتُ رَسُولَ اللهِ صلىٰ الله عليه وسلم يُصَلِّي فِي نَعْلَيْنِ مَخْصُوفَتَيْنِ».[١٠٩]

80. ʿAmr b. Ḥurayth ﷺ narrated: "I saw the Messenger of Allāh ﷺ praying while wearing a pair of sandals that had new soles sewn onto them."

ʿAbd al-Razzāq al-Badr said,

> The Prophet ﷺ used to sew the leather sole into his sandals by himself, as reported in the ḥadīth that al-Imām Ahmad documented in his *Musnad*. He reported that ʿĀ'ishah was asked, "What would the Prophet ﷺ do in his house?" She replied, "He would do just as any of you does. He repaired his sandals and patched his garments.[110]"

Al-Bājūrī said,

> The Prophet ﷺ had sandals that had one sole and sandals that had more than one sole.

٨١- حَدَّثنا إِسْحَاقُ بْنُ مُوسَىٰ الأَنْصَارِيُّ، قَالَ: حَدَّثَنَا مَعْنٌ، قَالَ: حَدَّثنا مَالِكٌ، عَنْ أَبِي الزِّنَادِ، عَنِ الأَعْرَجِ، عَنْ أَبِي هُرَيْرَةَ، أَنَّ رَسُولَ اللهِ صلىٰ الله عليه وسلم قَالَ: «لا يَمْشِيَنَّ أَحَدُكُمْ فِي نَعْلٍ وَاحِدَةٍ، لِيُنْعِلْهُمَا جَمِيعًا، أَوْ لِيُحْفِهِمَا جَمِيعًا».[١١١]

81. Abū Hurayrah ﷺ narrated that the Prophet ﷺ said: "One should not wear one shoe and walk. Either wear them both or remove them both."

---

109 *Al-Sunan al-Kubrā* of al-Nasā'ī (9719)

110 *Musnad al-Imām Aḥmad* (24749)

111 *Ṣaḥīḥ al-Bukhārī* (5855) and *Ṣaḥīḥ Muslim* (2097)

ʿAlī al-Qārī said,

> Al-Khaṭṭābī said that [it is disliked] because it would be difficult to walk whilst wearing one shoe, not to mention that it does not look good. Others said, it is [disliked] because it would make the person unjust between their own limbs, or because it would make people question their intellect and sensibility. Abū Bakr b. al-ʿArabī said, "It is disliked because it makes the person walk the walk of the Shayṭān. And it is said that it is disliked because it is immodest." Al-Bayhaqī said, "It is disliked because it makes the person known and famous and we are ordered not to attract the attention of others through our clothing or anything that may make us gain notoriety."

> Some scholars applied the same ruling on sleeves i.e. it is disliked to wear a shirt whilst having one arm in a sleeve and the other one bare.

٨٢- حَدَّثَنَا قُتَيْبَةُ، عَنْ مَالِكِ بْنِ أَنَسٍ، عَنْ أَبِي الزِّنَادِ نَحْوَهُ.

82. Abū Zinād reports the same.

٨٣- حَدَّثَنَا إِسْحَاقُ بْنُ مُوسَىٰ، قَالَ: حَدَّثَنَا مَعْنٌ، قَالَ: حَدَّثَنَا مَالِكٌ، عَنْ أَبِي الزُّبَيْرِ، عَنْ جَابِرٍ، ((أَنَّ النَّبِيَّ صلىٰ الله عليه وسلم نَهَىٰ أَنْ يَأْكُلَ - يَعْنِي الرَّجُلَ - بِشِمَالِهِ، أَوْ يَمْشِيَ فِي نَعْلٍ وَاحِدَةٍ)). ١١٢

83. Jābir b. ʿAbdillāh ☺ narrated: "The Prophet ﷺ prohibited people (lit. 'a man') from eating with the left hand and from wearing one sandal only."

ʿAbd al-Razzāq al-Badr said,

> **"Lit. 'a man'":** This does not mean that the ruling is specific to men. The word *rijāl* (men) is often used in the Prophetic narrations as usually, they were ones who were directly being addressed. However, the ruling applies equally to men and women.

> The prohibition of eating with the left hand applies to drinking as well.

Al-Bājūrī said,

---

112 *Ṣaḥīḥ Muslim* (2099)

The ruling on eating with the left hand without a necessity is that it is disliked according to the Shāfiʿī scholars and it is forbidden according to many Ḥanbalī and Mālikī scholars. The latter opinion was also held by some Shāfiʿīs.

٨٤- حَدَّثَنَا قُتَيْبَةُ، عَنْ مَالِكٍ، (ح) وَحَدَّثَنَا إِسْحَاقُ بْنُ مُوسَىٰ، قَالَ: حَدَّثَنَا مَعْنٌ، قَالَ: حَدَّثَنَا مَالِكٌ، عَنْ أَبِي الزِّنَادِ، عَنِ الأَعْرَجِ، عَنْ أَبِي هُرَيْرَةَ، أَنَّ النَّبِيَّ صلى الله عليه وسلم قَالَ: «إِذَا انْتَعَلَ أَحَدُكُمْ فَلْيَبْدَأْ بِالْيَمِينِ، وَإِذَا نَزَعَ فَلْيَبْدَأْ بِالشِّمَالِ، فَلْتَكُنِ الْيُمْنَىٰ أَوَّلَهُمَا تُنْعَلُ، وَآخِرَهُمَا تُنْزَعُ». ١١٣

84. Abū Hurayrah ؓ narrated that the Prophet ﷺ said: "Whenever one amongst you puts on their sandals, he should begin with the right, and when one of you removes them, the left one should be removed first. Let the right side be the first when putting them on and the last when removing them."

ʿAbd al-Razzāq al-Badr said,

> This shows the virtue of the right over the left in wearing shoes. It was the guidance of the Prophet ﷺ to start with the right in all that which is honoured and considered a matter of adornment and beauty such as wearing the shoes and clothes, grooming the hair etc. Whereas the left side is used to commence anything contrary to that such as removing the shoes, entering the toilet, and leaving the mosque etc.

Al-Bājūrī said,

> The right side is honoured and therefore it comes first in every matter that is intended to be perfect and good, whilst the left side is used in matters that imperfect the status. The right side is honoured because it is what Allāh prefers and likes in everything i.e. the dwellers of Paradise stand on the right side of the Throne on the Day of Judgement and receive their books with their right hands, the angel recording the good deeds is on the right side, the scale of good deeds are placed on the right side etc.

٨٥- حَدَّثَنَا أَبُو مُوسَىٰ مُحَمَّدُ بْنُ الْمُثَنَّىٰ، قَالَ: حَدَّثَنَا مُحَمَّدُ بْنُ جَعْفَرٍ، قَالَ:

---

113 *Ṣaḥīḥ al-Bukhārī* (5856) and *Ṣaḥīḥ Muslim* (2097)

حَدَّثَنَا شُعْبَةُ، قَالَ: حَدَّثَنَا أَشْعَثُ – هُوَ ابْنُ أَبِي الشَّعْثَاءِ –، عَنْ أَبِيهِ، عَنْ مَسْرُوقٍ، عَنْ عَائِشَةَ، قَالَتْ: «كَانَ رَسُولُ اللهِ صلى الله عليه وسلم يُحِبُّ التَّيَمُّنَ مَا اسْتَطَاعَ فِي تَرَجُّلِهِ، وَتَنَعُّلِهِ وَطُهُورِهِ.»١١٤

85. 'Ā'ishah ﷞ narrated: "The Prophet ﷺ liked to begin with the right side as much as possible: when he groomed his hair, wore his shoes and in his purification rites."

'Abd al-Razzāq al-Badr said,

This emphasises the meaning of the previous ḥadīth.

Al-Bājūrī said,

"The Prophet ﷺ liked to begin with the right side as much as possible": I.e. wherein this is possible. In instances where there is a necessity to do otherwise, it is not disliked (*makrūh*) to commence with the left.

٨٦ - حَدَّثَنَا مُحَمَّدُ بْنُ مَرْزُوقٍ أَبُو عَبْدِ اللهِ، قَالَ: حَدَّثَنَا عَبْدُ الرَّحْمَنِ بْنُ قَيْسٍ أَبُو مُعَاوِيَةَ، قَالَ: حَدَّثَنَا هِشَامٌ، عَنْ مُحَمَّدٍ، عَنْ أَبِي هُرَيْرَةَ، قَالَ: «كَانَ لِنَعْلِ رَسُولِ اللهِ صلى الله عليه وسلم قِبَالَانِ، وَأَبِي بَكْرٍ وَعُمَرَ، وَأَوَّلُ مَنْ عَقَدَ عَقْدًا وَاحِدًا عُثْمَانُ.»١١٥

86. Abū Hurayrah ﷞ narrated: "The sandals of Allāh's Messenger ﷺ had two upper straps, and so did the sandals of Abū Bakr ﷞ and 'Umar ﷞. However, 'Uthmān b. 'Affan ﷞ was the first one to use one strap."

'Abd al-Razzāq al-Badr said,

This action of 'Uthmān b. 'Affan ﷞ shows that the Prophet ﷺ had two straps due to his personal preference and not with the intention to draw closer to Allāh. This is because if it was done for this reason, 'Uthmān ﷞ would not have left it.

Al-Bājūrī said,

---

114 See ḥadīth 34
115 *Majma' al-Zawā'id wa Manba' al-Fawā'id* (5/141)

'Uthmān ؏ using one strap shows that the two straps were used because that was the custom and not because using one strap is disliked or not preferable. This illustrates that it is permissible to wear any type of shoes, because wearing sandals at that time was just the custom of people.

'Alī al-Qārī said,

> If 'Uthmān ؏ did not use the one strap it would have been assumed that using one strap is disliked. Thus, it shows that not wearing sandals and instead wearing anything else is permissible and not disliked.

باب ما جاء في ذكر خاتم رسول الله صلى الله عليه وسلم

[12] On Mention of the Ring (Seal) of Allāh's Messenger ﷺ

ʿAbd al-Razzāq al-Badr said,

> The Prophet ﷺ used the seal in the latter part of the sixth year of Hijrah when he started writing letters to the kings and leaders in which he called them to the religion of Allāh. This is because when he wanted to write to the Romans, he was advised that they do not read letters without seals on them. For that reason, he made a seal.

Al-Bājūrī said,

> The author used the word *dhikr* (mention of) in the chapter heading, contrary to his other chapter headings. This was done so as to differentiate between the *khātim al-nubuwwah* (the Prophetic seal between his shoulder blades) and the *khātim al-nabī* (the Prophet's seal/ring).

٨٧- حَدَّثَنَا قُتَيْبَةُ بْنُ سَعِيدٍ، وَغَيْرُ وَاحِدٍ، عَنْ عَبْدِ اللهِ بْنِ وَهْبٍ، عَنْ يُونُسَ، عَنِ ابْنِ شِهَابٍ، عَنْ أَنسِ بْنِ مَالِكٍ، قَالَ: «كَانَ خَاتَمُ النَّبِيِّ صلى الله عليه وسلم مِنْ وَرِقٍ، وَكَانَ فَصُّهُ حَبَشِيًّا».[١١٦]

87. Anas b. Mālik ؓ narrated: "The ring (i.e. seal) of Allāh's Messenger ﷺ was made of silver and its gem stone was Abyssinian."

ʿAbd al-Razzāq al-Badr said,

> This indicates that it is permissible for men to wear silver rings.

Al-Bājūrī said,

> The Prophet ﷺ had two seals that the reader of this book needs to distinguish; the seal of prophethood, which is the area of raised skin between his shoulders and the seal of the Prophet, which is the seal he

116 *Ṣaḥīḥ Muslim* (2094)

used to stamp his letters.

Ibn Ḥajar al-Haytamī said,

> It is permissible for men to wear rings; but it is disliked to wear more than two rings as stated by al-Dārimī (from our Shāfiʿī brethren), but the latter view is disputed over and this is not the appropriate place to expand on the matter.
>
> The gem stone was described as Abyssinian because it was agate, and it was said that it was termed so because its colour was black, or that the one who made it was an Abyssinian.

Al-Bājūrī said,

> The preference of the Prophet ﷺ to wear rings made of silver made some of the renowned Shāfiʿī scholars deduce that it is disliked to wear rings made of iron or copper and they relied on a number of ḥadīths, one of which is the ḥadīth wherein the Prophet ﷺ saw a man wearing a ring made of copper and said to him, "Why do I smell the scent of idols coming from you?!" So the man removed it and then he came wearing a ring made of iron so he said to him, "Why do you wear the jewellery of the people of Hell?" Upon which the man removed it.[117]
>
> Al-Bayhaqī said, after narrating the ḥadīths that talk about the gem stone of the Prophet ﷺ wherein some ḥadīths show that it was made of agate and others show that it was made of silver just like the ring, "These ḥadīths indicate that he had two rings, one of which the gem stone was Abyssinian and another of which the gem stone was silver."

٨٨- حَدَّثَنَا قُتَيْبَةُ، حَدَّثَنَا أَبُو عَوَانَةَ، عَنْ أَبِي بِشْرٍ، عَنْ نَافِعٍ، عَنِ ابْنِ عُمَرَ، «أَنَّ النَّبِيَّ صلى الله عليه وسلم اتَّخَذَ خَاتَمًا مِنْ فِضَّةٍ، فَكَانَ يَخْتِمُ بِهِ وَلا يَلْبَسُهُ».

قَالَ أَبُو عِيسَى: أَبُو بِشْرٍ اسْمُهُ: جَعْفَرُ بنُ أَبِي وَحْشِيَّةَ.[١١٨]

88. ʿAbdullāh b. ʿUmar ؓ narrated: "Allāh's Messenger ﷺ possessed a ring made of silver. He used it to stamp [his letters etc.], and did not wear it."

---

117 *Sunan al-Tirmidhī* (1785)
118 *Ṣaḥīḥ Ibn Ḥibbān* (5459)

Abū ʿĪsā said: Abū Bishr's name is Jaʿfar b. Abī Waḥshiyyah.

ʿAbd al-Razzāq al-Badr said,

> The last part of this ḥadīth opposes the many ḥadīths which state that the Prophet ﷺ wore the seal. However, some scholars reconciled this ḥadīth with the other ḥadīths by saying that the ring referred to in this ḥadīth was not made of silver only but rather had other materials that are not permissible to wear such as iron. Al-Imām Aḥmad reported that the Prophet ﷺ had a ring made of iron that had some silver on it that he threw away afterwards. Al-Hafiẓ Ibn Rajab commented on this ḥadīth in his book *Aḥkām al-Khawātim*, saying, "Perhaps, this was the ring that he used for stamping and sealing the letters but he never wore it." In any case, if this addition (the last part of the ḥadīth) is proven to be authentic, then it is understood to refer to a particular case. Some other scholars considered the addition odd and rejected it.

Al-Bājūrī said,

> The last part of this ḥadīth opposes the other ḥadīths which indicate that the Prophet ﷺ used to wear the ring on his right hand. However, this contradiction can be reconciled because [it appears] that he had two rings; one that had a gemstone with engraved words to stamp his letters, and this ring he did not wear, and another ring that he wore so that people follow his example. It is also possible that he did not wear it all the time or that he did not wear it at the beginning, and then wore it later to show the people that it is not intended for adornment.

٨٩- حَدَّثَنَا مَحْمُودُ بْنُ غَيْلانَ، قَالَ: حَدَّثَنَا حَفْصُ بْنُ عُمَرَ بْنِ عُبَيْدٍ - هُوَ الطَّنَافِسِيُّ -، قَالَ: حَدَّثَنَا زُهَيْرٌ أَبُو خَيْثَمَةَ، عَنْ حُمَيْدٍ، عَنْ أَنَسِ بْنِ مَالِكٍ قَالَ: «كَانَ خَاتَمُ النَّبِيِّ صلىٰ الله عليه وسلم مِنْ فِضَّةٍ فَصُّهُ مِنْهُ».[١١٩]

89. Anas b. Mālik ؓ narrated: "The Prophet ﷺ had a ring made of silver and its stone was also of silver."

ʿAlī al-Qārī said,

> The ring that had a gem stone made of silver was the ring that the Prophet ﷺ ordered to be made for him. Al-Dāraquṭnī reported that

---

119 *Ṣaḥiḥ al-Bukhārī* (5870)

Ya'lā b. Umayyah ﷺ said, "I myself made for the Prophet ﷺ a ring that no one else helped me with. I engraved on it, 'Muḥammad is the Messenger of Allāh.'"

Al-Bājūrī said,

The meaning of the last part of the ḥadīth is that the gemstone was part of the ring and not a separate stone added to it.

٩٠ - حَدَّثَنَا إِسْحَاقُ بْنُ مَنْصُورٍ، قَالَ: حَدَّثَنَا مُعَاذُ بْنُ هِشَامٍ، قَالَ: حَدَّثَنِي أَبِي، عَنْ قَتَادَةَ، عَنْ أَنَسِ بْنِ مَالِكٍ، قَالَ: «لَمَّا أَرَادَ رَسُولُ اللهِ صلىٰ الله عليه وسلم أَنْ يَكْتُبَ إِلَى الْعَجَمِ قِيلَ لَهُ: إِنَّ الْعَجَمَ لَا يَقْبَلُونَ إِلَّا كِتَابًا عَلَيْهِ خَاتَمٌ، فَاصْطَنَعَ خَاتَمًا، فَكَأَنِّي أَنْظُرُ إِلَىٰ بَيَاضِهِ فِي كَفِّهِ». ١٢٠

90. Anas b. Mālik ﷺ narrated: "When the Messenger of Allāh ﷺ intended to write letters to the leaders of the non-Arabs [to invite them to Islām], he was advised that they do not accept letters without a seal (stamp) on them. For that reason, he had a ring made for himself. It is as if the brightness of [the ring] which was on his hand is still before my eyes."

'Abd al-Razzāq al-Badr said,

This ḥadīth shows the reason behind the Prophet ﷺ wanting to have a ring (i.e. seal).

Ibn Ḥajar al-Haytamī said,

This incident took place after he ﷺ returned from Ḥudaybiyah. It is said that the person who advised the Prophet about the seal was a non-Arab or a person from the Quraysh.

The reason they did not accept unstamped letters was because it made them doubt the content or because the stamp indicated that the sender respected them, or that the stamp indicated that access to the contents of the letter was limited to certain people.

Al-Bājūrī said,

This ḥadīth indicates the permissibility of communication through

---

120 *Ṣaḥīḥ al-Bukhārī* (5875) and *Ṣaḥīḥ Muslim* (2092)

letters. Allāh made this a *sunnah* of His creation, adopted by the early generations and the later. The first person reported to have sent a letter was Prophet Sulaymān ﷺ when he sent the hoopoe to deliver his letter to Balqīs. The act of the Prophet ﷺ teaches us to do what people like and leave that which they dislike.

The part regarding the brightness of the ring indicates that it was made of silver, and it was said that it refers to the perfection of the ring.

٩١- حَدَّثَنَا مُحَمَّدُ بْنُ يَحْيَىٰ، قَالَ: حَدَّثَنَا مُحَمَّدُ بْنُ عَبْدِ اللهِ الأَنْصَارِيِّ، قَالَ: حَدَّثَنِي أَبِي، عَنْ ثُمَامَةَ، عَنْ أَنَسِ بْنِ مَالِكٍ، قَالَ: «كَانَ نَقْشُ خَاتَمِ رَسُولِ اللهِ صلىٰ الله عليه وسلم: مُحَمَّدٌ سَطْرٌ، وَرَسُولٌ: سَطْرٌ، وَاللهُ: سَطْرٌ.»[١٢١]

91. Anas b. Mālik ﷺ narrated: "The inscription engraved on the ring of Allāh's Messenger ﷺ was 'Muḥammad' on one line, 'Messenger' on the next, and 'Allāh' on the last."

ʿAbd al-Razzāq al-Badr said,

> This shows that the inscription engraved on the ring consisted of three words, each written on a separate line. The ring's small size may have been why the text was not written on one line, and Allāh knows best.

Al-Bājūrī said,

> The word "Muḥammad" was written on the first line at the top and the other words were written below. This is supported by another narration reported by al-Ismaʿīlī that explicitly stated the order of the lines, and it is also the apparent meaning of the narration reported by al-Bukhārī.

٩٢- حَدَّثَنَا نَصْرُ بْنُ عَلِيٍّ الْجَهْضَمِيُّ أَبُو عَمْرٍو، قَالَ: حَدَّثَنَا نُوحُ بْنُ قَيْسٍ، عَنْ خَالِدِ بْنِ قَيْسٍ، عَنْ قَتَادَةَ، عَنْ أَنَسِ بْنِ مَالِكٍ، أَنَّ النَّبِيَّ صلىٰ الله عليه وسلم كَتَبَ إِلَىٰ كِسْرَىٰ وَقَيْصَرَ وَالنَّجَاشِيِّ، فَقِيلَ لَهُ: إِنَّهُمْ لا يَقْبَلُونَ كِتَابًا إِلا بِخَاتَمٍ، فَصَاغَ رَسُولُ اللهِ صلىٰ الله عليه وسلم خَاتَمًا حَلْقَتُهُ فِضَّةٌ، وَنُقِشَ فِيهِ: مُحَمَّدٌ رَسُولُ

121 *Sahīh al-Bukhārī* (3106)

اللهِ». [١٢٢]

92. Anas b. Mālik ﷺ related: "Allāh's Messenger ﷺ [intended to] write letters to Kisrā (of the Persians), Caesar (of the Romans) and al-Najāshī (of the Abyssinians). The Prophet ﷺ was advised that they do not accept letters without a seal. For this reason, he ﷺ had a ring made of silver, and had 'Muḥammad is the Messenger of Allāh' engraved upon it."

Al-Bājūrī said,

> Kisrā was the title given to the kings of Persia. Caesar was the title given to the kings of the Romans. Al-Najāshī was the title given to the kings of Abyssinia. Pharaoh was the title given to the kings of the region of Copt in Egypt. Al-'Azīz was the title given to the kings of Egypt. Tubba' was the title given to the kings of the tribe of Ḥimyar. Khāqān was the title given to the kings of the Turks.

٩٣- حَدَّثَنَا إِسْحَاقُ بْنُ مَنْصُورٍ، قَالَ: حَدَّثَنَا سَعِيدُ بْنُ عَامِرٍ، وَالْحَجَّاجُ بْنُ مِنْهَالٍ، عَنْ هَمَّامٍ، عَنِ ابْنِ جُرَيْجٍ، عَنِ الزُّهْرِيِّ، عَنْ أَنَسٍ، «أَنَّ النَّبِيَّ صلى الله عليه وسلم كَانَ إِذَا دَخَلَ الْخَلاءَ نَزَعَ خَاتَمَهُ». [١٢٣]

93. Anas b. Mālik ﷺ related: "Whenever the Messenger of Allāh ﷺ entered the place where he relieved himself, he would remove his ring."

'Alī al-Qārī said,

> He ﷺ used to remove his ring before entering the place where he relieved himself because the ring had the name of Allāh engraved on it.
>
> Before gold was made forbidden for men to wear, the Prophet ﷺ had a ring made of gold and so the people began to wear golden rings in imitation of him. When he became aware of this, he removed it and said that he would not wear a golden ring again and so the people followed suit. Then he wore a ring made of silver as an adornment, so people followed him in that. However, he saw that this may lead to arrogance and pride so he removed it and so did the people. Later on, he needed to wear a ring for the purpose of stamping letters so he wore it but he said to the people, "I have made myself a ring and engraved on it some

---

122 See ḥadīth 90

123 *Sunan al-Tirmidhī* (1746)

words; so do not engrave on your rings [the same words I have used]."

Ibn Ḥajar al-Haytamī said,

> It is disliked to keep the Name of Allāh in ones possession whilst being in the place where people relieve themselves, and it was said that this is forbidden. It has also been said that keeping it on the left hand while performing *isinjāʾ* is also forbidden. The same ruling applies to anything that is glorified in religion such as the Qurʾān, the name of a prophet or an angel. As for names that people use that are also the names of prophets [or angels etc.] such as Muḥammad, then the ruling is based on the intention of the person. If the intention is that it is a normal person's name then it is permissible but if it is intended to refer to one who is glorified in the religion, then it is disliked.

٩٤- حَدَّثَنَا إِسْحَاقُ بْنُ مَنْصُورٍ، قَالَ: حَدَّثَنَا عَبْدُ اللهِ بْنُ نُمَيْرٍ، قَالَ: حَدَّثَنَا عُبَيْدُ اللهِ بْنُ عُمَرَ، عَنْ نَافِعٍ، عَنِ ابْنِ عُمَرَ، قَالَ: «اتَّخَذَ رَسُولُ اللهِ صلىٰ الله عليه وسلم، خَاتَمًا مِنْ وَرِقٍ، فَكَانَ فِي يَدِهِ ثُمَّ كَانَ فِي يَدِ أَبِي بَكْرٍ، وَيَدِ عُمَرَ، ثُمَّ كَانَ فِي يَدِ عُثْمَانَ، حَتَّىٰ وَقَعَ فِي بِئْرِ أَرِيسٍ، نَقْشُهُ: مُحَمَّدٌ رَسُولُ اللهِ».[١٢٤]

94. ʿAbdullāh b. ʿUmar ﵁ narrated: "The Messenger of Allāh ﷺ had a ring made of silver that he wore on his hand. Then, [after the death of the Prophet], Abū Bakr ﵁ wore it on his hand, and then [after the death of Abū Bakr] ʿUmar b. al-Khaṭṭāb ﵁ kept it and wore it on his hand. Then [after the death of ʿUmar], ʿUthmān b. ʿAffān ﵁ kept it and wore it until it fell into the well of Arīs. The inscription on the ring was 'Muḥammad is the Messenger of Allāh.'"

ʿAbd al-Razzāq al-Badr said,

> The well of Arīs is a well in a garden located near the Masjid Qubāʾ. The ring fell when ʿUthmān ﵁ was moving the ring on his finger while standing at the edge of the well. He spent three days, along with his companions, searching for it but they could not find it. Thus, claiming that the ring was found in present times is a baseless claim and to prove something is from the belongings of the Prophet ﷺ requires clear evidence.

---

124 *Ṣaḥīḥ al-Bukhārī* (5873) and *Ṣaḥīḥ Muslim* (2091)

Al-Bājūrī said,

> This ḥadīth shows that it is permissible to use a seal that has the name of someone else engraved on it after their death.

Ibn Ḥajar al-Haytamī said,

> The seal of the Prophet ﷺ was not from his inheritance because it was treated like his weapons that were allocated as a charity for the Muslims that the ruler would utilise in the way that serves their best interest. This is why Abū Bakr, ʿUmar and ʿUthmān used it as it was from the tools that the Caliphate needed.
>
> None of our fellow Shāfiʿī scholars discussed the weight of the ring, but some later scholars such as al-Adhraʿī stated that it is forbidden for it to exceed one *mithqāl* (a unit of mass equal to 4.25 grams) whilst other scholars said it is permissible, such as al-Ḥāfiẓ al-ʿIraqī who said that it is [not forbidden but rather] disliked for the ring to weigh one *mithqāl*. However, the appropriate, permissible weight depends on the norms of the people in their culture as the *mithqāl* was the norm of the people at that time.

باب ما جاء في أن النبي صلى الله عليه وسلم كان يتختم في يمينه

[13] On the Prophet's ﷺ Wearing of His Ring On the Right Hand

ʿAbd al-Razzāq al-Badr said,

> The title used for this chapter is intended to show that it is the Sunnah to wear the ring on the right hand. This is the view adopted by the author as he considered the ḥadīth wherein it states that he ﷺ wore the ring on the left hand to be weak. However, Ibn al-Qayyim said, "There are ḥadīths indicating that he wore his ring on the right hand and other ḥadīths stating that he wore it on the left hand, and the chains of all these ḥadīths are authentic."[125]
>
> Al-Nawawī said, "The scholars are in agreement that it is permissible to wear the ring on the right hand or the left hand as neither is disliked. However, they differed on what is better. Many of the *salaf* used to wear the ring on the right hand and many of them used to wear the ring on the left hand. Al-Imām Mālik preferred wearing the ring on the left hand and he disliked wearing it on the right hand. In our *madhhab* (Shāfiʿī) there are two views, but the most correct is that wearing the ring on the right hand is better because it is a form of adornment and the right hand is more deserving of being honoured and beautified."[126]

٩٥- حَدَّثَنَا مُحَمَّدُ بْنُ سَهْلِ بْنِ عَسْكَرٍ الْبَغْدَادِيُّ، وَعَبْدُ اللهِ بْنُ عَبْدِ الرَّحْمَنِ، قَالَا: أَخْبَرَنَا يَحْيَىٰ بْنُ حَسَّانَ، قَالَ: حَدَّثَنَا سُلَيْمَانُ بْنُ بِلَالٍ، عَنْ شَرِيكِ بْنِ عَبْدِ اللهِ بْنِ أَبِي نَمِرٍ، عَنْ إِبْرَاهِيمَ بْنِ عَبْدِ اللهِ بْنِ حُنَيْنٍ، عَنْ أَبِيهِ، عَنْ عَلِيِّ بْنِ أَبِي طَالِبٍ: «أَنَّ النَّبِيَّ صلىٰ الله عليه وسلم كَانَ يَلْبَسُ خَاتَمَهُ فِي يَمِينِهِ».[١٢٧]

95. ʿAlī b. Abī Ṭālib ؓ narrated: "The Messenger of Allāh ﷺ wore his

---

125 *Zād al-Maʿād* (1/134)

126 *Sharḥ Ṣaḥīḥ Muslim* (14/72-73)

127 *Sunan Abī Dāwūd* (4226)

ring on the right hand."

Al-Bājūrī said,

> The author (al-Tirmidhī) quoted al-Bukhārī who said, "The ḥadīths stating that he ﷺ wore the ring on his left hand are the most authentic ḥadīths on the subject."
>
> The differing ḥadīths can be reconciled i.e. he ﷺ had two rings, one he wore on his left hand and [on other occasions] he wore his other ring on his right hand, which goes in line with the ḥadīths that stated he had a ring with a gemstone made of silver and another from Abyssinia.

Ibn Ḥajar al-Haytamī said,

> Al-Imām Ahmad disliked wearing a ring on the index finger or the middle finger.

'Alī al-Qārī said,

> Ibn Ḥajar al-Asqalānī said, "If the ring is worn as an adornment then wearing it on the right hand is better but if it is worn to use for stamping letters, then wearing it on the left hand is better."

٩٦- حَدَّثَنَا مُحَمَّدُ بْنُ يَحْيَىٰ، قَالَ: حَدَّثَنَا أَحْمَدُ بْنُ صَالِحٍ، قَالَ: حَدَّثَنَا عَبْدُ اللهِ بْنُ وَهْبٍ، عَنْ سُلَيْمَانَ بْنِ بِلَالٍ، عَنْ شَرِيكِ بْنِ عَبْدِ اللهِ بْنِ أَبِي نَمِرٍ، نَحْوَهُ.

96. Sharīk b. 'Abdillāh b. Abū Namir reports the same.

٩٧- حَدَّثَنَا أَحْمَدُ بْنُ مَنِيعٍ، قَالَ: حَدَّثَنَا يَزِيدُ بْنُ هَارُونَ، عَنْ حَمَّادِ بْنِ سَلَمَةَ، قَالَ: رَأَيْتُ ابْنَ أَبِي رافِعٍ يَتَخَتَّمُ فِي يَمِينِهِ، فَسَأَلْتُهُ عَنْ ذَلِكَ، فَقَالَ: رَأَيْتُ عَبْدَ الله بْنَ جَعْفَرٍ يَتَخَتَّمُ فِي يَمِينِهِ، وقَالَ عَبْدُ اللهِ بْنُ جَعْفَرٍ: «كَانَ رَسُولُ اللهِ صلىٰ الله عليه وسلم يَتَخَتَّمُ فِي يَمِينِهِ». [١٢٨]

97. Ḥammād b. Salamah narrated that he saw Ibn Abī Rāfi' wearing a ring on his right hand. He inquired regarding the reason behind this and he replied: "I had seen 'Abdullāh b. Ja'far ؓ wearing a ring on his right hand, and he said that he had seen the Prophet ﷺ wear a

---

128 *Sunan al-Tirmidhī* (1744)

ring on his right hand."

Al-Bājūrī said,

> 'Abdullāh b. Ja'far was a companion, as was his father. He was the first child born in Islām. His birth was in the land of Abyssinia and his death was in Madīnah.

٩٨- حَدَّثَنَا يَحْيَىٰ بْنُ مُوسَىٰ، قَالَ: حَدَّثَنَا عَبْدُ اللهِ بْنُ نُمَيْرٍ، قَالَ: حَدَّثَنَا إِبْرَاهِيمُ بْنُ الْفَضْلِ، عَنْ عَبْدِ اللهِ بْنِ مُحَمَّدِ بْنِ عَقِيلٍ، عَنْ عَبْدِ اللهِ بْنِ جَعْفَرٍ: «أَنَّ النَّبِيَّ صلىٰ الله عليه وسلم كَانَ يَتَخَتَّمُ فِي يَمِينِهِ». [١٢٩]

98. 'Abdullāh b. Ja'far ﷺ narrates: "The Messenger of Allāh wore a ring on his right hand."

٩٩- حَدَّثَنَا أَبُو الْخَطَّابِ زِيَادُ بْنُ يَحْيَىٰ، قَالَ: حَدَّثَنَا عَبْدُ اللهِ بْنُ مَيْمُونٍ، عَنْ جَعْفَرِ بْنِ مُحَمَّدٍ، عَنْ أَبِيهِ، عَنْ جَابِرِ بْنِ عَبْدِ اللهِ: «أَنَّ النَّبِيَّ صلىٰ الله عليه وسلم كَانَ يَتَخَتَّمُ فِي يَمِينِهِ». [١٣٠]

99. Jābir b. 'Abdillāh ؓ narrated: "The Prophet ﷺ wore the ring on the right hand."

Al-Bājūrī said,

> These ḥadīths did not indicate what finger he ﷺ used to wear the ring on but the ḥadīths in the two *Ṣaḥīḥ* books show that he wore his ring on the pinkie. With that said, the Sunnah is to wear the ring on the pinkie only. The wisdom behind this is that the pinkie is far from the actions of the hand and [due to it being the furthest finger from the thumb,] it does not hinder the work of the hand unlike if it was worn on the index finger.

١٠٠- حَدَّثَنَا مُحَمَّدُ بْنُ حُمَيْدٍ الرَّازِيُّ، قَالَ: حَدَّثَنَا جَرِيرٌ، عَنْ مُحَمَّدِ بْنِ إِسْحَاقَ، عَنِ الصَّلتِ بْنِ عَبْدِ اللهِ، قَالَ: كَانَ ابْنُ عَبَّاسٍ يَتَخَتَّمُ فِي يَمِينِهِ وَلا إِخَالُهُ إِلا قَالَ:

---

129 *Musnad Aḥmad* (3/195)

130 *Al-'Ilal al-Kabīr* of al-Bukhārī (287) who said this report [from Jābir through this chain] is not authentic.

«كَانَ رَسُولُ اللهِ صلىٰ الله عليه وسلم يَتَخَتَّمُ فِي يَمِينِهِ».[١٣١]

100. Ṣalt b. ʿAbdullāh narrated: "Ibn ʿAbbās ﵄ wore a ring on the right hand, and as far as I can recall he used to say that the Prophet ﷺ wore it on the right hand."

١٠١ - حَدَّثَنَا مُحَمَّدُ بْنُ أَبِي عُمَرَ، قَالَ : حَدَّثَنَا سُفيان، عَنْ أَيُّوبَ بْنِ مُوسَىٰ، عَنْ نَافِعٍ، عَنِ ابْنِ عُمَرَ: «أَنَّ النَّبِيَّ صلىٰ الله عليه وسلم اتَّخَذَ خَاتَمًا مِنْ فِضَّةٍ، وَجَعَلَ فَصَّهُ مِمَّا يَلِي كَفَّهُ، وَنَقَشَ فِيهِ (مُحَمَّدٌ رَسُولُ اللهِ)، وَنَهَىٰ أَنْ يَنْقُشَ أَحَدٌ عَلَيْهِ، وَهُوَ الَّذِي سَقَطَ مِنْ مُعَيْقِيبٍ فِي بِئْرِ أَرِيسٍ».[١٣٢]

101. ʿAbdullāh b. ʿUmar ﵄ related: "The Prophet ﷺ had a ring made of silver which had its gemstone facing his palm. He [ordered] the words, 'Muḥammad is the Messenger of Allāh' to be engraved on it and prohibited people from putting the same inscription on their rings. This is the same ring that fell from the hands of Muʿayqīb ﵁ into the well of Arīs."

ʿAbd al-Razzāq al-Badr said,

> The Prophet ﷺ positioned its gemstone facing towards his palm so that it would not show, which indicates that the ring was for the purpose of sealing letters and not for adornment.
>
> This ḥadīth can be reconciled with the other ḥadīth where it stated that the ring fell from the hand of ʿUthmān ﵁: It is possible that ʿUthmān gave Muʿayqīb ﵁ the ring to use and then when he wanted to give it back to ʿUthmān, it fell from his hand. This is why both were referred to as the one from whom the ring fell down. Muʿayqīb is from the early companions. He witnessed all of the battles and he was given charge over the Muslim treasury (Bayt al-Māl) by ʿUmar.

ʿAlī al-Qārī said,

> Al-Nawawī said that the reason for keeping the gemstone of the ring towards the palm was because that would protect the inscription and because keeping it away from the eye would prevent showing off and pride.

---

131 *Sunan al-Tirmidhī* (1742) and *Sunan Abī Dāwūd* (4229)
132 *Ṣaḥīḥ Muslim* (2091)

Al-Bājūrī said,

> The Prophet ﷺ prohibited people from making this inscription on their rings to avert confusion and corruption. However, Ibn Jamāʿah and al-Zayn al-ʿIrāqī stated that this prohibition was only applicable during his life ﷺ, based on the presence of the aforementioned reasons.

١٠٢ – حَدَّثَنَا قُتَيْبَةُ بْنُ سَعِيدٍ، حَدَّثَنَا حَاتِمُ بْنُ إِسْمَاعِيلَ، عَنْ جَعْفَرِ بْنِ مُحَمَّدٍ عَنْ أَبِيهِ قَالَ: «كَانَ الحَسَنُ وَالحُسَيْنُ يَتَخَتَّمَانِ فِي يَسَارِهِمَا». ١٣٣

102. Muḥammad al-Bāqir related: "Al-Ḥasan and al-Ḥusayn ؓ wore their rings on their left hands."

Ibn Ḥajar al-Haytamī said,

> They wore their rings on the left hand to follow the example of the Prophet ﷺ who wore it on the left hand often. The reason the author included this narration though it opposes the title of the chapter is because he wanted to explain that such ḥadīths do not negate that wearing it on the right hand is better.

ʿAbd al-Razzāq al-Badr said,

> This shows that it is permissible to wear it on the left hand or the right hand. Doing so in either hand has been established in the Prophetic Sunnah.

١٠٣ – حَدَّثَنَا عَبْدُ اللهِ بْنُ عَبْدِ الرَّحْمَنِ، قَالَ: حَدَّثَنَا مُحَمَّدُ بْنُ عِيسَى – وَهُوَ ابْنُ الطَّبَّاعِ –، قَالَ: حَدَّثَنَا عَبَّادُ بْنُ الْعَوَّامِ، عَنْ سَعِيدِ بْنِ أَبِي عَرُوبَةَ، عَنْ قَتَادَةَ، عَنْ أَنَسِ بْنِ مَالِكٍ: «أَنَّهُ صلى الله عليه وسلم كَانَ يَتَخَتَّمُ فِي يَمِينِهِ». ١٣٤

103. Anas b. Mālik ؓ related: "The Prophet ﷺ wore a ring on his right hand."

وَقَالَ أَبُو عِيسَى: هَذَا حَدِيثٌ غَرِيبٌ، لَا نَعْرِفُهُ مِنْ حَدِيثِ سَعِيدِ بْنِ أَبِي عَرُوبَةَ، عَنْ قَتَادَةَ، عَنْ أَنَسٍ، عَنِ النَّبِيِّ صلى الله عليه وسلم نَحْوَ هَذَا إِلَّا مِنْ هَذَا الوَجْهِ.

133 *Sunan al-Tirmidhī* (1743)
134 *Sunan al-Nasāʾī* (5204)

Abū 'Īsā said: This ḥadīth is *gharīb*. We do not know a ḥadīth with this meaning from Sa'īd b. Abī 'Arūbah from Qatādah from Anas from the Prophet ﷺ except this.

وَرَوَىٰ بَعْضُ أَصْحَابِ قَتَادَةَ، عَنْ قَتَادَةَ، عَنْ أَنَسِ بْنِ مَالِكٍ، عَنِ النَّبِيِّ صلىٰ الله عليه وسلم أَنَّهُ كَانَ يَتَخَتَّمُ فِي يَسَارِهِ؛ وَهُوَ حَدِيثٌ لَا يَصِحُّ أَيْضًا.

Some of Qatādah's companions reported from him from Anas b. Mā-lik from the Prophet ﷺ that he would wear his ring on the left hand. It is also an unauthentic ḥadīth.

'Abd al-Razzāq al-Badr said,

> However, it is established in *Ṣaḥīḥ Muslim* via Thābit from Anas that he said, "The Prophet's ﷺ ring was here"–pointing towards the pinky finger of his left hand.

١٠٤ – حَدَّثَنَا مُحَمَّدُ بْنُ عُبَيْدِ اللهِ الْمُحَارِبِيُّ، قَالَ: حَدَّثَنَا عَبْدُ الْعَزِيزِ بْنُ أَبِي حَازِمٍ، عَنْ مُوسَىٰ بْنِ عُقْبَةَ، عَنْ نَافِعٍ، عَنِ ابْنِ عُمَرَ، قَالَ: «اتَّخَذَ رَسُولُ اللهِ صلىٰ الله عليه وسلم خَاتَمًا مِنْ ذَهَبٍ، فَكَانَ يَلْبَسُهُ فِي يَمِينِهِ، فَاتَّخَذَ النَّاسُ خَوَاتِيمَ مِنْ ذَهَبٍ فَطَرَحَهُ صلىٰ الله عليه وسلم، وَقَالَ: «لَا أَلْبَسُهُ أَبَدًا» فَطَرَحَ النَّاسُ خَوَاتِيمَهُمْ». ¹³⁵

104. 'Abdullāh b. 'Umar ؓ related: "The Prophet ﷺ possessed a ring made of gold which he wore on his right hand. [To follow the example of the Prophet ﷺ,] the companions also had gold rings made for themselves. Upon seeing this, the Prophet ﷺ removed the gold ring and said, 'I will never wear it again.' Accordingly, the people removed their gold rings too."

'Alī al-Qārī said,

> This ḥadīth refers to the period where gold was not yet made prohib-ited for men. The Prophet ﷺ removed the ring after it was revealed to him that gold was not allowed for men.

Al-Nawawī said,

> The scholars are in agreement that the Sunnah for men is to wear the

---

135 *Ṣaḥīḥ al-Bukhārī* (5865) and *Ṣaḥīḥ Muslim* (2091)

> ring on their pinky fingers whilst women can wear the ring on the finger of their choosing.

Al-Bājūrī said,

> He ﷺ removed it because he saw that people showed off with their gold rings and it coincided that the revelation came down to make gold forbidden for men.

باب ما جاء في صفة سَيْفِ رَسُولِ اللَّهِ صلى الله عليه وسلم

[14] On the Description of Allāh's Messenger's ﷺ Sword

ʿAbd al-Razzāq al-Badr said,

> This chapter and some subsequent chapters are dedicated to describing the weapons of the Prophet ﷺ that he used in battles and wars. There is a benefit that can be derived from the ordering of the chapters in that the author placed the chapter of the sword after the chapter of the ring. This ordering was deliberate and was to indicate that calling to Allāh using words comes before fighting with the sword. This is because the ring was used to stamp letters that were sent to disbelievers inviting them to Islām and so al-Tirmidhī placed it before the sword to show that preaching and advising people takes priority over calling them to Islām with the sword. And Allāh knows best.

Al-Bājūrī said,

> The Prophet ﷺ had many swords; the first sword he ever had was called "al-Mȧthūr" which he inherited from his father. The other swords he had were called: al-Qaḍīb, al-Qulaʿi, al-Battār, al-Ḥatf, al-Mikhḍham, al-Rasūb, al-Ṣamṣām, al-Laḥīf and Dhul-Fiqār.
>
> There are four ḥadīths in this chapter.

Ibn Ḥajar al-Haytamī said,

> The reason why the author started with the sword as the first weapon is because it was the most frequently used and most effective during battles.

١٠٥ - حَدَّثَنَا مُحَمَّدُ بْنُ بَشَّارٍ، قَالَ: حَدَّثَنَا وَهْبُ بْنُ جَرِيرٍ، قَالَ: حَدَّثَنَا أَبِي، عَنْ قَتَادَةَ، عَنْ أَنَسٍ، قَالَ: «كَانَتْ قَبِيعَةُ سَيْفِ رَسُولِ اللهِ صلىٰ الله عليه وسلم مِنْ فِضَّةٍ». ١٣٦

136 *Sunan al-Tirmidhī* (1691) and *Sunan Abī Dāwūd* (2583)

105. Anas b. Mālik ﵁ narrated: "The handle of the sword of the Messenger of Allāh ﷺ was made of silver."

'Alī al-Qārī said,

> This ḥadīth proves that it is permissible to adorn the sword and any other weapon with silver. As for adorning them with gold, this is forbidden.

Al-Bājūrī said,

> The sword referred to in this ḥadīth is the sword Dhul-Fiqār, which is the sword that the Prophet ﷺ always carried and had when he conquered Makkah.

١٠٦ – حَدَّثَنَا مُحَمَّدُ بْنُ بَشَّارٍ، قَالَ: حَدَّثَنَا مُعَاذُ بْنُ هِشَامٍ، قَالَ: حَدَّثَنِي أَبِي، عَنْ قَتَادَةَ، عَنْ سَعِيدِ بْنِ أَبِي الْحَسَنِ، قَالَ: «كَانَتْ قَبِيعَةُ سَيْفِ رَسُولِ اللهِ صلىٰ الله عليه وسلم مِنْ فِضَّةٍ».[137]

106. Sa'īd b. Abī al-Ḥasan related: "The handle of the sword of the Prophet ﷺ was made of silver."

Al-Bājūrī said,

> Sa'īd b. Abī al-Ḥasan is Ḥasan al-Baṣrī's brother, and he was a reliable and renowned narrator.

١٠٧ – حَدَّثَنَا أَبُو جَعْفَرٍ مُحَمَّدُ بْنُ صُدْرَانَ الْبَصْرِيُّ، قَالَ: حَدَّثَنَا طَالِبُ بْنُ حُجَيْرٍ، عَنْ هُودٍ – وَهُوَ ابْنُ عَبْدِ اللهِ بْنِ سَعْدٍ –، عَنْ جَدِّهِ، قَالَ: «دَخَلَ رَسُولُ اللهِ صلىٰ الله عليه وسلم مَكَّةَ يَوْمَ الْفَتْحِ وَعَلَىٰ سَيْفِهِ ذَهَبٌ وَفِضَّةٌ».

قَالَ طَالِبٌ: فَسَأَلْتُهُ عَنِ الْفِضَّةِ فَقَالَ : «كَانَتْ قَبِيعَةُ السَّيْفِ فِضَّةً».[138]

107. The grandfather of Hūd b. 'Abdillāh b. Sa'd narrated: "When the Prophet ﷺ entered Makkah on the day it was conquered, his sword was adorned with gold and silver. Ṭālib (who is one of the narrators of this ḥadīth) asked Hūd, 'On which part of the sword was

---

137 *Sunan Abī Dāwūd* (2584)
138 *Sunan Abī Dāwūd* (1690)

the silver?' He replied, 'The handle was made of silver.'"

Al-Bājūrī said,

> This ḥadīth is ruled as weak, as stated by al-Qaṭṭān, who deemed it a *munkar* ḥadīth. Hence, it cannot be used as evidence to allow adorning the weapons with gold.

Ibn Ḥajar al-Haytamī said,

> This ḥadīth does not contradict the ruling of prohibition regarding adorning weapons with gold because it is weak. It is incorrect to claim that the incident mentioned in this ḥadīth was before gold was made forbidden because this ruling occurred before the conquest of Makkah, as has been reported.

١٠٨ - حَدَّثَنَا مُحَمَّدُ بْنُ شُجَاعٍ الْبَغْدَادِيُّ، قال: حَدَّثَنَا أَبُو عُبَيْدَةَ الْحَدَّادُ، عَنْ عُثْمَانَ بْنِ سَعْدٍ، عَنِ ابْنِ سِيرِينَ، قَالَ: «صَنَعْتُ سَيْفِي عَلَىٰ سَيْفِ سَمُرَةَ بْنِ جُنْدُبٍ: وَزَعَمَ سَمُرَةُ أَنَّهُ صَنَعَ سَيْفَهُ عَلَىٰ سَيْفِ رَسُولِ اللهِ صلىٰ الله عليه وسلم وَكَانَ حَنَفِيًّا»[١٣٩].

108. Ibn Sīrīn narrated: "I based [the design of] my sword upon the sword of Samurah b. Jundub ﷺ because he said that he had his sword made like the sword of the Prophet ﷺ. The sword was the type used by the tribe of Banī Ḥanīfah."

ʿAbd al-Razzāq al-Badr said,

> The last part could be from the words of Ibn Sīrīn or Samurah and the sword was described as such because it was according to the sword design of the tribe of Banī Ḥanīfah – who were known for making exceptional swords, or because the one who made the sword was from the tribe of Banī Ḥanīfah.

١٠٩ - حَدَّثَنَا عُقْبَةُ بْنُ مُكْرَمٍ الْبَصْرِيُّ، قَالَ: حَدَّثَنَا مُحَمَّدُ بْنُ بَكْرٍ، عَنْ عُثْمَانَ بْنِ سَعْدٍ، بِهَذَا الإِسْنَادِ نَحْوَهُ.

109. ʿUthmān b. Saʿd reports similarly via the same chain.

---

139 *Sunan al-Tirmidhī* (1683)

باب ما جاء في صفة درع رَسُولِ اللهِ صلى الله عليه وسلم

[15] On the Description of Allāh's Messenger's ﷺ Armour

Ibn al-Qayyim said,

> The Prophet ﷺ had seven suits of armour, the names of which are: Dhāt al-Fuḍūl, which is the armour that he pawned for a year with a Jewish man for thirty *ṣāʿ* (a cubic measure) of barley and it was made of iron, Dhāt al-Wishāḥ, Dhāt al-Ḥawāshī, al-Saʿdiyyah, Fiḍḍah, al-Batrāʾ and al-Khirnaq.[140]

Al-Bājūrī said,

> This chapter is dedicated to describing the way the Prophet ﷺ used to wear his armour, rather than describing the suits of armour.
>
> There are two ḥadīths in the chapter.

١١٠ - حَدَّثَنَا أَبُو سَعِيدٍ عَبْدُ اللهِ بْنُ سَعِيدٍ الأَشَجُّ، قَالَ: حَدَّثَنَا يُونُسُ بْنُ بُكَيْرٍ، عَنْ مُحَمَّدِ بْنِ إِسْحَاقَ، عَنْ يَحْيَىٰ بْنِ عَبَّادِ بْنِ عَبْدِ اللهِ بْنِ الزُّبَيْرِ، عَنْ أَبِيهِ، عَنْ جَدِّهِ عَبْدِ اللهِ بْنِ الزُّبَيْرِ، عَنِ الزُّبَيْرِ بْنِ الْعَوَّامِ، قَالَ: «كَانَ عَلَىٰ النَّبِيِّ صلىٰ الله عليه وسلم يَوْمَ أُحُدٍ دِرْعَانِ، فَنَهَضَ إِلَىٰ الصَّخْرَةِ فَلَمْ يَسْتَطِعْ، فَأَقْعَدَ طَلْحَةَ تَحْتَهُ، وَصَعِدَ النَّبِيُّ صلىٰ الله عليه وسلم حَتَّىٰ اسْتَوَىٰ عَلَىٰ الصَّخْرَةِ»، قَالَ: سَمِعْتُ النَّبِيَّ صلىٰ الله عليه وسلم يَقُولُ: «أَوْجَبَ طَلْحَةُ»١٤١.

110. Al-Zubayr b. al-ʿAwwām ؓ related: "The Messenger of Allāh ﷺ wore two suits of armour during the Battle of Uhud. He tried to climb a rock but he could not do so. Thus, he requested Ṭalhah ؓ to sit and, with his aid, climbed the rock until he rose on it." Al-Zubayr ؓ said, "I heard the Prophet ﷺ say, 'Ṭalhah has necessitated Paradise for himself.'"

---

140 *Zād al-Maʿād* (1/130)
141 *Sunan al-Tirmidhī* (1692)

'Abd al-Razzāq al-Badr said,

> The two suits of armour that he ﷺ wore on that day were Dhāt al-Fuḍūl and Fiḍḍah, one over the other – which provides extra protection. The scholars concluded that the reality of reliance on Allāh lies in the heart and that a person is required to take the means [of protecting oneself] whilst the heart is fully dependent on the Causer and not the causes.

Al-Bājūrī said,

> The Prophet ﷺ wanted to climb the rock so that his army could see that he was still alive and gather around him[142].

Ibn Ḥajar al-Haytamī said,

> He ﷺ could not climb the rock because of the two suits of armour weighing him down. This (their thickness and weight) indicates how well made they were as it serves the ultimate purpose of wearing a suit of armour i.e. protection. This part [of the ḥadīth] provides a description of the suit of armour. However, some said that he could not climb the rock because of the wound he received on his noble head which resulted in losing a lot of blood.

'Alī al-Qārī said,

> Ṭalhah ؓ deserved Paradise because he sacrificed his life for the sake of the Prophet ﷺ as he kept protecting his body from arrows with his hand until his hand became paralysed and the rest of his body was wounded.

١١١ – حَدَّثَنَا مُحَمَّدُ بْنُ أَبِي عُمَرَ، قَالَ: حَدَّثَنَا سُفْيَانُ بْنُ عُيَيْنَةَ، عَنْ يَزِيدَ بْنِ خُصَيْفَةَ، عَنِ السَّائِبِ بْنِ يَزِيدَ، «أَنَّ رَسُولَ اللهِ صلى الله عليه وسلم كَانَ عَلَيْهِ يَوْمَ أُحُدٍ دِرْعَانِ، قَدْ ظَاهَرَ بَيْنَهُمَا».[١٤٣]

111. Al-Sā'ib b. Yazīd ؓ narrated: "In the Battle of Uhud, the Messenger of Allāh ﷺ wore two suits of armour. He wore them one over the other."

---

142 [Translator's Note] This was due to a rumour spreading during the battle that he had been martyred, causing confusion amongst the Muslim army.
143 *Sunan Ibn Mājah* (2806)

ʿAbd al-Razzāq al-Badr said,

> Al-Sāʾib b. Yazīd was the last companion who died in al-Madīnah; he died in 91 H.

Al-Bājūrī said,

> His wearing of two suits of armour indicates that reliance on Allāh should be accompanied by taking the means of protection.

بَابُ مَا جَاءَ فِي صِفَةِ مِغْفَرِ رَسُولِ اللَّهِ صَلَّى اللَّهُ عَلَيْهِ وَسَلَّمَ

[16] On the Description of Allāh's Messenger's ﷺ Mail Coif

Al-Bājūrī said,

> The mail coif is a flexible type of armour made of interlinked metal rings that is made to fit the size of the head and worn underneath the turban. It is considered to be from his weapons because a weapon refers to that which is used to fight and that which is used for protection.

There are two ḥadīths in the chapter.

١١٢ - حَدَّثَنَا قُتَيْبَةُ بْنُ سَعِيدٍ، قَالَ: حَدَّثَنَا مَالِكُ بْنُ أَنَسٍ، عَنِ ابْنِ شِهَابٍ، عَنْ أَنَسِ بْنِ مَالِكٍ: أَنَّ النَّبِيَّ صلى الله عليه وسلم دَخَلَ مَكَّةَ وَعَلَيْهِ مِغْفَرٌ، فَقِيلَ لَهُ: هَذَا ابْنُ خَطَلٍ مُتَعَلِّقٌ بِأَسْتَارِ الْكَعْبَةِ، فَقَالَ: «اقْتُلُوهُ». ١٤٤

112. Anas b. Mālik ؓ reported: "The Prophet ﷺ was wearing a mail coif when he entered Makkah. Someone came to him and said, 'O Messenger of Allāh, Ibn Khaṭal is holding the cover (black cloth) of the Kaʿbah.' The Prophet ﷺ replied, 'Kill him.'"

ʿAbd al-Razzāq al-Badr said,

> Ibn Khaṭal was one of those who the Prophet ﷺ ordered to be killed on the day of Makkah's conquest, wherever and whenever he was found. This was because he embraced Islām and had a Muslim servant but afterwards apostatised, killed the servant and started to defame the Prophet with foul language in his poetry and employed two female singers to sing his foul poetry against the Prophet and his companions.

Al-Bājūrī said,

> Ibn Khaṭal was holding the cover of the Kaʿbah because it was the

---

144 *Ṣaḥīḥ al-Bukhārī* (3044) and *Ṣaḥīḥ Muslim* (1357)

habit of the Arabs before Islām to give refuge to anyone who did this, regardless of their crimes.

Ibn Ḥajar al-Haytamī said,

> It is reported in *Ṣaḥīḥ Muslim* that the Prophet ﷺ said, "It is unlawful for anyone to carry a weapon in Makkah."[145] This appears contradictory to the incident narrated in this ḥadīth. However, there is no contradiction because it is proven authentic that Allāh made it lawful for the Prophet ﷺ to fight for one hour of a day in Makkah, and it is not permissible for anyone after him.[146]

ʿAlī al-Qārī said,

> There are four persons that the Prophet ﷺ ordered to be killed whenever and wherever they were found: al-Ḥuwayrith b. Nuqayd, Hilāl b. Khaṭal, Maqīs b. Ṣubābah and ʿAbdullāh b. Abī Sarḥ. The companion who killed Ibn Khaṭal is reported to be Saʿīd b. Ḥurayth but it was reported in a more authentic ḥadīth that the one who killed him was Abū Barzah al-Aslamī.

١١٣ - حَدَّثَنَا عِيسَىٰ بْنُ أَحْمَدَ، قَالَ: حَدَّثَنَا عَبْدُ اللهِ بْنُ وَهْبٍ، قَالَ: حَدَّثَنِي مَالِكُ بْنُ أَنَسٍ، عَنِ ابْنِ شِهَابٍ، عَنْ أَنَسِ بْنِ مَالِكٍ، أَنَّ رَسُولَ اللهِ صلىٰ الله عليه وسلم دَخَلَ مَكَّةَ عَامَ الْفَتْحِ، وَعَلَىٰ رَأْسِهِ الْمِغْفَرُ، قَالَ: فَلَمَّا نَزَعَهُ جَاءَهُ رَجُلٌ، فَقَالَ لَهُ: ابْنُ خَطَلٍ مُتَعَلِّقٌ بِأَسْتَارِ الْكَعْبَةِ، فَقَالَ: «اقْتُلُوهُ».

قَالَ ابْنُ شِهَابٍ: وَبَلَغَنِي أَنَّ رَسُولَ اللهِ صلىٰ الله عليه وسلم لَمْ يَكُنْ يَوْمَئِذٍ مُحْرِمًا.[١٤٧]

113. Anas b. Mālik ؓ narrated: "The Prophet ﷺ wore a mail coif on

145 *Ṣaḥīḥ Muslim* (1356)

146 Al-Ḥāfiẓ Ibn Ḥajar said in *Fatḥ al-Bārī*, commenting on this ḥadīth (no. 1737), "Al-Māwardī said, 'From the exclusive qualities of Makkah is that it is not allowed to fight its inhabitants. If they transgress and rebel against the Muslims, if their evil can be stopped without fighting then it is not allowed to fight them, and if fighting is the only solution then the majority said it is allowed because fighting the rebellious is from the rights of Allāh and cannot be overlooked whilst others said that they should be pressured until they become obedient again.'"

147 *Muwaṭṭá Mālik* (1271) – See ḥadīth 112

his head when he entered Makkah as a conqueror. After he removed it, a person came and said, 'O Messenger of Allāh, Ibn Khaṭal is clinging to the cover of the Kaʿbah.' The Prophet ﷺ replied, 'Kill him.'"

Ibn Shihāb (the one narrating from Anas) said, "I have been informed that the Prophet ﷺ was not in the state of *iḥrām* on that day."

ʿAbd al-Razzāq al-Badr said,

> The statement of Ibn Shihāb al-Zuhrī indicates that if a person is entering Makkah without intending to enter the state of *ihram*, then he is not required to wear the clothes of *iḥram* as this is only required for the one who wants to perform ʿUmrah or Ḥajj.

باب ما جاء في عمامة رسول الله صلى الله عليه وسلم

[17] On Allāh's Messenger's ﷺ Headdress

Ibn Ḥajar al-Haytamī said,

> The Prophet ﷺ had a turban called "al-Saḥāb" that he used to wear underneath a head cap.

Ibn al-Qayyim said,

> The size of the turban of the Prophet ﷺ was neither too large so as to make it a burden on the head nor too small so that it could not protect the head from heat and cold. Rather, it was moderate in size and indeed the best of things are those that are moderate and balanced.

Al-Bājūrī said,

> The term *'imāmah* refers to clothing wrapped around the head, but here it refers to all head covers besides the mail coif. This is indicated to by the fact that it has been addressed in the previous chapter. Wearing the *'imāmah* is a Sunnah, especially so in the prayer. The Sunnah is attained by wearing it on the head or over a cap.

١١٤ - حَدَّثَنَا مُحَمَّدُ بْنُ بَشَّارٍ، قَالَ: حَدَّثَنَا عَبْدُ الرَّحْمَنِ بْنُ مَهْدِيٍّ، عَنْ حَمَّادِ بْنِ سَلَمَةَ (ح) حَدَّثَنَا مَحْمُودُ بْنُ غَيْلَانَ، قَالَ: حَدَّثَنَا وَكِيعٌ، عَنْ حَمَّادِ بْنِ سَلَمَةَ، عَنْ أَبِي الزُّبَيْرِ، عَنْ جَابِرٍ، قَالَ: «دَخَلَ النَّبِيُّ صلى الله عليه وسلم مَكَّةَ يَوْمَ الْفَتْحِ وَعَلَيْهِ عِمَامَةٌ سَوْدَاءُ». [١٤٨]

114. Jābir b. 'Abdillāh ﷺ narrated: "When Makkah was conquered, the Messenger of Allāh ﷺ entered the city wearing a black turban."

'Abd al-Razzāq al-Badr said,

> It was mentioned in the preceding chapter that he ﷺ was wearing a mail coif on his head whereas this ḥadīth mentions that he was wear-

---

148 *Ṣaḥīḥ Muslim* (1358)

ing a black turban. There is no contradiction between the two ḥadīths as it is possible that he wore the mail coif underneath the turban as armour or that he removed the mail coif and then wore the black turban when things settled down.

Al-Bājūrī said,

> The reason why he ﷺ preferred the black turban over the white colour (though the latter is a praised colour) on that day was because the black colour indicates that Islām has prevailed and that Islām does not change, similar to how the colour black does not change to another colour.

١١٥ – حَدَّثَنَا ابْنُ أَبِي عُمَرَ، قَالَ: حَدَّثَنَا سُفْيَانُ، عَنْ مُسَاوِرٍ الْوَرَّاقِ، عَنْ جَعْفَرِ بْنِ عَمْرِو بْنِ حُرَيْثٍ، عَنْ أَبِيهِ، قَالَ: «رَأَيْتُ النَّبِيَّ صلى الله عليه وسلم يَخْطُبُ عَلَى الْمِنْبَرِ وَعَلَيْهِ عِمَامَةٌ سَوْدَاءُ».[١٤٩]

115. ʿAmr b. Ḥurayth ؓ narrated: "I once saw a black turban upon the head of the Messenger of Allāh ﷺ while he was on the pulpit delivering a sermon."

١١٦ – حَدَّثَنَا مَحْمُودُ بْنُ غَيْلَانَ، وَيُوسُفُ بْنُ عِيسَى، قَالَا: حَدَّثَنَا وَكِيعٌ، عَنْ مُسَاوِرٍ الْوَرَّاقِ، عَنْ جَعْفَرِ بْنِ عَمْرِو بْنِ حُرَيْثٍ، عَنْ أَبِيهِ، «أَنَّ النَّبِيَّ صلى الله عليه وسلم خَطَبَ النَّاسَ وَعَلَيْهِ عِمَامَةٌ سَوْدَاءُ».[١٥٠]

116. ʿAmr b. Ḥurayth ؓ narrated: "I had seen the Messenger of Allāh ﷺ address the people from the pulpit whilst wearing a black turban."

ʿAlī al-Qārī said,

> This ḥadīth proves that he ﷺ wore a black turban more than once because there was no pulpit when he gave his speech in Makkah as he gave it while standing in front of the gate of the Kaʿbah. This is why the author of *al-Maṣābīh* included this ḥadīth under the chapter of "Friday *Khutbah*".

Al-Nawawī said,

---

149 *Ṣaḥīḥ Muslim* (1359)
150 Ibid

It is permissible to wear black clothing when delivering the *Khutbah* on Friday but wearing white clothing is better.

١١٧ – حَدَّثَنَا هَارُونُ بْنُ إِسْحَاقَ الْهَمْدَانِيُّ، قَالَ: حَدَّثَنَا يَحْيَىٰ بْنُ مُحَمَّدٍ الْمَدَنِيُّ، عَنْ عَبْدِ الْعَزِيزِ بْنِ مُحَمَّدٍ، عَنْ عُبَيْدِ اللهِ بْنِ عُمَرَ، عَنْ نَافِعٍ، عَنِ ابْنِ عُمَرَ، قَالَ: «كَانَ النَّبِيُّ صلىٰ الله عليه وسلم إِذَا اعْتَمَّ سَدَلَ عِمَامَتَهُ بَيْنَ كَتِفَيْهِ».

قَالَ نَافِعٌ: وَكَانَ ابْنُ عُمَرَ يَفْعَلُ ذَلِكَ؛ قَالَ عُبَيْدُ اللهِ: وَرَأَيْتُ الْقَاسِمَ بْنَ مُحَمَّدٍ، وَسَالِمًا يَفْعَلَانِ ذَلِكَ.[١٥١]

117. ʿAbdullāh b. ʿUmar ﵄ reported: "Whenever Allāh's Messenger ﷺ wrapped his turban around his head, he made its loose end [in the form of a tail that he] hung down between his shoulders."

Nāfiʿ says, "I saw ʿAbdullāh b. ʿUmar ﵄ do it in the same manner." ʿUbaydullah, the student of Nāfiʿ, said, "In my time, al-Qāsim b. Muḥammad and Sālim did the same."

ʿAbd al-Razzāq al-Badr said,

> He ﷺ used to keep the loose end of the turban hanging down between his shoulders, behind his back.

Al-Bājūrī said,

> It can be concluded from this ḥadīth that wrapping the turban while leaving its loose end hanging down is recommended, and to have it hang down on the back between the shoulders is the best. However, if the tail was left to hang down on the front as Ṣūfīs and some people of knowledge do, it is debatable whether it is better to keep it hanging down from the left side or the right side. This is because there is a weak ḥadīth specifying that it should hang to the right side and the Ṣūfīs preferred the left side because it is the side where the heart is located (leaving it to hang on the left side is to remind them to keep the heart empty of everything but Allāh).
>
> Some of the Shāfiʿīs said that if one fears becoming prideful or something similar due to his turban hanging, he is not to be prohibited from doing so. Rather, he is to do it and fight against his inner incli-

151 *Sunan al-Tirmidhī* (1736)

> nations.

Ibn Ḥajar al-Haytamī said,

> He ﷺ made the ends of the turban of 'Abd al-Raḥmān b. 'Awf ؓ fall in front of him and behind him.

Abū 'Abdillāh b. al-Ḥāj said,

> It is a surprise that some late scholars considered leaving the ends hanging down to the front an innovation while there are explicit authentic ḥadīths citing that the early *salaf* did this.

١١٨ – حَدَّثَنَا يُوسُفُ بْنُ عِيسَىٰ، قَالَ: حَدَّثَنَا وَكِيعٌ، قَالَ: حَدَّثَنَا أَبُو سُلَيْمَانَ – وَهُوَ عَبْدُ الرَّحْمَنِ بْنُ الْغَسِيلِ –، عَنْ عِكْرِمَةَ، عَنِ ابْنِ عَبَّاسٍ: «أَنَّ النَّبِيَّ صلىٰ الله عليه وسلم خَطَبَ النَّاسَ وَعَلَيْهِ عِصَابَةٌ دَسْمَاءُ». [١٥٢]

118. 'Abdullāh b. 'Abbās ؓ reported: "The Prophet ﷺ was once delivering a sermon whilst wearing a black/oily turban."

'Abd al-Razzāq al-Badr said,

> There are no authentic ḥadīths from the Prophet ﷺ regarding the virtue of wearing a turban. The only authentic ḥadīths mention him wearing turbans. Anything else reported is either very weak or fabricated. Examples are, "Prayer in a turban is better than twenty-five prayers without wearing it", and, "The Friday prayer in a turban is better than seventy without wearing it."[153] It is not permissible to attribute such narrations to the Prophet ﷺ.
>
> Thus, a person should not oblige people to wear a particular dress. This is because a person should wear the normal clothes that are known in their society so long as the clothes are not unlawful to wear. A person should not wear that which makes him stand out because the Prophet ﷺ forbade people from wearing what would make an individual known or famous amongst people.

Ibn Ḥajar al-Haytamī said,

> This sermon was delivered whilst he was afflicted with the sickness of

152 *Ṣaḥīḥ al-Bukhārī* (927)

153 *Al-Maṣnū' fī Ma'rifat al-Ḥadīth al-Mawḍū'* (1/118)

which he died.

Al-Bājūrī said,

> The word *dasmāʾ* means black. It has also been said that it means stained by oil, caused by the oil he used in his hair.

ʿAlī al-Qārī said,

> Al-Haytamī in his commentary concerning the reason why the Prophet ﷺ preferred to keep the tail of his turban hang down behind his back, between his shoulders condemned and defamed Ibn al-Qayyim and Ibn Taymiyyah and accused them of advocating anthropomorphism! However, whoever reads the explanation of *Manāzil al-Sāʾirīn* will come to know that they (Ibn Taymiyyah and Ibn al-Qayyim) are from the esteemed major scholars of Ahl al-Sunnah wa al-Jamāʿah and from the pious ones of this nation. Shaykh al-Islām, ʿAbdullāh al-Anṣārī al-Ḥanbalī explains the great status and merits of Ibn Taymiyyah and that he is innocent from the accusations made by his enemies that he was an advocate of anthropomorphism but it is the habit of the enemies of the people of ḥadīth and Sunnah to falsely accuse. The Rāfiḍah accuse them of being Nawāṣib and the latter accuse them of being the former, and the Muʿtazilah accuse them of being agents of the Ḥashawiyyah.
>
> These accusations are the heritage that those deviated people received from the enemies of the Messenger of Allāh ﷺ who called the Prophet and his companions apostates and claimed that they invented a new religion!

باب ما جاء في صفة إزار رسول الله صلى الله عليه وسلم
[18] On the Description of Allāh's Messenger's ﷺ *Izār*

'Abd al-Razzāq al-Badr said,

> The *izār* refers to the voluminous garment that is wrapped around the lower part of the body.

Al-Bājūrī said,

> The title also refers to the *ridā*', which is the garment that covers the upper part of the body. This is similar to the use of the verse: **{And has made for you garments which protect you from the heat}**[154] which actually refers to the cold too.

١١٩ – حَدَّثَنَا أَحْمَدُ بْنُ مَنِيعٍ، قَالَ: حَدَّثَنَا إِسْمَاعِيلُ بْنُ إِبْرَاهِيمَ، قَالَ: حَدَّثَنَا أَيُّوبُ، عَنْ حُمَيْدِ بْنِ هِلَالٍ، عَنْ أَبِي بُرْدَةَ، قَالَ: «أَخْرَجَتْ إِلَيْنَا عَائِشَةُ كِسَاءً مُلَبَّدًا، وَإِزَارًا غَلِيظًا، فَقَالَتْ: قُبِضَ رُوحُ رَسُولِ اللهِ صلى الله عليه وسلم فِي هَذَيْنِ». [155]

119. Abū Burdah ؓ narrated: "'Ā'ishah ؓ showed us a patched garment that is worn to cover the upper part, and a coarse *izār*. She then said, 'The Messenger of Allāh ﷺ passed away whilst wearing these two garments.'"

'Abd al-Razzāq al-Badr said,

> The meaning of this ḥadīth is that he ﷺ passed away while he had these garments to wear.

Al-Bājūrī said,

> The reason 'Ā'ishah ؓ kept the two garments of the Prophet ﷺ was to seek blessing from his clothes. She ؓ also kept his *jubbah* (loose outer robe) and after she passed away, her sister Asmā' ؓ took it and kept it.

---

154 Qur'ān: 16:81
155 *Ṣaḥīḥ al-Bukhārī* (3108) and *Ṣaḥīḥ Muslim* (2080)

Ibn Ḥajar al-Haytamī said,

> The Prophet ﷺ wore these rough clothes despite the fact that he conquered many lands, subdued his enemies and had all the treasures before his hand. This is because he never cared about worldly pleasures and favoured the pleasures found in the Hereafter, and because he ﷺ wanted his nation to follow the example of his lifestyle (which no one perfected except him ﷺ), especially when they are old.

١٢٠ - حَدَّثَنَا مَحْمُودُ بْنُ غَيْلانَ، قَالَ: حَدَّثَنَا أَبُو دَاوُدَ، عَنْ شُعْبَةَ، عَنِ الأَشْعَثِ بْنِ سُلَيْمٍ، قَالَ: سَمِعْتُ عَمَّتِي تُحَدِّثُ عَنْ عَمِّهَا، قَالَ: «بَيْنَا أَنَا أَمْشِي بِالْمَدِينَةِ، إِذَا إِنْسَانٌ خَلْفِي يَقُولُ: «ارْفَعْ إِزَارَكَ، فَإِنَّهُ أَتْقَىٰ وَأَبْقَىٰ»، فَإِذَا هُوَ رَسُولُ اللهِ صلىٰ الله عليه وسلم، فَقُلْتُ: يَا رَسُولَ اللهِ! إِنَّمَا هِيَ بُرْدَةٌ مَلْحَاءُ، قَالَ: «أَمَا لَكَ فِيَّ أُسْوَةٌ؟» فَنَظَرْتُ فَإِذَا إِزَارُهُ إِلَىٰ نِصْفِ سَاقَيْهِ». ١٥٦

120. 'Ubayd b. Khālid ؓ narrated: "I was once walking in Madīnah and I then heard a person from behind me say, 'Lift your *izār* higher for that shows more piety and makes it last longer.' When I turned to see who this was, I saw that it was the Messenger of Allāh ﷺ. I said, 'O Messenger of Allāh! This is a black garment with white patterns!' He replied, 'Are you not taking me as your example?' I looked at him and I saw that his *izār* reached until the halfway point of his shins."

'Alī al-Qārī said,

> Lifting the garment up [above the ankles] negates the arrogance and showing off that a long garment [hanging below the ankles] entails, and so one follows the order of Allāh ﷻ. This is why the Prophet ﷺ said it shows more piety.

'Abd al-Razzāq al-Badr said,

> The reason why the companion ؓ stated the description of the wrap was to say that this kind of clothing cannot be used to show off or make one arrogant even if it reached below the ankle due to its simplicity.

Al-Bājūrī said,

---

156 *Musnad Aḥmad* (23086)

> The guidance of the Prophet ﷺ in respect to lifting the garment above the ankle applies to all types of clothes. This ruling is only applicable to men because it is recommended for women to let one hand span of their clothes drag on the floor.

Ibn Ḥajar al-Haytamī said,

> This ḥadīth shows us that a person should look after their clothes so that they do not become worn out as that equates to wasting money.

١٢١ - حَدَّثَنَا سُوَيْدُ بْنُ نَصْرٍ، قَالَ: حَدَّثَنَا عَبْدُ اللهِ بْنُ الْمُبَارَكِ، عَنْ مُوسَىٰ بْنِ عُبَيْدَةَ، عَنِ إِيَاسِ بْنِ سَلَمَةَ بْنِ الأَكْوَعِ، عَنْ أَبِيهِ، قَالَ: «كَانَ عُثْمَانُ بْنُ عَفَّانَ يَأْتَزِرُ إِلَىٰ أَنْصَافِ سَاقَيْهِ، وَقَالَ: هَكَذَا كَانَتْ إِزْرَةُ صَاحِبِي - يَعْنِي النَّبِيَّ صلىٰ الله عليه وسلم -». [١٥٧]

121. Salamah b. al-Akwaʿ ؓ narrated: "The *izār* of ʿUthmān b. ʿAffān would fall to the middle of his shins. ʿUthmān said, 'This is how my companion, the Messenger of Allāh ﷺ wore his *izār*.'"

١٢٢ - حَدَّثَنَا قُتَيْبَةُ بْنُ سَعِيدٍ، قَالَ: حَدَّثَنَا أَبُو الأَحْوَصِ، عَنْ أَبِي إِسْحَاقَ، عَنْ مُسْلِمِ بْنِ نَذِيرٍ، عَنْ حُذَيْفَةَ بْنِ الْيَمَانِ، قَالَ: «أَخَذَ رَسُولُ اللهِ صلىٰ الله عليه وسلم بِعَضَلَةِ سَاقِي أَوْ سَاقِهِ، فَقَالَ: هَذَا مَوْضِعُ الإِزَارِ، فَإِنْ أَبَيْتَ فَأَسْفَلَ، فَإِنْ أَبَيْتَ فَلَا حَقَّ لِلإِزَارِ فِي الْكَعْبَيْنِ». [١٥٨]

122. Ḥudhayfah b. al-Yamān ؓ reported: "The Messenger of Allāh ﷺ caught the calf of my leg/his leg (the narrator was unsure here) and said, 'This is where the *izār* should reach, and if not, then slightly lower, and if not, then it has no right to reach the ankles.'"

Al-Bājūrī said,

> **"Caught the calf of my leg/his leg":** This wording occurs in the report of the author and also Ibn Mājah. It is obvious that the doubt occurred from a narrator after Ḥudhayfah, due to the improbability of such a doubt arising from the direct participant of the incident.

---

157 *Muṣannaf Ibn Abī Shaybah* (24240)
158 *Sunan Ibn Mājah* (3572)

> **"And if not, then it has no right to reach the ankles":** A literal reading of this would denote that clothing reaching the ankles is prohibited. However, the literal reading of the wording from al-Bukhārī, "What goes beyond the ankles is in the fire" shows that it is permissible for the clothing to reach the ankles. Thus, the wording in this narration is interpreted as an emphatic *(mubālaghah)*, illustrating that one should be cautious in ensuring that the *izār* does not even reach the ankle so as to avoid it descending below it.

Ibn Ḥajar al-Haytamī said,

> The ruling on the length of clothes after considering all the ḥadīths is that the Sunnah is to keep it to the halfway-point of the shin, and that it is lawful to let it reach to the ankle, and that it is disliked to let it reach below the ankle if no showing off is intended, otherwise it would be forbidden.

باب ما جاء في مشية رسول الله صلى الله عليه وسلم

[19] On Allāh's Messenger's ﷺ Walking

ʿAbd al-Razzāq al-Badr said,

> The walking of the Prophet ﷺ was moderate (as he was in all things), in compliance with the guidance of the *āyah*: **{And be moderate in your pace...}**[159]

Al-Bājūrī said,

> There are three ḥadīths in this chapter.

١٢٣- حَدَّثَنَا قُتَيْبَةُ بْنُ سَعِيدٍ، قَالَ: حَدَّثَنَا ابْنُ لَهِيعَةَ، عَنْ أَبِي يُونُسَ، عَنْ أَبِي هُرَيْرَةَ، قَالَ: «وَلا رَأَيْتُ شَيْئًا أَحْسَنَ مِنْ رَسُولِ اللهِ صلى الله عليه وسلم؛ كَأَنَّ الشَّمْسَ تَجْرِي فِي وَجْهِهِ، وَمَا رَأَيْتُ أَحَدًا أَسْرَعَ فِي مِشْيَتِهِ مِنْ رَسُولِ اللهِ صلى الله عليه وسلم؛ كَأَنَّمَا الأَرْضُ تُطْوَىٰ لَهُ، إِنَّا لَنُجْهِدُ أَنْفُسَنَا وَإِنَّهُ لَغَيْرُ مُكْتَرِثٍ». ١٦٠

123. Abū Hurayrah ؓ narrated: "I have not seen anything more handsome than the Messenger of Allāh ﷺ. It was as if the brightness of the sun shone from his face. I have not seen anyone walk faster than the Messenger of Allāh ﷺ. It was as if the earth would fold up for him; we found it difficult to keep up the pace when we walked with him, yet he walked at his normal pace."

ʿAbd al-Razzāq al-Badr said,

> Abū Hurayrah ؓ intentionally used the word "anything" to include everything, meaning that his beauty surpassed the beauty of everything that a person can see such as humans, the sun, nature, the moon, and anything that is described as beautiful.
>
> The fast pace is indicative of his strong body.

---

159 Qurʾān: 31:19

160 *Sunan al-Tirmidhī* (3648)

Al-Bājūrī said,

> The reason that Abū Hurayrah ؓ referred to the face only to explain the beauty of the Prophet ﷺ is because the face is the focal point of a person's beauty and often the body conforms to the status of the face.

Ibn Ḥajar al-Haytamī said,

> Despite his fast pace, he walked in a manner that maintained his respect and status; hence his pace was moderate [for him].

١٢٤ - حَدَّثَنَا عَلِيُّ بْنُ حُجْرٍ، وَغَيْرُ وَاحِدٍ، قَالُوا: حَدَّثَنَا عِيسَىٰ بْنُ يُونُسَ، عَنْ عُمَرَ بْنِ عَبْدِ اللهِ مَوْلَىٰ غُفْرَةَ، قَالَ: أَخْبَرَنِي إِبْرَاهِيمُ بْنُ مُحَمَّدٍ مِنْ وَلَدِ عَلِيِّ بْنِ أَبِي طَالِبٍ، قَالَ: كَانَ عَلِيٌّ إِذَا وَصَفَ النَّبِيَّ صلىٰ الله عليه وسلم قَالَ: «كَانَ إِذَا مَشَىٰ تَقَلَّعَ كَأَنَّمَا يَنْحَطُّ مِنْ صَبَبٍ». [١٦١]

124. ʿAlī b. Abī Tālib ؓ used to describe the Messenger of Allāh ﷺ, saying: "When he walked, he lifted his legs with vigour; it seemed as if he was descending from a higher place."

Al-Bājūrī said,

> He ﷺ lifted his legs with vigour and did not lift them in an arrogant manner or slowly as that is the way women walk.

١٢٥ - حَدَّثَنَا سُفْيَانُ بْنُ وَكِيعٍ، قَالَ: حَدَّثَنَا أَبِي، عَنِ الْمَسْعُودِيِّ، عَنْ عُثْمَانَ بْنِ مُسْلِمِ بْنِ هُرْمُزَ، عَنْ نَافِعِ بْنِ جُبَيْرِ بْنِ مُطْعِمٍ، عَنْ عَلِيِّ بْنِ أَبِي طَالِبٍ قَالَ: «كَانَ النَّبِيُّ صلىٰ الله عليه وسلم إِذَا مَشَىٰ تَكَفَّأَ تَكَفُّؤًا، كَأَنَّمَا يَنْحَطُّ مِنْ صَبَبٍ». [١٦٢]

125. ʿAlī b. Abī Tālib ؓ narrated: "When the Messenger of Allāh ﷺ walked, he bent forward slightly as if he was descending from a high place."

ʿAlī al-Qārī said,

> This is to show that he did not drag his feet on the ground or walk in an arrogant manner.

161 See ḥadīth 7

162 See ḥadīth 5 and 6

باب ما جاء في تقنع رسول الله صلى الله عليه وسلم

[20] On Allāh's Messenger's ﷺ Head-veil

ʿAbd al-Razzāq al-Badr said,

> The head-veil referred to here is a cloth that is put over the head to protect clothes from the stains of oil.

Al-Bājūrī said,

> The head-veil (Arabic: *qināʿ*) refers, in its broader meaning, to the sheet that a person places over or under the turban and which partially covers the face to protect oneself from oil, heat, cold etc. However in the context of this chapter, it refers to the cloth worn underneath the turban to protect it from the stains of oil or the heat.

١٢٦ - حَدَّثَنَا يُوسُفُ بْنُ عِيسَىٰ، قَالَ: حَدَّثَنَا وَكِيعٌ، قَالَ: حَدَّثَنَا الرَّبِيعُ بْنُ صَبِيحٍ، عَنْ يَزِيدَ بْنِ أَبَانَ، عَنْ أَنَسِ بْنِ مَالِكٍ، قَالَ: «كَانَ رَسُولُ اللهِ صلىٰ الله عليه وسلم يُكْثِرُ الْقِنَاعَ كَأَنَّ ثَوْبَهُ ثَوْبُ زَيَّاتٍ».[١٦٣]

126. Anas b. Mālik ؓ narrated: "Allāh's Messenger ﷺ often wore a cloth on his head. This cloth[, because of its greasiness,] looked like that of an oil-seller."

Al-Bājūrī said,

> It has authentically been reported from Ibn Masʿūd – and it is ruled as a *marfūʿ* (raised) report that utilising a sheet to veil the head is from the ways of the Prophets. It states in a narration, "The head is not veiled except by one with complete wisdom in statement and action." It is derived from the above that it is imperative for the scholars to have hallmarks unique to them so that they can be identified, asked and then followed in their orders and prohibitions. This is the basis of [them] wearing garments such as the *ṭaylasān* (shawl).

---

163 See ḥadīth 33

The benefits of covering the turban with a sheet so that it covers most of the face are many, some of them are: it is a sign of one's shyness and fear of Allāh because it is the habit of the fearful to hide and cover themselves, it helps the heart to be more attentive to Allāh and not distracted by the surroundings, and it gives the person [the opportunity] to have a minor solitude, as some Ṣūfīs have said.

باب ما جاء في جلسته صلى الله عليه وسلم

[21] On the Prophet's ﷺ Sitting

ʿAbd al-Razzāq al-Badr said,

> This chapter is dedicated to describing the manner in which the Prophet ﷺ used to sit.

Al-Bājūrī said,

> There are three ḥadīths in the chapter.

١٢٧ - حَدَّثَنَا عَبْدُ بْنُ حُمَيْدٍ، قَالَ: حَدَّثَنَا عَفَّانُ بْنُ مُسْلِمٍ، قَالَ: حَدَّثَنَا عَبْدُ اللهِ بْنُ حَسَّانَ، عَنْ جَدَّتَيْهِ، عَنْ قَيْلَةَ بِنْتِ مَخْرَمَةَ، «أَنَّهَا رَأَتْ رَسُولَ اللهِ صلىٰ الله عليه وسلم فِي الْمَسْجِدِ وَهُوَ قَاعِدٌ الْقُرْفُصَاءَ، قَالَتْ: فَلَمَّا رَأَيْتُ رَسُولَ اللهِ صلىٰ الله عليه وسلم الْمُتَخَشِّعَ فِي الْجِلْسَةِ أُرْعِدْتُ مِنَ الْفَرَقِ». [١٦٤]

127. Qaylah bint Makhramah رضي الله عنها reported: "I saw the Messenger ﷺ in the masjid sitting in a *qurfuṣā'* posture. Whilst watching him [and observing his personality] I became overwhelmed due to his overwhelming tranquillity, and this caused me to shiver."

ʿAbd al-Razzāq al-Badr said,

> This ḥadīth is part of a longer one wherein Qaylah narrates the story of how she embraced Islām.

Al-Bājūrī said,

> *Qurfuṣā'* (also pronounced as *qarfaṣā'* and *qirfiṣā'*) is to sit on the ground with the thighs pressing against the stomach and the arms enfolding the legs. This position is also known as *al-iḥtibā*.

Ibn Ḥajar al-Haytamī said,

> He ﷺ was sitting in a humble state, gazing at the floor silently whilst

---

164 *Sunan Abī Dāwūd* (4847)

his body parts were calm and tranquil due to his abundant fear of Allāh, the Most High.

'Alī al-Qārī said,

> The sitting posture of the Prophet ﷺ manifested his true slavery to Allāh, the Most High as he said in a ḥadīth, "I sit like how a slave sits and I eat just like how a slave eats."[165] He did not sit in the manner of the arrogant and the proud. Qaylah was affected in the way she mentioned due to his overwhelming prestige and awe-inspiring personality that caused people to respect him highly and glorify him.

١٢٨ - حَدَّثَنَا سَعِيدُ بْنُ عَبْدِ الرَّحْمَنِ الْمَخْزُومِيُّ، وَغَيْرُ وَاحِدٍ قَالُوا: حَدَّثَنَا سُفْيَانُ، عَنِ الزُّهْرِيِّ، عَنْ عَبَّادِ بْنِ تَمِيمٍ، عَنْ عَمِّهِ، «أَنَّهُ رَأَى النَّبِيَّ صلىٰ الله عليه وسلم مُسْتَلْقِيًا فِي الْمَسْجِدِ وَاضِعًا إِحْدَىٰ رِجْلَيْهِ عَلَىٰ الأُخْرَىٰ». ١٦٦

128. 'Abdullāh b. Zayd ؓ reported: "I saw the Messenger of Allāh ﷺ lying on his back in the masjid with one leg placed upon the other."

'Abd al-Razzāq al-Badr said,

> This kind of posture is not common when a person is sitting with a group of people. Rather, a person adopts this posture when resting, when alone or whilst sitting in the company of a few people.

Al-Bājūrī said,

> This ḥadīth indicates that lying down is considered a form of sitting.

Ibn Ḥajar al-Haytamī said,

> It is reported in *Ṣaḥīḥ Muslim* that the Prophet ﷺ admonished this kind of posture. The reconciliation between his admonishment of sitting in such a position and his action [in the ḥadīth] is that his action shows that it is permissible to sit in that position when one is sure that his *'awrah* will not become uncovered.

'Alī al-Qārī said,

---

165 *Al-Mughnī 'An Ḥaml al-Asfār Fī Takhrīj Mā Fī al-Iḥyā min Akhbār* (1/187) (2/454)
166 *Ṣaḥīḥ al-Bukhārī* (6287) and *Ṣaḥīḥ Muslim* (2100)

Al-Khaṭṭābī said: "This indicates that the ḥadīth wherein the Prophet ﷺ prohibited this form of sitting is either abrogated or that it is prohibited only when the *ʿawrah* will show. This is because the *izār* could be tight and so placing the leg on the other would uncover the *ʿawrah*. It was also said that this incident happened before he ﷺ forbade this posture or that the prohibition does not apply to the case where one does it because of being tired or to rest, or that his action was to show that it is permissible. It is also said that resting one leg upon the other is done in two ways: (i) the two legs stretched out while one is on the other and this posture does not expose the *ʿawrah*, (ii) one leg is lifted and bent whilst the other leg is on it, and so the ḥadīth in this chapter refers to the first type while the prohibition [in *Ṣaḥīḥ Muslim*] refers to the second type.

١٢٩- حَدَّثَنَا سَلَمَةُ بْنُ شَبِيبٍ، قَالَ: حَدَّثَنَا عَبْدُ اللهِ بْنُ إِبْرَاهِيمَ الْمَدَنِيُّ، قَالَ: حَدَّثَنَا إِسْحَاقُ بْنُ مُحَمَّدٍ الأَنْصَارِيُّ، عَنْ رُبَيْحِ بْنِ عَبْدِ الرَّحْمَنِ بْنِ أَبِي سَعِيدٍ، عَنْ أَبِيهِ، عَنْ جَدِّهِ أَبِي سَعِيدٍ الْخُدْرِيِّ، قَالَ: «كَانَ رَسُولُ اللهِ صلىٰ الله عليه وسلم إِذَا جَلَسَ فِي الْمَسْجِدِ احْتَبَىٰ بِيَدَيْهِ».[١٦٧]

129. Abū Saʿīd al-Khudrī ؓ narrated: "When Allāh's Messenger ﷺ sat in the masjid, he did *iḥtibāʾ* with his hands."

Al-Bājūrī said,

> The exception to this posture is that which he ﷺ used to do after the prayer of *Fajr* where he used to sit with his legs crossed, as reported by Abū Dāwūd with an authentic chain of narrators.
>
> *Iḥtibāʾ* is the common posture of the Bedouins and it is to sit on the ground and to have the thighs pressing against the stomach by wrapping them with a turban and its likes [such as the arms] to give support to the back. The Bedouins used to do it as they had no walls to lean their backs upon.

---

167 *Al-Sunan al-Kubrā* of al-Bayhaqī (3/236)

باب ما جاء في تكأة رسول الله صلى الله عليه وسلم

[22] On Allāh's Messenger's ﷺ Leaning Cushion

'Abd al-Razzāq al-Badr said,

> This chapter is dedicated to describing that which the Prophet ﷺ used to rest on for support.

Al-Bājūrī said,

> There are four ḥadīths in the chapter.

١٣٠- حَدَّثَنَا عَبَّاسُ بْنُ مُحَمَّدٍ الدُّورِيُّ الْبَغْدَادِيُّ، قَالَ: حَدَّثَنَا إِسْحَاقُ بْنُ مَنْصُورٍ، عَنْ إِسْرَائِيلَ، عَنْ سِمَاكِ بْنِ حَرْبٍ، عَنْ جَابِرِ بْنِ سَمُرَةَ، قَالَ: «رَأَيْتُ رَسُولَ اللهِ صلى الله عليه وسلم مُتَّكِئًا عَلَىٰ وِسَادَةٍ عَلَىٰ يَسَارِهِ».[١٦٨]

130. Jābir b. Samurah ؓ narrated: "I saw the Messenger of Allāh ﷺ reclining upon a pillow which was on his left side."

Ibn Ḥajar al-Haytamī said,

> This ḥadīth describes the event and is not intended to restrict the side on which a person should lean on because it is allowed to lean towards both sides.

١٣١- حَدَّثَنَا حُمَيْدُ بْنُ مَسْعَدَةَ، قَالَ: حَدَّثَنَا بِشْرُ بْنُ الْمُفَضَّلِ، قَالَ: حَدَّثَنَا الْجُرَيْرِيُّ، عَنْ عَبْدِ الرَّحْمَنِ بْنِ أَبِي بَكْرَةَ، عَنْ أَبِيهِ، قَالَ: قَالَ رَسُولُ اللهِ صلى الله عليه وسلم: «أَلا أُحَدِّثُكُمْ بِأَكْبَرِ الْكَبَائِرِ؟» قَالُوا: بَلَىٰ يَا رَسُولَ اللهِ! قَالَ: «الإِشْرَاكُ بِاللهِ، وَعُقُوقُ الْوَالِدَيْنِ»، قَالَ: وَجَلَسَ رَسُولُ اللهِ صلى الله عليه وسلم وَكَانَ مُتَّكِئًا قَالَ: «وَشَهَادَةُ الزُّورِ» أَوْ «قَوْلُ الزُّورِ» قَالَ: فَمَا زَالَ رَسُولُ اللهِ صلى

168 *Sunan al-Tirmidhī* (2770) and *Sunan Abī Dāwūd* (4143)

الله عليه وسلم يَقُوْلُهَا حَتَّىٰ قُلْنَا: لَيْتَهُ سَكَتَ! ١٦٩

131. Abū Bakrah ☝ related: "The Messenger of Allāh ﷺ said, 'Shall I not inform you of the most severe of the major sins?' The Messenger of Allāh ﷺ asked this question thrice. We said, 'Yes, O Messenger of Allāh! [Please inform us.]' He said, 'Ascribing partners to Allāh, and being undutiful to your parents.' [Then] the Messenger of Allāh ﷺ sat up from his reclining position and said, '[And I warn you against] giving forged statements and false testimony.' The Messenger of Allāh ﷺ kept on repeating that warning until we wished he would stop."

'Abd al-Razzāq al-Badr said,

> **"Shall I not inform you of the most severe of the major sins":**
> This linguistic style was often used by the Prophet ﷺ as it attracts the attention of the audience and it is a good educational method.

Ibn Ḥajar al-Haytamī said,

> Ibn 'Abbās ☝ considered all that which Allāh has admonished and made forbidden to be major sins as he did not believe that there is a minor sin given the fact that the one being disobeyed is Allāh ﷻ. However, the most correct view is that sins are of two types, major and minor. The major sins are those that have been severely threatened against in the Qur'ān and Sunnah.

Al-Bājūrī said,

> The greatest of the major sins is disbelief but ascribing partners to Allāh is mentioned in this ḥadīth as it is the most common type of disbelief that people do. The second major sin is being undutiful to the parents and this includes all that which harms them in action or words. The mention of parents here also refers to the grandparents.

> This ḥadīth shows that it is permissible for a person to remember Allāh and teach others whilst reclining upon a pillow and that this act does not imperfect one's mannerisms. It also shows that the preacher should repeat the message until the audience becomes moved by the enthusiasm that they see.

---

169 *Ṣaḥīḥ al-Bukhārī* (2654) and *Ṣaḥīḥ Muslim* (87)

١٣٢ - حَدَّثَنَا قُتَيْبَةُ بْنُ سَعِيدٍ، قَالَ: حَدَّثَنَا شَرِيكٌ، عَنْ عَلِيِّ بْنِ الأَقْمَرِ، عَنْ أَبِي جُحَيْفَةَ، قَالَ: قَالَ رَسُولُ اللهِ صلى الله عليه وسلم: «أَمَّا أَنَا فَلا آكُلُ مُتَّكِئًا». ١٧٠

132. Abū Juḥayfah ﵁ reported: "The Messenger of Allāh ﷺ said, 'As for me, I do not eat whilst reclining.'"

ʿAlī al-Qārī said,

> The statement of the Prophet ﷺ was intended to condemn the practice of non-Muslims and leaders of the non-Arabs at that time as they used to eat while reclining to show their greatness, pride and arrogance. This statement hints that neither the Prophet ﷺ nor his followers would lean [on cushions etc.] when they ate, as Allāh ﷻ said: **{Say, "This is my way; I invite to Allāh with insight, I and those who follow me."}**[171]

Mīrak Shāh al-Ḥanafī said (as quoted by al-Qārī),

> Scholars explained that leaning/reclining is of four types: to lean/recline on one side, to place one of the hands on the floor and lean on it, sitting cross-legged on a pillow, resting the back against a pillow or its like. Adopting any of these positions whilst eating is prohibited as doing so indicates arrogance. The Sunnah is to eat while sitting down, leaning forward towards the food.

Al-Bayhaqī said,

> If a person is sick and cannot eat unless they are reclining, then it is permissible to eat in such a position.

Al-Bājūrī said,

> It is fine for a person to recline while eating nuts, based on the practice of ʿAlī b. Abī Ṭālib ﵁ and al-Ghazālī said, "Arabs may do that but eating while sitting down is better and it is not disliked to eat while standing. As for eating whilst sitting with crossed-legs, it is not the best position to eat in."

١٣٣ - حَدَّثَنَا مُحَمَّدُ بْنُ بَشَّارٍ، قَالَ: حَدَّثَنَا عَبْدُ الرَّحْمَنِ بْنُ مَهْدِيٍّ، قَالَ: حَدَّثَنَا

---

170 *Ṣaḥīḥ al-Bukhārī* (5389)
171 Qurʾān: 12:108

سُفْيَانُ، عَنْ عَلِيِّ بْنِ الأَقْمَرِ، قَالَ: سَمِعْتُ أَبَا جُحَيْفَةَ، يَقُولُ: قَالَ رَسُولُ اللهِ صلى الله عليه وسلم: «لَا آكُلُ مُتَّكِئًا». ١٧٢

133. Abū Juḥayfah ⬥ reported that Allāh's Messenger said, "I do not eat while reclining."

Al-Bājūrī said,

> **"I do not eat while reclining":** I.e. I do not eat while leaning to one side and resting on it solely, as clarified in the previous ḥadīth.

١٣٤ - حَدَّثَنَا يُوسُفُ بْنُ عِيسَىٰ، قَالَ: حَدَّثَنَا وَكِيعٌ، قَالَ: حَدَّثَنَا إِسْرَائِيلُ، عَنْ سِمَاكِ بْنِ حَرْبٍ، عَنْ جَابِرِ بْنِ سَمُرَةَ، قَالَ: «رَأَيْتُ النَّبِيَّ صلى الله عليه وسلم مُتَّكِئًا عَلَىٰ وِسَادَةٍ».

134. Jābir b. Samurah ⬥ narrated: "I saw the Messenger of Allāh reclining upon a pillow."

قَالَ أَبُو عِيسَىٰ: لَمْ يَذْكُرْ وَكِيعٌ «عَلَىٰ يَسَارِهِ»، وَهَكَذَا رَوَىٰ غَيْرُ وَاحِدٍ عَنْ إِسْرَائِيلَ نَحْوَ رِوَايَةِ وَكِيعٍ، وَلَا نَعْلَمُ أَحَدًا رَوَىٰ فِيهِ «عَلَىٰ يَسَارِهِ» إِلا مَا رَوَاهُ إِسْحَاقُ بْنُ مَنْصُورٍ، عَنْ إِسْرَائِيلَ. ١٧٣

Abū 'Īsā said: Wakī' (one of the narrators of this report) did not mention "to his left", and a number of others reported it the same from Isrā'īl. I do not know of anyone reporting it with "to his left" except Isḥāq b. Manṣūr from Isrā'īl (i.e. report 130 of this book).

Al-Bājūrī said,

> **"Abū 'Īsā said: Wakī' (one of the narrators of this report) did not mention 'to his left'...":** This refers to the addition [in report 130]. It means that this addition ("to his left") falls under the ḥadīth terminology term *gharīb* (strange), as the narrator Isḥāq solely mentioned it. It would have been more appropriate to place this current route of the narration (i.e. 134) after the route of Isḥāq b. Manṣūr (i.e. 130) which was mentioned at the start of the chapter.

---

172 See ḥadīth 132
173 See ḥadīth 130

باب ما جاء في اتكاء رسول الله صلى الله عليه وسلم

[23] On Allāh's Messenger's ﷺ Leaning/Reclining

ʿAbd al-Razzāq al-Badr said,

> This chapter describes the manner in which the Prophet ﷺ leaned whilst standing whereas the previous chapter described how he did so whilst sitting.

Mīrak Shāh said (as quoted by ʿAlī al-Qārī),

> The purpose of this chapter is to display the Prophet's leaning on one of his companions while walking, due to an illness or something similar. This can be understood by analysing the two ḥadīths placed here. The author's purpose was not apprehended by one individual, who claimed that the correct interpretation is that this chapter and the one preceding it should be combined.

Al-Bājūrī said,

> There are two ḥadīths in this chapter.

١٣٥ - حَدَّثَنَا عَبْدُ اللهِ بْنُ عَبْدِ الرَّحْمَنِ، قَالَ: حَدَّثَنَا عَمْرُو بْنُ عَاصِمٍ، قَالَ: حَدَّثَنَا حَمَّادُ بْنُ سَلَمَةَ، عَنْ حُمَيْدٍ، عَنْ أَنَسٍ: «أَنَّ النَّبِيَّ صلى الله عليه وسلم كَانَ شَاكِيًا فَخَرَجَ يَتَوَكَّأُ عَلَىٰ أُسَامَةَ بْنِ زَيْدٍ، وَعَلَيْهِ ثَوْبٌ قِطْرِيٌّ قَدْ تَوَشَّحَ بِهِ فَصَلَّىٰ بِهِمْ».[١٧٤]

135. Anas b. Mālik رضي الله عنه reported that he saw the Messenger of Allāh ﷺ, while he was sick, coming out of his room leaning upon Usāmah b. Zayd رضي الله عنه for support. He headed to the prayer leading the Muslims whilst wearing a Yemenī shawl that he put on his shoulders.

Al-Bājūrī said,

> This incident occurred during his final illness.

174 See ḥadīth 59

١٣٦ - حَدَّثَنَا عَبْدُ اللهِ بْنُ عَبْدِ الرَّحْمَنِ، قَالَ: حَدَّثَنَا مُحَمَّدُ بْنُ الْمُبَارَكِ، قَالَ: حَدَّثَنَا عَطَاءُ بْنُ مُسْلِمٍ الْخَفَّافُ الْحَلَبِيُّ، قَالَ: حَدَّثَنَا جَعْفَرُ بْنُ بُرْقَانَ، عَنْ عَطَاءِ بْنِ أَبِي رَبَاحٍ، عَنِ الْفَضْلِ بْنِ عَبَّاسٍ، قَالَ: دَخَلْتُ عَلَىٰ رَسُولِ اللهِ صلى الله عليه وسلم فِي مَرَضِهِ الَّذِي تُوُفِّيَ فِيهِ، وَعَلَىٰ رَأْسِهِ عِصَابَةٌ صَفْرَاءُ، فَسَلَّمْتُ عَلَيْهِ، فَقَالَ: «يَا فَضْلُ!»، قُلْتُ: لَبَّيْكَ يَا رَسُولَ اللهِ! قَالَ: «اشْدُدْ بِهَذِهِ الْعِصَابَةِ رَأْسِي»، قَالَ: فَفَعَلْتُ، ثُمَّ قَعَدَ فَوَضَعَ كَفَّهُ عَلَىٰ مَنْكِبِي، ثُمَّ قَامَ فَدَخَلَ فِي الْمَسْجِدِ.

وَفِي الْحَدِيثِ قِصَّةٌ.[175]

136. Al-Faḍl b. al-'Abbās ؓ narrated: "I came to Allāh's Messenger ﷺ during the time of his last illness before he passed away and I saw that a yellow band was around his head. I greeted him and [after replying,] he said, 'O Faḍl!' I replied, 'I am here for you, Allāh's Messenger!' He replied, 'Fasten this band around my head tightly.' I did so and then he sat. He placed his hands upon my shoulders, stood and then he entered the masjid."

The narration consists of a lengthy account.

Al-Bājūrī said,

> **"And I saw that a yellow band was around his head":** I.e. a cloth or yellow turban. This ḥadīth is the evidence used as the basis for wearing yellow turbans and the evidence for wearing black turbans is the ḥadīth that states that he ﷺ entered Makkah whilst wearing a black turban. However, the white turban is the best as we have explained before.
>
> The request of the Prophet ﷺ to fasten the band around his head was to relieve his headache. This shows that seeking treatment and medicine does not contradict full reliance on Allāh; rather it shows one's humility and need for Allāh.

175 *Mukhtaṣar al-Shamā'il* of al-Albānī (107)

باب ما جاء في أكل رسول الله صلى الله عليه وسلم
[24] On Allāh's Messenger's ﷺ Eating

'Abd al-Razzāq al-Badr said,

> This chapter describes the manner in which the Prophet ﷺ ate, sat down to eat and other reported etiquettes.

Al-Bājūrī said,

> There are five ḥadīths in this chapter.

١٣٧ - حَدَّثَنَا مُحَمَّدُ بْنُ بَشَّارٍ، قَالَ: حَدَّثَنَا عَبْدُ الرَّحْمَنِ بْنُ مَهْدِيٍّ، عَنْ سُفْيَانَ، عَنْ سَعْدِ بْنِ إِبْرَاهِيمَ، عَنِ ابْنٍ لِكَعْبِ بْنِ مَالِكٍ، عَنْ أَبِيهِ، «أَنَّ النَّبِيَّ صلى الله عليه وسلم كَانَ يَلْعَقُ أَصَابِعَهُ ثَلَاثًا».

137. Ka'b b. Mālik ؓ narrated: "The Messenger of Allāh ﷺ used to lick his fingers thrice [after eating]."

قَالَ أَبُو عِيسَىٰ: وَرَوَىٰ غَيْرُ مُحَمَّدِ بْنِ بَشَّارٍ هَذَا الْحَدِيثَ، قَالَ: «يَلْعَقُ أَصَابِعَهُ الثَّلَاثَ».[١٧٦]

Abū 'Īsā [al-Tirmidhī] said: "Other narrators of this ḥadīth besides Muḥammad b. Bashar cited the wording, "He ﷺ used to lick his three fingers."

'Abd al-Razzāq al-Badr said,

> The ḥadīth wherein it says that he ﷺ licked his fingers three times is an odd (*shādh*) narration. The preserved (*maḥfūẓ*) narration is that he licked his three fingers.

Al-Bājūrī said,

> The wisdom of licking the fingers is explained in another ḥadīth

176 *Ṣaḥīḥ Muslim* (2032)

wherein he said, "When one of you finishes eating, he should lick his fingers. Indeed, you do not know in which [part] of your food is the *barakah* (blessing)."[177]

Ibn Ḥajar al-Haytamī said,

> The reconciliation between this ḥadīth and the other one where it says that he licked his three fingers (rather than each finger thrice) is that he licked each of the three fingers thrice. The three fingers he used for eating were the thumb, index and middle fingers. The middle finger should be licked first after finishing the meal because it is the longest and so it will have more food stuck to it, then the index finger should be licked, followed by the thumb. It is the Sunnah to lick the fingers before washing them or wiping them.

Al-Qaḍī ʿIyāḍ said (as quoted by ʿAlī al-Qārī),

> The wisdom of licking the fingers is so that a person does not belittle the food and appreciates it even if it is little.

ʿAlī al-Qārī said,

> It is disliked to lick the fingers while eating because the fingers will then touch the food whilst having some traces of saliva upon them.

١٣٨ - حَدَّثَنَا الْحَسَنُ بْنُ عَلِيٍّ الْخَلالُ، قَالَ: حَدَّثَنَا عَفَّانُ، قَالَ: حَدَّثَنَا حَمَّادُ بْنُ سَلَمَةَ، عَنْ ثَابِتٍ، عَنْ أَنَسٍ، قَالَ: «كَانَ النَّبِيُّ صلىٰ الله عليه وسلم إِذَا أَكَلَ طَعَامًا لَعِقَ أَصَابِعَهُ الثَّلَاثَ».[١٧٨]

138. Anas b. Mālik ﵁ narrated: "The Messenger of Allāh ﷺ used to lick his three fingers after he finished eating."

ʿAbd al-Razzāq al-Badr said,

> This conveys the same meaning as the preceding report, displaying the aforementioned two etiquettes: (i) eating with three fingers. However, some scholars have said that eating with three fingers is not for soupy types of food i.e. it is for finger foods that can be collected in the three fingers, and (ii) licking the fingers after finishing the meal.

---

177 *Sunan al-Tirmidhī* (1801)

178 *Ṣaḥīḥ Muslim* (2034)

١٣٩ - حَدَّثَنَا الْحُسَيْنُ بْنُ عَلِيِّ بْنِ يَزِيدَ الصُّدَائِيُّ الْبَغْدَادِيُّ، قَالَ: حَدَّثَنَا يَعْقُوبُ بْنُ إِسْحَاقَ - يَعْنِي: الْحَضْرَمِيَّ -، قَالَ: حَدَّثَنَا شُعْبَةُ، عَنْ سُفْيَانَ الثَّوْرِيِّ، عَنْ عَلِيِّ بْنِ الأَقْمَرِ، عَنْ أَبِي جُحَيْفَةَ، قَالَ: قَالَ النَّبِيُّ صلى الله عليه وسلم: «أَمَّا أَنَا فَلا آكُلُ مُتَّكِئًا». ١٧٩

139. Abū Juḥayfah ﵁ narrated: "The Messenger of Allāh ﷺ said, 'As for me, I do not eat whilst I am reclining [upon something].'"

Al-Bājūrī said,

> This report was mentioned in the previous chapter, and it is repeated here due to mention of eating. It is narrated by Abū Shaybah from Mujāhid that the Prophet ate once while leaning. It is possible that this was to display its permissibility or that it took place before the prohibition. The latter is supported by the report of Shāhīn from ʿAṭā' that Jibrīl saw al-Muṣṭafā ﷺ eating while leaning and then prohibited it. From the wisdom of eating while leaning being detested (*makrūh*) is that it impacts digestion.

١٤٠ - حَدَّثَنَا مُحَمَّدُ بْنُ بَشَّارٍ، قَالَ: حَدَّثَنَا عَبْدُ الرَّحْمَنِ بْنُ مَهْدِيٍّ، قَالَ: حَدَّثَنَا سُفْيَانُ، عَنْ عَلِيِّ بْنِ الأَقْمَرِ نَحْوَهُ.

140. ʿAlī b. al-Aqmar reports the same.

Al-Bājūrī said,

> This is the same report via a *mursal* route, as the companion has been omitted.

١٤١ - حَدَّثَنَا هَارُونُ بْنُ إِسْحَاقَ الْهَمْدَانِيُّ، قَالَ: حَدَّثَنَا عَبْدَةُ بْنُ سُلَيْمَانَ عَنْ هِشَامِ بْنِ عُرْوَةَ عَنِ ابْنٍ لِكَعْبِ بْنِ مَالِكٍ عَنْ أَبِيهِ قَالَ: «كَانَ رَسُولُ اللهِ صلى الله عليه وسلم يَأْكُلُ بِأَصَابِعِهِ الثَّلاثِ وَيَلْعَقُهُنَّ». ١٨٠

141. Kaʿb b. Mālik ﵁ narrated: "The Messenger of Allāh ﷺ used to eat with his three fingers and lick them after finishing the meal."

Al-Bājūrī said,

179 See ḥadīth 130
180 *Muṣannaf Ibn Abī Shaybah* (23869)

It states in *al-Iḥyāʾ*, "Eating is of four types: (i) Eating with one finger, which is from detest, (ii) with two fingers, which is from pride, (iii) with three fingers, which is from the Sunnah, (iv) and with four or five fingers, which is from gluttony."

١٤٢ - حَدَّثَنَا أَحْمَدُ بْنُ مَنِيعٍ، قَالَ: حَدَّثَنَا الْفَضْلُ بْنُ دُكَيْنٍ، قَالَ: حَدَّثَنَا مُصْعَبُ بْنُ سُلَيْمٍ، قَالَ: سَمِعْتُ أَنَسَ بْنَ مَالِكٍ، يَقُولُ: «أُتِيَ رَسُولُ اللهِ صلى الله عليه وسلم بِتَمْرٍ فَرَأَيْتُهُ يَأْكُلُ وَهُوَ مُقْعٍ مِنَ الْجُوعِ».[١٨١]

142. Anas b. Mālik ﷺ said: "Dates were presented to the Messenger of Allāh ﷺ. I saw him hunched over due to hunger whilst eating the dates."

Ibn al-ʿUthaymīn said,

> The Prophet ﷺ ate like that so that he would not become too comfortable and eat too much. This is because, usually when a person sits in this manner, he does not feel too comfortable and this causes him to become unable to eat excessively. If he is not comfortable he will never eat to excess, but if he is comfortable he will.

ʿAbd al-Razzāq al-Badr said,

> This ḥadīth of Anas b. Mālik is fully narrated in the *Musnad* of al-Imām Aḥmad and its wording is: "Dates were presented to the Prophet ﷺ so he divided it equally to be distributed amongst the [needy] people and I was the one who was sent to give it away. After he finished, I saw him eating whilst sitting in a kneeling position and this made me realise that he was hungry."[182]
>
> This ḥadīth shows he gave priority to other persons who had a similar condition (i.e. hunger) despite the fact that he was hungry himself.

Ibn Ḥajar al-ʿAsqalānī said,

> The Sunnah when sitting to eat is to kneel down with the top of the feet resting upon the floor, or to sit with the right knee up, resting on the left foot.

---

181 *Ṣaḥīḥ Muslim* (2044)
182 *Musnad Aḥmad* (13101)

باب ما جاء في صفة خبز رسول الله صلى الله عليه وسلم
[25] On the Description of Allāh's Messenger's ﷺ Bread

Al-Bājūrī said,

There are eight ḥadīths in this chapter.

١٤٣ - حَدَّثَنَا مُحَمَّدُ بْنُ الْمُثَنَّىٰ، وَمُحَمَّدُ بْنُ بَشَّارٍ، قَالَا: حَدَّثَنَا مُحَمَّدُ بْنُ جَعْفَرٍ، قَالَ: حَدَّثَنَا شُعْبَةُ، عَنْ أَبِي إِسْحَاقَ، قَالَ: سَمِعْتُ عَبْدَ الرَّحْمَنِ بْنَ يَزِيدَ، يُحَدِّثُ عَنِ الْأَسْوَدِ بْنِ يَزِيدَ، عَنْ عَائِشَةَ، أَنَّهَا قَالَتْ: «مَا شَبِعَ آلُ مُحَمَّدٍ صلىٰ الله عليه وسلم مِنْ خُبْزِ الشَّعِيرِ يَوْمَيْنِ مُتَتَابِعَيْنِ حَتَّىٰ قُبِضَ رَسُولُ اللهِ صلىٰ الله عليه وسلم». ١٨٣

143. ʿĀ'ishah ؓ related: "The family of Muḥammad ﷺ never ate a full stomach of barley bread for two consecutive days until the day he passed away."

ʿAbd al-Razzāq al-Badr said,

This ḥadīth shows that the Prophet ﷺ used to eat little and that this worldly life held no weight upon his heart. He is the best of mankind but still he used to sleep hungry. This shows that the worldly life is trivial in the sight of Allāh. If it had any value, He would have endowed the best of His creation with all of its adornments and pleasures.

Al-Bājūrī said,

It is possible that the word 'family' mentioned in this ḥadīth is just an unnecessary addition i.e. if it is removed the meaning will still be the same. That is to say that the statement does not include the family of the Prophet ﷺ and the following ḥadīth confirms this meaning. It is also possible that the wording is an integral part of the ḥadīth and in

---

this case the word 'family' refers to those under the responsibility of the Prophet ﷺ, and not the family in its broader sense.

١٤٤ - حَدَّثَنَا عَبَّاسُ بْنُ مُحَمَّدٍ الدُّورِيُّ، قَالَ: حَدَّثَنَا يَحْيَىٰ بْنُ أَبِي بُكَيْرٍ، قَالَ: حَدَّثَنَا حَرِيزُ بْنُ عُثْمَانَ، عَنْ سُلَيْمِ بْنِ عَامِرٍ، قَالَ: سَمِعْتُ أَبَا أُمَامَةَ الْبَاهِلِيَّ يَقُولُ: «مَا كَانَ يَفْضُلُ عَنْ أَهْلِ بَيْتِ رَسُولِ اللهِ صلىٰ الله عليه وسلم خُبْزُ الشَّعِيرِ».[١٨٤]

144. Abū Umāmah al-Bāhilī ؓ stated: "The family of the Messenger of Allāh ﷺ never had any barley bread left over."

ʿAlī al-Qārī said,

> This is a way of saying that they were never full from food.

Mīrak said (as quoted by ʿAlī al-Qārī),

> This means that there was nothing on their dining spreads beyond the amount necessary for their meals.

١٤٥ - حَدَّثَنَا عَبْدُ اللهِ بْنُ مُعَاوِيَةَ الْجُمَحِيُّ، قَالَ: حَدَّثَنَا ثَابِتُ بْنُ يَزِيدَ، عَنْ هِلَالِ بْنِ خَبَّابٍ، عَنْ عِكْرِمَةَ، عَنِ ابْنِ عَبَّاسٍ، قَالَ: «كَانَ رَسُولُ اللهِ صلىٰ الله عليه وسلم يَبِيتُ اللَّيَالِيَ الْمُتَتَابِعَةَ طَاوِيًا هُوَ وَأَهْلُهُ، لا يَجِدُونَ عَشَاءً وَكَانَ أَكْثَرُ خُبْزِهِمْ خُبْزَ الشَّعِيرِ».[١٨٥]

145. ʿAbdullāh b. Abbās ؓ related: "The Messenger ﷺ and his family spent consecutive nights hungry as there would be no supper. Most often, their bread would be made of barley."

Al-Bājūrī said,

> This ḥadīth shows the noble character, dignity and self-esteem of the Prophet ﷺ as he took precautions so that none of his companions would know that he and his family slept hungry for several nights. This is evident, as it is certain that if they (the poor and the rich from them) were aware about it they would have raced each other to give him and his family priority over themselves and their families.

---

184 *Sunan al-Tirmidhī* (2359)
185 *Sunan al-Tirmidhī* (2359)

This indicates the virtue of the poor and directs people not to ask for food even when one is hungry.

١٤٦- حَدَّثَنَا عَبْدُ اللهِ بْنُ عَبْدِ الرَّحْمَنِ، قَالَ: حَدَّثَنَا عُبَيْدُ اللهِ بْنُ عَبْدِ الْمَجِيدِ الْحَنَفِيُّ، حَدَّثَنَا عَبْدُ الرَّحْمَنِ بْنُ عَبْدِ اللهِ بْنِ دِينَارٍ، قَالَ: حَدَّثَنَا أَبُو حَازِمٍ، عَنْ سَهْلِ بْنِ سَعْدٍ، أَنَّهُ قِيلَ لَهُ: «أَكَلَ رَسُولُ اللهِ صلى الله عليه وسلم النَّقِيَّ؟ - يَعْنِي الْحُوَّارَى - فَقَالَ سَهْلٌ: مَا رَأَى رَسُولُ اللهِ صلى الله عليه وسلم النَّقِيَّ حَتَّى لَقِيَ اللهَ عَزَّ وَجَلَّ، فَقِيلَ لَهُ: هَلْ كَانَتْ لَكُمْ مَنَاخِلُ عَلَى عَهْدِ رَسُولِ اللهِ صلى الله عليه وسلم؟ قَالَ: مَا كَانَتْ لَنَا مَنَاخِلُ؛ قِيلَ: كَيْفَ كُنْتُمْ تَصْنَعُونَ بِالشَّعِيرِ؟ قَالَ: كُنَّا نَنْفُخُهُ فَيَطِيرُ مِنْهُ مَا طَارَ ثُمَّ نَعْجِنُهُ».[١٨٦]

146. Someone asked Sahl b. Saʿd ﵁: "Did the Messenger of Allāh ﷺ ever eat bread made of white bran-free flour?" He replied, "The Messenger ﷺ never saw it in his lifetime." The questioner then asked, "Did you people use sieved flour in the time of the Messenger ﷺ?" He replied, "We did not have sieves." The questioner then asked, "How did you sieve the barley?" He replied, "We used to blow out the particles and then knead that which remained."

Al-Bājūrī said,

> **"Never saw it":** He answered the question by mentioning sight, despite the question being in regards to eating. This is because the absence of sighting dictates the absence of eating, and negating sighting is more emphatic than negating eating.

ʿAbd al-Razzāq al-Badr said,

> The reason why the questioner asked about barley is because it has grains that if they remain in the dough, the bread would be difficult to chew.

Ibn Ḥajar al-Haytamī said,

> This ḥadīth shows that the Prophet ﷺ was not fussy about food and so he ate the barley bread just like everyone else. It is only the fools and idle people who are fussy about food.

---

186 *Ṣaḥīḥ al-Bukhārī* (5413)

١٤٧ - حَدَّثَنَا مُحَمَّدُ بْنُ بَشَّارٍ، قَالَ: حَدَّثَنَا مُعَاذُ بْنُ هِشَامٍ، قَالَ: حَدَّثَنِي أَبِي، عَنْ يُونُسَ، عَنْ قَتَادَةَ، عَنْ أَنَسِ بْنِ مَالِكٍ، قَالَ: «مَا أَكَلَ نَبِيُّ اللهِ صلى الله عليه وسلم عَلَىٰ خِوَانٍ، وَلا فِي سُكُرَّجَةٍ، وَلا خُبِزَ لَهُ مُرَقَّقٌ».

قَالَ: فَقُلْتُ لِقَتَادَةَ: فَعَلامَ كَانُوا يَأْكُلُونَ؟ قَالَ: عَلَىٰ هَذِهِ السُّفَرِ[١٨٧].

قَالَ مُحَمَّدُ بْنُ بَشَّارٍ: يُونُسُ هَذَا الَّذِي رَوَىٰ عَنْ قَتَادَةَ هُوَ يُونُسُ الإِسْكَافُ.

147. Anas b. Mālik ﷺ reported: "The Messenger ﷺ never ate food from a table, nor from a *sukurrujah* (i.e. a small plate), nor was thin soft bread ever made for him."

Yūnus asked Qatādah (the narrator from Anas): "Then upon what did they eat their food?" He replied: "Upon these floor-sheets."

Muḥammad b. Bashshār said: "The Yūnus who narrated from Qatādah here is Yūnus al-Iskāf."

ʿAbd al-Razzāq al-Badr said,

> This shows the moderation of the Prophet ﷺ even in food as he ate neither from a table nor on the floor without placing a sheet underneath. This is because eating on the table was considered as a luxury whilst eating on the floor without placing anything underneath would expose the food to dirt. Thus, eating on the floor while having a sheet underneath is a humble way of eating that protects the food from dirt.

Al-Bājūrī said,

> Eating on dining tables was the practice followed by the prideful amongst the non-Arabs so that their heads would not lower while eating. Eating on it is an innovation, but it is allowed if there is no pride or arrogance involved.

Ibn Ḥajar al-Haytamī said,

> The *sukurrujah* is a small plate that is used for side dishes and appetisers.

---

187 *Ṣaḥīḥ al-Bukhārī* (5415)

١٤٨ - حَدَّثَنَا أَحْمَدُ بْنُ مَنِيعٍ، قَالَ: حَدَّثَنَا عَبَّادُ بْنُ عَبَّادٍ الْمُهَلَّبِيُّ، عَنْ مُجَالِدٍ، عَنِ الشَّعْبِيِّ، عَنْ مَسْرُوقٍ، قَالَ: دَخَلْتُ عَلَىٰ عَائِشَةَ، فَدَعَتْ لِي بِطَعَامٍ وَقَالَتْ: «مَا أَشْبَعُ مِنْ طَعَامٍ فَأَشَاءُ أَنْ أَبْكِيَ إِلا بَكَيتُ؛ قَالَ: قُلْتُ لِمَ؟ قَالَتْ: أَذْكُرُ الْحَالَ الَّتِي فَارَقَ عَلَيْهَا رَسُولُ اللهِ صلىٰ الله عليه وسلم الدُّنْيَا، وَاللهِ مَا شَبِعَ مِنْ خُبْزٍ وَلَحْمٍ مَرَّتَيْنِ فِي يَوْمٍ»[١٨٨].

148. Masrūq narrated: "I visited ʿĀ'ishah ﵂ and she ordered food for me and then said, 'I never eat to my full except that I wish to cry, then I begin to cry.' I asked, 'Why is that?' She replied, 'I remember the state of the Messenger of Allāh ﷺ upon which he left us for the next world. I swear by Allāh that he never filled his stomach twice in one day with meat or bread.'"

ʿAbd al-Razzāq al-Badr said,

> Masrūq was born during the lifetime of the Prophet ﷺ but never saw him as he was living in the city of Kufa in Iraq. He was a scholastic master amongst the major followers of the companions. The name Masrūq means "stolen", and it is said that he was given this name because he was kidnapped when he was a child and then later on his family managed to find him.

Ibn Ḥajar al-Haytamī said,

> The reason ʿĀ'ishah ﵂ used to cry every time she ate to her full was because she missed the hard life that she had experienced with the Prophet ﷺ. This is because that lifestyle was the highest level of virtuousness since it was the lifestyle that the Prophet chose for himself ﷺ and his family.

Al-Bājūrī said,

> He ﷺ never had a full stomach from either meat and bread [twice] in one day. Excessive enjoyment of the [lawful] cravings is disliked whereas minimalism is recommended, and humbleness is required.

١٤٩ - حَدَّثَنَا مَحْمُودُ بْنُ غَيْلانَ، قَالَ: حَدَّثَنَا أَبُو دَاوُدَ، قَالَ: حَدَّثَنَا شُعْبَةُ، عَنْ أَبِي إِسْحَاقَ، قَالَ: سَمِعْتُ عَبْدَ الرَّحْمَنِ بْنَ يَزِيدَ، يُحَدِّثُ عَنِ الأَسْوَدِ بْنِ يَزِيدَ، عَنْ

188 *Sunan al-Tirmidhī* (2356)

عَائِشَةَ، قَالَتْ: «مَا شَبِعَ رَسُولُ اللهِ صلى الله عليه وسلم مِنْ خُبْزِ الشَّعِيرِ يَوْمَيْنِ
مُتَتَابِعَيْنِ حَتَّىٰ قُبِضَ». ١٨٩

149. 'Ā'ishah ﵂ narrated: "The Messenger of Allāh ﷺ never filled his stomach with barley bread for two consecutive days until he passed away."

'Alī al-Qārī said,

> He ﷺ never filled his stomach with bread made of barley, let alone bread made of wheat. This was because he acted upon the decision he made when he was given the choice to either be a prophet who is a king in this world or just a slave of Allāh, and so he chose, "I prefer to be a Prophet who is a [true] slave of Allāh; I starve on one day so I bear it with patience and I eat well on another day so I praise Him."[190]

Al-Bājūrī said,

> He did not eat to his full twice in one day because he avoided that and preferred the state of hunger.

١٥٠ – حَدَّثَنَا عَبْدُ اللهِ بْنُ عَبْدِ الرَّحْمَنِ، قَالَ: حَدَّثَنَا عَبْدُ اللهِ بْنُ عَمْرٍو أَبُو مَعْمَرٍ،
حَدَّثَنَا عَبْدُ الْوَارِثِ، عَنْ سَعِيدِ بْنِ أَبِي عَرُوبَةَ، عَنْ قَتَادَةَ، عَنْ أَنَسٍ، قَالَ: «مَا أَكَلَ
رَسُولُ اللهِ صلى الله عليه وسلم عَلَىٰ خِوَانٍ، وَلَا أَكَلَ خُبْزًا مُرَقَّقًا حَتَّىٰ مَاتَ». ١٩١

150. Anas b. Mālik ﵁ narrated: "Until the end of his life, the Messenger of Allāh ﷺ never ate on a table and never ate thin soft bread."

Al-Bājūrī said,

> **"Until the end of his life"**: Meaning that he continuously did this until he left this world.

---

189 *Ṣaḥīḥ al-Bukhārī* (5416) and *Ṣaḥīḥ Muslim* (2970)
190 *Musnad Aḥmad* (12/143)
191 *Ṣaḥīḥ al-Bukhārī* (6450)

باب ما جاء في صفة إدام رسول الله صلى الله عليه وسلم

[26] On the Description of Allāh's Messenger's ﷺ *Idām*

Al-Bājūrī said,

> The *idām* refers to all that which is eaten with bread, be it liquid or solid, and so it includes dry food such as meat. The fact that meat is considered a type of *idām* is based on the linguistic meaning of the word but it is not considered an *idām* based on the norms of people.

Ibn Ḥajar al-Haytamī said,

> This is because the habit of people is to eat the *idām* to facilitate the eating of other food [i.e. it is used to eat the bread].

١٥١ - حَدَّثَنَا مُحَمَّدُ بْنُ سَهْلِ بْنِ عَسْكَرٍ، وَعَبْدُ اللهِ بْنُ عَبْدِ الرَّحْمَنِ، قَالا: حَدَّثَنَا يَحْيَىٰ بْنُ حَسَّانَ، قَالَ: حَدَّثَنَا سُلَيْمَانُ بْنُ بِلالٍ، عَنْ هِشَامِ بْنِ عُرْوَةَ، عَنْ أَبِيهِ، عَنْ عَائِشَةَ، أَنَّ رَسُولَ اللهِ صلىٰ الله عليه وسلم قَالَ: «نِعْمَ الإِدَامُ الْخَلُّ»، قَالَ عَبْدُ اللهِ بْنُ عَبْدِ الرَّحْمَنِ فِي حَدِيثِهِ: «نِعْمَ الإِدَامُ - أَوِ الأُدْمُ - الْخَلُّ».[١٩٢]

151. 'Ā'ishah ﵂ narrated: "The Messenger of Allāh ﷺ said, 'What an excellent *idām* vinegar is.'"

Ibn al-Qayyim said,

> This ḥadīth is intended to praise vinegar, given the circumstances of the event, and so it does not intend to prefer it over all other types of *idām*, as some ignorant people think. The context behind this statement is that he ﷺ went home and took a piece of bread. He then asked his family if there was an *idām* to eat with the bread and so they replied that they have nothing but vinegar. Upon that he praised the *idām*.[193]

Al-Bājūrī said,

192 *Ṣaḥīḥ Muslim* (2051)
193 *Zād al-Ma'ād* (4/219)

> The Prophet ﷺ praised vinegar to complement and bring comfort to the heart of the one presenting it to him. Otherwise if the available *idām* was milk or meat or honey, they would have been rightful to be praised instead.

١٥٢- حَدَّثَنَا قُتَيْبَةُ، قَالَ: حَدَّثَنَا أَبُو الأَحْوَصِ، عَنْ سِمَاكِ بْنِ حَرْبٍ، قَالَ: سَمِعْتُ النُّعْمَانَ بْنَ بَشِيرٍ، يَقُولُ: «أَلَسْتُمْ فِي طَعَامٍ وَشَرَابٍ مَا شِئْتُمْ؟ لَقَدْ رَأَيْتُ نَبِيَّكُمْ صلىٰ الله عليه وسلم وَمَا يَجِدُ مِنَ الدَّقَلِ مَا يَمْلأُ بَطْنَهُ».[١٩٤]

152. Al-Nuʿmān b. Bashīr ؓ said: "You are in enough luxury to eat and drink all that you wish! By Allāh, I have seen your Prophet ﷺ not having the worst type of dates to fill his stomach."

ʿAbd al-Razzāq al-Badr said,

> The purpose of al-Nuʿmān's statement was to remind the remaining companions and the generation that did not have the pleasure and honour to see the Prophet ﷺ of the blessings and favours of Allāh upon them.

Al-Bājūrī said,

> The purpose of al-Nuʿmān was to admonish those whom he addressed and advise them to suffice with the little that is enough and to follow the example of the Prophet ﷺ in this regard. The reason he said "your Prophet" was to emphasise the meaning of the advice that followed and to encourage them.

١٥٣- حَدَّثَنَا عَبْدَةُ بْنُ عَبْدِ اللهِ الْخُزَاعِيُّ، قَالَ: حَدَّثَنَا مُعَاوِيَةُ بْنُ هِشَامٍ، عَنْ سُفْيَانَ، عَنْ مُحَارِبِ بْنِ دِثَارٍ، عَنْ جَابِرِ بْنِ عَبْدِ اللهِ، قَالَ: قَالَ رَسُولُ اللهِ صلىٰ الله عليه وسلم: «نِعْمَ الإِدَامُ الْخَلُّ»[١٩٥].

153. Jābir b. ʿAbdillāh ؓ related: "The Messenger of Allāh ﷺ said, 'What a wonderful *idām* vinegar is.'"

Al-Bājūrī said,

194 *Ṣaḥīḥ Muslim* (2977)
195 *Sunan al-Tirmidhī* (1839)

> **"What a wonderful *idām* vinegar is":** We mentioned previously that this praise was according to the circumstances of that particular event, and not in an unrestricted sense. This ḥadīth is well-known *(mash-hūr)*, to the point of nearly being mass-transmitted *(mutawātir)*.

١٥٤ – حَدَّثَنَا هَنَّادٌ، قَالَ: حَدَّثَنَا وَكِيعٌ، عَنْ سُفْيَانَ، عَنْ أَيُّوبَ، عَنْ أَبِي قِلَابَةَ، عَنْ زَهْدَمٍ الْجَرْمِيِّ، قَالَ: «كُنَّا عِنْدَ أَبِي مُوسَىٰ الأَشْعَرِيِّ، فَأُتِيَ بِلَحْمِ دَجَاجٍ فَتَنَحَّىٰ رَجُلٌ مِنَ الْقَوْمِ، فَقَالَ: مَا لَكَ؟ فَقَالَ: إِنِّي رَأَيْتُهَا تَأْكُلُ شَيْئًا فَحَلَفْتُ أَنْ لَا آكُلَهَا، قَالَ: ادْنُ، فَإِنِّي رَأَيْتُ رَسُولَ اللهِ صلىٰ الله عليه وسلم يَأْكُلُ لَحْمَ دَجَاجٍ»[١٩٦].

154. Zahdam al-Jarmī narrated: "We were in the presence of Abū Mūsā al-Ashʿarī ﵁ when chicken was served to us. A person from among those present distanced himself from the gathering. Abū Mūsā ﵁ asked him the reason [for doing so]. He replied, 'I have seen the chicken eat something [unclean] so I swore that I would not eat it.' Abū Mūsā ﵁ said, 'Come, for I have seen the Messenger of Allāh ﷺ eat chicken meat.'"

Al-Bājūrī said,

> **"I have seen the chicken eat something":** I.e. something dirty. He insinuated this – instead of saying it explicitly – so those present would not feel disgusted and abstain from eating it.
>
> The direction of Abū Mūsa ﵁ given to the man was to indicate that it is better for him that he offers expiation for his oath and eats from the chicken to follow the example of the Prophet ﷺ based on the ḥadīth, "None of you shall believe until his desires are made to follow that which I brought."[197] It also indicates that the host serving the food should try to make the person break any similar oath if the reason for leaving a particular food is for a matter that is not disliked in religion (except in the case where the man made a conditional divorce).

Ibn Ḥajar al-Haytamī said,

> If the chicken is of the type that lives on dirt and garbage then one

196 *Ṣaḥīḥ al-Bukhārī* (5517) and *Ṣaḥīḥ Muslim* (1649)
197 *Al-Arbaʿūn al-Nawawiyyah* (41)

should not break his oath because it is forbidden to eat. However, it seems that the chicken was not from that type and it happened that it ate something dirty on that day.

ʿAbd al-Razzāq al-Badr said,

The man did not specify the type of dirt that he saw the chicken eating so that he would not make the people feel disgust towards the food. This is because it suffices for a person who dislikes a type of food just to state that he does not feel like eating it, thus following the guidance of the Prophet ﷺ in this kind of situation.

١٥٥ - حَدَّثَنَا الْفَضْلُ بْنُ سَهْلِ الْأَعْرَجُ الْبَغْدَادِيُّ، قَالَ: حَدَّثَنَا إِبْرَاهِيمُ بْنُ عَبْدِ الرَّحْمَنِ بْنِ مَهْدِيٍّ، عَنْ إِبْرَاهِيمَ بْنِ عُمَرَ بْنِ سَفِينَةَ، عَنْ أَبِيهِ، عَنْ جَدِّهِ، قَالَ: «أَكَلْتُ مَعَ رَسُولِ اللهِ صلى الله عليه وسلم لَحْمَ حُبَارَىٰ». ١٩٨

155. Safīna ؓ narrated: "I ate bustard meat with the Messenger of Allāh ﷺ."

Al-Bājūrī said,

Safīna is a nick name given to him. It means a ship because he carried a lot of luggage when travelling. He was one of the slaves that the Prophet ﷺ freed and his name is disputed over but some stated that his actual name is Mihrān.

١٥٦ - حَدَّثَنَا عَلِيُّ بْنُ حُجْرٍ، قَالَ: حَدَّثَنَا إِسْمَاعِيلُ بْنُ إِبْرَاهِيمَ، عَنْ أَيُّوبَ، عَنِ الْقَاسِمِ التَّمِيمِيِّ، عَنْ زَهْدَمٍ الْجَرْمِيِّ، قَالَ: كُنَّا عِنْدَ أَبِي مُوسَىٰ الْأَشْعَرِيِّ، قَالَ: فَقَدَّمَ طَعَامَهُ وَقَدَّمَ فِي طَعَامِهِ لَحْمَ دَجَاجٍ؛ وَفِي الْقَوْمِ رَجُلٌ مِنْ بَنِي تَيْمِ اللهِ أَحْمَرُ كَأَنَّهُ مَوْلَىٰ، قَالَ : فَلَمْ يَدْنُ، فَقَالَ لَهُ أَبُو مُوسَىٰ: ادْنُ، فَإِنِّي قَدْ رَأَيْتُ رَسُولَ اللهِ صلى الله عليه وسلم أَكَلَ مِنْهُ، فَقَالَ: إِنِّي رَأَيْتُهُ يَأْكُلُ شَيْئًا فَقَذِرْتُهُ فَحَلَفْتُ أَنْ لَا أَطْعَمَهُ أَبَدًا. ١٩٩

156. Zahdam al-Jarmī narrated: "We were present in a gathering with Abū Mūsa al-Ashʿarī ؓ and in the food that was served there

---

198 *Sunan Abī Dāwūd* (3797)
199 See ḥadīth 154.

was poultry. Among those present was a man from the tribe of Banī Taymillāh who was reddish in complexion and seemed to be a freed slave. He stayed away from the food. Abū Mūsā asked him to come near [and eat from the food] and related to him that he saw the Messenger ﷺ also eat chicken. He excused himself saying, 'I had seen it eating something [unclean.] For this reason I swore an oath that I would not eat it.'"[200]

Al-Bājūrī said,

This ḥadīth is repeated here via a different route.

١٥٧ - حَدَّثَنَا مَحْمُودُ بْنُ غَيْلَانَ، قَالَ: حَدَّثَنَا أَبُو أَحْمَدَ الزُّبَيْرِيُّ، وَأَبُو نُعَيْمٍ، قَالَا: حَدَّثَنَا سُفْيَانُ، عَنْ عَبْدِ اللهِ بْنِ عِيسَىٰ، عَنْ رَجُلٍ مِنْ أَهْلِ الشَّامِ يُقَالُ لَهُ: عَطَاءٌ، عَنْ أَبِي أَسِيدٍ قَالَ: قَالَ رَسُولُ اللهِ صلىٰ الله عليه وسلم: ﴿كُلُوا الزَّيْتَ وَادَّهِنُوا بِهِ، فَإِنَّهُ مِنْ شَجَرَةٍ مُبَارَكَةٍ﴾. ٢٠١

157. Abū Asīd ☆ narrated: "The Messenger of Allāh ﷺ said, 'Use olive oil as a food and for oiling [the hair/body], for it is from a blessed tree.'"

ʿAbd al-Razzāq al-Badr said,

The direction to eat olive oil relates to eating it with bread (i.e. using it as an *idām*).

Al-Bājūrī said,

"And for oiling": This should be moderate and not an excessive practice. Ibn al-Qayyim said, "Using oil in hot lands such as the region of Hejaz is good for one's health but it is harmful if it is used in cold lands."

ʿAlī al-Qārī said,

The olive tree is blessed because it grows in the blessed land (i.e. the region of al-Shām) and that makes its olives blessed. It was reported that the Prophet ﷺ encouraged using it as a medicine to treat haemorrhoids, and in another ḥadīth that olive oil cures seventy diseases.

---

200 Previously explained in ḥadīth 154.
201 *Sunan al-Tirmidhī* (1852)

١٥٨ - حَدَّثَنَا يَحْيَىٰ بْنُ مُوسَىٰ، قَالَ: حَدَّثَنَا عَبْدُ الرَّزَّاقِ، قَالَ: حَدَّثَنَا مَعْمَرٌ، عَنْ زَيْدِ بْنِ أَسْلَمَ، عَنْ أَبِيهِ، عَنْ عُمَرَ بْنِ الْخَطَّابِ، قَالَ: قَالَ رَسُولُ اللهِ صلى الله عليه وسلم: «كُلُوا الزَّيْتَ وَادَّهِنُوا بِهِ، فَإِنَّهُ مِنْ شَجَرَةٍ مُبَارَكَةٍ»[٢٠٢].

158. ʿUmar b. al-Khaṭṭāb ﷺ narrated: "The Messenger of Allāh ﷺ said, 'Use olive oil as a food and for oiling [the hair/body], for it is from a blessed tree.'"[203]

قَالَ أَبُو عِيسَىٰ: وعَبْدُ الرَّزَّاقِ يَضْطَرِبُ فِي هَذَا الْحَدِيثِ، فَرُبَّمَا أَسْنَدَهُ، وَرُبَّمَا أَرْسَلَهُ.

Abū ʿĪsā said, "ʿAbd al-Razzāq showed confusion in this ḥadīth, both reporting it with a full chain and also reporting it by omitting the companion (i.e. ʿUmar)."

Al-Bājūrī said,

> **"Reporting it with a full chain and also reporting it by omitting the companion":** He reported it with a full chain in this route (i.e. number 158) wherein he mentioned ʿUmar b. al-Khaṭṭab, and he omitted ʿUmar in the following route (i.e. number 159).

١٥٩ - حَدَّثَنَا السِّنْجِيُّ - وَهُوَ أَبُو دَاوُدَ سُلَيْمَانُ بْنُ مَعْبَدٍ السِّنْجِيُّ -، قَالَ: حَدَّثَنَا عَبْدُ الرَّزَّاقِ، عَنْ مَعْمَرٍ، عَنْ زَيْدِ بْنِ أَسْلَمَ، عَنْ أَبِيهِ، عَنِ النَّبِيِّ صلى الله عليه وسلم نَحْوَهُ، وَلَمْ يَذْكُرْ فِيهِ عَنْ عُمَرَ[٢٠٤].

159. Zayd b. Aslam reports the same from his father. ʿUmar was not mentioned in this route.

Al-Bājūrī said,

> **"ʿUmar was not mentioned in this route":** I.e. it was reported in *mursal* form.

---

202 *Sunan al-Tirmidhī* (1851) and *Sunan Ibn Mājah* (3319)
203 See ḥadīth 157
204 *Muṣannaf ʿAbd al-Razzāq* (19568)

١٦٠ - حَدَّثَنَا مُحَمَّدُ بْنُ بَشَّارٍ، قَالَ: حَدَّثَنَا مُحَمَّدُ بْنُ جَعْفَرٍ، وَعَبْدُ الرَّحْمَنِ بْنُ مَهْدِيٍّ، قَالَا: حَدَّثَنَا شُعْبَةُ، عَنْ قَتَادَةَ، عَنْ أَنَسِ بْنِ مَالِكٍ، قَالَ: «كَانَ النَّبِيُّ صلى الله عليه وسلم يُعْجِبُهُ الدُّبَّاءُ، فَأُتِيَ بِطَعَامٍ، أَوْ دُعِيَ لَهُ، فَجَعَلْتُ أَتَتَبَّعُهُ فَأَضَعُهُ بَيْنَ يَدَيْهِ لِمَا أَعْلَمُ أَنَّهُ يُحِبُّهُ»[٢٠٥].

160. Anas b. Mālik ﵁ narrated: "The Prophet ﷺ loved eating gourd. Once food was presented to him (or he attended an invitation) where gourd was served. As I knew that he loved it; I sought its pieces in the platter and then placed them in front of him so that he could eat them."

Al-Bājūrī said,

> The reason the Prophet ﷺ liked eating gourd is because it sharpens the mind, cures headaches, extinguishes thirst, it is good for the one who has a fever and is suitable for one who feels cold.

Ibn Ḥajar al-Haytamī said,

> The Prophet ﷺ liked gourd because he knew that this vine possesses hidden benefits since Allāh caused it to grow over his brother, Prophet Yūnus ﵇. Yūnus subsisted and lived under the shade of this vine [during his rehabilitation]. It was akin to a mother to him, nursing its young.
>
> One of the benefits concluded from this ḥadīth is that it is allowed for a person to reach for the food that is not in front of him if the food consists of different types.

١٦١ - حَدَّثَنَا قُتَيْبَةُ بْنُ سَعِيدٍ، قَالَ: حَدَّثَنَا حَفْصُ بْنُ غِيَاثٍ، عَنْ إِسْمَاعِيلَ بْنُ أَبِي خَالِدٍ، عَنْ حَكِيمِ بْنِ جَابِرٍ، عَنْ أَبِيهِ، قَالَ: دَخَلْتُ عَلَى النَّبِيِّ صلى الله عليه وسلم، فَرَأَيْتُ عِنْدَهُ دُبَّاءً يُقَطَّعُ، فَقُلْتُ: مَا هَذَا؟ قَالَ: «نُكَثِّرُ بِهِ طَعَامَنَا»[٢٠٦].

161. Jābir ﵁ narrated: "I visited the Prophet ﷺ and I observed that a gourd was being sliced. I inquired, 'What is the reason for cutting

---

205 *Musnad Aḥmad* (12811)
206 *Sunan Ibn Mājah* (3304)

it into pieces?' He replied, 'We use it to increase the quantity of our food.'"

قَالَ أَبُو عِيسَىٰ: وجَابِرٌ هَذَا: هُوَ جَابِرُ بنُ طَارِقٍ، وَيُقَالُ: ابْنُ أَبِي طَارِقٍ، وَهُوَ رَجُلٌ مِنْ أَصْحَابِ رَسُولِ اللهِ صلى الله عليه وسلم، وَلَا نَعْرِفُ لَهُ إِلَّا هَذَا الحَدِيثَ الوَاحِدَ، وأَبُو خالِدٍ اسْمُهُ: سَعْدٌ.

Abū 'Īsā said, "The Jābir mentioned is Jābir b. Ṭāriq, and it was also said: Ibn Abī Ṭāriq. He was a companion of Allāh's Messenger ﷺ. We only know of this solitary ḥadīth from him. The name of the Abū Khālid mentioned in the chain of narration is Sa'd.

'Abd al-Razzāq al-Badr said,

> This ḥadīth shows that gourd is from the *idām* that the Prophet ﷺ used.

Al-Bājūrī said,

> The slicing of the gourd into pieces indicates that one can take care in cooking as this does not contradict asceticism or reliance on Allāh, as one can live moderately in a manner that leads to contentment.

١٦٢ - حَدَّثَنَا قُتَيْبَةُ بْنُ سَعِيدٍ، عَنْ مَالِكِ بْنِ أَنَسٍ، عَنِ إِسْحَاقَ بْنِ عَبْدِ اللهِ بْنِ أَبِي طَلْحَةَ، أَنَّهُ سَمِعَ أَنَسَ بْنَ مَالِكٍ يَقُولُ: إِنَّ خَيَّاطًا دَعَا رَسُولَ اللهِ صلى الله عليه وسلم لِطَعَامٍ صَنَعَهُ، قَالَ أَنَسٌ: فَذَهَبْتُ مَعَ رَسُولِ اللهِ صلى الله عليه وسلم إِلَىٰ ذَلِكَ الطَّعَامِ، فَقَرَّبَ إِلَىٰ رَسُولِ اللهِ صلى الله عليه وسلم خُبْزًا مِنْ شَعِيرٍ وَمَرَقًا فِيهِ دُبَّاءٌ وَقَدِيدٌ، قَالَ أَنَسٌ: فَرَأَيْتُ النَّبِيَّ صلى الله عليه وسلم يَتَتَبَّعُ الدُّبَّاءَ حَوَالَيِ القَصْعَةِ فَلَمْ أَزَلْ أُحِبُّ الدُّبَّاءَ مِنْ يَوْمِئِذٍ.[٢٠٧]

162. Anas b. Mālik ﷺ narrated: "A tailor once invited the Messenger of Allāh ﷺ to a feast he had prepared. I went with Allāh's Messenger ﷺ and attended the gathering. The host presented the Messenger ﷺ with some bread made of barley and a broth with pieces of jerked meat and gourd in it. I saw the Messenger ﷺ look for pieces of gourd from all sides of the bowl. Thenceforth, I began loving gourd."

---

207 *Ṣaḥīḥ al-Bukhārī* (5379) and *Ṣaḥīḥ Muslim* (2041)

ʿAbd al-Razzāq al-Badr said,

> From the etiquettes of good hospitality is to place the food near the guest, as in Allāh's words concerning Ibrāhīm al-Khalīl's honouring of his guests: **{And he slipped away to his family and brought a fatted calf and set it before them. He said, "Will you not eat?"}**[208]

Al-Bājūrī said,

> Anas b. Mālik ﷺ attended the invitation with the Prophet ﷺ because he was his servant or because he was asked to.
>
> The fact that the Prophet ﷺ ate from all sides of the plate does not contradict his command that a person should eat only from in front of him. This is because the command was given so that other diners would not be harmed [by the person reaching], and no one would ever be harmed if the hand of the Prophet ﷺ reached in front of them because people seek blessing with that.

Ibn Ḥajar al-Haytamī said,

> This ḥadīth includes the following benefits:
>
> 1. It is recommended to accept the invitation of others even if the food made is little or the social status of the host is less than that of the invitee.
> 2. It is recommended to like gourd because the Prophet ﷺ liked it and the same applies to all of that which he ﷺ liked. This was mentioned by al-Nawawī.
> 3. It is recommended to eat with the servant. The Prophet ﷺ allowing his servant to accompany him and join him is an example of his humble character and kind treatment to the young companions.

١٦٣ - حَدَّثَنَا أَحْمَدُ بْنُ إِبْرَاهِيمَ الدَّوْرَقِيُّ، وَسَلَمَةُ بْنُ شَبِيبٍ، وَمَحْمُودُ بْنُ غَيْلَانَ، قَالُوا: حَدَّثَنَا أَبُو أُسَامَةَ، عَنْ هِشَامِ بْنِ عُرْوَةَ، عَنْ أَبِيهِ، عَنْ عَائِشَةَ قَالَتْ: «كَانَ النَّبِيُّ صلى الله عليه وسلم يُحِبُّ الْحَلْوَاءَ وَالْعَسَلَ»[٢٠٩].

208 Al-Dhāriyāt: 26-27

209 *Ṣaḥīḥ al-Bukhārī* (5431) and *Ṣaḥīḥ Muslim* (1473)

163. 'Ā'ishah ⬡ narrated: "The Prophet ⬡ loved *ḥalwā* and honey."

Ibn Ḥajar al-Haytamī said,

> *Ḥalwā* refers to all that which is sweet, and it can be used to refer to fruits. Al-Khaṭṭābī said that it refers to man-made sweets. Al-Tha'ālibī said that the *ḥalwā* that the Prophet ⬡ liked was a mixture of dates that is knead with milk.

> Al-Khaṭṭābī said, "He ⬡ did not like *ḥalwā* in the sense that he used to crave for it but rather he would like to eat more of it when it was presented to him and that is how it was known that he liked it."

١٦٤ - حَدَّثَنَا الْحَسَنُ بْنُ مُحَمَّدٍ الزَّعْفَرَانِيُّ، قَالَ: حَدَّثَنَا الْحَجَّاجُ بْنُ مُحَمَّدٍ، قَالَ: قَالَ ابْنُ جُرَيْجٍ: أَخْبَرَنِي مُحَمَّدُ بْنُ يُوسُفَ، أَنَّ عَطَاءَ بْنَ يَسَارٍ، أَخْبَرَهُ أَنَّ أُمَّ سَلَمَةَ أَخْبَرَتْهُ: «أَنَّهَا قَرَّبَتْ إِلَىٰ رَسُولِ اللهِ صلىٰ الله عليه وسلم جَنْبًا مَشْوِيًّا فَأَكَلَ مِنْهُ، ثُمَّ قَامَ إِلَىٰ الصَّلَاةِ وَمَا تَوَضَّأَ»٢١٠.

164. Umm Salamah ⬡ related: "I presented a grilled side portion of sheep to the Messenger of Allāh ⬡. He ate from it and then prayed without performing ablution."

'Abd al-Razzāq al-Badr said,

> The last practice of the Prophet ⬡ was not to perform ablution after eating meat cooked on fire except for camel meat, according to the most correct view of scholars.

Al-Bājūrī said,

> Mentioning the meat after *ḥalwā* and honey indicates that these are the three best types of food. It is reported from 'Alī that meat refines the body and one's nature, and that if one abstains from it for forty days he will spoil his nature. However, Ibn al-Qayyim mentioned that one should not eat meat all the time as that can cause illness. Hippocrates (the Greek physician) said, "Do not make your stomachs the graveyards of animals."

١٦٥ - حَدَّثَنَا قُتَيْبَةُ، قَالَ: حَدَّثَنَا ابْنُ لَهِيعَةَ، عَنْ سُلَيْمَانَ بْنِ زِيَادٍ، عَنْ عَبْدِ اللهِ بْنِ

---
210 *Sunan al-Tirmidhī* (1829)

الْحَارِثِ، قَالَ: «أَكَلْنَا مَعَ رَسُولِ اللهِ صلى الله عليه وسلم شِوَاءً فِي الْمَسْجِدِ».[٢١١]

165. ʿAbdullāh b. al-Ḥārith ﵁ narrated: "We ate grilled meat with the Messenger of Allāh ﷺ whilst in the masjid."

Al-Bājūrī said,

> The *Sunan* of Ibn Mājah includes the following addition to the ḥadīth, "Then, he got up and prayed and we prayed with him. We did not do anything after finishing the meal more than wiping our hands with stones." It is possible that this incident took place during their *ʿitikāf*, though it is permissible to eat in the masjid if one can assure that the food will not cause mess.

١٦٦ - حَدَّثَنَا مَحْمُودُ بْنُ غَيْلَانَ، قَالَ: حَدَّثَنَا وَكِيعٌ، قَالَ: حَدَّثَنَا مِسْعَرٌ، عَنْ أَبِي صَخْرَةَ جَامِعِ بْنِ شَدَّادٍ، عَنِ الْمُغِيرَةِ بْنِ عَبْدِ اللهِ، عَنِ الْمُغِيرَةِ بْنِ شُعْبَةَ، قَالَ: ضِفْتُ مَعَ رَسُولِ اللهِ صلى الله عليه وسلم ذَاتَ لَيْلَةٍ، فَأُتِيَ بِجَنْبٍ مَشْوِيٍّ، ثُمَّ أَخَذَ الشَّفْرَةَ فَجَعَلَ يَحُزُّ، فَحَزَّ لِي بِهَا مِنْهُ، قَالَ: فَجَاءَ بِلَالٌ يُؤْذِنُهُ بِالصَّلَاةِ فَأَلْقَى الشَّفْرَةَ، فَقَالَ: «مَا لَهُ تَرِبَتْ يَدَاهُ؟»، قَالَ: وَكَانَ شَارِبُهُ قَدْ وَفَى، فَقَالَ لَهُ: «أَقُصُّهُ لَكَ عَلَى سِوَاكٍ»، أَوْ «قُصُّهُ عَلَى سِوَاكٍ»[٢١٢].

166. Al-Mughīrah b. Shuʿbah ﵁ narrated: "One night, I and the Messenger of Allāh ﷺ were the guests of an individual. The host served us a grilled side portion of sheep and then he ﷺ took a knife and started cutting pieces from it and he cut some for me to eat. During this period, Bilāl ﵁ came and began the call to prayer, and so the Prophet ﷺ put down the knife and said, 'May both his hands be in dust. What made him call out for the prayer at this moment?'"

Al-Mughīrah said that his moustache had grown long and so the Messenger of Allāh ﷺ said to him, "Come let me put a *siwāk* on it and then trim the hair that goes below its level."

Ibn Ḥajar al-Haytamī said,

> The Messenger of Allāh ﷺ cutting the meat for al-Mughīrah shows his modesty and it was an action done to show kindness to al-Mughīrah

---

211 *Sunan Ibn Mājah* (3311)
212 *Sunan Abī Dāwūd* (188)

who had recently embraced Islām at that time. His high status did not prevent him from serving his companions; even the juniors amongst them.

The Messenger of Allāh ﷺ blamed Bilal for calling him to the prayer in the presence of food when there was still time remaining for the time of the prayer.[213]

ʿAlī al-Qārī said,

> The statement of the Messenger of Allāh ﷺ to Bilal could be interpreted either in the sense of blame or praise. To assume it is intended to mean the latter, then it was said to praise Bilal for notifying him of the prayer. If it is the former then, it was said because delaying the prayer of *ʿIshā* is better than praying it at the beginning of its time.

Ibn Ḥajar al-Haytamī said,

> The scholars differed on whether it is better to trim the moustache or to shave it. Some scholars held the view that shaving the moustache is better based on a ḥadīth but the majority stated that trimming it is better.

١٦٧ - حَدَّثَنَا وَاصِلُ بْنُ عَبْدِ الأَعْلَى، قَالَ: حَدَّثَنَا مُحَمَّدُ بْنُ فُضَيْلٍ، عَنْ أَبِي حَيَّانَ التَّيْمِيِّ، عَنْ أَبِي زُرْعَةَ، عَنْ أَبِي هُرَيْرَةَ، قَالَ: «أُتِيَ النَّبِيُّ صلى الله عليه وسلم بِلَحْمٍ فَرُفِعَ إِلَيْهِ الذِّرَاعُ، وَكَانَتْ تُعْجِبُهُ فَنَهَسَ مِنْهَا»٢١٤.

167. Abū Hurayrah ؓ narrated: "Someone sent the Messenger of Allāh ﷺ some meat. From it the forearm was presented to him as he loved this portion of the meat, and so he ate a morsel of it with his front teeth."

Al-Qāḍī ʿIyyād said,

> He ﷺ liked the meat of the forearm because it is delicious, quick to cook, easy to chew and swallow, and it is far from the parts of the animal that are exposed to dirt and harm.[215]

---

213 The Prophet ﷺ said: When the supper is brought and the *prayer* begins, one should first take *food." [Ṣaḥīḥ Muslim]*

214 *Ṣaḥīḥ al-Bukhārī* (4712) and *Ṣaḥīḥ Muslim* (194)

215 Transmitted by al-Nawawī in his commentary on *Ṣaḥīḥ Muslim* (3/65).

Al-Bājūrī said,

> This indicates that one should avoid eating ravenously. This is because the Prophet ﷺ – despite his love for forearm meat – took a morsel with his front teeth and not a full bite.

١٦٨ - حَدَّثَنَا مُحَمَّدُ بْنُ بَشَّارٍ، قَالَ: حَدَّثَنَا أَبُو دَاوُدَ، عَنْ زُهَيْرٍ - يَعْنِي ابْنَ مُحَمَّدٍ -، عَنِ أَبِي إِسْحَاقَ، عَنْ سَعْدِ بْنِ عِيَاضٍ، عَنِ ابْنِ مَسْعُودٍ، قَالَ: «كَانَ النَّبِيُّ صلىٰ الله عليه وسلم يُعْجِبُهُ الذِّرَاعُ، قَالَ: وَسُمَّ فِي الذِّرَاعِ، وَكَانَ يَرَىٰ أَنَّ الْيَهُودَ سَمُّوهُ»[٢١٦].

168. ʿAbdullāh b. Masʿūd ؓ narrated: "The Messenger of Allāh ﷺ loved the meat of the forearm." He also narrated: "He ﷺ was given poison in the forearm portion of the meat and it was believed that the Jews poisoned him."

Al-Bājūrī said,

> In another ḥadīth, it mentions that he loved the shoulder. He ﷺ also liked the meat of the neck because it is similar to the meat of the forearm in that it is far from the places of harm.
>
> Ibn ʿUmar ؓ narrated that he ﷺ disliked eating seven things from the sheep: (i) the gall bladder, (ii) the bladder, (iii) the testicles, (iv) the penis, (v) the vagina, (vi) the blood, (vii) and the gland.

ʿAlī al-Qārī said,

> The lethal poisoned meat did not harm the Prophet ﷺ when he ate it but it used to affect him every year until he ﷺ died because of it. This was in order to double his reward. It was narrated that he ﷺ only ate one bite of it and then Jibrīl ؑ informed him about the poison upon which he ﷺ informed his companions to refrain from eating it. However, one of them (Bishr b. al-Barāʾ) passed away. In another ḥadīth, it was the poisoned forearm that informed the Prophet ﷺ about it. The Jewish woman who did this was questioned about her motives and she answered that she believed if he ﷺ was a Prophet then the poison would not harm him and for that he ﷺ forgave her and the woman embraced Islām after she saw the outcome of her test. However, later

216 *Sunan Abī Dāwūd* (3780)

on she was executed because her poison led to the death of one of the other companions who ate from the meat. The wisdom behind Jibrīl and the forearm (according to the other narration) not informing him ﷺ until after he ate from the meat was to manifest the truthfulness of his status as a Prophet, to be a reason for the Jewish woman to embrace Islām, and to be an evidence against anyone who insists after that on disbelief.

ʿAbd al-Razzāq al-Badr said,

> After the Jewish woman confessed, the Prophet ﷺ did not seek anything against her. However, Bishr b. al-Barā' ate from the meat and died. His family sought her life as a blood retribution for his murder and so she was executed.

١٦٩ - حَدَّثَنَا مُحَمَّدُ بْنُ بَشَّارٍ، قَالَ: حَدَّثَنَا مُسْلِمُ بْنُ إِبْرَاهِيمَ، قَالَ: حَدَّثَنَا أَبَانُ بْنُ يَزِيدَ، عَنْ قَتَادَةَ، عَنْ شَهْرِ بْنِ حَوْشَبٍ، عَنْ أَبِي عُبَيْدَةَ، قَالَ: طَبَخْتُ لِلنَّبِيِّ صلى الله عليه وسلم قِدْرًا وَقَدْ كَانَ يُعْجِبُهُ الذِّرَاعُ فَنَاوَلْتُهُ الذِّرَاعَ ثُمَّ قَالَ: «نَاوِلْنِي الذِّرَاعَ»، فَنَاوَلْتُهُ، ثُمَّ قَالَ: «نَاوِلْنِي الذِّرَاعَ»، فَقُلْتُ: يَا رَسُولَ اللهِ، وَكَمْ لِلشَّاةِ مِنْ ذِرَاعٍ، فَقَالَ: «وَالَّذِي نَفْسِي بِيَدِهِ لَوْ سَكَتَّ لَنَاوَلْتَنِي الذِّرَاعَ مَا دَعَوْتُ»[٢١٧].

169. Abū ʿUbaydah رضي الله عنه narrated: "I once prepared food for the Messenger of Allāh ﷺ. Because he loved the forearm portion of the meat, I served him that portion. He then ordered another one, I served the second one. He then ordered one again. I replied, 'O Messenger of Allāh! The lamb has only two forearms!' To that he said, 'I swear by the One in whose Hand is my soul, if you kept quiet, you could have served me every time I requested one from you.'"

ʿAbd al-Razzāq al-Badr said,

> This is a ḥadīth that shows one of the miracles of the Messenger of Allāh ﷺ and signs of his truthfulness.

Ibn Ḥajar al-Haytamī said,

> The reason why the inquisitive statement of the companion resulted in not witnessing this miracle is because witnessing such a miracle is

---

217 *Al-Bidāyah wa al-Nihāyah* (6/127)

an honour by itself and only a person whose submission is perfect and free of any personal desire or opinion deserves to witness it.

١٧٠ - حَدَّثَنَا الْحَسَنُ بْنُ مُحَمَّدٍ الزَّعْفَرَانِيُّ، قَالَ: حَدَّثَنَا يَحْيَىٰ بْنُ عَبَّادٍ، عَنْ فُلَيْحِ بْنِ سُلَيْمَانَ، قَالَ: حَدَّثَنِي رَجُلٌ مِنْ بَنِي عَبَّادٍ، يُقَالُ لَهُ: عَبْدُ الْوَهَّابِ بْنُ يَحْيَىٰ بْنُ عَبَّادٍ، عَنْ عَبْدِ اللهِ بْنِ الزُّبَيْرِ، عَنْ عَائِشَةَ، قَالَتْ: مَا كَانَتِ الذِّرَاعُ أَحَبَّ اللَّحْمِ إِلَىٰ رَسُولِ اللهِ صلىٰ الله عليه وسلم وَلَكِنَّهُ كَانَ لا يَجِدُ اللَّحْمَ إلا غِبًّا، وَكَانَ يَعْجَلُ إِلَيْهَا، لأَنَّهَا أَعْجَلُهَا نُضْجًا[٢١٨].

170. ʿĀʾishah ﵂ narrated: "The Messenger of Allāh ﷺ did not like the forearm portion of meat the best (i.e. due to its taste). Rather, as meat was only available occasionally, and as this portion of the meat cooked quickly, he liked it."

ʿAlī al-Qārī said,

> This is supported by the statement of ʿĀʾishah ﵂ that it would pass a whole month without them having anything to cook and that they would live on dates and water unless they received some meat. This ḥadīth also shows that he ﷺ liked other portions of meat such as the meat of the back (the meat that is along the backbone of the animal), as stated in the next ḥadīth.

Ibn Ḥajar al-Haytamī said,

> The statement of ʿĀʾishah ﵂ negating that he ﷺ liked forearm meat as a personal preference seems to be given to indicate that the noble status of the Prophet ﷺ transcended any inclination to the worldly pleasures. Thus she explained that he liked it because it cooks fast and that saved him time so he could return quickly to his commitments and look after the affairs of Muslims. However, to love forearm meat as a personal preference does not contravene his perfection because imperfection is to work hard to attain a worldly pleasure or feeling sorry for missing it.

١٧١ - حَدَّثَنَا مَحْمُودُ بْنُ غَيْلانَ، قَالَ: حَدَّثَنَا أَبُو أَحْمَدَ، قَالَ: حَدَّثَنَا مِسْعَرٌ، قَالَ:

---

218 *Sunan al-Tirmidhī* (1838)

سَمِعْتُ شَيْخًا مِنْ فَهْمٍ، قَالَ: سَمِعْتُ عَبْدَ اللهِ بْنَ جَعْفَرٍ، يَقُولُ: سَمِعْتُ رَسُولَ اللهِ صلى الله عليه وسلم يَقُولُ: «إِنَّ أَطْيَبَ اللَّحْمِ لَحْمُ الظَّهْرِ»٢١٩.

171. ʿAbdullāh b. Jaʿfar ﷺ narrated: "I heard the Prophet ﷺ saying, 'The best meat is the meat of the back (the meat that is along the backbone of the animal).'"

ʿAbd al-Razzāq al-Badr said,

> This praise shows that the Prophet ﷺ ate the meat of the back as well.

Al-Bājūrī said,

> **"The best meat is the meat of the back":** I.e. the best tasting meat is that of the back. The suitability of this report to the chapter is that such a praise dictates that the Prophet ﷺ ate it some times.

١٧٢- حَدَّثَنَا سُفْيَانُ بْنُ وَكِيعٍ، قَالَ: حَدَّثَنَا زَيْدُ بْنُ الْحُبَابِ، عَنْ عَبْدِ اللهِ بْنِ الْمُؤَمَّلِ، عَنِ ابْنِ أَبِي مُلَيْكَةَ، عَنْ عَائِشَةَ: أَنَّ النَّبِيَّ صلى الله عليه وسلم قَالَ: «نِعْمَ الإِدَامُ الْخَلُّ»٢٢٠.

172. ʿĀ'ishah ﷺ narrated that the Prophet ﷺ said: "Vinegar is an excellent *idām*."[221]

Al-Bājūrī said,

> Details concerning this were mentioned at the start of the chapter.

١٧٣- حَدَّثَنَا أَبُو كُرَيْبٍ مُحَمَّدُ بْنُ الْعَلاءِ، قَالَ: حَدَّثَنَا أَبُو بَكْرِ بْنُ عَيَّاشٍ، عَنْ ثَابِتٍ أَبِي حَمْزَةَ الثُّمَالِيِّ، عَنِ الشَّعْبِيِّ، عَنْ أُمِّ هَانِئٍ، قَالَتْ: دَخَلَ عَلَيَّ النَّبِيُّ صلى الله عليه وسلم فَقَالَ: «أَعِنْدَكِ شَيْءٌ؟» فَقُلْتُ: لا إِلا خُبْزٌ يَابِسٌ وَخَلٌّ، فَقَالَ: «هَاتِي، مَا أَقْفَرَ بَيْتٌ مِنْ أُدُمٍ فِيهِ الخل»٢٢٢.

173. Umm Hānī' ﷺ related: "The Messenger of Allāh ﷺ came to my house and asked if there was something to eat. I replied, 'Nothing

219 *Sunan Ibn Mājah* (3308)
220 *Sunan Abī Dāwūd* (3820)
221 Previously explained in ḥadīth 151.
222 *Sunan al-Tirmidhī* (1841)

besides dry bread and vinegar.' The Messenger of Allāh ﷺ said, 'Bring it. The house that has vinegar in it is not a house devoid of an *idām*.'"

ʿAlī al-Qārī said,

> This incident happened on the day that Makkah was conquered.
>
> It was said that the statement of Umm Hānī' began with a negative word to indicate that there was no food in the house even though there was some. This was because she glorified the status of the Prophet ﷺ and thought that dry bread and vinegar were not suitable foods to be served to a person with such a high, noble status.
>
> The meaning of the statement of the Prophet ﷺ is that a house that has vinegar will not be in need of another *idām*.

Ibn Ḥajar al-Haytamī said,

> Benefits derived from this ḥadīth include:
>
> 1. Encouraging not belittling bread and vinegar as a food.
> 2. It is permissible to ask someone for food if the relationship is strong enough that the questioner will not feel embarrassment when asking.

١٧٤ - حَدَّثَنَا مُحَمَّدُ بْنُ الْمُثَنَّىٰ، قَالَ: حَدَّثَنَا مُحَمَّدُ بْنُ جَعْفَرٍ، قَالَ: حَدَّثَنَا شُعْبَةُ، عَنْ عَمْرِو بْنِ مُرَّةَ، عَنْ مُرَّةَ الْهَمْدَانِيِّ، عَنْ أَبِي مُوسَىٰ الْأَشْعَرِيِّ، عَنِ النَّبِيِّ صلى الله عليه وسلم قَالَ: «فَضْلُ عَائِشَةَ عَلَىٰ النِّسَاءِ كَفَضْلِ الثَّرِيدِ عَلَىٰ سَائِرِ الطَّعَامِ»[٢٢٣].

174. Abū Mūsa al-Ashʿarī ﵁ narrated: "The Messenger of Allāh ﷺ said, 'The excellence of ʿĀ'ishah ﵂ over other women is like the excellence of *tharīd* over all other foods.'"

Al-Bājūrī said,

> This description of ʿĀ'ishah ﵂ is a merit she earned due to her good character, eloquence in speech, sensibility and wisdom, and her constant efforts to please her husband. This ḥadīth is intended to mean that she was the best of his wives because the best of women are in the following order: Maryam bint ʿImrān, Fāṭimah al-Zahrā' (daughter of

223 *Ṣaḥīḥ al-Bukhārī* (5418) and *Ṣaḥīḥ Muslim* (2431)

the Prophet ﷺ), Khadījah bint Khuwaylid (the first wife of the Prophet ﷺ) and then comes 'Ā'ishah, who was declared innocent by Allāh. This was the view of many of the *salaf* and many of the later scholars.

Ibn Ḥajar al-Haytamī said,

Tharīd is a dish made of pieces of bread in meat broth. This dish does not always include pieces of meat.

١٧٥ - حَدَّثَنَا عَلِيُّ بْنُ حُجْرٍ، قَالَ: حَدَّثَنَا إِسْمَاعِيلُ بْنُ جَعْفَرٍ، قَالَ: حَدَّثَنَا عَبْدُ اللهِ بْنُ عَبْدِ الرَّحْمَنِ بْنِ مَعْمَرٍ الأَنْصَارِيُّ أَبُو طُوَالَةَ، أَنَّهُ سَمِعَ أَنَسَ بْنَ مَالِكٍ، يَقُولُ: قَالَ رَسُولُ اللهِ صلى الله عليه وسلم: «فَضْلُ عَائِشَةَ عَلَى النِّسَاءِ كَفَضْلِ الثَّرِيدِ عَلَى سَائِرِ الطَّعَامِ»[٢٢٤].

175. Anas b. Mālik ؓ narrated: "The Messenger of Allāh ﷺ said, 'The excellence of 'Ā'ishah ؓ over other women is like the excellence of *tharīd* over all other foods.'"

'Abd al-Razzāq al-Badr said,

This was covered in the previous narration.

١٧٦ - حَدَّثَنَا قُتَيْبَةُ بْنُ سَعِيدٍ، قَالَ: حَدَّثَنَا عَبْدُ الْعَزِيزِ بْنُ مُحَمَّدٍ، عَنْ سُهَيْلِ بْنِ أَبِي صَالِحٍ، عَنِ أَبِيهِ، عَنْ أَبِي هُرَيْرَةَ، «أَنَّهُ رَأَى رَسُولَ اللهِ صلى الله عليه وسلم تَوَضَّأَ مِنْ أَكْلِ ثَوْرِ أَقِطٍ، ثُمَّ رَآهُ أَكَلَ مِنْ كَتِفِ شَاةٍ، ثُمَّ صَلَّى وَلَمْ يَتَوَضَّأْ»[٢٢٥].

176. Abū Hurayrah ؓ narrated: "He once saw the Messenger of Allāh ﷺ performing ablution after he ate a piece of hard dry yoghurt (made from ewe or goat's milk), and he saw him on another occasion eating from the shoulder of a lamb, and then he prayed without performing ablution."

'Abd al-Razzāq al-Badr said,

The word ablution (Arabic: *wuḍū*) is used in this ḥadīth twice but each mention entails a different meaning; the linguistic meaning and the religious meaning. The word was used in reference to eating dry

224 *Ṣaḥīḥ al-Bukhārī* (5428) and *Ṣaḥīḥ Muslim* (2446)
225 *Musnad Aḥmad* (9050)

yoghurt to mean that he ﷺ washed his hands after he ate it, and the word was used in the second instance to refer to the actual ablution. Thus, the meaning of the ḥadīth is that he ﷺ washed his hands after eating the first meal, and he did not perform ablution after eating from the sheep because it does not invalidate one's ablution.

١٧٧ - حَدَّثَنَا ابْنُ أَبِي عُمَرَ ، قَالَ : حَدَّثَنَا سُفْيَانُ بْنُ عُيَيْنَةَ ، عَنْ وَائِلِ بْنِ دَاوُدَ، عَنِ ابْنِهِ - وَهُوَ بَكْرُ بْنُ وَائِلٍ -، عَنِ الزُّهْرِيِّ، عَنْ أَنَسِ بْنِ مَالِكٍ قَالَ: «أَوْلَمَ رَسُولُ اللهِ صلّىٰ الله عليه وسلم عَلَىٰ صَفِيَّةَ بِتَمْرٍ وَسَوِيقٍ»٢٢٦.

177. Anas b. Mālik ❀ reported: "The Messenger of Allāh ﷺ had his wedding feast in celebration of his marriage with Ṣafiyyah ❁ with dates and *sawīq*."

ʿAbd al-Razzāq al-Badr said,

> Mother of the Believers Ṣafiyyah was the daughter of Ḥuyayy b. Akhtab and she was from the captives (slaves) but the Prophet ﷺ freed her and married her, making her freedom her wedding gift (*mahr*). The *sawīq* is a meal made of wheat or barley. However, in *Ṣaḥīḥ al-Bukhārī* it states that the feast was a meal made of dates, *ghee* and dried milk or wheat.[227]

Al-Bājūrī said,

> The father of Ṣafiyyah was the master of the Jewish tribe Banī al-Naḍīr and his daughter was one of the female captives on the day of Khaybar. Before she was captured and entered Islām, she saw a dream that the moon fell upon her lap. When she told her father about the dream he hit her hard on the face, leaving a mark on it and he said to her, "You will keep looking high until you become the woman of the king of the Arabs."

١٧٨ - حَدَّثَنَا الْحُسَيْنُ بْنُ مُحَمَّدٍ الْبَصْرِيُّ، قَالَ: حَدَّثَنَا الْفُضَيْلُ بْنُ سُلَيْمَانَ، قَالَ: حَدَّثَنِي فَائِدٌ مَوْلَىٰ عُبَيْدِ اللهِ بْنِ عَلِيِّ بْنِ أَبِي رَافِعٍ مَوْلَىٰ رَسُولِ اللهِ صلّىٰ الله عليه وسلم، قَالَ: حَدَّثَنِي عُبَيْدُ اللهِ بْنُ عَلِيٍّ، عَنْ جَدَّتِهِ سَلْمَىٰ، أَنَّ الْحَسَنَ بْنَ عَلِيٍّ،

---

226 *Sunan Abī Dāwūd* (3744) and *Sunan Ibn Mājah* (1909)
227 Al-Bukhārī, reported by Anas b. Mālik (5169).

وَابْنَ عَبَّاسٍ، وَابْنَ جَعْفَرٍ أَتَوْهَا فَقَالُوا لَهَا: «اصْنَعِي لَنَا طَعَامًا مِمَّا كَانَ يُعْجِبُ رَسُولَ اللهِ صلى الله عليه وسلم وَيُحْسِنُ أَكْلَهُ، فَقَالَتْ: يَا بُنَيَّ! لا تَشْتَهِيهِ الْيَوْمَ، قَالَ: بَلَى اصْنَعِيهِ لَنَا؛ قَالَ: فَقَامَتْ فَأَخَذَتْ مِنْ شَعِيرٍ فَطَحَنَتْهُ، ثُمَّ جَعَلَتْهُ فِي قِدْرٍ، وَصَبَّتْ عَلَيْهِ شَيْئًا مِنْ زَيْتٍ وَدَقَّتِ الْفُلْفُلَ وَالتَّوَابِلَ فَقَرَّبَتْهُ إِلَيْهِمْ، فَقَالَتْ: هَذَا مِمَّا كَانَ يُعْجِبُ رَسُولَ اللهِ صلى الله عليه وسلم وَيُحْسِنُ أَكْلَهُ»[٢٢٨].

178. Salmā ﵂, the grandmother of ʿUbayd Allāh b. ʿAlī narrated that Al-Ḥasan b. ʿAlī, Ibn ʿAbbās and Ibn Jaʿfar ﵃ visited her and asked her to make them a food that the Messenger of Allāh ﷺ liked and ate with pleasure. However, she replied, "O my children, you will not like it now." They replied, "We will surely like it." She stood up and gathered some barley, crushed it and put it in a pot, poured a little olive oil over it, then crushed some pepper and spices and added that to the pot and served it whilst saying, "This is from the food that the Messenger of Allāh ﷺ liked and ate with pleasure."

Al-Bājūrī said,

> The grandmother of ʿUbayd Allāh b. ʿAlī was the one who helped deliver Ibrāhīm, the son of the Prophet ﷺ. She was the servant of the Prophet ﷺ and the one who cooked for him. This is why she was approached and asked about the food he ﷺ used to like.
>
> Her stating that they would not like the food was meant to indicate that it would not meet their personal preferences in terms of what constitutes a good food. This was due to this food being eaten during difficult times whereas the food they (the companions who visited her) were now accustomed to was far more diverse as life had become more comfortable.

ʿAlī al-Qārī said,

> Their answering that they will like it meant that they will surely like it since the Prophet ﷺ liked it and they were seeking the blessings of following the example of the Prophet ﷺ.

١٧٩ - حَدَّثَنَا مَحْمُودُ بْنُ غَيْلانَ، قَالَ: حَدَّثَنَا أَبُو أَحْمَدَ، قَالَ: حَدَّثَنَا سُفْيَانُ، عَنِ

228 *Al-Targhīb wa al-Tarhīb* (4/173)

الْأَسْوَدِ بْنِ قَيْسٍ، عَنْ نُبَيْحٍ الْعَنَزِيِّ، عَنْ جَابِرِ بْنِ عَبْدِ اللهِ، قَالَ: «أَتَانَا النَّبِيُّ صلى الله عليه وسلم فِي مَنْزِلِنَا فَذَبَحْنَا لَهُ شَاةً، فَقَالَ: كَأَنَّهُمْ عَلِمُوا أَنَّا نُحِبُّ اللَّحْمَ» وَفِي الْحَدِيثِ قِصَّةٌ. ٢٢٩

179. Jābir b. ʿAbdullāh ☙ narrated: "The Messenger of Allāh ﷺ came to our house and we slaughtered a sheep in his honour. He ﷺ said, 'It is as if they knew we like meat.'"

[Al-Imām al-Tirmidhī said:] "There is a story behind the visit of the Prophet ﷺ."

Al-Bājūrī said,

> The statement of the Messenger of Allāh ﷺ was intended to compliment the hosts and make them happy, not to show his admiration for meat. This ḥadīth teaches us that the host should serve that which the guest likes, if he knows about it, and that the guest should mention to his host the food he likes (unless he knows that it would burden the host).

ʿAbd al-Razzāq al-Badr said,

> The reason behind the visit of the Prophet ﷺ to the house of Jābir ☙ is explained in the ḥadīth documented in the *Musnad* of al-Imām Aḥmad wherein it states that Jābir asked the Prophet ﷺ to help him pay the debts of his father, so he ﷺ said that he would pay a visit to his house. Then Jābir went home and told his wife not to talk to or ask the Prophet ﷺ for anything. So, when he ﷺ visited them, he slaughtered for him a sheep and so he ﷺ said, "It is as if they knew we like meat." But, when he ﷺ went out, Jābir's wife asked the Prophet ﷺ to pray on her and her husband so the Prophet ﷺ said, "O Allāh, may your *ṣalāh* be upon them." This made Jābir chastise his wife for disobeying him but she said, "Did you want him ﷺ to enter our house and leave without supplicating for us!"[230]

١٨٠ - حَدَّثَنَا ابْنُ أَبِي عُمَرَ، قَالَ: حَدَّثَنَا سُفْيَانُ، قَالَ: حَدَّثَنَا عَبْدُ اللهِ بْنُ مُحَمَّدِ بْنِ عَقِيلٍ، أَنَّهُ سَمِعَ جَابِرًا، قَالَ سُفْيَانُ: وَحَدَّثَنَا مُحَمَّدُ بْنُ الْمُنْكَدِرِ، عَنْ جَابِرٍ قَالَ:

229 *Al-Ajwibah al-Murḍiyyah* (1/177)
230 *Musnad Aḥmad* (14245)

«خَرَجَ رَسُولُ اللهِ صلى الله عليه وسلم وَأَنَا مَعَهُ فَدَخَلَ عَلَى امْرَأَةٍ مِنَ الأَنْصَارِ،
فَذَبَحَتْ لَهُ شَاةً، فَأَكَلَ مِنْهَا، وَأَتَتْهُ بِقِنَاعٍ مِنْ رُطَبٍ، فَأَكَلَ مِنْهُ، ثُمَّ تَوَضَّأَ لِلظُّهْرِ
وَصَلَّى، صلى الله عليه وسلم، ثُمَّ انْصَرَفَ، فَأَتَتْهُ بِعُلَالَةٍ مِنْ عُلَالَةِ الشَّاةِ، فَأَكَلَ ثُمَّ
صَلَّى الْعَصْرَ وَلَمْ يَتَوَضَّأْ»٢٣١.

180. Jābir ﷺ narrated: "The Messenger of Allāh ﷺ went out to the house of a woman from among the Anṣār and I accompanied him. The hostess slaughtered a sheep for the Messenger of Allāh ﷺ and so he ate from it. She then served him fresh dates upon a tray made of palm leaves. The Messenger of Allāh ﷺ ate some from it, then performed ablution and prayed *Ẓuhr*. After returning from the prayer, she served him some of the remaining meat. The Messenger of Allāh ﷺ ate from it and then prayed '*Aṣr* without performing ablution."

'Abd al-Razzāq al-Badr said,

The statement of Jābir when he said, "I accompanied him" demonstrates the high level of politeness and good etiquette of the companions when talking about the Prophet ﷺ as their choice of words always implied that they were following the Prophet ﷺ.

Al-Bājūrī said,

This ḥadīth shows us that the Prophet ﷺ ate meat twice in one day and this does not contradict the statement of 'Ā'ishah ﷺ wherein she mentioned that he ﷺ never had a full stomach from meat. This is because eating meat twice on the same say does not necessitate that he had a full stomach.

Ibn Ḥajar al-Haytamī said,

This ḥadīth teaches us that it is allowed to eat twice even if the food from the first time has not yet fully digested if one knows that he will not overeat, or if the food served first was little.

١٨١ - حَدَّثَنَا الْعَبَّاسُ بْنُ مُحَمَّدٍ الدُّورِيُّ، قَالَ: حَدَّثَنَا يُونُسُ بْنُ مُحَمَّدٍ، قَالَ:
حَدَّثَنَا فُلَيْحُ بْنُ سُلَيْمَانَ، عَنْ عُثْمَانَ بْنِ عَبْدِ الرَّحْمَن، عَنْ يَعْقُوبَ بْنِ أَبِي يَعْقُوبَ،
عَنْ أُمِّ الْمُنْذِرِ، قَالَتْ: «دَخَلَ عَلَيَّ رَسُولُ اللهِ صلى الله عليه وسلم وَمَعَهُ عَلِيٌّ، وَلَنَا

دَوَالٍ مُعَلَّقَةٌ، قَالَتْ: فَجَعَلَ رَسُولُ اللهِ صلى الله عليه وسلم يَأْكُلُ وَعَلِيٌّ مَعَهُ يَأْكُلُ، فَقَالَ رَسُولُ اللهِ صلى الله عليه وسلم لِعَلِيٍّ: مَهْ يَا عَلِيُّ! فَإِنَّكَ نَاقِهٌ، قَالَتْ: فَجَلَسَ عَلِيٌّ وَالنَّبِيُّ صلى الله عليه وسلم يَأْكُلُ، قَالَتْ: فَجَعَلْتُ لَهُمْ سِلْقًا وَشَعِيرًا، فَقَالَ النَّبِيُّ صلى الله عليه وسلم لِعَلِيٍّ: مِنْ هَذَا فَأَصِبْ؛ فَإِنَّ هَذَا أَوْفَقُ لَكَ»[٢٣٢].

181. Umm al-Mundhir ﵂ narrated: "Allāh's Messenger ﷺ visited me and ʿAlī ﵁ was with him. We had some dates hanging and the Messenger of Allāh ﷺ began eating from them and so did ʿAlī ﵁. The Messenger of Allāh ﷺ stopped him saying, 'You have not fully recovered from your illness and should not eat this.' ʿAlī ﵁ stopped and Allāh's Messenger ﷺ continued eating. Then I prepared for them some barley and chard. The Messenger of Allāh ﷺ said to ʿAlī ﵁, 'Eat of this, for it is more suitable for you.'"

ʿAbd al-Razzāq al-Badr said,

> It is said that Umm al-Mundhir was one of the maternal aunts of the Prophet ﷺ.

Al-Bājūrī said,

> The directions of the Prophet ﷺ show that it is prescribed to seek medication and that this does not contradict reliance on Allāh.

١٨٢ - حَدَّثَنَا مَحْمُودُ بْنُ غَيْلَانَ، قَالَ: حَدَّثَنَا بِشْرُ بْنُ السَّرِيِّ، عَنْ سُفْيَانَ، عَنْ طَلْحَةَ بْنِ يَحْيَىٰ، عَنْ عَائِشَةَ بِنْتِ طَلْحَةَ، عَنْ عَائِشَةَ أُمِّ الْمُؤْمِنِينَ، قَالَتْ: «كَانَ النَّبِيُّ صلى الله عليه وسلم يَأْتِينِي فَيَقُولُ: أَعِنْدَكِ غَدَاءٌ؟ فَأَقُولُ: لا قَالَتْ: فَيَقُولُ: إِنِّي صَائِمٌ، قَالَتْ: فَأَتَانِي يَوْمًا، فَقُلْتُ: يَا رَسُولَ اللهِ! إِنَّهُ أُهْدِيَتْ لَنَا هَدِيَّةٌ، قَالَ: وَمَا هِيَ؟ قُلْتُ: حَيْسٌ، قَالَ: أَمَا إِنِّي أَصْبَحْتُ صَائِمًا قَالَتْ: ثُمَّ أَكَلَ»[٢٣٣].

182. ʿĀʾishah, the mother of the believers ﵂, narrated: "The Messenger of Allāh ﷺ used to come to me and ask if there was any food available for lunch. When I would say no, he would reply, 'In that case, I make the intention to fast.' On one occasion he came and enquired, I replied, 'We have received a gift.' He asked, 'What is it?' I replied,

232 *Sunan Al-Tirmidhī* (2037)
233 *Ṣaḥīḥ Muslim* (1154)

'*Ḥays* (dates mixed with ghee and dry yoghurt or ghee and wheat).' He said, 'I woke up with the intention of fasting.' He then ate some from it."

'Abd al-Razzāq al-Badr said,

> It is not a condition of voluntary fasting to establish the intention to fast before the time of *Fajr*. Thus, if a person wakes up and did not eat or drink, he can make the intention to fast during the day.

Al-Bājūrī said,

> The wives of the Prophet ﷺ are called the mothers of the believers because they are unlawful for the Muslims to marry. It is said so because it is obligatory to look after them and respect them [as mothers].
>
> The statement of the Prophet ﷺ wherein he disclosed his intention to fast shows that it is fine to show others your voluntary good deeds if the purpose is to educate them.

Ibn Ḥajar al-Haytamī said,

> The act of the Prophet ﷺ where he ate whilst he was fasting indicates that it is allowed for a person to break his voluntary fast and this view is supported by a number of other ḥadīths.

١٨٣ - حَدَّثَنَا عَبْدُ اللهِ بْنُ عَبْدِ الرَّحْمَنِ، قَالَ: حَدَّثَنَا عُمَرُ بْنُ حَفْصِ بْنِ غِيَاثٍ، قَالَ: حَدَّثَنَا أَبِي، عَنْ مُحَمَّدِ بْنِ أَبِي يَحْيَىٰ الأَسْلَمِيِّ، عَنْ يَزِيدَ بْنِ أَبِي أُمَيَّةَ الأَعْوَرِ، عَنْ يُوسُفَ بْنِ عَبْدِ اللهِ بْنِ سَلامٍ، قَالَ: رَأَيْتُ النَّبِيَّ صلىٰ الله عليه وسلم أَخَذَ كِسْرَةً مِنْ خُبْزِ الشَّعِيرِ فَوَضَعَ عَلَيْهَا تَمْرَةً، وَقَالَ: «هَذِهِ إِدَامُ هَذِهِ» وأكل[٢٣٤].

183. Yūsuf b. 'Abdullāh b. Salām ﵁ narrated: "I once saw the Messenger of Allāh ﷺ taking a piece of bread made of barley and putting a date on it. He then said, 'This [date] is the *idām* for this [bread].' He then ate it."

'Alī al-Qārī said,

> This ḥadīth teaches us to utilise the resources available to have good nutrition, for the bread made of barley is cold and dry whilst the date

234 *Sunan Abī Dāwūd* (3260)

is warm and moist. It also teaches that one should be self-content with whatever one has.

١٨٤ - حَدَّثَنَا عَبْدُ اللهِ بْنُ عَبْدِ الرَّحْمَنِ، قَالَ: حَدَّثَنَا سَعِيدُ بْنُ سُلَيْمَانَ، عَنْ عَبَّادِ بْنِ الْعَوَّامِ، عَنْ حُمَيْدٍ، عَنْ أَنَسٍ: «أَنَّ رَسُولَ اللهِ صلى الله عليه وسلم كَانَ يُعْجِبُهُ الثَّفْلُ»، قَالَ عَبْدُ اللهِ: يَعْنِي مَا بَقِيَ مِنَ الطَّعَامِ²³⁵.

184. Anas b. Mālik ۞ narrated: "The Messenger of Allāh ۞ liked to eat the remains of food."

ʿAbdullāh said, "The word *al-thuflu* means left over food."

ʿAbd al-Razzāq al-Badr said,

> The remains of food refers to the food that remains in the bottom of the pot as it is the most cooked and tastiest of the food cooked in the pot.

Al-Bājūrī said,

> This displays his humbleness and contentment with little. Many wealthy people are too proud to eat from leftovers, whereas Allāh placed immense wisdom in his ۞ statements and actions. Therefore, glad tidings to those who comprehend his value and follow his way.

---

235 *Musnad Aḥmad* (13300)

باب ما جاء في صفة وضوء رسول الله صلى الله عليه وسلم عند الطعام

[27] On the Description of Allāh's Messenger's ﷺ *Wuḍū* at the Time of Eating

Al-Bājūrī said,

The word "*wuḍū*" used in the title of this chapter is used in its linguistic and religious sense. The former means to wash and cleanse the hands and the latter means to perform ablution.

This chapter is dedicated to explaining that ablution is neither obligatory nor recommended at the time of eating and that washing the hands is recommended.

١٨٥ - حَدَّثَنَا أَحْمَدُ بْنُ مَنِيعٍ، قَالَ: حَدَّثَنَا إِسْمَاعِيلُ بْنُ إِبْرَاهِيمَ، عَنْ أَيُّوبَ، عَنِ ابْنِ أَبِي مُلَيْكَةَ، عَنِ ابْنِ عَبَّاسٍ، أَنَّ رَسُولَ اللهِ صلى الله عليه وسلم خَرَجَ مِنَ الْخَلَاءِ فَقُرِّبَ إِلَيْهِ الطَّعَامُ، فَقَالُوا: أَلَا نَأْتِيكَ بِوَضُوءٍ؟ قَالَ: «إِنَّمَا أُمِرْتُ بِالْوُضُوءِ إِذَا قُمْتُ إِلَى الصَّلَاةِ».²³⁶

185. 'Abdullāh b. 'Abbās ؓ narrated: "Once after the Messenger of Allāh ﷺ finished relieving himself from the call of nature, food was served to him. He was asked if the water for ablution should be brought. He replied, 'I have only been commanded to perform ablution when I want to pray.'"

'Abd al-Razzāq al-Badr said,

The statement of the Messenger of Allāh ﷺ was to explain to the companions that ablution is not required when a person wants to eat; rather only when one wants to pray.

Al-Bājūrī said,

The command that the Messenger of Allāh ﷺ referred to is in the

---

236 *Sunan Abī Dāwūd* (3760) and *Sunan al-Tirmidhī* (1847)

āyah: **{O you who have believed, when you rise to [perform] prayer, wash your faces and your forearms to the elbows and wipe over your heads and wash your feet to the ankles.}**[237]

Al-Walī al-ʿIrāqī said, "This ḥadīth is a proof that the Messenger of Allāh ﷺ liked to perform ablution before each prayer, whether he was in a state of purity or not, except on the day Makkah was conquered as he prayed the five daily prayers with one ablution. This made ʿUmar b. al-Khaṭṭāb ؓ exclaim saying, 'I saw you today doing something you never did before.' The Prophet ﷺ replied, 'O ʿUmar! I did that intentionally.'"[238]

١٨٦ - حَدَّثَنَا سَعِيدُ بْنُ عَبْدِ الرَّحْمَنِ الْمَخْزُومِيُّ، قَالَ: حَدَّثَنَا سُفْيَانُ بْنُ عُيَيْنَةَ، عَنْ عَمْرِو بْنِ دِينَارٍ، عَنْ سَعِيدِ بْنِ الْحُوَيْرِثِ، عَنِ ابْنِ عَبَّاسٍ قَالَ: «خَرَجَ رَسُولُ اللهِ صلىٰ الله عليه وسلم مِنَ الْغَائِطِ فَأُتِيَ بِطَعَامٍ، فَقِيلَ لَهُ: أَلا تَتَوَضَّأُ؟ فَقَالَ: أَأُصَلِّي، فَأَتَوَضَّأُ؟!»[٢٣٩].

186. ʿAbdullāh b. ʿAbbās ؓ narrated: "Once after the Messenger of Allāh ﷺ finished relieving himself from the call of nature, food was served to him. He was asked if he was going to perform ablution. He replied, 'Am I going to offer a prayer so that I need to perform ablution?'"

١٨٧ - حَدَّثَنَا يَحْيَىٰ بْنُ مُوسَىٰ، قَالَ: حَدَّثَنَا عَبْدُ اللهِ بْنُ نُمَيْرٍ، قَالَ: حَدَّثَنَا قَيْسُ بْنُ الرَّبِيعِ، (ح) وَحَدَّثَنَا قُتَيْبَةُ، قَالَ: حَدَّثَنَا عَبْدُ الْكَرِيمِ الْجُرْجَانِيُّ، عَنْ قَيْسِ بْنِ الرَّبِيعِ، عَنْ أَبِي هَاشِمٍ، عَنْ زَاذَانَ، عَنْ سَلْمَانَ، قَالَ: قَرَأْتُ فِي التَّوْرَاةِ أَنَّ بَرَكَةَ الطَّعَامِ الْوُضُوءُ بَعْدَهُ، فَذَكَرْتُ ذَلِكَ لِلنَّبِيِّ صلىٰ الله عليه وسلم، وَأَخْبَرْتُهُ بِمَا قَرَأْتُ فِي التَّوْرَاةِ، فَقَالَ رَسُولُ اللهِ صلىٰ الله عليه وسلم: «بَرَكَةُ الطَّعَامِ الْوُضُوءُ قَبْلَهُ، وَالْوُضُوءُ بَعْدَهُ»[٢٤٠].

187. Salmān al-Fārisī ؓ narrated: "I have read in the Torah that

237 Qur'ān: 5:6
238 *Ṣaḥīḥ al-Nasā'ī* (133)
239 *Ṣaḥīḥ Muslim* (374)
240 *Sunan Abī Dāwūd* (3761) and *Sunan al-Tirmidhi* (1846)

to attain the blessings from food one should wash the hands after eating. I mentioned this to the Messenger of Allāh ﷺ and so he said, 'The blessing in food is attained when washing the hands before and after eating.'"

ʿAbd al-Razzāq al-Badr said,

> **"I have read in the Torah":** It is possible that this reading occurred before he became a Muslim. This is because the [lay] Muslim is not allowed to read the Torah and Bible, nor other books abrogated by the Qur'ān.
>
> Al-Imām Aḥmad reports from ʿUmar b. al-Khaṭṭāb that he brought forth a scripture to the Prophet ﷺ which he took from a Christian or Jew. He read it to the Prophet ﷺ and he became angry, replying, "Are you confused in the religion O Ibn al-Khaṭṭāb? By the One who holds my soul in His hand, I have brought it forth to you clear and pure. Do not ask them anything. They may state to you something truthful and you may reject it, or something false and you may believe it. By the One who holds my soul in His hand, if Mūsā was alive, he would have no option except to follow me."[241]
>
> Furthermore, when ʿĪsā descends in the end times, he will rule by the Qur'ān and not the Bible. The Qur'ān abrogates the books which preceded it, and thus it is not permissible to read them. However, if a Muslim firmly grounded in knowledge is required to study these books to refute doubts, defend the religion or highlight false beliefs, it is allowed to do so.

ʿAlī al-Qārī said,

> **"The blessing in food is attained when washing the hands before and after eating":** It is possible that he is indicating towards the Torah's distortion, and also that his religion increased upon it so as to gain blessings of purity, in line with the narration, "I have come to perfect good manners."

Al-Bājūrī said,

> It is recommended to allow the children to wash their hands first before old people as the hands of children are more likely to be dirty

241 *Musnad al-Imām Aḥmad* (15156).

compared to the hands of old people and water may run out if the old people take the lead. This is recommended before eating and the opposite is the case after eating, meaning the old people should be given priority to wash their hands over the youngsters to show respect to their age. As for the host, he takes the priority to wash his hands first before everyone but should be the last to wash his hands. It is recommended to dry the washed hands after eating but not before eating. This is because if the towel has some dirt on it and hands were dried using it before eating, then the dirt may transfer to the hands, and also because wet hands will prevent the ghee (butter) from sticking to the hands.

Al-Qurṭubī said,

> If the one who reads it (the Qur'ān) will have a tenfold reward or more for each letter, according to what we mentioned in the introduction to this book, then turning away from it and towards other scriptures is misguidance and loss, and this is a poor trade off and waste of time.

Ibn Ḥajar al-'Asqalānī said,

> It is important to note that in the case of those who are not well-versed in knowledge and are lacking in faith, it is not permissible for them to read any of those books.

باب ما جاء في قول رسول الله صلى الله عليه وسلم قبل الطعام وعند الفراغ منه

[28] On Allāh's Messenger's ﷺ Words Before Eating and Afterwards

Al-Bājūrī said,

> This chapter includes all of that which the Messenger of Allāh ﷺ used to say before and after eating and drinking.

١٨٨ - حَدَّثَنَا قُتَيْبَةُ، قَالَ: حَدَّثَنَا ابْنُ لَهِيعَةَ، عَنْ يَزِيدَ بْنِ أَبِي حَبِيبٍ، عَنْ رَاشِدِ بْنِ جَنْدَلٍ الْيَافِعِيِّ، عَنْ حَبِيبِ بْنِ أَوْسٍ، عَنْ أَبِي أَيُّوبَ الأَنْصَارِيِّ، قَالَ: كُنَّا عِنْدَ النَّبِيِّ صلى الله عليه وسلم يَوْمًا، فَقَرَّبَ إِلَيْهِ طَعَامًا، فَلَمْ أَرَ طَعَامًا كَانَ أَعْظَمَ بَرَكَةً مِنْهُ أَوَّلَ مَا أَكَلْنَا، وَلا أَقَلَّ بَرَكَةً فِي آخِرِهِ، قُلْنَا: يَا رَسُولَ اللهِ، كَيْفَ هَذَا؟ قَالَ: «إِنَّا ذَكَرْنَا اسْمَ اللهِ حِينَ أَكَلْنَا، ثُمَّ قَعَدَ مَنْ أَكَلَ وَلَمْ يُسَمِّ اللهَ تَعَالَىٰ فَأَكَلَ مَعَهُ الشَّيْطَانُ»[٢٤٢].

188. Abū Ayyūb al-Anṣārī ؓ narrated: "We were once sitting with the Messenger of Allāh ﷺ. Food was presented to him and I have never seen any food that had such a large amount of blessings at the beginning and less blessings left in the food at the end. We therefore asked, 'O Messenger of Allāh ﷺ! How did this happen?' He replied, 'In the beginning we all mentioned the name of Allāh before we began eating. Then someone in the end joined us, and did not recite '*Bismillāh*' and so Satan ate with him.'"

'Abd al-Razzāq al-Badr said,

> The statement of Abū Ayyūb ؓ at the beginning demonstrates the perfect manners of the companions when talking about the Prophet ﷺ as they used statements that indicated that they were his followers.

242 *Musnad Aḥmad* (23522)

Al-Bājūrī said,

The answer of the Messenger of Allāh ﷺ proves that saying *'Bismillāh'* is enough to fulfil the Sunnah of mentioning the name of Allāh before eating, which is the reason why the food had so much blessing in it. However, al-Ghazālī, al-Nawawī and others said that adding *'al-Raḥmān al-Raḥīm'* to *'Bismillāh'* is better and closer to perfection. This is recommended to say even if the woman is menstruating or in postpartum, or when the person is in a state of major impurity due to intercourse. However, it is stipulated that they do not intend to say this with the intention to recite from the Qur'ān.

Ibn Ḥajar al-Haytamī said,

It is recommended to say *'Bismillāh'* before commencing anything that is important and virtuous except in the case of remembrance of Allāh and supplications (i.e. it is not prescribed for us to say *Bismillāh* before we invoke Allāh or before reciting any *dhikr*). It is also not recommended for *makrūh* (detested) and *ḥarām* (prohibited) acts.

١٨٩ - حَدَّثَنَا يَحْيَىٰ بْنُ مُوسَىٰ، قَالَ: حَدَّثَنَا أَبُو دَاوُدَ، قَالَ: حَدَّثَنَا هِشَامٌ الدَّسْتُوَائِيُّ، عَنْ بُدَيْلٍ الْعُقَيْلِيِّ، عَنْ عَبْدِ اللهِ بْنِ عُبَيْدِ بْنِ عُمَيْرٍ، عَنْ أُمِّ كُلْثُومٍ، عَنْ عَائِشَةَ، قَالَتْ: قَالَ رَسُولُ اللهِ صلى الله عليه وسلم: «إِذَا أَكَلَ أَحَدُكُمْ فَنَسِيَ أَنْ يَذْكُرَ اللهَ تَعَالَىٰ عَلَىٰ طَعَامِهِ، فَلْيَقُلْ: بِسْمِ اللهِ أَوَّلَهُ وَآخِرَهُ»٢٤٣.

189. 'Ā'ishah ﷺ narrated: "The Messenger of Allāh ﷺ said, 'When a person eats and has forgotten to recite 'Bismillāh' [before starting to eat], then one should recite, 'Bismillāhi awwalahu wa ākhirahu" ('Bismillāh at the beginning and at the end')."

'Abd al-Razzāq al-Badr said,

This is a direction to those who may forget to mention the name of Allāh before eating and then remember it before they finish eating. In such a case, the person should say, *"Bismillāhi awwalahu wa ākhirahu"* in order to attain the blessings of the food, by the will of Allāh. This is from the mercy of Allāh.

Al-Bājūrī said,

243 See *Ṣaḥīḥ al-Jāmi'* (1323)

The statement "*Bismillāh* at the beginning and at the end" includes all that comes in the middle and it is possible that it refers to the first half and second half of the time spent eating. In other words, it means "*Bismillāh* throughout the time spent eating."

١٩٠- حَدَّثَنَا عَبْدُ اللهِ بْنُ الصَّبَّاحِ الْهَاشِمِيُّ الْبَصْرِيُّ، قَالَ: حَدَّثَنَا عَبْدُ الْأَعْلَىٰ، عَنْ مَعْمَرٍ، عَنْ هِشَامِ بْنِ عُرْوَةَ، عَنْ أَبِيهِ، عَنْ عُمَرَ بْنِ أَبِي سَلَمَةَ، أَنَّهُ دَخَلَ عَلَىٰ رَسُولِ اللهِ صلىٰ الله عليه وسلم، وَعِنْدَهُ طَعَامٌ، فَقَالَ: «ادْنُ يَا بُنَيَّ، فَسَمِّ اللهَ تَعَالَىٰ، وَكُلْ بِيَمِينِكَ، وَكُلْ مِمَّا يَلِيكَ»٢٤٤.

190. ʿUmar b. Abī Salamah ☀ narrated: "I entered the presence of Allāh's Messenger ☀ whilst some food had been served to him. He ☀ said, 'O my son! Come near, say *Bismillāh*, and eat with your right hand from that which is in front of you.'"

ʿAbd al-Razzāq al-Badr said,

> This ḥadīth teaches us that it is allowed to call those other than one's own children "son" and it includes three etiquettes pertaining to food:
>
> 1. To say *Bismillāh* before eating.
>
> 2. To eat with the right hand.
>
> 3. To eat from the portion in front of you.

Al-Bājūrī said,

> The ruling on eating with the right hand is that it is recommended but other scholars stated that it is obligatory due to the existence of the ḥadīth wherein the Prophet ☀ admonished the person who ate with his left hand.

Ibn Ḥajar al-Haytamī said,

> This ḥadīth teaches us the following:
>
> 1. It is recommended for the elders to be kind with the youth, especially when food is served so as to break the ice since there can

---

244 *Sunan Ibn Mājah* (3265) and *Sunan al-Tirmidhī* (1857)

be elements of shyness on such occasions.

2. It is recommended to say *Bismillāh* audibly so others can hear it.

3. It is obligatory on the person to eat from the portion in front of themselves except in the case of fruits.

4. It is recommended for a person to teach others who eat about any of the etiquettes of food if a person does not act upon them.

١٩١- حَدَّثَنَا مَحْمُودُ بْنُ غَيْلاَنَ، قَالَ: حَدَّثَنَا أَبُو أَحْمَدَ الزُّبَيْرِيُّ، قَالَ: حَدَّثَنَا سُفْيَانُ الثَّوْرِيُّ، عَنْ أَبِي هَاشِمٍ، عَنِ إِسْمَاعِيلَ بْنِ رِيَاحٍ، عَنْ أَبِيهِ رِيَاحِ بْنِ عَبِيدَةَ، عَنْ أَبِي سَعِيدٍ الْخُدْرِيِّ، قَالَ: كَانَ رَسُولُ اللهِ صلى الله عليه وسلم إِذَا فَرَغَ مِنْ طَعَامِهِ، قَالَ: «الْحَمْدُ لِلَّهِ الَّذِي أَطْعَمَنَا، وَسَقَانَا، وَجَعَلَنَا مُسْلِمِينَ»²⁴⁵.

191. Abū Saʿīd al-Khudrī ❧ narrated: "After the Messenger of Allāh ❧ finished eating he recited, 'All praise is due only to Allāh, who has fed us, granted us something to drink and has made us Muslims.'"

'Abd al-Razzāq al-Badr said,

There are different statements that the Prophet ❧ used to say to praise Allāh after eating and it is prescribed for a person to recite these various phrases of praise at different times so that on a certain occasion one is said and at another time something else and so forth. The minimum one can say is "*Alḥamdulillah*" – as will follow shortly – but it is better to memorise what one is able to from the Prophetic supplications and then vary their usage.

Al-Bājūrī said,

Praising Allāh for the food after finishing a meal is to show gratefulness and appreciation to Allāh who has blessed us with that. The reason why he mentioned food before the drink is because drinks complement the food, not the other way around. The reason behind praising Allāh for making us Muslims is to combine praising Him for that which we receive in this world and that which we will receive in the Hereafter. It also indicates that one who praises Allāh for a

---

245 *Sunan Abī Dāwūd* (3850) and *Sunan al-Tirmidhī* (3457)

worldly matter should praise Him for the blessings of Islām because through Islām we learnt to praise Him.

١٩٢ - حَدَّثَنَا مُحَمَّدُ بْنُ بَشَّارٍ، قَالَ: حَدَّثَنَا يَحْيَىٰ بْنُ سَعِيدٍ، قَالَ: حَدَّثَنَا ثَوْرُ بْنُ يَزِيدَ، عَنْ خَالِدِ بْنِ مَعْدَانَ، عَنْ أَبِي أُمَامَةَ، قَالَ: كَانَ رَسُولُ اللهِ صلىٰ الله عليه وسلم إِذَا رُفِعَتِ الْمَائِدَةُ مِنْ بَيْنِ يَدَيْهِ يَقُولُ: «الْحَمْدُ لِلَّهِ حَمْدًا كَثِيرًا طَيِّبًا مُبَارَكًا فِيهِ، غَيْرَ مُودَعٍ، وَلا مُسْتَغْنًىٰ عَنْهُ رَبَّنَا»[٢٤٦].

192. Abū Umāmah ؓ narrated: "The Messenger of Allāh ﷺ used to say after the food was removed, 'All praise is due to Allāh alone; praise which is abundant, good and blessed that is neither insufficient, nor abandoned, nor ignored from our Lord.'"

ʿAlī al-Qārī said,

> The Sunnah is not to say "*Alḥamdulillah*" aloud after finishing the meal whist other people are still eating as that may make them stop eating.
>
> The meaning of "praise which is abundant, good and blessed" is a praise that is endless just like how His blessings and favours upon us are endless, with sincerity and no element of showing off, and a praise that is ceaseless and blessed.
>
> The Prophet ﷺ used to supplicate for the person at whose house he ate before leaving. The Sunnah is not to leave the food even if one is full until the other people in the group finish too. This is so that they do not feel embarrassed and leave the food whilst they still wish to eat.

١٩٣ - حَدَّثَنَا أَبُو بَكْرٍ مُحَمَّدُ بْنُ أَبَانَ، قَالَ: حَدَّثَنَا وَكِيعٌ، عَنْ هِشَامٍ الدَّسْتُوَائِيِّ، عَنْ بُدَيْلِ بْنِ مَيْسَرَةَ الْعُقَيْلِيِّ، عَنْ عَبْدِ اللهِ بْنِ عُبَيْدِ بْنِ عُمَيْرٍ، عَنْ أُمِّ كُلْثُومٍ، عَنْ عَائِشَةَ، قَالَتْ: كَانَ النَّبِيُّ صلىٰ الله عليه وسلم يَأْكُلُ الطَّعَامَ فِي سِتَّةٍ مِنْ أَصْحَابِهِ، فَجَاءَ أَعْرَابِيٌّ فَأَكَلَهُ بِلُقْمَتَيْنِ، فَقَالَ رَسُولُ اللهِ صلىٰ الله عليه وسلم: «لَوْ سَمَّىٰ لَكَفَاكُمْ»[٢٤٧].

---

246 *Ṣaḥīḥ al-Bukhārī* (5458)
247 *Sunan al-Tirmidhī* (1858)

193. 'Ā'ishah ﷺ related: "While six of the companions were eating with the Messenger of Allāh ﷺ, a Bedouin came and ate all the food in two bites. The Messenger of Allāh ﷺ said, 'If he had said '*Bismillāh*' it would have been sufficient for all of you.'"

'Abd al-Razzāq al-Badr said,

> This shows that leaving off saying *Bismillāh* removes the blessings of the food.

١٩٤ - حَدَّثَنَا هَنَّادٌ، وَمَحْمُودُ بْنُ غَيْلَانَ، قَالَا: حَدَّثَنَا أَبُو أُسَامَةَ، عَنْ زَكَرِيَّا بْنِ أَبِي زَائِدَةَ، عَنْ سَعِيدِ بْنِ أَبِي بُرْدَةَ، عَنْ أَنَسِ بْنِ مَالِكٍ قَالَ: قَالَ رَسُولُ اللهِ صلى الله عليه وسلم: «إِنَّ اللهَ لَيَرْضَىٰ عَنِ الْعَبْدِ أَنْ يَأْكُلَ الأَكْلَةَ، أَوْ يَشْرَبَ الشَّرْبَةَ فَيَحْمَدَهُ عَلَيْهَا»[٢٤٨].

194. Anas b. Mālik ﷺ related: "The Messenger of Allāh ﷺ said, 'Allāh is pleased with His slave who praises Him after eating a morsel of food or taking a sip of a beverage.'"

'Abd al-Razzāq al-Badr said,

> The author kept this ḥadīth until the end of the chapter because it includes the reward of praising Allāh for one's food and drink: gaining the pleasure of Allāh.

Al-Bājūrī said,

> The Sunnah is attained via any wording derived from *al-ḥamd* (praise) and the aforementioned wordings of praise reported from the Prophet ﷺ are cited to display the perfect form.

---

248 *Ṣaḥīḥ Muslim* (2734)

باب ما جاء في قدح رسول الله صلى الله عليه وسلم

[29] On Allāh's Messenger's ﷺ Cup

ʿAbd al-Razzāq al-Badr said,

> *Al-qadḥ* (the cup) refers to all that which is used to drink from. Here, it refers to the vessel from which the Prophet ﷺ drank water, *nabīdh*, juice, milk etc. from.

١٩٥ - حَدَّثَنَا الْحُسَيْنُ بْنُ الأَسْوَدِ الْبَغْدَادِيُّ، قَالَ: حَدَّثَنَا عَمْرُو بْنُ مُحَمَّدٍ، قَالَ: حَدَّثَنَا عِيسَىٰ بْنُ طَهْمَانَ، عَنْ ثَابِتٍ، قَالَ: «أَخرَجَ إِلَيْنَا أَنَسُ بْنُ مَالِكٍ، قَدَحَ خَشَبٍ، غَلِيظًا، مُضَبَّبًا بِحَدِيدٍ، فَقَالَ: يَا ثَابِتُ! هَذَا قَدَحُ رَسُولِ اللهِ صلىٰ الله عليه وسلم»[٢٤٩].

195. Thābit narrated: "Anas ؓ presented to us a thick wooden cup which was lined with iron, and said, 'O Thābit, this is the cup of the Messenger of Allāh ﷺ.'"

Mīrak Shāh al-Ḥanafī said (as quoted by ʿAlī al-Qārī),

> It is proven in the authentic ḥadīth that the cup of the Prophet ﷺ that Anas b. Mālik ؓ possessed was a good cup with a length shorter than its width, and that this cup had a crack in it so the Prophet ﷺ fixed it with a silver chain.

Ibn Ḥajar al-Haytamī said,

> This cup was purchased from the estate of al-Naḍr b. Anas for eight hundred thousand [dirhams]. Al-Bukhārī said that he saw it in Baṣrah and drank from it.

١٩٦ - حَدَّثَنَا عَبْدُ اللهِ بْنُ عَبْدِ الرَّحْمَنِ، قَالَ: أَنْبَأَنَا عَمْرُو بْنُ عَاصِمٍ، قَالَ: أَنْبَأَنَا حَمَّادُ بْنُ سَلَمَةَ، قَالَ: أَنْبَأَنَا حُمَيْدٌ، وَثَابِتٌ، عَنْ أَنَسٍ، قَالَ: «لَقَدْ سَقَيْتُ رَسُولَ اللهِ

---

249 *Sharḥ al-Sunnah* of al-Baghawī (2935)

صلّى الله عليه وسلم بِهَذَا الْقَدَح الشَّرَابَ كُلَّهُ، الْمَاءَ وَالنَّبِيذَ وَالْعَسَلَ وَاللَّبَنَ﴾ ٢٥٠.

**196. Anas b. Mālik ❀ narrated: "I presented the Messenger of Allāh
❀ with drinks in this cup from all forms; water, *nabīdh*, honey and
milk."**

'Abd al-Razzāq al-Badr said,

> *Nabīdh* is water that has had something like dates or grapes put in it
> and left overnight. By morning the water becomes sweetened with
> the taste of dates or grapes.

Al-Bājūrī said,

> If something remained from his *nabīdh*, he would give it to his serv-
> ant if it was not feared that the drink had fermented. If such a fear
> was present, he would order it to be spilled. This drink is effective in
> strengthening the body.

---

250 *Ṣaḥīḥ Muslim* (2008)

باب ما جاء في صفة فاكهة رسول الله صلى الله عليه وسلم

[30] On the Description of Allāh's Messenger's ﷺ Fruit

١٩٧ - حَدَّثَنَا إِسْمَاعِيلُ بْنُ مُوسَىٰ الْفَزَارِيُّ، قَالَ: حَدَّثَنَا إِبْرَاهِيمُ بْنُ سَعْدٍ، عَنْ أَبِيهِ، عَنْ عَبْدِ اللهِ، قَالَ: «كَانَ النَّبِيُّ صلىٰ الله عليه وسلم يَأْكُلُ الْقِثَّاءَ بِالرُّطَبِ»[٢٥١].

197. ʿAbdullāh b. Jaʿfar ﷺ narrated: "The Messenger of Allāh ﷺ ate *qithā'* with ripe dates (*ruṭab*)."

ʿAbd al-Razzāq al-Badr said,

> *Qithā'* is a type of cucumber that is larger than the normal cucumber.

Al-Bājūrī said,

> He ﷺ combined between dates and cucumber to attain the benefits and avert the harms of each. This is because the hotness of dates neutralises the coolness of cucumber i.e. dates neutralise the negative effects of cucumber and the latter neutralises the negative effects of dates.

Ibn Ḥajar al-Haytamī said,

> You should know that the Messenger of Allāh ﷺ used to eat from the fruits grown in his town and never refrained from it. This is a means of maintaining one's health.
>
> This ḥadīth teaches us that it is allowed to combine between two or more types of *idām* and the ḥadīth does not state that both are chewed at once. Rather, it means that both are eaten one after another so they are both in the digestive tract.

١٩٨ - حَدَّثَنَا عَبْدَةُ بْنُ عَبْدِ اللهِ الْخُزَاعِيُّ الْبَصْرِيُّ، قَالَ: حَدَّثَنَا مُعَاوِيَةُ بْنُ هِشَامٍ، عَنْ سُفْيَانَ، عَنْ هِشَامِ بْنِ عُرْوَةَ، عَنْ أَبِيهِ، عَنْ عَائِشَةَ: «أَنَّ النَّبِيَّ صلىٰ الله عليه

---

251 *Ṣaḥīḥ al-Bukhārī* (5440) and *Ṣaḥīḥ Muslim* (2043)

وسلم كَانَ يَأْكُلُ الْبِطِّيخَ بِالرُّطَبِ»٢٥٢.

198. ʿĀ'ishah ﵂ narrated: "The Messenger of Allāh ﷺ ate watermelon with ripe dates (*ruṭab*)."

ʿAbd al-Razzāq al-Badr said,

> Ibn al-Qayyim said in *Zad al-Maʿād*, "All the ḥadīths about the virtue of watermelon are fabricated or very weak except this ḥadīth."[253]

Al-Bājūrī said,

> The combination of fruits that he ﷺ used to eat shows that he followed the logic of medicine i.e. he ate that which would neutralise the bad effects of the other food.

١٩٩ - حَدَّثَنَا إِبْرَاهِيمُ بْنُ يَعْقُوبَ، قَالَ: حَدَّثَنَا وَهْبُ بْنُ جَرِيرٍ، قَالَ: حَدَّثَنَا أَبِي قَالَ: سَمِعْتُ حُمَيْدًا - أَوْ قَالَ: حَدَّثَنِي حُمَيْدٌ - قَالَ وَهْبٌ: وَكَانَ صَدِيقًا لَهُ، عَنْ أَنسِ بْنِ مَالِكٍ قَالَ: «رَأَيْتُ رَسُولَ اللهِ صلى الله عليه وسلم يَجْمَعُ بَيْنَ الْخِرْبِزِ وَالرُّطَبِ»٢٥٤.

199. Anas b. Mālik ﵁ reported: "I saw the Messenger of Allāh ﷺ eating muskmelon together with ripe dates *(ruṭab)*."

٢٠٠ - حَدَّثَنَا مُحَمَّدُ بْنُ يَحْيَى، قَالَ: حَدَّثَنَا مُحَمَّدُ بْنُ عَبْدِ الْعَزِيزِ الرَّمْلِيُّ، قَالَ: حَدَّثَنَا عَبْدُ اللهِ بْنُ يَزِيدَ بْنِ الصَّلْتِ، عَنْ مُحَمَّدِ بْنِ إِسْحَاقَ، عَنْ يَزِيدَ بْنِ رُومَانَ، عَنْ عُرْوَةَ، عَنْ عَائِشَةَ: «أَنَّ النَّبِيَّ صلى الله عليه وسلم أَكَلَ الْبِطِّيخَ بِالرُّطَبِ»٢٥٥.

200. ʿĀ'ishah ﵂ narrated: "The Messenger of Allāh ﷺ ate watermelon with ripe dates (*ruṭab*)."

ʿAlī al-Qārī said,

> The author's purpose [of repeating this narration] is to show that it has many routes to ʿĀ'ishah and others.

---

252 *Sunan Abī Dāwūd* (3836) and *Sunan al-Tirmidhī* (1843)
253 *Zad al-Maʿād* (4/287)
254 *Musnad Aḥmad* (12460)
255 See ḥadīth 195

٢٠١ - حَدَّثَنَا قُتَيْبَةُ بْنُ سَعِيدٍ، عَنْ مَالِكِ بْنِ أَنَسٍ، (ح) وَحَدَّثَنَا إِسْحَاقُ بْنُ مُوسَىٰ، قَالَ: حَدَّثَنَا مَعْنٌ، قَالَ: حَدَّثَنَا مَالِكٌ، عَنْ سُهَيْلِ بْنِ أَبِي صَالِحٍ، عَنْ أَبِيهِ، عَنْ أَبِي هُرَيْرَةَ، قَالَ: كَانَ النَّاسُ إِذَا رَأَوْا أَوَّلَ الثَّمَرِ جَاءُوا بِهِ إِلَىٰ رَسُولِ اللهِ صلىٰ الله عليه وسلم، فَإِذَا أَخَذَهُ رَسُولُ اللهِ صلىٰ الله عليه وسلم قَالَ: «اللَّهُمَّ بَارِكْ لَنَا فِي ثِمَارِنَا، وَبَارِكْ لَنَا فِي مَدِينَتِنَا، وَبَارِكْ لَنَا فِي صَاعِنَا، وَفِي مُدِّنَا، اللَّهُمَّ إِنَّ إِبْرَاهِيمَ عَبْدُكَ وَخَلِيلُكَ وَنَبِيُّكَ، وَإِنِّي عَبْدُكَ وَنَبِيُّكَ، وَإِنَّهُ دَعَاكَ لِمَكَّةَ، وَإِنِّي أَدْعُوكَ لِلْمَدِينَةِ بِمِثْلِ مَا دَعَاكَ بِهِ لِمَكَّةَ وَمِثْلِهِ مَعَهُ»، قَالَ: ثُمَّ يَدْعُو أَصْغَرَ وَلِيدٍ يَرَاهُ فَيُعْطِيهِ ذَلِكَ الثَّمَرَ.[٢٥٦]

201. Abū Hurayrah ﵁ narrated: "When people saw their new fruit, they would present it to the Messenger of Allāh ﷺ. He ﷺ then would take it and supplicate, 'O Allāh! Bless us in our fruits. Bless our city. Bless us in our *ṣāʿ*, and bless us in our *mudd* (these are two units of measurement used to measure dates). O Allāh! Ibrāhīm ﵇ is Your slave, close friend, and Prophet, and I am Your slave and Prophet. And, he supplicated to You for Makkah and I supplicate to You for Madīnah for the like of what He prayed to You for Makkah and one more.' Then, he would call the youngest child he could see and give him that fruit."

ʿAbd al-Razzāq al-Badr said,

> This ḥadīth shows an allowed type of intercession - that is intercession through one's state as a slave of Allāh and humility before Him.
>
> It was his perfect manners, kindness and mercy that made him give the fruit to the youngest child present because children long the most for fruits.

Al-Bājūrī said,

> The Prophet ﷺ is also the *khalīl* of Allāh (i.e. close friend of Allāh) but he did not mention it either out of reverence for Ibrāhīm ﵇ or because he was granted a higher level of love and closeness to Allāh.
>
> **"And, he supplicated to You for Makkah and I supplicate to You for Madīnah for the like of what He prayed to You for**

256 *Ṣaḥīḥ Muslim* (2038)

> **Makkah and one more":** Ibrāhīm's supplication for Makkah was accepted, and likewise was the Prophet's ﷺ for Madīnah. All types of fruits from the east and the west were gathered therein.
>
> The fact that the Prophet ﷺ did not eat the fruit brought to him and instead gave it to a child demonstrates that noble people with pure souls and high manners do not long to eat something until after everyone else can have it.
>
> The scholars are in agreement that Makkah and Madīnah are the best places on earth, and the three *imāms* hold the view that Makkah is better than Madīnah whereas al-Imām Mālik stated otherwise. However, the dispute is not over the noble area where he ﷺ is buried for it is indeed better than the heavens and the earth.

Ibn Ḥajar al-Haytamī said,

> The people brought the fruits to the Prophet ﷺ because they favoured him over themselves and to seek his blessings.

٢٠٢- حَدَّثَنَا مُحَمَّدُ بْنُ حُمَيْدٍ الرَّازِيُّ، قَالَ: حَدَّثَنَا إِبْرَاهِيمُ بْنُ الْمُخْتَارِ، عَنْ مُحَمَّدِ بْنِ إِسْحَاقَ، عَنْ أَبِي عُبَيْدَةَ بْنِ مُحَمَّدِ بْنِ عَمَّارِ بْنِ يَاسِرٍ، عَنِ الرُّبَيِّعِ بِنْتِ مُعَوِّذِ بْنِ عَفْرَاءَ، قَالَتْ: «بَعَثَنِي مُعَاذُ بْنُ عَفْرَاءَ بِقِنَاعٍ مِنْ رُطَبٍ وَعَلَيْهِ أَجْرٍ مِنْ قِثَّاءٍ زُغْبٍ، وَكَانَ النَّبِيُّ صلى الله عليه وسلم يُحِبُّ الْقِثَّاءَ، فَأَتَيْتُهُ بِهِ وَعِنْدَهُ حِلْيَةٌ قَدْ قَدِمَتْ عَلَيْهِ مِنَ الْبَحْرَيْنِ، فَمَلأَ يَدَهُ مِنْهَا فَأَعْطَانِيهِ»[٢٥٧].

202. Al-Rubayyi' bint Mu'awwidh b. 'Afrā ﵂ narrated: "Mu'ādh b. 'Afrā sent me with a plate of ripe dates (*ruṭab*), which had small cucumbers upon it, to the Messenger of Allāh ﷺ. He ﷺ liked cucumbers. I took the plate to him and when I entered on him, I saw jewellery that was sent to him from Baḥrayn. He took hold of a handful from it and gave it to me."

'Abd al-Razzāq al-Badr said,

> He ﷺ gave her from the jewellery because it was suitable for women.

Al-Bājūrī said,

---

257 *Sharḥ al-Sunnah* of al-Baghawī (2897)

Muʿādh b. ʿAfrā was the uncle of al-Rubayyiʿ and he and his brother Muʿawwidh participated in the killing of Abū Jahl during the battle of Badr. The death blow was delivered by Ibn Masʿūd, who found him wounded and still able to speak.

The word *ḥilyah* refers to money and pieces of jewellery.

Baḥrayn is the region between Baṣrah and Oman, and it is a part of the Najd area.

٢٠٣- حَدَّثَنَا عَلِيُّ بْنُ حُجْرٍ، قَالَ: حَدَّثَنَا شَرِيكٌ، عَنْ عَبْدِ اللهِ بْنِ مُحَمَّدِ بْنِ عَقِيلٍ، عَنِ الرُّبَيِّعِ بِنْتِ مُعَوِّذِ بْنِ عَفْرَاءَ، قَالَتْ: «أَتَيْتُ النَّبِيَّ صلى الله عليه وسلم بِقِنَاعٍ مِنْ رُطَبٍ، وَأَجْرِ زُغْبٍ، فَأَعْطَانِي مِلْءَ كَفِّهِ حُلِيًّا أَوْ قَالَتْ: ذَهَبًا»²⁵⁸.

203. Al-Rubayyiʾ bint Muʿawwidh b. ʿAfrā ⬥ narrated: "I took a plate of ripe dates (*ruṭab*) and small cucumbers to the Messenger of Allāh ⬥. He gifted me with a handful of jewellery, or a handful of gold."

Al-Bājūrī said,

This is a different route of the previous ḥadīth with a conciser wording.

---

258 *Musnad Aḥmad* (27020)

باب ما جاء في صفة شراب رسول الله صلى الله عليه وسلم

[31] On the Description of Allāh's Messenger's ﷺ Drinks

ʿAbd al-Razzāq al-Badr said,

> This chapter is dedicated to describing that which the Prophet ﷺ used to drink and the following chapter will describe the manner in which he used to drink.

Al-Bājūrī said,

> This chapter includes two ḥadīths.

٢٠٤- حَدَّثَنَا ابْنُ أَبِي عُمَرَ، قَالَ: حَدَّثَنَا سُفْيَانُ، عَنْ مَعْمَرٍ، عَنِ الزُّهْرِيِّ، عَنْ عُرْوَةَ، عَنْ عَائِشَةَ، قَالَتْ: «كَانَ أَحَبَّ الشَّرَابِ إِلَىٰ رَسُولِ اللهِ صلىٰ الله عليه وسلم الْحُلْوُ الْبَارِدُ»[٢٥٩].

204. ʿĀ'ishah ﵂ narrated: "The drink most liked by the Messenger of Allāh ﷺ was that which was sweet and cold."

Ibn Ḥajar al-Haytamī said,

> **"That which was sweet and cold":** I.e. cold water. It has been said that it means cold water mixed with honey, dates or raisins.

Al-Bājūrī said,

> Liking the drink to be sweet and cold does not contradict asceticism as it is intended to witness and observe more of the graces of Allāh and accordingly to show sincere gratitude.

Ibn Baṭṭāl said (as quoted by ʿAlī al-Qārī),

> Drinking sweetened water does not contravene asceticism and it is not included in the admonished types of luxury, contrary to scenting the water with something like musk. Furthermore, there is no benefit

---

259 *Sunan al-Tirmidhī* (1895)

or virtue in salty water. Allāh made a likeness of the disbeliever with salty water and of the believer with sweet water: **{And not alike are the two bodies of water. One is fresh and sweet, palatable for drinking, and one is salty and bitter.}**[260]

'Alī al-Qārī said,

> It was said that the sweet water mentioned in this ḥadīth refers to water mixed with honey because the Prophet ﷺ did not use sugar at all, not to mention that honey is a cure in and of itself.

٢٠٥ – حَدَّثَنَا أَحْمَدُ بْنُ مَنِيعٍ، قَالَ: حَدَّثَنَا إِسْمَاعِيلُ بْنُ إِبْرَاهِيمَ، قَالَ: حَدَّثَنَا عَلِيُّ بْنُ زَيْدٍ، عَنْ عُمَرَ هُوَ ابْنُ أَبِي حَرْمَلَةَ، عَنِ ابْنِ عَبَّاسٍ، قَالَ: دَخَلْتُ مَعَ رَسُولِ اللهِ صلىٰ الله عليه وسلم أَنَا وَخَالِدُ بْنُ الْوَلِيدِ عَلَىٰ مَيْمُونَةَ، فَجَاءَتْنَا بِإِنَاءٍ مِنْ لَبَنٍ، فَشَرِبَ رَسُولُ اللهِ صلىٰ الله عليه وسلم وَأَنَا عَلَىٰ يَمِينِهِ وَخَالِدٌ عَلَىٰ شِمَالِهِ، فَقَالَ لِي: «الشَّرْبَةُ لَكَ، فَإِنْ شِئْتَ آثَرْتَ بِهَا خَالِدًا»، فَقُلْتُ: مَا كُنْتُ لأُوثِرَ عَلَىٰ سُؤْرِكَ أَحَدًا، ثُمَّ قَالَ رَسُولُ اللهِ صلىٰ الله عليه وسلم: «مَنْ أَطْعَمَهُ اللهُ طَعَامًا، فَلْيَقُلِ: اللَّهُمَّ بَارِكْ لَنَا فِيهِ، وَأَطْعِمْنَا خَيْرًا مِنْهُ، وَمَنْ سَقَاهُ اللهُ عَزَّ وَجَلَّ لَبَنًا، فَلْيَقُلِ: اللَّهُمَّ بَارِكْ لَنَا فِيهِ، وَزِدْنَا مِنْهُ»، ثُمَّ قَالَ: قَالَ رَسُولُ اللهِ صلىٰ الله عليه وسلم: «لَيْسَ شَيْءٌ يُجْزِئُ مَكَانَ الطَّعَامِ وَالشَّرَابِ غَيْرُ اللَّبَنِ»[٢٦١].

205. 'Abdullāh b. 'Abbās رضي الله عنه narrated: "Khālid b. al-Walīd and I both accompanied Allāh's Messenger ﷺ to the house of Maymūnah. There, she presented us with milk in a vessel and Allāh's Messenger ﷺ drank from it. I was upon his right and Khālid to his left. The Messenger of Allāh ﷺ said to me, 'You possess the right of drinking but if you wish, you could give your right to Khālid.' I replied that I would not give up his leftovers to anyone else. After that, the Messenger of Allāh ﷺ said, 'Whenever Allāh feeds someone anything, the following supplication should be recited, 'O Allāh grant us blessings in it, and feed us something better than it,' and whenever Allāh gives someone milk to drink, one should read, 'O Allāh grant us blessing in it and increase it for us.' Then, the Messenger of Allāh ﷺ added, 'There is nothing that

260 Qur'ān: 35:12

261 *Sunan Abī Dāwūd* (3730) and *Sunan al-Tirmidhī* (2455)

serves the place of both food and drink except for milk.'"

قَالَ أَبُو عِيسَىٰ: وَمَيْمُونَةُ بِنْتُ الْحَارِثِ زَوْجُ النَّبِيِّ صَلَّى اللهُ عَلَيْهِ وَسَلَّمَ هِيَ خَالَةُ خَالِدِ بْنِ الْوَلِيدِ، وَخَالَةُ ابْنِ عَبَّاسٍ، وَخَالَةُ يَزِيدَ بْنِ الْأَصَمِّ، وَاخْتَلَفَ النَّاسُ فِي رِوَايَةِ هَذَا الْحَدِيثِ، عَنْ عَلِيِّ بْنِ زَيْدِ بْنِ جُدْعَانَ، فَرَوَىٰ بَعْضُهُمْ عَنْ عَلِيِّ بْنِ زَيْدٍ، عَنْ عُمَرَ بْنِ أَبِي حَرْمَلَةَ، وَرَوَىٰ شُعْبَةُ عَنْ عَلِيِّ بْنِ زَيْدٍ، فَقَالَ: عَنْ عَمْرِو بْنِ حَرْمَلَةَ، وَالصَّحِيحُ عُمَرُ بْنُ أَبِي حَرْمَلَةَ.

Al-Tirmidhī said: "Maymūnah bint al-Ḥārith ◉ is the wife of the Messenger of Allāh ◉, the maternal aunt of Ibn ʿAbbās and Khālid b. al-Walīd and the paternal aunt of Yazīd b. al-Aṣamm."

The ḥadīth masters differed in the narration of this ḥadīth from ʿAlī b. Zayd b. Judʿān. Some of them narrated it as ʿAlī b. Zayd from ʿUmar b. Abī Ḥarmalah, whereas Shuʿbah narrated it as ʿAlī b. Zayd from ʿAmr b. Ḥarmalah. The correct route is from ʿUmar b. Abī Ḥarmalah.

ʿAbd al-Razzāq al-Badr said,

This ḥadīth shows that the one to the right of the person has more right to be served first than the one on the left. It also shows that it is permissible for the one on the right to give his right to the person on the left.

Al-Bājūrī said,

There is a narration from Anas reported by Mālik, Aḥmad and the authors of the six *Sunan* which states, "The one to the right and then to the right." A secret within this precedence given to the one on the right is because he is next to the angel of the right.

The Sunnah of giving preference to the one on the right applies to food, drink, clothing etc. The Prophet ◉ explained that Ibn ʿAbbās had the right to drink first because he was on the right side but as Khālid was older than Ibn ʿAbbās and a leader in his tribe as well as being a new Muslim at that time, he informed Ibn ʿAbbās that he could give Khālid this right to show Khālid that he was not being disrespected or overlooked.

Ibn Ḥajar al-Haytamī said,

> The response of Ibn 'Abbās began with the excuse of not wanting to give that right to anyone so that it would not give the impression that he was refusing to comply.

باب ما جاء في شرب رسول الله صلى الله عليه وسلم

[32] On the Description of Allāh's Messenger's ﷺ Drinking

ʿAbd al-Razzāq al-Badr said,

> This chapter describes how the Prophet ﷺ drank; standing or sitting, how many breaths he took into the vessel etc.

Al-Bājūrī said,

> There are ten ḥadīths in this chapter.

٢٠٦- حَدَّثَنَا أَحْمَدُ بْنُ مَنِيعٍ، قَالَ: حَدَّثَنَا هُشَيْمٌ، قَالَ: حَدَّثنا عَاصِمٌ الأَحْوَلُ، وَمُغِيرَةُ، عَنِ الشَّعْبِيِّ، عَنِ ابْنِ عَبَّاسٍ: «أَنَّ النَّبِيَّ صلى الله عليه وسلم شَرِبَ مِنْ زَمْزَمَ، وَهُوَ قَائِمٌ». [٢٦٢]

206. ʿAbdullāh b. ʿAbbās ؓ narrated: "The Prophet ﷺ drank Zamzam water whilst standing."

Al-Bājūrī said,

> Zamzam is the famous well in Makkah. One view of why it is given that name is because Hājar said, "*Zamī, zamī* (constrict, constrict)" when its water gushed excessively.

Ibn al-Qayyim said,

> The guidance of the Prophet ﷺ in drinking was to drink whilst sitting down and it is proven authentic that he forbade people to drink while they are standing but at the same time it is proven authentic that he drank while he was standing. Some scholars reconciled between the two, stating that the latter abrogated the former, and other scholars stated that the order not to drink while standing was to show that it is not the best thing to do, and some scholars said that there is no need for reconciliation at all as he drank while he was standing be-

262 *Ṣaḥīḥ al-Bukhārī* (5617) and *Ṣaḥīḥ Muslim* (2027)

> cause the situation required that. This was because, as he ﷺ arrived to the well of Zamzam, people were drinking and he was handed a bottle of Zamzam water.

Ibn Ḥajar al-Haytamī said,

> The reason he ﷺ drank while he was standing (despite his normal manner being to drink sitting) was to show that this is permissible as he ordered people [at an earlier point] to only drink while they are sitting down.

٢٠٧- حَدَّثَنَا قُتَيْبَةُ بْنُ سَعِيدٍ، قَالَ: حَدَّثَنَا مُحَمَّدُ بْنُ جَعْفَرٍ، عَنْ حُسَيْنٍ الْمُعَلِّمِ، عَنْ عَمْرِو بْنِ شُعَيْبٍ، عَنْ أَبِيهِ، عَنْ جَدِّهِ قَالَ: «رَأَيْتُ رَسُولَ اللهِ صلىٰ الله عليه وسلم يَشْرَبُ قَائِمًا وَقَاعِدًا». [٢٦٣]

207. ʿAbdullāh b. ʿAmr رضي الله عنه related: "I saw the Messenger of Allāh ﷺ drink while standing and also whilst sitting."

Ibn Ḥajar al-Haytamī said,

> He ﷺ drank while he was sitting many times and he drank while he was standing one time to display its permissibility. His ﷺ known practice was to drink while he was sitting.

Al-Bājūrī said,

> Man has eight positions: Standing, sitting, walking, leaning on a support, bowing, prostrating, reclining and lying. Though it is possible to drink in all of these positions, the easiest and most common position to drink in is while sitting, followed by standing. [...] Preceding with the word "standing" in ḥadīths like this one is to emphasise that it is not prohibited, and not due to its performance being more than whilst sitting (as some falsely assumed).

٢٠٨- حَدَّثَنَا عَلِيُّ بْنُ حُجْرٍ، قَالَ: حَدَّثَنَا ابْنُ الْمُبَارِكِ، عَنْ عَاصِمٍ الأَحْوَلِ، عَنِ الشَّعْبِيِّ، عَنِ ابْنِ عَبَّاسٍ، قَالَ: «سَقَيْتُ النَّبِيَّ صلىٰ الله عليه وسلم مِنْ زَمْزَمَ فَشَرِبَ وَهُوَ قَائِمٌ» [٢٦٤].

---

263 *Sunan Abī Dāwūd* (653) and *Sunan al-Tirmidhī* (1883)
264 See ḥadīth 206

208. ʿAbdullāh b. ʿAbbās ﵁ narrated: "I gave the Prophet ﷺ Zamzam water to drink, so he drank it while he was standing."

ʿAbd al-Razzāq al-Badr said,

> This was mentioned at the start of the chapter, and it is cited here via a different route.

٢٠٩- حَدَّثَنَا أَبُو كُرَيْبٍ مُحَمَّدُ بْنُ الْعَلاءِ، وَمُحَمَّدُ بْنُ طَرِيفٍ الْكُوفِيُّ، قَالا: حَدَّثَنَا ابْنُ الْفُضَيْلِ، عَنِ الأَعْمَشِ، عَنْ عَبْدِ الْمَلِكِ بْنِ مَيْسَرَةَ، عَنِ النَّزَّالِ بْنِ سَبْرَةَ قَالَ: أَتَىٰ عَلِيٌّ بِكُوزٍ مِنْ مَاءٍ وَهُوَ فِي الرَّحْبَةِ، فَأَخَذَ مِنْهُ كَفًّا فَغَسَلَ يَدَيْهِ وَمَضْمَضَ وَاسْتَنْشَقَ، وَمَسَحَ وَجْهَهُ وَذِرَاعَيْهِ وَرَأْسَهُ، ثُمَّ شَرِبَ وَهُوَ قَائِمٌ، ثُمَّ قَالَ: هَذَا وُضُوءُ مَنْ لَمْ يُحْدِثْ، هَكَذَا رَأَيْتُ رَسُولَ اللهِ صلىٰ الله عليه وسلم فَعَلَ.[٢٦٥]

209. Al-Nazzāl b. Sabrah ﵁ related: "Water in a clay pot was brought to ʿAlī b. Abī Ṭālib ﵁ whilst he was in the courtyard of the *masjid*. He took a handful from this water and used it to wash his hands. Then he rinsed his mouth, sniffed the water to clean his nose and washed his face, forearms and head. Thereafter, he stood and drank from it. He then said, 'This is the ablution of a person who is not ritually impure. I have observed the Messenger of Allāh ﷺ perform it so.'"

Al-Bājūrī said,

> The word *raḥbah* either refers to the place in Kūfah with that name – where he would sit to give rulings or preach, or the courtyard of a *masjid*.

Ibn Ḥajar al-Haytamī said,

> This ḥadīth describes how to renew the ablution without being in a state of impurity. This ablution is intended for cleansing and not to remove the state of ritual impurity.

ʿAbd al-Razzāq al-Badr said,

> The relevant part in this ḥadīth to the chapter is that he ﵁ drank the water whilst he was standing.

265 *Ṣaḥīḥ al-Bukhārī* (5615)

ʿAlī al-Qārī said,

In another version it added, "And he washed his feet."

٢١٠- حَدَّثَنَا قُتَيْبَةُ بْنُ سَعِيدٍ، وَيُوسُفُ بْنُ حَمَّادٍ، قَالَا: حَدَّثَنَا عَبْدُ الْوَارِثِ بْنُ

سَعِيدٍ، عَنْ أَبِي عِصَامَ، عَنْ أَنَسِ بْنِ مَالِكٍ، أَنَّ النَّبِيَّ صلى الله عليه وسلم: «كَانَ

يَتَنَفَّسُ فِي الْإِنَاءِ ثَلَاثًا إِذَا شَرِبَ، وَيَقُولُ: هُوَ أَمْرَأُ وَأَرْوَى»٢٦٦.

210. Anas b. Mālik 🕮 **narrated: "The Messenger of Allāh** 🕮 **drank water from the vessel in three breaths (i.e. in three sips) and used to say, 'It is more pleasing and thirst quenching in this manner.'"**

ʿAlī al-Qārī said,

The practice that is admonished is to breathe in the bottle or vessel and then drink because this changes the nature of the water in addition to the benefits mentioned in this ḥadīth. It is also admonished to drink the contents of the vessel all at once because the Prophet 🕮 stated it is the way Shayṭān drinks, not to mention that this could cause the person to choke and block the throat.

٢١١- حَدَّثَنَا عَلِيُّ بْنُ خَشْرَمٍ، قَالَ: حَدَّثَنَا عِيسَى بْنُ يُونُسَ، عَنْ رِشْدِينِ بْنِ

كُرَيْبٍ، عَنْ أَبِيهِ، عَنِ ابْنِ عَبَّاسٍ: «أَنَّ النَّبِيَّ صلى الله عليه وسلم كَانَ إِذَا شَرِبَ

تَنَفَّسَ مَرَّتَيْنِ»٢٦٧.

211. ʿAbdullāh b. ʿAbbās 🕮 **narrated: "The Prophet** 🕮 **drank water in two breaths."**

ʿAbd al-Razzāq al-Badr said,

This ḥadīth is not an explicit evidence that he 🕮 drank water in two breaths because it is possible that the narrator did not count the last breath, which is bound to happen by default, and only described the two pauses that happened while drinking.

٢١٢- حَدَّثَنَا ابْنُ أَبِي عُمَرَ، قَالَ: حَدَّثَنَا سُفْيَانُ، عَنْ يَزِيدَ بْنِ يَزِيدَ بْنِ جَابِرٍ، عَنْ

---

266 *Ṣaḥīḥ Muslim* (2028)
267 *Sunan Ibn Mājah* (3417) and *Sunan al-Tirmidhī* (1886)

عَبْدِ الرَّحْمَنِ بْنِ أَبِي عَمْرَةَ، عَنْ جَدَّتِهِ كَبْشَةِ، قَالَتْ: «دَخَلَ عَلَيَّ النَّبِيُّ صلىٰ الله عليه وسلم فَشَرِبَ مِنْ قِرْبَةٍ مُعَلَّقَةٍ قَائِمًا»، فَقُمْتُ إِلَىٰ فِيهَا فَقَطَعْتُهُ[٢٦٨].

212. Kabshah bint Thābit ﵄ narrated: "The Prophet ﷺ once visited me at home and he drank while he was standing from a leather water bag that was suspended. Then, I got up and cut out the mouth [part] of the bag."

ʿAbd al-Razzāq al-Badr said,

> Kabshah bint Thābit is the sister of Ḥassān b. Thābit, the poet of the Prophet ﷺ.

ʿAlī al-Qārī said,

> Him ﷺ drinking while standing shows that his order not to drink while standing was to display it as being not preferred, and not that it is forbidden.
>
> She cut out the mouth part of the bag after he ﷺ drank from it in order to preserve the place where the Prophet ﷺ placed his mouth upon and to keep it for seeking its blessings.

٢١٣- حَدَّثَنَا مُحَمَّدُ بْنُ بَشَّارٍ، قَالَ: حَدَّثَنَا عَبْدُ الرَّحْمَنِ بْنُ مَهْدِيٍّ، قَالَ: حَدَّثَنَا عُزْرَةُ بْنُ ثَابِتٍ الأَنْصَارِيُّ، عَنْ ثُمَامَةَ بْنِ عَبْدِ اللهِ، قَالَ: كَانَ أَنَسُ بْنُ مَالِكٍ، يَتَنَفَّسُ فِي الإِنَاءِ ثَلاثًا، وَزَعَمَ أَنَسٌ «أَنَّ النَّبِيَّ صلىٰ الله عليه وسلم كَانَ يَتَنَفَّسُ فِي الإِنَاءِ ثَلاثًا»[٢٦٩].

213. Thumāmah b. ʿAbdullāh ﵁ narrated: "Anas b. Mālik ﵁ used to drink water in three breaths, and he stated that the Prophet ﷺ drank water in the same manner."

ʿAbd al-Razzāq al-Badr said,

> This shows how keen the companions ﵃ were to follow the Sunnah and adhere to the beautiful manners and etiquettes of the Prophet ﷺ.

٢١٤- حَدَّثَنَا عَبْدُ اللهِ بْنُ عَبْدِ الرَّحْمَنِ، قَالَ: حَدَّثَنَا أَبُو عَاصِمٍ، عَنِ ابْنِ جُرَيْجٍ،

268 *Sunan Ibn Mājah* (3423) and *Sunan al-Tirmidhī* (1892)
269 *Ṣaḥīḥ al-Bukhārī* (5631) and *Ṣaḥīḥ Muslim* (2028)

عَنْ عَبْدِ الْكَرِيمِ، عَنِ الْبَرَاءِ بْنِ زَيْدٍ - ابْنِ ابْنَةِ أَنَسِ بْنِ مَالِكٍ -، عَنْ أَنَسِ بْنِ مَالِكٍ: «أَنَّ النَّبِيَّ صلى الله عليه وسلم، دَخَلَ عَلَى أُمِّ سُلَيْمٍ، وَقِرْبَةٌ مُعَلَّقَةٌ، فَشَرِبَ مِنْ فَمِ الْقِرْبَةِ وَهُوَ قَائِمٌ، فَقَامَتْ أُمُّ سُلَيْمٍ إِلَى رَأْسِ الْقِرْبَةِ فَقَطَعَتْهَا»[٢٧٠].

214. Anas b. Mālik narrated: "The Prophet once visited Umm Sulaym at her home and he drank while he was standing, from a leather water bag that was suspended. Then, she got up and cut out the mouth [part] of the bag."

Al-Bājūrī said,

> Umm Sulaym is Anas b. Mālik's mother.

٢١٥ - حَدَّثَنَا أَحْمَدُ بْنُ نَصْرٍ النَّيْسَابُورِيُّ، قَالَ: حَدَّثَنَا إِسْحَاقُ بْنُ مُحَمَّدٍ الْفَرْوِيُّ، قَالَ: حَدَّثَتْنَا عَبِيدَةُ بِنْتُ نَائِلٍ، عَنْ عَائِشَةَ بِنْتِ سَعْدِ بْنِ أَبِي وَقَّاصٍ، عَنْ أَبِيهَا «أَنَّ النَّبِيَّ صلى الله عليه وسلم كَانَ يَشْرَبُ قَائِمًا»،[٢٧١] قَالَ أَبُو عِيسَى: وَقَالَ بَعْضُهُمْ: عُبَيْدَةُ بِنْتُ نَابِلٍ.

215. Sa'd b. Abī Waqqāṣ narrated: "The Prophet used to drink whilst standing."

Abū 'Īsā said, "Some mentioned [in the chain of narration]: 'Ubaydah bint Nābil (instead of Nā'il)."

Al-Bājūrī said,

> Sa'd b. Abī Waqqāṣ was one of the ten people who were given the glad tidings of Paradise, the first person in Islām who shot an arrow in Allāh's path and he witnessed all the battles [of his time], so he was called the Knight of Islām.
>
> As it was explained, the common practice of the Prophet was to drink while he was sitting and on some rare occasions he drank while standing.

---

270 *Musnad Aḥmad* (12188)

271 *Mukhtaṣar al-Shamā'il* of al-Albānī (184)

باب ما جاء في تعطر رسول الله صلى الله عليه وسلم

[33] On Allāh's Messenger's ﷺ Perfuming

ʿAbd al-Razzāq al-Badr said,

> This chapter is dedicated to describing the guidance of the Prophet ﷺ in respect to perfume.

Ibn al-Qayyim said,

> The Prophet ﷺ liked applying perfume and he always wore it. His scent was the best and the scent of his perspiration was even better than that of perfume.[272]

Al-Bājūrī said,

> It is more emphasised for men to wear perfume on Fridays, days of Eid, when entering the state of *iḥrām*, attending a congregation, attending gatherings, reciting the Qur'ān, learning and teaching knowledge, and remembrance of Allāh. It is also recommended for the husband and wife to perfume themselves before being intimate. (Quoted from ʿAlī al-Qārī)

٢١٦- حَدَّثَنَا مُحَمَّدُ بْنُ رَافِعٍ، وَغَيْرُ وَاحِدٍ، قَالُوا: حَدَّثَنَا أَبُو أَحْمَدَ الزُّبَيْرِيُّ قَالَ: حَدَّثَنَا شَيْبَانُ، عَنْ عَبْدِ اللهِ بْنِ الْمُخْتَارِ، عَنْ مُوسَىٰ بْنِ أَنَسِ بْنِ مَالِكٍ، عَنْ أَبِيهِ، قَالَ: «كَانَ لِرَسُولِ اللهِ صلىٰ الله عليه وسلم سُكَّةٌ يَتَطَيَّبُ مِنْهَا»[273].

216. Anas b. Mālik ؓ narrated: "The Messenger of Allāh ﷺ had a container that he would apply perfume from."

Al-Bājūrī said,

> Based on the context of the ḥadīth, *sukkah* refers here to the perfume bottle, though one of its meanings is a perfume that is made of a mixture of elements.

---

272 *Zād al-Maʿād* (4/239)
273 *Sunan Abī Dāwūd* (4162)

٢١٧ - حَدَّثَنَا مُحَمَّدُ بْنُ بَشَّارٍ، قَالَ: حَدَّثَنَا عَبْدُ الرَّحْمَنِ بْنُ مَهْدِيٍّ، قَالَ: حَدَّثَنَا عَزْرَةُ بْنُ ثَابِتٍ، عَنْ ثُمَامَةَ بْنِ عَبْدِ اللهِ، قَالَ: كَانَ أَنَسُ بْنُ مَالِكٍ لا يَرُدُّ الطِّيبَ، وَقَالَ أَنَسٌ: «إِنَّ النَّبِيَّ صلىٰ الله عليه وسلم كَانَ لا يَرُدُّ الطِّيبَ»[٢٧٤].

217. Thumāmah b. 'Abdullāh ﷺ narrated: "Anas b. Mālik ﷺ never refused accepting perfume whenever it was offered and he said, 'The Messenger of Allāh ﷺ never refused perfume whenever it was offered to him.'"

'Abd al-Razzāq al-Badr said,

> Anas b. Mālik ﷺ never rejected perfume so as to follow the example of the Messenger of Allāh ﷺ. The reason why he ﷺ never rejected an offering of perfume was because it is light in weight and has a good smell.

Abū Bakr b. al-'Arabī said,

> The reason why he ﷺ never rejected an offering of perfume was because he liked it and needed it more than anyone else as he was always receiving revelation from his Lord.

٢١٨ - حَدَّثَنَا قُتَيْبَةُ بْنُ سَعِيدٍ، قَالَ: حَدَّثَنَا ابْنُ أَبِي فُدَيْكٍ، عَنْ عَبْدِ اللهِ بْنِ مُسْلِمِ بْنِ جُنْدُبٍ، عَنْ أَبِيهِ، عَنِ ابْنِ عُمَرَ، قَالَ: قَالَ رَسُولُ اللهِ صلىٰ الله عليه وسلم: «ثَلاثٌ لا تُرَدُّ: الْوَسَائِدُ، وَالدُّهْنُ، وَاللَّبَنُ»[٢٧٥].

218. 'Abdullāh b. 'Umar ﷺ narrated: "The Messenger of Allāh ﷺ said, 'Three things should not be refused: cushions (pillows), [scented] oil and milk.'"

Al-Bājūrī said,

> This ḥadīth can be understood in two ways: that these gifts are not refused to avoid the gift giver feeling hurt by the rejection and this is the apparent meaning, or that the guest should not refuse any of these three things when the host offers them.
>
> This applies to all of that which people do not consider a favour con-

274 *Ṣaḥīḥ al-Bukhārī* (5929)
275 *Sunan al-Tirmidhī* (2790)

ferred upon others i.e. it applies to all items and gifts that do not cause the recipient to feel like he will owe a favour to the individual who gifted him.

Al-Suyūṭī said (as quoted by al-Bājūrī),

> The Sunnah is to accept and not to refuse seven things when they are offered: sweets, milk, [scented] oil, cushions, provision given to a person in need, perfume and basil.

٢١٩ – حَدَّثَنَا مَحْمُودُ بْنُ غَيْلانَ، قَالَ: حَدَّثَنَا أَبُو دَاوُدَ الْحَفَرِيُّ، عَنْ سُفْيَانَ، عَنِ الْجُرَيْرِيِّ، عَنْ أَبِي نَضْرَةَ، عَنْ رَجُلٍ، عَنْ أَبِي هُرَيْرَةَ، قَالَ: قَالَ رَسُولُ اللهِ صلى الله عليه وسلم: «طِيبُ الرِّجَالِ: مَا ظَهَرَ رِيحُهُ وَخَفِيَ لَوْنُهُ، وَطِيبُ النِّسَاءِ: مَا ظَهَرَ لَوْنُهُ وَخَفِيَ رِيحُهُ»[٢٧٦].

219. Abū Hurayrah ﵁ narrated: "The Messenger of Allāh ﷺ said: 'The perfume of men is that which possesses a fragrance that spreads yet is colourless, and the perfume of women is that which has a colour yet its fragrance does not spread.'"

ʿAlī al-Qārī said,

> Qatādah said that scholars understood the perfume prescribed for women in this ḥadīth as that which she wears when she wants to go outside her house, and she can wear any type of perfume she wants when she is with her husband. It was reported that Abū Mūsā ﵁ narrated that the Prophet ﷺ said, "The eye is liable to commit adultery; and the woman who wears perfume and then passes by people, she is considered an adulteress."[277]

Al-Bājūrī said,

> The perfume of men is of types such as musk, rosewater, amber and camphor and the perfume of women is of types such as saffron and sandalwood.

٢٢٠ – حَدَّثَنَا عَلِيُّ بْنُ حُجْرٍ، قَالَ: أَنْبَأَنَا إِسْمَاعِيلُ بْنُ إِبْرَاهِيمَ، عَنِ الْجُرَيْرِيِّ،

---

276 *Sunan Abī Dāwūd* (2174) and *Sunan al-Tirmidhī* (2787)

277 Reported by al-Tirmidhī

عَنْ أَبِي نَضْرَةَ، عَنِ الطُّفَاوِيِّ، عَنْ أَبِي هُرَيْرَةَ، عَنِ النَّبِيِّ صلى الله عليه وسلم مِثْلَهُ بِمَعْنَاهُ[٢٧٨].

220. Abū Hurayrah ﷺ narrated a similar report with the same meaning.

Al-Bājūrī said,

> **"With the same meaning":** This is for emphasis. He mentioned the narration again with this chain of narration to increase confidence in it.
>
> **"A similar report":** I.e. to the previous report in wording and meaning.

٢٢١ - حَدَّثَنَا مُحَمَّدُ بْنُ خَلِيفَةَ، وَعَمْرُو بْنُ عَلِيٍّ، قَالا: حَدَّثَنَا يَزِيدُ بْنُ زُرَيْعٍ، قَالَ: حَدَّثَنَا حَجَّاجٌ الصَّوَّافُ، عَنْ حَنَانٍ، عَنْ أَبِي عُثْمَانَ النَّهْدِيِّ، قَالَ: قَالَ رَسُولُ اللهِ صلى الله عليه وسلم: «إِذَا أُعْطِيَ أَحَدُكُمُ الرَّيْحَانَ فَلا يَرُدُّهُ، فَإِنَّهُ خَرَجَ مِنَ الْجَنَّةِ»[٢٧٩].

221. Abū 'Uthmān al-Nahdī narrated: "The Messenger of Allāh ﷺ said, 'If one is given fragrance of basil, he should not refuse it, because it originated from Paradise.'"

Abū 'Īsā said, "We only know of this ḥadīth from Ḥannān."

Al-Qāḍī 'Iyāḍ said,

> I find it possible to interpret the use of basil here in this context to refer to all types of perfume.[280]

Al-Nawawī said,

> This ḥadīth shows that it is disliked to refuse fragrance of basil unless there is a reason to reject it (i.e. a person cannot handle its smell etc.).[281]

'Alī al-Qārī said,

---

278 See ḥadīth 219
279 *Sunan al-Tirmidhī* (2791)
280 *Ikmāl al-Mu'lim bi Fawā'id Muslim* (7/194)
281 *Al-Minhāj Sharḥ Ṣaḥīḥ Muslim b. al-Hajjāj* (15/10)

"Because it originated from Paradise": The origin of the nice scent is from Paradise. Allāh has created the good scents in this worldly life to remind His creation of the scents of the Hereafter. This is to make them want to enter Paradise and thus increase in good deeds. The meaning here is not that the good scents in this world emanate from Paradise, though it is possible that its seed emanated from there.

٢٢٢- حَدَّثَنَا عُمَرُ بْنُ إسماعيلَ بْنِ مُجَالِدِ بْنِ سَعِيدٍ الْهَمَذَانِيُّ، قَالَ: حَدَّثنا أَبِي، عَنْ بَيَانٍ، عَنْ قَيسِ بْنِ أَبِي حَازِمٍ، عَنْ جَرِيرِ بْنِ عَبْدِ اللهِ، قَالَ: عُرِضْتُ بَيْنَ يَدَيْ عُمَرُ بْنِ الْخِطَابِ، فَأَلْقَىٰ جَرِيرٌ رِدَاءَهُ وَمَشَىٰ فِي إِزَارٍ، فَقَالَ لَهُ: خُذْ رِدَاءَكَ؛ فَقَالَ عُمَرُ لِلْقَوْمِ: مَا رَأَيْتُ رَجُلًا أَحْسَنَ صُورَةٍ مِنْ جَرِيرٍ إِلَّا مَا بَلَغَنَا مِنْ صُورَةِ يُوسُفَ عَلَيْهِ السُّلَّامَ. [٢٨٢]

222. Jarīr b. ʿAbdillāh ﷺ related that he was presented to ʿUmar b. al-Khaṭṭāb ﷺ and then he threw off his top cloak and walked in his *izār* only. ʿUmar told him to take his top cloak and put it back on and then addressed the people saying, "I have not seen anyone more handsome than Jarīr except what has been reported to us about Yūsuf ﷺ."

Al-Bājūrī said,

> The reason Jarīr ﷺ was presented to ʿUmar ﷺ was so ʿUmar ﷺ could check if he was physically fit to join the army.

Ibn Ḥajar al-Haytamī said,

> Jarīr was known for his inability to remain on the back of the horse until the Prophet ﷺ hit him on his chest and asked Allāh to rid him of this fault. This incident happened forty nights before the death of the Prophet ﷺ. He took off his upper garment to show his strength and skills.

ʿAbd al-Razzāq al-Badr said,

> The reason why this ḥadīth was included in this chapter though it does not mention anything regarding perfume was to hint that being good looking necessitates smelling good as well.
>
> It is known that there is no one more handsome than the Prophet

282 *Musnad al-Fārūq* of Ibn Kathīr (2/682)

ﷺ and the statement of 'Umar ؓ was said in respect to the physical build of Jarīr ؓ, since he made that statement after Jarīr took off his top cloak.

باب كيف كان كلام رسول الله صلى الله عليه وسلم

[34] On Allāh's Messenger's ﷺ Speech

ʿAbd al-Razzāq al-Badr said,

> This chapter is dedicated to describing how the Prophet ﷺ used to talk.

Al-Bājūrī said,

> There are three ḥadīths in the chapter.

٢٢٣- حَدَّثَنَا حُمَيْدُ بْنُ مَسْعَدَةَ الْبَصْرِيُّ، قَالَ: حَدَّثَنَا حُمَيْدُ بْنُ الأَسْوَدِ، عَنِ أُسَامَةَ بْنِ زَيْدٍ، عَنِ الزُّهْرِيِّ، عَنْ عُرْوَةَ، عَنْ عَائِشَةَ قَالَتْ: «مَا كَانَ رَسُولُ اللهِ صلى الله عليه وسلم يَسْرُدُ سَرْدَكُمْ هَذَا، وَلَكِنَّهُ كَانَ يَتَكَلَّمُ بِكَلَامٍ بَيِّنٍ فَصْلٍ، يَحْفَظُهُ مَنْ جَلَسَ إِلَيْهِ»[٢٨٣].

223. ʿĀ'ishah رضي الله عنها related: "The speech of the Messenger of Allāh ﷺ was not fast paced as that of yours. He spoke clearly, enunciating each word properly so that anyone sitting with him would remember what he said."

ʿAbd al-Razzāq al-Badr said,

> This shows that due to his eloquence and concise use of words, anyone sitting with him would easily remember all that he ﷺ said.

Al-Bājūrī said,

> Enunciating each word slowly ensures the clearness of the sentence and it leaves no room for doubts. It also helps the listener memorise that which he has heard.

٢٢٤- حَدَّثَنَا مُحَمَّدُ بْنُ يَحْيَى، قَالَ: حَدَّثَنَا أَبُو قُتَيْبَةَ سَلْمُ بْنُ قُتَيْبَةَ، عَنْ عَبْدِ اللهِ بْنِ

---

283 *Sunan al-Tirmidhī* (3639)

الْمُثَنَّىٰ، عَنْ ثُمَامَةَ، عَنْ أَنَسِ بْنِ مَالِكٍ، قَالَ: «كَانَ رَسُولُ اللهِ صلىٰ الله عليه وسلم يُعِيدُ الْكَلِمَةَ ثَلاثًا لِتُعْقَلَ عَنْهُ»[٢٨٤].

224. Anas b. Mālik ﷺ related: "The Messenger of Allāh ﷺ used to repeat a word thrice, in order that they (his listeners) could understand what was said correctly."

Ibn Ḥajar al-Haytamī said,

> The Messenger of Allāh ﷺ used to repeat the word or the sentence for a variety of reasons: to ensure he had the attention of the people, to ensure the audience understood the meaning or when the audience was increasing around him, to ensure everybody heard what he said. This exhibits the perfection of his compassion and mercy for his nation.
>
> Based on this ḥadīth and what preceded it, it is recommended for the teacher to talk slowly and repeat his words to ensure the audience understands him.

٢٢٥- حَدَّثَنَا سُفْيَانُ بْنُ وَكِيعٍ، قَالَ: حَدَّثَنَا جُمَيْعُ بْنُ عُمَرَ بْنِ عَبْدِ الرَّحْمَنِ الْعِجْلِيُّ، قَالَ: حَدَّثَنِي رَجُلٌ مِنْ بَنِي تَمِيمٍ مِنْ وَلَدِ أَبِي هَالَةَ زَوْجِ خَدِيجَةَ يُكْنَىٰ أَبَا عَبْدِ اللهِ، عَنِ ابْنٍ لأَبِي هَالَةَ، عَنِ الْحَسَنِ بْنِ عَلِيٍّ، قَالَ: سَأَلْتُ خَالِي هِنْدَ بْنَ أَبِي هَالَةَ، وَكَانَ وَصَّافًا، فَقُلْتُ: صِفْ لِي مَنْطِقَ رَسُولِ اللهِ صلىٰ الله عليه وسلم قَالَ: «كَانَ رَسُولُ اللهِ صلىٰ الله عليه وسلم مُتَوَاصِلَ الأَحْزَانِ، دَائِمَ الْفِكْرَةِ، لَيْسَتْ لَهُ رَاحَةٌ، طَوِيلُ السَّكْتِ، لا يَتَكَلَّمُ فِي غَيْرِ حَاجَةٍ، يَفْتَتِحُ الْكَلامَ، وَيَخْتِمُهُ بِاسْمِ اللهِ تَعَالَىٰ، وَيَتَكَلَّمُ بِجَوَامِعِ الْكَلِمِ، كَلامُهُ فَصْلٌ، لا فُضُولَ، وَلا تَقْصِيرَ، لَيْسَ بِالْجَافِي، وَلا الْمُهِينِ، يُعَظِّمُ النِّعْمَةَ وَإِنْ دَقَّتْ، لا يَذُمُّ مِنْهَا شَيْئًا، غَيْرَ أَنَّهُ لَمْ يَكُنْ يَذُمُّ ذَوَّاقًا وَلا يَمْدَحُهُ، وَلا تُغْضِبُهُ الدُّنْيَا، وَلا مَا كَانَ لَهَا، فَإِذَا تُعُدِّيَ الْحَقُّ لَمْ يَقُمْ لِغَضَبِهِ شَيْءٌ حَتَّىٰ يَنْتَصِرَ لَهُ، وَلا يَغْضَبُ لِنَفْسِهِ، وَلا يَنْتَصِرُ لَهَا، إِذَا أَشَارَ أَشَارَ بِكَفِّهِ كُلِّهَا، وَإِذَا تَعَجَّبَ قَلَبَهَا، وَإِذَا تَحَدَّثَ اتَّصَلَ بِهَا، وَضَرَبَ بِرَاحَتِهِ الْيُمْنَىٰ بَطْنَ إِبْهَامِهِ الْيُسْرَىٰ، وَإِذَا غَضِبَ أَعْرَضَ وَأَشَاحَ، وَإِذَا فَرِحَ غَضَّ طَرْفَهُ، جُلُّ

---

284 *Ṣaḥīḥ al-Bukhārī* (6244)

ضَحِكِهِ التَّبَسُّمُ، يَفْتَرُّ عَنْ مِثْلِ حَبِّ الْغَمَامِ»[٢٨٥].

225. Al-Ḥasan b. 'Alī ﷺ narrated: "I asked my maternal uncle Hind b. Abī Hālah, who was known as one who would describe the features of the Prophet ﷺ, to describe to me the manner in which the Messenger of Allāh ﷺ spoke. He replied, 'The Messenger of Allāh ﷺ was in a continual state of worry, constantly thoughtful and his mind was never at rest.

He would remain silent for long periods and he would not speak without need. He used to begin and end his speech with the name of Allāh, and it was concise yet comprehensive, and clearly articulated. There was no excess in his speech, nor was there deficiency. He was not rude or unkind, nor did he disgrace anyone. He always glorified and appreciated the blessings of Allāh, however little, and never faulted any of it. He did not criticise food and drink, nor over-praise it. He was never angered for anything worldly. However if someone transgressed the limits in religious matters, he would not calm down until he avenged it. He neither became angry for a personal matter nor avenged for himself.

If he wanted to make a gesture or point at something, he would do so with his full hand. Whenever he was surprised by something, he turned his hands upside down, and when he spoke he moved his hands. He would hit the palm of his right hand with the inside part of his left thumb. When he became angry with someone, he would direct his attention away from that person. When he was happy he would gaze down. The laugh of his was mostly a smile and at that moment his teeth glittered like shining hailstones piercing the clouds.'"

'Abd al-Razzāq al-Badr said,

> Ibn al-Qayyim stated in *Madārij al-Sālikīn* that this ḥadīth is not authentic and it has some parts that are questionable.[286]

Al-Bājūrī said,

> The state of worry refers to his constant fear of Allāh and this is a common trait of all Prophets. It is also a trait of deep understanding. However, in public he used to maintain a smile on his face for the

285 See ḥadīth 8
286 *Madārij al-Sālikīn* (1/412)

people, to soften their hearts.

He glorified and appreciated the blessings of Allāh, those which are hidden, those which are apparent and those which are related to this world and the Hereafter. He did that by praising Allāh with his tongue and using these blessings in obeying Him.

Ibn Taymiyyah said,

The state of worry mentioned is intended to mean that he was always alert and attentive to what he received and this involves the heart and the eyes whilst silence and thoughtfulness involve the tongue and the heart. It is factual that he was never worried or concerned about a worldly matter.

Ibn Ḥajar al-Haytamī said,

He ﷺ never rested because he was always busy in good deeds. He started and ended his speeches with the name of Allāh, meaning he mostly started with *bismillāh* and ended them with *alḥamdulillāh* or something similar like *astaghfirullāh*. This was with the intention of making his speeches engulfed with the blessings of His Name.

'Alī al-Qārī said,

He ﷺ never became angry for a worldly matter, following the divine order: **{And do not extend your eyes toward that by which We have given enjoyment to [some] categories of them, [its being but] the splendour of worldly life by which We test them. And the provision of your Lord is better and more enduring.}**[287]

He neither became angry for a personal matter nor avenged for himself as he always encountered insult with forbearance, and harm with forgiveness, following the divine order: **{Enjoin what is good, and turn away from the ignorant.}**[288]

He pointed out using his full hand because pointing out with some fingers is from the acts of the arrogant.

287 Qur'ān: 20:131
288 Qur'ān: 7:199

باب ما جاء في ضحك رسول الله صلى الله عليه وسلم

[35] On Allāh's Messenger's ﷺ Laughter

ʿAbd al-Razzāq al-Badr said,

> The guidance of the Prophet ﷺ in respect to laughing was to be moderate just as he was moderate in all of his affairs. On most occasions, his laugh was just a smile and if he laughed audibly, he would not laugh boisterously, instead making a noise that only those close-by could hear.

Al-Bājūrī said,

> The chapter contains nine ḥadīths.

٢٢٦- حَدَّثَنَا أَحْمَدُ بْنُ مَنِيعٍ، قَالَ: حَدَّثَنَا عَبَّادُ بْنُ الْعَوَّامِ، قَالَ أَخْبَرَنَا الْحَجَّاجُ وَهُوَ ابْنُ أَرْطَاةَ، عَنْ سِمَاكِ بْنِ حَرْبٍ، عَنْ جَابِرِ بْنِ سَمُرَةَ، قَالَ: «كَانَ فِي سَاقَيْ رَسُولِ اللهِ صلىٰ الله عليه وسلم حُمُوشَةٌ، وَكَانَ لا يَضْحَكُ إِلا تَبَسُّمًا، فَكُنْتُ إِذَا نَظَرْتُ إِلَيْهِ قُلْتُ: أَكْحَلُ الْعَيْنَيْنِ، وَلَيْسَ بِأَكْحَلَ»[٢٨٩].

226. Jābir b. Samurah ؓ narrated: "The legs of the Messenger of Allāh ﷺ were slightly thin. His laugh was only that of a smile. Every time I looked at him, I would think that kohl had been applied to his eyes even though it had not."

ʿAbd al-Razzāq al-Badr said,

> The slight thinness in his legs befitted the structure of his body and so it is a characteristic that people praise.

Al-Bājūrī said,

> The statement that **'his laugh was only that of a smile'** does not mean that he never laughed but rather it is to state that most of the time he used to smile. This is because it was reported that the Messen-

289 *Sunan al-Tirmidhi* (3645)

ger of Allāh ﷺ laughed until his molars showed. Some scholars offered a nice explanation to highlight the difference between the reasons that made him laugh and the reasons that made him smile. This explanation is that the Messenger of Allāh ﷺ smiled in matters related to this worldly life and laughed in matters related to the Hereafter.

Ibn Ḥajar al-Haytamī said,

> The eyelashes of the Messenger of Allāh ﷺ were dark enough to give the impression that he had applied kohl.

٢٢٧- حَدَّثَنَا قُتَيْبَةُ بْنُ سَعِيدٍ، قَالَ: أَخْبَرَنَا ابْنُ لَهِيعَةَ، عَنْ عُبَيْدِ اللهِ بْنِ الْمُغِيرَةِ، عَنْ عَبْدِ اللهِ بْنِ الْحَارِثِ بْنِ جَزْءٍ، أَنَّهُ قَالَ: «مَا رَأَيْتُ أَحَدًا أَكْثَرَ تَبَسُّمًا مِنْ رَسُولِ اللهِ صلى الله عليه وسلم».[٢٩٠]

227. 'Abdullāh b. al-Ḥārith b. Jaz' ؓ narrated: "I never saw a person who smiled more than the Messenger of Allāh ﷺ."

Al-Bājūrī said,

> This is a characteristic that indicates his perfection as he used to smile in the face of people despite the feelings of concern regarding the Hereafter that he concealed in his heart.

'Abd al-Razzāq al-Badr said,

> A Muslims smile towards his brother is a form of charity he does for him. This is because it is a means towards entering happiness in his heart, and it creates a desire for him to hear his speech and to sit in his presence.

٢٢٨- حَدَّثَنَا أَحْمَدُ بْنُ خَالِدٍ الْخَلالُ، قَالَ: حَدَّثَنَا يَحْيَىٰ بْنُ إِسْحَاقَ السَّيْلَحَانِيُّ، قَالَ: حَدَّثَنَا لَيْثُ بْنُ سَعْدٍ، عَنْ يَزِيدَ بْنِ أَبِي حَبِيبٍ، عَنْ عَبْدِ اللهِ بْنِ الْحَارِثِ، قَالَ: «مَا كَانَ ضَحِكُ رَسُولِ اللهِ صلى الله عليه وسلم إِلا تَبَسُّمًا»[٢٩١].

228. 'Abdullāh b. al-Ḥārith narrated: "The laughter of the Messenger of Allāh ﷺ was naught but a smile."

---

290 *Sunan al-Tirmidhī* (3641)
291 *Sunan al-Tirmidhī* (3642)

قَالَ أَبُو عِيسَىٰ: هَذَا حَدِيثٌ غَرِيبٌ مِنْ حَدِيثِ لَيْثِ بْنِ سَعْدٍ.

Abū ʿĪsā said: This ḥadīth is a *gharīb* report of Layth b. Saʿd.

Al-Bājūrī said,

> **"This ḥadīth is a *gharīb* report of Layth b. Saʿd":** I.e. due to al-Layth solely reporting it. This occurs in the chain of narration and not the text of the ḥadīth, so it does not negate its authenticity.

٢٢٩- حَدَّثَنَا أَبُو عَمَّارٍ الْحُسَيْنُ بْنُ حُرَيْثٍ، قَالَ: حَدَّثَنَا وَكِيعٌ، قَالَ: حَدَّثَنَا الْأَعْمَشُ، عَنِ الْمَعْرُورِ بْنِ سُوَيْدٍ، عَنْ أَبِي ذَرٍّ، قَالَ: قَالَ رَسُولُ اللهِ صلى الله عليه وسلم: «إِنِّي لَأَعْلَمُ أَوَّلَ رَجُلٍ يَدْخُلُ الْجَنَّةَ، وَآخَرَ رَجُلٍ يَخْرُجُ مِنَ النَّارِ، يُؤْتَىٰ بِالرَّجُلِ يَوْمَ الْقِيَامَةِ فَيُقَالُ: اعْرِضُوا عَلَيْهِ صِغَارَ ذُنُوبِهِ وَيُخَبَّأُ عَنْهُ كِبَارُهَا، فَيُقَالُ لَهُ: عَمِلْتَ يَوْمَ كَذَا وَكَذَا كَذَا، وَهُوَ مُقِرٌّ لَا يُنْكِرُ، وَهُوَ مُشْفِقٌ مِنْ كِبَارِهَا، فَيُقَالُ: أَعْطُوهُ مَكَانَ كُلِّ سَيِّئَةٍ عَمِلَهَا حَسَنَةً، فَيَقُولُ: إِنَّ لِي ذُنُوبًا مَا أَرَاهَا هَهُنَا!»، قَالَ أَبُو ذَرٍّ: «فَلَقَدْ رَأَيْتُ رَسُولَ اللهِ صلى الله عليه وسلم ضَحِكَ حَتَّىٰ بَدَتْ نَوَاجِذُهُ».²⁹²

229. Abū Dharr ◉ narrated: "The Messenger of Allāh ◉ said, 'I know the person who will enter Paradise first and also the last person to be taken out of the Hellfire. On the Day of Judgment, a person will be brought forward and then it shall be commanded that all the minor sins of that person be put forward to him and the major sins be concealed. Then, it will be said to him, 'On such a day you did this and on such a day you did this.' He will attest to this without protest whilst being filled with anxiety due to the pending disclosure of his major sins. Then, it shall be commanded that for every sin of that person he be given a good deed. Upon hearing this, the person says, 'I still have many sins left to account for that I do not find here!'"

Abū Dharr ◉ then stated: "[By Allāh,] I saw Allāh's Messenger ◉ laughing [because of the response of the person] until his molar teeth began to show."

ʿAbd al-Razzāq al-Badr said,

The first person who will enter Paradise is the Messenger of Allāh ◉

---

292 *Ṣaḥīḥ Muslim* (190)

> and the last person who is taken out from the Hellfire will be the last person to enter Paradise, leaving behind in the Hellfire all those who will remain there forever. The ones who will remain there forever are the disbelievers because the sinners (i.e. who perform sins below the grade of *shirk*/polytheism) amongst the believers will eventually leave Hell.

Al-Bājūrī said,

> The story of the person in the ḥadīth is separate from the statement wherein he ﷺ mentioned the first and last person to enter Paradise.
>
> The reason that he was given a good deed for every misdeed is due to his sincere repentance. Allāh the Most High says: **{Except for those who repent, believe and do righteous work. For them Allāh will replace their evil deeds with good. And ever is Allāh Forgiving and Merciful.}**[293]
>
> The reason the Prophet ﷺ laughed was because he was astonished [at what this man will be granted]. The man was anxious at first because he feared his major sins being exposed but after he saw that his minor sins turned into good deeds, he started looking forward to seeing his major sins too. Abū Dharr swore that he saw the Prophet ﷺ laughing so no one would doubt his statement since his ﷺ laugh was known to be like a smile.

Ibn Ḥajar al-Haytamī said,

> The response of the man was because he was overwhelmed with the great Mercy that Allāh bestowed upon him so he wanted to find more sins hoping that they will be replaced with good deeds too.

٢٣٠- حَدَّثَنَا أَحْمَدُ بْنُ مَنِيعٍ، قَالَ: حَدَّثَنَا مُعَاوِيَةُ بْنُ عَمْرٍو، قَالَ: حَدَّثَنَا زَائِدَةُ، عَنْ بَيَانٍ، عَنْ قَيْسِ بْنِ أَبِي حَازِمٍ، عَنْ جَرِيرِ بْنِ عَبْدِ اللهِ قَالَ: «مَا حَجَبَنِي رَسُولُ اللهِ صلىٰ الله عليه وسلم مُنْذُ أَسْلَمْتُ، وَلا رَآنِي إِلا ضَحِكَ»[٢٩٤].

230. Jarīr b. ʿAbdullāh ؓ narrated: "From the day I accepted Islām, the Messenger of Allāh ﷺ never prevented me from entering upon

293 Qur'ān: 25:70
294 *Ṣaḥiḥ al-Bukhārī* (3035) and *Ṣaḥiḥ Muslim* (2475)

him and every time he saw me, he would laugh."

Al-Bājūrī said,

> Jarīr b. ʿAbdullāh ﵁ embraced Islām forty days before the death of the Messenger of Allāh ﷺ.

Ibn Ḥajar al-Haytamī said,

> **"The Messenger of Allāh ﷺ never prevented me from entering upon him":** I.e. the Messenger of Allāh ﷺ never prevented him from entering his presence in his house when he was with his close companions and aides. This shows the special status of Jarīr.

٢٣١- حَدَّثَنَا أَحْمَدُ بْنُ مَنِيعٍ، قَالَ: حَدَّثَنَا مُعَاوِيَةُ بْنُ عَمْرٍو، قَالَ: حَدَّثَنَا زَائِدَةُ، عَنْ إِسْمَاعِيلَ بْنِ أَبِي خَالِدٍ، عَنْ قَيْسٍ، عَنْ جَرِيرٍ، قَالَ: «مَا حَجَبَنِي رَسُولُ اللهِ صلى الله عليه وسلم وَلا رَآنِي مُنْذُ أَسْلَمْتُ إِلا تَبَسَّمَ»[٢٩٥].

231. Jarīr b. ʿAbdullāh ﵁ narrated: "From the day I accepted Islām, the Messenger of Allāh ﷺ never prevented me from entering upon him and every time he saw me, he would smile."

Ibn Ḥajar al-Haytamī said,

> This ḥadīth explains that the meaning intended with 'laughing' mentioned in the previous ḥadīth referred to smiling i.e. he ﷺ used to smile whenever he saw Jarīr ﵁.

٢٣٢- حَدَّثَنَا هَنَّادُ بْنُ السَّرِيِّ ، قَالَ: حَدَّثَنَا أَبُو مُعَاوِيَةَ، عَنِ الأَعْمَشِ، عَنِ إِبْرَاهِيمَ، عَنْ عَبِيدَةَ السَّلْمَانِيِّ، عَنْ عَبْدِ اللهِ بْنِ مَسْعُودٍ، قَالَ: قَالَ رَسُولُ اللهِ صلى الله عليه وسلم: «إِنِّي لأَعْرِفُ آخِرَ أَهْلِ النَّارِ خُرُوجًا، رَجُلٌ يَخْرُجُ مِنْهَا زَحْفًا، فَيُقَالُ لَهُ: انْطَلِقْ فَادْخُلِ الْجَنَّةَ، قَالَ: فَيَذْهَبُ لِيَدْخُلَ الْجَنَّةَ، فَيَجِدُ النَّاسَ قَدْ أَخَذُوا الْمَنَازِلَ، فَيَرْجِعُ فَيَقُولُ: يَا رَبِّ، قَدْ أَخَذَ النَّاسُ الْمَنَازِلَ، فَيُقَالُ لَهُ: أَتَذْكُرُ الزَّمَانَ الَّذِي كُنْتَ فِيهِ، فَيَقُولُ: نَعَمْ، قَالَ: فَيُقَالُ لَهُ: تَمَنَّ، قَالَ: فَيَتَمَنَّى، فَيُقَالُ لَهُ: فَإِنَّ لَكَ الَّذِي تَمَنَّيْتَ وَعَشَرَةَ أَضْعَافِ الدُّنْيَا، قَالَ: فَيَقُولُ: تَسْخَرُ بِي وَأَنْتَ الْمَلِكُ! قَالَ:

---

295 *Sunan al-Tirmidhī* (3821)

فَلَقَدْ رَأَيْتُ رَسُولَ اللهِ صلىٰ الله عليه وسلم ضَحِكَ حَتَّىٰ بَدَتْ نَوَاجِذُهُ»[٢٩٦].

232. 'Abdullāh b. Mas'ūd ﵁ narrated: "The Messenger of Allāh ﷺ said, 'I know the last of the people of Hell to be brought forth, and the last of the people of Paradise to enter therein. It will be a man who will emerge crawling from Hell, and Allāh will say to him, 'Go and enter Paradise.' He will come to it and it will appear to him that all the abodes were taken. He will go back and say, 'O Lord, the people have taken the abodes.' Allāh will say to him, 'Do you remember your time before [on Earth]?' The man answers, 'Yes, I do.' Allāh will say to him, 'Make a wish,' and so the man makes a wish and then Allāh says to him, 'You will have that which you wished and ten times the worldly.' He will say, 'Are You mocking me, yet You are the King [and Sovereign]?'"

'Abdullāh b. Mas'ūd said: "And I saw the Messenger of Allāh ﷺ laugh so that his molars appeared."

Ibn Ḥajar al-Haytamī said,

> The statement of the man, **"Are You mocking me, yet You are the King [and Sovereign],"** was said due to the overwhelming surprise felt by the man. This made him unaware of his words in a similar manner to the incident reported in the ḥadīth of the man who lost all of his provisions and his camel and then awaited death as he was in the middle of desert. When he saw that his camel had returned, he said out of overwhelming surprise, "O Lord, you are my slave and I am your Lord!"[297]

Al-Bājūrī said,

> The reason the man returned after he reached Paradise was because his thought process was according to the rules of this worldly life, his understanding caused him to believe that Paradise only accommodates a specific number of people and so it was full.
>
> Allāh, the Most High, asked the man to make a wish in order to show him that the rules of the worldly life do not apply to Paradise, and thus he could wish for what he likes. Life in Paradise cannot be made comparison of with the worldly life, for the latter is restricted and full

296 *Ṣaḥīḥ al-Bukhārī* (6571) and *Ṣaḥīḥ Muslim* (186)
297 *Ṣaḥīḥ Muslim* (2747)

of trials, whereas the former is a place of abundance and reward.

٢٣٣- حَدَّثَنَا قُتَيْبَةُ بْنُ سَعِيدٍ، قَالَ: حَدَّثَنَا أَبُو الأَحْوَصِ، عَنْ أَبِي إِسْحَاقَ، عَنْ عَلِيِّ بْنِ رَبِيعَةَ، قَالَ: شَهِدْتُ عَلِيًّا، أُتِيَ بِدَابَّةٍ لِيَرْكَبَهَا فَلَمَّا وَضَعَ رِجْلَهُ فِي الرِّكَابِ، قَالَ: بِسْمِ اللهِ! فَلَمَّا اسْتَوَىٰ عَلَىٰ ظَهْرِهَا، قَالَ: الْحَمْدُ لِلَّهِ، ثُمَّ قَالَ: ﴿سُبْحَانَ الَّذِي سَخَّرَ لَنَا هَٰذَا وَمَا كُنَّا لَهُ مُقْرِنِينَ وَإِنَّا إِلَىٰ رَبِّنَا لَمُنْقَلِبُونَ﴾، ثُمَّ قَالَ: الْحَمْدُ لِلَّهِ ثَلَاثًا، وَاللهُ أَكْبَرُ ثَلَاثًا، سُبْحَانَكَ إِنِّي ظَلَمْتُ نَفْسِي، فَاغْفِرْ لِي فَإِنَّهُ لَا يَغْفِرُ الذُّنُوبَ إِلَّا أَنْتَ، ثُمَّ ضَحِكَ فَقُلْتُ: مِنْ أَيِّ شَيْءٍ ضَحِكْتَ يَا أَمِيرَ الْمُؤْمِنِينَ؟ قَالَ: رَأَيْتُ رَسُولَ اللهِ صلى الله عليه وسلم صَنَعَ كَمَا صَنَعْتُ ثُمَّ ضَحِكَ، فَقُلْتُ: مِنْ أَيِّ شَيْءٍ ضَحِكْتَ يَا رَسُولَ اللهِ؟ قَالَ: إِنَّ رَبَّكَ لَيَعْجَبُ مِنْ عَبْدِهِ إِذَا قَالَ: رَبِّ اغْفِرْ لِي ذُنُوبِي، إِنَّهُ لَا يَغْفِرُ الذُّنُوبَ غَيْرُكَ.[٢٩٨]

233. ʿAlī b. Rabīʿah ﵁ narrated: "I was present when an animal (i.e. a horse or a donkey) was brought to ʿAlī b. Abī Ṭālib ﵁. When he put his feet on the stirrup, he recited *'Bismillāh'* and after he had mounted it, he said *'Alḥamdulillāh'* and supplicated: '*Subḥān* (glorified be) *Allāh* who has subjected this to us, and we could not have [otherwise] subdued it. And indeed we, to our Lord, will [surely] return. *Alḥamdulillāh, Alḥamdulillāh, Alḥamdulillāh, Allāhu Akbar, Allāhu Akbar, Allāhu Akbar. Subḥānak*, I have wronged myself so forgive me as no one can forgive sins save You.' Then, he laughed and I asked him, 'O Chief of Believers! What is the reason for you laughing?' He replied, 'The Messenger of Allāh ﷺ also did as I did and thereafter laughed. I inquired from him the reason for laughing. The Messenger of Allāh ﷺ said, 'Your Lord becomes pleased when His servants say, 'My Lord, forgive my sins. No one can forgive sins save You.'"

Al-Bājūrī said,

> *Bismillah* is recited to mean, "By the blessings of the name of Allāh I mount." The basis for saying *bismillah* when mounting is from the statement of Nūḥ ﵇ when he mounted the ship, as reported in the Qur'ān.

298 *Sunan al-Tirmidhī* (3446)

> The reason for saying after mounting, "*and indeed we, to our Lord, will surely return,*" is because a person may fall off and die and so the statement is to remind the person that he will return to Allāh. It is for this reason that it is recommended for a person who takes a means that could lead to death (translator's note: such as the various forms of modern transport) to repent and turn to Allāh during the trip.

'Alī al-Qārī said,

> The praise is said to praise Allāh, the Most High, for the blessing of having a means of transport.
>
> The statement, 'Exalted be He' is to reflect on how the strong horse and camel is tamed to serve the humans who have weak bodies when compared to these animals.
>
> Repeating the praise three times is to show one's gratitude for the blessing and repeating *Allāhu Akbar* is to glorify the perfection of Allāh manifested in His creation.

'Abd al-Razzāq al-Badr said,

> **"I have wronged myself so forgive me,"** is said to acknowledge one's shortcomings as opposed to the blessings that one has been granted. Thus, with all these blessings it befits that one asks for Allāh's forgiveness.

٢٣٤- حَدَّثَنَا مُحَمَّدُ بْنُ بَشَّارٍ، قَالَ: حَدَّثَنَا مُحَمَّدُ بْنُ عَبْدِ اللهِ الأَنْصَارِيُّ، قَالَ: حَدَّثَنَا عَبْدُ اللهِ بْنُ عَوْنٍ، عَنْ مُحَمَّدِ بْنِ مُحَمَّدِ بْنِ الأَسْوَدِ، عَنْ عَامِرِ بْنِ سَعْدٍ، قَالَ: قَالَ سَعْدٌ: «لَقَدْ رَأَيْتُ النَّبِيَّ صلى الله عليه وسلم ضَحِكَ يَوْمَ الْخَنْدَقِ حَتَّى بَدَتْ نَوَاجِذُهُ؛ قَالَ: قُلْتُ: كَيْفَ كَانَ؟ قَالَ: كَانَ رَجُلٌ مَعَهُ تُرْسٌ، وَكَانَ سَعْدٌ رَامِيًا، وَكَانَ يَقُولُ كَذَا وَكَذَا بِالتُّرْسِ يُغَطِّي جَبْهَتَهُ، فَنَزَعَ لَهُ سَعْدٌ بِسَهْمٍ، فَلَمَّا رَفَعَ رَأْسَهُ رَمَاهُ فَلَمْ يُخْطِئْ هَذِهِ مِنْهُ - يَعْنِي جَبْهَتَهُ - وَانْقَلَبَ الرَّجُلُ، وَشَالَ بِرِجْلِهِ، فَضَحِكَ النَّبِيُّ صلى الله عليه وسلم حَتَّى بَدَتْ نَوَاجِذُهُ؛ قَالَ: قُلْتُ: مِنْ أَيِّ شَيْءٍ ضَحِكَ؟ قَالَ: مِنْ فِعْلِهِ بِالرَّجُلِ»[٢٩٩].

299 *Musnad Aḥmad* (1620)

234. ʿĀmir b. al-Aswad narrated from Saʿd b. Abī Waqqāṣ ﵁ that: "[Saʿd said] 'The Messenger of Allāh ﷺ laughed on the day of the Battle of the Trench until his teeth showed.' I asked Saʿd, 'What caused him to laugh?' He replied, 'A disbeliever had a shield, and Saʿd was an archer. He was swaying the shield from side to side to protect his forehead, whilst making derogatory remarks. Saʿd took an arrow and kept it ready in the bow. When the disbeliever exposed his head, he quickly aimed at his forehead and did not miss the target. The enemy immediately fell down with his legs rising into the air. On that the Messenger of Allāh ﷺ laughed until his molar teeth were displayed.' I asked, 'Why did the Messenger of Allāh ﷺ laugh?' He replied, 'Because of what Saʿd did to the man.'"

ʿAbd al-Razzāq al-Badr said,

> The Messenger of Allāh ﷺ laughed because he was happy that an enemy of Allāh was killed and not because of how the man fell down. This was because that disbeliever caused a lot of harm.

باب ما جاء في صفة مزاح رسول الله صلى الله عليه وسلم

[36] On the Description of Allāh's Messenger's ﷺ Humour

'Abd al-Razzāq al-Badr said,

> The jokes of the Prophet ﷺ were always truthful and intended to bring forth affability. He joked with his companions only according to the need. For this reason, one should be moderate in his sense of humour and refrain from insulting and mocking others.
>
> Joking should be treated like salt in food: In its absence, food will not be accepted nor deemed tasty, and when it is excessive, the food will not benefit. Joking should be treated the same.

Al-Nawawi said,

> Scholars have stated that the forbidden type of joking is that which is immoderate and highly frequent for this hardens the heart and makes laughing a habit of the person, distracting him from the remembrance of Allāh and giving attention to the important religious matters. Not to mention that excessive joking can often lead to hurting the feelings of others, thereby inducing hatred and compromising one's dignity and respect before the people. If the joke is free of all these defects, then it is the lawful joking that the Prophet ﷺ did.[300]

Al-Bājūrī said,

> There are six ḥadīths in this chapter.

٢٣٥- حَدَّثَنَا مَحْمُودُ بْنُ غَيْلانَ، قَالَ: حَدَّثَنَا أَبُو أُسَامَةَ، عَنْ شَرِيكٍ، عَنْ عَاصِمٍ الأَحْوَلِ، عَنْ أَنَسِ بْنِ مَالِكٍ، أَنَّ النَّبِيَّ صلىٰ الله عليه وسلم قَالَ لَهُ: «يَا ذَا الأُذُنَيْنِ»[٣٠١].

300 *Kitāb al-Adkhār* (1/327)
301 *Sunan Abī Dāwūd* (5002) and *Sunan al-Tirmidhī* (1992)

قَالَ مَحْمُودٌ: قَالَ أَبُو أُسَامَةَ: يَعْنِي يُمَازِحُهُ.

235. Anas b. Mālik ﷺ narrated that the Prophet ﷺ called him, "O two eared one!"

Maḥmūd said that Abū 'Usāmah said: "This was intended as a humorous statement."

'Abd al-Razzāq al-Badr said,

> The statement of the Messenger of Allāh ﷺ to Anas ﷺ was to joke with him and it shows his humbleness as he joked with his servant.

Al-Bājūrī said,

> The statement of the Messenger of Allāh ﷺ was said to praise Anas for being an attentive listener who understands the words he hears accurately. The humorous aspect of the statement is that it gives the impression that the person possesses no sense except for that which emanates from the ears.

'Alī al-Qārī said,

> **"Maḥmūd said that Abū 'Usāmah said"**: The former is the author's teacher and the latter is the teacher's teacher.

٢٣٦ - حَدَّثَنَا هَنَّادُ بْنُ السَّرِيِّ، قَالَ: حَدَّثَنَا وَكِيعٌ، عَنْ شُعْبَةَ، عَنْ أَبِي التَّيَّاحِ، عَنْ أَنَسِ بْنِ مَالِكٍ، قَالَ: إِنْ كَانَ رَسُولُ اللهِ صلى الله عليه وسلم لَيُخَالِطُنَا حَتَّىٰ يَقُولَ لِأَخٍ لِي صَغِيرٍ: ﴿يَا أَبَا عُمَيْرٍ! مَا فَعَلَ النُّغَيْرُ؟﴾. ٣٠٢

236. Anas b. Mālik ﷺ narrated: "The Messenger of Allāh ﷺ used to mix with us (i.e. me and my family) to the extent that he said to my younger brother, 'Abū 'Umayr, what happened to the Nughayr?'"

قَالَ أَبُو عِيسَىٰ: وَفِقْهُ هَذَا الْحَدِيثِ أَنَّ النَّبِيَّ صلى الله عليه وسلم كَانَ يُمَازِحُ، وَفِيهِ أَنَّهُ كَنَّىٰ غُلَامًا صَغِيرًا، فَقَالَ لَهُ: ﴿يَا أَبَا عُمَيْرٍ﴾. وَفِيهِ أَنَّهُ لَا بَأْسَ أَنْ يُعْطَىٰ الصَّبِيُّ الطَّيْرَ لِيَلْعَبَ بِهِ وَإِنَّمَا قَالَ لَهُ النَّبِيُّ صلى الله عليه وسلم: يَا أَبَا عُمَيْرٍ، مَا فَعَلَ النُّغَيْرُ؟﴾ لِأَنَّهُ كَانَ لَهُ نُغَيْرٌ يَلْعَبُ بِهِ فَمَاتَ، فَحَزِنَ الْغُلَامُ عَلَيْهِ فَمَازَحَهُ النَّبِيُّ صلى

---

302 *Ṣaḥīḥ al-Bukhārī* (6129) and *Ṣaḥīḥ Muslim* (2150)

الله عليه وسلم فَقَالَ: «يَا أَبَا عُمَيْرٍ، مَا فَعَلَ النُّغَيْرُ؟»

Abū ʿĪsā said: "This ḥadīth shows that the Prophet ﷺ used to joke with others, that he called a young boy 'the father of ʿUmayr' and that it is allowed to give young children birds to play with. Furthermore, the Prophet's ﷺ statement, 'Abū ʿUmayr, what happened to the Nughayr?' was because he had a small bird which he used to play with that died, thus he became saddened and so the Prophet tried to lighten his mood."

Ibn Ḥajar al-Haytamī said,

> Al-Nughayr is a type of bird and the Prophet ﷺ used a *kunyah* to call the young child to bring joy to his heart as he knew that his bird had died.

Al-Baghawī said, "This ḥadīth shows that it is allowed to rhyme if it is natural and intended."

The following can be derived from this ḥadīth:

1. It is allowed to have birds in a cage to enjoy their colour, sound or play with so long as they are fed and looked after.

2. It is allowed to call children with a *kunyah* (i.e. the father of so and so).

3. It is allowed to joke so long as the joke does not involve sins.

4. It shows the kind manners and compassion of the Prophet ﷺ.

5. It is from the recommended good manners to look after the vulnerable ones and bring happiness to their hearts.

٢٣٧ - حَدَّثَنَا عَبَّاسُ بْنُ مُحَمَّدٍ الدُّورِيُّ، قَالَ: حَدَّثَنَا عَلِيُّ بْنُ الْحَسَنِ بْنِ شَقِيقٍ، قَالَ: أَنْبَأَنَا عَبْدُ اللهِ بْنُ الْمُبَارَكِ، عَنْ أُسَامَةَ بْنِ زَيْدٍ، عَنْ سَعِيدٍ الْمَقْبُرِيِّ، عَنْ أَبِي هُرَيْرَةَ، قَالَ: قَالُوا: يَا رَسُولَ اللهِ، إِنَّكَ تُدَاعِبُنَا؟ قَالَ: «إِنِّي لَا أَقُولُ إِلَّا حَقًّا»٣٠٣.

237. Abū Hurayrah ﷺ narrated: "The companions ﷺ said, 'O Messenger of Allāh ﷺ! Verily, you joke with us!' He said, 'Yes, except I do not say but the truth.'"

---

303 *Sunan al-Tirmidhī* (1990)

'Abd al-Razzāq al-Badr said,

> The Prophet ﷺ joked but his jokes did not include anything unlawful as all of his statements were truthful.

Al-Bājūrī said,

> It was said to Sufyān b. 'Uyaynah, "Humour is a trial." He replied, "No, it is a Sunnah in the case of one who does so well and appropriately."

٢٣٨- حَدَّثَنَا قُتَيْبَةُ بْنُ سَعِيدٍ، قَالَ: حَدَّثَنَا خَالِدُ بْنُ عَبْدِ اللهِ، عَنْ حُمَيْدٍ، عَنْ أَنَسِ بْنِ مَالِكٍ، أَنَّ رَجُلًا اسْتَحْمَلَ رَسُولَ اللهِ صلىٰ الله عليه وسلم فَقَالَ: «إِنِّي حَامِلُكَ عَلَىٰ وَلَدِ نَاقَةٍ»، فَقَالَ: يَا رَسُولَ اللهِ! مَا أَصْنَعُ بِوَلَدِ النَّاقَةِ؟ فَقَالَ صلىٰ الله عليه وسلم: «وَهَلْ تَلِدُ الإِبِلَ إِلا النُّوقُ». ٣٠٤

238. Anas b. Mālik ﷺ narrated: "A man requested from the Messenger of Allāh ﷺ a means of transport. The Messenger of Allāh ﷺ said, 'I will give you the baby of a camel to ride.' The man said, 'O Messenger of Allāh! What shall I do with the baby camel?' He replied, '[Do you not know that] every camel is the baby of a camel?'"

Al-Bājūrī said,

> The response of the Prophet ﷺ to the reaction of the man teaches us that one should contemplate the words he hears and not rush to respond and reject a statement or offering until after it is understood well.

٢٣٩- حَدَّثَنَا إِسْحَاقُ بْنُ مَنْصُورٍ، قَالَ: حَدَّثَنَا عَبْدُ الرَّزَّاقِ، قَالَ: حَدَّثَنَا مَعْمَرٌ، عَنْ ثَابِتٍ، عَنْ أَنَسِ بْنِ مَالِكٍ، أَنَّ رَجُلا مِنْ أَهْلِ الْبَادِيَةِ كَانَ اسْمُهُ زَاهِرًا وَكَانَ يُهْدِي إِلَىٰ النَّبِيِّ صلىٰ الله عليه وسلم هَدِيَّةً مِنَ الْبَادِيَةِ، فَيُجَهِّزُهُ النَّبِيُّ صلىٰ الله عليه وسلم إِذَا أَرَادَ أَنْ يَخْرُجَ، فَقَالَ النَّبِيُّ صلىٰ الله عليه وسلم: إِنَّ زَاهِرًا بَادِيَتُنَا وَنَحْنُ حَاضِرُوهُ، وَكَانَ صلىٰ الله عليه وسلم يُحِبُّهُ وَكَانَ رَجُلا دَمِيمًا، فَأَتَاهُ النَّبِيُّ صلىٰ الله عليه وسلم يَوْمًا وَهُوَ يَبِيعُ مَتَاعَهُ وَاحْتَضَنَهُ مِنْ خَلْفِهِ وَهُوَ لا يُبْصِرُهُ،

304 *Sunan Abī Dāwūd* (4998) and *Sunan al-Tirmidhī* (1991)

فَقَالَ: مَنْ هَذَا؟ أَرْسِلْنِي فَالْتَفَتَ فَعَرَفَ النَّبِيُّ صلّى الله عليه وسلم فَجَعَلَ لا

يَأْلُو مَا أَلْصَقَ ظَهْرَهُ بِصَدْرِ النَّبِيِّ صلّى الله عليه وسلم حِينَ عَرَفَهُ، فَجَعَلَ النَّبِيُّ

صلّى الله عليه وسلم يَقُولُ: «مَنْ يَشْتَرِي هَذَا الْعَبْدَ؟» فَقَالَ: يَا رَسُولَ اللهِ، إِذًا وَاللهِ

تَجِدُنِي كَاسِدًا، فَقَالَ النَّبِيُّ صلّى الله عليه وسلم: «لَكِنْ عِنْدَ اللهِ لَسْتَ بِكَاسِدٍ»، أَوْ

قَالَ: «أَنْتَ عِنْدَ اللهِ غَالٍ». ٣٠٥

239. Anas b. Mālik ❀ narrated: "There was a resident of the desert whose name was Zāhir, whenever he visited the Messenger of Allāh ❀ he brought with him a present from the desert and when he intended to leave Madīnah, the Messenger of Allāh ❀ used to present him with provisions [of the city.] Once the Messenger of Allāh ❀ said, 'Zāhir is our desert, and we are his city.' The Messenger of Allāh ❀ had a strong bond with him though he had an unpleasant appearance. One day, the Messenger of Allāh ❀ approached him while he was selling his merchandise in the market and caught him in between the arms from the back in such a manner that he could not be seen. Zāhir ❀ said, 'Who is this? Let me go.' But when he turned and saw with the corner of his eye that it was the Messenger of Allāh ❀, he straightened his back and began pressing it to the chest of the Messenger of Allāh ❀. The Prophet ❀ then said, 'Who will purchase this slave?' Zāhir ❀ replied, 'O Messenger of Allāh, if you shall sell me, you will be selling something defective.' The Messenger of Allāh ❀ replied, 'No, you are not defective in the sight of Allāh, but very valuable.'"

ʿAbd al-Razzāq al-Badr said,

> Zāhir ❀ used to gift the Messenger of Allāh ❀ from the items that the Bedouins used to make such as dry milk, ghee etc. In return, the Messenger of Allāh ❀ used to reciprocate with a better gift when Zāhir wanted to leave Madīnah.

> The statement of the Prophet ❀ that, **"Zāhir is our desert and we are his city"** was to show that both sets of people complete each other as the people in the desert need the ones in the city and the people in the city need the ones living in the desert.

> This ḥadīth shows that joking is not limited to words but can also include action as can be seen from the act of the Messenger of Allāh

---

305 *Musnad Aḥmad* (12669)

ﷺ when he held Zāhir from the back. This is if it will bring about happiness and friendliness.

"Who will purchase this slave?": This is intended as a joke.

The reason Anas ؓ mentioned Zāhir's appearance was to clarify the reason why Zāhir described himself as defective merchandise that no one would want to buy.

The statement of the Prophet ﷺ to Zāhir shows the virtue of this companion and at the same time goes in line with the other ḥadīth, "Allāh does not look at your image and wealth, rather He looks at your deeds and hearts."[306] The virtue of a person depends on his piety and not his physical appearance.

٢٤٠ - حَدَّثَنَا عَبْدُ بْنُ حُمَيْدٍ، قَالَ: حَدَّثَنَا مُصْعَبُ بْنُ الْمِقْدَامِ، قَالَ: حَدَّثَنَا الْمُبَارِكُ بْنُ فَضَالَةَ، عَنِ الْحَسَنِ، قَالَ: أَتَتْ عَجُوزٌ إِلَىٰ النَّبِيِّ صلىٰ الله عليه وسلم، فَقَالَتْ: يَا رَسُولَ اللهِ، ادْعُ اللهَ أَنْ يُدْخِلَنِي الْجَنَّةَ، فَقَالَ: «يَا أُمَّ فُلانٍ، إِنَّ الْجَنَّةَ لا تَدْخُلُهَا عَجُوزٌ»، قَالَ: فَوَلَّتْ تَبْكِي، فَقَالَ: «أَخْبِرُوهَا أَنَّهَا لا تَدْخُلُهَا وَهِيَ عَجُوزٌ، إِنَّ اللهَ تَعَالَىٰ يَقُولُ: ﴿إِنَّا أَنْشَأْنَاهُنَّ إِنْشَاءً ﴿٣٥﴾ فَجَعَلْنَاهُنَّ أَبْكَارًا ﴿٣٦﴾ عُرُبًا أَتْرَابًا﴾».[٣٠٧]

240. Al-Ḥasan al-Basrī narrated: "An old woman came to the Messenger of Allāh ﷺ and said, 'O Messenger of Allāh! Ask Allāh to grant me entrance into Paradise.' Allāh's Messenger ﷺ replied, 'O mother of so and so! No old women will enter Paradise.' The woman started crying and began to leave. Allāh's Messenger ﷺ said, 'Say to the woman that she will not enter Paradise in a state of old age. Allāh ﷻ says: {Lo! We have created them a [new] creation and made them virgins, lovers, equal in age.}[308]'"

Al-Bājūrī said,

> The statement of the Prophet ﷺ was intended to teach the woman in a humorous manner that old women will be created anew and their age when they enter Paradise will be thirty or thirty three as stated in the ḥadīth reported by Mu'ādh b. Jabal ؓ and documented in the

306 *Ṣaḥiḥ Muslim* (4657)
307 *Ma'ālim al-Tanzīl* (1203)
308 Qur'ān: 35-37

Musnad of al-Imām Aḥmad.

باب ما جاء في صفة كلام رسول الله صلى الله عليه وسلم في الشعر

[37] On the Description of Allāh's Messenger's ﷺ Recitation of Poetry

ʿAbd al-Razzāq al-Badr said,

> Poetry takes the same ruling as any other speech: that which is good is allowed and can be recited, but that which is otherwise, it is not allowed to recite it or listen to it. The Prophet ﷺ said that some poetry contains wisdom. This shows that not all poetry is good; hence you find poetry that encourages sins, innovation and superstition, and some that encourages guidance and promotes the truth.

Al-Bājūrī said,

> There are nine ḥadīths in this chapter.

٢٤١- حَدَّثَنَا عَلِيُّ بْنُ حُجْرٍ، قَالَ: حَدَّثَنَا شَرِيكٌ، عَنِ الْمِقْدَامِ بْنِ شُرَيْحٍ، عَنْ أَبِيهِ، عَنْ عَائِشَةَ، قَالَتْ: قِيلَ لَهَا: هَلْ كَانَ النَّبِيُّ صلى الله عليه وسلم يَتَمَثَّلُ بِشَيْءٍ مِنَ الشِّعْرِ؟ قَالَتْ: «كَانَ يَتَمَثَّلُ بِشِعْرِ ابْنِ رَوَاحَةَ، وَيَتَمَثَّلُ بِقَوْلِهِ: يَأْتِيكَ بِالأَخْبَارِ مَنْ لَمْ تُزَوِّدِ»[٣٠٩].

241. ʿĀʾishah ﵂ was asked: "Did the Prophet ﷺ quote from poetry that which he used as a proverb?" She replied: "He recited a line of poetry of Ibn Rawāḥah [but without following its structure and rhyme.] He recited this couplet of his, 'News is brought to you by a person whom you have not compensated.'"

Ibn Ḥajar al-Haytamī said,

> It was narrated that the most disliked of speech to him ﷺ was poetry but he would quote some proverbs taken from poetry on occasion. Such as when he recited a line of poetry of the brother of Qays b. Ṭurfah whilst changing the order of the words i.e. he did not follow

309 *Sunan al-Tirmidhī* (2848)

the order of words in the line so he said, "News is brought to you by a person whom you have not compensated." Abū Bakr ؓ said, "O Messenger of Allāh! The couplet is not as you have recited!" The Messenger of Allāh ﷺ replied, "I am not a poet." Meaning that he only intended to mention the message of the words and not to recite the poem.

'Abdullāh b. Rawāḥah ؓ was one of the poets who defended the Prophet ﷺ but the most active influential poets who defended him were Ka'b b. Mālik and Ḥassān b. Thābit ؓ.

٢٤٢- حَدَّثَنَا مُحَمَّدُ بْنُ بَشَّارٍ، قَالَ: حَدَّثَنَا عَبْدُ الرَّحْمَنِ بْنُ مَهْدِيٍّ، قَالَ: حَدَّثَنَا سُفْيَانُ الثَّوْرِيُّ، عَنْ عَبْدِ الْمَلِكِ بْنِ عُمَيْرٍ، قَالَ: حَدَّثَنَا أَبُو سَلَمَةَ، عَنْ أَبِي هُرَيْرَةَ قَالَ: قَالَ رَسُولُ اللهِ صلى الله عليه وسلم: «إِنَّ أَصْدَقَ كَلِمَةٍ قَالَهَا الشَّاعِرُ كَلِمَةُ لَبِيدٍ: أَلا كُلُّ شَيْءٍ مَا خَلا اللهَ بَاطِلٌ»، وَكَادَ أُمَيَّةُ بْنُ أَبِي الصَّلْتِ أَنْ يُسْلِمَ»٣١٠.

242. Abū Hurayrah ؓ narrated: "The Messenger of Allāh ﷺ said, 'The most truthful statement said by a poet is that of Labīd, 'Indeed, be aware, everything besides Allāh is false.' Umayyah b. Abī al-Ṣalt was close to accepting Islām.'"

Al-Bājūrī said,

Labīd b. Rabī'ah al-'Āmirī was one of the renowned poets, he embraced Islām and did not recite any poetry from that point on as he said, "The Qur'ān suffices me."

The meaning of the line is that everything else besides Allāh is doomed to perish.

'Alī al-Qārī said,

The reason he ﷺ described these words as being the most truthful statement a poet has ever said was because the statement conforms to the *āyah*: {**Everything will be destroyed except His Face**}³¹¹ and this is the core of monotheism.

Umayyah b. Abī al-Ṣalt was a poet whose poems conformed to the

---

310 *Ṣaḥīḥ al-Bukhārī* (6147) and *Ṣaḥīḥ Muslim* (3841)
311 Qur'ān: 28:88

tenets of Islām and he believed in the Resurrection and was a wor-
shipper but he did not embrace Islām, though he died after the emer-
gence of Islām.

٢٤٣ - حَدَّثَنَا مُحَمَّدُ بْنُ الْمُثَنَّى، قَالَ: حَدَّثَنَا مُحَمَّدُ بْنُ جَعْفَرٍ، قَالَ: حَدَّثَنَا شُعْبَةُ،
عَنِ الْأَسْوَدِ بْنِ قَيْسٍ، عَنْ جُنْدُبِ بْنِ سُفْيَانَ الْبَجَلِيِّ، قَالَ: أَصَابَ حَجَرٌ أُصْبُعَ
رَسُولِ اللهِ صلى الله عليه وسلم فَدَمِيَتْ، فَقَالَ: «هَلْ أَنْتِ إِلا أُصْبُعٌ دَمِيتِ وَفِي
سَبِيلِ اللهِ مَا لَقِيتِ»٣١٢.

243. Jundub b. Sufyān ⬥ narrated: "Once a rock fell upon the toe of
the Messenger of Allāh ⬥ and caused it to bleed. Thereupon, he recited this couplet, 'You are but a toe that has bled. This is not fruitless,
for reward has been obtained in the path of Allāh.'"

ʿAbd al-Razzāq al-Badr said,

> The bleeding was caused by the toe of the Messenger of Allāh ⬥ hit-
> ting a stone while he was walking. This ḥadīth is evidence that the
> Muslim is rewarded for every difficulty and test he goes through if he
> shows patience and seeks the reward of Allāh.

٢٤٤ - حَدَّثَنَا ابْنُ أَبِي عُمَرَ، قَالَ: حَدَّثَنَا سُفْيَانُ بْنُ عُيَيْنَةَ، عَنِ الْأَسْوَدِ بْنِ قَيْسٍ،
عَنْ جُنْدُبِ بْنِ عَبْدِ اللهِ الْبَجَلِيِّ، نَحْوَهُ.٣١٣

244. The same is reported through another route.

٢٤٥ - حَدَّثَنَا مُحَمَّدُ بْنُ بَشَّارٍ، قَالَ: حَدَّثَنَا يَحْيَى بْنُ سَعِيدٍ، قَالَ: حَدَّثَنَا سُفْيَانُ
الثَّوْرِيُّ، قَالَ: أَنْبَأَنَا أَبُو إِسْحَاقَ، عَنِ الْبَرَاءِ بْنِ عَازِبٍ، قَالَ: قَالَ لَهُ رَجُلٌ: أَفَرَرْتُمْ
عَنْ رَسُولِ اللهِ صلى الله عليه وسلم يَا أَبَا عُمَارَةَ؟ فَقَالَ: لا، وَاللهِ مَا وَلَّى رَسُولُ اللهِ
صلى الله عليه وسلم، وَلَكِنْ وَلَّى سَرَعَانُ النَّاسِ تَلَقَّتْهُمْ هَوَازِنُ بِالنَّبْلِ، وَرَسُولُ
اللهِ صلى الله عليه وسلم عَلَى بَغْلَتِهِ، وَأَبُو سُفْيَانَ بْنُ الْحَارِثِ بْنِ عَبْدِ الْمُطَّلِبِ
آخِذٌ بِلِجَامِهَا، وَرَسُولُ اللهِ يَقُولُ: أَنَا النَّبِيُّ لا كَذِبْ أَنَا ابْنُ عَبْدِ الْمُطَّلِبْ»٣١٤.

---

312 Ṣaḥīḥ al-Bukhārī (2802) and Ṣaḥīḥ Muslim (1796)

313 See ḥadīth 243

314 Ṣaḥīḥ al-Bukhārī (2824) and Ṣaḥīḥ Muslim (1776)

245. A man asked al-Barā' b. 'Āzib ؓ: "O Abū 'Umārah! Did you all flee the battle [leaving] Allāh's Messenger [exposed]?" He replied, "No, not all of us. The Messenger of Allāh ﷺ did not turn away but [some] people in the army were hasty as the tribe of Hawāzin showered arrows at them. The Messenger of Allāh ﷺ was upon his mule and Abū Sufyān b. al-Ḥārith b. 'Abd al-Muṭṭalib ؓ was leading it by its reins. The Messenger of Allāh ﷺ was reciting the following couplet, 'Verily, I am the Prophet, and it is no lie. I am from the children [grandsons] of 'Abd al-Muṭṭalib.'"

Al-Bājūrī said,

> The answer of al-Barā' that not everyone fled the battle on that day required him to state that he ﷺ did not turn away to show that the major companions remained with him too. However, al-Barā' did not use the term "flee" when talking about the Prophet ﷺ to avoid attributing him with such an ugly defective characteristic. This is because it is forbidden to describe him with such a trait and it would nullify one's Islām to call him as such if he intends to degrade him, and if no degrading is intended then the person deserves severe punishment according al-Shāfi'ī and execution according to Mālik. This is because the term "turn away" can be used to show that the person is changing his tactics whereas the term "flee" necessitates cowardice and fear.

Ibn Ḥajar al-Haytamī said,

> The hasty ones refer to those in whose hearts Islām was not established deeply such as the new Muslims, those who embraced Islām after the conquest of Makkah and those like them.
>
> The battle referred to here is the battle of Ḥunayn, which happened after the conquest of Makkah when the tribes of Hawāzin and Thaqīf agreed to unite to fight the Muslims. In light of this, the Prophet ﷺ led a force of ten thousand persons from Madīnah and two thousand from those who embraced Islām after Makkah was conquered (who are the ones who the Prophet ﷺ freed on that day) and eighty disbelievers, including Ṣafwān b. Umayyah as he ﷺ borrowed one hundred shields from him to use in the battle.
>
> This battle was amongst the toughest that the Prophet ﷺ participated in because after some of the army fled, the Prophet ﷺ asked al-'Abbās

to call the Anṣār and those who gave the pledge under the tree, and his voice was heard from the distance of eight miles, upon which the army returned to the battle swiftly. Then, after they engaged in the fight and it became extremely heated, the Prophet ﷺ picked up some pebbles from the ground and threw them in the air and said, "May their faces be deformed!" Subsequently, the pebbles entered the eyes of the disbelievers and the Muhajirūn and Anṣār engaged in the battle fiercely, causing the disbelievers to flee the battle and be defeated.

Angels fought alongside the Muslims in the battle of Badr and the battle of Ḥunayn only, where in the latter they wore red turbans.

The reason why the Prophet ﷺ was riding his white mule although he had horses and riding a mule in battle is not suitable for engagement, was to show the Muslims that victory was guaranteed from Allāh so that their hearts would be filled with tranquillity and they would return to the battle. This action of the Prophet ﷺ shows his great courage and bravery.

The meaning of the couplet is that he is truthfully the Prophet ﷺ and thus he will not run away and will not be defeated, and it is no lie because a Prophet does not lie and so he was certain of victory.

٢٤٦- حَدَّثَنَا إِسْحَاقُ بْنُ مَنْصُورٍ، قَالَ: حَدَّثَنَا عَبْدُ الرَّزَّاقِ، قَالَ: حَدَّثَنَا جَعْفَرُ بْنُ سُلَيْمَانَ، قَالَ: حَدَّثَنَا ثَابِتٌ، عَنْ أَنَسٍ: أَنَّ النَّبِيَّ صلىٰ الله عليه وسلم دَخَلَ مَكَّةَ فِي عُمْرَةِ الْقَضَاءِ، وَابْنُ رَوَاحَةَ يَمْشِي بَيْنَ يَدَيْهِ، وَهُوَ يَقُولُ: خَلُّوا بَنِي الْكُفَّارِ عَنْ سَبِيلِهِ، الْيَوْمَ نَضْرِبُكُمْ عَلَىٰ تَنْزِيلِهِ، ضَرْبًا يُزِيلُ الْهَامَ عَنْ مَقِيلِهِ، وَيُذْهِلُ الْخَلِيلَ عَنْ خَلِيلِهِ، فَقَالَ لَهُ عُمَرُ: يَا ابْنَ رَوَاحَةَ، بَيْنَ يَدَيْ رَسُولِ اللهِ صلىٰ الله عليه وسلم، وَفِي حَرَمِ اللهِ تَقُولُ الشِّعْرَ! فَقَالَ صلىٰ الله عليه وسلم: «خَلِّ عَنْهُ يَا عُمَرُ، فَلَهِيَ أَسْرَعُ فِيهِمْ، مِنْ نَضْحِ النَّبْلِ»[٣١٥].

246. Anas b. Mālik ؓ narrated: "The Messenger of Allāh ﷺ entered Makkah for ʿUmrat al-Qaḍā' while ʿAbdullāh b. Rawāḥah ؓ was walking ahead of him reciting these couplets:

O non-believers clear his path and leave today, for today we shall

315 *Sunan al-Tirmidhī* (2847)

strike you upon his arrival,

Such a strike that we will separate the head from its body, and will cause a friend to forget his friend.

'Umar ﷺ said, 'O Ibn Rawāḥah! How do you recite poetry in the presence of the Messenger of Allāh ﷺ and in the Sacred Precinct of Allāh?' The Messenger of Allāh ﷺ said, 'O 'Umar, leave him! These couplets have more impact than showering arrows onto them.'"

'Abd al-Razzāq al-Badr said,

> The statement of the Messenger of Allāh ﷺ shows that poetry can scare the enemy and trouble them, strengthening the believers to avert the harm of the disbelievers and protect the religion of Allāh.

'Alī al-Qārī said,

> *'Umrat al-Qaḍā'* refers to the 'Umrah that the Messenger of Allāh ﷺ wanted to make up as he could not perform it due to the truce signed between the Muslims and disbelievers on the day of Ḥudaybiyah that made the Muslims agree not to perform 'Umrah on that day. This is evidence that if a person intended to perform 'Umrah or Ḥajj and after entering the state of *iḥrām* could not continue it, he should make it up.
>
> The couplets were said after the day of Ḥudaybiyah to celebrate this victory of the Muslims and to threaten the disbelievers of what will happen to them should they breach the truce.
>
> The reason behind the statement of 'Umar was because he thought poetry was condemned in all cases as he read it in the Qur'ān and heard it from the Messenger of Allāh ﷺ. The response of the Messenger of Allāh ﷺ was to show that not all poetry is condemned and admonished.

٢٤٧- حَدَّثَنَا عَلِيُّ بْنُ حُجْرٍ، قَالَ: حَدَّثَنَا شَرِيكٌ، عَنْ سِمَاكِ بْنِ حَرْبٍ، عَنْ جَابِرِ بْنِ سَمُرَةَ، قَالَ: «جَالَسْتُ النَّبِيَّ صلى الله عليه وسلم أَكْثَرَ مِنْ مِائَةِ مَرَّةٍ، وَكَانَ أَصْحَابُهُ يَتَنَاشَدُونَ الشِّعْرَ، وَيَتَذَاكَرُونَ أَشْيَاءَ مِنْ أَمْرِ الْجَاهِلِيَّةِ، وَهُوَ سَاكِتٌ

وَرُبَّمَا تَبَسَّمَ مَعَهُمْ»[٣١٦].

247. Jābir b. Samurah ﷺ narrated: "I sat with the Prophet ﷺ more than a hundred times. His companions ﷺ would recite poetry and relate certain stories from the days of Jāhiliyyah. The Prophet ﷺ listened to them silently and at times he smiled with them."

ʿAbd al-Razzāq al-Badr said,

> The reason he ﷺ mentioned the number of times was to assure the listener that the statement he was about to narrate was true.

Al-Bājūrī said,

> This ḥadīth teaches us that it is allowed to recite poetry and listen to it even if it includes mentioning the days before Islām and events, on the condition that it has nothing that is considered as disliked or unlawful in the religion.

٢٤٨- حَدَّثَنَا عَلِيُّ بْنُ حُجْرٍ، قَالَ: حَدَّثَنَا شَرِيكٌ، عَنْ عَبْدِ الْمَلِكِ بْنِ عُمَيْرٍ، عَنْ أَبِي سَلَمَةَ، عَنْ أَبِي هُرَيْرَةَ، عَنِ النَّبِيِّ صلى الله عليه وسلم، قَالَ: «أَشْعَرُ كَلِمَةٍ تَكَلَّمَتْ بِهَا الْعَرَبُ كَلِمَةُ لَبِيدٍ: أَلَا كُلُّ شَيْءٍ مَا خَلَا اللهَ بَاطِلُ»[٣١٧].

248. Abū Hurayrah ﷺ narrated: "The Messenger of Allāh ﷺ said: 'The best words that the Arabs ever recited is that of Labīd, 'Indeed, be aware, everything besides Allāh is false.'''"

٢٤٩- حَدَّثَنَا أَحْمَدُ بْنُ مَنِيعٍ، قَالَ: حَدَّثَنَا مَرْوَانُ بْنُ مُعَاوِيَةَ، عَنْ عَبْدِ اللهِ بْنِ عَبْدِ الرَّحْمَنِ الطَّائِفِيِّ، عَنْ عَمْرِو بْنِ الشَّرِيدِ، عَنْ أَبِيهِ، قَالَ: كُنْتُ رِدْفَ النَّبِيِّ صلى الله عليه وسلم فَأَنْشَدْتُهُ مِائَةَ قَافِيَةٍ مِنْ قَوْلِ أُمَيَّةَ بْنِ أَبِي الصَّلْتِ الثَّقَفِيِّ، كُلَّمَا أَنْشَدْتُهُ بَيْتًا قَالَ لِيَ النَّبِيُّ صلى الله عليه وسلم: «هِيهْ» حَتَّى أَنْشَدْتُهُ مِائَةً - يَعْنِي بَيْتًا -، فَقَالَ النَّبِيُّ صلى الله عليه وسلم: «إِنْ كَادَ لَيُسْلِمُ»[٣١٨].

249. ʿAmr b. Sharīd reported that his father ﷺ said: "I once rode behind the Prophet ﷺ. I recited for him one hundred couplets of

---

316 *Sunan al-Tirmidhī* (2850)
317 See ḥadīth 242
318 *Ṣaḥiḥ Muslim* (2255)

Umayyah b. Abī Salṭ al-Thaqafi's poetry. After reciting each couplet, he asked me to continue until I recited a hundred couplets. In the end, he said, 'He (Umayyah) came close to accepting Islām.'"

Ibn Ḥajar al-Haytamī said,

> The liking that the Prophet ﷺ took to the poetry of Umayyah and his request to hear more of it is evidence that poetry is recommended if it includes affirmation of Allāh's Oneness and fine gems and wisdoms.

Al-Bājūrī said,

> Umayyah is the famous poet Umayyah b. Abī al-Ṣalt al-Thaqafī, of whom it is said that Allāh ﷻ revealed an *āyah* regarding: **{And recite to them, [O Muḥammad], the news of him to whom we gave [knowledge of] Our signs, but he detached himself from them; so Satan pursued him, and he became of the deviators.}**[319] He read the Torah and the Bible before the emergence of Islām, and knew that a prophet would appear. However, he desired for himself to be that prophet and that was the reason why he rejected the Prophet ﷺ and caused him to envy him and disbelieve.
>
> The statement of the Prophet ﷺ was said after he heard the content of the poem as it included words indicating monotheism and good wisdom.

٢٥٠- حَدَّثَنَا إِسْمَاعِيلُ بْنُ مُوسَىٰ الْفَزَارِيُّ، وَعَلِيُّ بْنُ حُجْرٍ، وَالْمَعْنَىٰ وَاحِدٌ، قَالا: حَدَّثَنَا عَبْدُ الرَّحْمَنِ بْنُ أَبِي الزِّنَادِ، عَنْ هِشَامِ بْنِ عُرْوَةَ، عَنْ أَبِيهِ، عَنْ عَائِشَةَ، قَالَتْ: كَانَ رَسُولُ اللهِ صلىٰ الله عليه وسلم يَضَعُ لِحَسَّانَ بْنِ ثَابِتٍ مِنْبَرًا فِي الْمَسْجِدِ يَقُومُ عَلَيْهِ قَائِمًا يُفَاخِرُ عَنْ رَسُولِ اللهِ صلىٰ الله عليه وسلم - أَوْ قَالَ: يُنَافِحُ - عَنْ رَسُولِ اللهِ صلىٰ الله عليه وسلم وَيَقُولُ صلىٰ الله عليه وسلم: «إِنَّ اللهَ يُؤَيِّدُ حَسَّانَ بِرُوحِ الْقُدُسِ مَا يُنَافِحُ - أَوْ يُفَاخِرُ - عَنْ رَسُولِ اللهِ صلىٰ الله عليه وسلم»[٣٢٠].

250. 'Ā'ishah ؓ narrated: "The Messenger of Allāh ﷺ would place something high in the *Masjid* for Ḥassān b. Thābit ؓ, so that he

319 Qur'ān: 7:175

320 *Sunan Abī Dāwūd* (5015) and *Sunan al-Tirmidhī* (2846)

could stand upon it and recite poetry praising the Messenger of Allāh ﷺ (or it was said: defending the Messenger of Allāh ﷺ). He ﷺ would say, 'Verily, Allāh aids Ḥassān with the *Rūḥ al-Qudus* as long as he defends or praises the Messenger of Allāh ﷺ.'"

Al-Bājūrī said,

> *Rūḥ al-Qudus* (the Holy Spirit) refers to Jibrīl ﵇ and he was referred to as the "spirit" because the spirit (soul) brings life to the heart and because he is the one who delivers the revelations that provide eternal life to the Prophets.
>
> He (Ḥassān) defended the Prophet ﷺ in response to the false accusations and abuse of the disbelievers.

٢٥١- حَدَّثَنَا إِسْمَاعِيلُ بْنُ مُوسَىٰ، وَعَلِيُّ بْنُ حُجْرٍ، قَالا: حَدَّثَنَا ابْنُ أَبِي الزِّنَادِ، عَنْ أَبِيهِ، عَنْ عُرْوَةَ، عَنْ عَائِشَةَ، عَنِ النَّبِيِّ صلىٰ الله عليه وسلم مِثْلَهُ.

251. ʿĀ'ishah ﵂ reported a similar ḥadīth through a different route.

باب ما جاء في كلام رسول الله صلى الله عليه وسلم في السمر

[38] On Allāh's Messenger's ﷺ Speech in the Night

Al-Bājūrī said,

This chapter contains two ḥadīths.

٢٥٢- حَدَّثَنَا الْحَسَنُ بْنُ صَبَّاحِ الْبَزَّارُ، قَالَ: حَدَّثَنَا أَبُو النَّضْرِ، قَالَ: حَدَّثَنَا أَبُو عَقِيلٍ الثَّقَفِيُّ عَبْدُ اللهِ بْنُ عَقِيلٍ، عَنْ مُجَالِدٍ، عَنِ الشَّعْبِيِّ، عَنْ مَسْرُوقٍ، عَنْ عَائِشَةَ، قَالَتْ: حَدَّثَ رَسُولُ اللهِ صلى الله عليه وسلم ذَاتَ لَيْلَةٍ نِسَاءَهُ حَدِيثًا، فَقَالَتِ امْرَأَةٌ مِنْهُنَّ: كَأَنَّ الْحَدِيثَ حَدِيثُ خُرَافَةَ، فَقَالَ: «أَتَدْرُونَ مَا خُرَافَةُ؟ إِنَّ خُرَافَةَ كَانَ رَجُلًا مِنْ عُذْرَةَ، أَسَرَتْهُ الْجِنُّ فِي الْجَاهِلِيَّةِ فَمَكَثَ فِيهِمْ دَهْرًا، ثُمَّ رَدُّوهُ إِلَى الْإِنْسِ، فَكَانَ يُحَدِّثُ النَّاسَ بِمَا رَأَى فِيهِمْ مِنَ الْأَعَاجِيبِ، فَقَالَ النَّاسُ: حَدِيثُ خُرَافَةَ»٣٢١.

252. 'Ā'ishah ﴾ reported: "One night, the Messenger of Allāh ﷺ related an [astonishing] story to his wives. One of his wives commented, 'This story is as astonishing as the stories of Khurāfah.' The Messenger of Allāh ﷺ said, 'Do you know the original story of Khurāfah? He was a man from the tribe of 'Udhrah, whom the Jinn kidnapped. They kept him for a long time, and then they returned him to the people. He began to relate the wonders and strange things that he saw during his stay with them. Thenceforth, the people began to call every story that was incredible or too much for the mind to handle, a story of Khurāfah.'"

'Abd al-Razzāq al-Badr said,

Khurāfah is the name of a man who was kidnapped by the Jinn during the pre-Islamic era and after some time they brought him back to the people. He used to relate strange stories about matters that people

---

321 *Musnad Aḥmad* (25244)

had never heard of or saw in their lifetimes, which made them feel astonished. From that time, it became a proverb to describe any unbelievable story as being a story of Khurāfah.

Al-Bājūrī said,

> The purpose of the Prophet ﷺ entertaining his wives at night was to make them happy and show them kindness. As for the ḥadīths concerning disallowing talking after praying '*Ishā*, they refer to the talk that has no benefit in it.

٢٥٣ - حَدَّثَنَا عَلِيُّ بْنُ حُجْرٍ، قَالَ: حَدَّثَنَا عِيسَىٰ بْنُ يُونُسَ، عَنْ هِشَامِ بْنِ عُرْوَةَ، عَنْ أَخِيهِ عَبْدِ اللهِ بْنِ عُرْوَةَ، عَنْ عُرْوَةَ، عَنْ عَائِشَةَ، قَالَتْ: جَلَسَتْ إِحْدَىٰ عَشْرَةَ امْرَأَةً فَتَعَاهَدْنَ وَتَعَاقَدْنَ أَنْ لَا يَكْتُمْنَ مِنْ أَخْبَارِ أَزْوَاجِهِنَّ شَيْئًا:

فَقَالَتِ الْأُولَىٰ: زَوْجِي لَحْمُ جَمَلٍ غَثٍّ، عَلَىٰ رَأْسِ جَبَلٍ وَعْرٍ، لَا سَهْلٌ فَيُرْتَقَىٰ، وَلَا سَمِينٌ فَيُنْتَقَلُ.

قَالَتِ الثَّانِيَةُ : زَوْجِي لَا أَبُثُّ خَبَرَهُ، إِنِّي أَخَافُ أَنْ لَا أَذَرَهُ، إِنْ أَذْكُرْهُ أَذْكُرْ عُجَرَهُ وَبُجَرَهُ.

قَالَتِ الثَّالِثَةُ: زَوْجِي الْعَشَنَّقُ، إِنْ أَنْطِقْ أُطَلَّقْ، وَإِنْ أَسْكُتْ أُعَلَّقْ.

قَالَتِ الرَّابِعَةُ: زَوْجِي كَلَيْلِ تِهَامَةَ، لَا حَرٌّ وَلَا قُرٌّ، وَلَا مَخَافَةَ وَلَا سَآمَةَ.

قَالَتِ الْخَامِسَةُ: زَوْجِي إِنْ دَخَلَ فَهِدَ، وَإِنْ خَرَجَ أَسِدَ، وَلَا يَسْأَلُ عَمَّا عَهِدَ.

قَالَتِ السَّادِسَةُ: زَوْجِي إِنْ أَكَلَ لَفَّ، وَإِنْ شَرِبَ اشْتَفَّ، وَإِنِ اضْطَجَعَ الْتَفَّ، وَلَا يُولِجُ الْكَفَّ لِيَعْلَمَ الْبَثَّ.

قَالَتِ السَّابِعَةُ: زَوْجِي عَيَايَاءُ - أَوْ غَيَايَاءُ - طَبَاقَاءُ، كُلُّ دَاءٍ لَهُ دَاءٌ، شَجَّكِ أَوْ فَلَّكِ، أَوْ جَمَعَ كُلًا لَكِ.

قَالَتِ الثَّامِنَةُ: زَوْجِي الْمَسُّ مَسُّ أَرْنَبٍ، وَالرِّيحُ رِيحُ زَرْنَبٍ.

قَالَتِ التَّاسِعَةُ: زَوْجِي رَفِيعُ الْعِمَادِ، طَوِيلُ النِّجَادِ، عَظِيمُ الرَّمَادِ، قَرِيبُ الْبَيْتِ مِنَ النَّادِ.

قَالَتِ الْعَاشِرَةُ: زَوْجِي مَالِكٌ وَمَا مَالِكٌ! مَالِكٌ خَيْرٌ مِنْ ذَلِكِ، لَهُ إِبِلٌ كَثِيرَاتُ الْمَبَارِكِ، قَلِيلاتُ الْمَسَارِحِ، إِذَا سَمِعْنَ صَوْتَ الْمِزْهَرِ، أَيْقَنَّ أَنَّهُنَّ هَوَالِكُ.

قَالَتِ الْحَادِيَةَ عَشْرَةَ: زَوْجِي أَبُو زَرْعٍ وَمَا أَبُو زَرْعٍ؟ أَنَاسَ مِنْ حُلِيٍّ أُذُنَيَّ، وَمَلأَ مِنْ شَحْمٍ عَضُدَيَّ، وَبَجَّحَنِي، فَبَجِحَتْ إِلَيَّ نَفْسِي، وَجَدَنِي فِي أَهْلِ غُنَيْمَةٍ بِشِقٍّ، فَجَعَلَنِي فِي أَهْلِ صَهِيلٍ، وَأَطِيطٍ، وَدَائِسٍ، وَمُنَقٍّ، فَعِنْدَهُ أَقُولُ: فَلا أُقَبَّحُ، وَأَرْقُدُ فَأَتَصَبَّحُ، وَأَشْرَبُ فَأَتَقَمَّحُ.

أُمُّ أَبِي زَرْعٍ فَمَا أُمُّ أَبِي زَرْعٍ؟! عُكُومُهَا رَدَاحٌ، وَبَيْتُهَا فَسَاحٌ.

ابْنُ أَبِي زَرْعٍ، فَمَا ابْنُ أَبِي زَرْعٍ؟! مَضْجَعُهُ كَمَسَلِّ شَطْبَةٍ، وَتُشْبِعُهُ ذِرَاعُ الْجَفْرَةِ.

بِنْتُ أَبِي زَرْعٍ، فَمَا بِنْتُ أَبِي زَرْعٍ؟! طَوْعُ أَبِيهَا وَطَوْعُ أُمِّهَا، مِلْءُ كِسَائِهَا، وَغَيْظُ جَارَتِهَا.

جَارِيَةُ أَبِي زَرْعٍ، فَمَا جَارِيَةُ أَبِي زَرْعٍ؟! لا تَبُثُّ حَدِيثَنَا تَبْثِيثًا، وَلا تُنَقِّثُ مِيرَتَنَا تَنْقِيثًا، وَلا تَمْلأُ بَيْتَنَا تَعْشِيشًا.

قَالَتْ: خَرَجَ أَبُو زَرْعٍ وَالأَوْطَابُ تُمْخَضُ، فَلَقِيَ امْرَأَةً مَعَهَا وَلَدَانِ لَهَا كَالْفَهْدَيْنِ، يَلْعَبَانِ مِنْ تَحْتِ خَصْرِهَا بِرُمَّانَتَيْنِ، فَطَلَّقَنِي وَنَكَحَهَا، فَنَكَحْتُ بَعْدَهُ رَجُلا سَرِيًّا، رَكِبَ شَرِيًّا، وَأَخَذَ خَطِّيًّا، وَأَرَاحَ عَلَيَّ نَعَمًا ثَرِيًّا، وَأَعْطَانِي مِنْ كُلِّ رَائِحَةٍ زَوْجًا، وَقَالَ: كُلِي أُمَّ زَرْعٍ، وَمِيرِي أَهْلَكِ، فَلَوْ جَمَعْتُ كُلَّ شَيْءٍ أَعْطَانِيهِ، مَا بَلَغَ أَصْغَرَ آنِيَةِ أَبِي زَرْعٍ.

قَالَتْ عَائِشَةُ: فَقَالَ لِي رَسُولُ اللهِ صلىٰ الله عليه وسلم: «كُنْتُ لَكِ كَأَبِي زَرْعٍ لأُمِّ زَرْعٍ»[٣٢٢].

322 *Ṣaḥiḥ al-Bukhārī* (5189) and *Ṣaḥiḥ Muslim* (2448)

253. 'Ā'ishah ﵂ reported:

[One day] there sat together eleven women making an explicit promise amongst themselves that they would conceal nothing about their spouses.

The first one said, "My husband is like the meat of a lean, weak camel which is kept on the top of a mountain which is neither easy to climb, nor is the meat fat, so that one might put up with the trouble of fetching it."

The second one said, "I shall not relate my husband's news, for I fear that I may not be able to finish his story, for if I describe him, I will mention all of his defects and bad traits."

The third one said, "My husband is a lanky man [who is useless due to being thick-headed and ill-mannered]; if I describe him [and he hears of that] he will divorce me, and if I keep quiet, he will neither divorce me nor treat me as a wife."

The fourth one said, "My husband is a moderate person like the night of Tihāma which is neither hot nor cold. I am neither afraid of him, nor am I discontented with him."

The fifth one said, "My husband, when entering [the house] is a leopard, and when he is outside he is a lion. He does not ask about the state of his home."

The sixth one said, "If my husband eats. he eats too much [leaving the dishes empty], and if he drinks he leaves nothing, and if he sleeps he sleeps alone [away from me] covered in garments and he does not stretch his hands to avoid touching my body as he may see my grief."

The seventh one said, "My husband is an impotent wrong-doer, weak and foolish. All the defects are present in him. He may injure your head, your body or may do both."

The eighth one said, "My husband is soft to the touch like a rabbit and smells like a *zarnab* (a kind of good smelling grass)."

The ninth one said, "My husband is a tall generous man wearing a long strap for carrying his sword. His ashes are abundant and his house is near to the people who can easily consult him."

The tenth one said, "My husband is Mālik, and what is Mālik? Mālik is greater than whatever I can say about him. Most of his camels are kept at home [ready to be slaughtered for the guests] and only a few are taken to the pastures. When the camels hear the sound of the lute (or the tambourine) they realise that they are going to be slaughtered for the guests."

The eleventh one said, "My husband is Abū Zarʿ and what is Abū Zarʿ (i.e. what should I say about him)? He has given me many ornaments and my ears are heavily loaded with them and my arms have become fat. And he has pleased me, and I have become so happy that I feel proud of myself. He found me with my family who were mere owners of a few sheep and living in poverty, and brought me to a respected family having horses, camels, threshing cows and purifying grain. Whatever I say, he does not rebuke or insult me. When I sleep, I sleep till late in the morning, and when I drink water (or milk), I drink to my fill.

The mother of Abū Zarʿ, what could one say in praise of the mother of Abū Zarʿ? Her saddle bags were always full of provision and her house was spacious.

As for the son of Abū Zarʿ, what could one say about the son of Abū Zarʿ? His bed is as narrow as an unsheathed sword and an arm of a lamb [of four months] satisfies his hunger.

As for the daughter of Abū Zarʿ, what could one say about the daughter of Abū Zarʿ? She is obedient to her father and to her mother. She has a fat, well-built body and that arouses the jealousy of her husband's other wife.

As for the slave girl of Abū Zarʿ, what could one say about the slave girl of Abū Zarʿ? She does not disclose our secrets but keeps them, and does not waste our provisions and does not leave the rubbish scattered everywhere in our house."

The eleventh woman added, "One day it so happened that Abū Zarʿ went out at the time when the milk was being milked from the animals, and he saw a woman who had two sons like two leopards playing under her waist with two pomegranate [like lumps]. [On seeing her] he divorced me and married her.

Thereafter I married a noble man who used to ride a fast tireless horse and keep a spear in his hand. He gave me many things, and also a pair of every kind of livestock and said, 'Eat (of this), O Umm Zarʿ, and give provision to your relatives.'" She added, "Yet, all those things which my second husband gave me could not fill the smallest utensil of Abū Zarʿ."

'Ā'ishah then said: "Allāh's Messenger ﷺ said to me, 'I am to you as Abū Zarʿ was to Umm Zarʿ.'"

'Abd al-Razzāq al-Badr said,

> The author listed this ḥadīth to show how the Prophet ﷺ used to interact with his wives in a manner that brought joy to their hearts and how he used to give pleasant remarks and comments.
>
> This is a famous ḥadīth that some scholars dedicated books to due to the many gems and benefits it possesses. From the scholars who covered this ḥadīth in one book is al-Qāḍī 'Iyāḍ in his book "*Bughyatu al-Rā'id lima Taḍamanahu Ḥadīth Umm Zarʿ min al-Fawā'id*" and from the scholars who explained this ḥadīth in depth is al-Ḥāfiẓ Ibn Ḥajar in his book "*Fatḥ al-Bārī*".

Al-Bājūrī said,

> **"I am to you as Abū Zarʿ was to Umm Zarʿ.":** I.e. in terms kindness and giving, but not in terms of the separation [i.e. via divorce].
>
> To summarise: 'Ā'ishah mentioned some unnamed women, and some of these women mentioned the defects of their husbands who were not known, not through identification nor name. Such a case is not deemed to be back-biting, [in addition to the fact that] they were people from the pre-Islamic era of ignorance.

باب في نوم رسول الله صلى الله عليه وسلم

[39] On Allāh's Messenger's ﷺ Sleeping

ʿAbd al-Razzāq al-Badr said,

> Sleeping is one of the great signs of Allāh ﷻ that indicates Allāh's Oneness, Perfect Power and Arrangement of this Universe. It is a mercy from Allāh ﷻ to His slaves and one of His favours. Allāh ﷻ said: **{And of His signs are your sleep by night and day and your seeking of His bounty. Indeed in that are signs for a people who listen.}**[323] **{And out of His mercy He made for you the night and the day that you may rest therein and [by day] seek from His bounty and [that] perhaps you will be grateful.}**[324]

Ibn Ḥajar al-Haytamī said,

> Know that he ﷺ used to sleep at the beginning of the night, wake up in the second half of the night and then cleanse his teeth with a *siwāk*, perform ablution and pray until a sixth of the night remained. Then, he would sleep or talk with his wives until *Fajr*. He did not oversleep nor did he deny himself from his required amount. He ﷺ would sleep with a light stomach and on his right side, remembering Allāh until he fell into the state of sleep. Sometimes he would sleep on bedding stuffed with palm-fibre, sometimes on a leather mat, sometimes on a straw mat and sometimes on the ground.

Al-Bājūrī said,

> As sleeping follows one's speaking during the night, it was appropriate to place this chapter after the preceding one.
>
> This chapter contains six ḥadīths.

٢٥٤- حَدَّثَنَا مُحَمَّدُ بْنُ الْمُثَنَّى، قَالَ: حَدَّثَنَا عَبْدُ الرَّحْمَنِ بْنُ مَهْدِيٍّ، قَالَ: حَدَّثَنَا

323 Qurʾān: 30:23
324 Qurʾān: 28:73

إِسْرَائِيلُ، عَنْ أَبِي إِسْحَاقَ، عَنْ عَبْدِ اللهِ بْنِ يَزِيدَ، عَنِ الْبَرَاءِ بْنِ عَازِبٍ، أَنَّ النَّبِيَّ
صلى الله عليه وسلم كَانَ إِذَا أَخَذَ مَضْجَعَهُ وَضَعَ كَفَّهُ الْيُمْنَى تَحْتَ خَدِّهِ الْأَيْمَنِ،
وَقَالَ: «رَبِّ قِنِي عَذَابَكَ يَوْمَ تَبْعَثُ عِبَادَكَ»٣٢٥.

254. Al-Barā' b. al-'Āzib ؓ narrated: "When the Prophet ﷺ used to lie
down [to sleep], he would put his right hand under his right cheek,
and recite, 'O Allāh, save me from Your Punishment on the Day of
Judgment.'"

'Abd al-Razzāq al-Badr said,

This ḥadīth provides us with three etiquettes related to sleep:

1.   Lie down on the right side.

2.   Put the right hand under the right cheek.

3.   Supplicate: "*O Allāh, save me from Your Punishment on the Day
      of Resurrection.*"

Al-Bājūrī said,

The Prophet ﷺ recited this supplication, despite his high rank and
infallibility, to show humility before Allāh and to give Him His due
right as the Lord of mankind. He ﷺ recited such so that his nation
would follow his example. [Reciting this *du'ā*] ensures that the words
of remembrance of Allāh are the last words uttered before sleeping.
Furthermore, the words of this specific *du'ā* are said to seek protection
from one's shortcomings that necessitate punishment as it is possible
that the individual may never wake up from his sleep. The mention of
the Day of Resurrection indicates that death is the twin of sleep and
waking up is similar to the state of resurrection. This is why he ﷺ used
to say after waking up, "*All praise be to Allāh Who restored life into us
after He took our souls, and to Him we shall be resurrected,*" as shall be
mentioned later in the book.

٢٥٥- حَدَّثَنَا مُحَمَّدُ بْنُ الْمُثَنَّى، قَالَ: حَدَّثَنَا عَبْدُ الرَّحْمَنِ، قَالَ: حَدَّثَنَا إِسْرَائِيلُ،
عَنْ أَبِي إِسْحَاقَ، عَنْ أَبِي عُبَيْدَةَ عَنْ عَبْدِ اللهِ، مِثْلَهُ وَقَالَ: «يَوْمَ تَجْمَعُ عِبَادَكَ»٣٢٦.

---

325 *Musnad Aḥmad* (18672)
326 *Musnad Aḥmad* (3664)

255. ʿAbdullāh b. Masʿūd ﷺ narrated the same but with the end of the supplication as: "On the Day where You will gather your slaves."

٢٥٦- حَدَّثَنَا مَحْمُودُ بْنُ غَيْلانَ، قَالَ: حَدَّثَنَا عَبْدُ الرَّزَّاقِ، قَالَ: حَدَّثَنَا سُفْيَانُ، عَنْ عَبْدِ الْمَلِكِ بْنِ عُمَيْرٍ، عَنْ رِبْعِيِّ بْنِ حِرَاشٍ، عَنْ حُذَيْفَةَ، قَالَ: كَانَ النَّبِيُّ صلى الله عليه وسلم إِذَا أَوَىٰ إِلَىٰ فِرَاشِهِ، قَالَ: «اللَّهُمَّ بِاسْمِكَ أَمُوتُ وَأَحْيَا»، وَإِذَا اسْتَيْقَظَ قَالَ: «الْحَمْدُ لِلَّهِ الَّذِي أَحْيَانَا بَعْدَمَا أَمَاتَنَا وَإِلَيْهِ النُّشُورُ»[٣٢٧].

256. Ḥudhayfah ﷺ narrated: "When the Prophet ﷺ used to lie down on his bed, he would say, 'O Allāh! On [the remembrance of] Your Name, I die and I live.' Then upon waking he would say, 'All praise be to Allāh Who restored life into us after He took our souls, and to Him we shall be resurrected.'"

Ibn Ḥajar al-Haytamī said,

> **"I die and I live":** The reason sleeping is resembled to death is because a person loses control over all their senses just like it is the case in death. Also, a life can be described as such when it is spent in good deeds and obedience; otherwise the disobedient spends his life as a dead person.
>
> Praising Allāh for life is because this is from the most important blessings as it distinguishes the human from the non-human and whereby one comes to learn about Allāh and His worship.
>
> The last part of the supplication recited after waking up is to remind us that just as we awake to life at the cessation of sleep, there will be resurrection after death and then people will be judged.
>
> The wisdom behind reciting these supplications is so the last deed of the day consists of the remembrance of Allāh and the first deed a statement of monotheism and *taqwa*. This reminds the person that it is important to be conscious of Allāh and His Grandeur throughout the day and not to utter anything unless it is good.

٢٥٧- حَدَّثَنَا قُتَيْبَةُ بْنُ سَعِيدٍ، قَالَ: حَدَّثَنَا الْمُفَضَّلُ بْنُ فَضَالَةَ، عَنْ عُقَيْلٍ، أُرَاهُ

327 *Ṣaḥīḥ al-Bukhārī* (6312)

عَنِ الزُّهْرِيِّ، عَنْ عُرْوَةَ، عَنْ عَائِشَةَ قَالَتْ: «كَانَ رَسُولُ اللهِ صلى الله عليه وسلم إِذَا أَوَىٰ إِلَىٰ فِرَاشِهِ كُلَّ لَيْلَةٍ جَمَعَ كَفَّيْهِ فَنَفَثَ فِيهِمَا، وَقَرَأَ فِيهِمَا ﴿قُلْ هُوَ اللَّهُ أَحَدٌ﴾ وَ﴿قُلْ أَعُوذُ بِرَبِّ الْفَلَقِ﴾ وَ﴿قُلْ أَعُوذُ بِرَبِّ النَّاسِ﴾، ثُمَّ مَسَحَ بِهِمَا مَا اسْتَطَاعَ مِنْ جَسَدِهِ، يَبْدَأُ بِهِمَا رَأْسَهُ وَوَجْهَهُ، وَمَا أَقْبَلَ مِنْ جَسَدِهِ، يَصْنَعُ ذَلِكَ ثَلَاثَ مَرَّاتٍ»[٣٢٨].

257. ʿĀʾishah ؓ narrated: "Every night before the Messenger of Allāh ﷺ slept upon his bed he would join his hands, lightly blow into them and recite the last three sūrahs of the Qurʾān (i.e. Sūrah al-Ikhlāṣ, Sūrah al-Falaq, and Sūrah al-Nās). He would then wipe his hands over whatever parts of his body he could. He began with the head and face, and then the front part of his body. He did so thrice."

ʿAbd al-Razzāq al-Badr said,

> The regular practice of this indicates the keenness of the Prophet ﷺ to do so, to the extent that he ordered ʿĀʾishah ؓ to do so on his behalf during his sickness whereof he died.
>
> The Prophet ﷺ passed his hands over wherever he could reach to attain the blessings of the *ayāt* as this protects the person from the devil and other harmful things.
>
> It is important that a person understands and contemplates the meanings of these verses by reading the *tafsīr* of Ibn Kathīr or the *tafsīr* of al-Saʿdī, for example. This is because the person who recites them while understanding their meaning is not like the one who recites them without this knowledge.

Al-Bājūrī said,

> **"He did so thrice":** I.e. all of the aforementioned: gathering the hands, blowing in them, reciting and wiping. Doing so thrice is the complete Sunnah, while the foundational act is attained by doing it once (as is the case in other acts).

٢٥٨- حَدَّثَنَا مُحَمَّدُ بْنُ بَشَّارٍ، حَدَّثَنَا عَبْدُ الرَّحْمَنِ بْنُ مَهْدِيٍّ، حَدَّثَنَا سُفْيَانُ، عَنْ سَلَمَةَ بْنِ كُهَيْلٍ، عَنْ كُرَيْبٍ، عَنِ ابْنِ عَبَّاسٍ: أَنَّ رَسُولَ اللهِ صلى الله عليه

328 *Ṣaḥīḥ al-Bukhārī* (5017)

وسلم نَامَ حَتَّىٰ نَفَخَ، وَكَانَ إِذَا نَامَ نَفَخَ، فَأَتَاهُ بِلَالٌ فَآذَنَهُ بِالصَّلَاةِ، فَقَامَ وَصَلَّىٰ وَلَمْ يَتَوَضَّأْ، وَفِي الْحَدِيثِ قِصَّةٌ[٣٢٩].

258. ʿAbdullāh b. ʿAbbās ؓ narrated: "Once the Messenger of Allāh ﷺ slept and began to blow. It was the nature of the Messenger of Allāh ﷺ that he blew when he slept. Bilāl ؓ came and gave the call for the prayer. The Messenger of Allāh ﷺ awakened and offered the prayer without performing the ablution." This ḥadīth has a detailed story behind it.

Al-Bājūrī said,

> Blowing is a sign of deep sleep and knowing that it was the nature of the Messenger of Allāh ﷺ, we know that blowing while sleeping is not something that is dispraised.
>
> The Messenger of Allāh ﷺ did not perform ablution though he entered a state of deep sleep. This is an exclusive quality of his due to his heart always remaining awake (i.e. conscious) as he stated in the ḥadīth, "We Prophets, the eyes close in sleep whilst the hearts remain awake."[330] Therefore this is a special trait he holds amongst his nation but it is shared quality amongst the Prophets.
>
> The detailed story of this ḥadīth will be mentioned in the fifth report within the chapter detailing his worship.

٢٥٩ - حَدَّثَنَا إِسْحَاقُ بْنُ مَنْصُورٍ، قَالَ: حَدَّثَنَا عَفَّانُ، قَالَ: حَدَّثَنَا حَمَّادُ بْنُ سَلَمَةَ، عَنْ ثَابِتٍ، عَنْ أَنَسِ بْنِ مَالِكٍ، أَنَّ رَسُولَ اللهِ صلىٰ الله عليه وسلم كَانَ إِذَا أَوَىٰ إِلَىٰ فِرَاشِهِ، قَالَ: «الْحَمْدُ لِلَّهِ الَّذِي أَطْعَمَنَا وَسَقَانَا وَكَفَانَا وَآوَانَا، فَكَمْ مِمَّنْ لا كَافِيَ لَهُ وَلا مُؤْوِيَ»[٣٣١].

259. Anas b. Mālik ؓ narrated: "When the Messenger of Allāh ﷺ would lie down on his bed, he would say, 'All praise is for Allāh, Who fed us and gave us drink, and Who is sufficient for us, and has sheltered us, for how many have none to suffice them or shelter them!'"

ʿAlī al-Qārī said,

---

329 *Ṣaḥiḥ al-Bukhārī* (138)
330 *Musnad Aḥmad* (24171)
331 *Ṣaḥiḥ Muslim* (2715)

> The Prophet ﷺ praised Allāh for providing food and drink before he slept because without these three, one's life cannot be sustained, and because sleeping occurs after one eats and drinks (i.e. it is difficult to sleep when one is hungry and thus easier to sleep when one has eaten and drunk).
>
> Al-Muẓhir describes Allāh's sufficiency and shelter as meaning that He averts the harm of people and facilitates for one shelter. So all praise be to Allāh for making us from amongst the protected for there are many people who Allāh does not protect against the harm of evil people and they are left to fend for themselves against the evil, and thus the vile people overcome them. Likewise, there are many people bereft of shelter and so He left them to be harmed by the elements.

Al-Nawawī said (as quoted by 'Alī al-Qārī),

> The meaning of the last part of the supplication means that many people have no one to have mercy on them, to be compassionate with them and many have no shelter to stay in.

٢٦٠- حَدَّثَنَا الْحُسَيْنُ بْنُ مُحَمَّدٍ الْجُرَيْرِيُّ، قَالَ: حَدَّثَنَا سُلَيْمَانُ بْنُ حَرْبٍ، قَالَ: حَدَّثَنَا حَمَّادُ بْنُ سَلَمَةَ، عَنْ حُمَيْدٍ، عَنْ بَكْرِ بْنِ عَبْدِ اللهِ الْمُزَنِيِّ، عَنْ عَبْدِ اللهِ بْنِ رَبَاحٍ، عَنْ أَبِي قَتَادَةَ: «أَنَّ النَّبِيَّ صلىٰ الله عليه وسلم كَانَ إِذَا عَرَّسَ بِلَيْلٍ اضْطَجَعَ عَلَىٰ شِقِّهِ الأَيْمَنِ، وَإِذَا عَرَّسَ قُبَيْلَ الصُّبْحِ نَصَبَ ذِرَاعَهُ، وَوَضَعَ رَأْسَهُ عَلَىٰ كَفِّهِ»[٣٣٢].

260. Abū Qatādah ؓ narrated: "When the Prophet ﷺ was journeying and stopped for rest and there was enough time in the night, he slept on his right side. However, if he stopped close to the time of the morning, he would lift his right arm, put his head upon his palm and sleep."

'Abd al-Razzāq al-Badr said,

> This shows the concern he had for performing the prayer of *Fajr* as sleeping in that position would make it difficult for the person to enter the state of deep sleep.

332 *Ṣaḥīḥ Muslim* (2715)

Al-Bājūrī said,

> If the prayer time is close, it is essential that if one requires sleep, he does so in a manner wherein he could quickly wake. This is so as to attain the virtues of the early part of the prayer time and to emulate the Prophet ﷺ.

ʿAlī al-Qārī said,

> It could be that the wisdom of lying in this fashion was to teach his nation in the case where sleep could overpower the individual and cause one to miss the morning prayer's time.

باب ما جاء في عبادة النبي صلى الله عليه وسلم

[40] On the Prophet's ﷺ Worship

ʿAbd al-Razzāq al-Badr said,

> Though the title of the chapter is general, the ḥadīths included in this chapter relate to the night prayer.

Al-Bājūrī said,

> This chapter was placed after the chapter of sleep because his ﷺ sleep was to aid his acts of worship and obedience.
>
> There are fourteen ḥadīths in this chapter.

٢٦١- حَدَّثَنَا قُتَيْبَةُ بْنُ سَعِيدٍ، وَبِشْرُ بْنُ مُعَاذٍ، قَالا: حَدَّثَنَا أَبُو عَوَانَةَ، عَنْ زِيَادِ بْنِ عِلاقَةَ، عَنِ الْمُغِيرَةِ بْنِ شُعْبَةَ قَالَ: صَلَّىٰ رَسُولُ اللهِ صلى الله عليه وسلم حَتَّىٰ انْتَفَخَتْ قَدَمَاهُ، فَقِيلَ لَهُ: أَتَتَكَلَّفُ هَذَا وَقَدْ غَفَرَ اللهُ لَكَ مَا تَقَدَّمَ مِنْ ذَنْبِكَ وَمَا تَأَخَّرَ؟ قَالَ: «أَفَلا أَكُونُ عَبْدًا شَكُورًا»[٣٣٣].

261. Al-Mughīrah b. Shuʿbah ؓ narrated: "The Messenger of Allāh ﷺ performed prayers of such length that his feet would become swollen. It was said to him, 'You exert yourself to such a degree yet Allāh has forgiven your past and future sins?' The Messenger of Allāh ﷺ said, 'Should I not be a grateful servant?'"

Ibn Ḥajar al-Haytamī said,

> This response of the Messenger of Allāh ﷺ could be expanded in other words as: "Praying at night is to show appreciation and thankfulness for Allāh's forgiveness; hence how could it be possible for me to stop this!"
>
> If a person fears becoming bored due to excessive worship, then he should not force himself to do it. If otherwise, one should push him-

333 *Ṣaḥiḥ al-Bukhārī* (1130) and *Ṣaḥiḥ Muslim* (2819)

self to worship as much as possible.

Ibn 'Allān al-Shafi'ī said,

> The companion thought that the reason the Messenger of Allāh ﷺ underwent such difficulties in worship was because he feared the punishment of his sins or hoped for the reward [of the prayers]. But the Messenger of Allāh ﷺ clarified that the reason was nobler and higher: to show appreciation, gratitude and acknowledgement of one's servitude.[334]

'Alī al-Qārī said,

> The Messenger of Allāh ﷺ is infallible and the sins referred to in this ḥadīth are not understood at face value because the good deeds of the pious are viewed as sins for the ones in higher ranks (meaning: the inability of a person to praise, worship, thank Allāh and give Him His due right is looked upon as a shortcoming that equals sins for those who are at a higher state).[335]

٢٦٢ - حَدَّثَنَا أَبُو عَمَّارٍ الْحُسَيْنُ بْنُ حُرَيْثٍ، قَالَ: حَدَّثَنَا الْفَضْلُ بْنُ مُوسَىٰ، عَنْ مُحَمَّدِ بْنِ عَمْرٍو، عَنْ أَبِي سَلَمَةَ، عَنْ أَبِي هُرَيْرَةَ، قَالَ: كَانَ رَسُولُ اللهِ صَلَّىٰ الله عليه وسلم يُصَلِّي حَتَّىٰ تَرِمَ قَدَمَاهُ، قَالَ: فَقِيلَ لَهُ: أَتَفْعَلُ هَذَا وَقَدْ جَاءَكَ أَنَّ اللهَ قَدْ غَفَرَ لَكَ مَا تَقَدَّمَ مِنْ ذَنْبِكَ وَمَا تَأَخَّرَ؟ قَالَ: «أَفَلَا أَكُونُ عَبْدًا شَكُورًا».[336]

262. Abū Hurayrah ؓ narrated: "The Messenger of Allāh ﷺ used to pray at night until his feet became swollen. It was said to him, 'You do this although Allāh has forgiven your past and future sins?' The Messenger of Allāh ﷺ replied, 'Should I not be a grateful servant?'"

٢٦٣ - حَدَّثَنَا عِيسَىٰ بْنُ عُثْمَانَ بْنِ عِيسَىٰ بْنِ عَبْدِ الرَّحْمَنِ الرَّمْلِيُّ، قَالَ: حَدَّثَنَا عَمِّي يَحْيَىٰ بْنُ عِيسَىٰ الرَّمْلِيُّ، عَنِ الْأَعْمَشِ، عَنْ أَبِي صَالِحٍ، عَنْ أَبِي هُرَيْرَةَ، قَالَ: كَانَ رَسُولُ اللهِ صَلَّىٰ الله عليه وسلم يَقُومُ يُصَلِّي حَتَّىٰ تَنْتَفِخَ قَدَمَاهُ فَيُقَالُ لَهُ: يَا رَسُولَ اللهِ، تَفْعَلُ هَذَا وَقَدْ غَفَرَ اللهُ لَكَ مَا تَقَدَّمَ مِنْ ذَنْبِكَ وَمَا تَأَخَّرَ؟ قَالَ: «أَفَلَا

---

334 *Dalīl al-Fāliḥīn li Ṭuruq Riyāḍ al-Ṣāliḥīn*
335 *Sharḥ Musnad Abī Ḥanīfah*
336 See ḥadīth 261

أَكُونُ عَبْدًا شَكُورًا»[٣٣٧].

263. Abū Hurayrah ﷺ narrated: "The Messenger of Allāh ﷺ performed such lengthy prayers that his feet became swollen. It was said to him, 'You do this although Allāh has forgiven your past and future sins?' The Messenger of Allāh ﷺ said, 'Should I not be a grateful servant?'"

Al-Bājūrī said,

> The author mentioned this ḥadīth with three chains of narration so as to emphasise and strengthen it.

٢٦٤- حَدَّثَنَا مُحَمَّدُ بْنُ بَشَّارٍ، قَالَ: حَدَّثَنَا مُحَمَّدُ بْنُ جَعْفَرٍ، قَالَ: حَدَّثَنَا شُعْبَةُ، عَنْ أَبِي إِسْحَاقَ، عَنِ الأَسْوَدِ بْنِ يَزِيدَ، قَالَ: سَأَلْتُ عَائِشَةَ، عَنْ صَلاةِ رَسُولِ اللهِ صلى الله عليه وسلم بِاللَّيْلِ؟ فَقَالَتْ: «كَانَ يَنَامُ أَوَّلَ اللَّيْلِ ثُمَّ يَقُومُ، فَإِذَا كَانَ مِنَ السَّحَرِ أَوْتَرَ، ثُمَّ أَتَى فِرَاشَهُ، فَإِذَا كَانَ لَهُ حَاجَةٌ أَلَمَّ بِأَهْلِهِ، فَإِذَا سَمِعَ الأَذَانَ وَثَبَ، فَإِنْ كَانَ جُنُبًا أَفَاضَ عَلَيْهِ مِنَ الْمَاءِ، وَإِلا تَوَضَّأَ وَخَرَجَ إِلَى الصَّلاةِ»[٣٣٨].

264. Al-Aswad b. Yazīd enquired from ʿĀʾishah ﷺ regarding the prayer of the Messenger of Allāh ﷺ at night. She replied: "The Messenger of Allāh ﷺ used to sleep for the first half portion of the night. He would then wake up and pray at night but when the time of the last sixth of the night entered, he would pray the *witr* and then go to his bed. If he had a desire, he would approach his wife. And, when he would hear the call for prayer, he would get up actively. If he was in a state of major ritual impurity, he performed *ghusl*. If not, he performed ablution and then went to pray."

ʿAbd al-Razzāq al-Badr said,

> The beginning of the night starts from sunset but the time intended in this ḥadīth refers to after the prayer of *ʿIshā* because the Prophet ﷺ disliked sleeping before *ʿIshā* and disliked talking after it, so he would sleep right after praying *ʿIshā*.
>
> He ﷺ used to wake up after the middle of the night as explained in the authentic ḥadīth found in *Ṣaḥīḥ al-Bukharī* (1131) and *Ṣaḥīḥ Mus-*

337 See ḥadīth 261
338 *Ṣaḥīḥ al-Bukhārī* (1146) and *Ṣaḥīḥ Muslim* (739)

lim (1159).

Al-Bājūrī said,

> The intention of the question regarding his prayer at night was to ask about the time that he used to pray the night prayers and *witr*.

> It is possible that he ﷺ performed ablution because his ablution was nullified for a reason other than sleeping or that he renewed his ablution. This ḥadīth teaches us to care for the acts of worship, not to be lazy in sleep and to perform the worship whilst being active and energetic.

٢٦٥- حَدَّثَنَا قُتَيْبَةُ بْنُ سَعِيدٍ، عَنْ مَالِكِ بْنِ أَنَسٍ (ح) وَحَدَّثَنَا إِسْحَاقُ بْنُ مُوسَىٰ الْأَنْصَارِيُّ، قَالَ: حَدَّثَنَا مَعْنٌ، عَنْ مَالِكٍ، عَنْ مَخْرَمَةَ بْنِ سُلَيْمَانَ، عَنْ كُرَيْبٍ، عَنِ ابْنِ عَبَّاسٍ، «أَنَّهُ أَخْبَرَهُ، أَنَّهُ بَاتَ عِنْدَ مَيْمُونَةَ وَهِيَ خَالَتُهُ، قَالَ: فَاضْطَجَعْتُ فِي عَرْضِ الْوِسَادَةِ، وَاضْطَجَعَ رَسُولُ اللَّهِ صلى الله عليه وسلم فِي طُولِهَا، فَنَامَ رَسُولُ اللَّهِ صلى الله عليه وسلم حَتَّىٰ إِذَا انْتَصَفَ اللَّيْلُ أَوْ قَبْلَهُ بِقَلِيلٍ أَوْ بَعْدَهُ بِقَلِيلٍ، فَاسْتَيْقَظَ رَسُولُ اللَّهِ صلى الله عليه وسلم فَجَعَلَ يَمْسَحُ النَّوْمَ عَنْ وَجْهِهِ، ثُمَّ قَرَأَ الْعَشْرَ الْآيَاتِ الْخَوَاتِيمَ مِنْ سُورَةِ آلِ عِمْرَانَ، ثُمَّ قَامَ إِلَىٰ شَنٍّ مُعَلَّقٍ فَتَوَضَّأَ مِنْهَا، فَأَحْسَنَ الْوُضُوءَ، ثُمَّ قَامَ يُصَلِّي، قَالَ عَبْدُ اللَّهِ بْنُ عَبَّاسٍ: فَقُمْتُ إِلَىٰ جَنْبِهِ فَوَضَعَ رَسُولُ اللَّهِ صلى الله عليه وسلم يَدَهُ الْيُمْنَىٰ عَلَىٰ رَأْسِي ثُمَّ أَخَذَ بِأُذُنِي الْيُمْنَىٰ فَفَتَلَهَا فَصَلَّىٰ رَكْعَتَيْنِ ثُمَّ رَكْعَتَيْنِ، ثُمَّ رَكْعَتَيْنِ، ثُمَّ رَكْعَتَيْنِ، ثُمَّ رَكْعَتَيْنِ - قَالَ مَعْنٌ: سِتَّ مَرَّاتٍ - ثُمَّ أَوْتَرَ، ثُمَّ اضْطَجَعَ، حَتَّىٰ جَاءَهُ الْمُؤَذِّنُ فَقَامَ فَصَلَّىٰ رَكْعَتَيْنِ خَفِيفَتَيْنِ، ثُمَّ خَرَجَ فَصَلَّى الصُّبْحَ».[339]

265. 'Abdullāh b. 'Abbās ؓ reported that he once slept at the house of his maternal aunt Maymūnah ؓ. He said: "I slept on the width of the cushion and the Messenger of Allāh ﷺ slept on the length of the cushion and he slept until the middle of the night, or a little before or after that. He ﷺ then awoke, began wiping off the signs of sleep from his face and then recited the last ten *ayāt* of Sūrah Āl 'Imrān.

---

339 See ḥadīth 258

He then stood and used the water he found in a water skin that was hanging to perform his ablution. He performed his ablution thoroughly and commenced the prayer."

ʿAbdullāh b. ʿAbbās ⬥ added: "I stood next to him [on his left]. The Messenger of Allāh ﷺ put his right hand on my head, took a hold of my ear and twisted it. He performed two units, then two units, then two units, then two units, then two units, then two units. [Maʿn (a narrator of this ḥadīth from Ibn ʿAbbās) says that it was six times (a total of twelve units)].

The Messenger of Allāh ﷺ then performed the *witr* and lied down [for a short period] until the *muʾadhdhin* came to inform him of the *Fajr* prayer. He then prayed two short units and headed for the *masjid*."

Al-Bājūrī said,

> The reason Ibn ʿAbbās ⬥ slept at the house of his maternal aunt was because his father, al-ʿAbbās (the uncle of the Prophet) wanted to know the worship of the Prophet ﷺ at night so he could follow his guidance.
>
> **"And then recited the last ten *ayāt* of Sūrah Āl ʿImrān":** When one awakes, it is recommended for him to recite a portion of the Qurʾān as it causes laziness to dissipate and invigorates the individual for worship. Furthermore, these specific verses are recommended upon waking.
>
> **"Took a hold of my ear and twisted it":** It is said that a teacher twisting the ear of his student causes him to understand better. Al-Rabīʿ said, "[I was walking with] al-Shāfiʿī while he was riding and I leaned against his saddle so he twisted my ear. I viewed this action gravely until I came across Ibn ʿAbbās's report that he ﷺ did the same to him. Upon this, I understood that the *imām* did not do anything unless it was based on a precedent."

The Prophet ﷺ normally slept upon a bed besides one of his wives and this was his habit. However, whenever he wanted to perform worship he would leave his wives and focus on his worship. This way he fulfilled the rights of his wives and did justice to the rights of his Lord.

Ibn Ḥajar al-Haytamī said,

> It can be extracted from this ḥadīth that it is recommended to recite the last ten *ayāt* of Sūrah Āl 'Imrān after waking up and that it is allowed to recite the Qur'ān in a state of minor ritual impurity.
>
> He ﷺ twisted the ear of Ibn 'Abbās ؓ either to notify him that he was not following the Sunnah when he stood on his left side, to keep him alert so that he could memorise the Sunnah or to remove his sleepiness.
>
> The habit of the Prophet ﷺ was to pray the *witr* at the end of the night but sometimes he prayed it at the mid-point and sometimes at the beginning. The variation most likely occurred due to the necessities of different situations, as it is possible that he prayed the *witr* at the beginning of the night due to sickness and at the middle of the night because he was travelling.
>
> Benefits derived from this ḥadīth include:
>
> 1. It is recommended in a congregation made of two that the person following the *imām* stands to his right side, and to move to the right side if he was standing on the left side. If he does not move to the correct side, it is recommended for the *imām* to move him to his right side.
> 2. It is recommended for the *imām* to physically instruct the person praying behind him to the Sunnah if he notices him not following it. This shows that a small amount of physical action in the prayer does not nullify the prayer, and it can be the Sunnah in some cases, as exemplified in this ḥadīth.
> 3. The congregation is valid with a young boy and he takes the same ruling as adults in congregation.
> 4. It is valid to pray a voluntary prayer in congregation.
> 5. It is recommended to pray the *witr* and voluntary prayers, two units by two units.
> 6. It is recommended for the *mu'adhdhin* to notify the *imām* in person to come to the prayer.
> 7. It is recommended to make the Sunnah units of *Fajr* short.

٢٦٦ - حَدَّثَنَا أَبُو كُرَيْبٍ مُحَمَّدُ بْنُ الْعَلَاءِ، قَالَ: حَدَّثَنَا وَكِيعٌ، عَنْ شُعْبَةَ، عَنْ أَبِي جَمْرَةَ، عَنِ ابْنِ عَبَّاسٍ، قَالَ: «كَانَ النَّبِيُّ صلى الله عليه وسلم يُصَلِّي مِنَ اللَّيْلِ ثَلَاثَ عَشْرَةَ رَكْعَةً»٣٤٠.

266. ʿAbdullāh b. ʿAbbās ☙ **narrated: "The Prophet** ☙ **used to pray during the night thirteen units."**

ʿAbd al-Razzāq al-Badr said,

> There are other ḥadīths stating that he ☙ prayed eleven units and nine units. However, scholars understood these ḥadīths in the context that each refers to a different situation and incident.

Al-Bājūrī said,

> The thirteen units mentioned consist of two units as the Sunnah of *ʿIshā* or the Sunnah of ablution and eleven units as *witr*.

٢٦٧ - حَدَّثَنَا قُتَيْبَةُ بْنُ سَعِيدٍ، قَالَ: حَدَّثَنَا أَبُو عَوَانَةَ، عَنْ قَتَادَةَ، عَنْ زُرَارَةَ بْنِ أَوْفَى، عَنْ سَعْدِ بْنِ هِشَامٍ، عَنْ عَائِشَةَ: أَنَّ النَّبِيَّ صلى الله عليه وسلم كَانَ إِذَا لَمْ يُصَلِّ بِاللَّيْلِ مَنَعَهُ مِنْ ذَلِكَ النَّوْمُ، أَوْ غَلَبَتْهُ عَيْنَاهُ، صَلَّى مِنَ النَّهَارِ ثِنْتَيْ عَشْرَةَ رَكْعَةً٣٤١.

267. ʿĀʾishah ☙ **reported: "Whenever the Prophet** ☙ **could not pray the night prayers due to sleep or excessive fatigue; he would pray twelve units during the daytime."**

ʿAbd al-Razzāq al-Badr said,

> This shows that the Prophet ☙ did not pray *witr* (odd units) during the daytime. It teaches us that if a person misses his regular night prayers, it is prescribed for him to make them up during the day.

Al-Bājūrī said,

> The night prayers mentioned in the ḥadīth refer to the *tahajjud* and *witr*.
>
> The reason the Prophet ☙ did not pray at night, based on the wording

---

340 *Ṣaḥīḥ al-Bukhārī* (1138) and *Ṣaḥīḥ Muslim* (764)
341 *Ṣaḥīḥ Muslim* (746)

> of the ḥadīth, shows that the narrator was uncertain as he mentioned two possibilities, each of which gives a different meaning i.e. if the reason was that he slept, that means he made the choice to sleep though he could stay awake, but if the reason was that he was too fatigued, it means that he was in a state where he could not stay awake.

٢٦٨- حَدَّثَنَا مُحَمَّدُ بْنُ الْعَلاءِ، قَالَ: حَدَّثَنَا أَبُو أُسَامَةَ، عَنْ هِشَامٍ - يَعْنِي ابْنَ حَسَّانَ -، عَنْ مُحَمَّدِ بْنِ سِيرِينَ، عَنْ أَبِي هُرَيْرَةَ، عَنِ النَّبِيِّ صلى الله عليه وسلم قَالَ: «إِذَا قَامَ أَحَدُكُمْ مِنَ اللَّيْلِ فَلْيَفْتَتِحْ صَلاتَهُ بِرَكْعَتَيْنِ خَفِيفَتَيْنِ»[٣٤٢].

268. Abū Hurayrah ﷺ narrated: "The Prophet ﷺ said: 'When one awakes at night, let him begin [his night prayers] with two short units of prayer.'"

Al-Bājūrī said,

> These two units are recommended to be an introduction to the *witr* so that one can pray the *witr* actively while being fully awake. This is similar to how it is recommended to precede the obligatory prayer with the Sunnah prayer.

٢٦٩- حَدَّثَنَا قُتَيْبَةُ بْنُ سَعِيدٍ، عَنْ مَالِكِ بْنِ أَنَسٍ (ح) وَحَدَّثَنَا إِسْحَاقُ بْنُ مُوسَى، قَالَ: حَدَّثَنَا مَعْنٌ قَالَ: حَدَّثَنَا مَالِكٌ، عَنْ عَبْدِ اللهِ بْنِ أَبِي بَكْرٍ، عَنْ أَبِيهِ، أَنَّ عَبْدَ اللهِ بْنَ قَيْسِ بْنِ مَخْرَمَةَ، أَخْبَرَهُ عَنْ زَيْدِ بْنِ خَالِدٍ الْجُهَنِيِّ، أَنَّهُ قَالَ: «لأَرْمُقَنَّ صَلاةَ النَّبِيِّ صلى الله عليه وسلم، فَتَوَسَّدْتُ عَتَبَتَهُ، أَوْ فُسْطَاطَهُ فَصَلَّى رَسُولُ اللهِ صلى الله عليه وسلم رَكْعَتَيْنِ خَفِيفَتَيْنِ، ثُمَّ صَلَّى رَكْعَتَيْنِ طَوِيلَتَيْنِ، طَوِيلَتَيْنِ، طَوِيلَتَيْنِ، ثُمَّ صَلَّى رَكْعَتَيْنِ وَهُمَا دُونَ اللَّتَيْنِ قَبْلَهُمَا، ثُمَّ صَلَّى رَكْعَتَيْنِ وَهُمَا دُونَ اللَّتَيْنِ قَبْلَهُمَا، ثُمَّ صَلَّى رَكْعَتَيْنِ وَهُمَا دُونَ اللَّتَيْنِ قَبْلَهُمَا، ثُمَّ صَلَّى رَكْعَتَيْنِ وَهُمَا دُونَ اللَّتَيْنِ قَبْلَهُمَا، ثُمَّ أَوْتَرَ فَذَلِكَ ثَلاثَ عَشْرَةَ رَكْعَةً»[٣٤٣].

269. Zayd b. Khālid al-Juhanī ﷺ narrated: "I decided that I would closely observe how the Prophet ﷺ performed his prayers. Thus, I lied down on the threshold [of his house or his tent]. The Messenger of

---

342 *Ṣaḥiḥ Muslim* (768)
343 *Ṣaḥiḥ Muslim* (765)

Allāh ﷺ first prayed two short units, and then he prayed two long, long, long units. He then prayed two units shorter than the previous ones, and then prayed two more units shorter than the ones before. And again, he prayed two more units shorter than the previous ones. He again prayed two units shorter than the previous ones. He then prayed the *witr*. They amounted to thirteen units of prayer in total."

Al-Bājūrī said,

> The narrator doubted whether it was the threshold of his house or his tent, and it is most likely the latter because the Prophet ﷺ would be with his wives in his house and so it is inappropriate to say that Zayd stood there watching him inside in such circumstances. However, during his travels, he ﷺ would be in his tent and not with his wives so Zayd could remain on the threshold of his tent and watch.
>
> The reason Zayd repeated thrice that the first two units were long was to show how lengthy they were, as if they were equivalent in length to six long units. The reason why he ﷺ made these units very long was because a person is more active and possesses more energy at the beginning of the prayer as opposed to the end. This is why it is recommended to make the first unit of the prayer longer than the second one in obligatory prayers.
>
> The thirteen units mentioned include the introductory two units and the remaining eleven units are *witr* prayer.

٢٧٠ - حَدَّثَنَا إِسْحَاقُ بْنُ مُوسَىٰ، قَالَ: حَدَّثَنَا مَعْنٌ، قَالَ: حَدَّثَنَا مَالِكٌ، عَنْ سَعِيدِ بْنِ أَبِي سَعِيدٍ الْمَقْبُرِيِّ، عَنْ أَبِي سَلَمَةَ بْنِ عَبْدِ الرَّحْمَنِ، أَنَّهُ أَخْبَرَهُ أَنَّهُ سَأَلَ عَائِشَةَ، كَيْفَ كَانَتْ صَلاةُ رَسُولِ اللهِ صلىٰ الله عليه وسلم فِي رَمَضَانَ؟ فَقَالَتْ: مَا كَانَ رَسُولُ اللهِ صلىٰ الله عليه وسلم لِيَزِيدَ فِي رَمَضَانَ وَلا فِي غَيْرِهِ عَلَىٰ إِحْدَىٰ عَشْرَةَ رَكْعَةً، يُصَلِّي أَرْبَعًا لا تَسْأَلْ عَنْ حُسْنِهِنَّ وَطُولِهِنَّ، ثُمَّ يُصَلِّي أَرْبَعًا لا تَسْأَلْ عَنْ حُسْنِهِنَّ وَطُولِهِنَّ، ثُمَّ يُصَلِّي ثَلاثًا، قَالَتْ عَائِشَةُ: قُلْتُ: يَا رَسُولَ اللهِ، أَتَنَامُ قَبْلَ أَنْ تُوتِرَ؟ فَقَالَ: «يَا عَائِشَةُ، إِنَّ عَيْنَيَّ تَنَامَانِ وَلا يَنَامُ قَلْبِي»[٣٤٤].

270. Abū Salamah b. ʿAbd al-Raḥmān asked ʿĀʾishah ﷺ to describe

344 *Ṣaḥiḥ al-Bukhārī* (1147) and *Ṣaḥiḥ Muslim* (738)

for him the prayer of the Messenger of Allāh ﷺ during Ramaḍān so she said: "The Messenger of Allāh ﷺ did not pray more than eleven units, whether he prayed in the month of Ramaḍān or outside of it. He used to pray four units and it is too difficult to describe their length and earnestness. Then, in the same manner he prayed four more units. After that he prayed three units of prayer." 'Ā'ishah ﵂ said, "I asked him, 'O Messenger of Allāh. How come you sleep before praying the *witr*?' He replied, 'O 'Ā'ishah, my eyes sleep but my heart does not.'"

'Abd al-Razzāq al-Badr said,

> This ḥadīth does not contradict the other ḥadīths by stating that he ﷺ prayed eleven units of prayer. This is because 'Ā'ishah ﵂ did not count the two introductory units that he ﷺ prayed at the beginning as can be noted when she detailed how the units were divided four by four.

Al-Bājūrī said,

> Each set of four units were prayed two by two and not as the apparent meaning of the statement of 'Ā'ishah ﵂. This way, the ḥadīth conforms to the previous ḥadīth narrated by Zayd. The reason the four units were mentioned as a whole is because the two sets of two units were similar in length and performance.
>
> This ḥadīth shows that prolonging the standing in prayer is better than praying a higher quantity of short units. The ḥadīth about the closeness to our Lord in prostration[345] teaches us that supplications are more likely to be answered therein. The last three units were not described in the same manner as the preceding ones to show that they were short.
>
> The reason 'Ā'ishah ﵂ asked the question [regarding sleeping before *witr*] is because it was known that he ﷺ ordered some of his companions such as Abū Hurayrah ﵁ not to sleep before praying *witr* due to fearing that they may oversleep and miss it. The answer of the Prophet ﷺ came to show that the possibility to miss the *Fajr* is inapplicable in his case as his heart is awake. Thus, it is recommended for the one

345 "The closest a servant comes to his Lord is in *Sujūd*; therefore make excessive *du'ā*, for it is most likely to be answered." Collected in *Ṣaḥīḥ Muslim*.

who is certain that he will wake up before *Fajr* to postpone the *witr* and pray it after waking up, if otherwise he should pray it before.

٢٧١- حَدَّثَنَا إِسْحَاقُ بْنُ مُوسَىٰ، قَالَ: حَدَّثَنَا مَعْنٌ، قَالَ: حَدَّثَنَا مَالِكٌ، عَنِ ابْنِ شِهَابٍ، عَنْ عُرْوَةَ، عَنْ عَائِشَةَ: «أَنَّ رَسُولَ اللهِ صلىٰ الله عليه وسلم كَانَ يُصَلِّي مِنَ اللَّيْلِ إِحْدَىٰ عَشْرَةَ رَكْعَةً يُوتِرُ مِنْهَا بِوَاحِدَةٍ، فَإِذَا فَرَغَ مِنْهَا اضْطَجَعَ عَلَىٰ شِقِّهِ الأَيْمَنِ»٣٤٦.

271. ʿĀʾishah ؇ narrated: "The Messenger of Allāh ؈ used to pray eleven units at night, one of which was a unit of *witr*. After he finished, he would lie down on his right side."

ʿAbd al-Razzāq al-Badr said,

> Some scholars extracted a gem from this ḥadīth: The number of units that he ؈ prayed at night was exactly the same as the units performed for the daytime obligatory prayers, which are *Ẓuhr*, *ʿAṣr* and *Maghrib*.

Ibn Ḥajar al-Haytamī said,

> This is an explicit statement to show that the least number of units for *witr* is one, and that a prayer of one unit is valid.

٢٧٢- حَدَّثَنَا ابْنُ أَبِي عُمَرَ، قَالَ: حَدَّثَنَا مَعْنٌ، عَنْ مَالِكٍ، عَنِ ابْنِ شِهَابٍ، نَحْوَهُ (ح)، وَحَدَّثَنَا قُتَيْبَةُ، عَنْ مَالِكٍ، عَنِ ابْنِ شِهَابٍ، نَحْوَهُ.

272. Ibn Shihāb reported the same through two different routes.

٢٧٣- حَدَّثَنَا هَنَّادٌ، قَالَ: حَدَّثَنَا أَبُو الأَحْوَصِ، عَنِ الأَعْمَشِ، عَنْ إِبْرَاهِيمَ، عَنِ الأَسْوَدِ، عَنْ عَائِشَةَ، قَالَتْ: «كَانَ رَسُولُ اللهِ صلىٰ الله عليه وسلم يُصَلِّي مِنَ اللَّيْلِ تِسْعَ رَكَعَاتٍ»٣٤٧.

273. ʿĀʾishah ؇ narrated: "The Messenger of Allāh ؈ used to pray nine units during the night."

---

346 *Ṣaḥīḥ al-Bukhārī* (994) and *Ṣaḥīḥ Muslim* (736)
347 *Sunan Ibn Mājah* (1360) and *Sunan al-Tirmidhī* (443)

٢٧٤ - حَدَّثَنَا مَحْمُودُ بْنُ غَيْلَانَ، قَالَ: حَدَّثَنَا يَحْيَىٰ بْنُ آدَمَ، قَالَ: حَدَّثَنَا سُفْيَانُ
الثَّوْرِيُّ، عَنِ الأَعْمَشِ، نَحْوَهُ.

274. Al-Aʿmash reported the same through a different route.

٢٧٥ - حَدَّثَنَا مُحَمَّدُ بْنُ الْمُثَنَّىٰ، قَالَ: حَدَّثَنَا مُحَمَّدُ بْنُ جَعْفَرٍ، قَالَ: حَدَّثَنَا شُعْبَةُ،
عَنْ عَمْرِو بْنِ مُرَّةَ، عَنْ أَبِي حَمْزَةَ، رَجُلٍ مِنَ الأَنْصَارِ، عَنْ رَجُلٍ مِنْ بَنِي عَبْسٍ، عَنْ
حُذَيْفَةَ بْنِ الْيَمَانِ، «أَنَّهُ صَلَّىٰ مَعَ النَّبِيِّ صلى الله عليه وسلم مِنَ اللَّيْلِ، قَالَ: فَلَمَّا
دَخَلَ فِي الصَّلَاةِ، قَالَ: اللهُ أَكْبَرُ ذُو الْمَلَكُوتِ وَالْجَبَرُوتِ وَالْكِبْرِيَاءِ وَالْعَظَمَةِ،
قَالَ: ثُمَّ قَرَأَ الْبَقَرَةَ، ثُمَّ رَكَعَ رُكُوعَهُ نَحْوًا مِنْ قِيَامِهِ، وَكَانَ يَقُولُ: سُبْحَانَ رَبِّيَ
الْعَظِيمِ، سُبْحَانَ رَبِّيَ الْعَظِيمِ ثُمَّ رَفَعَ رَأْسَهُ فَكَانَ قِيَامُهُ نَحْوًا مِنْ رُكُوعِهِ، وَكَانَ
يَقُولُ: لِرَبِّيَ الْحَمْدُ، لِرَبِّيَ الْحَمْدُ ثُمَّ سَجَدَ فَكَانَ سُجُودُهُ نَحْوًا مِنْ قِيَامِهِ، وَكَانَ
يَقُولُ: سُبْحَانَ رَبِّيَ الأَعْلَىٰ، سُبْحَانَ رَبِّيَ الأَعْلَىٰ ثُمَّ رَفَعَ رَأْسَهُ، فَكَانَ مَا بَيْنَ
السَّجْدَتَيْنِ نَحْوًا مِنَ السُّجُودِ، وَكَانَ يَقُولُ: رَبِّ اغْفِرْ لِي، رَبِّ اغْفِرْ لِي حَتَّىٰ قَرَأَ
الْبَقَرَةَ وَآلَ عِمْرَانَ، وَالنِّسَاءَ، وَالْمَائِدَةَ، أَوِ الأَنْعَامَ» شُعْبَةُ الَّذِي شَكَّ فِي الْمَائِدَةِ
وَالأَنْعَامِ.٣٤٨

275. Ḥudhayfah b. al-Yamān ⬥ narrated: "I prayed with the Prophet ﷺ during the night. He commenced the prayer with the following statement, *'Allāhu Akbaru dhu' l-Malakūtī wa 'l-Jabarūtī wa 'l-Kibriyā wa 'l-ʿAẓamah.'* Then he recited Sūrah al-Baqarah (after al-Fātiḥah) and proceeded to bow. The length of the bowing was as long as the standing posture, during which he said repeatedly, *'Subḥāna rabbiya 'l-Aẓīm.'* Then, he raised his torso and the length of his standing was like that of his bowing, during which he said repeatedly, *'Li-Rabbiya 'l-Ḥamd.'* Then, he prostrated and the length of his prostration was similar to his standing, during which he said repeatedly, *'Subḥāna Rabbiya 'l-Alā.'* Then he raised himself from prostration. The length of the sitting posture was similar to the prostration, during which he repeatedly said, *'Rabbi 'ghfir lī.'* He prayed each unit in the same manner and in that prayer he recited al-Baqarah, Āl ʿImrān, al-Nisāʾ and [al-Māʾidah or al-Anʿām]."

348 *Sunan Abī Dāwūd* (874)

قَالَ أَبُو عِيسَىٰ: وَأَبُو حَمْزَةَ اسْمُهُ: طَلْحَةُ بْنُ يَزِيدَ، وَأَبُو جَمْرَةَ الضُّبَعِيُّ اسْمُهُ: نَصْرُ بْنُ عِمْرَانَ.

Abū ʿĪsā said: Abū Ḥamzah in the chain of narration is Ṭalḥah b. Yazīd. Abū Jamrah al-Ḍubaʿī is Naṣr b. ʿImrān.

Al-Bājūrī said,

> Regarding the meaning of the opening statement: *Dhu 'l-Malakūt* means the One with Dominion and Pride. *Dhu 'l-Jabarūtī* means the Subduer and Surmounter. *Dhul Kibriyā* means the One who transcends all defects and shortcomings while everything submits to Him. None are described with these two attributes except Allāh. *Dhu 'l-ʿAẓamah* means the One Who nothing can encompass. It is said that *Kibriyā* refers to the perfection of His essence while *ʿAẓamah* refers to the beauty of His Attributes.
>
> He recited al-Baqarah in the first unit, Āl ʿImrān in the second unit, al-Nisā' in the third unit and the narrator doubted whether it was al-Mā'idah or al-Anʿām that was recited in the fourth unit.

٢٧٦- حَدَّثَنَا أَبُو بَكْرٍ مُحَمَّدُ بْنُ نَافِعٍ الْبَصْرِيُّ، قَالَ: حَدَّثَنَا عَبْدُ الصَّمَدِ بْنُ عَبْدِ الْوَارِثِ، عَنْ إِسْمَاعِيلَ بْنِ مُسْلِمٍ الْعَبْدِيِّ، عَنْ أَبِي الْمُتَوَكِّلِ، عَنْ عَائِشَةَ، قَالَتْ: «قَامَ رَسُولُ اللهِ صلى الله عليه وسلم بِآيَةٍ مِنَ الْقُرْآنِ لَيْلَةً»[٣٤٩].

276. ʿĀ'ishah ﵂ narrated: "The Messenger of Allāh ﷺ stood in a [complete] night's prayer reciting one verse of the Qur'ān."

ʿAbd al-Razzāq al-Badr said,

> The verse mentioned is: **{If You should punish them - indeed they are Your servants; but if You forgive them - indeed it is You who is the Exalted in Might, the Wise.}**[350] As stated in the ḥadīth collected in the *Musnad* of al-Imām Aḥmad.[351]

Ibn al-Qayyim said,

> If people knew the benefits of reciting the Qur'ān with contempla-

349 *Sunan al-Tirmidhī* (448)
350 Qur'ān: 5:118
351 #21328

tion they would busy themselves with it and leave everything else. A person should recite the Qur'ān with contemplation and if he comes across a verse that touches his heart, repeat it one hundred times or even the whole night to attain its benefit. The recitation of a verse with contemplation and understanding is better than reciting the whole Qur'ān without understanding and contemplating it. It is certainly more beneficial to the heart and increases one's faith in it. Furthermore, it lets the person taste the sweetness of the Qur'ān. This was the habit of the *salaf* who used to repeat one verse until the time of *Fajr*.[352]

٢٧٧- حَدَّثَنَا مَحْمُودُ بْنُ غَيْلَانَ، قَالَ: حَدَّثَنَا سُلَيْمَانُ بْنُ حَرْبٍ، قَالَ: حَدَّثَنَا شُعْبَةُ، عَنِ الأَعْمَشِ، عَنْ أَبِي وَائِلٍ، عَنْ عَبْدِ اللهِ بْنِ مَسْعُودٍ، قَالَ: «صَلَّيْتُ لَيْلَةً مَعَ رَسُولِ اللهِ صلى الله عليه وسلم فَلَمْ يَزَلْ قَائِمًا حَتَّى هَمَمْتُ بِأَمْرِ سُوءٍ، قِيلَ لَهُ: وَمَا هَمَمْتَ بِهِ؟ قَالَ: هَمَمْتُ أَنْ أَقْعُدَ وَأَدَعَ النَّبِيَّ صلى الله عليه وسلم»[٣٥٣].

277. 'Abdullāh b. Mas'ūd ﷺ narrated: "Once at night I prayed in congregation with the Messenger of Allāh ﷺ wherein he stood for such a long time that I intended to do a bad deed." Someone asked: "What deed did you intend to do?" He replied: "I was about to sit down and leave the Prophet ﷺ standing alone."

'Abd al-Razzāq al-Badr said,

> This displays how long the night prayer of the Prophet ﷺ was.

٢٧٨- حَدَّثَنَا سُفْيَانُ بْنُ وَكِيعٍ، قَالَ: حَدَّثَنَا جَرِيرٌ، عَنِ الأَعْمَشِ، نَحْوَهُ.

278. A similar report is narrated through a different route from al-A'mash.

٢٧٩- حَدَّثَنَا إِسْحَاقُ بْنُ مُوسَى الأَنْصَارِيُّ، قَالَ: حَدَّثَنَا مَعْنٌ، قَالَ: حَدَّثَنَا مَالِكٌ، عَنْ أَبِي النَّضْرِ، عَنْ أَبِي سَلَمَةَ، عَنْ عَائِشَةَ: «أَنَّ النَّبِيَّ صلى الله عليه وسلم كَانَ يُصَلِّي جَالِسًا فَيَقْرَأُ وَهُوَ جَالِسٌ، فَإِذَا بَقِيَ مِنْ قِرَاءَتِهِ قَدْرُ مَا يَكُونُ ثَلَاثِينَ أَوْ أَرْبَعِينَ

---

352 *Miftāḥ Dār al-Sa'ādah* (1/187)

353 *Ṣaḥīḥ al-Bukhārī* (1135) and *Ṣaḥīḥ Muslim* (773)

آيَةً، قَامَ فَقَرَأَ وَهُوَ قَائِمٌ، ثُمَّ رَكَعَ وَسَجَدَ، ثُمَّ صَنَعَ فِي الرَّكْعَةِ الثَّانِيَةِ مِثْلَ ذَلِكَ»[٣٥٤].

279. ʿĀʾishah narrated: "The Prophet ﷺ prayed in a sitting posture until about thirty or forty verses were remaining. At this point he stood up and completed them standing. He then bowed and prostrated. He would subsequently do the same in the second unit."

Al-Bājūrī said,

> This was the case when he ﷺ became old in age, as ʿĀʾishah explicitly stated in the ḥadīth documented in *Ṣaḥīḥ al-Bukhārī* and *Ṣaḥīḥ Muslim*.
>
> It shows that it is allowed to pray while sitting and standing in voluntary prayers.

٢٨٠- حَدَّثَنَا أَحْمَدُ بْنُ مَنِيعٍ، قَالَ: حَدَّثَنَا هُشَيْمٌ، قَالَ: حَدَّثَنَا خَالِدٌ الْحَذَّاءُ، عَنْ عَبْدِ اللهِ بْنِ شَقِيقٍ، قَالَ: سَأَلْتُ عَائِشَةَ عَنْ صَلاةِ رَسُولِ اللهِ صلى الله عليه وسلم عَنْ تَطَوُّعِهِ، فَقَالَتْ: «كَانَ يُصَلِّي لَيْلا طَوِيلا قَائِمًا وَلَيْلا طَوِيلا قَاعِدًا، فَإِذَا قَرَأَ وَهُوَ قَائِمٌ رَكَعَ وَسَجَدَ وَهُوَ قَائِمٌ، وَإِذَا قَرَأَ وَهُوَ جَالِسٌ رَكَعَ وَسَجَدَ وَهُوَ جَالِسٌ»[٣٥٥].

280. ʿAbdullāh b. Shaqīq asked ʿĀʾishah about the voluntary prayer of the Messenger of Allāh ﷺ. She said: "He used to pray lengthy periods of the night whilst standing and lengthy periods of the night whilst sitting. If he prayed standing, he would bow and prostrate whilst standing, and if he prayed whilst sitting, he would bow and prostrate from the sitting posture."

ʿAbd al-Razzāq al-Badr said,

> The reward for praying while sitting down is half of praying while standing. However, this does not apply to the Prophet ﷺ as he himself stated in the ḥadīth documented in *Ṣaḥīḥ Muslim*: ʿAbdullāh b. ʿAmr reported, "It was narrated to me that the Messenger of Allāh ﷺ had said, 'The prayer observed by a person sitting is half of the prayer.' I came to him ﷺ and found him praying in a sitting position. I placed my hand on his head. He said, 'O ʿAbdullāh b. ʿAmr, what is the matter with you?' I replied, 'Messenger of Allāh, it has been narrated to

354 *Ṣaḥīḥ al-Bukhārī* (1119) and *Ṣaḥīḥ Muslim* (731)
355 *Ṣaḥīḥ Muslim* (730)

me that you said, 'The prayer of a man in a sitting position is half of the prayer,' and you are observing the prayer sitting.' He ﷺ said, 'Yes, it is so, but I am not like anyone amongst you.'"[356]

٢٨١ - حَدَّثَنَا إِسْحَاقُ بْنُ مُوسَىٰ الْأَنْصَارِيُّ، قَالَ: حَدَّثَنَا مَعْنٌ، قَالَ: حَدَّثَنَا مَالِكٌ، عَنِ ابْنِ شِهَابٍ، عَنِ السَّائِبِ بْنِ يَزِيدَ، عَنِ الْمُطَّلِبِ بْنِ أَبِي وَدَاعَةَ السَّهْمِيِّ، عَنْ حَفْصَةَ، زَوْجِ النَّبِيِّ صلىٰ الله عليه وسلم قَالَتْ: «كَانَ رَسُولُ اللهِ يُصَلِّي فِي سُبْحَتِهِ قَاعِدًا وَيَقْرَأُ بِالسُّورَةِ وَيُرَتِّلُهَا حَتَّىٰ تَكُونَ أَطْوَلَ مِنْ أَطْوَلَ مِنْهَا»[٣٥٧].

281. The Prophet's ﷺ wife, Ḥafṣah رضي الله عنها narrated: "The Messenger of Allāh ﷺ prayed voluntary prayers whilst sitting. He would recite with slow, distinct and clear intonation, such that the *sūrah* became longer than a *sūrah* that was actually lengthier."

ʿAbd al-Razzāq al-Badr said,

> He prayed most of the time whilst sitting towards the end of his life as he was sick and could not stand for long durations as he used to.
>
> The manner in which he ﷺ recited was to recite slowly, contemplating the verses. If there was a verse about punishment, he would take refuge in Allāh from it, and if a verse contained *tasbīḥ*, he would glorify Allāh, and if a verse contained a mercy, he would ask Allāh for His mercy. This would make a *sūrah* seem longer than other lengthier ones.

Al-Bājūrī said,

> It is recommended to recite with *tartīl* (a measured manner) during the prayer and to recite a *sūrah* over a single unit. It is better than reading the same amount from part of a *sūrah*, though this is also virtuous and not disliked at all.

٢٨٢ - حَدَّثَنَا الْحَسَنُ بْنُ مُحَمَّدٍ الزَّعْفَرَانِيُّ، قَالَ: حَدَّثَنَا الْحَجَّاجُ بْنُ مُحَمَّدٍ، عَنِ ابْنِ جُرَيْجٍ، قَالَ: أَخْبَرَنِي عُثْمَانُ بْنُ أَبِي سُلَيْمَانَ، أَنَّ أَبَا سَلَمَةَ بْنَ عَبْدِ الرَّحْمَنِ أَخْبَرَهُ أَنَّ عَائِشَةَ أَخْبَرَتْهُ «أَنَّ النَّبِيَّ صلىٰ الله عليه وسلم لَمْ يَمُتْ حَتَّىٰ كَانَ أَكْثَرُ

356 *Ṣaḥīḥ Muslim* (735)
357 *Ṣaḥīḥ Muslim* (733)

صَلَاتِهِ وَهُوَ جَالِسٌ».٣٥٨

282. ʿĀʾishah ⲅ reported: "The Prophet ⲅ, towards the end of his life, would perform most of his prayers whilst sitting."

ʿAbd al-Razzāq al-Badr said,

> This was close to the time of his death and due to the toll inflicted by age and his illness.

Ibn Ḥajar al-Haytamī said,

> This refers to the voluntary prayers.

Al-Bājūrī said,

> Evidence of this referring to the voluntary prayer is the report of Umm Salamah, "By the One who holds my soul in His hand, Allāh's Messenger did not die ⲅ until most of his prayer were performed whilst sitting, except for the [five] prescribed prayers."[359]

٢٨٣- حَدَّثَنَا أَحْمَدُ بْنُ مَنِيعٍ، قَالَ: حَدَّثَنَا إِسْمَاعِيلُ بْنُ إِبْرَاهِيمَ، قَالَ: حَدَّثَنَا أَيُّوبَ، عَنْ نَافِعٍ، عَنِ ابْنِ عُمَرَ، قَالَ: «صَلَّيْتُ مَعَ النَّبِيِّ صلى الله عليه وسلم رَكْعَتَيْنِ قَبْلَ الظُّهْرِ، وَرَكْعَتَيْنِ بَعْدَهَا، وَرَكْعَتَيْنِ بَعْدَ الْمَغْرِبِ فِي بَيْتِهِ، وَرَكْعَتَيْنِ بَعْدَ الْعِشَاءِ فِي بَيْتِهِ».٣٦٠

283. ʿAbdullāh b. ʿUmar ⲅ narrated: "I prayed with the Prophet ⲅ two units before and after *Ẓuhr*, two units after *Maghrib* in his house, and [also] two units after *ʿIshāʾ* in his house."

ʿAbd al-Razzāq al-Badr said,

> This ḥadīth talks about the regular Sunnah units associated with the obligatory prayers while the previous ḥadīth was regarding optional prayers.

Al-Bājūrī said,

> It is derived from this ḥadīth that the house is a better place for vol-

---

358 *Muṣannaf ʿAbd al-Razzāq* (3959)
359 *Sunan al-Nasāʾī* (1655), *Sunan Ibn Mājah* (1225) and *Musnad Aḥmad* (26599)
360 *Ṣaḥīḥ al-Bukhārī* (937) and *Ṣaḥīḥ Muslim* (729)

untary prayers [than the mosque] except for prayers wherein there is an exception found. This would be the case even if it was performed within the midst of the Ka'bah. The wisdom behind this is that it entails discreetness, so it draws one closer to sincerity and away from showing off.

٢٨٤- حَدَّثَنَا أَحْمَدُ بْنُ مَنِيعٍ، قَالَ: حَدَّثَنَا إِسْمَاعِيلُ بْنُ إِبْرَاهِيمَ، قَالَ: حَدَّثَنَا أَيُّوبُ، عَنْ نَافِعٍ، عَنِ ابْنِ عُمَرَ، قَالَ: حَدَّثَتْنِي حَفْصَةُ: «أَنَّ رَسُولَ اللهِ صلى الله عليه وسلم كَانَ يُصَلِّي رَكْعَتَيْنِ حِينَ يَطْلُعُ الْفَجْرُ وَيُنَادِي الْمُنَادِي».

قَالَ أَيُّوبُ: وَأُرَاهُ ، قَالَ: خَفِيفَتَيْنِ.[٣٦١]

284. 'Abdullāh b. 'Umar ﵁ narrated: "Ḥafṣah related to me that the Messenger of Allāh ﷺ used to pray two units upon the commencement of *Fajr*, when the call to prayer was made."

Ayyūb (one of the narrators) said: "I think he said: 'Short units.'"

'Abd al-Razzāq al-Badr said,

> This ḥadīth talks about the supererogatory prayers of the Prophet ﷺ that he prayed before *Fajr* and with these two units, the total number of the units is ten. Ibn 'Umar ﵁ saw him pray eight units and then his sister Ḥafṣah ﵂, the wife of the Prophet, informed him of the other two units which he prayed at home. The Sunnah is to keep these two voluntary units short, and to recite "al-Kāfirūn" in the first unit and "al-Ikhlāṣ" in the second unit.

Al-Bājūrī said,

> The two short units referred to here are the Sunnah of *Fajr*.
>
> Ayyūb is referring to Nāfi', the one who narrated from 'Abdullāh b. 'Umar.

٢٨٥- حَدَّثَنَا قُتَيْبَةُ بْنُ سَعِيدٍ، قَالَ: حَدَّثَنَا مَرْوَانُ بْنُ مُعَاوِيَةَ الْفَزَارِيُّ، عَنْ جَعْفَرِ بْنِ بُرْقَانَ، عَنْ مَيْمُونِ بْنِ مِهْرَانَ، عَنِ ابْنِ عُمَرَ، قَالَ: «حَفِظْتُ مِنْ رَسُولِ اللهِ صلى الله عليه وسلم ثَمَانِيَ رَكَعَاتٍ: رَكْعَتَيْنِ قَبْلَ الظُّهْرِ، وَرَكْعَتَيْنِ بَعْدَهَا، وَرَكْعَتَيْنِ

361 Part of ḥadīth 283

بَعْدَ الْمَغْرِبِ، وَرَكْعَتَيْنِ بَعْدَ الْعِشَاءِ، قَالَ ابْنُ عُمَرَ: وَحَدَّثَتْنِي حَفْصَةُ بِرَكْعَتِي
الْغَدَاةِ، وَلَمْ أَكُنْ أَرَاهُمَا مِنَ النَّبِيِّ صلىٰ الله عليه وسلم»٣٦٢.

285. ʿAbdullāh b. ʿUmar ﷺ narrated: "I memorised from the Messenger of Allāh ﷺ eight units of prayer; two before *Ẓuhr* and two after it; two units after *Maghrib* and two after *ʿIshāʾ*. Ḥafṣah related to me about the two units before *Fajr*, which I did not observe from the Prophet ﷺ."

Ibn Ḥajar al-Haytamī said,

> This shows that he ﷺ prayed the regular Sunnah of the obligatory prayers in the *masjid*; therefore Ibn ʿUmar saw them. Unlike the Sunnah of *Fajr* which he always prayed at home.

٢٨٦ - حَدَّثَنَا أَبُو سَلَمَةَ يَحْيَىٰ بْنُ خَلَفٍ، قَالَ: حَدَّثَنَا بِشْرُ بْنُ الْمُفَضَّلِ، عَنْ خَالِدٍ
الْحَذَّاءِ، عَنْ عَبْدِ اللهِ بْنِ شَقِيقٍ، قَالَ: سَأَلْتُ عَائِشَةَ عَنْ صَلَاةِ النَّبِيِّ صلىٰ الله عليه
وسلم قَالَتْ: «كَانَ يُصَلِّي قَبْلَ الظُّهْرِ رَكْعَتَيْنِ وَبَعْدَهَا رَكْعَتَيْنِ، وَبَعْدَ الْمَغْرِبِ
رَكْعَتَيْنِ، وَبَعْدَ الْعِشَاءِ رَكْعَتَيْنِ، وَقَبْلَ الْفَجْرِ ثِنْتَيْنِ»٣٦٣.

286. ʿAbdullāh b. Shaqīq asked ʿĀʾishah ﷺ about the [optional] prayers of the Prophet ﷺ. She replied: "He used to pray two units before and two after *Ẓuhr*, two units after *Maghrib*, two units after *ʿIshāʾ* and two before *Fajr*."

Ibn Ḥajar al-Haytamī said,

> These units of prayer are the emphasised regular Sunnah prayers (i.e. those which are prayed alongside the obligatory prayers). This is because the Prophet ﷺ consistently performed them, as covered above.
>
> It is noted that Muslim has reported from ʿĀʾishah that she said, "He prayed four units in his home before *Ẓuhr*."[364] Furthermore, the two *shaykhs* reported the narration, "He would not leave off the four units before *Ẓuhr*."[365] This clear textual proof emphasising four units be-

---

362 See ḥadīth 283
363 See ḥadīth 280
364 *Ṣaḥīḥ Muslim* (105)
365 *Ṣaḥīḥ al-Bukhārī* (1182), *Sunan Abī Dāwūd* (1253), *Sunan al-Nasāʾī* (3/251), *Musnad Aḥmad* (6/63 and 148) and *Sharḥ al-Sunnah* (3/447).

fore *Ẓuhr* may make our scholars' deeming of the two units only being emphasised seem problematic. However, it is possible that the four units were an independent prayer performed after noon, of which the next ḥadith details. This would negate any discrepancy between the authentic ḥadīth from Ibn 'Umar, "I prayed with the Prophet two units before *Ẓuhr* and two after it", and the report from 'Ā'ishah, "He would not leave off four before *Ẓuhr*." The former units were from the recommended prayer of *Ẓuhr*, and the latter units were from the recommended prayer of *Zawāl*. It is also possible that the former units were those he would pray if he was in the mosque, and the latter units were those he would pray if he was in his house.

٢٨٧ - حَدَّثَنَا مُحَمَّدُ بْنُ الْمُثَنَّىٰ، قَالَ: حَدَّثَنَا مُحَمَّدُ بْنُ جَعْفَرٍ، قَالَ: حَدَّثَنَا شُعْبَةُ، عَنْ أَبِي إِسْحَاقَ، قَالَ: سَمِعْتُ عَاصِمَ بْنَ ضَمْرَةَ، يَقُولُ: سَأَلْنَا عَلِيًّا عَنْ صَلاةِ رَسُولِ اللهِ صلىٰ الله عليه وسلم مِنَ النَّهَارِ، فَقَالَ: «إِنَّكُمْ لا تُطِيقُونَ ذَلِكَ، قَالَ: فَقُلْنَا: مَنْ أَطَاقَ ذَلِكَ مِنَّا صَلَّىٰ، فَقَالَ: كَانَ إِذَا كَانَتِ الشَّمْسُ مِنْ هَهُنَا كَهَيْئَتِهَا مِنْ هَهُنَا عِنْدَ الْعَصْرِ صَلَّىٰ رَكْعَتَيْنِ، وَإِذَا كَانَتِ الشَّمْسُ مِنْ هَهُنَا كَهَيْئَتِهَا مِنْ هَهُنَا عِنْدَ الظُّهْرِ صَلَّىٰ أَرْبَعًا، وَيُصَلِّي قَبْلَ الظُّهْرِ أَرْبَعًا، وَبَعْدَهَا رَكْعَتَيْنِ، وَقَبْلَ الْعَصْرِ أَرْبَعًا، يَفْصِلُ بَيْنَ كُلِّ رَكْعَتَيْنِ بِالتَّسْلِيمِ عَلَىٰ الْمَلائِكَةِ الْمُقَرَّبِينَ وَالنَّبِيِّينَ، وَمَنْ تَبِعَهُمْ مِنَ الْمُؤْمِنِينَ وَالْمُسْلِمِينَ»[٣٦٦].

287. 'Āṣim b. Ḍamrah narrated: "We asked 'Alī b. Abī Ṭālib ﵁ about the optional prayers that the Messenger of Allāh ﷺ performed during the daytime. 'Alī replied, 'You do not have the capability to perform them.' We replied, 'Whoever from amongst us that possesses the capability will do so.' 'Alī said, 'In the morning when the sun rose [eastward] to the height, the same as it is [westward] at the time for *'Aṣr*, at that time he performed two units. When the sun rose [in the east] to a similar height as it is [in the west] at the time of *Ẓuhr*, he performed four units. He performed four units before *Ẓuhr* and two after. Four units were performed before *'Aṣr*. He would separate between each pair of two units by sending salutations to the close angels, Prophets, and those who followed them from the devoted believers and Muslims.'"

366 *Sunan al-Tirmidhī* (599)

Ibn Ḥajar al-Haytamī said,

> **"You do not have the capability to perform them":** I.e. in terms of doing so consistently, especially so considering what his worship entailed of devotion and tranquillity.

ʿAbd al-Razzāq al-Badr said,

> The inquiry of ʿĀsim shows the keen interest of the *salaf* towards learning the guidance of the Prophet ﷺ and following it.
>
> The first set of two units mentioned in the ḥadīth refers to the *Ḍuḥā* prayer.
>
> The first set of four units mentioned in the ḥadīth refers to – as explained by some commentators – the prayer of *awwābīn* which is offered when the pebbles become overheated (i.e. when the temperature is high).
>
> The second set of four units mentioned in the ḥadīth refers to the regular Sunnah preceding the prayer of *Ẓuhr*, which concords with the aforementioned ḥadīth of ʿĀ'ishah ("He would not leave off four before *Ẓuhr*") and that of Umm Ḥabībah[367].
>
> The two units performed after *Ẓuhr* and four units before *ʿAṣr* are not the regular Sunnah associated with these two prayers. These prayers have a great reward, as in the report mentioned by al-Imām Aḥmad and others from Ibn ʿUmar that the Prophet ﷺ said, "Allāh's mercy be upon the man who prays four units before *ʿAṣr*."[368]

"He would separate between each pair of two units by sending salutations to the close angels, Prophets, and those who followed them from the devoted believers and Muslims": This statement could be the *taslīm* with which he concluded the prayer or the *tashahhud* wherein salutations are sent to all pious slaves of Allāh, which includes angels and the Prophets. However, the former is more likely to be the case and more obvious in the context of this ḥadīth and other ḥadīths.

---

367 *Ṣaḥīḥ Muslim* (728)
368 *Musnad Aḥmad* (5980)

باب صلاة الضحى

[41] The *Ḍuḥā* Prayer (Forenoon Prayer)

Al-Sanʿāni said,

> Ibn al-Qayyim compiled all the views of the scholars regarding the ruling on praying the *Ḍuḥā* prayer, and they totalled to six different views, as follows:
>
> 1. It is a recommended Sunnah.
> 2. It is not prescribed unless there is a reason for it.
> 3. It is not recommended.
> 4. It is recommended to pray it but not on a regular basis.
> 5. It is preferable to pray it at home.
> 6. It is an innovation.
>
> The most correct view of these is that it is a recommended Sunnah, as stated by Ibn Daqīq al-ʿĪd.[369]

Al-Bājūrī said,

> There are eight ḥadīths in this chapter.

٢٨٨- حَدَّثَنَا مَحْمُودُ بْنُ غَيْلَانَ، قَالَ: حَدَّثَنَا أَبُو دَاوُدَ الطَّيَالِسِيُّ، قَالَ: حَدَّثَنَا شُعْبَةُ، عَنْ يَزِيدَ الرِّشْكِ، قَالَ: سَمِعْتُ مُعَاذَةَ، قَالَتْ: «قُلْتُ لِعَائِشَةَ: أَكَانَ النَّبِيُّ صلى الله عليه وسلم يُصَلِّي الضُّحَى؟ قَالَتْ: نَعَمْ، أَرْبَعَ رَكَعَاتٍ وَيَزِيدُ مَا شَاءَ اللهُ عَزَّ وَجَلَّ»[٣٧٠].

288. Muʿādhah narrated: "I asked ʿĀ'ishah ﵂, 'Did the Prophet ﷺ pray the *Ḍuḥā* prayer?' She replied, 'Yes, he prayed four units, and

---

369 *Subul al-Salām*

370 *Sahīh Muslim* (719)

would also increase upon that [number] whatever Allāh willed.'"

Ibn Baṭṭāl said,

> Masrūq said: "We used to recite Qur'ān [after *Fajr*] in the *masjid* and would remain in the *masjid* after Ibn Mas'ūd ﷺ would leave, and then [later we would] perform the *Ḍuḥā* prayer. The news reached Ibn Mas'ūd and so he said to us, 'Why do you dictate upon people that which Allāh did not oblige them to do. If you want to pray it, then do so at home.'"
>
> The *salaf* preferred praying the *Ḍuḥā* prayer in secret and not in view of the public, lest they assume that it is obligatory.[371]

Al-Sindī said,

> The affirmative answer of 'Ā'ishah ﷺ indicates that he ﷺ prayed it sometimes. This is because she related in other ḥadīths that he did not pray it; thus to reconcile between these ḥadīths, it appears she meant that he did not pray it all the time or that she did not see him pray it but was then informed by someone at a later point that he did pray it.[372]

Al-Ḥāfiẓ al-'Irāqī said,

> Al-Nawawī and al-Bayhaqī said that scholars understood the ḥadīths indicating that the Prophet ﷺ did not pray it to mean that he did not pray it regularly as he feared that it may become obligatory. This is evident in the statement of 'Ā'ishah ﷺ wherein she said, "The Messenger of Allāh ﷺ would not do an act of worship he liked to perform just out of fear that the people would follow suit and accordingly, it would become obligatory."[373]

Al-Munāwī said,

> This ḥadīth was used as evidence by some scholars that the number of its units is open.[374]

٢٨٩- حَدَّثَنَا مُحَمَّدُ بْنُ الْمُثَنَّى، قَالَ: حَدَّثَنِي حَكِيمُ بْنُ مُعَاوِيَةَ الزِّيَادِيُّ، قَالَ:

---

371 *Sharḥ Ṣaḥīḥ al-Bukhārī*

372 *Ḥāshiyat al-Sindi 'alā Sunan Ibn Mājah*

373 *Ṭarḥ al-Tathrīb Sharḥ al-Taqrīb*

374 *Al-Taysīr bi Sharḥ al-Jāmi' al-Ṣaghīr*

حَدَّثَنَا زِيَادُ بْنُ عُبَيْدِ اللهِ بْنِ الرَّبِيعِ الزِّيَادِيُّ، عَنْ حُمَيْدٍ الطَّوِيلِ، عَنْ أَنَسِ بْنِ مَالِكٍ: «أَنَّ النَّبِيَّ صلى الله عليه وسلم كَانَ يُصَلِّي الضُّحَى سِتَّ رَكَعَاتٍ»[٣٧٥].

289. Anas b. Mālik ﷺ narrated: "The Prophet ﷺ used to pray six units as the *Ḍuḥā* prayer."

Al-Bājūrī said,

> **"The Prophet ﷺ used to pray six units as the *Ḍuḥā* prayer":** I.e. on some occasions. There is no conflict between the narrations.

Al-Munāwī said,

> The *Ḍuḥā* prayer is an established Sunnah. The Shafiʿī scholars stated that the minimum number of its units is two, the best is eight units and the maximum is twelve (based on the ḥadīths narrating the number of units of this prayer).

٢٩٠ - حَدَّثَنَا مُحَمَّدُ بْنُ الْمُثَنَّى، قَالَ: حَدَّثَنَا مُحَمَّدُ بْنُ جَعْفَرٍ، قَالَ: حَدَّثَنَا شُعْبَةُ، عَنْ عَمْرِو بْنِ مُرَّةَ، عَنْ عَبْدِ الرَّحْمَنِ بْنِ أَبِي لَيْلَى، قَالَ: مَا أَخْبَرَنِي أَحَدٌ أَنَّهُ رَأَى النَّبِيَّ صلى الله عليه وسلم يُصَلِّي الضُّحَى إِلا أُمُّ هَانِئٍ، فَإِنَّهَا حَدَّثَتْ «أَنَّ رَسُولَ اللهِ صلى الله عليه وسلم دَخَلَ بَيْتَهَا يَوْمَ فَتْحِ مَكَّةَ فَاغْتَسَلَ فَسَبَّحَ ثَمَانِيَ رَكَعَاتٍ، مَا رَأَيْتُهُ صلى الله عليه وسلم صَلَّى صَلاةً قَطُّ أَخَفَّ مِنْهَا، غَيْرَ أَنَّهُ كَانَ يُتِمُّ الرُّكُوعَ وَالسُّجُودَ»[٣٧٦].

290. ʿAbd al-Raḥmān b. Abī Laylah narrated: "None had informed me that they had observed the Prophet ﷺ pray the *Ḍuḥā* prayer besides Umm Hānīʾ ﷺ, for she related, 'The Messenger of Allāh ﷺ came to my house on the day Makkah was conquered, and there he performed *ghusl* and then prayed eight units that I did not observe him perform any prayer shorter than, but he still bowed and prostrated his normal length.'"

Al-Bājūrī said,

> **"None had informed me that they had observed the Prophet ﷺ pray the *Ḍuḥā* prayer besides Umm Hānīʾ ﷺ":** This negation is

375 *Al-Muʿjam al-Awsaṭ* (1276)
376 *Ṣaḥīḥ al-Bukhārī* (1103) and *Ṣaḥīḥ Muslim* (336)

specific to 'Abd al-Raḥmān b. Abī Laylah, i.e. no one reported this to him besides Umm Hāni'. Nineteen major companions reported that the Prophet prayed it. Abū Zur'ah said, "Many famous, authentic ḥadiths have been related concerning it." Ibn Jarīr said, "They reach the level of mass-transmission."

'Alā al-Dīn al-Baghdādī said,

> Ibn 'Abbās ﷺ said: "I did not know the *Ḍuḥā* prayer was mentioned in the verse: **{Indeed, We subjected the mountains [to praise] with him, exalting [Allāh] in the [late] afternoon <u>and [after] sunrise.</u>}**[377] until I heard Umm Hānī' tell me that the Messenger of Allāh visited her and asked for water to perform ablution and then prayed the *Ḍuḥā* prayer. After he finished, he said to her, 'O Umm Hānī'! This is the *Ḍuḥā* prayer.'"[378] [379]

Ibn Ḥajar al-'Asqalānī said,

> Though this ḥadīth indicates that it is prescribed to shorten the *Ḍuḥā* prayer, this is something debatable due to the possibility that he ﷺ shortened it due to the multitude of tasks he was burdened with when Makkah was conquered, particularly as it is proven that he ﷺ prayed lengthy *Ḍuḥā* prayers at other times. However, al-Qāḍī 'Iyyād reported from some scholars that the prayer mentioned in this ḥadīth is the prayer of conquest which Khālid b. al-Walīd ﷺ prayed in some of his conquests.
>
> Al-Tirmidhī narrated from al-Imām Aḥmad that the most authentic ḥadīth about the *Ḍuḥā* prayer is the ḥadīth of Umm Hānī', and it is as he stated. This is the reason al-Nawawī said that the best number of units to pray are eight, while the maximum is twelve (though many other scholars did not place a restriction on the maximum number of units).[380]

٢٩١- حدثنا ابن أبي عمر، قَالَ: حدثنا وَكِيعٌ، قَالَ: حدثنا كَهْمَسُ بْنُ الحَسَنِ، عَنْ عَبْدِ الله بْنِ شَقِيقٍ، قَالَ: قُلتُ لِعَائِشَةَ: «أَكَانَ النَّبِيُّ صلى الله عليه وسلم يُصَلِّي

---

377 Qur'ān: 38:18
378 *Tafsīr al-Khāzin*
379 *Al-Mu'jam al-Awsaṭ* (4/296)
380 *Fatḥ al-Bārī*

الضُّحَىٰ ؟ قَالَتْ: لَا، إِلَّا أَنْ يَجِيءَ مِنْ مَغِيبِهِ»٣٨١.

291. 'Abdullāh b. Shaqīq related: "I asked 'Ā'ishah ﵂, 'Did the Prophet ﷺ pray the *Ḍuḥā* prayer?' She replied, 'No. He did not perform it except when he would return from a journey.'"

Ibn Ḥajar al-'Asqalānī said,

> He ﷺ prayed it after his return from travelling because he admonished arriving home from a journey at night and so he would arrive early in the morning and the first thing he would do was to go to the *masjid* and pray two units, then sit there.[382]

Al-Suyūṭī said,

> This clarifies the other ḥadīth of 'Ā'ishah ﵂ wherein she negated that the Prophet ﷺ prayed the *Ḍuḥā* prayer as she meant that he did not pray it regularly.[383]

٢٩٢- حَدَّثَنَا زِيَادُ بْنُ أَيُّوبَ الْبَغْدَادِيُّ، قَالَ: حَدَّثَنَا مُحَمَّدُ بْنُ رَبِيعَةَ، عَنْ فُضَيْلِ بْنِ مَرْزُوقٍ، عَنْ عَطِيَّةَ، عَنْ أَبِي سَعِيدٍ الْخُدْرِيِّ، قَالَ: «كَانَ النَّبِيُّ صلى الله عليه وسلم يُصَلِّي الضُّحَىٰ حَتَّىٰ نَقُولَ: لا يَدَعُهَا، وَيَدَعُهَا حَتَّىٰ نَقُولَ: لا يُصَلِّيهَا»٣٨٤.

292. Abū Sa'īd al-Khudrī ﵁ narrated: "The Prophet ﷺ used to pray the *Ḍuḥā* prayer with such regularity that we thought he would not leave it. And, he would not pray it [for such a lengthy period of time], that we thought he would not pray it again."

Ibn Ḥajar al-Haytamī said,

> Benefit: From the benefits of the *Ḍuḥā* prayer is that it suffices for the mornings' charity due on the human joints, as reported by Muslim, wherein it states, "Two units of *Ḍuḥā* suffice for that." Al-Ḥāfiẓ Abū al-Faḍl al-Zayn al-'Irāqī reported that a common misunderstanding among the laity was that cutting off praying it causes one to become blind, so many of them completely leave off[385] praying it for that rea-

381 *Ṣaḥīḥ Muslim* (336)
382 *Fatḥ al-Bārī*
383 *Sharḥ Sunan Ibn Mājah*
384 *Sunan al-Tirmidhī* (477)
385 In the Arabic text, this is "do not leave off", which appears to be a typo.

> son. What they say has no basis, rather it appears that it is something the devil has cast upon their souls to deprive them of great goodness, especially as it suffices for the charity [mentioned in the narration]. Al-Ḥākim reports, "Allāh's Messenger ﷺ ordered us to pray the *Ḍuḥā* prayer with chapters including *'[w]al-shamsi wa ḍuḥahā'*, and *'[w] al-ḍuḥā'...'*" The appropriateness [of these chapters] is clear.

Ibn Ḥajar al-Asqalānī said,

> 'Ikrimah related that Ibn 'Abbās ؓ used to pray it for ten days and then leave it for ten days. Sufyān al-Thawrī related that Manṣūr said, "They (the *salaf*) disliked praying the *Ḍuḥā* prayer on a regular basis just like they observe the obligatory prayer." Sa'īd b. Jubayr said, "I do not pray it [sometimes] though I like praying it, as I fear I might start obliging myself to pray it."[386]

Zayn al-Dīn al-'Iraqī said,

> The reason he ﷺ did not pray it on a regular basis was because he feared it becoming obligatory upon his nation. However, as he ﷺ passed away and the religion is now complete and perfect, one should try to pray it as much as possible.

٢٩٣- حَدَّثَنَا أَحْمَدُ بْنُ مَنِيعٍ، عَنْ هُشَيْمٍ، قَالَ: حَدَّثَنَا عُبَيْدَةُ، عَنِ إِبْرَاهِيمَ، عَنْ سَهْمِ بْنِ مِنْجَابٍ، عَنْ قَرْثَعٍ الضَّبِّيِّ، أَوْ عَنْ قَزَعَةَ، عَنْ قَرْثَعٍ، عَنْ أَبِي أَيُّوبَ الأَنْصَارِيِّ، «أَنَّ النَّبِيَّ صلىٰ الله عليه وسلم كَانَ يُدْمِنُ أَرْبَعَ رَكَعَاتٍ عِنْدَ زَوَالِ الشَّمْسِ، فَقُلْتُ: يَا رَسُولَ اللهِ! إِنَّكَ تُدْمِنُ هَذِهِ الأَرْبَعَ رَكَعَاتٍ عِنْدَ زَوَالِ الشَّمْسِ، فَقَالَ: إِنَّ أَبْوَابَ السَّمَاءِ تُفْتَحُ عِنْدَ زَوَالِ الشَّمْسِ فَلا تُرْتَجُ حَتَّىٰ تُصَلَّىٰ الظُّهْرُ، فَأُحِبُّ أَنْ يَصْعَدَ لِي فِي تِلْكَ السَّاعَةِ خَيْرٌ، قُلْتُ: أَفِي كُلِّهِنَّ قِرَاءَةٌ؟ قَالَ: نَعَمْ، قُلْتُ: هَلْ فِيهِنَّ تَسْلِيمٌ فَاصِلٌ؟ قَالَ: لا»[٣٨٧].

293. Abū Ayyūb al-Anṣārī ؓ narrated: "The Prophet ﷺ always prayed four units when the sun passed the zenith. I said, 'O Messenger of Allāh! You constantly pray these four units when the sun passes the zenith.' The Messenger ﷺ replied, 'The doors of the heavens open

---

386 *Fatḥ al-Bārī*
387 *Musnad Aḥmad* (23532)

from the time the sun passes the zenith until the *Ẓuhr* prayer is performed; hence I like that a good deed of mine reaches the heavens at that time.' I asked, 'Is there a recital in every unit?' He replied, 'Yes.' I enquired, 'Is there a *taslīm* separating in between?' He replied, 'No.'"

ʿUbayd al-Raḥmān al-Mubārakfūrī said,

> These four units are known as the Sunnah of *Zawāl* which is different to the four units of Sunnah preceding the *Ẓuhr* prayer and they are linked to the time of the sun passing the zenith. The wisdom for praying it at that time is because the time of midday mirrors the time of midnight; the doors of the heavens are open at midday and Allāh ﷻ descends after midnight; thus both times are times of mercy.
>
> Ibn al-Qayyim said that the Prophet ﷺ prayed these four units after the sun passed its zenith.[388]

ʿAbdullāh b. Saʿīd al-Ḥaḍramī al-Makkī said,

> The inquiry about whether these units included any Qurʾān recitation refers to anything in addition to Sūrah al-Fātiḥah. This is because a prayer is not accepted without reciting al-Fātiḥah even if it is an optional prayer, and this is something well known.
>
> The inquiry about the *taslīm* was to find out whether the four units are prayed with one *taslīm* or prayed two units by two. This ḥadīth was used as evidence by the scholars who hold the view that the optional prayers of the daytime should consist of four units with one *taslīm*. However, other scholars understood the statement of the Prophet ﷺ to mean that the *taslīm* is not obligatory. Meaning one is not obligated to pray them two units by two and so it does not contradict that the best manner of praying the optional prayers is two by two.[389]

٢٩٤- حدثنا أَحْمَدُ بْنُ مَنِيعٍ، قَالَ: حَدَّثَنَا أَبُو مُعَاوِيَةَ، قَالَ: حَدَّثَنَا عُبَيْدَةُ، عَنْ إِبْرَاهِيمَ، عَنْ سَهْمِ بْنِ مِنْجَابٍ، عَنْ قَزَعَةَ، عَنْ قَرْثَعٍ، عَنْ أَبِي أَيُّوبَ الأَنْصَارِيِّ، عَنِ النَّبِيِّ صلى الله عليه وسلم نَحْوَهُ.

388 *Mirʿāt al-Mafātīḥ Sharḥ Mishkāt al-Maṣābīḥ*
389 *Muntahā al-Suʾl ʿalā Wasāʾil al-Wuṣūl ilā Shamāʾil al-Rasūl*

294. Abū Ayyūb al-Anṣārī ﷺ narrated from the Prophet ﷺ a similar narration through a different route.

٢٩٥- حَدَّثَنَا مُحَمَّدُ بْنُ الْمُثَنَّىٰ، قَالَ: حَدَّثَنَا أَبُو دَاوُدَ، قَالَ: حَدَّثَنَا مُحَمَّدُ بْنُ مُسْلِمِ بْنِ أَبِي الْوَضَّاحِ، عَنْ عَبْدِ الْكَرِيمِ الْجَزَرِيِّ، عَنْ مُجَاهِدٍ، عَنْ عَبْدِ اللهِ بْنِ السَّائِبِ، «أَنَّ رَسُولَ اللهِ صلى الله عليه وسلم كَانَ يُصَلِّي أَرْبَعًا بَعْدَ أَنْ تَزُولَ الشَّمْسُ قَبْلَ الظُّهْرِ، وَقَالَ: إِنَّهَا سَاعَةٌ تُفْتَحُ فِيهَا أَبْوَابُ السَّمَاءِ، فَأُحِبُّ أَنْ يَصْعَدَ لِي فِيهَا عَمَلٌ صَالِحٌ»[٣٩٠].

295. ʿAbdullāh b. al-Sā'ib ﷺ narrated: "The Messenger of Allāh ﷺ used to pray four units at the time of the sun's passing the zenith before the *Ẓuhr* prayer, and he ﷺ said, 'The doors of the heavens open at this moment; therefore I like that a good deed of mine ascends at this moment.'"

٢٩٦- حَدَّثَنَا أَبُو سَلَمَةَ يَحْيَىٰ بْنُ خَلَفٍ، قَالَ: حَدَّثَنَا عُمَرُ بْنُ عَلِيٍّ الْمُقَدَّمِيُّ، عَنْ مِسْعَرِ بْنِ كِدَامٍ، عَنْ أَبِي إِسْحَاقَ، عَنْ عَاصِمِ بْنِ ضَمْرَةَ، عَنْ عَلِيٍّ، «أَنَّهُ كَانَ يُصَلِّي قَبْلَ الظُّهْرِ أَرْبَعًا، وَذَكَرَ أَنَّ رَسُولَ اللهِ صلى الله عليه وسلم كَانَ يُصَلِّيهَا عِنْدَ الزَّوَالِ وَيَمُدُّ فِيهَا»[٣٩١].

296. ʿAlī b. Abī Ṭālib ﷺ used to pray four units before the *Ẓuhr* prayer and he mentioned that the Messenger of Allāh ﷺ used to pray these four units when the sun passed the zenith and he would make the units long in duration.

Al-Bājūrī said,

> **"When the sun passed the zenith":** I.e. after it.
>
> **"And he would make the units long in duration":** E.g. by lengthening the recitation.

Ibn Ḥajar al-Haytamī said,

> This shows that it is recommended to prolong the *Ḍuḥā* prayer.

390 *Sunan al-Tirmidhī* (478)
391 *Al-Targhīb fī Faḍā'il al-Aʿmāl (82)*

باب صلاة التطوع في البيت

[42] Praying Voluntary Prayers at Home

Al-Bājūrī said,

> This refers to prayers besides the obligatory ones, and it encompasses the emphasised prayers and others.
>
> **"At home":** I.e. not in the *masjid*, for prayer in the home entails a presence of sincerity and an absence of showing off. Ibn 'Umar narrates from Allāh's Messenger ﷺ, "Perform some of your prayers within your homes and do not leave them as graveyards."
>
> This chapter contains one ḥadīth.

'Abd al-Razzāq al-Badr said,

> It is more rewarding to pray voluntary prayers at home than in the *masjid* even if the *masjid* is one of the three wherein the reward is multiplied. Praying at home brings life to it and whenever a home is devoid of prayer then it is devoid of life. From the benefits of praying voluntary prayers at home is that it encourages the children to pray, expels devils from the home and brings tranquillity and peace therein.

٢٩٧- حَدَّثَنَا عَبَّاسٌ الْعَنْبَرِيُّ، قَالَ: حَدَّثَنَا عَبْدُ الرَّحْمَنِ بْنُ مَهْدِيٍّ، عَنْ مُعَاوِيَةَ بْنِ صَالِحٍ، عَنِ الْعَلَاءِ بْنِ الْحَارِثِ، عَنْ حَرَامِ بْنِ مُعَاوِيَةَ، عَنْ عَمِّهِ عَبْدِ اللهِ بْنِ سَعْدٍ قَالَ: سَأَلْتُ رَسُولَ اللهِ صلى الله عليه وسلم عَنِ الصَّلَاةِ فِي بَيْتِي وَالصَّلَاةِ فِي الْمَسْجِدِ قَالَ: «قَدْ تَرَى مَا أَقْرَبَ بَيْتِي مِنَ الْمَسْجِدِ، فَلَأَنْ أُصَلِّيَ فِي بَيْتِي أَحَبُّ إِلَيَّ مِنْ أَنْ أُصَلِّيَ فِي الْمَسْجِدِ إِلا أَنْ تَكُونَ صَلَاةً مَكْتُوبَةً»[٣٩٢].

297. 'Abdullāh b. Sa'd ﷺ related: "I asked the Messenger of Allāh ﷺ which is more meritorious, praying at home or praying at the *masjid*?" He replied, "You can see that my house is very close to the

392 *Sunan Abī Dāwūd* (311) and *Sunan Ibn Mājah* (651)

***masjid* yet besides the five obligatory prayers, I prefer to pray in my house rather than in the *masjid*."**

Muḥammad al-Amīn al-Shanqīṭī said,

> The scholars differed on whether it is better to pray the supererogatory prayers at home or at the *masjid* of the Prophet ﷺ because each group understood the overall texts differently. The views of the scholars are as follows:
>
> Al-Imām Abū Ḥanīfah said that praying voluntary prayers at home is better and there would be no difference in reward if they were prayed at the *masjid* of the Prophet ﷺ.
>
> Al-Imām al-Shāfiʿī had two views reported from him, as noted in *Sharḥ Ṣaḥīḥ Muslim* of al-Nawawī and *al-Majmūʿ* of the same author.
>
> Mālikī scholars hold the view that praying voluntary prayers in the *masjid* of the Prophet ﷺ is better than praying them at home.
>
> It should be noted that the reward for women praying at home is greater than them praying at the *masjid*, be it voluntary prayers or obligatory prayers.[393]

Al-Nabhānī said,

> The reason he ﷺ preferred to offer voluntary prayers at home was so the blessings of prayer encompass the home and the household members, and through this angels enter the house and devils leave it.[394]

---

393 *Aḍwā' al-Bayān*
394 *Al-Wasā'il al-Wuṣūl ilā Shamā'il al-Rasūl*

باب ما جاء في صوم رسول الله صلى الله عليه وسلم

[43] On Allāh's Messenger's ﷺ Fasting

ʿAbd al-Razzāq al-Badr said,

This chapter is dedicated to clarifying the recommended and obligatory fasting of the Prophet ﷺ – that which he repeated every week such as the fast of Mondays and Thursdays, and that which he repeated every month such as the three days of each month, and that which he repeated every year such as the month of Ramaḍān (which is a pillar of Islām) and the day of ʿĀshūrā.

The linguistic meaning of the Arabic word '*ṣawm*' is abstaining and refraining. In its religious context, it means refraining from food, drink and sexual activities during the day from the time of *Fajr* until sunset.

Fasting is a tool for religious development which the believers use to gain deep insights and spiritual lessons. This is why Allāh states: **{O believers! Fasting has been prescribed upon you like it was for those before you so that you can be wary/mindful.}**[395] It is a lofty act of obedience which grows mindfulness of Allāh within the hearts. It kindles in the heart a connection to Allāh, sending the soul away from the forbidden and sinfulness. It is a shield for the one who performs it.

Fasting is of two types, the first of which is to refrain from food, drink and sexual activities and this must be observed by Muslims during each day of the month of Ramaḍān, from *Fajr* until sunset. The other type of fasting is to refrain from sins and this must be observed all of the time. It is for this reason that each bodily limb must fast, the ears must refrain from listening to the forbidden, the tongue must refrain from uttering the forbidden and so forth.

Al-Bājūrī said,

395 Al-Baqarah: 183

This chapter contains sixteen ḥadīths.

٢٩٨- حَدَّثَنَا قُتَيْبَةُ بْنُ سَعِيدٍ، قَالَ: حَدَّثَنَا حَمَّادُ بْنُ زَيْدٍ، عَنْ أَيُّوبَ، عَنْ عَبْدِ اللهِ بْنِ شَقِيقٍ، قَالَ: سَأَلْتُ عَائِشَةَ، عَنْ صِيَامِ رَسُولِ اللهِ صلى الله عليه وسلم، قَالَتْ: «كَانَ يَصُومُ حَتَّىٰ نَقُولَ قَدْ صَامَ، وَيُفْطِرُ حَتَّىٰ نَقُولَ قَدْ أَفْطَرَ، قَالَتْ: وَمَا صَامَ رَسُولُ اللهِ صلى الله عليه وسلم شَهْرًا كَامِلا مُنْذُ قَدِمَ الْمَدِينَةَ إِلا رَمَضَانَ»[٣٩٦].

298. 'Abdullāh b. Shaqīq ﷺ narrated: "I inquired from 'Ā'ishah ﷺ regarding Allāh's Messenger's ﷺ voluntary fasting. She replied, 'At times he would fast continuous days to the point that we thought he would not cease fasting. And at times he would not fast, until we began thinking he would continue to not fast. The Messenger of Allāh ﷺ did not fast a whole month from the time he entered Madīnah, except the month of Ramaḍān.'"

Al-Nawawī said,

> This ḥadīth shows that it is recommended for a person to fast a day or more from each month, and that optional fasting does not have a specific time as it can be offered anytime during the year except the month of Ramaḍān, 'Īd days and the days of *Tashrīq*.[397]

Ibn Ḥajar al-Haytamī said,

> The reason it was mentioned that this was his practice from the day he entered Madinah is because most of the rulings were revealed after immigration.
>
> This is a proof that optional fasting during the month of Ramaḍān is invalid.

٢٩٩- حَدَّثَنَا عَلِيُّ بْنُ حُجْرٍ، قَالَ: حَدَّثَنَا إِسْمَاعِيلُ بْنُ جَعْفَرٍ، عَنْ حُمَيْدٍ، عَنْ أَنَسِ بْنِ مَالِكٍ، أَنَّهُ سُئِلَ عَنْ صَوْمِ النَّبِيِّ صلى الله عليه وسلم، فَقَالَ: «كَانَ يَصُومُ مِنَ الشَّهْرِ حَتَّىٰ نَرَىٰ أَنْ لا يُرِيدَ أَنْ يُفْطِرَ مِنْهُ، وَيُفْطِرُ مِنْهُ حَتَّىٰ نَرَىٰ أَنْ لا يُرِيدَ أَنْ يَصُومَ مِنْهُ شَيْئًا وَكُنْتَ لا تَشَاءُ أَنْ تَرَاهُ مِنَ اللَّيْلِ مُصَلِّيًا إِلا رَأَيْتَهُ مُصَلِّيًا، وَلا نَائِمًا

---

396 *Ṣaḥīḥ Muslim* (1156)
397 *Sharḥ Ṣaḥīḥ Muslim*

إِلَّا رَأَيْتَهُ نَائِمًا».٣٩٨

299. Anas b. Mālik ؓ was asked about the Prophet's ﷺ fasting. He replied: "It was his habit that in some months he fasted for so many days, that it was thought he would continue fasting the whole month. In other months, he did not fast to the point that it was thought he would not fast any day from the month. If anyone wanted to observe him praying at a time of night, it was possible, and if one wanted to observe him sleeping, this too was possible."

Yaḥyā b. Yaḥyā al-ʿĀmirī said,

> You should know that fasting is from the best acts of worship and it is an act of striving. Its virtues have been reported in many ḥadīths, the loftiest of which is the ḥadīth mentioned in *Ṣaḥīḥ al-Bukhārī* and *Ṣaḥīḥ Muslim* wherein Allāh ﷻ said on the Prophet's ﷺ tongue, "Every deed of the son of Ādam is for him except fasting; it is for Me and I shall reward him for it."[399] [400]

Al-Bājūrī said,

> **"If anyone wanted to observe him praying at a time of night, it was possible, and if one wanted to observe him sleeping, this too was possible":** I.e. because he did not specify a time for prayer and a time for sleep. Rather, his prayer time during some nights was his sleeping time in others, and vice versa. He performed his night prayer according to his circumstances. Furthermore, the night prayer's being performed at the early part of night or the late does not negate one's persistence on an act. This is akin to when the obligatory prayer is sometimes performed during the early part of the prayer time and sometimes at the later time, this does not negate one's persistence on it.

> Prayer was mentioned in the answer despite the question specifically mentioning fasting. This was an indication towards the questioner that he should also give care to the prayer.

> To summarise: The Prophet's fasting and prayer ﷺ were of the utmost balance, they neither bore excess or neglect.

---

398 *Ṣaḥīḥ al-Bukhārī* (1141)
399 *Ṣaḥīḥ al-Bukhārī* (1780) and *Ṣaḥīḥ Muslim* (1949)
400 *Bahjat al-Maḥāfil*

ʿAbd al-Raḥmān al-Mubārakfūrī said,

> Al-Ḥāfiẓ Ibn Ḥajar said that the meaning of this ḥadīth is that he ﷺ did not follow a particular pattern in his worship. An example of this is that he used to pray night prayers at the beginning of the night, some other times in the middle of the night and some other times at the end of the night. Likewise, he used to fast the beginning of the month, and some other times in the middle of the month and some other times at the end of the month. Thus, if a person wanted to observe his worship, he would certainly be able to see him either fasting or praying.[401]

٣٠٠- حَدَّثَنَا مَحْمُودُ بْنُ غَيْلانَ، قَالَ: حَدَّثَنَا أَبُو دَاوُدَ قَالَ: حَدَّثَنَا شُعْبَةُ، عَنْ أَبِي بِشْرٍ، قَالَ: سَمِعْتُ سَعِيدَ بْنَ جُبَيْرٍ، عَنِ ابْنِ عَبَّاسٍ قَالَ: «كَانَ النَّبِيُّ صلىٰ الله عليه وسلم يَصُومُ حَتَّىٰ نَقُولَ مَا يُرِيدُ أَنْ يُفْطِرَ مِنْهُ، وَيُفْطِرُ حَتَّىٰ نَقُولَ مَا يُرِيدُ أَنْ يَصُومَ، وَمَا صَامَ شَهْرًا كَامِلا مُنْذُ قَدِمَ الْمَدِينَةَ إِلا رَمَضَانَ»[٤٠٢].

300. ʿAbdullāh b. ʿAbbās ﷺ narrated: "The Prophet ﷺ at times would fast continuously to such an extent that we began to think that he would not discontinue fasting. And, at times he would not fast to such an extent that we began thinking he would not restart fasting. The Messenger of Allāh ﷺ did not fast a whole month from the time he entered Madīnah, except the month of Ramaḍān."

ʿAbd al-Razzāq al-Badr said,

> Ibn ʿAbbās's ḥadīth is similar in meaning to the previous ḥadīths of ʿĀ'ishah and Anas.

٣٠١- حَدَّثَنَا مُحَمَّدُ بْنُ بَشَّارٍ، قَالَ: حَدَّثَنَا عَبْدُ الرَّحْمَنِ بْنُ مَهْدِيٍّ، عَنْ سُفْيَانَ، عَنْ مَنْصُورٍ، عَنْ سَالِمِ بْنِ أَبِي الْجَعْدِ، عَنْ أَبِي سَلَمَةَ، عَنْ أُمِّ سَلَمَةَ، قَالَتْ: مَا رَأَيْتُ النَّبِيَّ صلىٰ الله عليه وسلم يَصُومُ شَهْرَيْنِ مُتَتَابِعَيْنِ إِلا شَعْبَانَ وَرَمَضَانَ[٤٠٣].

301. Umm Salamah ﷺ narrated: "I did not see the Prophet ﷺ fast two consecutive months except the months of Shaʿbān and Ramaḍān."

---

401 *Tuḥfat al-Aḥwadhī*
402 *Sahīh al-Bukhārī* (1971) and *Ṣaḥīḥ Muslim* (1157)
403 *Sunan Abī Dāwūd* (2336) and *Sunan Ibn Mājah* (1648)

قَالَ أَبُو عِيسَىٰ: هَذَا إِسنَادٌ صَحِيحٌ وَهَكَذَا قَالَ: عَنْ أَبِي سَلَمَةَ، عَنْ أُمِّ سَلَمَةَ، وَرَوَىٰ هَذَا الْحَدِيثَ غَيْرُ وَاحِدٍ، عَنْ أَبِي سَلَمَةَ، عَنْ عَائِشَةَ، عَنِ النَّبِيِّ صلىٰ الله عليه وسلم، وَيُحْتَمَلُ أَنْ يَكُونَ أَبُو سَلَمَةَ بْنُ عَبْدِ الرَّحْمَنِ قَدْ رَوَىٰ الْحَدِيثَ عَنْ عَائِشَةَ وَأُمِّ سَلَمَةَ جَمِيعًا، عَنِ النَّبِيِّ صلىٰ الله عليه وسلم.

Abū ʿĪsā said: This chain of narration from Abū Salamah from Umm Salamah is authentic. A number of other people reported this ḥadīth from Abū Salamah from ʿĀ'ishah from the Prophet ﷺ. It is possible that Abū Salamah b. ʿAbd al-Raḥmān reported this ḥadīth from both ʿĀ'ishah and Umm Salamah together.

Ibn ʿAbd al-Barr said,

> ʿAbdullāh b. al-Mubārak said, "In the Arabic language saying 'fasted the whole month' can refer to someone fasting most of the month."[404]

Ibn Rajab said,

> The Prophet ﷺ used to fast during the month of Shaʿbān more than any other months. The most correct view is that he ﷺ fasted most of the month as evidenced in many other explicit ḥadīths. Ibn ʿAbbās ﷺ used to forbid people from fasting a whole month (except the month of Ramaḍān). The month of Shaʿbān is the most virtuous month after the month of Ramaḍān due to the fact that it is the closest month to the month of Ramaḍān. Thus when one offers optional fasting in Shaʿbān and then follows it with obligatory fasting in Ramaḍān, it is like the regular Sunnah prayers preceding and following the obligatory prayers.[405]

Al-Bājūrī said,

> **"It is possible that Abū Salamah b. ʿAbd al-Raḥmān reported this ḥadīth from both ʿĀ'ishah and Umm Salamah together":** The author mentions this here to display that both routes are authentic. This is further strengthened by the fact that Abū Salamah would sometimes report [it] from Umm Salamah and sometimes from ʿĀ'ishah.

---

404 *Al-Istidhkār*
405 *Laṭā'if al-Maʿārif*

٣٠٢- حَدَّثَنَا هَنَّادٌ، قَالَ: حَدَّثَنَا عَبْدَةُ، عَنْ مُحَمَّدِ بْنِ عَمْرٍو، قَالَ: حَدَّثَنَا أَبُو سَلَمَةَ، عَنْ عَائِشَةَ، قَالَتْ: «لَمْ أَرَ رَسُولَ اللهِ صلى الله عليه وسلم يَصُومُ فِي شَهْرٍ أَكْثَرَ مِنْ صِيَامِهِ لِلَّهِ فِي شَعْبَانَ، كَانَ يَصُومُ شَعْبَانَ إِلا قَلِيلا، بَلْ كَانَ يَصُومُهُ كُلَّهُ»٤٠٦.

302. 'Ā'ishah ﵂ narrated: "I did not see the Messenger of Allāh ﷺ fast in a month [excluding Ramaḍān] more than he did in Sha'bān. He fasted the month except for a few days; rather he fasted the full month."

Ibn al-Qayyim said,

> The statement of 'Ā'ishah ﵂ indicates that he nearly fasted the whole month of Sha'bān and the days he left out were insignificant in number. Al-Nawawī said that the Prophet ﷺ did not fast a whole month except Ramaḍān so people would not make this act of his obligatory.[407]

Al-Shawkānī said,

> The first part of the statement of 'Ā'ishah ﵂ seems to contradict her last statement and scholars reconciled the meanings of the two statements by concluding that she meant that he nearly fasted the whole month. However, al-Ṭībī dismissed such a reconciliation based on the meanings of the word "*kul*" (English: whole) mentioned in the ḥadīth, and so he stated that she meant that he fasted the whole month of Sha'bān one year and most of it another year so that people would not think that it is obligatory to fast it.[408]

٣٠٣- حَدَّثَنَا الْقَاسِمُ بْنُ دِينَارٍ الْكُوفِيُّ، قَالَ: حَدَّثَنَا عُبَيْدُ اللهِ بْنُ مُوسَىٰ، وَطَلْقُ بْنُ غَنَّامٍ، عَنْ شَيْبَانَ، عَنْ عَاصِمٍ، عَنْ زِرِّ بْنِ حُبَيْشٍ، عَنْ عَبْدِ اللهِ، قَالَ: «كَانَ رَسُولُ اللهِ صلى الله عليه وسلم يَصُومُ مِنْ غُرَّةِ كُلِّ شَهْرٍ ثَلاثَةَ أَيَّامٍ، وَقَلَّمَا كَانَ يُفْطِرُ يَوْمَ الْجُمُعَةِ»٤٠٩.

303. 'Abdullāh b. Mas'ūd ﵁ narrated: "The Messenger of Allāh ﷺ fasted for three days at the beginning of every month, and rarely would he miss fasting on Fridays."

---

406 *Ṣaḥīḥ al-Bukhārī* (1969) and *Ṣaḥīḥ Muslim* (1156)
407 *Ḥāshiyat Ibn al-Qayyim 'alā Sunan Abī Dāwūd*
408 *Nayl al-Awṭār*
409 *Sunan Abī Dāwūd* (2450) and *Sunan Ibn Mājah* (1725)

Ibn Ḥajar al-ʿAsqalanī said,

> Reconciling all the ḥadīths related to fasting on Friday, it is disliked to single out Friday for fasting and the wisdom behind that is because Friday is a day of celebration and such days are not fasted. However, the counterargument is that the Prophet ﷺ allowed its fasting if Thursday or Saturday is fasted with it, and Ibn al-Qayyim and other scholars responded saying that fasting another day with it negates the intention of fasting Friday in particular.[410]

Al-Shawkānī said,

> This ḥadīth entails that he ﷺ fasted Friday along with Thursday or Saturday.[411]

٣٠٤- حَدَّثَنَا أَبُو حَفْصٍ عَمْرُو بْنُ عَلِيٍّ، قَالَ: حَدَّثَنَا عَبْدُ اللهِ بْنُ دَاوُدَ، عَنْ ثَوْرِ بْنِ يَزِيدَ، عَنْ خَالِدِ بْنِ مَعْدَانَ، عَنْ رَبِيعَةَ الْجُرَشِيِّ، عَنْ عَائِشَةَ، قَالَتْ: «كَانَ النَّبِيُّ صلىٰ الله عليه وسلم يَتَحَرَّىٰ صَوْمَ الاثْنَيْنِ وَالْخَمِيسِ»[٤١٢].

304. ʿĀʾishah ؓ narrated: "The Prophet ﷺ was keen to fast on Mondays and Thursdays."

Ibn ʿAllān al-Shafiʿī said,

> He ﷺ used to fast these two days due to their great virtue.[413]

Al-Bājūrī said,

> **"The Prophet ﷺ was keen to fast on Mondays and Thursdays":** This was because the deeds are presented on these days, as will be mentioned in the next report.

ʿAbd al-Raḥmān al-Mubarakfūrī said,

> This shows that he ﷺ had great keenness towards the fasting of these two days.[414]

---

410 *Fatḥ al-Bārī*
411 *Nayl al-Awṭār*
412 *Sunan Ibn Mājah* (1649) and *Sunan al-Tirmidhī* (745)
413 *Dalīl al-Fāliḥīn li Ṭuruq Riyāḍ al-Ṣāliḥīn*
414 *Tuḥfat al-Aḥwadhī*

٣٠٥- حَدَّثَنَا مُحَمَّدُ بْنُ يَحْيَىٰ، قَالَ: حَدَّثَنَا أَبُو عَاصِمٍ، عَنْ مُحَمَّدِ بْنِ رِفَاعَةَ، عَنْ سُهَيْلِ بْنِ أَبِي صَالِحٍ، عَنْ أَبِيهِ، عَنْ أَبِي هُرَيْرَةَ، أَنَّ النَّبِيَّ صلىٰ الله عليه وسلم قَالَ: «تُعْرَضُ الأَعْمَالُ يَوْمَ الاثْنَيْنِ وَالْخَمِيسِ، فَأُحِبُّ أَنْ يُعْرَضَ عَمَلِي وَأَنَا صَائِمٌ».[٤١٥]

305. Abū Hurayrah رضي الله عنه narrated: "The Prophet ﷺ said, 'Deeds are presented before Allāh جل جلاله on Mondays and Thursdays; therefore I like for my [good] deeds to be presented whilst I am fasting.'"

Ibn al-ʿUthaymīn said,

> The virtue of the day of Monday is established in other ḥadīths wherein he ﷺ mentioned that it was the day on which he was born, the day he was sent to people and also the day on which he received the first revelation. Fasting the day of Thursday is a Sunnah but it is less virtuous than the day of Monday. However, the most virtuous kind of fasting is the fasting of Prophet Dāwūd عليه السلام which is to fast alternate days.[416]

Al-Bājūrī said,

> The wisdom behind presenting the deeds is so that Allāh can display [proudly] the obedient servants' [deeds] to the angels. Otherwise, He is transcendent of needing the presentation, for He is more aware of His servants than the angels.

٣٠٦- حَدَّثَنَا مَحْمُودُ بْنُ غَيْلَانَ، قَالَ: حَدَّثَنَا أَبُو أَحْمَدَ، وَمُعَاوِيَةُ بْنُ هِشَامٍ، قَالَا: حَدَّثَنَا سُفْيَانُ، عَنْ مَنْصُورٍ، عَنْ خَيْثَمَةَ، عَنْ عَائِشَةَ، قَالَتْ: «كَانَ النَّبِيُّ صلىٰ الله عليه وسلم يَصُومُ مِنَ الشَّهْرِ السَّبْتَ وَالأَحَدَ وَالاثْنَيْنَ، وَمِنَ الشَّهْرِ الآخَرِ الثُّلَاثَاءَ وَالأَرْبَعَاءَ وَالْخَمِيسَ»[٤١٧].

306. ʿĀ'ishah رضي الله عنها narrated: "The Prophet ﷺ used to fast in one month Saturdays, Sundays and Mondays, and in the following month he would fast on Tuesdays, Wednesdays and Thursdays."

Ibn Ḥajar al-ʿAsqalānī said,

> The purpose of dividing his fasting was so that he could be able to fast

415 *Sunan al-Tirmidhī* (747)
416 *Sharḥ Riyāḍ al-Ṣāliḥīn*
417 *Sunan al-Tirmidhī* (746)

most of the days of the week.[418]

Al-Ṣanʿanī said,

> The reason behind him ﷺ fasting Saturdays and Sundays is explained in another ḥadīth wherein he mentioned that he fasted them because they are the ʿĪd days of the disbelievers. Subsequently, he wanted to oppose them by fasting these days since on their days of ʿĪd the disbelievers would be indulging in feasts, drinks and merriment.[419]

Ibn al-Qayyim said,

> It is disliked to single out Saturday for fasting and this ḥadīth can be reconciled with other ḥadīths as the ruling of "disliked" is removed when another day is fasted with it (i.e. Friday or Sunday). The reason it is disliked to single out Saturday is so that the day venerated by the Jews as a day of rest is not glorified [by the Muslims].[420]

٣٠٧- حَدَّثَنَا أَبُو مُصْعَبٍ الْمَدِينِيُّ، عَنْ مَالِكِ بْنِ أَنَسٍ، عَنْ أَبِي النَّضْرِ، عَنْ أَبِي سَلَمَةَ بْنِ عَبْدِ الرَّحْمَنِ، عَنْ عَائِشَةَ، قَالَتْ: «مَا كَانَ رَسُولُ اللهِ صلى الله عليه وسلم يَصُومُ فِي شَهْرٍ أَكْثَرَ مِنْ صِيَامِهِ فِي شَعْبَانَ»٤٢١.

307. ʿĀʾishah ﵂ narrated: "The Messenger of Allāh ﷺ did not fast in any month more than he did in the month of Shaʿbān."

ʿAbd al-Razzāq al-Badr said,

> This explains ʿĀʾishah's previous ḥadīth wherein she stated that the Prophet ﷺ fasted most of Shaʿbān.

٣٠٨- حَدَّثَنَا مَحْمُودُ بْنُ غَيْلَانَ، قَالَ: حَدَّثَنَا أَبُو دَاوُدَ، قَالَ: حَدَّثَنَا شُعْبَةُ، عَنْ يَزِيدَ الرِّشْكِ، قَالَ: سَمِعْتُ مُعَاذَةَ، قَالَتْ: قُلْتُ لِعَائِشَةَ: «أَكَانَ رَسُولُ اللهِ صلى الله عليه وسلم يَصُومُ ثَلَاثَةَ أَيَّامٍ مِنْ كُلِّ شَهْرٍ؟ قَالَتْ: نَعَمْ، قُلْتُ: مِنْ أَيِّهِ كَانَ يَصُومُ؟ قَالَتْ: كَانَ لَا يُبَالِي مِنْ أَيِّهِ صَامَ»٤٢٢.

---

418 *Fatḥ al-Bārī*
419 *Subul al-Salām*
420 *Ḥāshiyat Ibn al-Qayyim*
421 See ḥadīth 302
422 *Ṣaḥīḥ Muslim* (1160)

308. Muʿādhah narrated: "I asked ʿĀ'ishah ﷺ whether the Messenger of Allāh ﷺ used to fast three days of each month and she ﷺ confirmed that. Thus, I asked her, 'On which days of the month did he fast?' She replied, 'He did not specify any particular days.'"

قَالَ أَبُو عِيسىٰ: يَزِيدُ الرِّشْكُ هُوَ يَزِيدُ الضُّبَعِيُّ الْبَصْرِيُّ، وَهُوَ ثِقَةٌ، رَوَىٰ عَنْهُ شُعْبَةُ، وَعَبْدُ الْوَارِثِ بْنُ سَعِيدٍ، وَحَمَّادُ بْنُ زَيْدٍ، وَإِسْمَاعِيلُ بْنُ إِبْرَاهِيمَ، وَغَيْرُ وَاحِدٍ مِنَ الأَئِمَةِ، وَهُوَ يَزِيدُ الْقَاسِمُ، وَيُقَالُ: الْقَسَّامُ، وَالرِّشْكُ بِلُغَةِ أَهْلِ الْبَصْرَةِ هُوَ الْقَسَّامُ.

Abū ʿĪsā said: Yazīd al-Rishk is Yazīd al-Ḍubaʿī al-Baṣrī. He is a reliable narrator. Shuʿbah, ʿAbd al-Wārith b. Saʿīd, Ḥammād b. Zayd, Ismāʿīl b. Ibrāhīm and others amongst the ḥadīth masters reported from him. His name is Yazīd al-Qāsim, and it was also said as al-Qassām. Al-Rishk in the dialect of the Baṣrans means al-Qassām.

Ibn Rajab said,

> This ḥadīth shows that he ﷺ did not have any specific days selected to fast the three days from each month.[423]

Al-Bājūrī said,

> **"He did not specify any particular days":** I.e. fasting in the early part of the month, the middle part and the end part was equal to him.
>
> **"Abū ʿĪsā said":** The author is mentioning the biography of Yazīd al-Rishk so as to certify his reliability, refuting those who falsely view him as being weak in ḥadīth. Criticism was levelled over the author's choice of mentioning this here. This is because he mentioned Yazīd al-Rishk earlier in the Chapter of *Ṣalāṭ al-Ḍuḥā*, and so it was more appropriate to certify his reliability there. Ibn Ḥajar replied to this by positing that the report here could be said to contradict the preceding reports that the Prophet ﷺ fasted the early part of the month and Mondays and Thursdays etc. Thus a critic may have levied an accusation on Yazīd due to this contradiction, and so the author chose to certify him as reliable here.

٣٠٩- حَدَّثَنَا هَارُونُ بْنُ إِسْحَاقَ الْهَمْدَانِيُّ، قَالَ: حَدَّثَنَا عَبْدَةُ بْنُ سُلَيْمَانَ،

---

423 *Laṭā'if al-Maʿārif*

عَنْ هِشَامِ بْنِ عُرْوَةَ، عَنْ أَبِيهِ، عَنْ عَائِشَةَ، قَالَتْ: «كَانَ عَاشُورَاءُ يَوْمًا تَصُومُهُ قُرَيْشٌ فِي الْجَاهِلِيَّةِ، وَكَانَ رَسُولُ اللهِ صلى الله عليه وسلم يَصُومُهُ، فَلَمَّا قَدِمَ الْمَدِينَةَ صَامَهُ وَأَمَرَ بِصِيَامِهِ، فَلَمَّا افْتُرِضَ رَمَضَانُ كَانَ رَمَضَانُ هُوَ الْفَرِيضَةَ وَتُرِكَ عَاشُورَاءُ، فَمَنْ شَاءَ صَامَهُ وَمَنْ شَاءَ تَرَكَهُ»[٤٢٤].

309. ʿĀʾishah ﵂ narrated: "The day of ʿĀshūrā was a day that the Quraysh used to fast before Islām and the Messenger of Allāh ﷺ observed this fast too. When he came to Madīnah he observed its fast and commanded others to fast it too. However, when the command to fast the month of Ramaḍān was revealed, it became the obligatory fasting and the fast of ʿĀshūrā was left; whoever wished, observed its fast and whoever did not, left it."

ʿAbd al-Raḥmān al-Mubārakfūrī said,

> This shows that the fast of ʿĀshūrā[425] was made obligatory but the ruling was abrogated when it was revealed that the fast of Ramaḍān is obligatory.[426]

ʿAbdullāh b. Saʿīd al-Ḥaḍramī al-Makkī said,

> Al-Qāḍī ʿIyyād said that it is possible that he ﷺ fasted the day of ʿĀshūrā to incline the hearts of the Jews to Islām just as he did when he prayed toward their *qiblah* (Jerusalem). However, when Makkah was conquered and Islām spread, he preferred to oppose them and so he said that he will fast another day with the day of ʿĀshūrā.
>
> According to some scholars the best manner of fasting the day of ʿAshūrā is by fasting it with the day that precedes it and the day that follows it. Then, to fast ʿĀshūrā and the day before it, and the last in rank is to fast the day alone.[427]

Al-Bājūrī said,

---

424 *Ṣaḥīḥ al-Bukhari* (1592) and *Ṣaḥīḥ Muslim* (1125)

425 Ibn ʿAbbās narrated that the Prophet ﷺ came to Madīnah and saw the Jews fasting on the day of ʿĀshūrā. He said, "What is this?" They said, "This is a good day, this is the day when Allāh saved the Children of Israel from their enemy and Mūsā fasted on this day." He ﷺ said, "We are closer to Mūsā than you." So he fasted on this day and told the people to fast. (*Ṣaḥīḥ al-Bukhārī* (1865))

426 *Tuḥfat al-Aḥwadhī*

427 *Muntahā al-Suʾl ʿalā Wasāʾil al-Wuṣūl ilā Shamāʾil al-Rasūl*

"That the Quraysh used to fast before Islām": I.e. a practice taken from the People of the Scripture. Al-Qurṭubī said, "It is possible that they based this fasting on the legislation of Ibrāhīm or Nūh. It is reported that it was the day wherein the ark came to rest on the Mount Judi, and so Nūḥ fasted it out of thanks."

It states in *Ṣaḥīḥ Muslim* that fasting 'Āshūrā expiates a year's sins, whereas fasting 'Arafah does so for two years' worth. The wisdom behind this is that 'Āshūrā is a Mūsawi (i.e. Prophet Mūsā's) tradition whereas the day of 'Arafah is a Muḥammadi tradition.

٣١٠- حَدَّثَنَا مُحَمَّدُ بْنُ بَشَّارٍ، قَالَ: حَدَّثَنَا عَبْدُ الرَّحْمَنِ بْنُ مَهْدِيٍّ، قَالَ: حَدَّثَنَا سُفْيَانُ، عَنْ مَنْصُورٍ، عَنِ إِبْرَاهِيمَ، عَنْ عَلْقَمَةَ، قَالَ: سَأَلْتُ عَائِشَةَ، «أَكَانَ رَسُولُ اللهِ صلىٰ الله عليه وسلم يَخُصُّ مِنَ الأَيَّامِ شَيْئًا؟ قَالَتْ: كَانَ عَمَلُهُ دِيمَةً، وَأَيُّكُمْ يُطِيقُ مَا كَانَ رَسُولُ اللهِ صلىٰ الله عليه وسلم يُطِيقُ»[٤٢٨].

310. 'Alqamah narrated: "I asked 'Ā'ishah ﵂, 'Did the Messenger of Allāh ﷺ set aside particular days for worship?' She replied, 'The worship of the Prophet ﷺ was of a continuous nature, and who amongst you would have the strength that the Messenger of Allāh ﷺ possessed?'"

Ibn Baṭṭāl said,

> This means that he did not specify an act of worship to a particular day but it was narrated that his optional fasting was increased during the month of Sha'bān and that he encouraged fasting Mondays and Thursdays. We understand this by stating that he ﷺ fasted according to his energy level and so it happened that the fasting often coincided with the days he preferred.[429]

Ibn Rajab said,

> The Prophet ﷺ admonished discontinuing good deeds when they have become routine for the individual as noted in the ḥadīth wherein he addressed 'Abdullāh b. 'Umar ﵁, "Do not be like so and so, he used

428 *Ṣaḥīḥ al-Bukhārī* (1987) and *Ṣaḥīḥ Muslim* (783)
429 *Sharḥ Ṣaḥīḥ al-Bukhārī*

to offer night prayers and then he stopped."[430] [431]

Ibn Ḥajar al-ʿAsqalānī said,

> The virtue of continuing to do a good deed after it becomes habitual is so the individual does not become a person who breaks contact with his beloved. A person like that deserves admonishment. A similar case is the one who memorises from the Qur'ān and forgets it; there are many ḥadīths admonishing this. In this ḥadīth lies an encouragement for people to spare no efforts in worship, striving to reach their maximum individual capacity, provided that the exertion does not reach to the degree that will cause the person to leave the worship due to reasons such as boredom.[432]

Al-Ghazālī said,

> It was narrated that if Allāh accustoms a person to an act of worship but later on he stops it out of boredom, Allāh will despise him. This is why it is reported that the Prophet ﷺ continuously prayed the two units after *ʿAṣr* to make up the two units he missed after the *Ẓuhr* prayer due to his visitors.[433] However, he prayed them in his house

430 *Fatḥ al-Bārī* of Ibn Rajab
431 *Ṣaḥīḥ al-Bukhārī* (1090)
432 *Fatḥ al-Bārī*
433 Kurayb, the freed slave of Ibn ʿAbbās stated: "Ibn ʿAbbās, ʿAbd al-Raḥmān b. Azhar and al-Miswar b. Makhramah sent me to ʿĀ'ishah saying, "Pay her our greetings and ask her about our offering of the two units after *ʿAṣr* prayer, and tell her that we have been informed that you offer these two units while we have heard that the Prophet ﷺ had forbidden their offering." Ibn ʿAbbās said, "I and ʿUmar used to beat the people for their offering of them." I entered upon her and delivered their message to her. She said, "Ask Umm Salamah." So, I informed them [of ʿĀ'ishah's answer] and they sent me to Umm Salamah for the same purpose as they sent me to ʿĀ'ishah. Umm Salamah replied, "I heard the Prophet ﷺ forbidding the offering of these two units. Once the Prophet ﷺ offered the *ʿAṣr* prayer, and then came to me. And at that time an Anṣāri women from the tribe of Banū Ḥarām was with me. Then [the Prophet ﷺ] offered those two units, and I sent my [lady] servant to him, saying, "Stand beside him and say [to him]: "Umm Salamah says, "O Allāh's Apostle! Didn't I hear you forbidding the offering of these two units [after the *ʿAṣr* prayer] yet I see you offering them?" And if he beckons to you with his hand, then wait behind." So the lady slave did that and the Prophet ﷺ beckoned to her with his hand, and she stayed behind. When the Prophet ﷺ finished his prayer, he said, "O the daughter of Abū Umayyah (i.e. Umm Salamah), you were asking me about these two units after the *ʿAsr* prayer. In fact, some people from the tribe of ʿAbd al-Qays came to me to embrace Islām and busied me so much

and not outside so that the people would not imitate him in this matter.[434]

Al-Bājūrī said,

To summarise: He had a routine most of the time and left it due to prudence.

٣١١- حَدَّثَنَا هَارُونُ بْنُ إِسْحَاقَ، قَالَ: حَدَّثَنَا عَبْدَةُ، عَنْ هِشَامِ بْنِ عُرْوَةَ، عَنْ أَبِيهِ، عَنْ عَائِشَةَ، قَالَتْ: دَخَلَ عَلَيَّ رَسُولُ اللهِ صلى الله عليه وسلم وَعِنْدِي امْرَأَةٌ، فَقَالَ: «مَنْ هَذِهِ؟» قُلْتُ: فُلَانَةُ لَا تَنَامُ اللَّيْلَ، فَقَالَ رَسُولُ اللهِ صلى الله عليه وسلم: «عَلَيْكُمْ مِنَ الْأَعْمَالِ مَا تُطِيقُونَ، فَوَاللهِ لَا يَمَلُّ اللهُ حَتَّى تَمَلُّوا»، وَكَانَ أَحَبَّ ذَلِكَ إِلَى رَسُولِ اللهِ صلى الله عليه وسلم الَّذِي يَدُومُ عَلَيْهِ صَاحِبُهُ[435].

311. 'Ā'ishah ؓ narrated: "The Messenger of Allāh ﷺ once came home while a woman was present at that time. He inquired, 'Who is this woman?' I told him the name of the woman and then said, 'She does not sleep at night.' The Messenger ﷺ said, 'One should offer deeds that befit one's capacity. By Allāh! Allāh will not get bored until you get bored [from the act of worship].'" ['Ā'ishah added], "The most beloved of deeds to the Messenger ﷺ were those that were performed with consistency."

Al-Bājūrī said,

"She does not sleep at night": I.e. she spends the night engaged in prayer, remembrance, recitation of the Qur'ān etc.

Ibn 'Abd al-Barr said,

The scholars understand the part, "Allāh will not get bored until you

---

that I did not offer the two units that are offered after the *Ẓuhr* compulsory prayer, and these two units [you have seen me offering] make up for those." (*Ṣaḥīḥ al-Bukhārī*: 4370)

Abū Salamah narrated that he asked 'Ā'ishah about the two prostrations (i.e. units) that the Messenger of Allah ﷺ used to pray after *'Aṣr*. She said, "He used to pray them before *'Aṣr*, but if he got distracted or forgot them, he would pray them after *'Aṣr*, and if he performed a prayer he would be consistent in it." (*Sunan al-Nasā'ī*: 578)

434 *Iḥyā 'Ulūm al-Dīn*
435 *Ṣaḥīḥ al-Bukhārī* (43) and *Ṣaḥīḥ Muslim* (785)

> get bored" to mean that Allāh will continue to reward the individual until he becomes bored of offering the good deed. Boredom in worship arises when one overburdens himself with that which he cannot bear.[436]

Ibn al-Qayyim said,

> Extremism in worship is of two types. The first type is that which negates the nature of the act of worship. Subsequently, the act is no longer considered to be an act of obedience. Examples of such cases are: a person who adds one unit to an obligatory prayer, fasts everyday or [during the days of *tashrīq*] instead of throwing pebbles, one throws big rocks. The second type is that which causes the person to cease his habitual acts of worship such as praying all night without sleeping, fasting every day except the forbidden days and overburdening oneself with anything similar.[437]

Ibn Rajab said,

> Performing a good deed that the body can bear throughout its anointed time, during one's weakness and strength will uphold the right path, and whoever performs a deed he cannot bear during weakness and sickness may end up discontinuing it.[438]

٣١٢- حَدَّثَنَا أَبُو هِشَامٍ مُحَمَّدُ بْنُ يَزِيدَ الرِّفَاعِيُّ، قَالَ: حَدَّثَنَا ابْنُ فُضَيْلٍ، عَنِ الأَعْمَشِ، عَنْ أَبِي صَالِحٍ، قَالَ: سَأَلْتُ عَائِشَةَ، وَأُمَّ سَلَمَةَ، «أَيُّ الْعَمَلِ كَانَ أَحَبَّ إِلَىٰ رَسُولِ اللهِ صلىٰ الله عليه وسلم؟ قَالَتَا: مَا دِيمَ عَلَيْهِ، وَإِنْ قَلَّ»٤٣٩.

312. Abū Ṣāliḥ narrated: "I enquired from ʿĀ'ishah and Umm Salamah ﷺ about the act that was the most beloved to the Messenger of Allāh ﷺ. Both answered, 'That deed which was practiced continuously, regardless of its size.'"

ʿAbd al-Razzāq al-Badr said,

> This is similar in meaning to what preceded. It entails a great maxim in acts of obedience, which is that one should betake acts of worship

436 *Al-Tamhīd*
437 *Madārij al-Sālikīn*
438 *Laṭā'if al-Maʿārif*
439 *Sunan al-Tirmidhī* (2856)

that he is capable of performing consistently.

٣١٣- حَدَّثَنَا مُحَمَّدُ بْنُ إِسْمَاعِيلَ، قَالَ: حَدَّثَنَا عَبْدُ اللهِ بْنُ صَالِحٍ، قَالَ: حَدَّثَنِي مُعَاوِيَةُ بْنُ صَالِحٍ، عَنْ عَمْرِو بْنِ قَيْسٍ، أَنَّهُ سَمِعَ عَاصِمَ بْنَ حُمَيْدٍ، قَالَ: سَمِعْتُ عَوْفَ بْنَ مَالِكٍ يَقُولُ: «كُنْتُ مَعَ رَسُولِ اللهِ صلىٰ الله عليه وسلم لَيْلَةً فَاسْتَاكَ ثُمَّ تَوَضَّأَ ثُمَّ قَامَ يُصَلِّي، فَقُمْتُ مَعَهُ فَبَدَأَ فَاسْتَفْتَحَ الْبَقَرَةَ فَلا يَمُرُّ بِآيَةِ رَحْمَةٍ إِلا وَقَفَ فَسَأَلَ، وَلا يَمُرُّ بِآيَةِ عَذَابٍ، إِلا وَقَفَ فَتَعَوَّذَ، ثُمَّ رَكَعَ فَمَكَثَ رَاكِعًا بِقَدْرِ قِيَامِهِ، وَيَقُولُ فِي رُكُوعِهِ: سُبْحَانَ ذِي الْجَبَرُوتِ وَالْمَلَكُوتِ وَالْكِبْرِيَاءِ وَالْعَظَمَةِ، ثُمَّ سَجَدَ بِقَدْرِ رُكُوعِهِ، وَيَقُولُ فِي سُجُودِهِ: سُبْحَانَ ذِي الْجَبَرُوتِ وَالْمَلَكُوتِ وَالْكِبْرِيَاءِ وَالْعَظَمَةِ ثُمَّ قَرَأَ آلَ عِمْرَانَ ثُمَّ سُورَةً يَفْعَلُ مِثْلَ ذَلِكَ»".

313. 'Awf b. Mālik ﷺ related: "I spent a night with the Messenger of Allāh ﷺ. He brushed his teeth with a *siwāk*, performed ablution and then stood up to commence the prayer, and so I joined him in the prayer. He began reciting Sūrah al-Baqarah [after al-Fātiḥah] and whenever he came across a verse about Allāh's mercy, he paused and beseeched Allāh for His Mercy. Likewise, when he came across a verse regarding His punishment, he paused and sought refuge in Allāh from His punishment. Then, he bowed and remained bowing for as long as he had spent in the standing posture. He recited whilst bowing, *'Subḥāna dhi 'l-Jabarūti wa 'l-Malakūti wa 'l-Kibriyā wa 'l-'Aẓamah.'* Then he prostrated for a similar length to the bowing and recited the same in the prostration. Then, he recited [in the second unit] Sūrah Āl 'Imrān and kept doing the same, proceeding chapter by chapter [in each subsequent unit.]"

Al-Bājūrī said,

Dhu 'l-Malakūt means the One with dominion and benevolence. *Dhu 'l-Jabarūt* means the One who subdues and surmounts. *Dhu 'l-Kibriyā* means the One who transcends all defects and shortcomings whilst everything submits to Him. *Dhu 'l-'Aẓamah* means the One whom nothing can encompass. It is said that *Kibriyā* refers to the perfection of His essence while *'Aẓamah* refers to the beauty of His attributes.

---

440 *Sunan Abī Dāwūd* (873)

"And kept doing the same": I.e. keeping the aforementioned traits related to seeking mercy and forgiveness, and the duration of the bowing and prostration.

"Proceeding chapter by chapter": I.e. he recited Sūrah al-Nisāʾ in the third unit and then al-Māʾidah in the fourth.

Ibn Sayyid al-Nās said,

This is one of the ḥadīths that provide a vivid insight into his fear of his Lord ﷻ and his worship.[441]

---

441 *ʿUyūn al-Athar*

باب ما جاء في قراءة رسول الله صلى الله عليه وسلم

[44] On Allāh's Messenger's ﷺ Recitation

Ibn al-Qayyim said,

> The Prophet ﷺ used to recite the Qur'ān whilst standing, sitting and lying down. He recited it with ablution and without ablution. The only thing that prevented him from reciting it was the state of major impurity.

Al-Bājūrī said,

> There are eight ḥadīths in this chapter.

٣١٤- حَدَّثَنَا قُتَيْبَةُ بْنُ سَعِيدٍ، قَالَ: حَدَّثَنَا اللَّيْثُ، عَنِ ابْنِ أَبِي مُلَيْكَةَ، عَنْ يَعلَىٰ بْنِ مَمْلَكٍ «أَنَّهُ سَأَلَ أُمَّ سَلَمَةَ، عَنْ قِرَاءَةِ رَسُولِ اللهِ صلىٰ الله عليه وسلم فَإِذَا هِيَ تَنْعَتُ قِرَاءَةً مُفَسَّرَةً حَرْفًا حَرْفًا»[٤٤٢].

314. Ya'lā b. Mamlak narrated that he asked Umm Salamah ﵂ about the way the Messenger of Allāh ﷺ recited the Qur'ān, and she described his recitation as clear, thoughtful and slow, letter by letter.

Al-Ghazālī said,

> The recommended way to recite the Qur'ān is to recite it slowly and clearly (Arabic: *tartīl*). It was narrated that Ibn 'Abbās ﵁ said, "I prefer to recite Sūrah al-Baqarah and Āl 'Imrān slowly with contemplation than reciting the whole Qur'ān hastily."[443]

٣١٥- حَدَّثَنَا مُحَمَّدُ بْنُ بَشَّارٍ، قَالَ: حَدَّثَنَا وَهْبُ بْنُ جَرِيرِ بْنِ حَازِمٍ، قَالَ: حَدَّثَنَا أَبِي، عَنْ قَتَادَةَ، قَالَ: قُلْتُ لأَنَسِ بْنِ مَالِكٍ: «كَيْفَ كَانَتْ قِرَاءَةُ رَسُولِ اللهِ صلىٰ

---

442 *Sunan Abī Dāwūd* (1466) and *Sunan al-Tirmidhī* (2923)

443 *Iḥyā' 'Ulūm al-Dīn*

الله عليه وسلم؟ فَقَالَ: مَدًّا»٤٤٤.

315. Qatādah narrated: "I asked Anas b. Mālik ◉, 'How was the recitation of the Messenger of Allāh ◉?' He replied, 'He prolonged the recitation of Qur'ān.'"

Al-Ṭībī said,

> The letters that are prolonged in the recitation of the Qur'ān are three letters, namely (ي – و – ا) and the length of the prolonged letter depends on the letter that follows and whether it is paused or not.[445]

Al-Bājūrī said,

> **"He prolonged the recitation of Qur'ān":** This relates to where lengthening is appropriate, whether that be long, short or medium. This does not mean exaggerating in lengthening wherein it is not appropriate, as done by reciters of our era and even the *imāms* of our prayers.

٣١٦- حَدَّثَنَا عَلِيُّ بْنُ حُجْرٍ، قَالَ: حَدَّثَنَا يَحْيَىٰ بْنُ سَعِيدٍ الأُمَوِيُّ، عَنِ ابْنِ جُرَيْجٍ، عَنِ ابْنِ أَبِي مُلَيْكَةَ، عَنْ أُمِّ سَلَمَةَ، قَالَتْ: «كَانَ النَّبِيُّ صلى الله عليه وسلم يَقْطَعُ قِرَاءَتَهُ يَقُولُ: ﴿الْحَمْدُ لِلَّهِ رَبِّ الْعَٰلَمِينَ ٢﴾ ثُمَّ يَقِفُ، ثُمَّ يَقُولُ: ﴿الرَّحْمَٰنِ الرَّحِيمِ ٣﴾ ثُمَّ يَقِفُ، وَكَانَ يَقْرَأُ ﴿مَٰلِكِ يَوْمِ الدِّينِ ٤﴾»٤٤٦

316. Umm Salamah ◉ narrated: "The Prophet ◉ recited every verse separately; he recited *'Alḥamdulillāhī rabbi 'l-'ālamīn'* and paused, then recited *'Al-raḥmāni 'l-raḥīm'* and paused, and then he recited *'Māliki yawmi 'l-dīn.'"*

Al-Sakhāwī said,

> This is evidence that he ◉ used to recite Sūrah al-Fātiḥah audibly.[447]

Ibn Baṭṭāl said,

> He ◉ used to recite in this way to fulfil the command of Allāh to recite the Qur'ān slowly and thoughtfully. Thus, he ◉ recited in such a

---

444 *Ṣaḥīḥ al-Bukhārī* (5045)
445 *Sharḥ Mishkāt al-Maṣābīḥ*
446 *Sunan al-Tirmidhī* (2927)
447 *Jamāl al-Qurrā' wa Kamāl al-Iqrā'*

manner to teach his nation the way to recite the Qurʾān and how to contemplate it.[448]

Ibn al-Qayyim said,

> The method of recitation mentioned in this ḥadīth is the most recommended way. It is better to pause after each verse even if the following verse depends on the verse that precedes it.[449]

Al-Bājūrī said,

> **"And paused":** I.e. he would stop reciting for a moment and then recite the next verse. He would do so until the end of the chapter.

٣١٧- حَدَّثَنَا قُتَيْبَةُ، قَالَ: حَدَّثَنَا اللَّيْثُ، عَنْ مُعَاوِيَةَ بْنِ صَالِحٍ، عَنْ عَبْدِ اللهِ بْنِ أَبِي قَيْسٍ، قَالَ: سَأَلْتُ عَائِشَةَ، عَنْ قِرَاءَةِ النَّبِيِّ صلى الله عليه وسلم أَكَانَ يُسِرُّ بِالْقِرَاءَةِ أَمْ يَجْهَرُ؟ قَالَتْ: «كُلُّ ذَلِكَ قَدْ كَانَ يَفْعَلُ، قَدْ كَانَ رُبَّمَا أَسَرَّ وَرُبَّمَا جَهَرَ، فَقُلْتُ: الْحَمْدُ لِلَّهِ الَّذِي جَعَلَ فِي الأَمْرِ سَعَةً»٤٥٠.

317. ʿAbdullāh b. Abī Qays ﷺ reported: "I inquired from ʿĀʾishah ﷺ about the recital of the Prophet ﷺ: whether he recited quietly or audibly. She replied, 'He recited in both ways; he recited quietly and audibly.' I said, 'Praise be to Allāh, who has accorded ease in this matter.'"

Al-Bājūrī said,

> **"About the recital of the Prophet ﷺ":** I.e. at night. This is shown by the author's listing of this narration in his *Jāmiʿ* (i.e. his famous, large ḥadīth compendium) under the chapter "Recitation During the Night" with the same chain of narration and the additional wording, "I inquired from ʿĀʾishah ﷺ about the recital of the Prophet ﷺ at night."
>
> **"He recited in both ways; he recited quietly and audibly":** The most appropriate choice is that which increases one's tranquillity and averts showing off.

---

448 *Sharḥ Ṣaḥīḥ al-Bukhārī*
449 *Zād al-Maʿād*
450 *Sunan Abī Dāwūd* (226)

"Praise be to Allāh, who has accorded ease in this matter": This is because if one form was specified, the soul might not kindle to it and thus the reward would be prohibited. Allāh's giving of scope in a religious duty is a blessing which should be met with thanks.

Al-Nabhānī said,

> Ibn 'Abbās ﷺ said, "When the Prophet ﷺ recited the Qur'ān in his house, those in the same house would be able to hear his recital but he would not let it reach [to the ears of those] outside his house."[451]

٣١٨- حَدَّثَنَا مَحْمُودُ بْنُ غَيْلَانَ، قَالَ: حَدَّثَنَا وَكِيعٌ، قَالَ: حَدَّثَنَا مِسْعَرٌ، عَنْ أَبِي الْعَلَاءِ الْعَبْدِيِّ، عَنْ يَحْيَىٰ بْنِ جَعْدَةَ، عَنْ أُمِّ هَانِئٍ، قَالَتْ: «كُنْتُ أَسْمَعُ قِرَاءَةَ النَّبِيِّ صلىٰ الله عليه وسلم بِاللَّيْلِ وَأَنَا عَلَىٰ عَرِيشِي»[452].

318. Umm Hānī' ﵂ narrated: "I heard the Prophet ﷺ reciting the Qur'ān at night, whilst I was upon my bed."

Al-Qāsim b. Sallām said,

> Umm Hānī' intended to mean that she heard his recitation during the night.[453]

'Abdullāh b. Sa'īd al-Ḥaḍramī al-Makkī said,

> This ḥadīth refers to an instance when the Prophet ﷺ was in Makkah and he was offering his night prayers next to the Ka'bah. This happened before the migration (Hijrah).[454]

٣١٩- حَدَّثَنَا مَحْمُودُ بْنُ غَيْلَانَ، قَالَ: حَدَّثَنَا أَبُو دَاوُدَ، قَالَ: حَدَّثَنَا شُعْبَةُ، عَنْ مُعَاوِيَةَ بْنِ قُرَّةَ، قَالَ: سَمِعْتُ عَبْدَ اللهِ بْنَ مُغَفَّلٍ يَقُولُ: «رَأَيْتُ النَّبِيَّ صلىٰ الله عليه وسلم عَلَىٰ نَاقَتِهِ يَوْمَ الْفَتْحِ وَهُوَ يَقْرَأُ: ﴿إِنَّا فَتَحْنَا لَكَ فَتْحًا مُّبِينًا ۝ لِّيَغْفِرَ لَكَ ٱللَّهُ مَا تَقَدَّمَ مِن ذَنبِكَ وَمَا تَأَخَّرَ﴾ [الفتح ١-٢]، قَالَ: فَقَرَأَ وَرَجَّعَ».

---

451 *Al-Wasā'il al-Wuṣūl ilā Shamā'il al-Rasūl*
452 *Sunan Ibn Mājah* (1349)
453 *Faḍā'il al-Qur'ān*
454 *Muntahā al-Su'l 'alā Wasā'il al-Wuṣūl ilā Shamā'il al-Rasūl*

قَالَ: وَقَالَ مُعَاوِيَةُ بْنُ قُرَّةَ: لَوْلا أَنْ يَجْتَمِعَ النَّاسُ عَلَيَّ لأَخَذْتُ لَكُمْ فِي ذَلِكَ الصَّوْتِ أَوْ قَالَ: اللَّحْنِ.[٤٥٥]

319. ʿAbdullāh b. Mughaffal ﷺ narrated: "I saw the Prophet ﷺ riding his camel on the day of the conquest and he was reciting, {Indeed, We have given you, [O Muḥammad], a clear conquest, that Allāh may forgive for you what preceded of your sin and what will follow.}[456] He ﷺ recited it and did *tarjīʿ*[457]."

Muʿāwiyah b. Qurrah ﷺ (a narrator of this ḥadīth) said, "If I did not fear that people would gather around me, I would have recited it for you in the same tone."

Al-Bājūrī said,

> **"And he was reciting":** This displays the Prophet's ﷺ diligence towards worship, even in times when he was riding and travelling.
>
> **"If I did not fear that people would gather around me, I would have recited it for you in the same tone":** It can be derived from this that doing an action which causes the people to gather is detested (*makrūh*) if it would lead to *fitnah* (tribulation) or a decrease in one's reputation.

ʿAbdullāh b. Saʿīd al-Ḥaḍramī al-Makkī said,

> This indicates that reciting audibly is better than reciting inaudibly in some places especially when it is to glorify Allāh and awake the heedless. The conquest referred to is either the conquest of Makkah, as reported from Anas b. Mālik, or Khaybar, as reported from Mujāhid, or the Ḥudaybiyah Truce as reported from the majority because it was the basis of all the conquests that followed.
>
> He ﷺ recited the entirety of Sūrah al-Fatḥ, as stated in the ḥadīth reported by al-Bukharī. *Tarjīʿ* means the coming and going of sound

455 *Ṣaḥīḥ al-Bukhārī* (4281) and *Ṣaḥīḥ Muslim* (794)

456 Qurʾān: 48:1-2

457 Translator Note: The scholars differed on the actual meaning of "*tarjī*", some said it refers to the coming and going of sound in the larynx, or technically speaking, rolling of the sound in it, and some said it means beautifying the voice, and some said it happens unwillingly due to joy, and some said it happened when he ﷺ was riding his camel so it happened unwillingly due to the movement of the camel, and some said it means repeating the words in a lower tone.

and it often happens due to joy, as it happened to the Prophet ﷺ on that day.[458]

٣٢٠- حَدَّثَنَا قُتَيْبَةُ بْنُ سَعِيدٍ، قَالَ: حَدَّثَنَا نُوحُ بْنُ قَيْسٍ الْحُدَّانِيُّ، عَنْ حُسَامِ بْنِ مِصَكٍّ، عَنْ قَتَادَةَ قَالَ: «مَا بَعَثَ اللهُ نَبِيًّا إِلا حَسَنَ الْوَجْهِ، حَسَنَ الصَّوْتِ، وَكَانَ نَبِيُّكُمْ صلى الله عليه وسلم حَسَنَ الْوَجْهِ، حَسَنَ الصَّوْتِ، وَكَانَ لا يُرَجِّعُ».[459]

320. Qatādah ؓ said: "Allāh blessed every Prophet that He had sent with a beautiful face and beautiful voice. Your Prophet ﷺ had a beautiful face and a beautiful voice, and did not recite with *tarjīʿ*."

Al-Bājūrī said,

> **"With a beautiful face and beautiful voice":** So his outward beauty indicates his beautiful interior, for the outward is an embodiment of the inward.

Ibn al-Athīr said,

> This refers to his recital when he was not riding since the instance of the *tarjīʿ* happened while he was riding.[460]

Muḥammad b. Yūsuf al-Shāmī said,

> Ibn al-Munīr, al-Zarkashī and others commented on the statement of the Prophet ﷺ wherein he mentioned that Prophet Yūsuf ؑ was given half of the beauty, saying, "Some people think that the other half of beauty, based on this ḥadīth, is divided among the rest of people while, in fact, it means that Prophet Yūsuf was given half of the beauty given to Prophet Muḥammad ﷺ.[461]

٣٢١- حَدَّثَنَا عَبْدُ اللهِ بْنُ عَبْدِ الرَّحْمَنِ، قَالَ: حَدَّثَنَا يَحْيَىٰ بْنُ حَسَّانَ، قَالَ: حَدَّثَنَا عَبْدُ الرَّحْمَنِ بْنُ أَبِي الزِّنَادِ، عَنْ عَمْرِو بْنِ أَبِي عَمْرٍو، عَنْ عِكْرِمَةَ، عَنِ ابْنِ عَبَّاسٍ قَالَ: «كَانَتْ قِرَاءَةُ النَّبِيِّ صلى الله عليه وسلم رُبَّمَا يَسْمَعُهَا مَنْ فِي الْحُجْرَةِ وَهُوَ

---

458 *Muntahā al-Suʾl ʿalā Wasāʾil al-Wuṣūl ilā Shamāʾil al-Rasūl*
459 *Tabaqāt Ibn Saʿd* (879)
460 *Al-Nihāyah fī Gharīb al-Ḥadīth*
461 *Subul Hudā wa al-Rashād*

فِي الْبَيْتِ»٤٦٢.

321. **ʿAbdullāh b. ʿAbbās** ❧ narrated: "The recitation of the Prophet
❧ was audible enough that it might have been possible that if he recited in the house, those in the courtyard would be able to hear it."

ʿAbd al-Razzāq al-Badr said,

> This explains the previous ḥadīths regarding the audibility of his rec-
> itation, which is to state that if he recited audibly in the night then it
> would be loud enough to be heard by those who were near to him,
> meaning he did not recite very loudly.

---

462 *Sunan Abī Dāwūd* (1327)

[45] On Allāh's Messenger's ﷺ Crying

Ibn al-Qayyim said.

The nature of his crying was similar to that of his laughing; he neither laughed out loud nor did he laugh boisterously. Likewise when he cried, he neither wailed nor was his breath taken away due to it. Rather, his eyes would shed tears and a sound would emit from his chest; he cried out of his mercy for the deceased and sometimes he cried out of his concern and mercy for his nation. Sometimes he would cry due to his fear of Allāh, and sometimes when he heard the Qurʾān, due to his love of Allāh. Thus embodying the required combination of love and fear of Allāh.[463]

Al-Bājūrī said,

There are six ḥadīths in this chapter.

٣٢٢- حَدَّثَنَا سُوَيْدُ بْنُ نَصْرٍ، قَالَ: حَدَّثَنَا عَبْدُ اللهِ بْنُ الْمُبَارَكِ، عَنْ حَمَّادِ بْنِ سَلَمَةَ، عَنْ ثَابِتٍ، عَنْ مُطَرِّفٍ وَهُوَ ابْنُ عَبْدِ اللهِ بْنِ الشِّخِّيرِ، عَنْ أَبِيهِ، قَالَ: أَتَيْتُ رَسُولَ اللهِ صلى الله عليه وسلم وَهُوَ يُصَلِّي وَلِجَوْفِهِ أَزِيزٌ كَأَزِيزِ الْمِرْجَلِ مِنَ الْبُكَاءِ[464].

322. ʿAbdullāh b. Shikhīr ؓ narrated: "I entered upon the Messenger of Allāh ﷺ whilst he was praying. Due to his crying, humming emitted from his chest like that of a cauldron."

ʿAlī al-Qārī said,

"Due to his crying": This is proof of his perfect fearfulness, awe and humility in his worship. It is from this aspect that he said, "If you knew what I know, you would laugh less and weep more." And he also said, "I am the most knowledgeable of Allāh amongst you and the most in awe (*khashyah*) of Him." Both of these were report-

---

463 *Zād al-Maʿād* (1/183)
464 *Sunan Abī Dāwūd* (904)

ed by al-Bukhārī. And Muslim reported, "By the One whose hand Muḥammad's soul is in, if you saw what I saw you would laugh little and weep plenty." They asked, "What did you see O Allāh's Messenger?" He replied, "I saw paradise and the fire." Thus, Allāh gathered within him the knowledge of certainty (*'ilm al-yaqīn*) and the eye of certainty (*'ayn al-yaqīn*), rather He gathered with that the attestation of certainty (*ḥaqq al-yaqīn*).

Al-khashyah is more specific than fear, as it is fear connected to respect derived from complete knowledge. This is why Allāh states: **{It is those of His servants who have knowledge who stand in true awe of Allāh.}**[465]

Abd al-Karīm al-Khuḍayr said,

This description given by the narrator is to show the high level of humility and piety of the Prophet ﷺ from the effect of the Qur'ān. However, it is unfortunate that many people enter the prayer and end it without being affected by the Qur'ān they recite. The description given in this ḥadīth is what happens to those who follow the Prophet's example which results from the fear of Allāh that one feels whilst standing before Him in the prayer.

You find some people who are touched by the recitation of some individuals but never feel anything when the same verses are recited by someone else. This could be due to the beauty of the voice but one ought to be blamed if he only becomes touched by particular voices and does not get touched if the Qur'ān is recited beautifully by other people. This is because a person should feel touched and impacted by the words of the Qur'ān themselves, and so the beauty of the voice should serve to help the person to increase this feeling and not be that which makes the person cry.

Sometimes, there are individuals who we hear cry aloud in the prayer. If this happens because the person is overwhelmed and cannot control himself, then the person is not blamed. It is noticed that the effect on some people is short i.e. they cry when they come across a verse and after the verse ends, they return to their normal status. It should be noted that the real crying that affects the heart is that which does not end quickly. It was reported that many of the righteous prede-

465 Qur'ān: 35:26

> cessors would fall sick in the next morning because of their crying in the night while praying. Thus, the heart which cannot maintain this effect is indicative of the effect being weak upon it. I saw during the last Ramaḍān someone who was weeping out loud in the prayer and after the prayer ended he entered into a verbal altercation with other people over some issue. This shows that the heart is still taken away by this worldly life and the sins are not yet cleansed.[466]

٣٢٣- حَدَّثَنَا مَحْمُودُ بْنُ غَيْلَانَ، قَالَ: حَدَّثَنَا مُعَاوِيَةُ بْنُ هِشَامٍ، قَالَ: حَدَّثَنَا سُفْيَانُ، عَنِ الأَعْمَشِ، عَنِ إِبْرَاهِيمَ، عَنْ عُبَيْدَةَ، عَنْ عَبْدِ اللهِ بْنِ مَسْعُودٍ، قَالَ: قَالَ لِي رَسُولُ اللهِ صلىٰ الله عليه وسلم: اقْرَأْ عَلَيَّ فَقُلْتُ: يَا رَسُولَ اللهِ! أَقَرَأُ عَلَيْكَ وَعَلَيْكَ أُنْزِلَ؟ قَالَ: إِنِّي أُحِبُّ أَنْ أَسْمَعَهُ مِنْ غَيْرِي، فَقَرَأْتُ سُورَةَ النِّسَاءِ، حَتَّىٰ بَلَغْتُ ﴿وَجِئْنَا بِكَ عَلَىٰ هَٰٓؤُلَآءِ شَهِيدًا ﴿٤١﴾﴾، قَالَ: فَرَأَيْتُ عَيْنَيْ رَسُولِ اللهِ تَهمِلَانِ[٤٦٧].

323. ʿAbdullāh b. Masʿūd ﷺ related: "The Messenger of Allāh ﷺ once asked me to recite the Qurʿān to him. I said, 'O Messenger of Allāh! How could I recite it to you when it has been revealed to you?' He ﷺ said, 'I love to hear it from other people.' Thereupon I began reciting Sūrah al-Nisāʾ and when I reached, {But how [will it be with them] when We bring of every people a witness, and We bring thee [O Muḥammad] a witness against these?}[468] I saw tears begin to flow from the eyes of the Messenger of Allāh ﷺ."

Al-Qasṭallānī said,

> This effect is what a person would have when listening to the Qur'ān with his heart and not just his ears. Allāh ﷻ said: **{And when they hear what has been revealed to the Messenger, you see their eyes overflowing with tears because of what they have recognized of the truth.}**[469] [470]

Al-Bājūrī said,

> **"How could I recite it to you when it has been revealed to you?":**

466 *Sharḥ al-Muḥarrar fi al-Ḥadīth*
467 *Ṣaḥīḥ al-Bukhārī* (4582) and *Ṣaḥīḥ Muslim* (800)
468 Qur'ān: 4:41
469 Qur'ān: 5:83
470 *Al-Mawāhib al-Laduniyah bi al-Minaḥ al-Muḥammadiyyah*

Ibn Masʿūd was surprised at this request because he understood it as the Prophet ﷺ wishing to enjoy his recitation and not to test his accuracy.

From the benefits of this ḥadīth is to notify the superior that he should not turn his nose to benefiting from the junior/inferior. Many of the pious predecessors (*salaf*) would take benefit from their students.

ʿAlī al-Qārī said,

> Ibn Baṭṭāl said: "It is possible that he ﷺ requested to hear the Qur'ān from Ibn Masʿūd ؓ to show that listening to the Qur'ān is a Sunnah (even if the person has memorised it) or to contemplate it and reflect upon it because the listener is more focused and more able to contemplate than the reciter who is busy reciting."

Abū Ḥafs al-Suhrawardī said,

> This is indeed the truthful manner for listening to the Qur'ān. It is a truthfulness that no two believers would ever dispute over its truthfulness, and evidence testifying to the guidance of the person who is listening in such a lofty manner. The ignited flame of this thoughtful listening overcomes the coldness of certainty, causing the eyes to be flushed with tears. The combination of the element of certainty with the element of attentive and thoughtful listening brings forth different emotions; sometimes it produces grief, which is an enkindled emotion, and some other times it brings forth the flames of yearning, which is an enkindled emotion, and sometimes it sets the fire of regret, which is also an enkindled emotion. If listening to the Qur'ān manages to call forth these emotions from a heart that is filled with the coolness of certainty, the eyes will have no power but to release the tears therein because water is a result of the engagement between heat and cold. When the heat of listening emerges into the layers of the heart, its effect reflects on the bodily limbs through goose bumps; Allāh ﷻ said: **{Allāh has sent down the best statement: a consistent Book wherein is reiteration. The skins shiver there from of those who fear their Lord.}**[471] And when its effect escalates, it reaches into the brain causing the eyes to drop its tears, and when its effect crosses the borders and reaches into the soul, the waves can no longer be constrained within and so crying and disturbance manifest

471 Qur'ān: 29:23

upon the body. Each person, depending on his level, experiences these conditions.[472]

٣٢٤- حَدَّثَنَا قُتَيْبَةُ، قَالَ: حَدَّثنا جَرِيرٌ، عَنْ عَطَاءِ بْنِ السَّائِبِ، عَنْ أَبِيهِ، عَنْ عَبْدِ اللهِ بْنِ عَمْرٍو، قَالَ: «انْكَسَفَتِ الشَّمْسُ يَوْمًا عَلَىٰ عَهْدِ رَسُولِ اللهِ صلىٰ الله عليه وسلم فَقَامَ رَسُولُ اللهِ صلىٰ الله عليه وسلم يُصَلِّي، حَتَّىٰ لَمْ يَكَدْ يَرْكَعُ ثُمَّ رَكَعَ، فَلَمْ يَكَدْ يَرْفَعُ رَأْسَهُ، ثُمَّ رَفَعَ رَأْسَهُ، فَلَمْ يَكَدْ أَنْ يَسْجُدَ، ثُمَّ سَجَدَ، فَلَمْ يَكَدْ أَنْ يَرْفَعَ رَأْسَهُ، ثُمَّ رَفَعَ رَأْسَهُ، فَلَمْ يَكَدْ أَنْ يَسْجُدَ، ثُمَّ سَجَدَ فَلَمْ يَكَدْ أَنْ يَرْفَعَ رَأْسَهُ، فَجَعَلَ يَنْفُخُ وَيَبْكِي، وَيَقُولُ: رَبِّ أَلَمْ تَعِدْنِي أَنْ لا تُعَذِّبَهُمْ وَأَنَا فِيهِمْ؟ رَبِّ أَلَمْ تَعِدْنِي أَنْ لا تُعَذِّبَهُمْ وَهُمْ يَسْتَغْفِرُونَ؟ وَنَحْنُ نَسْتَغْفِرُكَ، فَلَمَّا صَلَّىٰ رَكْعَتَيْنِ انْجَلَتِ الشَّمْسُ، فَقَامَ فَحَمِدَ اللهَ تَعَالَىٰ وَأَثْنَىٰ عَلَيْهِ، ثُمَّ قَالَ: إِنَّ الشَّمْسَ وَالْقَمَرَ آيَتَانِ مِنْ آيَاتِ اللهِ لا يَنْكَسِفَانِ لِمَوْتِ أَحَدٍ وَلا لِحَيَاتِهِ، فَإِذَا انْكَسَفَا فَافْزَعُوا إِلَىٰ ذِكْرِ اللهِ تَعَالَىٰ»[٤٧٣].

324. ʿAbdullāh b. ʿAmr رضي الله عنه narrated: "In the time of the Messenger of Allāh ﷺ there once occurred a solar eclipse. Subsequently, the Messenger of Allāh ﷺ began to pray and he stood for such a period that it seemed that he did not intend to bow and then he did so. He then remained bowing to such an extent that it seemed that he did not intend to rise and then he did so. Then in the same manner after standing up from bowing, he stood for such a long period that it seemed that he did not intend to prostrate and then he did so. He remained in the position of prostration for such a long period that it seemed that he did not intend to raise his head and then he did so. In this manner he did the same after lifting his head and sitting between the two prostrations. He did the same [as he did in the first prostration] in the second one. After he arose from the prostration he began breathing heavily and crying whilst pleading, 'O Allāh! You have promised me that you will not punish them so long as I am among them. O Allāh! You have promised me that you will not punish them while they seek forgiveness. O Allāh! We beseech you for your forgiveness.'

When he ﷺ completed the prayer, the sun had already cleared. There-

472 *ʿAwārif al-Maʿārif*
473 *Musnad Aḥmad* (6483)

upon, he ﷺ delivered a sermon wherein he praised and exalted Allāh ﷻ then he said, 'Indeed, the sun and moon are from the signs of Allāh that do not eclipse because of the death or birth of anyone. Whenever eclipses happen, hasten to resort to the remembrance of Allāh.'"

'Abd al-Karīm al-Khudayr said,

> The Prophet ﷺ refuted the claim of the disbelievers before Islām that eclipses occur because of the death of persons who possess great status. This great sign is taken lightly today because the people perceive it as a mere natural phenomenon whose time of occurrence can be expected based on calculation. In other words, people have started to look at it through the lens of science to the extent that they will buy sunglasses and travel to other countries just to watch an eclipse while they should fear Allāh and rush to perform prayers in light of the guidance of the Prophet ﷺ in this regard.[474]

Muḥib al-Dīn al-Ṭabarī said,

> It coincided on this day that the son of the Prophet ﷺ died. The sun would often eclipse, according to their observations, on the twenty eighth or twenty ninth of the month. Thus, when they saw it had eclipsed on the tenth they said it must have eclipsed due to the death of the son of the Prophet ﷺ.[475]

Abū al-Ḥasan al-Nadwī said,

> Had this emotional sad event (i.e. the death of the son of the Prophet ﷺ) happened to any other leader, ruler or preacher, the least they would have done is to remain silent so as not to negate the speculations of people about the relation between the event and the occurrence of the eclipse. This is because the occurrence would serve their cause and movements and would allow them to enforce a layer of glorification that would make people trust them more. However, in this great event, the position of the Prophet ﷺ stands out, drawing the line between Prophets and all other leaders due to his refusal to take advantage of any event to attract more praise and glorification. This is why Allāh ﷻ prescribed to pray upon the occurrence of this event so as to prevent any opportunity for this deviated notion to grow in

---

474 *Sharḥ al-Muḥarrar fi al-Ḥadīth*

475 *Dhakhā'ir al-'Uqbā fi Manāqib Dhawil Qurbā*

the hearts of people and to strengthen the bond between the people and Allāh ﷻ.[476]

Al-Bājūrī said,

> Al-Nawawī mentioned that this was the only occasion that he ﷺ prayed the solar eclipse prayer.

٣٢٥- حَدَّثَنَا مَحْمُودُ بْنُ غَيْلانَ، قَالَ: حَدَّثَنَا أَبُو أَحْمَدَ، قَالَ: حَدَّثَنَا سُفْيَانُ، عَنْ عَطَاءِ بْنِ السَّائِبِ، عَنْ عِكْرِمَةَ، عَنِ ابْنِ عَبَّاسٍ، قَالَ: أَخَذَ رَسُولُ اللهِ صلىٰ الله عليه وسلم ابْنَةً لَهُ تَقْضِي فَاحْتَضَنَهَا فَوَضَعَهَا بَيْنَ يَدَيْهِ فَمَاتَتْ وَهِيَ بَيْنَ يَدَيْهِ، وَصَاحَتْ أُمُّ أَيْمَنَ فَقَالَ - يَعْنِي صلىٰ الله عليه وسلم -: «أَتَبْكِينَ عِنْدَ رَسُولِ اللهِ؟» فَقَالَتْ: أَلَسْتُ أَرَاكَ تَبْكِي؟ قَالَ: «إِنِّي لَسْتُ أَبْكِي، إِنَّمَا هِيَ رَحْمَةٌ، إِنَّ الْمُؤْمِنَ بِكُلِّ خَيْرٍ عَلَىٰ كُلِّ حَالٍ، إِنَّ نَفْسَهُ تُنْزَعُ مِنْ بَيْنِ جَنْبَيْهِ، وَهُوَ يَحْمَدُ اللهَ تعالىٰ»[٤٧٧].

325. ʿAbdullāh b. ʿAbbās ؓ related: "One of the daughters of the Messenger of Allāh ﷺ was on her death bed. He picked her up and placed her before him. Thus she passed away whilst in front of him. Umm Ayman began wailing aloud at her passing. The Messenger of Allāh ﷺ said, 'Are you crying in the presence of the Messenger of Allāh!?' She said, 'Do I not see you cry?' He replied, 'The tears you see are not from crying, but rather they are a mercy from Allāh. A believer is in a good state at all times, his soul is taken out whilst still praising Allāh ﷻ.'"

Al-Bājūrī said,

> **"Are you crying in the presence of the Messenger of Allāh!?":** I.e. the forbidden form of crying which is coupled with wailing that indicates despondency. He intended to reject and rebuke this. He said "In the presence of the Messenger of Allāh" instead of "In my presence" as that is more emphatic in rebuking and in preventing exiting religious boundaries.
>
> **"The tears you see are not from crying":** I.e. the forbidden form of crying like yours. Rather, my crying is of the eyes only.

---

476 *Al-Sīrat al-Nabawiyyah*
477 *Musnad Aḥmad* (2412)

'Abdullāh b. Sa'īd al-Ḥaḍramī al-Makkī said,

> It is prohibited to wail loudly but as she saw him shedding tears she thought what she did was permissible. This is why when he ﷺ admonished her act, she replied, "I saw you crying." Meaning, "I followed your guidance and I thought it is allowed to wail along with shedding the tears." The response of the Prophet ﷺ was to teach her that he was not crying due to an inability to be patient or due to panic but rather his tears fell due to the mercy that Allāh had planted in his heart. This ḥadīth does not contradict the ḥadīth wherein 'Ā'ishah رضي الله عنها mentioned that, "The Prophet ﷺ never cried over a dead person; the most he would do was to hold his own beard." This is because she meant that he never cried due to grieving over the deceased but his tears were due to his mercy for his nation.[478]

٣٢٦- حَدَّثَنَا مُحَمَّدُ بْنُ بَشَّارٍ، قَالَ: حَدَّثَنَا عَبْدُ الرَّحْمَنِ بْنُ مَهْدِيٍّ قَالَ: حَدَّثَنَا سُفْيَانُ، عَنْ عَاصِمِ بْنِ عُبَيْدِ اللهِ، عَنِ الْقَاسِمِ بْنِ مُحَمَّدٍ، عَنْ عَائِشَةَ: «أَنَّ رَسُولَ اللهِ صلى الله عليه وسلم قَبَّلَ عُثْمَانَ بْنَ مَظْعُونٍ وَهُوَ مَيِّتٌ وَهُوَ يَبْكِي، أَوْ قَالَ: عَيْنَاهُ تَهْرَاقَانِ»٤٧٩.

326. 'Ā'ishah رضي الله عنها narrated: "The Messenger of Allāh ﷺ kissed [the forehead] of 'Uthmān b. Maẓ'ūn رضي الله عنه [after his death] and his eyes were shedding tears whilst he was doing so."

Al-Bājūrī said,

> **"And his eyes were shedding tears":** I.e. he wept, and it is reported in *al-Mishkāt* that his tears fell onto 'Uthmān's face.

'Abd al-Muḥsin al-'Abbād said,

> This shows that kissing the dead is permissible and there are other ḥadīths that indicate this permissibility.[480]

Ibn al-Qayyim said,

> From the guidance of the Prophet ﷺ is to cover the face and body of

478 *Muntahā al-Su'l 'alā Wasā'il al-Wuṣūl ilā Shamā'il al-Rasūl*
479 *Sunan Abī Dāwūd* (3163) and *Sunan Ibn Mājah* (1456)
480 *Sharḥ Sunan Abī Dāwūd*

the deceased and to close the eyes of the person. Sometimes he would kiss the deceased just as he did with ʿUthmān b. Maẓʿūn.

٣٢٧- حَدَّثَنَا إِسْحَاقُ بْنُ مَنْصُورٍ، قَالَ: أَخْبَرَنَا أَبُو عَامِرٍ، قَالَ: حَدَّثَنَا فُلَيْحٌ وَهُوَ ابْنُ سُلَيْمَانَ، عَنْ هِلَالِ بْنِ عَلِيٍّ، عَنْ أَنَسِ بْنِ مَالِكٍ، قَالَ: «شَهِدْنَا ابْنَةً لِرَسُولِ اللهِ صلى الله عليه وسلم وَرَسُولُ اللهِ جَالِسٌ عَلَى الْقَبْرِ، فَرَأَيْتُ عَيْنَيْهِ تدمَعَانِ، فَقَالَ: أَفِيكُمْ رَجُلٌ لَمْ يُقَارِفِ اللَّيْلَةَ؟ قَالَ أَبُو طَلْحَةَ: أَنَا قَالَ: انْزِلْ فَنَزَلَ فِي قَبْرِهَا»[٤٨١].

327. Anas b. Mālik ؓ reported: "We witnessed with the Messenger of Allāh ﷺ the burial of one of his daughters. He was sitting next to the grave whilst the tears flowed from his eyes. The Messenger of Allāh ﷺ said, 'Is there any person here who did not have sexual relations today.' Abū Ṭalhah ؓ replied, 'I did not.' The Prophet ﷺ told him to enter the grave and so he entered her grave and buried her."

Al-Bājūrī said,

> **"Of one of his daughters":** This was Umm Kulthūm.
>
> **"The Prophet ﷺ told him to enter the grave":** It can be derived from this that the guardian of the deceased can give a non-relative permission to enter a female's grave, and that such a case is permissible (i.e. when permission is given).

ʿAbd al-Muḥsin al-ʿAbbād said,

> This ḥadīth indicates that a person who has sexual relations on the same day should not enter the grave to bury the deceased.[482]

Al-Qasṭallānī said,

> The reason Abū Ṭalhah ؓ was given precedence over ʿUthmān ؓ (the husband of Umm Kulthūm ؓا) was because ʿUthmān had sexual intercourse with one of his women that night and so the Prophet ﷺ did not want him to enter the grave of his wife. This was because he ﷺ did not like that he left his wife on her death bed to fulfil his desires. It is possible that the sickness of his wife was long and ʿUthmān needed to fulfil his desire that night and did not think that she would die on the

---

481 *Ṣaḥīḥ al-Bukhārī* (1285)
482 *Sharḥ Sunan Abī Dāwūd*

same night.[483]

483 *Irshād al-Sārī Sharḥ Ṣaḥīḥ al-Bukhārī*

باب ما جاء في فراش رسول الله صلى الله عليه وسلم

[46] On Allāh's Messenger's ﷺ Bed

Al-Bājūrī said,

> I.e. on the reports displaying its roughness, so that this can be emulated. There are two ḥadīths in this chapter.

'Abd al-Razzāq al-Badr said,

> The Prophet ﷺ slept only to provide his body with rest and thus he would not oversleep, sufficing with the amount of sleep that provided this. It is for this reason that he did not sleep upon luxurious mattresses or beds. This is because he had great things to achieve in his lifetime, for he is the Messenger of Allāh and the role model for mankind.

٣٢٨- حَدَّثَنَا عَلِيُّ بْنُ حُجْرٍ، قَالَ: حَدَّثَنَا عَلِيُّ بْنُ مُسْهِرٍ، عَنْ هِشَامِ بْنِ عُرْوَةَ، عَنْ أَبِيهِ، عَنْ عَائِشَةَ، قَالَتْ: «إِنَّمَا كَانَ فِرَاشُ رَسُولِ اللهِ صلى الله عليه وسلم الَّذِي يَنَامُ عَلَيْهِ مِنْ أَدَمٍ، حَشْوُهُ لِيفٌ»٤٨٤.

328. 'Ā'ishah ﵂ narrated: "The bed on which the Messenger of Allāh ﷺ slept upon was made of leather stuffed with the fibre of palm trees."

Al-Qaḍı 'Iyaḍ said,

> This indicates the permissibility of pillows, sleeping pads and to have sleeping pads that are made of leather and stuffed.[485]

Ibn al-Jawzī said,

> 'Ā'ishah ﵂ narrated, "A woman from the Anṣār visited me and saw that the pad on which the Prophet ﷺ used to lie on was a folded robe so she left and returned with a pad filled with wool. The Messenger of Allāh ﷺ came afterwards and saw it so he asked about it. I mentioned to him what happened so he told me to return it three times but as

484 *Ṣaḥīḥ al-Bukhārī* (6456) and *Ṣaḥīḥ Muslim* (2082)
485 *Ikmāl al-Mu'lim bi Fawā'id Muslim*

> he saw that I liked it and wanted to keep it he said, 'O 'Ā'ishah, return it for by Allāh if I wanted, Allāh would have given me mountains of gold and silver.'"[486] [487]

٣٢٩- حَدَّثَنَا أَبُو الْخَطَّابِ زِيَادُ بْنُ يَحْيَىٰ الْبَصْرِيُّ، قَالَ: حَدَّثَنَا عَبْدُ اللهِ بْنُ مَيْمُونٍ، قَالَ: حَدَّثَنَا جَعْفَرُ بْنُ مُحَمَّدٍ، عَنْ أَبِيهِ قَالَ: سُئِلَتْ عَائِشَةُ، مَا كَانَ فِرَاشُ رَسُولِ اللهِ صلىٰ الله عليه وسلم فِي بَيْتِكِ؟ قَالَتْ: مِنْ أَدَمٍ حَشْوُهُ مِنْ لِيفٍ.

وَسُئِلَتْ حَفْصَةُ، مَا كَانَ فِرَاشُ رَسُولِ اللهِ صلىٰ الله عليه وسلم فِي بَيْتِكِ؟ قَالَتْ: مِسْحًا نَثْنِيهِ ثَنِيَّتَيْنِ فَيَنَامُ عَلَيْهِ، فَلَمَّا كَانَ ذَاتَ لَيْلَةٍ ، قُلْتُ: لَوْ ثَنَيْتَهُ أَرْبَعَ ثَنِيَاتٍ لَكَانَ أَوْطَأَ لَهُ فَثَنَيْنَاهُ لَهُ بِأَرْبَعِ ثَنِيَاتٍ، فَلَمَّا أَصْبَحَ، قَالَ: مَا فَرَشْتُمْ لِيَ اللَّيْلَةَ؟ قَالَتْ: قُلْنَا: هُوَ فِرَاشُكَ إِلا أَنَّا ثَنَيْنَاهُ بِأَرْبَعِ ثَنِيَاتٍ، قُلْنَا: هُوَ أَوْطَأُ لَكَ، قَالَ: رُدُّوهُ لِحَالَتِهِ الأُولَىٰ، فَإِنَّهُ مَنَعَتْنِي وَطَاءَتُهُ صَلاتِيَ اللَّيْلَةَ[٤٨٨].

329. Muḥammad al-Bāqir narrated that someone asked 'Ā'ishah ﵂: "How was the bed of the Messenger of Allāh ﷺ in your house?" She replied: "It was made of leather stuffed with the fibre of palm trees."

Ḥafṣah ﵂ was asked: "How was the bed of the Messenger of Allāh ﷺ in your house?" She replied: "It was a rough canvas made of wool folded into two, which was spread for him to sleep on. On one night I thought if I folded it into four and spread it, it would become more comfortable and so we folded it and spread it that way. In the morning, he asked, 'What did you spread out for me last night?' We replied, 'It was your bedding but I folded it into four so that it may become softer.' He ﷺ said, 'Leave it in its original state. Its softness prevented me from praying the night prayers.'"

'Abdullāh b. Sa'īd al-Ḥaḍramī al-Makkī said,

> The Prophet ﷺ thought that his sleeping pad was changed as he noticed it felt softer and he asked his wife to fold it into two layers (the manner in which he was accustomed to) because a softer bed can

486 *Al-Mu'jam al-Awsaṭ* (6195)
487 *Al-Wafā bi Ta'rīf Faḍā'il al-Musṭafā*
488 *Akhlāq al-Nabi* (454)

cause one to fall into deep sleep.[489]

489 *Muntahā al-Su'l ʿalā Wasā'il al-Wuṣūl ilā Shamā'il al-Rasūl*

باب ما جاء في تواضع رسول الله صلى الله عليه وسلم

[47] On Allāh's Messenger's ﷺ Humility

'Abd al-Razzāq al-Badr said,

> Humility is to show kindness in treatment and interaction, and also to refrain from false pride and arrogance. The humility of the Prophet ﷺ manifested in his mannerisms, character and dealings with people as will be explained in this chapter.

Al-Bājūrī said,

> There are thirteen ḥadīths in this chapter.

٣٣٠- حَدَّثَنَا أَحْمَدُ بْنُ مَنِيعٍ، وَسَعِيدُ بْنُ عَبْدِ الرَّحْمَنِ الْمَخْزُومِيُّ، وَغَيْرُ وَاحِدٍ قَالُوا: حَدَّثَنَا سُفْيَانُ بْنُ عُيَيْنَةَ، عَنِ الزُّهْرِيِّ، عَنْ عُبَيْدِ اللهِ، عَنِ ابْنِ عَبَّاسٍ، عَنْ عُمَرَ بْنِ الْخَطَّابِ قَالَ: قَالَ رَسُولُ اللهِ صلى الله عليه وسلم: «لا تُطْرُونِي كَمَا أَطْرَتِ النَّصَارَىٰ ابْنَ مَرْيَمَ، إِنَّمَا أَنَا عَبْدٌ فَقُولُوا: عَبْدُ اللهِ وَرَسُولُهُ»[٤٩٠].

330. 'Umar b. al-Khaṭṭab ﷺ narrated: "The Messenger of Allāh ﷺ said, 'Do not over praise me as the Christians over praised 'Īsa b. Maryam, for I am just a slave of Allāh, so call me the slave of Allāh and His Messenger.'"

Al-Bājūrī said,

> **"For I am just a slave of Allāh":** I.e. I am a slave and not a deity, thus do not believe anything which would negate my servitude.
>
> **"So call me the slave of Allāh and His Messenger":** I.e. because I am described with servitude and as a messenger, thus do not describe me with any characteristics of lordship or divinity that would negate this.

Ibn Shāmah said,

490 *Ṣaḥīḥ al-Bukhārī* (2462) and *Ṣaḥīḥ Muslim* (1691)

Apart from the fact that the Mawlid is an innovation, it often includes other wrongdoings such as mixing between men and women, songs, musical instruments, liquor and drugs. However, what is even worse is the major *shirk* committed when they go to extremes towards the Messenger of Allāh ﷺ or any of the *awliyā'* by seeking his or their help and believing he knows the future and such similar acts of disbelief that people do when they celebrate the Prophet's ﷺ birthday. They do such acts even though they have been ordered not to go to extremes in praise for him ﷺ as reported in the ḥadīth.

The irony is that many people are enthusiastic, energetic and keen to attend these innovated celebrations whilst you will find them too slack and lazy to attend that which Allāh has dictated for them to attend such as the congregational and Friday prayers and still they do not find their slackness as a serious issue. Evidently, this is due to their weak *īmān*, poor insight of their hearts and the many sins that cover their hearts. We ask Allāh to protect us from all of that, for us and all Muslims.[491]

Ibn Ḥajar al-'Asqalānī said,

The admonished over praise that is mentioned in this ḥadīth refers to that which is false praise. This is similar to how the Christians praise Jesus عليه السلام with false praise when they claim that he is the son of God.[492]

٣٣١- حَدَّثَنَا عَلِيُّ بْنُ حُجْرٍ، قَالَ: حَدَّثَنَا سُوَيْدُ بْنُ عَبْدِ الْعَزِيزِ، عَنْ حُمَيْدٍ، عَنْ أَنَسِ بْنِ مَالِكٍ، أَنَّ امْرَأَةً جَاءَتْ إِلَىٰ النَّبِيِّ صلىٰ الله عليه وسلم، فَقَالَتْ لَهُ: إِنَّ لِي إِلَيْكَ حَاجَةً، فَقَالَ: «اجْلِسِي فِي أَيِّ طَرِيقِ الْمَدِينَةِ شِئْتِ أَجْلِسْ إِلَيْكِ»[٤٩٣].

331. Anas b. Mālik رضي الله عنه reported: "A woman came to the Prophet ﷺ and said, 'I wish to speak to you in private.' He replied, 'Choose any pathway of Madīnah and I will come there and listen to you.'"

Al-Bājūrī said,

This shows that non-*maḥram* relatives of the opposite gender should not be secluded. Rather, if the female has any need, he should sit/as-

491 *Al-Bā'ith 'alā Inkār al-Bida' wa al-Ḥawādith*
492 *Fatḥ al-Bārī*
493 *Sunan Abī Dāwūd* (4818)

sociate with her in a place wherein he would not face any accusation, e.g. in the street. Furthermore, it shows that the ruler should give importance to the needs of the needy and not tarry in doing so.

Al-Nawawī said,

> This ḥadīth shows the closeness of the Prophet ﷺ to his people and his desire to help people have their rights fulfilled and guide those who need guidance, so that people can see his actions and follow his example. This ḥadīth does not condone sitting with women in privacy as [the Prophet ﷺ made it a point to meet her in public]. They met on the road and though people were passing by, no one could hear her question as she wanted to ask it in private.[494]

٣٣٢- حَدَّثَنَا عَلِيُّ بْنُ حُجْرٍ، قَالَ: حَدَّثَنَا عَلِيُّ بْنُ مُسْهِرٍ، عَنْ مُسْلِمٍ الأَعْوَرِ، عَنْ أَنَسِ بْنِ مَالِكٍ، قَالَ: «كَانَ رَسُولُ اللهِ صلىٰ الله عليه وسلم يَعُودُ الْمَرِيضَ، وَيَشْهَدُ الْجَنَائِزَ، وَيَرْكَبُ الْحِمَارَ، وَيُجِيبُ دَعْوَةَ الْعَبْدِ، وَكَانَ يَوْمَ بَنِي قُرَيْظَةَ عَلَىٰ حِمَارٍ مَخْطُومٍ بِحَبْلٍ مِنْ لِيفٍ، وَعَلَيْهِ إِكَافٌ مِنْ لِيفٍ»[٤٩٥].

332. Anas b. Mālik ؓ related: "The Messenger of Allāh ﷺ would visit the sick, attend funerals, ride donkeys and accept the invitations of slaves. On the day of the battle of Banu Qurayẓah, he rode upon a donkey, the reigns of which were made of date palm fibre, and the saddle was also made of date palm fibre."

Al-Bājūrī said,

> This ḥadīth shows that the noble person's riding of a donkey ([t] i.e. a cheap ride) does not reduce his respectability.

ʿAbdullāh b. Saʿīd al-Ḥaḍramī al-Makkī said,

> Some people preferred solitude and that made them lose the immense reward of these good deeds despite the fact that their solitude brought forth great benefit to them.
>
> The guidance of the Prophet ﷺ when visiting the sick is to sit near one's head and then inquire about the condition of the person's

494 *Sharḥ Ṣaḥīḥ Muslim*
495 *Sunan Ibn Mājah* (2296) and *Sunan al-Tirmidhī* (1017)

health.

He used to attend the *janāzah* and witness the burial of the deceased. The way of the Prophet ﷺ when walking in funerals was that his sadness would manifest upon him, he would speak little and he would be engaged in contemplation of the event.[496]

٣٣٣- حَدَّثَنَا وَاصِلُ بْنُ عَبْدِ الأَعْلَىٰ الْكُوفِيُّ، قَالَ: حَدَّثَنَا مُحَمَّدُ بْنُ فُضَيْلٍ، عَنِ الأَعْمَشِ، عَنْ أَنَسِ بْنِ مَالِكٍ، قَالَ: كَانَ النَّبِيُّ صلىٰ الله عليه وسلم يُدْعَىٰ إِلَىٰ خُبْزِ الشَّعِيرِ وَالإِهَالَةِ السَّنِخَةِ فَيُجِيبُ، وَلَقَدْ كَانَ لَهُ دِرْعٌ عِنْدَ يَهُودِيٍّ، فَمَا وَجَدَ مَا يَفُكُّهَا حَتَّىٰ مَاتَ٤٩٧.

333. Anas b. Mālik ؓ narrated: "The Messenger of Allāh ﷺ accepted and attended invitations to places where bread made of barley and days old stale fat was served. Thc armour he possessed had been pawned to a Jew. [He passed away] without possessing a sufficient amount to release it.'"

'Abdullāh b. Sa'īd al-Ḥaḍramī al-Makkī said,

> This shows that it is allowed to eat old food so long as it does not cause harm. The story of the armour is that he ﷺ pawned it for thirty *ṣā'* of barley as stated in *Ṣaḥīḥ al-Bukharī*, and the name of the armour was "Dhāt al-Fuḍūl" as stated by Ibn al-Qayyim. The reason he ﷺ went to the Jewish man instead of his companions was to show that dealing with Jews and pawnbrokers is permissible and because the companions would not agree to take money from him ﷺ or accept it as a pawn type agreement. The armour was released by Abū Bakr [after the Prophet's ﷺ death] and handed to Alī b. Abī Ṭālib. The ḥadīth also shows the rigorous self-discipline employed by the Prophet ﷺ.[498]

٣٣٤- حَدَّثَنَا مَحْمُودُ بْنُ غَيْلَانَ، قَالَ: حَدَّثَنَا أَبُو دَاوُدَ الْحَفَرِيُّ، عَنْ سُفْيَانَ، عَنِ الرَّبِيعِ بْنِ صَبِيحٍ، عَنْ يَزِيدَ بْنِ أَبَانَ، عَنْ أَنَسِ بْنِ مَالِكٍ، قَالَ: «حَجَّ رَسُولُ اللهِ صلىٰ الله عليه وسلم عَلَىٰ رَحْلٍ رَثٍّ، وَعَلَيْهِ قَطِيفَةٌ لا تُسَاوِي أَرْبَعَةَ دَرَاهِمَ، فَقَالَ:

---

496 *Muntahā al-Su'l 'alā Wasā'il al-Wuṣūl ilā Shamā'il al-Rasūl*
497 *Musnad Aḥmad* (11993)
498 *Muntahā al-Su'l 'alā Wasā'il al-Wuṣūl ilā Shamā'il al-Rasūl*

اللَّهُمَّ اجْعَلْهُ حَجًّا لا رِيَاءَ فِيهِ وَلا سُمْعَةَ»٤٩٩.

334. Anas b. Mālik ﷺ narrated: "The Messenger of Allāh ﷺ performed Ḥajj upon an old and worn saddle. On it was a piece of cloth, the value of which did not equate to four Dirhams. He ﷺ supplicated, 'O Allāh! Make this Ḥajj one that has no element of showing off or seeking fame.'"

Al-Bājūrī said,

> **"O Allāh! Make this Ḥajj one that has no element of showing off or seeking fame":** He said this out of humility and to teach his nation, as he was infallible in this regard. Furthermore, such only occurs to those who perform Ḥajj on luxurious rides and in fancy clothing, as done by people during our time and especially by some scholars.

Al-Zarqanī said,

> Despite the infallibility of the Prophet ﷺ and the impossibility that he would do an act for fame or showing off, he asked Allāh to make his Ḥajj free from these two traits due to his great humility and his consideration of himself as just a normal person. This is because ostentation and seeking fame can easily creep upon someone mounting a fancy ride and wearing fancy garments.[500]

ʿAbdullāh b. Saʿīd al-Ḥaḍramī al-Makkī said,

> Given that Ḥajj entails detachment from all worldly pleasures, it befitted the most that he ﷺ manifested the highest level of humility in this event.[501]

٣٣٥- حَدَّثَنَا عَبْدُ اللهِ بْنُ عَبْدِ الرَّحْمَنِ، قَالَ: حَدَّثَنَا عَفَّانُ، قَالَ: حَدَّثَنَا حَمَّادُ بْنُ سَلَمَةَ، عَنْ حُمَيْدٍ، عَنْ أَنَسِ بْنِ مَالِكٍ، قَالَ: «لَمْ يَكُنْ شَخْصٌ أَحَبَّ إِلَيْهِمْ مِنْ رَسُولِ اللهِ صلى الله عليه وسلم قَالَ: وَكَانُوا إِذَا رَأَوْهُ لَمْ يَقُومُوا، لِمَا يَعْلَمُونَ مِنْ كَرَاهِيَتِهِ لِذَلِكَ»٥٠٢.

---

499 *Sunan Ibn Mājah* (2890)
500 *Sharḥ al-Zarqānī ʿalā al-Mawāhib*
501 *Muntahā al-Su'l ʿalā Wasā'il al-Wuṣūl ilā Shamā'il al-Rasūl*
502 *Sunan al-Tirmidhi* (2754)

335. Anas b. Mālik ﵁ narrated: "There was no individual more beloved to the companions than the Messenger of Allāh ﷺ. When they saw him they would not stand up as they knew that he disliked it."

Al-Bājūrī said,

> **"There was no individual more beloved to the companions than the Messenger of Allāh ﷺ":** This is because he took them out of waywardness and guided them towards bliss. This was to the extent that 'Umar said, "O Allāh's Messenger, you are more beloved to me than everything besides myself." He ﷺ replied, "Your faith is not perfected until I am more loved to you than your own self." 'Umar remained silent for a while and then said, "Than my own self." He replied, "Now your faith is complete O 'Umar." This love was proven by such instances as Abū 'Ubaydah killing his father due to his harming the Prophet ﷺ and Abū Bakr's wishing to fight his son 'Abd al-Raḥmān during the Battle of Badr.

Ibn Ḥajar al-'Asqalānī said,

> Al-Nawawī said that the reason he ﷺ disliked them standing up for him is he feared that this would lead to them over glorifying him just as he stated, "Do not over praise me." However, he did not dislike that they stand up for each other because he stood up for some of his companions and they stood up for other people in his presence and he did not object to this. The other reason is that the level of love and bond between him and his companions was perfect to the extent that standing up would not have manifested more love or honouring.[503]

٣٣٦- حَدَّثَنَا سُفْيَانُ بْنُ وَكِيعٍ، قَالَ: حَدَّثَنَا جُمَيْعُ بْنُ عُمَيْرِ بْنِ عَبْدِ الرَّحْمَنِ الْعِجْلِيُّ، قَالَ: أَنْبَأَنَا رَجُلٌ مِنْ بَنِي تَمِيمٍ مِنْ وَلَدِ أَبِي هَالَةَ زَوْجِ خَدِيجَةَ يُكْنَىٰ أَبَا عَبْدِ اللهِ، عَنِ ابْنٍ لأَبِي هَالَةَ، عَنِ الْحَسَنِ بْنِ عَلِيٍّ، قَالَ: سَأَلْتُ خَالِي هِنْدَ بْنَ أَبِي هَالَةَ، - وَكَانَ وَصَّافًا - عَنْ حِلْيَةِ رَسُولِ اللهِ صلىٰ الله عليه وسلم، وَأَنَا أَشْتَهِي أَنْ يَصِفَ لِي مِنْهَا شَيْئًا، فَقَالَ: كَانَ رَسُولُ اللهِ صلىٰ الله عليه وسلم فَخْمًا مُفَخَّمًا، يَتَلَأْلأُ وَجْهُهُ تَلَأْلُؤَ الْقَمَرِ لَيْلَةَ الْبَدْرِ، فَذَكَرَ الْحَدِيثَ بِطُولِهِ، قَالَ الْحَسَنُ: فَكَتَمْتُهَا الْحُسَيْنَ زَمَانًا، ثُمَّ حَدَّثْتُهُ فَوَجَدْتُهُ قَدْ سَبَقَنِي إِلَيْهِ، فَسَأَلَهُ عَمَّا سَأَلْتُهُ عَنْهُ، وَوَجَدْتُهُ

503 *Fatḥ al-Bārī*

قَدْ سَأَلَ أَبَاهُ عَنْ مَدْخَلِهِ وَمَخْرَجِهِ وَشَكْلِهِ فَلَمْ يَدَعْ مِنْهُ شَيْئًا.

قَالَ الْحُسَيْنُ: فَسَأَلْتُ أَبِي، عَنْ دُخُولِ رَسُولِ اللهِ صَلَّىٰ اللهُ عَلَيْهِ وَسَلَّمَ فَقَالَ: كَانَ إِذَا أَوَىٰ إِلَىٰ مَنْزِلِهِ جَزَّأَ دُخُولَهُ ثَلَاثَةَ أَجْزَاءٍ، جُزْءًا لِلَّهِ، وَجُزْءًا لِأَهْلِهِ، وَجُزْءًا لِنَفْسِهِ، ثُمَّ جَزَّأَ جُزْأَهُ بَيْنَهُ وَبَيْنَ النَّاسِ، فَيَرُدُّ ذَلِكَ بِالْخَاصَّةِ عَلَىٰ الْعَامَّةِ، وَلَا يَدَّخِرُ عَنْهُمْ شَيْئًا، وَكَانَ مِنْ سِيرَتِهِ فِي جُزْءِ الْأُمَّةِ إِيثَارُ أَهْلِ الْفَضْلِ بِإِذْنِهِ، وَقَسْمُهُ عَلَىٰ قَدْرِ فَضْلِهِمْ فِي الدِّينِ، فَمِنْهُمْ ذُو الْحَاجَةِ، وَمِنْهُمْ ذُو الْحَاجَتَيْنِ، وَمِنْهُمْ ذُو الْحَوَائِجِ، فَيَتَشَاغَلُ بِهِمْ وَيَشْغَلُهُمْ فِيمَا يُصْلِحُهُمْ وَالْأُمَّةَ مِنْ مُسَاءَلَتِهِمْ عَنْهُ وَإِخْبَارِهِمْ بِالَّذِي يَنْبَغِي لَهُمْ، وَيَقُولُ: لِيُبَلِّغِ الشَّاهِدُ مِنْكُمُ الْغَائِبَ، وَأَبْلِغُونِي حَاجَةَ مَنْ لَا يَسْتَطِيعُ إِبْلَاغَهَا، فَإِنَّهُ مَنْ أَبْلَغَ سُلْطَانًا حَاجَةَ مَنْ لَا يَسْتَطِيعُ إِبْلَاغَهَا ثَبَّتَ اللهُ قَدَمَيْهِ يَوْمَ الْقِيَامَةِ، لَا يُذْكَرُ عِنْدَهُ إِلَّا ذَلِكَ، وَلَا يُقْبَلُ مِنْ أَحَدٍ غَيْرِهِ، يَدْخُلُونَ رُوَّادًا وَلَا يَفْتَرِقُونَ إِلَّا عَنْ ذَوَاقٍ، وَيُخْرِجُونَ أَدِلَّةً يَعْنِي عَلَىٰ الْخَيْرِ.

قَالَ: فَسَأَلْتُهُ عَنْ مَخْرَجِهِ كَيْفَ يَصْنَعُ فِيهِ؟ قَالَ: كَانَ رَسُولُ اللهِ صلىٰ الله عليه وسلم يَخْزِنُ لِسَانَهُ إِلَّا فِيمَا يَعْنِيهِ، وَيُؤَلِّفُهُمْ وَلَا يُنَفِّرُهُمْ، وَيُكْرِمُ كَرِيمَ كُلِّ قَوْمٍ وَيُوَلِّيهِ عَلَيْهِمْ، وَيَحْذَرُ النَّاسَ وَيَحْتَرِسُ مِنْهُمْ مِنْ غَيْرِ أَنْ يَطْوِيَ عَنْ أَحَدٍ مِنْهُمْ بِشْرَهُ وَخُلُقَهُ، وَيَتَفَقَّدُ أَصْحَابَهُ، وَيَسْأَلُ النَّاسَ عَمَّا فِي النَّاسِ، وَيُحَسِّنُ الْحَسَنَ وَيُقَوِّيهِ، وَيُقَبِّحُ الْقَبِيحَ وَيُوَهِّيهِ، مُعْتَدِلَ الْأَمْرِ غَيْرَ مُخْتَلِفٍ، لَا يَغْفُلُ مَخَافَةَ أَنْ يَغْفُلُوا أَوْ يَمِيلُوا، لِكُلِّ حَالٍ عِنْدَهُ عَتَادٌ، لَا يُقَصِّرُ عَنِ الْحَقِّ وَلَا يُجَاوِزُهُ الَّذِينَ يَلُونَهُ مِنَ النَّاسِ خِيَارُهُمْ، أَفْضَلُهُمْ عِنْدَهُ أَعَمُّهُمْ نَصِيحَةً، وَأَعْظَمُهُمْ عِنْدَهُ مَنْزِلَةً أَحْسَنُهُمْ مُوَاسَاةً وَمُؤَازَرَةً.

قَالَ: فَسَأَلْتُهُ عَنْ مَجْلِسِهِ، فَقَالَ: كَانَ رَسُولُ اللهِ صلىٰ الله عليه وسلم لَا يَقُومُ وَلَا يَجْلِسُ إِلَّا عَلَىٰ ذِكْرٍ، وَإِذَا انْتَهَىٰ إِلَىٰ قَوْمٍ جَلَسَ حَيْثُ يَنْتَهِي بِهِ الْمَجْلِسُ، وَيَأْمُرُ بِذَلِكَ، يُعْطِي كُلَّ جُلَسَائِهِ بِنَصِيبِهِ، لَا يَحْسَبُ جَلِيسُهُ أَنَّ أَحَدًا أَكْرَمُ عَلَيْهِ مِنْهُ، مَنْ جَالَسَهُ أَوْ فَاوَضَهُ فِي حَاجَةٍ صَابَرَهُ حَتَّىٰ يَكُونَ هُوَ الْمُنْصَرِفُ عَنْهُ، وَمَنْ سَأَلَهُ حَاجَةً لَمْ يَرُدَّهُ إِلَّا بِهَا، أَوْ بِمَيْسُورٍ مِنَ الْقَوْلِ، قَدْ وَسِعَ النَّاسَ بَسْطُهُ وَخُلُقُهُ، فَصَارَ

لَهُمْ أَبًا وَصَارُوا عِنْدَهُ فِي الْحَقِّ سَوَاءً، مَجْلِسُهُ مَجْلِسُ عِلْمٍ وَحِلْمٍ وَحَيَاءٍ وَأَمَانَةٍ وَصَبْرٍ، لا تُرْفَعُ فِيهِ الأَصْوَاتُ، وَلا تُؤْبَنُ فِيهِ الْحُرَمُ، وَلا تُثَّنَى فَلَتَاتُهُ، مُتَعَادِلِينَ، بَلْ كَانُوا يَتَفَاضَلُونَ فِيهِ بِالتَّقْوَى، مُتَوَاضِعِينَ يُوَقِّرُونَ فِيهِ الْكَبِيرَ، وَيَرْحَمُونَ فِيهِ الصَّغِيرَ، وَيُؤْثِرُونَ ذَا الْحَاجَةِ، وَيَحْفَظُونَ الْغَرِيبَ"[504].

336. Al-Ḥasan b. ʿAlī ؓ reported: "I asked my maternal uncle, Hind b. Abī Hālah ؓ, who was known for his skill of describing, about the awe-inspiring characteristics and features of the Prophet ﷺ, whilst hoping he could describe to me some of his features to be well acquainted with his description. My maternal uncle described the Prophet ﷺ by saying, 'His qualities and attributes were the acme of beauty, and his companions and whoever saw him held him in high esteem. His face used to shine like the full moon... [To the end of the ḥadīth].'

I withheld this information from al-Ḥusayn ؓ but when I shared it with him I realised that he had inquired about it before me and I found out that he had asked our father about the interaction of the Prophet ﷺ both outside and within his house and his features, leaving nothing to inquire about."

Al-Ḥusayn [b. ʿAlī b. Abī Ṭālib ؓ] narrated: "I asked my father about what the Prophet ﷺ did when he was at home. He said: "He ﷺ distributed his time into three portions; one portion for Allāh, another portion for his family and a portion for himself. Then, he distributed his personal portion in two, one for himself and one for the people; in such a manner that he communicated knowledge to the masses through his close companions when they visited him and he did not conceal anything from them. During the portion he dedicated for people, he gave preference to the people of greater piety and status to enter upon him and he distributed this time according to their level of piety. From among those who visited him, some had one need, some had two needs, and some had many needs. He ﷺ sacrificed the time to fulfil all their requirements and busied them in things that would rectify them and the entire nation. When they inquired on matters related to religion, he replied to them in a manner that benefited them and he used to say, 'Those that are present, should convey to those that are absent [regarding these beneficial matters.]'

504 See ḥadīth 8

He also used to say, 'Those people who for some reason cannot bring forth their needs, you should inform me about them. This is because the person who conveys to a ruler the need of another, who is unable to do so himself, Allāh ﷻ will keep that person firm on the Day of Judgment.' No issues besides those of importance and benefit were presented to him in his gatherings and he did not accept listening to anything besides that. The companions came to his assemblies for their religious and lawful needs and they did not depart without enjoying the taste of his knowledge, and they left with guidance for the people.'

I then asked him about his interaction with people outside his house. He replied, 'The Messenger of Allāh ﷺ controlled his tongue, only speaking regarding that which concerned him. He brought unity amongst the people and did not alienate them. He honoured the esteemed ones of every group and made them the leaders of their groups. He warned the people and was cautious when dealing with people to preserve his status among them but he never lacked courtesy towards others.

He inquired about his companions if one of them was absent and he made himself aware about the affairs and conditions of people. He praised good deeds and encouraged them and admonished misdeeds and discouraged them. He was moderate and consistent in all matters. He did not neglect guiding the people out of fear that they become either heedless or inclined to the worldly pleasures. He was prepared for every scenario, and he established the rights of others in all matters, and did not exceed the limits in this.

Those who were close to him were the best of people, the best of whom in his eyes were the ones who wished everybody well, and the ones with the highest status in his eyes were the ones with the most compassion, who aided the creation the most.'

I then asked my father regarding his gatherings. He replied, 'The Messenger of Allāh ﷺ did not stand nor sit except with the remembrance of Allāh. When he came to a gathering, he sat where there was space available, and instructed the people to do the same. He gave every attendee his due respect and rights to a degree that led every individual present to think that he ﷺ was honouring him the most. When an individual came to sit with him or came regarding

some issue, he ﷺ would remain seated until that person began to rise. Whenever he was asked for something, he would fulfil that request, and did not refuse it; [if he did not possess that which was required] he would advise the person with soft and kind words. His affection and good manners were for all and not restricted to certain people. He was like a father to them and he was just and fair with each one of them.

His gatherings were the gatherings of knowledge, humility, patience and trustworthiness. In his gatherings, voices were not raised and vile and unlawful topics were refrained from. If anyone committed a fault, it was not publicised. All were regarded as equals amongst themselves and superiority was according to the piety possessed. Therein the old were respected, the young were loved, the needy were given preference, and strangers and travellers were cared for and his gems were observed attentively and memorised.'"

'Abdullāh b. Sa'īd al-Ḥaḍramī al-Makkī said,

> The Prophet ﷺ did not talk unless there was a need, be it related to religion or worldly affairs, following the guidance of the verse: **{And they who turn away from idle speech}**[505] and he would repeat his speech twice or thrice to ensure the listeners understood and memorised his statements.
>
> He ﷺ used to bring the hearts of people together and removed all disputes and animosity from their hearts so that they became like one person and he did not do anything that could cause dispute due to his overwhelming compassion and forgiveness.
>
> He ﷺ inquired about the affairs of people to see if there were cases of injustice to be removed, rights to be restored or oppressed people to help. This manner should be followed by the rulers, scholars and pious people and anyone who has followers as they should follow up the news of their followers to avoid neglecting them.
>
> He ﷺ drew close to the best of his people because they would benefit the most from his knowledge and learn it. The teacher should make his best students stay close to him because this will ensure that those who will be entrusted with knowledge are those whose piety is trust-

---

505 Qur'ān 23:3

ed.[506]

ʿAbd al-Razzāq al-Badr said,

> Al-Ḥasan did not inform al-Ḥusayn about his inquiry about the description of the Prophet ﷺ but later on he found out that al-Ḥusayn had already enquired about it. So he asked him regarding what he had acquired since al-Ḥusayn had collected more information than him.
>
> The Prophet ﷺ was cautious in his interactions due to the fact that people are of different natures; there are the rude, the aggressive, the kind and the well-mannered etc. Thus, he dealt with each individual in a suitable and appropriate manner to keep everyone close to him.
>
> This ḥadīth proves that the virtue of the companions differs from one to another. The best of them was Abū Bakr, then ʿUmar, then ʿUthmān, then ʿAlī, and then the ten companions who were given the glad tidings of Paradise.
>
> Fatherhood is of two types, religious and biological. The former is established for the Prophet ﷺ, meaning he is the father of all believers and the latter is negated, as stated in the Qurʾān: **{Muḥammad is not the father of [any] one of your men, but [he is] the Messenger of Allah and last of the prophets. And ever is Allah, of all things, Knowing.}**[507]

٣٣٧- حَدَّثَنَا مُحَمَّدُ بْنُ عَبْدِ اللهِ بْنِ بَزِيعٍ، قَالَ: حَدَّثَنَا بِشْرُ بْنُ الْمُفَضَّلِ، قَالَ: حَدَّثَنَا سَعِيدٌ، عَنْ قَتَادَةَ، عَنْ أَنَسِ بْنِ مَالِكٍ، قَالَ: قَالَ رَسُولُ اللهِ صلى الله عليه وسلم: «لَوْ أُهْدِيَ إِلَيَّ كُرَاعٌ لَقَبِلْتُ، وَلَوْ دُعِيتُ عَلَيْهِ لَأَجَبْتُ»٥٠٨.

337. Anas b. Mālik ﷺ reported: "The Messenger of Allāh ﷺ said, 'Even if thc foot of a goat was gifted to me, I would accept it, and if I was invited to eat from it, I would surely accept that invitation.'"

Al-Bājūrī said,

> **"Even if the foot of a goat was gifted to me, I would accept it":** This is because it brings about mutual love and harmony. However, if

506 *Muntahā al-Su'l ʿalā Wasāʾil al-Wuṣūl ilā Shamāʾil al-Rasūl*
507 Qurʾān 33:40
508 *Sunan al-Tirmidhī* (1338)

the gift is rejected, this brings about estrangement and enmity. Thus, it is recommended to accept gifts even if it is something small (and the same is the case for invitations).

Ibn Baṭṭāl said,

> Al-Muhallab said, "This ḥadīth shows that one should show humility, refrain from arrogance and bring the hearts together by accepting the invitation even if it is for something minute and by accepting gifts. This is because these acts confirm the bond between people and invitations for food cannot be given unless this bond of affability pre-exists between people. It is for these reasons that the Prophet ﷺ encouraged accepting the gift [even if it is little] and answering the invitation of people.[509]

٣٣٨- حَدَّثَنَا مُحَمَّدُ بْنُ بَشَّارٍ، قَالَ: حَدَّثَنَا عَبْدُ الرَّحْمَنِ، قَالَ: حَدَّثَنَا سُفْيَانُ، عَنْ مُحَمَّدِ بْنِ الْمُنْكَدِرِ، عَنْ جَابِرٍ، قَالَ: «جَاءَنِي رَسُولُ اللهِ صلى الله عليه وسلم لَيْسَ بِرَاكِبِ بَغْلٍ، وَلا بِرْذَوْنٍ»[٥١٠].

338. Jabir ؓ narrated: "The Messenger of Allāh ﷺ came to visit me [while I was sick] and he did not come on the back of a mule or on a Turkish horse."

Al-Bājūrī said,

> **"And he did not come on the back of a mule":** Out of humility, he would visit his companions walking. This means that riding was not his customary practice, which does not negate the possibility that he rode on some occasions.

Ibn Baṭṭāl said,

> This ḥadīth teaches us that visiting the sick whether on a ride or by foot is a rewarding deed when the intention is sincerely for the sake of Allāh alone, even if the effort required to reach the sick is minimal.[511]

Badr al-Din al-ʿAynī said,

509 *Sharḥ Ṣaḥīḥ al-Bukhārī*
510 *Ṣaḥīḥ al-Bukhārī* (194) and *Ṣaḥīḥ Muslim* (1616)
511 *Sharḥ Ṣaḥīḥ al-Bukhārī*

> This ḥadīth shows the virtue of walking over riding when visiting the sick as it shows more humility.[512]

٣٣٩- حَدَّثَنَا عَبْدُ اللهِ بْنُ عَبْدِ الرَّحْمَنِ، قَالَ: حَدَّثَنَا أَبُو نُعَيْمٍ، قَالَ: أَنْبَأَنَا يَحْيَىٰ بْنُ أَبِي الْهَيْثَمِ الْعَطَّارُ، قَالَ: سَمِعْتُ يُوسُفَ بْنَ عَبْدِ اللهِ بْنِ سَلَامٍ، قَالَ: «سَمَّانِي رَسُولُ اللهِ صلىٰ الله عليه وسلم يُوسُفَ، وَأَقْعَدَنِي فِي حِجْرِهِ، وَمَسَحَ عَلَىٰ رَأْسِي»٥١٣.

339. Yūsuf b. ʿAbdullāh b. Salām ﵁ reported: "The Messenger of Allāh ﷺ named me Yūsuf and he put me on his lap and then wiped his hand over my head."

Ibn Ḥajar al-Haytamī said,

> It is recommended for a person of high esteem, whose example is followed to name the children of his companions and to choose for them good names. This ḥadīth also shows that the names of the Prophets are good names.

Al-Bājūrī said,

> We can see that it is recommended to sit infants in the lap, as done so by the Prophet ﷺ, displaying his perfect humbleness and good nature.

٣٤٠- حَدَّثَنَا إِسْحَاقُ بْنُ مَنْصُورٍ، قَالَ: حَدَّثَنَا أَبُو دَاوُدَ الطَّيَالِسِيُّ، قَالَ: حَدَّثَنَا الرَّبِيعُ وَهُوَ ابْنُ صَبِيحٍ، قَالَ: حَدَّثَنَا يَزِيدُ الرَّقَاشِيُّ، عَنْ أَنَسِ بْنِ مَالِكٍ، «أَنَّ رَسُولَ اللهِ صلىٰ الله عليه وسلم حَجَّ عَلَىٰ رَحْلٍ رَثٍّ وَقَطِيفَةٍ، كُنَّا نَرَىٰ ثَمَنَهَا أَرْبَعَةَ دَرَاهِمَ، فَلَمَّا اسْتَوَتْ بِهِ رَاحِلَتُهُ قَالَ: لَبَّيْكَ بِحَجَّةٍ لَا سُمْعَةَ فِيهَا وَلَا رِيَاءَ»٥١٤.

340. Anas b. Mālik ﵁ narrated: "The Messenger of Allāh ﷺ performed Ḥajj upon an old and worn saddle. Upon it was a piece of cloth, the value of which we think was less than four dirhams. When his mount rose, he ﷺ supplicated, 'At your service O Allāh! Make this Ḥajj one that has no element of showing off or seeking fame.'"

ʿAbd al-Razzāq al-Badr said,

---

512 *Sharḥ Sunan Abī Dāwūd*

513 *Musnad Aḥmad* (16404)

514 See ḥadīth 334

This is a different route for the ḥadīth mentioned earlier.

٣٤١- حَدَّثَنَا إِسْحَاقُ بْنُ مَنْصُورٍ، قَالَ: حَدَّثَنَا عَبْدُ الرَّزَّاقِ، قَالَ: حَدَّثَنَا مَعْمَرٌ، عَنْ ثَابِتٍ الْبُنَانِيِّ، وَعَاصِمٍ الأَحْوَلِ، عَنْ أَنَسِ بْنِ مَالِكٍ، «أَنَّ رَجُلًا خَيَّاطًا دَعَا رَسُولَ اللهِ صلىٰ الله عليه وسلم فَقَرَّبَ مِنْهُ ثَرِيدًا عَلَيْهِ دُبَّاءُ ، قَالَ: فَكَانَ رَسُولُ اللهِ صلىٰ الله عليه وسلم يَأْخُذُ الدُّبَّاءَ، وَكَانَ يُحِبُّ الدُّبَّاءَ»[٥١٥].

قَالَ ثَابِتٌ: فَسَمِعْتُ أَنَسًا يَقُولُ: فَمَا صُنِعَ لِي طَعَامٌ أَقْدِرُ عَلَىٰ أَنْ يُصْنَعَ فِيهِ دُبَّاءُ إِلَّا صُنِعَ.

341. Anas b. Mālik ﷺ reported: "A tailor once invited the Messenger of Allāh ﷺ to his home. *Tharīd* was served, in which gourd was added, and he ﷺ began eating it as he liked the gourd." Anas ﷺ added, "After that, whenever food was prepared for me, if gourd could be added to it, it was added."

Ibn Ḥajar al-Haytamī said,

> *Tharīd* is a dish made of pieces of bread in meat broth. This dish may or may not include pieces of meat. This ḥadīth shows that it is recommended to like all of that which the Prophet ﷺ liked.

٣٤٢- حَدَّثَنَا مُحَمَّدُ بْنُ إِسْمَاعِيلَ، قَالَ: حَدَّثَنَا عَبْدُ اللهِ بْنُ صَالِحٍ، قَالَ: حَدَّثَنَا مُعَاوِيَةُ بْنُ صَالِحٍ، عَنْ يَحْيَىٰ بْنِ سَعِيدٍ، عَنْ عَمْرَةَ ، قَالَتْ: قِيلَ لِعَائِشَةَ: مَاذَا كَانَ يَعْمَلُ رَسُولُ اللهِ صلىٰ الله عليه وسلم فِي بَيْتِهِ؟ قَالَتْ: «كَانَ بَشَرًا مِنَ الْبَشَرِ، يَفْلِي ثَوْبَهُ، وَيَحْلُبُ شَاتَهُ، وَيَخْدُمُ نَفْسَهُ»[٥١٦].

342. ʿAmrah ﷺ reported that someone asked ʿĀ'ishah ﷺ: "What was the normal routine of the Messenger of Allāh ﷺ at home?" She replied: "He was a man from amongst men. He himself removed anything that was attached to his clothing, milked his goats, and did all of his work himself."

Al-Bājūrī said,

515 *Ṣaḥīḥ Muslim* (2041)
516 *Al-Adab al-Mufrad* (541)

> **"And did all of his work himself":** It states in other narrations: "He sewed his garments and mended his sandals", "He would patch his garment and do the tasks which men do in their homes" and: "He did work around the house, and most of what a tailor does."

Abū Bakr b. al-ʿArabī said,

> The best work that a person can do individually without the help of others is the acts of worship so that they are all sincerely for Allāh alone. This includes doing everything that leads to these acts of worship as that will amplify the reward.[517]

Al-Ṭībī said,

> The reason ʿĀ'ishah ﵂ mentioned first that he ﷺ was a man is because disbelievers believed that it does not befit the status of Prophets to do what normal people do. Their belief was mentioned in the Qur'ān wherein Allāh ﷻ said: **{And they say, "What is this messenger that eats food and walks in the markets?"}**[518] And so she wanted to show that he ﷺ was simply a man from the sons of Ādam whom Allāh honoured with Prophethood and the Message. Thus, he was like all other humans and humble in all of his affairs.[519]

---

517 *Aḥkām al-Qur'ān*
518 Qur'ān 25:7
519 *Al-Kāshif ʿan Ḥaqā'iq al-Sunan*

باب ما جاء في خلق رسول الله صلى الله عليه وسلم

[48] On Allāh's Messenger's ﷺ Character

'Abd al-Razzāq al-Badr said,

The character consists of inward etiquettes such as shyness, patience and generosity, and outward etiquettes such as cheerful countenance, good treatment, and honesty in speech.

The character of the Prophet ﷺ is the most perfect of all characters for his character resembled the Qur'ān.

٣٤٣ - حَدَّثَنَا عَبَّاسُ بْنُ مُحَمَّدٍ الدُّورِيُّ، قَالَ: حَدَّثَنَا عَبْدُ اللهِ بْنُ يَزِيدَ الْمُقْرِئُ، قَالَ: حَدَّثَنَا لَيْثُ بْنُ سَعْدٍ، قَالَ: حَدَّثَنِي أَبُو عُثْمَانَ الْوَلِيدُ بْنُ أَبِي الْوَلِيدِ، عَنْ سُلَيْمَانَ بْنِ خَارِجَةَ، عَنْ خَارِجَةَ بْنِ زَيْدِ بْنِ ثَابِتٍ، قَالَ: دَخَلَ نَفَرٌ عَلَىٰ زَيْدِ بْنِ ثَابِتٍ، فَقَالُوا لَهُ: حَدِّثْنَا أَحَادِيثَ رَسُولِ اللهِ صلىٰ الله عليه وسلم، قَالَ: «مَاذَا أُحَدِّثُكُمْ؟ كُنْتُ جَارَهُ فَكَانَ إِذَا نَزَلَ عَلَيْهِ الْوَحْيُ بَعَثَ إِلَيَّ فَكَتَبْتُهُ لَهُ، فَكُنَّا إِذَا ذَكَرْنَا الدُّنْيَا ذَكَرَهَا مَعَنَا، وَإِذَا ذَكَرْنَا الْآخِرَةَ ذَكَرَهَا مَعَنَا، وَإِذَا ذَكَرْنَا الطَّعَامَ ذَكَرَهُ مَعَنَا، فَكُلُّ هَذَا أُحَدِّثُكُمْ عَنْ رَسُولِ اللهِ صلىٰ الله عليه وسلم» ٥٢٠.

343. Khārijah b. Zayd b. Thābit related: "A group of people came to Zayd b. Thābit ؓ and requested him to tell them about the Messenger of Allāh ﷺ. He replied, 'What should I tell you? I was his neighbour and he used to send for me every time something was revealed to him, so that I could transcribe it for him. If we entered into discussion regarding worldly affairs, he would join us in doing so. If we entered into discussion regarding the Hereafter, he would join us in doing so. If we entered into discussion regarding food, he also did so. All of this that I have stated to you regarding him is factual.'"

Al-Bājūrī said,

> There were nine scribes of the revelation: Zayd, ʿUthmān, ʿAlī, Ubayy, Muʿāwiyah, Khālid b. Saʿīd, Ḥanzalah b. al-Rabīʿ, al-ʿAlāʾ b. al-Ḥaḍramī and Abān b. Saʿīd.

ʿAlī al-Qārī said,

> Zayd b. Thābit was one of the scribes of the Qurʾān who transcribed it directly from the mouth of the Prophet ﷺ. He was the most knowledgeable companion in the science of inheritance and one of the most esteemed Qurʾān reciters.
>
> He ﷺ mentioned that he was the neighbour of the Prophet ﷺ to show his closeness to him in terms of location and companionship and to indicate that he was more familiar with him than other companions.
>
> The Prophet ﷺ joined their conversations because this life is the farmland of deeds where people plant their seeds to reap the harvest in the Hereafter. Thus, he would join them in order to help them survive this life and to reach the Hereafter safe. This is why he joined their conversations regarding the Hereafter, to inspire them towards the attainment of good deeds. The mention of food indicates that he ﷺ showed them its benefits and etiquettes.
>
> In summary he ﷺ used to join them in conversation so that they would not become bored and share with them through the means of conversation, religious rulings and exhortations.[521]

٣٤٤- حَدَّثَنَا إِسْحَاقُ بْنُ مُوسَىٰ، قَالَ: حَدَّثَنَا يُونُسُ بْنُ بُكَيْرٍ، عَنْ مُحَمَّدِ بْنِ إِسْحَاقَ، عَنْ زِيَادِ بْنِ أَبِي زِيَادٍ، عَنْ مُحَمَّدِ بْنِ كَعْبٍ الْقُرَظِيِّ، عَنْ عَمْرِو بْنِ الْعَاصِ، قَالَ: «كَانَ رَسُولُ اللهِ صلىٰ الله عليه وسلم يُقْبِلُ بِوَجْهِهِ وَحَدِيثِهِ عَلَىٰ أَشَرِّ الْقَوْمِ يَتَأَلَّفُهُمْ بِذَلِكَ فَكَانَ يُقْبِلُ بِوَجْهِهِ وَحَدِيثِهِ عَلَيَّ حَتَّىٰ ظَنَنْتُ أَنِّي خَيْرُ الْقَوْمِ، فَقُلْتُ: يَا رَسُولَ اللهِ، أَنَا خَيْرٌ أَوْ أَبُو بَكْرٍ؟ قَالَ: أَبُو بَكْرٍ، فَقُلْتُ: يَا رَسُولَ اللهِ، أَنَا خَيْرٌ أَوْ عُمَرُ؟ فَقَالَ: عُمَرُ، فَقُلْتُ: يَا رَسُولَ اللهِ، أَنَا خَيْرٌ أَوْ عُثْمَانُ؟ قَالَ: عُثْمَانُ، فَلَمَّا سَأَلْتُ رَسُولَ اللهِ صلىٰ الله عليه وسلم فَصَدَقَنِي فَلَوَدِدْتُ أَنِّي لَمْ أَكُنْ

---

521 *Mirqāt al-Mafātīḥ*

سَأَلْتُهُ ﴾٥٢٣﴿.

344. ʿAmr b. al-ʿĀṣ ☺ reported: "The Messenger of Allāh ﷺ spoke directly to vile people [with a cheerful countenance] to soften their hearts. He used to embrace me and speak to me in a manner that made me feel that I was the best amongst the people. I asked, 'O Messenger of Allāh! Who is better, me or Abū Bakr ☺?' He replied, 'Abū Bakr.' I then asked, 'Am I better, or is ʿUmar ☺?' He replied, "Umar.' I asked, 'Am I better or is ʿUthmān ☺?' He replied, "Uthmān.' After I asked him these questions and he told me the truth, I wished I had not asked him such."

ʿAbdullāh b. Saʿīd al-Ḥaḍramī al-Makkī said,

> The Prophet ﷺ used to embrace people with a cheerful countenance to either make them more inclined towards Islām, to aid them in remaining steadfast in religion or to avoid their evil. It is allowed to avoid the evil of bad people by showing them a cheerful countenance but it is not allowed to praise the evil people as this constitutes lying.

> The extra attention he ﷺ gave them does not contradict the fact that he gave equal attention to all of his companions. This is because that (i.e. giving them equal attention) was the case in normal circumstances when there was no necessity or need to show more attention. From the benefits of meeting vile people with a cheerful countenance is that it prevents arrogance and pride.

> The reason why the Prophet ﷺ showed more attention to ʿAmr b. al-ʿĀṣ ☺ was because he was new to Islām and from the leaders of his tribe.

> The reason he ☺ regretted enquiring such is because he thought the attention and good treatment he received was due to his status in the religion but then he realised it was to soften his heart. It is for this reason a person should not ask about a matter before verifying it, in order to avoid embarrassment.

> The kind of mannerisms mentioned in this ḥadīth reflects the verse: **{So by mercy from Allāh, [O Muḥammad], you were lenient with them. And if you had been rude [in speech] and harsh in heart, they would have disbanded from about you. So par-**

don them and ask forgiveness for them and consult them in the matter.}[524] [523]

٣٤٥- حَدَّثَنَا قُتَيْبَةُ بْنُ سَعِيدٍ، قَالَ: حَدَّثَنَا جَعْفَرُ بْنُ سُلَيْمَانَ الضُّبَعِيُّ، عَنْ ثَابِتٍ، عَنْ أَنَسِ بْنِ مَالِكٍ، قَالَ: «خَدَمْتُ رَسُولَ اللهِ صلىٰ الله عليه وسلم عَشْرَ سِنِينَ، فَمَا قَالَ لِي أُفٍّ قَطُّ، وَمَا قَالَ لِشَيْءٍ صَنَعْتُهُ لِمَ صَنَعْتَهُ، وَلا لِشَيْءٍ تَرَكْتُهُ لِمَ تَرَكْتَهُ، وَكَانَ رَسُولُ اللهِ صلىٰ الله عليه وسلم مِنْ أَحْسَنِ النَّاسِ خُلُقًا، وَلا مَسَسْتُ خَزًّا وَلا حَرِيرًا، وَلا شَيْئًا كَانَ أَلْيَنَ مِنْ كَفِّ رَسُولِ اللهِ صلىٰ الله عليه وسلم، وَلا شَمَمْتُ مِسْكًا قَطُّ، وَلا عِطْرًا كَانَ أَطْيَبَ مِنْ عَرَقِ رسول الله صلىٰ الله عليه وسلم»[٥٢٥].

345. Anas b. Mālik ﷺ related: "I served the Messenger of Allāh ﷺ for ten years. He never once said *uff* to me and he never asked me the reason behind anything I did, nor did he ever ask me the reason behind anything that I left. The Messenger of Allāh ﷺ was the most beautiful of people in character. I have never felt any fabric, pure silk or anything else softer than his palm. Nor did I smell any musk or any other fragrance, with a sweeter scent than the perspiration of the Messenger of Allāh ﷺ."

Al-Bājūrī said,

> **"I served the Messenger of Allāh ﷺ for ten years":** I.e. at home and while travelling. His age at that time was also ten.

Ibn Ḥajar al-'Asqalānī said,

> The act of refraining from asking others regarding things that have been done or not done shows that one should avoid blaming others for things that have already occurred. It shows that one should safeguard his tongue from admonishing and rebuking others [for actions that have no religious implications] and that one should soften the heart of the servant by not admonishing him if it is regarding something personal (i.e. worldly) but issues related to religion must be addressed.

---

523 Qur'ān 3:159

524 *Muntahā al-Su'l 'alā Wasā'il al-Wuṣūl ilā Shamā'il al-Rasūl*

525 *Ṣaḥīḥ al-Bukhārī* (6041) and *Ṣaḥīḥ Muslim* (2330)

> The softness of his hands and pleasant scent of his body indicates the perfect character and features of the Prophet ﷺ, for the pleasant scent he possessed was due to his interactions with angels.[526]

٣٤٦- حَدَّثَنَا قُتَيْبَةُ بْنُ سَعِيدٍ، وَأَحْمَدُ بْنُ عَبْدَةَ هُوَ الضَّبِّيُّ، وَالْمَعْنَىٰ وَاحِدٌ، قَالا: حَدَّثَنَا حَمَّادُ بْنُ زَيْدٍ، عَنْ سَلْمٍ الْعَلَوِيِّ، عَنْ أَنَسِ بْنِ مَالِكٍ، «عَنْ رَسُولِ اللهِ صلى الله عليه وسلم أَنَّهُ كَانَ عِنْدَهُ رَجُلٌ بِهِ أَثَرُ صُفْرَةٍ، قَالَ: وَكَانَ رَسُولُ اللهِ صلى الله عليه وسلم لا يَكَادُ يُوَاجِهُ أَحَدًا بِشَيْءٍ يَكْرَهُهُ، فَلَمَّا قَامَ قَالَ لِلْقَوْمِ: لَوْ قُلْتُمْ لَهُ يَدَعُ هَذِهِ الصُّفْرَةَ»[٥٢٧].

346. Anas b. Mālik ﷺ reported: "A man with traces of saffron on him sat with the Messenger of Allāh ﷺ and the habit of the Messenger of Allāh ﷺ was that he would often avoid bluntly expressing things that other people would dislike. After the man left, he said to those who were present, 'It would have been better if you told him to rid himself of this saffron.'"

Ibn Ḥajar al-Haytamī said,

> The Prophet ﷺ tended to avoid saying or doing something to an individual if that was something that the person would dislike.
>
> The reason he ﷺ did not ask the individual to remove it directly was because that trace was not prohibited, otherwise he ﷺ would not have postponed giving the advice. This is supported by another ḥadīth wherein the Prophet ﷺ saw ʿAmr b. al-ʿĀṣ ﷺ wearing saffron-dyed garments and ordered him to remove them right away. If someone asks why the Prophet ﷺ ordered ʿAmr directly but delegated this task to the other companions in the case of the man mentioned in this ḥadīth, the answer is: ʿAmr was wearing something that was deemed unlawful while it was not the case for the other man. And, if we assume that wearing saffron-dyed clothing is not forbidden, then the answer is: it could be that the man was a new Muslim, and he ﷺ feared that such a direct order would lead to an undesired outcome whilst in the case of ʿAmr, he would be very happy to hasten to obey the Messenger ﷺ.

---

526 *Fatḥ al-Bārī*

527 *Sunan Abī Dāwūd* (4182)

The argument of some who said that he ﷺ disliked the colour yellow because it is a distinguishing sign of the Jews is incorrect. This is because this colour was made as the sign that distinguishes them from Muslims only recently as it happened in some countries like Egypt. Ibn Abī Ḥajlah mentioned that the Christians wore blue turbans, the Jews wore yellow turbans and the Samaritans wore red turbans in 701 H. The reason they wore such distinctive colours is because it happened that one day a man from Morocco was sitting at the door of a castle and a Christian man came wearing a white turban. Thereupon, the Moroccan man got up and stood in respect thinking he was a Muslim. However after he realised that he was a Christian, he went to the Sultan, al-Nāṣir Muḥammad b. Qalāwūn and requested the change of the dress code of the non-Muslims living in the lands of Islām so that they could be distinguished from the Muslims and he accepted his request.

٣٤٧- حَدَّثَنَا مُحَمَّدُ بْنُ بَشَّارٍ، قَالَ: حَدَّثَنَا مُحَمَّدُ بْنُ جَعْفَرٍ، قَالَ: حَدَّثَنَا شُعْبَةُ، عَنْ أَبِي إِسْحَاقَ، عَنْ أَبِي عَبْدِ اللهِ الْجَدَلِيِّ – وَاسْمُهُ عَبْدُ بْنُ عَبْدٍ –، عَنْ عَائِشَةَ، أَنَّهَا قَالَتْ: «لَمْ يَكُنْ رَسُولُ اللهِ صلىٰ الله عليه وسلم فَاحِشًا وَلا مُتَفَحِّشًا وَلا صَخَّابًا فِي الأَسْوَاقِ، وَلا يَجْزِي بِالسَّيِّئَةِ السَّيِّئَةَ وَلَكِنْ يَعْفُو وَيَصْفَحُ»[٥٢٨].

347. 'Ā'ishah رضي الله عنها narrated: "The Messenger of Allāh ﷺ was not indecent or offensive. Nor did he shout in the market. He did not respond to a bad deed with a bad deed. Rather, he forgave and pardoned."

Al-Bājūrī said,

"Rather, he forgave and pardoned": It suffices for us to mention his pardoning of his enemies who waged war upon him, and went to excess in harming him to the point of breaking his tooth and injuring his face. There is not a patient person except that he is known to have slips or lapses which stop him from having complete patience. The exception is the Chosen One ﷺ, for no matter the level of ignorance and harm he faced, he met it with forgiveness and pardon. This is in accordance to the words of Allāh: **{Overlook this and pardon them.}**[529]

---

528 *Sunan al-Tirmidhī* (2016)

529 Qur'ān 5: 13

Bakr Abū Zayd said,

> The Prophet ﷺ was selective in his words and he was always keen to use the most respectful and kindest words which were far from the words used by rude and vulgar people. He disliked giving respectful titles to those who did not deserve them and also using insulting words against those who should be honoured. For example, he ﷺ prevented people from addressing the hypocrite with the title "master" and from calling Abū Jahl with the *kunyah* Abu 'l-Ḥakam, or a slave person from calling his master 'my lord' and a master calling his slave "my slave". Rather, he directed the master to say "my boy" or "my girl" and the slave to say to their masters "my master" etc.[530]

٣٤٨- حَدَّثَنَا هَارُونُ بْنُ إِسْحَاقَ الْهَمْدَانِيُّ، قَالَ: حَدَّثَنَا عَبْدَةُ، عَنْ هِشَامِ بْنِ عُرْوَةَ، عَنْ أَبِيهِ، عَنْ عَائِشَةَ، قَالَتْ: «مَا ضَرَبَ رَسُولُ اللهِ صلىٰ الله عليه وسلم بِيَدِهِ شَيْئًا قَطُّ إِلَّا أَنْ يُجَاهِدَ فِي سَبِيلِ اللهِ، وَلَا ضَرَبَ خَادِمًا وَلَا امْرَأَةً»[531].

348. ʿĀishah ؓ narrated: "The Messenger of Allāh ﷺ never hit anything or anyone with his hands, unless he was fighting in the Path of Allāh, and he did not hit a servant or a woman."

Ibn ʿAbd al-Barr said,

> This ḥadīth indicates that it is recommended for rulers and scholars not to avenge themselves. By doing so, they follow the example of the Prophet ﷺ by forgiving those who were unjust to them.[532]

Al-Bājūrī said,

> Abstaining from hitting slaves and women – wherever possible – is an act of virtuosity, especially for the chivalrous and noble people. More emphatic than this is the aforementioned report of Anas that he never reprimanded him.

٣٤٩- حَدَّثَنَا أَحْمَدُ بْنُ عَبْدَةَ الضَّبِّيُّ، قَالَ: حَدَّثَنَا فُضَيْلُ بْنُ عِيَاضٍ، عَنْ مَنْصُورٍ، عَنِ الزُّهْرِيِّ، عَنْ عُرْوَةَ، عَنْ عَائِشَةَ، قَالَتْ: «مَا رَأَيْتُ رَسُولَ اللهِ صلىٰ الله عليه

---

530 *Muʿjam al-Manāhī al-Lafẓiyyah*
531 *Ṣaḥīḥ Muslim* (2328)
532 *Al-Istidkhār*

وسلم مُنْتَصِرًا مِنْ مَظْلَمَةٍ ظُلِمَهَا قَطُّ مَا لَمْ يُنْتَهَكْ مِنْ مَحَارِمِ اللهِ تَعَالَىٰ شَيْءٌ، فَإِذَا انْتُهِكَ مِنْ مَحَارِمِ اللهِ شَيْءٌ كَانَ مِنْ أَشَدِّهِمْ فِي ذَلِكَ غَضَبًا، وَمَا خُيِّرَ بَيْنَ أَمْرَيْنِ إِلَّا اخْتَارَ أَيْسَرَهُمَا مَا لَمْ يَكُنْ مَأْثَمًا»[٥٣٣].

349. 'Ā'ishah ﵂ narrated: "I have never seen the Messenger of Allāh ﷺ avenge the injustice he was subjected to unless there was a case where the laws of Allāh were transgressed or broken. If the laws of Allāh were transgressed, there was no one angrier than him. If the situation arose where he was given a choice between two things, he always chose the one that was easier, unless it was sinful."

Al-Bājūrī said,

> He would only avenge religious transgressions due to his firmness in the religion. Overlooking such transgressions would entail weakness and spinelessness.

Ibn 'Abd al-Barr said,

> There are three benefits concluded from this ḥadīth:
>
> 1. It is recommended for rulers and scholars not to avenge themselves, thereby following the example of the Prophet ﷺ and to forgive those who show injustice towards them. The scholars agreed that the judge cannot judge in a case in which he is involved.
>
> 2. It is allowed to take concessions.
>
> 3. The Messenger ﷺ never avenged in personal matters related to worldly affairs. As for the cases where he was abused verbally, then it is mandatory to avenge because this is from the rights of Allāh and it is an act of disbelief. If a person apostates then he cannot be left without a punishment.[534]

٣٥٠- حَدَّثَنَا ابْنُ أَبِي عُمَرَ، قَالَ: حَدَّثَنَا سُفْيَانُ، عَنْ مُحَمَّدِ بْنِ الْمُنْكَدِرِ، عَنْ عُرْوَةَ، عَنْ عَائِشَةَ، قَالَتِ: «اسْتَأْذَنَ رَجُلٌ عَلَىٰ رَسُولِ اللهِ صلىٰ الله عليه وسلم وَأَنَا عِنْدَهُ، فَقَالَ: بِئْسَ ابْنُ الْعَشِيرَةِ أَوْ أَخُو الْعَشِيرَةِ، ثُمَّ أَذِنَ لَهُ، فَأَلَانَ لَهُ الْقَوْلَ، فَلَمَّا

533 *Ṣaḥīḥ al-Bukhārī* (3560) and *Ṣaḥīḥ Muslim* (2327)
534 *Al-Masālik fī Sharḥ Muwaṭṭá Mālik*

خَرَجَ قُلْتُ: يَا رَسُولَ اللهِ، قُلْتَ مَا قُلْتَ ثُمَّ أَلَنْتَ لَهُ الْقَوْلَ؟ فَقَالَ: يَا عَائِشَةُ، إِنَّ مِنْ شَرِّ النَّاسِ مَنْ تَرَكَهُ النَّاسُ أَوْ وَدَعَهُ النَّاسُ اتِّقَاءَ فُحْشِهِ»[٥٣٥].

350. ʿĀʾishah ﵂ narrated: "A man sought permission from the Messenger of Allāh ﷺ to enter his presence whilst I was with him. He ﷺ said, 'What a wretched person is he amongst his community,' and then he gave him permission to enter. After the person entered, he spoke in a kind manner to him. When the man left I said, 'O Messenger of Allāh! You said what you said before he entered and then you spoke so kindly to him?' The Messenger ﷺ said, 'O ʿĀʾishah! Indeed, from the vilest are those who people avoid to avert their wickedness.'"

Al-Khaṭṭābī said,

> The fact that the Prophet ﷺ mentioned the bad trait of this man in his absence does not make it an act of backbiting. This is because this kind of statement is intended to warn people from the person and admonish others from following his ways. It is possible that the wickedness of the man was done in public and in religion mentioning the wrongdoing of a person who does it in public is not considered backbiting.[536]

Ibn Baṭṭāl said,

> Whoever Allāh has guided to take the path of sensibility to accustom his tongue to saying good words follows the example of the Prophets. They are indeed the best role models that all should follow. This ḥadīth shows that it is not considered backbiting when mentioning the public sins of a *fāsiq* (a person who does sins in public). It also indicates that kindness should be employed towards the *fāsiq* if there is a benefit hoped from him. The person mentioned in this ḥadīth is ʿUyaynah b. Badr al-Fazārī who was the leader of his people and he was known as, "The idiot who people obey." The Prophet ﷺ hoped with his kind treatment towards him that he would embrace Islām and subsequently his people would follow suit in doing so.[537]

٣٥١- حَدَّثَنَا سُفْيَانُ بْنُ وَكِيعٍ، قَالَ: حَدَّثَنَا جُمَيْعُ بْنُ عُمَرَ بْنِ عَبْدِ الرَّحْمَنِ

535 *Ṣaḥīḥ al-Bukhārī* (6032) and *Ṣaḥīḥ Muslim* (2591)
536 *Maʿālim al-Sunan*
537 *Sharḥ Ṣaḥīḥ al-Bukhārī*

الْعِجْلِيُّ، قَالَ: أَنْبَأَنَا رَجُلٌ مِنْ بَنِي تَمِيمٍ مِنْ وَلَدِ أَبِي هَالَةَ زَوْجِ خَدِيجَةَ وَيُكْنَىٰ أَبَا عَبْدِ اللهِ، عَنِ ابْنٍ لأَبِي هَالَةَ، عَنِ الْحَسَنِ بْنِ عَلِيٍّ، قَالَ: قَالَ الْحُسَيْنُ: سَأَلْتُ أَبِي عَنْ سِيرَةِ النَّبِيِّ صلىٰ الله عليه وسلم فِي جُلَسَائِهِ، فَقَالَ: كَانَ رَسُولُ اللهِ صلىٰ الله عليه وسلم دَائِمَ الْبِشْرِ، سَهْلَ الْخُلُقِ، لَيِّنَ الْجَانِبِ، لَيْسَ بِفَظٍّ وَلا غَلِيظٍ، وَلا صَخَّابٍ وَلا فَحَّاشٍ، وَلا عَيَّابٍ وَلا مُشَاحٍّ، يَتَغَافَلُ عَمَّا لا يَشْتَهِي، وَلا يُؤْيِسُ مِنْهُ رَاجِيهِ وَلا يُخَيَّبُ فِيهِ، قَدْ تَرَكَ نَفْسَهُ مِنْ ثَلاثٍ: الْمِرَاءِ وَالإِكْثَارِ وَمَا لا يَعْنِيهِ، وَتَرَكَ النَّاسَ مِنْ ثَلاثٍ: كَانَ لا يَذُمُّ أَحَدًا وَلا يَعِيبُهُ، وَلا يَطْلُبُ عَوْرَتَهُ، وَلا يَتَكَلَّمُ إِلَّا فِيمَا رَجَا ثَوَابَهُ، وَإِذَا تَكَلَّمَ أَطْرَقَ جُلَسَاؤُهُ كَأَنَّمَا عَلَىٰ رُؤُوسِهِمُ الطَّيْرُ، فَإِذَا سَكَتَ تَكَلَّمُوا لا يَتَنَازَعُونَ عِنْدَهُ الْحَدِيثَ، وَمَنْ تَكَلَّمَ عِنْدَهُ أَنْصَتُوا لَهُ حَتَّىٰ يَفْرُغَ، حَدِيثُهُمْ عِنْدَهُ حَدِيثُ أَوَّلِهِمْ، يَضْحَكُ مِمَّا يَضْحَكُونَ مِنْهُ، وَيَتَعَجَّبُ مِمَّا يَتَعَجَّبُونَ مِنْهُ، وَيَصْبِرُ لِلْغَرِيبِ عَلَىٰ الْجَفْوَةِ فِي مَنْطِقِهِ وَمَسْأَلَتِهِ، حَتَّىٰ إِنْ كَانَ أَصْحَابُهُ لَيَسْتَجْلِبُونَهُمْ وَيَقُولُ: إِذَا رَأَيْتُمْ طَالِبَ حَاجَةٍ يَطْلُبُهَا فَأَرْفِدُوهُ، وَلا يَقْبَلُ الثَّنَاءَ إِلَّا مِنْ مُكَافِئٍ وَلا يَقْطَعُ عَلَىٰ أَحَدٍ حَدِيثَهُ حَتَّىٰ يَجُوزَ فَيَقْطَعُهُ بِنَهْيٍ أَوْ قِيَامٍ»[٥٣٨].

351. Al-Ḥasan b. 'Alī ﵁ narrated that al-Ḥusayn b. 'Alī ﵁ said: "I inquired from my father regarding the conduct of the Prophet ﷺ with his company. He replied, 'The Messenger of Allāh ﷺ maintained a cheerful countenance and he was easy mannered. He was soft-natured; neither rude nor harsh, and neither stone-hearted nor loud or offensive in his speech. He did not mention the faults of anything and he was not narrow-minded or argumentative. If he heard or saw something he disliked he would turn his attention away as if he did not notice it. He did not make people fall into despair or feel disheartened, and he did not respond negatively to the requests that he disliked. He refrained from three traits related to himself: stubbornness in arguments (in some versions: pretension), excessiveness (in some versions: pride), and that which did not concern him. He refrained from three traits related to people: he did not disgrace or insult anyone, nor look for the hidden faults of others; he only spoke that from which reward was hoped.

When he spoke, those present bowed their heads in such a manner,

538 See ḥadīth 8

as if birds were perched upon them. When he was silent, the others would begin speaking. They would not dispute in his presence regarding anything and whenever a person spoke to him the others would keep quiet and listen until he would finish. They would speak in order (i.e. the first person to arrive would be the first person to speak and so forth). When those around him laughed due to some reason, he would laugh as well and he would show surprise at the things that surprised the people. He exercised patience at the crude and indecent questions of the traveller and his companions would bring travellers to his assemblies. He used to say to his companions, 'When you see a person in need, always help that person.' If someone praised him, he would detest it unless it came from someone, who in the process of giving thanks praised him commensurately. He did not interrupt someone speaking. However, if one exceeded the limits he would stop him or would get up and leave."

Al-Bājūrī said,

> **"He exercised patience at the crude and indecent questions of the traveller and his companions would bring travellers to his assemblies":** Patience upon the harm and crudeness of people is amongst its greatest forms. It has been reported that the believer who mixes with people and bears patience with their harm is more virtuous than one who secludes himself from them. The Prophet has the highest degree in this matter.
>
> **"And his companions would bring travellers to his assemblies":** I.e. so that they could benefit from the issues they brought up. This is because the companions were intimidated of posing some questions whilst the travellers were not. Thus, the Prophet bore patience with their excessiveness in questioning.
>
> **"If someone praised him, he would detest it unless it came from someone, who in the process of giving thanks praised him commensurately":** This is because Allāh censured the one who loves to be praised for things he did not do in His statement: **{Do not think [O Prophet] that those who exult in what they have done and seek praise for things they have not done will escape the torment; agonizing torment awaits them.}**[539]

539 Qurʾān 3: 188

'Abdullāh b. Sa'īd al-Ḥaḍramī al-Makkī said,

> The cheerful countenance of the Prophet ﷺ does not negate the sad state of his heart due to his concern about the Hereafter and his nation.
>
> He ﷺ never uttered a word or did something that hurt others without any lawful right. He was merciful and soft-hearted with the believers. He never dispraised a food or anything lawful and this does not contradict that he dispraised the forbidden and admonished it.
>
> If someone asked him for something that he disliked, he would not make the person hopeful to achieve it nor resigned to give up on it. Rather, he would remain silent.
>
> This ḥadīth manifests the perfect character of the Prophet ﷺ.[540]

٣٥٢- حَدَّثَنَا مُحَمَّدُ بْنُ بَشَّارٍ، قَالَ: حَدَّثَنَا عَبْدُ الرَّحْمَنِ بْنُ مَهْدِيٍّ، قَالَ: حَدَّثَنَا سُفْيَانُ، عَنْ مُحَمَّدِ بْنِ الْمُنْكَدِرِ، قَالَ: سَمِعْتُ جَابِرَ بْنَ عَبْدِ اللهِ، يَقُولُ: «مَا سُئِلَ رَسُولُ اللهِ صلىٰ الله عليه وسلم شَيْئًا قَطُّ فَقَالَ: لا»[٥٤١].

352. Jābir b. 'Abdillāh ﷺ narrated: "The Messenger of Allāh ﷺ was never asked of something to which he replied 'No.'"

Al-Nawawī said,

> This shows the excessive generosity of the Prophet ﷺ for he was never asked for anything from this worldly life except that he agreed to give it away.[542]

Ibn al-'Uthaymīn said,

> This ḥadīth along with other ḥadīths encourages us to spend for the sake of Allāh for Allāh has provided people with money to test them. Allāh ﷻ said: **{Your wealth and your children are but a trial and Allāh has with Him a great reward.}**[543] Thus, some people spend it to fulfil their unlawful desires and pleasures which keep them distant from Allāh whilst some other people spend it in the path of Allāh

540 *Muntahā al-Su'l 'alā Wasā'il al-Wuṣūl ilā Shamā'il al-Rasūl*
541 *Ṣaḥīḥ al-Bukhārī* (6034) and *Ṣaḥīḥ Muslim* (2311)
542 *Sharḥ Ṣaḥīḥ Muslim*
543 Qur'ān 64:15

seeking His reward. As for those who spend it in matters that are neither prescribed in religion nor forbidden, then they have just wasted their wealth.[544]

٣٥٣- حَدَّثَنَا عَبْدُ اللهِ بْنُ عِمْرَانَ أَبُو الْقَاسِمِ الْقُرَشِيُّ الْمَكِّيُّ، قَالَ: حَدَّثَنَا إِبْرَاهِيمُ بْنُ سَعْدٍ، عَنِ ابْنِ شِهَابٍ، عَنْ عُبَيْدِ اللهِ، عَنِ ابْنِ عَبَّاسٍ، قَالَ: «كَانَ رَسُولُ اللهِ صلى الله عليه وسلم أَجْوَدَ النَّاسِ بِالْخَيْرِ، وَكَانَ أَجْوَدَ مَا يَكُونُ فِي شَهْرِ رَمَضَانَ، حَتَّىٰ يَنْسَلِخَ فَيَأْتِيهِ جِبْرِيلُ فَيَعْرِضُ عَلَيْهِ الْقُرْآنَ، فَإِذَا لَقِيَهُ جِبْرِيلُ كَانَ رَسُولُ اللهِ صلى الله عليه وسلم أَجْوَدَ بِالْخَيْرِ مِنَ الرِّيحِ الْمُرْسَلَةِ»[٥٤٥].

353. ʿAbdullāh b. ʿAbbās ؓ narrated: "The Messenger of Allāh ﷺ was the most generous amongst the people in good. He would increase in generosity during the month of Ramaḍān until the month's end. In this month Jibrīl ؑ used to visit him and recite the Qur'ān to him. Every time Jibrīl met him, the generosity of the Messenger of Allāh ﷺ was more than that of a wind that brings forth heavy rains."

Al-Bājūrī said,

> **"The Messenger of Allāh ﷺ was the most generous amongst the people":** To summarise his state: He gave like a king and lived like a pauper. He tied a stone on his stomach to curb hunger and a month or multiple would pass without fire being lit in his house.
>
> **"He would increase in generosity during the month of Ramaḍān until the month's end":** This is because it is the season of goodness and proliferation of it, for in this month Allāh endows His servants with things not present in other months. Thus, the Prophet ﷺ followed in the manner of his Lord.

Ibn Baṭṭāl said,

> Al-Muhallab said, "This ḥadīth shows the benefits and blessings of being in the company of pious and righteous people as this reminds the person to do good deeds and increase his share from good deeds. This is why the Prophet ﷺ ordered us to sit with the learned ones and spend time in the gatherings of Allāh's remembrance and gave the

544 *Riyāḍ al-Ṣāliḥīn*

545 *Ṣaḥīḥ al-Bukhari* (1902) and *Ṣaḥīḥ Muslim* (2308)

example of the righteous friend as the perfume seller. It also shows the blessings attained through good deeds and that a good deed leads to another i.e. the blessing of fasting, meeting Jibrīl and reciting the Qur'ān increased the generosity of the Prophet ﷺ.[546]

٣٥٤- حَدَّثَنَا قُتَيْبَةُ بْنُ سَعِيدٍ، قَالَ: أَخْبَرَنَا جَعْفَرُ بْنُ سُلَيْمَانَ، عَنْ ثَابِتٍ، عَنْ أَنَسِ بْنِ مَالِكٍ قَالَ: «كَانَ النَّبِيُّ صلى الله عليه وسلم لا يَدَّخِرُ شَيْئًا لِغَدٍ»[٥٤٧].

354. Anas b. Mālik ﷺ narrated: "The Prophet ﷺ would not store anything for the following day."

Al-Bājūrī said,

> This is due to his perfect reliance on Allāh (*tawakkul*). This is in specific to himself, and it does not negate that he would store a year's worth of [basic] sustenance for his dependants. This is because they did not possess the same level of *tawakkul*.
>
> This narration is appropriate for this chapter as the absence of storage dictates a great level of *tawakkul*, which is amongst the greatest character traits.

Al-Qasṭallānī said,

> It is permissible to store food for one's wife and children and this does not negate reliance on Allāh because the Prophet ﷺ did it and he is the master of those who rely on Allāh ﷻ. This is because taking the means (whilst the reliance on Allāh is established in the heart) does not contradict one's reliance. The fact that he ﷺ stored for his family their sustenance for one year does not contradict that he did not store anything for the next day because this was either before he ﷺ had access to sustenance or it means that he did not store anything for himself.[548]

٣٥٥- حَدَّثَنَا هَارُونُ بْنُ مُوسَىٰ بْنِ أَبِي عَلْقَمَةَ الْمَدِينِيُّ، قَالَ: حَدَّثَنِي أَبِي، عَنْ هِشَامِ بْنِ سَعْدٍ، عَنْ زَيْدِ بْنِ أَسْلَمَ، عَنْ أَبِيهِ، عَنْ عُمَرَ بْنِ الْخَطَّابِ، أَنَّ رَجُلًا جَاءَ

---

546 *Sharḥ Ṣaḥīḥ al-Bukhārī*
547 *Sunan al-Tirmidhī* (2362)
548 *Irshād al-Sārī*

إِلَىٰ النَّبِيِّ صلىٰ الله عليه وسلم فَسَأَلَهُ أَنْ يُعْطِيَهُ، فَقَالَ النَّبِيُّ صلىٰ الله عليه وسلم: مَا عِنْدِي شَيْءٌ وَلَكِنِ ابْتَعْ عَلَيَّ، فَإِذَا جَاءَنِي شَيْءٌ قَضَيْتُهُ، فَقَالَ عُمَرُ: يَا رَسُولَ اللهِ، قَدْ أَعْطَيْتَهُ فَمَّا كَلَّفَكَ اللهُ مَا لا تَقْدِرُ عَلَيْهِ، فَكَرِهَ النَّبِيُّ صلىٰ الله عليه وسلم قَوْلَ عُمَرَ، فَقَالَ رَجُلٌ مِنَ الأَنْصَارِ: يَا رَسُولَ اللهِ، أَنْفِقْ وَلا تَخَفْ مِنْ ذِي الْعَرْشِ إِقْلَالًا، فَتَبَسَّمَ رَسُولُ اللهِ صلىٰ الله عليه وسلم وَعُرِفَ فِي وَجْهِهِ الْبِشْرُ لِقَوْلِ الأَنْصَارِيِّ، ثُمَّ قَالَ: بِهَذَا أُمِرْتُ[٥٤٩].

355. ʿUmar b. al-Khaṭṭāb ﷺ narrated: "A man came to the Prophet ﷺ asking for something. The Prophet ﷺ replied, 'I do not have anything at present but go and purchase something on my name and I will pay for it when I have sufficient money.' ʿUmar ﷺ said, 'O Messenger of Allāh! You have already given him that which you had and Allāh ﷻ did not make you responsible for that which is beyond your means.' The Messenger ﷺ disliked this statement of ʿUmar ﷺ. A man from the Anṣār said, 'O Messenger of Allāh! Spend whatever you wish, and do not fear any diminution from the Lord of the Throne.' The Messenger ﷺ smiled and the happiness could be seen on his face due to the statement of the man. He ﷺ then said, 'With this I have been ordered.'"

ʿAbdullāh b. Saʿīd al-Ḥaḍramī al-Makkī said,

> The statement of ʿUmar either meant that he ﷺ gave to that person before, therefore there was no need to promise him more since he ﷺ did not have anything at that time or that he ﷺ answered the man in a kind manner when he explained that he did not have anything to give away. The reason why the Prophet ﷺ disliked the statement of ʿUmar is that it made the man feel disappointed and that the promise made was not considered a burden given that he ﷺ used to be lavished with the blessings of Allāh.[550]

Al-Bājūrī said,

> **"With this I have been ordered":** I.e. with the giving ordered by the Anṣārī man and not the withholding ordered by ʿUmar.

549 *Al-Aḥādīth al-Mukhtarah* (78)
550 *Muntahā al-Su'l ʿalā Wasā'il al-Wuṣūl ilā Shamā'il al-Rasūl*

٣٥٦- حَدَّثَنَا عَلِيُّ بْنُ حُجْرٍ، قَالَ: أَخْبَرَنَا شَرِيكٌ، عَنْ عَبْدِ اللهِ بْنِ مُحَمَّدِ بْنِ عَقِيلٍ، عَنِ الرُّبَيِّعِ بِنْتِ مُعَوِّذِ بْنِ عَفْرَاءَ، قَالَتْ: «أَتَيْتُ النَّبِيَّ صلى الله عليه وسلم، بِقِنَاعٍ مِنْ رُطَبٍ وَأَجْرٍ زُغْبٍ فَأَعْطَانِي مِلْءَ كَفِّهِ حُلِيًّا وَذَهَبًا»[٥٥١].

356. Al-Rubayyi' bint Mu'awwidh b. 'Afrā' ﵄ narrated: "I took a plate of ripe dates (*ruṭab*) and small cucumbers to the Messenger of Allāh ﷺ. He gave me a handful of jewellery, or a handful of gold."

Al-Bājūrī said,

> **"He gave me":** I.e. in exchange for accepting her gift and rewarding her for it, or due to her presence whilst he was dividing the wealth.
>
> This narration was mentioned earlier in the chapter detailing fruits. It is repeated here to evidence his ﷺ perfect generosity and good nature.

٣٥٧- حَدَّثَنَا عَلِيُّ بْنُ خَشْرَمٍ، وَغَيْرُ وَاحِدٍ، قَالُوا: حَدَّثَنَا عِيسَى بْنُ يُونُسَ، عَنْ هِشَامِ بْنِ عُرْوَةَ، عَنْ أَبِيهِ، عَنْ عَائِشَةَ: «أَنَّ النَّبِيَّ صلى الله عليه وسلم كَانَ يَقْبَلُ الْهَدِيَّةَ وَيُثِيبُ عَلَيْهَا»[٥٥٢].

357. 'Ā'ishah ﵂ narrated: "The Messenger of Allāh ﷺ accepted gifts and would reciprocate in return."

Al-Khaṭṭābī said,

> Accepting gifts is a form of generosity and from the kind manners that bring hearts together and it was reported that he ﷺ ordered people to exchange gifts as that will bring forth love between people. The acceptance of gifts was one of the signs of his prophethood mentioned in previous scriptures wherein he was described as a person who accepts gifts and does not take charity. The Prophet ﷺ used to reward those who gave him gifts so that no one could have the upper hand over him or hold favours over him. Allāh ﷻ said: **{O my people, I do not ask you for it any reward. My reward is only from the one who created me. Then will you not reason?}**[553] And if he ﷺ accepted gifts without rewarding those who presented the gifts, it would have been as if he was receiving rewards for his mission. It is

551 See ḥadīth 203
552 *Ṣaḥīḥ al-Bukhārī* (2585)
553 Qur'ān 11:51

> for this reason, giving gifts to rulers is considered a form of bribery because it was not allowed for the Messenger ﷺ to accept gifts without reciprocating or to take without giving, and he is the leader and master of all humanity.[554]

Al-Bājūrī said,

> It should be noted here that the Prophet's ﷺ manners, guidance and *sīrah* (way/biography) are the ultimate litmus test. Things are weighed against them, and that which concords with them is accepted, whereas that which is contrary to them is rejected.

---

554 *Maʿālim al-Sunan*

باب ما جاء في حياء رسول الله صلى الله عليه وسلم

[49] On Allāh's Messenger's ﷺ Modesty and Shyness

ʿAbd al-Razzāq al-Badr said,

> The quality of *ḥayāʾ* is an attribute that brings forth nothing but good and it is one of the parts of *īmān*. It induces the person to do the good in all of his affairs, be it related to worship, etiquettes or social life. It also keeps the person away from the ugly sins, wrongdoings and ill-manners.

Al-Bājūrī said,

> It is obvious that *ḥayāʾ* falls under good character. It has been given its own independent chapter to emphasise its great station, as it leads to good social interactions and truthful dealings.

٣٥٨- حَدَّثَنَا مَحْمُودُ بْنُ غَيْلَانَ، قَالَ: حَدَّثَنَا أَبُو دَاوُدَ، قَالَ: حَدَّثَنَا شُعْبَةُ، عَنْ قَتَادَةَ، قَالَ: سَمِعْتُ عَبْدَ اللهِ بْنَ أَبِي عُتْبَةَ، يُحَدِّثُ عَنْ أَبِي سَعِيدٍ الْخُدْرِيِّ، قَالَ: «كَانَ النَّبِيُّ صلى الله عليه وسلم أَشَدَّ حَيَاءً مِنَ الْعَذْرَاءِ فِي خِدْرِهَا، وَكَانَ إِذَا كَرِهَ شَيْئًا عَرَفْنَاهُ فِي وَجْهِهِ»[555].

358. Abū Saʿīd al-Khudrī ؓ narrated: "The Prophet ﷺ was the most modest, more so than a maiden in her private quarters. If he did not like something, we could notice that on his face."

Al-Bājūrī said,

> **"The Prophet ﷺ was the most modest, more so than a maiden in her private quarters":** Shyness is praiseworthy so long as it does not lead to weakness, cowardice, diverting from the truth or leaving off the application of fixed punishments (*ḥudūd*). If otherwise, it is dispraised. Due to the Prophet's ﷺ strong shyness, he would only bathe behind rocks and no one ever saw his *ʿawrah* (i.e. private area, from

---

555 *Ṣaḥīḥ al-Bukhārī* (3562) and *Ṣaḥīḥ Muslim* (2320)

the naval to the privates).

"If he did not like something, we could notice that on his face": During his life, he did not explicitly exclaim his dislike of anything, rather it would be noticed from his face. This is akin to the maiden within her chamber, she does not explicitly mention her dislike of things, rather it is seen on her face. This parallel displays the connection between this sentence and the one that preceded it.

Ibn Ḥajar al-'Asqalānī said,

> Al-Qāḍī 'Iyād said, "Shyness and modesty were made part of *īmān* though it is a human instinct. For a characteristic to fall in line with the guidelines of religion [rather than being a mere human instinct], one would need to establish the intention, endeavour and possess the knowledge to do so. As for stating that shyness brings about nothing but goodness, it is found problematic because someone may argue that sometimes shyness prevents one from facing and stopping a wrongdoer or not fulfilling rights and obligations. The answer to this is that there are two types of shyness; one that conforms to religion and that does not lead to the aforementioned weakness whilst the other type is given the same name (i.e. shyness) because it shares the trait of preventing one from low and ugly acts.
>
> Abū al-'Abbās al-Qurṭubī said that cultivated shyness is the type of shyness that Allāh has made part of *īmān* and the characteristic that people ought to acquire. However, the instinctual type of shyness could support the attained shyness and it could integrate with the attained shyness until the prescribed shyness becomes an innate nature and the Prophet ﷺ enjoyed both types; his instinctual shyness made him more modest than a maiden in her private quarters and his attained shyness elevated him to the highest status.[556]

٣٥٩- حَدَّثَنَا مَحْمُودُ بْنُ غَيْلانَ، قَالَ: حَدَّثَنَا وَكِيعٌ، قَالَ: حَدَّثَنَا سُفْيَانُ، عَنْ مَنْصُورٍ، عَنْ مُوسَىٰ بْنِ عَبْدِ اللهِ بْنِ يَزِيدَ الْخَطْمِيِّ، عَنْ مَوْلًى لِعَائِشَةَ، قَالَ: قَالَتْ عَائِشَةُ: «مَا نَظَرْتُ إِلَىٰ فَرْجِ رَسُولِ اللهِ صلىٰ الله عليه وسلم»، أَوْ قَالَتْ: «مَا رَأَيْتُ

556 *Fatḥ al-Bārī*

فَرْجَ رَسُولِ اللهِ صلىٰ الله عليه وسلم قَطُّ»٥٥٧.

359. ʿĀ'ishah ﷺ reported: "I never looked towards the private parts of the Messenger of Allāh ﷺ, [or she said] that I never saw the private parts of the Messenger of Allāh ﷺ."

Ibn Ḥajar al-Haytamī said,

> This ḥadīth manifests the perfect level of shyness possessed by the Prophet ﷺ because he did not do anything that would allow her to look at his private parts. This is because a woman would not dare to see the private parts of her husband unless he would allow it and give his consent.

557 *Sunan Ibn Mājah* (662)

باب ما جاء في حجامة رسول الله صلى الله عليه وسلم

[50] On Allāh's Messenger's ﷺ Cupping

ʿAbd al-Razzāq al-Badr said,

> Cupping is a medical treatment that the Prophet ﷺ had administered upon himself many times and he paid the cupper for it. He also encouraged it and stated that it is a cure. Ibn ʿAbbas narrated that the Prophet ﷺ said "Healing is in three things: In the incision of the cupper, in drinking honey, and in cauterizing with fire, but I forbid my Ummah (nation) from cauterization (branding with fire)."[558]

٣٦٠- حَدَّثَنَا عَلِيُّ بْنُ حُجْرٍ، قَالَ: حَدَّثَنَا إِسْمَاعِيلُ بْنُ جَعْفَرٍ، عَنْ حُمَيْدٍ، قَالَ: سُئِلَ أَنَسُ بْنُ مَالِكٍ عَنْ كَسْبِ الْحَجَّامِ، فَقَالَ: «احْتَجَمَ رَسُولُ اللهِ صلىٰ الله عليه وسلم، حَجَمَهُ أَبُو طَيْبَةَ، فَأَمَرَ لَهُ بِصَاعَيْنِ مِنْ طَعَامٍ، وَكَلَّمَ أَهْلَهُ فَوَضَعُوا عَنْهُ مِنْ خَرَاجِهِ، وَقَالَ: إِنَّ أَفْضَلَ مَا تَدَاوَيْتُمْ بِهِ الْحِجَامَةُ، أَوْ إِنَّ مِنْ أَمْثَلِ دَوَائِكُمُ الْحِجَامَةَ»[٥٥٩].

360. Anas b. Mālik ؓ was asked about the ruling on the income of the cupper. He said: "The Messenger of Allāh ﷺ had the treatment of cupping administered upon him by Abū Ṭaybah ؓ. In return, he ﷺ gave Abū Ṭaybah two *ṣāʿ* of food, and interceded on his behalf with his masters that the stipulated labour tax imposed upon him be reduced. He also said, 'Indeed the best of treatments is cupping.'"

ʿAbd al-Raḥmān al-Mubārakfūrī said,

> This ḥadīth shows that it is allowed to charge fees for medical treatment and it is recommended to intercede for people so that the person receiving the request reduces some of their rights and becomes easy with others in this regard. It shows that it is permissible for the master to let his slave work independently in return of a fixed pay-

558 *Ṣaḥīḥ al-Bukhārī* (3436)
559 *Ṣaḥīḥ al-Bukhārī* (2102) and *Ṣaḥīḥ Muslim* (1577)

ment with the rest of the earnings going to the slave.

The scholars differed on the ruling of the income of the cupper, the majority stated that it is lawful, as stated by al-Ḥāfiẓ Ibn Ḥajar.[560]

٣٦١- حَدَّثَنَا عَمْرُو بْنُ عَلِيٍّ، قَالَ: حَدَّثَنَا أَبُو دَاوُدَ، قَالَ: حَدَّثَنَا وَرْقَاءُ بْنُ عُمَرَ، عَنْ عَبْدِ الْأَعْلَىٰ، عَنْ أَبِي جَمِيلَةَ، عَنْ عَلِيٍّ: «أَنَّ النَّبِيَّ صلى الله عليه وسلم احْتَجَمَ وَأَمَرَنِي فَأَعْطَيْتُ الْحَجَّامَ أَجْرَهُ»[561].

361. 'Alī ☙ narrated: "The Prophet ﷺ had the treatment of cupping administered upon him and ordered me to pay the cupper his fees, so I did."

'Alī al-Qārī said,

> Ibn al-Jawzī mentioned that the Prophet ﷺ disliked the income of cuppers because cupping is from the things that Muslims ought to offer for free when it is required by fellow Muslims.

٣٦٢- حَدَّثَنَا هَارُونُ بْنُ إِسْحَاقَ الْهَمْدَانِيُّ، قَالَ: حَدَّثَنَا عَبْدَةُ، عَنْ سُفْيَانَ الثَّوْرِيِّ، عَنْ جَابِرٍ، عَنِ الشَّعْبِيِّ، عَنِ ابْنِ عَبَّاسٍ، قَالَ: «إِنَّ النَّبِيَّ صلى الله عليه وسلم احْتَجَمَ فِي الْأَخْدَعَيْنِ وَبَيْنَ الْكَتِفَيْنِ، وَأَعْطَىٰ الْحَجَّامَ أَجْرَهُ، وَلَوْ كَانَ حَرَامًا لَمْ يُعْطِهِ»[562].

362. 'Abdullāh b. 'Abbās ☙ narrated: "The Prophet ﷺ had the treatment of cupping administered on both sides of his neck and the top area between his shoulders, and paid the cupper his fees. Had it been forbidden to charge fees for cupping, he would not have paid it."

'Alī al-Qārī said,

> It is proven in many ḥadīths that he had cupping administered on different parts of his body depending on the treatment needed on each occasion. The majority of scholars relied on this ḥadīth amongst others to state that the income of cuppers is lawful.

---

560 *Tuḥfat al-Aḥwadhī*
561 *Sunan Ibn Mājah* (2163)
562 See *Ṣaḥīḥ al-Bukhārī* (2103) and *Ṣaḥīḥ Muslim* (1202)

Al-Bājūrī said,

> **"Had it been forbidden to charge fees for cupping, he would not have paid it":** I.e. because this would be aiding in the forbidden, and he ﷺ would never do so.

٣٦٣- حَدَّثَنَا هَارُونُ بْنُ إِسْحَاقَ، قَالَ: حَدَّثَنَا عَبْدَةُ، عَنِ ابْنِ أَبِي لَيْلَىٰ، عَنْ نَافِعٍ، عَنِ ابْنِ عُمَرَ، «أَنَّ النَّبِيَّ صلىٰ الله عليه وسلم دَعَا حَجَّامًا فَحَجَمَهُ، وَسَأَلَهُ: كَمْ خَرَاجُكَ؟ فَقَالَ: ثَلَاثَةُ آصُعٍ، فَوَضَعَ عَنْهُ صَاعًا وَأَعْطَاهُ أَجْرَهُ»[٥٦٣].

363. ʿAbdullāh b. ʿUmar ؓ narrated: "The Prophet ﷺ requested a cupper to treat him. After he finished, he ﷺ inquired from him regarding the amount of labour tax he paid his master. The cupper replied, 'Three *ṣāʿ*.' So he ﷺ had it reduced to two *ṣāʿ*, and gave him his remuneration."

Ibn Ḥajar al-Haytamī said,

> The name of the cupper mentioned in this ḥadīth is said to be Abū Ṭaybah, as mentioned in the previous ḥadīth.

٣٦٤- حَدَّثَنَا عَبْدُ الْقُدُّوسِ بْنُ مُحَمَّدٍ الْعَطَّارُ الْبَصْرِيُّ، قَالَ: حَدَّثَنَا عَمْرُو بْنُ عَاصِمٍ، قَالَ: حَدَّثَنَا هَمَّامٌ، وَجَرِيرُ بْنُ حَازِمٍ، قَالَا: حَدَّثَنَا قَتَادَةُ، عَنْ أَنَسِ بْنِ مَالِكٍ قَالَ: «كَانَ رَسُولُ اللهِ صلىٰ الله عليه وسلم يَحْتَجِمُ فِي الْأَخْدَعَيْنِ وَالْكَاهِلِ، وَكَانَ يَحْتَجِمُ لِسَبْعَ عَشْرَةَ، وَتِسْعَ عَشْرَةَ وَإِحْدَىٰ وَعِشْرِينَ»[٥٦٤].

364. Anas b. Mālik ؓ narrated: "The Messenger of Allāh ﷺ used to have the treatment of cupping administered upon both sides of his neck and between the two shoulders. He used to take this treatment on the seventeenth, nineteenth or the twenty first [of the lunar month]."

Ibn Mufliḥ said,

> The reason why the Prophet ﷺ cupped the top area between the shoulders is because this is the closest area to the heart which can be

563 See *al-Muʿjam al-Kabīr* (12427)
564 *Sunan Abī Dāwūd* (3860) and *Sunan Ibn Mājah* (3483)

cupped.[565]

Ibn al-Qayyim said,

> The administration of cupping on both sides of the neck can treat sicknesses related to the head and its parts such as the face, teeth, ears, eyes, nose and throat if the sickness is due to excessive or corrupted blood.[566]

'Abdullāh b. Sa'īd al-Ḥaḍramī al-Makkī said,

> The companions ﷺ used to follow his example in choosing the time for cupping as they liked doing it on the odd nights of the month. This is due to the virtue of odd numbers as Allāh loves odd numbers. The best day to have cupping administered is on a Monday if it coincides with the seventeenth, nineteenth or twenty first of the month.[567]

٣٦٥- حَدَّثَنَا إِسْحَاقُ بْنُ مَنْصُورٍ، قَالَ: أَنْبَأَنَا عَبْدُ الرَّزَّاقِ، عَنْ مَعْمَرٍ، عَنْ قَتَادَةَ، عَنْ أَنَسِ بْنِ مَالِكٍ: «أَنَّ رَسُولَ اللهِ صلىٰ الله عليه وسلم احْتَجَمَ وَهُوَ مُحْرِمٌ بِمَلَلٍ عَلىٰ ظَهْرِ الْقَدَمِ»٥٦٨.

365. Anas b. Mālik ﷺ narrated: "The Messenger of Allāh ﷺ had cupping administered upon the top of his foot at a place called Malal whilst he was in the state of *iḥrām*."

'Abd al-Razzāq al-Badr said,

> **"Upon the top of his foot":** Al-Imām Aḥmad added, "Due to a pain he felt."[569] Cupping is a useful aid in reducing pain.

Ibn Ḥajar al-Haytamī said,

> Malal is a place between Makkah and Madīnah. It is about seventeen miles away from Madīnah.
>
> It is allowed to administer cupping whilst a person is still in the state of *iḥrām* if the treatment does not include removing hair; otherwise

565 *Al-'Ādāb al-Shar'iyyah*
566 *Al-Ṭibb al-Nabawī*
567 *Muntahā al-Su'l 'alā Wasā'il al-Wuṣūl ilā Shamā'il al-Rasūl*
568 *Sunan Abī Dāwūd* (1837)
569 *Al-Musnad* (12682)

it is considered to be forbidden unless there is a necessity and in such a case the person is required to slaughter a sacrifice as expiation.

باب ما جاء في أسماء رسول الله صلى الله عليه وسلم

[51] On Allāh's Messenger's ﷺ Names

ʿAbd al-Razzāq al-Badr said,

> The names of the Prophet ﷺ are more than just names as they reflect his character and nature.

Al-Bājūrī said,

> [It is said that] there is a maxim: An abundance of names indicates the eminence of the named.

٣٦٦- حَدَّثَنَا سَعِيدُ بْنُ عَبْدِ الرَّحْمَنِ الْمَخْزُومِيُّ، وَغَيْرُ وَاحِدٍ، قَالُوا: حَدَّثَنَا سُفْيَانُ، عَنِ الزُّهْرِيِّ، عَنْ مُحَمَّدِ بْنِ جُبَيْرِ بْنِ مُطْعِمٍ، عَنْ أَبِيهِ، قَالَ: قَالَ رَسُولُ اللهِ صلى الله عليه وسلم: «إِنَّ لِي أَسْمَاءً أَنَا مُحَمَّدٌ، وَأَنَا أَحْمَدُ، وَأَنَا الْمَاحِي الَّذِي يَمْحُو اللهُ بِيَ الْكُفْرَ، وَأَنَا الْحَاشِرُ الَّذِي يُحْشَرُ النَّاسُ عَلَى قَدَمِي، وَأَنَا الْعَاقِبُ» وَالْعَاقِبُ: الَّذِي لَيْسَ بَعْدَهُ نَبِيٌّ[٥٧٠].

366. Jubayr b. Muṭʿim ؓ narrated: "The Messenger of Allāh ﷺ said, 'I have many names. I am Muḥammad, I am Aḥmad. I am al-Māḥī [the obliterator] with whom Allāh obliterates disbelief. I am al-Ḥāshir [the gatherer] as the people will be gathered after I am gathered [on the Day of Resurrection], and I am al-ʿĀqib [i.e. the one who succeeds the other Prophets in bringing about good]." Al-ʿĀqib means: After whom there will come no prophet.

Ibn Ḥajar al-ʿAsqalānī said,

> The Prophet ﷺ will be the first one to be resurrected as stated in the authentic ḥadīth. His other agreed upon names that are mentioned in the Qurʾān are: al-Shāhid (the witness), al-Mubashshir (giver of glad tidings), al-Nadhīr al-Mubīn (the evident warner), al-Dāʿī ila Allāh

570 *Ṣaḥīḥ al-Bukhārī* (3532) and *Ṣaḥīḥ Muslim* (2354)

(caller to Allāh), al-Sirāj al-Munīr (enlightening luminary), al-Mudhakkir (the reminder), al-Raḥmah (the mercy), al-Niʿmah (the grace), al-Hādī (the guide), al-Amīn (the trustworthy), al-Muzzamil (enwrapped in his raiment), and al-Muddaththir (the one shrouded in his mantle).

٣٦٧- حَدَّثَنَا مُحَمَّدُ بْنُ طَرِيفٍ الْكُوفِيُّ، قَالَ: حَدَّثَنَا أَبُو بَكْرِ بْنُ عَيَّاشٍ، عَنْ عَاصِمٍ، عَنْ أَبِي وَائِلٍ، عَنْ حُذَيْفَةَ، قَالَ: لَقِيتُ النَّبِيَّ صلى الله عليه وسلم فِي بَعْضِ طُرُقِ الْمَدِينَةِ فَقَالَ: «أَنَا مُحَمَّدٌ، وَأَنَا أَحْمَدُ، وَأَنَا نَبِيُّ الرَّحْمَةِ، وَنَبِيُّ التَّوْبَةِ، وَأَنَا الْمُقَفَّى، وَأَنَا الْحَاشِرُ، وَنَبِيُّ الْمَلَاحِمِ»⁵⁷¹.

367. Ḥudhayfah ☙ narrated: "I once met the Messenger of Allāh ﷺ in one of the roads of Madīnah. He said, 'I am Muḥammad, and I am Aḥmad, and I am the Prophet of Mercy, the Prophet of Repentance, I am Muqaffā (the last Prophet), I am al-Hāshir (the first one to be gathered), and the Prophet of the battlefield.'"

Ibn al-Jawzī said,

Ibn Qutaybah said, "From the signs and evidences regarding the coming of the Prophet Muḥammad ﷺ is that his name (i.e. Aḥmad or Muḥammad) was prophesied in the previous scriptures and yet no one was given it before him. This was so that Allāh could protect this name and avert any doubts and false claims should someone be named with it. Thus, when his time came and the People of the Book spread the news that he was about to come out, his name was given." [572]

Al-Ṭībī said,

He is the Prophet of the battlefield because of his keenness for *jihad* and the great courage he possessed on the battlefield. [573]

٣٦٨- حَدَّثَنَا إِسْحَاقُ بْنُ مَنْصُورٍ، قَالَ: حَدَّثَنَا النَّضْرُ بْنُ شُمَيْلٍ، قَالَ: أَنْبَأَنَا حَمَّادُ بْنُ سَلَمَةَ، عَنْ عَاصِمٍ، عَنْ زِرٍّ، عَنْ حُذَيْفَةَ، عَنِ النَّبِيِّ صلى الله عليه وسلم نَحْوَهُ بِمَعْنَاهُ.

---

571 *Musnad Aḥmad* (23445)
572 *Al-Wafāʾ bi Aḥwāl al-Muṣṭafā*
573 *Sharḥ al-Mishkāt*

هَكَذَا قَالَ حَمَّادُ بْنُ سَلَمَةَ، عَنْ عَاصِمٍ، عَنْ زِرٍّ، عَنْ حُذَيْفَةَ.

368. The same is reported from Ḥudhayfah ﷺ through another route.

باب ما جاء في عيش رسول الله صلى الله عليه وسلم

[52] On Allāh's Messenger's ﷺ Manner of Living

ʿAbd al-Razzāq al-Badr said,

> The subject of this chapter has already been addressed in chapter nine under which two ḥadīths were listed, and it is addressed here again to emphasise his ﷺ concern regarding the Hereafter and his disinterest regarding the worldly pleasures.

٣٦٩- حَدَّثَنَا قُتَيْبَةُ بْنُ سَعِيدٍ، قَالَ: حَدَّثَنَا أَبُو الأَحْوَصِ، عَنْ سِمَاكِ بْنِ حَرْبٍ قَالَ: سَمِعْتُ النُّعْمَانَ بْنَ بَشِيرٍ يَقُولُ: «أَلَسْتُمْ فِي طَعَامٍ وَشَرَابٍ مَا شِئْتُمْ؟ لَقَدْ رَأَيْتُ نَبِيَّكُمْ صلى الله عليه وسلم وَمَا يَجِدُ مِنَ الدَّقَلِ مَا يَمْلأُ بَطْنَهُ»[٥٧٤].

369. Al-Nuʿmān b. Bashīr said: "You are in enough luxury to eat and drink all that you wish! By Allāh, I have seen your Prophet ﷺ not having the worst type of dates to fill his stomach."

Al-Bājūrī said,

> **"You are in enough luxury to eat and drink all that you wish!":** This is intended as a rebuke of excess in eating and drinking. Al-Ṭabarānī reported, "The people of full [bellies] are the people of hunger in the hereafter." It states in a ḥadīth, "The fullest of you in this world will be the hungriest of you in the hereafter." Some of the wise said, "Starve yourselves for the feast in al-Firdaws (the highest level of Paradise)."
>
> What is rebuked is the heavy fullness that dictates lethargy which prevents the attainment of knowledge and action. As for the eating which helps in worship, it is sought after, especially if it is done with the intention of giving strength upon obedience [to Allāh]. Allāh says: **{O messengers,[575] eat of the good foods and do righteous-**

574 See hadīth 152

575 [T] In the printed version, this is (يا أيها الذين آمنوا) "O you who believe". Which is

ness.}[576]

٣٧٠- حَدَّثَنَا هَارُونُ بْنُ إِسْحَاقَ، قَالَ: حَدَّثَنَا عَبْدَةُ، عَنْ هِشَامِ بْنِ عُرْوَةَ، عَنْ أَبِيهِ، عَنْ عَائِشَةَ، قَالَتْ: «إِنْ كُنَّا آلَ مُحَمَّدٍ نَمكُثُ شَهْرًا مَا نَسْتَوْقِدُ بِنَارٍ، إِنْ هُوَ إِلَّا التَّمْرُ وَالْمَاءُ»٥٧٧.

370. 'Ā'ishah ﷺ narrated: "We, the family of Muḥammad would pass a whole month without kindling a fire in our homes. [During this time] we would sustain ourselves on dates and water."

Al-Bājūrī said,

> The appropriateness of this narration being included in this chapter is because his ﷺ state can be understood from theirs, [and his state would be more harsher] as he was the most patient and most able to endure amongst them.

Abū Bakr b. al-'Arabī said,

> Al-Tirmidhī reported from al-Zubayr b. al-'Awwām ﷺ that when the *āyah*: **{Then you will surely be asked that Day about the delight [you indulged in, in this world]!}**[578] was revealed, he asked, "O Messenger of Allāh! What delight will we be asked about when all that we have is just dates and water?" The Prophet ﷺ replied, "Indeed, it will happen."[579] [580]

Ibn Baṭṭāl said,

> This shows the rigorous self-denial and self-restraint of the Prophet ﷺ and his favouring of the Hereafter over the worldly pleasures. This is because when he was given the choice between receiving the pleasures of this worldly life and the pleasures of the Hereafter, he chose the latter, and when he was given the choice either to be a Prophet and a slave to Allāh or a Prophet who is a king, he chose the former. It is

---

a typo.

576 Al-Mu'minūn: 50

577 *Ṣaḥīḥ al-Bukhārī* (6458) and *Ṣaḥīḥ Muslim* (2971)

578 Qur'ān 102:8

579 *Sunan al-Tirmidhī* (3356)

580 *Aḥkām al-Qur'ān*

also an evidence for those who favour poverty over possessing riches.[581]

٣٧١- حَدَّثَنَا عَبْدُ اللهِ بْنُ أَبِي زِيَادٍ، قَالَ: حَدَّثَنَا سَيَّارٌ، قَالَ: حَدَّثَنَا سَهْلُ بْنُ أَسْلَمَ، عَنْ يَزِيدَ بْنِ أَبِي مَنْصُورٍ، عَنْ أَنَسٍ، عَنْ أَبِي طَلْحَةَ، قَالَ: شَكَوْنَا إِلَىٰ رَسُولِ اللهِ صلىٰ الله عليه وسلم الْجُوعَ وَرَفَعْنَا عَنْ بُطُونِنَا عَنْ حَجَرٍ حَجَرٍ، فَرَفَعَ رَسُولُ اللهِ صلىٰ الله عليه وسلم عَنْ بَطْنِهِ عَنْ حَجَرَيْنِ[٥٨٢].

371. Abū Ṭalḥah ﵁ narrated: "We complained to the Messenger of Allāh ﷺ regarding the hunger we suffered, and showed him the stones fastened on our stomachs. Thereupon, he ﷺ raised his garment and revealed two stones that he had fastened onto his stomach."

قَالَ أَبُو عِيسَىٰ: هَذَا حَدِيثٌ غَرِيبٌ مِنْ حَدِيثِ أَبِي طَلْحَةَ لا نَعْرِفُهُ إِلَّا مِنْ هَذَا الْوَجْهِ، وَمَعْنَىٰ قَوْلِهِ: وَرَفَعْنَا عَنْ بُطُونِنَا عَنْ حَجَرٍ حَجَرٍ»، كَانَ أَحَدُهُمْ يَشُدُّ فِي بَطْنِهِ الْحَجَرَ مِنَ الْجُهْدِ وَالضَّعْفِ الَّذِي بِهِ مِنَ الْجُوعِ.

Abū ʿĪsā said: "This is a *gharīb* (strange) ḥadīth from Abū Ṭalḥah and we only know of it from this way. They fastened stones on their stomachs due to the severe exhaustion and hunger they suffered from."

ʿAlī al-Qārī said,

> It was said that the benefit of fastening a stone onto the stomach is that it averts intestinal emphysema, gives support to the back and thus allows easy movement. Al-Ḥāfiẓ Ibn Ḥajar mentioned that this was the habit of Arabs or the people of Madīnah.

Al-Bājūrī said,

> **"This is a *gharīb* (strange) ḥadīth from Abū Ṭalḥah and we only know of it from this way":** Despite this, its narrators are all *thiqāt* (reliable), and thus its strangeness does not affect its authenticity because *gharīb* reports can be *ḥasan* (fair) and *ṣaḥīḥ* (authentic). A report being *gharīb* means that a single narrator reported it from the men who transmitted it.

581 *Sharḥ Ṣaḥīḥ al-Bukhārī*
582 *Sunan al-Tirmidhī* (2371)

٣٧٢- حَدَّثَنَا مُحَمَّدُ بْنُ إِسْمَاعِيلَ، قَالَ: حَدَّثَنَا آدَمُ بْنُ أَبِي إِيَاسٍ، قَالَ: حَدَّثَنَا شَيْبَانُ أَبُو مُعَاوِيَةَ، قَالَ: حَدَّثَنَا عَبْدُ الْمَلِكِ بْنُ عُمَيْرٍ، عَنْ أَبِي سَلَمَةَ بْنِ عَبْدِ الرَّحْمَنِ، عَنْ أَبِي هُرَيْرَةَ، قَالَ: خَرَجَ رَسُولُ اللهِ صلىٰ الله عليه وسلم فِي سَاعَةٍ لا يَخْرُجُ فِيهَا، وَلا يَلْقَاهُ فِيهَا أَحَدٌ، فَأَتَاهُ أَبُو بَكْرٍ، فَقَالَ: «مَا جَاءَ بِكَ يَا أَبَا بَكْرٍ؟» قَالَ: خَرَجْتُ أَلْقَىٰ رَسُولَ اللهِ صلىٰ الله عليه وسلم وَأَنْظُرُ فِي وَجْهِهِ، وَالتَّسْلِيمَ عَلَيْهِ، فَلَمْ يَلْبَثْ أَنْ جَاءَ عُمَرُ، فَقَالَ: «مَا جَاءَ بِكَ يَا عُمَرُ؟» قَالَ: الْجُوعُ يَا رَسُولَ اللهِ! قَالَ صلىٰ الله عليه وسلم: «وَأَنَا قَدْ وَجَدْتُ بَعْضَ ذَلِكَ»، فَانْطَلَقُوا إِلَىٰ مَنْزِلِ أَبِي الْهَيْثَمِ بْنِ التَّيْهَانِ الْأَنْصَارِيِّ، وَكَانَ رَجُلا كَثِيرَ النَّخْلِ وَالشَّاءِ، وَلَمْ يَكُنْ لَهُ خَدَمٌ، فَلَمْ يَجِدُوهُ، فَقَالُوا لامْرَأَتِهِ: أَيْنَ صَاحِبُكِ؟ فَقَالَتِ: انْطَلَقَ يَسْتَعْذِبُ لَنَا الْمَاءَ، فَلَمْ يَلْبَثُوا أَنْ جَاءَ أَبُو الْهَيْثَمِ بِقِرْبَةٍ يَزْعَبُهَا، فَوَضَعَهَا ثُمَّ جَاءَ يَلْتَزِمُ النَّبِيَّ صلىٰ الله عليه وسلم وَيُفَدِّيهِ بِأَبِيهِ وَأُمِّهِ، ثُمَّ انْطَلَقَ بِهِمْ إِلَىٰ حَدِيقَتِهِ فَبَسَطَ لَهُمْ بِسَاطًا، ثُمَّ انْطَلَقَ إِلَىٰ نَخْلَةٍ فَجَاءَ بِقِنْوٍ فَوَضَعَهُ، فَقَالَ النَّبِيُّ صلىٰ الله عليه وسلم: «أَفَلا تَنَقَّيْتَ لَنَا مِنْ رُطَبِهِ؟» فَقَالَ: يَا رَسُولَ اللهِ، إِنِّي أَرَدْتُ أَنْ تَخْتَارُوا، أَوْ تَخَيَّرُوا مِنْ رُطَبِهِ وَبُسْرِهِ، فَأَكَلُوا وَشَرِبُوا مِنْ ذَلِكَ الْمَاءِ فَقَالَ صلىٰ الله عليه وسلم: «هَذَا وَالَّذِي نَفْسِي بِيَدِهِ مِنَ النَّعِيمِ الَّذِي تُسْأَلُونَ عَنْهُ يَوْمَ الْقِيَامَةِ ظِلٌّ بَارِدٌ، وَرُطَبٌ طَيِّبٌ، وَمَاءٌ بَارِدٌ»، فَانْطَلَقَ أَبُو الْهَيْثَمِ لِيَصْنَعَ لَهُمْ طَعَامًا فَقَالَ النَّبِيُّ صلىٰ الله عليه وسلم: «لا تَذْبَحَنَّ ذَاتَ دَرٍّ»، فَذَبَحَ لَهُمْ عَنَاقًا أَوْ جَدْيًا، فَأَتَاهُمْ بِهَا فَأَكَلُوا، فَقَالَ صلىٰ الله عليه وسلم: «هَلْ لَكَ خَادِمٌ؟»، قَالَ: لا، قَالَ: «فَإِذَا أَتَانَا سَبْيٌ فَأْتِنَا»، فَأُتِيَ النَّبِيُّ صلىٰ الله عليه وسلم بِرَأْسَيْنِ لَيْسَ مَعَهُمَا ثَالِثٌ، فَأَتَاهُ أَبُو الْهَيْثَمِ، فَقَالَ النَّبِيُّ صلىٰ الله عليه وسلم: «اخْتَرْ مِنْهُمَا» فَقَالَ: يَا رَسُولَ اللهِ، اخْتَرْ لِي فَقَالَ النَّبِيُّ صلىٰ الله عليه وسلم: «إِنَّ الْمُسْتَشَارَ مُؤْتَمَنٌ، خُذْ هَذَا فَإِنِّي رَأَيْتُهُ يُصَلِّي، وَاسْتَوْصِ بِهِ مَعْرُوفًا» فَانْطَلَقَ أَبُو الْهَيْثَمِ إِلَىٰ امْرَأَتِهِ، فَأَخْبَرَهَا بِقَوْلِ رَسُولِ اللهِ صلىٰ الله عليه وسلم، فَقَالَتِ امْرَأَتُهُ: مَا أَنْتَ بِبَالِغٍ حَقَّ مَا قَالَ فِيهِ النَّبِيُّ صلىٰ الله عليه وسلم إِلَّا بِأَنْ تَعْتِقَهُ، قَالَ: فَهُوَ عَتِيقٌ، فَقَالَ صلىٰ الله عليه وسلم: «إِنَّ اللهَ لَمْ يَبْعَثْ نَبِيًّا وَلا خَلِيفَةً إِلَّا وَلَهُ بِطَانَتَانِ: بِطَانَةٌ تَأْمُرُهُ بِالْمَعْرُوفِ وَتَنْهَاهُ عَنِ الْمُنْكَرِ، وَبِطَانَةٌ لا تَأْلُوهُ

خَبَالا، وَمَنْ يُوقَ بِطَانَةَ السُّوءِ فَقَدْ وُقِيَ»[٥٨٣].

372. Abu Hurayrah ﷺ narrated: "Once, the Messenger of Allāh ﷺ exited [his house] at such a time that he would not normally leave his home, a time at which people would not meet him. Abū Bakr came to him and so he ﷺ asked, 'O Abū Bakr! Why have you come out?' Abū Bakr replied, 'I came out to meet the Messenger of Allāh, to look at his face and greet him.'

Soon after, 'Umar came and so he ﷺ said, 'O 'Umar! Why have you come out?' 'Umar replied, 'O Messenger of Allāh, due to hunger!' The Messenger of Allāh ﷺ said, 'I too am slightly hungry.' They then proceeded to the house of Abū al-Haytham b. al-Tayhān al-Anṣārī. He owned many date palm trees and sheep, but he did not have any servants. However, after arriving, they did not find him present. They asked his wife, 'Where is your husband?' She replied, 'He has gone to bring us fresh water.' It was not long until he arrived whilst carrying a water bag with difficulty. He placed it to the ground, embraced the Prophet ﷺ and said, 'May my father and mother be sacrificed for you.'

He then invited them to his garden where he spread out for them a mat to sit upon and then went to a palm tree and brought a large cluster of dates, placing it before his guests. The Prophet ﷺ said, 'Why did you not just pick for us the ripe ones [rather than bringing forth a whole cluster?]' The host replied, 'O Messenger of Allāh! I wanted that you could eat what pleases you from it.' They ate and drank from the water [he brought]. The Messenger of Allāh ﷺ said, 'I swear by the One in whose Hand is my soul that this is also included amongst those blessings of which one will be asked on the Day of Judgment; the cool shadow, fresh and pure dates, and cold water.'

Abū al-Haytham ﷺ then went to prepare some food, and the Prophet ﷺ said to him, 'Do not slaughter a sheep that gives milk.' So, he slaughtered for them a sheep that had not yet reached four months. After they ate, the Prophet ﷺ asked the host, 'Do you have any servants?' He replied, 'No.' The Prophet ﷺ replied, 'When we receive captives of war, remind us.'

Thus at a later point, two slaves were brought to the Messenger ﷺ upon which Abū al-Haytham ﷺ came to the Prophet ﷺ who said to

583 *Sunan Abī Dāwūd* (5128) and *Sunan Ibn Mājah* (2745)

him, 'Pick from them.' He ﷺ said, 'O Messenger of Allāh! I would prefer if you chose for me.' The Prophet ﷺ said, 'The one whose advice is sought ought to be honest in his advice. I hence choose this slave for you, as I saw him praying. My advice to you is to treat him well.'

Abū al-Haytham went to his wife and told her what the Messenger ﷺ had advised him to do with the slave. His wife said, 'You will not be able to fulfil that which the Prophet ﷺ has commanded except by freeing him.' He said, 'Then, he is free.' The Prophet ﷺ said, 'Allāh has not sent a Prophet or a vicegerent except that He ﷻ made for them two types of close advisers. One of which ordains the good and forbids the evil. The other tries to corrupt the individual. The one that is saved from the corrupt advisor is saved from ruin and destruction.'"

Ibn Ḥajar al-Haytamī said,

> It is evident that the Prophet ﷺ experienced periods of time when he had nothing and periods of time when he possessed riches but it was his habit to distribute the wealth he received between the needy ones and spending upon the army and delegates etc.
>
> Al-Ḥalīmī said in *Shu'ab al-Īmān* that the Prophet ﷺ should be given his due respect by not describing him as a poor person. Al-Badr al-Zarkashī quoted some later jurists who said that the Prophet ﷺ was not poor; rather he was rich for Allāh sufficed him in his worldly life.

The following can be derived from this ḥadīth:

- It is permissible to express one's pain and hunger if it is intended to help oneself to endure it. This is because if the intent is to complain, it is ugly and disliked.
- It is allowed to drink fresh water and look for it and that does not contradict *zuhd*.
- Serving one's family is from the good manners and humbleness.
- It is recommended to honour the guest and show happiness for hosting them.
- It is recommended to eat fruit before food due to it digesting

quicker and to hasten serving the food that can be eaten right away, especially if the host believes the guest is hungry. Some of the *salaf* disliked the host burdening himself with that which is beyond his capacity as that will affect one's sincerity and may result in showing worry.

- The host should serve the best food he has even if this may take more time to cook.

- It is allowed to eat to a full stomach and the ḥadīths condemning overeating relate to when it is harmful or when it becomes regular as this hardens the heart and makes one forget about the needy ones.

- Al-Nawawī said, "The mention of the questioning on the Day of Judgement regarding the bounties that Allāh has bestowed upon us, which is mentioned in the ḥadīth, was to draw attention to His favours upon us and it was not intended for the purpose of condemnation or questioning."

- The advisor should mind the best interest of the one asking for advice and must not withhold information that may benefit him.

- It shows that those who pray are better than those who do not pray.

- It is from evil to remain silent about evil and being good requires the person to order the good and forbid the wrong.

٣٧٣- حَدَّثَنَا عُمَرُ بْنُ إِسْمَاعِيلَ بْنِ مُجَالِدِ بْنِ سَعِيدٍ، حَدَّثَنِي أَبِي عَنْ بَيَانِ بْنِ بِشْرٍ عَنْ قَيْسِ بْنِ أَبِي حَازِمٍ، قَالَ: سَمِعْتُ سَعْدَ بْنَ أَبِي وَقَّاصٍ يَقُولُ: إِنِّي لأَوَّلُ رَجُلٍ أَهْرَاقَ دَمًا فِي سَبِيلِ اللهِ وَإِنْي لأَوَّلُ رَجُلٍ رَمَىٰ بِسَهْمٍ فِي سَبِيلِ اللهِ، لَقَدْ رَأَيْتُنِي أَغْزُو فِي الْعِصَابَةَ مِنْ أَصْحَابِ مُحَمْدٍ عَلَيْهِ الصَّلَاةُ وَالسَّلَام - مَا نَأْكُلْ إِلاَّ وَرَقَ الشَجَرِ وَالْحُبْلَةَ حَتَّىٰ تَقَرَحَتْ أَشْدَاقُنَا وَإِنْ أَحَدَنَا لَيَضَعُ كَمَا تَضَعُ الشَّاةُ وَالبَعِيرُ، وَأَصْبَحَتْ بَنُو أَسَدٍ يَعْزُرُونِي فِي الدِّينِ، لَقَدْ خِبْتُ إِذَنْ وَخَسِرْتُ إِذًا

وَضَلَّ عَمَلِي.[٥٨٤]

373. Sa'd b. Abī Waqqāṣ ﷺ reported: "I was the first man to spill blood in the path of Allāh, and I was the first man to shoot an arrow in the path of Allāh. I found myself fighting besides a regiment from the companions of Muḥammad ﷺ and we were in such a state where we ate nothing except the leaves of trees and shrubs. As a result, the corners of our mouths were sore and when we relieved ourselves, what came out appeared as if a camel or sheep had relieved itself. And now, the people of Banū Asad come to criticise my prayer. Indeed, I am ruined and in loss of my actions if their [false] claim is true."

'Alī al-Qārī said,

> The companions ﷺ used to pray in secret and it happened that some disbelievers saw Sa'd with a few other companions praying in secret. Thus, they started to abuse them and the dispute escalated so Sa'd hit one of them and made him bleed.
>
> The battle referred to in the ḥadīth is the battle of al-Khabaṭ which happened in the eighth year. The number of companions was three hundred and their leader was Abū 'Ubaydah ﷺ. Before they left Madīnah, the Prophet ﷺ gave them a bag of dates and so Abū 'Ubaydah ﷺ used to divide it between the companions and reduce the share of each until it dwindled down to one date per person. After they finished the dates and endured a great degree of suffering, Allāh gave them from the sea an extremely large fish that they lived on for approximately one month. It was said that the battle that Sa'd referred to was a battle that the Prophet ﷺ participated in, which is reported in *Ṣaḥīḥ al-Bukhārī* and *Ṣaḥīḥ Muslim*. Regardless of which battle it was, the relevance of this ḥadīth in the context of this chapter is that it indicates the minimal resources that the Prophet ﷺ possessed, because if he had more he would have given his companions more.
>
> The reason Sa'd b. Abī Waqqāṣ ﷺ was upset with Banī Asad is because he was appointed as the ruler of Basra during the time of 'Umar ﷺ and they falsely claimed that he did not know how to pray. So he expressed his objection to this, indicating to them the absurdity of their claim when he was from the first ones who embraced Islām and accompanied the Prophet ﷺ for such a long time.

584 *Ṣaḥīḥ al-Bukhārī* (3728) and *Ṣaḥīḥ Muslim* (2966)

٣٧٤- حَدَّثَنَا مُحَمَّدُ بْنُ بَشَّارٍ، قَالَ: حَدَّثَنَا صَفْوَانُ بْنُ عِيسَىٰ، قَالَ: حَدَّثَنَا عَمْرُو بْنُ عِيسَىٰ أَبُو نَعَامَةَ العَدَوِيُّ، قَالَ: سَمِعْتُ خَالِدَ بْنَ عُمَيْرٍ، وَشُوَيْسًا أَبَا الرُّقَادِ، قَالَا: بَعَثَ عُمَرُ بْنُ الخَطَّابِ عُتْبَةَ بْنَ غَزْوَانَ وقَالَ: انْطَلِقْ أَنْتَ وَمَنْ مَعَكَ حَتَّىٰ إِذَا كُنْتُمْ فِي أَقْصَىٰ بِلَادِ العَرَبِ وَأَدْنَىٰ بِلَادِ العَجَمِ، فَأَقْبَلُوا حَتَّىٰ إِذَا كَانُوا بِالمِرْبَدِ وَجَدُوا هَذَا الكَذَّانَ، فَقَالُوا: مَا هَذِهِ؟ قَالُوا: هَذِهِ البَصْرَةُ فَسَارُوا حَتَّىٰ إِذَا بَلَغُوا حِيَالَ الجِسْرِ الصَّغِيرِ، فَقَالُوا: هَهُنَا أُمِرْتُمْ، فَنَزَلُوا - فَذَكَرُوا الحَدِيثَ بِطُولِهِ -.

قَالَ: فَقَالَ عُتْبَةُ بْنُ غَزْوَانَ: لَقَدْ رَأَيْتُنِي وَإِنِّي لَسَابِعَ سَبْعَةٍ مَعَ رَسُولِ اللهِ صلىٰ الله عليه وسلم مَا لَنَا طَعَامٌ إِلَّا وَرَقُ الشَّجَرِ، حَتَّىٰ تَقَرَّحَتْ أَشْدَاقُنَا، فَالْتَقَطْتُ بُرْدَةً قَسَمْتُهَا بَيْنِي وَبَيْنَ سَعْدٍ، فَمَا مِنَّا مِنْ أُولَئِكَ السَّبْعَةِ أَحَدٌ إِلَّا وَهُوَ أَمِيرُ مِصْرٍ مِنَ الأَمْصَارِ وَسَتُجَرِّبُونَ الأُمَرَاءَ بَعْدَنَا»٥٨٥.

374. Khālid b. ʿUmayr and Shuwaysā narrated: "ʿUmar b. al-Khaṭṭāb ﵁ instructed ʿUtbah b. Ghazwān and those under his command to travel to the farthest point of the lands of the Arabs and the nearest part of the lands of the non-Arabs and camp there. The army embarked on the journey and when they reached al-Mirbad, they saw some strange white stones. They asked, 'What is this?' The people replied, 'This is Basra.' Then, they proceeded until they reached a small bridge. The people said, 'This is the place that ʿUmar ﵁ had ordered us to set up our camp.'" [The narrator mentioned the story in its totality.]

ʿUtbah b. Ghazwān ﵁ said: "By Allāh, I was the seventh of the seven with the Messenger of Allāh ﷺ, eating nothing but the leaves of trees until the corners of our mouths were sore. I picked up [from the floor] a garment and then I split it into two halves and gave one half to Saʿd and I wore the other half. Each one from the seven became a leader of a city from amongst the cities. After us, you will find leaders that are in no way similar to us."

ʿAbd al-Razzāq al-Badr said,

> ʿUmar b. al-Khaṭṭāb ﵁ sent ʿUtbah b. Ghazwān with a group of people to guard the boarders from where the attacks of the disbelievers

585 *Al-Muʿjam al-Awsaṭ* (4/243)

were feared. He appointed for them the location where they needed to set up their camp in.

Al-Tirmidhī did not include the full story due its irrelevance to the chapter; thus he skipped to the parts that are related to the title of the chapter.

The reason 'Utbah b. Ghazwān ؓ mentioned that he and the other six companions became rulers eventually was to show them how life was difficult at that time and how it changed afterwards.

The full incident is mentioned in *Ṣaḥīḥ Muslim*[586] and part of the remaining statement of 'Utbah ؓ was, "I seek refuge in Allāh from being great in this world whilst being small in His sight."

٣٧٥ - حَدَّثَنَا عَبْدُ اللهِ بْنُ عَبْدِ الرَّحْمَنِ، قَالَ: حَدَّثَنَا رَوْحُ بْنُ أَسْلَمَ أَبُو حَاتِمٍ الْبَصْرِيُّ، قَالَ: حَدَّثَنَا حَمَّادُ بْنُ سَلَمَةَ، قَالَ: حَدَّثَنَا ثَابِتٌ، عَنْ أَنَسٍ، قَالَ: قَالَ رَسُولُ اللهِ صلى الله عليه وسلم: «لَقَدْ أُخِفْتُ فِي اللهِ وَمَا يَخَافُ أَحَدٌ، وَلَقَدْ أُوذِيتُ فِي اللهِ وَمَا يُؤْذَى أَحَدٌ، وَلَقَدْ أَتَتْ عَلَيَّ ثَلَاثُونَ مِنْ بَيْنِ لَيْلَةٍ وَيَوْمٍ وَمَا لِي وَلِبِلَالٍ طَعَامٌ يَأْكُلُهُ ذُو كَبِدٍ إِلَّا شَيْءٌ يُوَارِيهِ إِبْطُ بِلَالٍ».[587]

375. Anas b. Mālik ؓ narrated: "The Messenger of Allāh ﷺ said: 'I was made to fear [for striving] in the path of Allāh at a time when no one else feared. I was harmed [for striving] in the path of Allāh at a time when no one else experienced harm. Thirty consecutive nights and days passed wherein I and Bilāl ؓ had no food that a being with a liver could eat, except for the minute [that could be] hidden under the arm of Bilāl ؓ.'"

Ibn Ḥajar al-'Asqalānī said,

Narrated 'Ā'ishah ؓ: "I asked the Prophet ﷺ, 'Have you encountered a day harder than the day [of the battle] of Uhud?' The Prophet ﷺ replied, 'Your tribes have troubled me a lot, and the worst trouble was the trouble on the day of 'Aqabah when I presented myself to Ibn 'Abd Yālayl b. 'Abd Kulāl and he did not respond to my request. So I departed, overwhelmed with sorrow and proceeded on. I could not

---

586 *Ṣaḥīḥ Muslim* (2967)
587 *Sunan Ibn Mājah* (151) and *Sunan al-Tirmidhī* (2372)

relax until I found myself at Qarn al-Thaʿālib where I lifted my head towards the sky to see a cloud shading me unexpectedly. I looked up and saw Jibrīl in it. He called me saying, 'Allāh has heard your people's words to you, and what they have replied back to you, Allāh has sent the Angel of the Mountains to you so that you may order him to do whatever you wish to these people.' The Angel of the Mountains called and greeted me, and then said, 'O Muḥammad! Order what you wish. If you like, I will let al-Akhshabayn (i.e. two mountains) fall upon them.' I said, 'No but I hope that Allāh will let them beget children who will worship Allah alone, and will worship none besides Him.'""[588] [589]

Ibn Ḥajar al-Haytamī said,

Al-Tirmidhī said that this was during the period when the Prophet ﷺ left Makkah.

٣٧٦- حَدَّثَنَا عَبْدُ اللهِ بْنُ عَبْدِ الرَّحْمَنِ، قَالَ: حَدَّثَنَا عَفَّانُ بْنُ مُسْلِمٍ، قَالَ: حَدَّثَنَا أَبَانُ بْنُ يَزِيدَ الْعَطَّارُ، قَالَ: حَدَّثَنَا قَتَادَةُ، عَنْ أَنَسِ بْنِ مَالِكٍ: أَنَّ النَّبِيَّ صلى الله عليه وسلم لَمْ يَجْتَمِعْ عِنْدَهُ غَدَاءٌ وَلا عَشَاءٌ مِنْ خُبْزٍ وَلَحْمٍ إِلَّا عَلَى ضَفَفٍ[٥٩٠].

قَالَ عَبْدُ اللهِ: قَالَ بَعْضُهُمْ : هُوَ كَثْرَةُ الأَيْدِي.

376. Anas b. Mālik ﵁ narrated: "The Messenger of Allāh ﷺ would not consume bread or meat in the morning or evening twice in one day, except amongst guests."

ʿAbdullāh said, "Some said that it means amongst many hands."

Al-Bājūrī said,

"ʿAbdullāh said": I.e. Ibn ʿAbd al-Raḥmān, the teacher of al-Tirmidhī.

"Some said": I.e. some of the ḥadīth masters and linguists.

"That it means": I.e. the word *al-ḍafaf*.

588 *Ṣaḥīḥ al-Bukhārī* (3010) and *Ṣaḥīḥ Muslim* (3358)
589 *Fatḥ al-Bārī*
590 *Musnad Aḥmad* (13859)

> **"Amongst many hands":** I.e. the hands of many guests. This is the meaning here. Though the word has different meanings, most of them are not appropriate here. It is used to refer to an abundance of dependants, arduous times, intense poverty and people congregating over a meal as guests or hosts.

٣٧٧- حَدَّثَنَا عَبْدُ بْنُ حُمَيْدٍ، قَالَ: حَدَّثَنَا مُحَمَّدُ بْنُ إِسْمَاعِيلَ بْنِ أَبِي فُدَيْكٍ، قَالَ: حَدَّثَنَا ابْنُ أَبِي ذِئْبٍ، عَنْ مُسْلِمِ بْنِ جُنْدُبٍ، عَنْ نَوْفَلِ بْنِ إِيَاسٍ الْهُذَلِيِّ، قَالَ: كَانَ عَبْدُ الرَّحْمَنِ بْنُ عَوْفٍ لَنَا جَلِيسًا، وَكَانَ نِعْمَ الْجَلِيسُ، وَإِنَّهُ انْقَلَبَ بِنَا ذَاتَ يَوْمٍ حَتَّىٰ إِذَا دَخَلْنَا بَيْتَهُ وَدَخَلَ فَاغْتَسَلَ، ثُمَّ خَرَجَ وَأُتِينَا بِصَحْفَةٍ فِيهَا خُبْزٌ وَلَحْمٌ، فَلَمَّا وُضِعَتْ بَكَىٰ عَبْدُ الرَّحْمَنِ فَقُلْتُ: يَا أَبَا مُحَمَّدٍ، مَا يُبْكِيكَ؟ فَقَالَ: هَلَكَ رَسُولُ اللهِ صلىٰ الله عليه وسلم وَلَمْ يَشْبَعْ هُوَ وَأَهْلُ بَيْتِهِ مِنْ خُبْزِ الشَّعِيرِ فَلا أَرَانَا أُخِّرْنَا لِمَا هُوَ خَيْرٌ لَنَا[٥٩١].

377. Nawfal b. Iyās al-Hudhalī narrated: "ʿAbd al-Raḥmān b. al-ʿAwf ﷺ would host gatherings for us, and verily he was a good host. Once we were returning from a place with him. On returning we went with him to his house. When we entered his home he first took a bath and then came to us. Bread and meat was served upon a large platter. Thereupon he began to cry. I asked, 'O Abā Muḥammad! What causes you to cry?' He said, 'Until the demise of Allāh's Messenger ﷺ, he and his family members did not fill their stomachs with [something as little as] the bread made of barley. I never thought that we would be delayed from that which is better for us.'"

ʿAbdullāh b. Saʿīd al-Ḥaḍramī al-Makkī said,

> The crying of ʿAbd al-Raḥmān b. al-ʿAwf ﷺ was due to his concern regarding the consequences of the ease which had come to engulf their lives. This is because the simple lifestyle of the best of mankind ﷺ was such that he could not eat to his full even with the barley bread. The first generation used to become worried and concerned when life became easy for them as they feared that Allāh had made their reward in this worldly life instead of the Hereafter.[592]

591 *Musnad ʿAbd b. Ḥumayd* (161)
592 *Muntahā al-Suʾl ʿalā Wasāʾil al-Wuṣūl ilā Shamāʾil al-Rasūl*

Al-Bājūrī said,

> **"I asked, 'O Abā Muḥammad!":** This is the *kunyah* (nickname) of ʿAbd al-Raḥmān b. ʿAwf.
>
> **"Until the demise of Allāh's Messenger ﷺ, he and his family members did not fill their stomachs with [something as little as] the bread made of barley":** I.e. for two consecutive days, as in ʿĀ'ishah's narration. It is possible that the content of the platter was enough to fill them, thus it caused him to cry.

باب ما جاء في سن رسول الله صلى الله عليه وسلم

[53] On Allāh's Messenger's ﷺ Age

Al-Bājūrī said,

> This chapter covers the different narrations which report his ﷺ age.

٣٧٨- حَدَّثَنَا أَحْمَدُ بْنُ مَنِيعٍ، قَالَ: حَدَّثَنَا رَوْحُ بْنُ عُبَادَةَ، قَالَ: حَدَّثَنَا زَكَرِيَّا بْنُ إِسْحَاقَ، قَالَ: حَدَّثَنَا عَمْرُو بْنُ دِينَارٍ، عَنِ ابْنِ عَبَّاسٍ قَالَ: مَكَثَ النَّبِيُّ صلى الله عليه وسلم بِمَكَّةَ ثَلاثَ عَشْرَةَ سَنَةً يُوحَىٰ إِلَيْهِ، وَ بِالْمَدِينَةِ عَشْرًا، وَتُوُفِّيَ وَهُوَ ابْنُ ثَلاثٍ وَسِتِّينَ»٥٩٣.

378. 'Abdullāh b. 'Abbās ؓ narrated: "The Prophet ﷺ remained in Makkah for thirteen years during which he received revelation, and in Madīnah for ten years. He passed away at the age of sixty three."

Ibn Ḥajar al-'Asqalānī said,

> The Prophet ﷺ was forty years old when he received the revelation on the first occasion and it was mentioned previously in the chapter of revelation that the revelation was in the month of Ramaḍān. The most famous and correct view is that he was born in the month of Rabī' al-Awwal.[594]

'Abd al-Raḥmān al-Mubārakfūrī said,

> Al-Tirmidhī reported three narrations regarding the age of the Prophet ﷺ at the time of his passing. The first ḥadīth states that he passed away when he was sixty three years old, the next ḥadīth states that he was sixty years old and the last ḥadīth states that he was sixty five years old. Al-Nawawī offered a good reconciliation between these three ḥadīths as he stated, "The most correct and most widely accepted view is that he ﷺ was sixty three years old when he passed and the

---

593 *Ṣaḥīḥ al-Bukhārī* (3903) and *Ṣaḥīḥ Muslim* (2351)
594 *Fatḥ al-Bārī*

ḥadīth stating his age as sixty was mentioned in respect to decades and not to give an exact number. The other ḥadīth was just a confusion on the part of Ibn 'Abbās 🙣 for 'Urwah 🙣 rejected this statement of his and said that Ibn 'Abbās erred as he did not accompany the Prophet 🙻 as much as other companions and did not witness the beginning of his prophethood." The scholars agreed that he 🙻 was born on a Monday and died on a Monday but they differed upon which day of the month he was born, whether it was the second, eighth, tenth or twelfth of Rabī' al-Awwal.[595]

Al-Bājūrī said,

The view of his age being sixty five is based on adding the year he was born in and the year he died in.

٣٧٩ - حَدَّثَنَا مُحَمَّدُ بْنُ بَشَّارٍ، قَالَ: حَدَّثَنَا مُحَمَّدُ بْنُ جَعْفَرٍ، عَنْ شُعْبَةَ، عَنْ أَبِي إِسْحَاقَ، عَنْ عَامِرِ بْنِ سَعْدٍ، عَنْ جَرِيرٍ، عَنْ مُعَاوِيَةَ، أَنَّهُ سَمِعَهُ يَخْطُبُ، قَالَ: «مَاتَ رَسُولُ اللهِ صلى الله عليه وسلم وَهُوَ ابْنُ ثَلَاثٍ وَسِتِّينَ وَأَبُو بَكْرٍ وَعُمَرُ، وَأَنَا ابْنُ ثَلَاثٍ وَسِتِّينَ سنة»[596].

379. Jarīr narrated that he heard Mu'āwiyah 🙣 saying in a sermon: "The Messenger of Allāh 🙻 passed away at the age of sixty three. Likewise, Abū Bakr and 'Umar 🙣 passed away at the same age. I am [currently] sixty three."

'Alī al-Qārī said,

Given the age of passing of the Prophet 🙻 and his two companions 🙣, Mu'āwiyah expected to die at the same age. In *Jāmi' al-Uṣūl* it is stated that Mu'āwiyah passed away at the age of seventy eight and it was said at eighty six years old. Mīrak said, "He hoped to die at the age of sixty three just like the Prophet 🙻 and his two companions but that did not happen as he died when he was nearly eighty years old."[597]

Al-Bājūrī said,

"Likewise, Abū Bakr and 'Umar 🙣 passed away at the same

---

[595] *Tuḥfat al-Aḥwadhī*
[596] *Ṣaḥīḥ Muslim* (2352)
[597] *Mirqāt al-Mafātīḥ*

age": There is unanimous agreement on this being Abū Bakr's age. As for ʿUmar, it has been said that his age was fifty one, fifty six, fifty seven and fifty eight.

He did not mention ʿUthmān, who was killed at eighty two, and it has also been said that he was eighty eight. He also did not mention ʿAlī, of whom the preponderant view is that he was killed at sixty three, and it has also been said that he was sixty five, seventy and fifty eight.

٣٨٠- حَدَّثَنَا حُسَيْنُ بْنُ مَهْدِيٍّ الْبَصْرِيُّ، قَالَ: حَدَّثَنَا عَبْدُ الرَّزَّاقِ، عَنِ ابْنِ جُرَيْجٍ، عَنِ الزُّهْرِيِّ، عَنْ عُرْوَةَ، عَنْ عَائِشَةَ: «أَنَّ النَّبِيَّ صلى الله عليه وسلم مَاتَ وَهُوَ ابْنُ ثَلاثٍ وَسِتِّينَ سَنَةً»[٥٩٨].

380. ʿĀʾishah ﵂ narrated: "The Prophet ﷺ passed away when he was sixty three years of age."

ʿAbd al-Razzāq al-Badr said,

> This concords with the two previous narrations of Ibn ʿAbbās and Muʿāwiyah.

٣٨١- حَدَّثَنَا أَحْمَدُ بْنُ مَنِيعٍ، وَيَعْقُوبُ بْنُ إِبْرَاهِيمَ الدَّوْرَقِيُّ، قَالا: حَدَّثَنَا إِسْمَاعِيلُ بْنُ عُلَيَّةَ، عَنْ خَالِدٍ الْحَذَّاءِ، قَالَ: أَنْبَأَنَا عَمَّارٌ مَوْلَى بَنِي هَاشِمٍ قَالَ: سَمِعْتُ ابْنَ عَبَّاسٍ يَقُولُ: تُوُفِّيَ رَسُولُ الله صلى الله عليه وسلم وَهُوَ ابْنُ خَمْسٍ وَسِتِّينَ[٥٩٩].

381. ʿAbdullāh b. ʿAbbās ﵄ narrated: "The Messenger of Allāh ﷺ passed away when he was sixty five years old."

ʿAbd al-Razzāq al-Badr said,

> The relied upon report – as attested to by the scholars – is that he was sixty three. That which has been attributed to Ibn ʿAbbās citing the age to be sixty five is either *shādh* (irregular) or can be given an interpretation.

Al-Bājūrī said,

> [If we assume that this is authentic, the interpretation given is that]

598 *Sahīh al-Bukhārī* (3536) and *Ṣaḥīḥ Muslim* (2349)
599 *Ṣaḥīḥ Muslim* (2353)

this is in addition to the year of his birth and death, as mentioned earlier.

٣٨٢- حَدَّثَنَا مُحَمَّدُ بْنُ بَشَّارٍ، وَمُحَمَّدُ بْنُ أَبَانَ، قَالا: حَدَّثَنَا مُعَاذُ بْنُ هِشَامٍ، قَالَ: حَدَّثَنِي أَبِي، عَنْ قَتَادَةَ، عَنِ الْحَسَنِ، عَنْ دَغْفَلِ بْنِ حَنْظَلَةَ: «أَنَّ النَّبِيَّ صلى الله عليه وسلم قُبِضَ وَهُوَ ابْنُ خَمْسٍ وَسِتِّينَ».

382. Daghfal b. Ḥanẓalah narrated: "The Prophet ﷺ passed away when he was sixty five years of age."

قَالَ أَبُو عِيسَى: «وَدَغْفَلُ لا نَعْرِفُ لَهُ سَمَاعًا مِنَ النَّبِيِّ صلى الله عليه وسلم، وَكَانَ فِي زَمَنِ النَّبِيِّ صلى الله عليه وسلم رَجُلًا»[٦٠٠].

Abū ʿĪsā said: "Daghfal did not hear any reports from the Prophet ﷺ directly, though we know that he lived during the lifetime of the Prophet ﷺ."

Al-Bājūrī said,

> **"The Prophet ﷺ passed away when he was sixty five years of age":** This has been explained in the previous narration.

ʿAbd al-Razzāq al-Badr said,

> **"Daghfal did not hear any reports from the Prophet ﷺ directly, though we know that he lived during the lifetime of the Prophet ﷺ":** He stated this so as to note that the establishment of his companionship is questionable. This is because he was a man present during the life of the Prophet ﷺ but there is nothing that would establish his hearing from the Prophet ﷺ.

٣٨٣- حَدَّثَنَا إِسْحَاقُ بْنُ مُوسَى الأَنْصَارِيُّ، قَالَ: حَدَّثَنَا مَعْنٌ، حَدَّثَنَا مَالِكُ بْنُ أَنَسٍ، عَنْ رَبِيعَةَ بْنِ أَبِي عَبْدِ الرَّحْمَنِ، عَنْ أَنَسِ بْنِ مَالِكٍ، أَنَّهُ سَمِعَهُ يَقُولُ: «كَانَ رَسُولُ اللهِ صلى الله عليه وسلم لَيْسَ بِالطَّوِيلِ الْبَائِنِ، وَلا بِالْقَصِيرِ، وَلا بِالأَبْيَضِ الأَمْهَقِ، وَلا بِالآدَمِ، وَلا بِالْجَعْدِ الْقَطَطِ، وَلا بِالسَّبْطِ، بَعَثَهُ اللهُ تَعَالَى عَلَى رَأْسِ

600 See ḥadīth 381

أَرْبَعِينَ سَنَةً، فَأَقَامَ بِمَكَّةَ عَشْرَ سِنِينَ، وَبِالْمَدِينَةِ عَشْرَ سِنِينَ، وَتَوَفَّاهُ اللهُ عَلَى رَأْسِ سِتِّينَ سَنَةً وَلَيْسَ فِي رَأْسِهِ وَلِحْيَتِهِ عِشْرُونَ شَعَرَةً بَيْضَاءَ»[٦٠١].

383. Narrated by Rabīʿah b. Abī ʿAbd al-Raḥmān ﷺ: "I heard Anas b. Mālik describing the Prophet ﷺ saying, 'He was neither too tall nor short; neither absolutely white nor brown; his hair was neither very frizzy nor completely lank. The divine revelation was revealed to him when he was forty years old. He stayed ten years in Makkah, and stayed in Madīnah for ten more years. When he died, he was sixty years old and had [approximately] twenty grey hairs in his head and beard."

Al-Bājūrī said,

> **"He stayed ten years in Makkah":** I.e. after the cessation of revelation, thus this does not negate that he stayed there for three additional years.
>
> **"When he died, he was sixty years old":** I.e. by omitting the single years, which does not negate that he passed away at sixty three, as mentioned above.

٣٨٤- حَدَّثَنَا قُتَيْبَةُ بْنُ سَعِيدٍ، عَنْ مَالِكِ بْنِ أَنَسٍ، عَنْ رَبِيعَةَ بْنِ أَبِي عَبْدِ الرَّحْمَنِ، عَنْ أَنَسِ بْنِ مَالِكٍ، نَحْوَهُ.

384. Anas b. Mālik ﷺ reports the same through a different route.

ʿAbd al-Razzāq al-Badr said,

> This narration was mentioned at the start of the book, and it was repeated here due to the words, **"When he died, he was sixty years old."** Though this states the age as sixty, the correct [interpretation] is that the extra years were omitted by a narrator. This is supported by the fact that al-Imām Muslim reported Anas being in accordance to the majority, wherein Anas said, "Allāh's Messenger ﷺ was taken at the age of sixty three."[602]

---

601 See ḥadīth 1
602 *Ṣaḥīḥ Muslim* (2348)

باب ما جاء في وفاة رسول الله صلى الله عليه وسلم

[54] On Allāh's Messenger's ﷺ Death

ʿAbd al-Razzāq al-Badr said,

> The author wanted to highlight the death of the Prophet ﷺ after he finished the chapters related to his description as his death was indeed the greatest calamity that befell the Muslims.
>
> The most famous remark made upon the death of the Prophet ﷺ was said during the state of confusion that overtook the Muslims. They could not believe the news and were under the shock of it. Then Abū Bakr addressed the people, "Whoever worships Allāh, then know that Allāh is alive and does not die, and whoever worships Muḥammad, then Muḥammad has died."

Al-Bājūrī said,

> There are fourteen ḥadīths in this chapter.

٣٨٥- حَدَّثَنَا أَبُو عَمَّارٍ الْحُسَيْنُ بْنُ حُرَيْثٍ، وَقُتَيْبَةُ بْنُ سَعِيدٍ، وَغَيْرُ وَاحِدٍ، قَالُوا: حَدَّثَنَا سُفْيَانُ بْنُ عُيَيْنَةَ، عَنِ الزُّهْرِيِّ، عَنْ أَنَسِ بْنِ مَالِكٍ قَالَ: «آخِرُ نَظْرَةٍ نَظَرْتُهَا إِلَىٰ رَسُولِ اللهِ صلى الله عليه وسلم كَشْفُ السِّتَارَةِ يَوْمَ الاثْنَيْنِ، فَنَظَرْتُ إِلَىٰ وَجْهِهِ كَأَنَّهُ وَرَقَةُ مُصْحَفٍ وَالنَّاسُ خَلْفَ أَبِي بَكْرٍ، فَكَادَ النَّاسُ أَنْ يَضْطَرِبُوا، فَأَشَارَ إِلَىٰ النَّاسِ أَنِ اثْبُتُوا، وَأَبُو بَكْرٍ يَؤُمُّهُمْ وَأَلْقَىٰ السِّجْفَ، وَتُوُفِّيَ رَسُولُ اللهِ صلى الله عليه وسلم مِنْ آخِرِ ذَلِكَ الْيَوْمِ»[٦٠٣].

385. Anas b. Mālik ؓ narrated: "The last glimpse I laid upon the Messenger of Allāh ﷺ was on a Monday when the curtain of his house was lifted (the people had aligned [in rows] for the prayer). I looked at his face and it was as if it was a page of a *muṣḥaf* (Qur'ān copy). We were behind Abū Bakr, and upon seeing the Prophet ﷺ, we were

603 *Ṣaḥīḥ al-Bukhārī* (680) and *Ṣaḥīḥ Muslim* (419)

about to leave the prayer [due to the overwhelming joy of seeing him]. However, he ﷺ beckoned to us to complete the prayer. Abū Bakr ؓ led the people in prayer and he let the curtain fall. Towards the end of that day the Messenger of Allāh ﷺ passed away."

'Abd al-Razzāq al-Badr said,

This ḥadīth explains that the death of the Prophet ﷺ was on a Monday. On that day, the sickness of the Prophet ﷺ became severe and so Abū Bakr ؓ led the *Fajr* prayer. Upon the brief moment that the Prophet ﷺ lifted the curtain and saw his companions standing in lines with humility ready for the prayer, he rejoiced at witnessing that scene and smiled, as stated in the ḥadīth in *Ṣaḥīḥ al-Bukhārī* and *Ṣaḥīḥ Muslim*.[604]

The concern and worry of the Prophet ﷺ regarding the prayer did not stop there for his last words upon his death bed were to remind the people to observe the prayer and he mentioned it twice, as stated in *Sunan Ibn Mājah*.[605] This shows the great status of the prayer in Islām.

The correct view is that the Prophet ﷺ passed away during the time of *Ḍuḥā* and it seems that the meaning of Anas was that people verified the news of his death towards the end of the day. It happened when they inquired from Abū Bakr ؓ regarding the authenticity of such news. He confirmed the news, recited the verse: {**Indeed you will pass and they will also pass**}[606] kissed the Prophet ﷺ between his eyes and delivered a speech to the people to inform them about it.

٣٨٦- حَدَّثَنَا حُمَيْدُ بْنُ مَسْعَدَةَ الْبَصْرِيُّ، قَالَ: حَدَّثَنَا سُلَيْمُ بْنُ أَخْضَرَ، عَنِ ابْنِ عَوْنٍ، عَنْ إِبْرَاهِيمَ، عَنِ الْأَسْوَدِ، عَنْ عَائِشَةَ، قَالَتْ: «كُنْتُ مُسْنِدَةَ النَّبِيَّ صلى الله عليه وسلم إِلَى صَدْرِي - أَوْ قَالَتْ: إِلَى حِجْرِي - فَدَعَا بِطَسْتٍ لِيَبُولَ فِيهِ، ثُمَّ بَالَ، فَمَاتَ»[٦٠٧].

386. 'Ā'ishah ؓ narrated: "The Prophet ﷺ was resting against my

---

604 *Ṣaḥīḥ al-Bukhārī* (680) and *Ṣaḥīḥ Muslim* (419)
605 *Sunan Ibn Mājah* [585]
606 Qur'ān: 39:30
607 *Ṣaḥīḥ al-Bukhārī* (741) and *Ṣaḥīḥ Muslim* (1636)

chest, [or she said: in my lap]. He asked for a wash-basin to relieve himself. He relieved himself and thereafter, he passed away."

Ibn Kathīr said,

> It is reported in the two *Ṣaḥīḥ* books that in the presence of ʿĀʾishah some people mentioned that the Prophet ﷺ had appointed ʿAlī by will as his successor. ʿĀʾishah said, "When did he appoint him by will? Verily when he died he was resting against my chest (or she said: in my lap), he asked for a wash-basin and then collapsed whilst in that state. I could not even perceive that he had died, so when did he appoint him by will?"
>
> Ṭalḥah b. Muṣarrif related, "I asked ʿAbdullāh b. Abī Awfā, 'Did the Messenger of Allāh ﷺ have a will?' He replied, 'No.' I said, 'If he did not do so, why did he order us to write our own wills?' He said, 'His will was that we do not overlook the book of Allah.'"[608]

ʿAbd al-Razzāq al-Badr said,

> The other ḥadīths indicate that he ﷺ was resting against her chest. The Prophet ﷺ asked the permission of his wives to be treated in the house of ʿĀʾishah رضي الله عنها and he used to lead the prayer until he could no longer do so due to his sickness. The last prayer he led was a Friday prayer and then Abū Bakr رضي الله عنه began leading the prayer from that Friday until the *Fajr* prayer on Monday.
>
> Due to his sickness, he could not get up from his bed and this is why he asked for the container.

٣٨٧- حَدَّثَنَا قُتَيْبَةُ، قَالَ: حَدَّثَنَا اللَّيْثُ، عَنِ ابْنِ الْهَادِ، عَنْ مُوسَىٰ ابْنِ سَرْجِسَ، عَنِ الْقَاسِمِ بْنِ مُحَمَّدٍ، عَنْ عَائِشَةَ، أَنَّهَا قَالَتْ: رَأَيْتُ رَسُولَ اللهِ صلىٰ الله عليه وسلم وَهُوَ بِالْمَوْتِ وَعِنْدَهُ قَدَحٌ فِيهِ مَاءٌ، وَهُوَ يُدْخِلُ يَدَهُ فِي الْقَدَحِ ثُمَّ يَمْسَحُ وَجْهَهُ بِالْمَاءِ، ثُمَّ يَقُولُ: «اللَّهُمَّ أَعِنِّي عَلَىٰ مُنْكَرَاتِ - أَوْ قَالَ: عَلَىٰ سَكَرَاتِ - الْمَوْتِ»[٦٠٩].

387. ʿĀʾishah رضي الله عنها narrated: "I saw the Messenger of Allāh ﷺ just before

---

608 *Tafsīr Ibn Kathīr*
609 *Sunan al-Tirmidhī* (978)

he passed away placing his hands into a cup of water. He would wipe his face with it whilst saying, 'O Allāh help me endure the agonies of death.'"

Al-Bājūrī said,

> **"He would wipe his face with it":** I.e. because he was losing consciousness due to his severe sickness, and this would revitalise him. It is recommended to do this when one approaches death, and if one cannot do it himself, then someone does it for him (unless there is a sign that he dislikes this). If it becomes apparent that he is in need of this, it is recommended – rather, obligatory – to do so [for him].

'Abd al-Razzāq al-Badr said,

> The Prophet ﷺ repeated the statement, "There is no god worthy of worship besides Allāh" and then said, "Death possesses agony." Then he stretched his hand, raised it and said, "I choose to be with the company of the higher companion" until he died and his hand fell down.

Ibn Ḥajar al-'Asqalānī said,

> Al-Suhaylī said, "The reason why these ("O Allāh, [with] the higher companion") were the last words of the Prophet ﷺ is because they refer both to *tawḥīd* and to *dhikr* in the heart. It offers comfort to those who are unable to speak [when dying], because some people may not be able to speak out loud for some reason, but that does not matter if their hearts are steadfast in remembering Allāh."[610]

٣٨٨- حَدَّثَنَا الْحَسَنُ بْنُ الصَّبَّاحِ الْبَزَّازُ، قَالَ: حَدَّثَنَا مُبَشِّرُ بْنُ إِسْمَاعِيلَ، عَنْ عَبْدِ الرَّحْمَنِ بْنِ الْعَلاءِ، عَنْ أَبِيهِ، عَنِ ابْنِ عُمَرَ، عَنْ عَائِشَةَ، قَالَتْ: «لا أَغْبِطُ أَحَدًا بِهَوْنِ مَوْتٍ بَعْدَ الَّذِي رَأَيْتُ مِنْ شِدَّةِ مَوْتِ رَسُولِ اللهِ صلىٰ الله عليه وسلم»[٦١١].

388. 'Ā'ishah ؓ said: "I no longer rejoice at anyone experiencing an easy death after having witnessed the difficulties in death endured by the Messenger ﷺ of Allāh."

Ibn Ḥajar al-'Asqalānī said,

610 *Fatḥ al-Bārī*

611 *Sunan al-Tirmidhī* (979)

> This shows that experiencing hardship and agony at the time of death does not indicate a lower status of *īmān*; rather it is a means whereby the good deeds of the believers increase or the bad deeds of the believers are erased.[612]

Al-Sindī said,

> This ḥadīth proves that ʿĀ'ishah ﵂ knew that the more agony a person experiences at the time of death, the more good deeds he receives. [This is from] observing the extreme level of suffering the Prophet ﷺ endured upon his death bed.[613]

Al-Bājūrī said,

> To summarise the matter, a hard death is not [necessarily] a bad sign nor the opposite, and an easy death is not [necessarily] a good sign nor the opposite.

٣٨٩- حَدَّثَنَا أَبُو كُرَيْبٍ مُحَمَّدُ بْنُ الْعَلَاءِ، قَالَ: حَدَّثَنَا أَبُو مُعَاوِيَةَ، عَنْ عَبْدِ الرَّحْمَنِ بْنِ أَبِي بَكْرٍ وَهُوَ ابْنُ الْمُلَيْكِيِّ، عَنِ ابْنِ أَبِي مُلَيْكَةَ، عَنْ عَائِشَةَ، قَالَتْ: «لَمَّا قُبِضَ رَسُولُ اللهِ صلىٰ الله عليه وسلم اخْتَلَفُوا فِي دَفْنِهِ، فَقَالَ أَبُو بَكْرٍ: سَمِعْتُ مِنْ رَسُولِ اللهِ صلىٰ الله عليه وسلم شَيْئًا مَا نَسِيتُهُ قَالَ: «مَا قَبَضَ اللهُ نَبِيًّا إِلَّا فِي الْمَوْضِعِ الَّذِي يُحِبُّ أَنْ يُدْفَنَ فِيهِ»، ادْفِنُوهُ فِي مَوْضِعِ فِرَاشِهِ»[٦١٤].

389. ʿĀ'ishah ﵂ related: "After the demise of Allāh's Messenger ﷺ, the people disagreed regarding his burial. Abū Bakr ﵁ said, 'I heard something from the Messenger of Allāh ﷺ that I did not forget. He ﷺ said, 'Allāh does not take the life of His Prophets except in the location He [or the Prophet] wishes them buried." Thus he was buried in the place where his bed was."

Al-Bājūrī said,

> **"After the demise of Allāh's Messenger ﷺ, the people disagreed regarding his burial":** I.e. in regards to whether he should be buried at all; whether he should be buried in his mosque, in al-Baqīʿ with his

612 *Fatḥ al-Bārī*
613 *Ḥāshiyat al-Sindī ʿalā Sunan Ibn Mājah*
614 *Sunan al-Tirmidhī* (1018)

companions, in the Levant with his father Ibrāhīm, or in his home-land Makkah.

"Allāh does not take the life of His Prophets except in the location He [or the Prophet] wishes them buried": This is not negated by Mūsā moving Yūsuf from Egypt to his fathers in Palestine. This is due to the possibility that his wish to be buried in Egypt was temporary, as there was no one who could transfer him. This is based on the apparent fact that Mūsā performed this based on revelation. It is also reported that 'Īsā will be buried next to the Prophet ﷺ in the empty space between him and the two *shaykhs*. Some [scholars] derived from this that 'Īsā will pass away there.

'Alī al-Qārī said,

The companions differed regarding the location where they should bury the Prophet ﷺ, some suggested to bury him in his *masjid*, some said in al-Baqī' where his companions were buried, and some suggested in Makkah.[615]

Al-Zarqānī said,

Indeed, there was no darker day than the day in which he ﷺ died. Upon his death, he moved to another place that has the pleasure of receiving him, and to celebrate his coming Paradise wore its best adornment to welcome his soul.

After the death of the Prophet ﷺ, it is reported that his donkey showed sadness until it fell in a well and died. Also, his camel refused to eat and drink anything after his death until it died.[616]

٣٩٠- حَدَّثَنَا مُحَمَّدُ بْنُ بَشَّارٍ، وَعَبَّاسٌ العَنْبَرِيُّ، وَسَوَّارُ بْنُ عَبْدِ الله، وَغَيْرُ وَاحِدٍ قَالُوا: حَدَّثَنَا يَحْيَىٰ بْنُ سَعِيدٍ، عَنْ سُفْيَانَ الثَّوْرِيِّ، عَنْ مُوسَىٰ بْنِ أَبِي عَائِشَةَ، عَنْ عُبَيْدِ الله بْنِ عَبْدِ الله، عَنِ ابْنِ عَبَّاسٍ، وَعَائِشَةَ، أَنَّ أَبَا بَكْرٍ قَبَّلَ النَّبِيَّ صلىٰ الله عليه وسلم بَعْدَمَا مَاتَ».[617]

390. 'Abdullāh b. 'Abbās and 'Ā'ishah ؓ both narrated: "Abū Bakr ؓ

---

615 *Mirqāt al-Mafātīḥ*
616 *Sharḥ al-Zarqānī 'alā al-Mawāhib*
617 *Ṣaḥīḥ al-Bukhārī* (4451)

kissed the Prophet ﷺ after he passed away.”

Al-Bājūrī said,

> **“Abū Bakr ؓ kissed the Prophet ﷺ”:** On his forehead, so as to obtain blessings and to follow his ﷺ way.

٣٩١- حَدَّثَنَا نَصْرُ بْنُ عَلِيٍّ الجَهْضَمِيُّ، قَالَ: حَدَّثنا مَرْحُومُ بْنُ عَبْدِ العَزِيزِ العَطَّارُ، عَنِ أَبِي عِمْرَانَ الجَوْنِيِّ، عَنِ يَزِيدَ بْنِ بَابَنُوسَ، عَنْ عَائِشَةَ، أَنَّ أَبَا بَكْرٍ دَخَلَ عَلَىٰ النَّبِيِّ صلىٰ الله عليه وسلم بَعْدَ وَفَاتِهِ فَوَضَعَ فَمَهُ بَيْنَ عَيْنَيْهِ، وَوَضَعَ يَدَيْهِ عَلَىٰ سَاعِدَيْهِ، وَقَالَ: وَانَبِيَّاهُ! وَاصَفِيَّاهُ، وَاخَلِيلَاهُ![٦١٨].

391. ʿĀʾishah ؓ narrated: “Abū Bakr ؓ entered upon the Prophet ﷺ after his death. He kissed him ﷺ between his eyes, put his hands upon his forearms and said, ‘O my Prophet! O my close companion! O my best friend!’”

Ibn al-Qayyim said,

> It is permissible to express one’s sadness over someone’s death if the statement is simple and truthful and is not intended to wail or to show discontentment as this does not contradict the patience that one is obliged to show in such events, as can be noted in this ḥadīth.[619]

Ibn Ḥajar al-Haytamī said,

> Abū Bakr ؓ cried and kissed the forehead of the Prophet ﷺ to follow the example that he ﷺ set when he kissed ʿUthmān b. Maẓʿūn ؓ after his death. It shows that it is recommended to kiss the face of the deceased pious person.

٣٩٢- حَدَّثَنَا بِشْرُ بْنُ هِلَالٍ الصَّوَّافُ الْبَصْرِيُّ، قَالَ: حَدَّثَنَا جَعْفَرُ بْنُ سُلَيْمَانَ، عَنْ ثَابِتٍ، عَنْ أَنَسٍ قَالَ: «لَمَّا كَانَ الْيَوْمُ الَّذِي دَخَلَ فِيهِ رَسُولُ اللهِ صلىٰ الله عليه وسلم الْمَدِينَةَ أَضَاءَ مِنْهَا كُلُّ شَيْءٍ، فَلَمَّا كَانَ الْيَوْمُ الَّذِي مَاتَ فِيهِ أَظْلَمَ مِنْهَا كُلُّ شَيْءٍ، وَمَا نَفَضْنَا أَيْدِينَا مِنَ التُّرَابِ، وَإِنَّا لَفِي دَفْنِهِ صلىٰ الله عليه وسلم حَتَّىٰ

---

618 *Sunan Abī Dāwūd* (2137)
619 *ʿUddat al-Ṣābirīn wa Dhakirat al-Shākirīn*

أَنْكَرْنَا قُلُوبَنَا»."٦٢٠

392. Anas b. Mālik ؓ narrated: "The day the Messenger of Allāh ﷺ arrived at Madīnah, everything became illuminated. The day that the Messenger of Allāh ﷺ passed away, everything darkened. We had not yet dusted off the earth [of his burial] from our hands, yet we felt a change in our hearts."

Al-Bājūrī said,

> **"Yet we felt a change in our hearts":** I.e. their softness and serenity changed due to the halting of the teaching they would receive. This does not mean that they lost strength in faith, as their faith did not decrease upon his ﷺ death.

Ibn Ḥajar al-ʿAsqalānī said,

> After the burial of the Prophet ﷺ, Fāṭimah ؓ chastised the companions, including Anas b. Mālik ؓ for having the heart to place the Prophet ﷺ down in his grave [and bury him] as she knew their extreme love towards him. In response, Anas ؓ remained silent given the emotional state he was in at that time as if to indicate that they disliked doing so but they had to subdue their hearts to comply with his command.

> The statement where he ﷺ said that they felt a change in their hearts meant that they did not find their hearts to be upon the same degree of purity, serenity and softness as before the Prophet's death, when revelation was still being revealed to him, and when he was still teaching them.[621]

Ibn ʿAbd al-Barr said,

> Indeed, the death of the Prophet ﷺ made all other calamities and hardships look small and trivial. How could it not be when by his passing the divine revelation ceased descending to the earth!

> The Prophet ﷺ said that there is no Muslim who is afflicted with a calamity and says that which Allāh has enjoined, *"Innā lillāhi wa inna ilayhi rājiʿūn. Allāhumma ajurni fi muṣībati wakhluf li khayran minha"* (Verily to Allāh we belong and to Him we will return.

---

620 *Sunan Ibn Mājah* (1631) and *Sunan al-Tirmidhī* (3618)
621 *Fatḥ al-Bārī*

> O Allāh, reward me for my calamity and compensate me with something better than it), but Allāh will compensate him with something better than it.[622]

٣٩٣- حَدَّثَنَا مُحَمَّدُ بْنُ حَاتِمٍ، قَالَ: حَدَّثَنَا عَامِرُ بْنُ صَالِحٍ ، عَنْ هِشَامِ بْنِ عُرْوَةَ، عَنْ أَبِيهِ، عَنْ عَائِشَةَ، قَالَتْ: «تُوُفِّيَ رَسُولُ اللهِ صلىٰ الله عليه وسلم يَوْمَ الاثْنَيْنِ»٦٢٣.

393. ʿĀʾishah ﵂ narrated: "The Messenger of Allāh ﷺ passed away on a Monday."

٣٩٤- حَدَّثَنَا مُحَمَّدُ بْنُ أَبِي عُمَرَ، قَالَ: حَدَّثَنَا سُفْيَانُ بْنُ عُيَيْنَةَ، عَنْ جَعْفَرِ بْنِ مُحَمَّدٍ، عَنْ أَبِيهِ، قَالَ: قُبِضَ رَسُولُ اللهِ صلىٰ الله عليه وسلم يَوْمَ الاثْنَيْنِ، فَمَكَثَ ذَلِكَ الْيَوْمَ وَلَيْلَةَ الثُّلاثَاءِ، وَدُفِنَ مِنَ اللَّيْلِ٦٢٤.

وَقَالَ سُفْيَانُ: وَقَالَ غَيْرُهُ: يُسْمَعُ صَوْتُ الْمَسَاحِي مِنْ آخِرِ اللَّيْلِ.

394. Muḥammad al-Bāqir ﵀ narrated: "The Messenger of Allah ﷺ passed away on a Monday. His burial waited until the day of Monday and night of Tuesday had passed, and then he was buried on the night of Wednesday. (The night between Wednesday and Thursday)."

Sufyān (a narrator of this ḥadīth) said: "In other narrations it is stated that the sound of spades could be heard in the latter portion of the night."

Ibn al-Qayyim said,

> It is permissible to bury the deceased at night. Al-Imām Aḥmad was asked about the ruling on burying the deceased during the night and he did not object to it and said, "Abū Bakr was buried at night, and ʿAlī b. Abī Ṭālib buried Fāṭimah ﵂ at night."[625]

Ibn Ḥajar al-Haytamī said,

---

622 *Al-Istidkhār*
623 *Sunan al-Tirmidhi* (996)
624 *Muṣannaf ʿAbd al-Razzāq* (6209)
625 *Zād al-Maʿād*

> The reason why the companions ﷺ delayed his burial was either due to the fact that some of them did not believe that he had passed away, because they differed upon where to bury him or because of their busyness with the succession of the Prophet ﷺ so as to avert any possible disputes that may have arisen if there was a delay in the decision being made and the pledge being given. The burial was decided after the intervention of Abū Bakr ﷺ whose statement settled the dispute.

Ibn Baṭṭāl said,

> It is narrated that 'Ā'ishah ﷺ said, "We did not know of the burial of the Messenger of Allāh ﷺ until we heard the sound of spades in the latter portion of the night of Wednesday."[626]
>
> 'Uqbah b. 'Āmir ﷺ narrated, "There are three times at which the Messenger of Allāh ﷺ forbade us to pray or to bury our dead: when the sun has clearly started to rise until it is fully risen, when it is directly overhead at midday until it has passed its zenith, and when the sun starts to set until it has fully set."[627]

Al-Bājūrī said,

> The burial preparation began on Tuesday and the burial finished during the latter part of the night of Wednesday. This can reconcile the reports stating he was buried on Tuesday and the reports stating he was buried on Wednesday.

٣٩٥- حَدَّثَنَا قُتَيْبَةُ بْنُ سَعِيدٍ، قَالَ: حَدَّثَنَا عَبْدُ الْعَزِيزِ بْنُ مُحَمَّدٍ، عَنْ شَرِيكِ بْنِ عَبْدِ اللهِ بْنِ أَبِي نَمِرٍ، عَنْ أَبِي سَلَمَةَ بْنِ عَبْدِ الرَّحْمَنِ بْنِ عَوْفٍ، قَالَ: «تُوُفِّيَ رَسُولُ اللهِ صلىٰ الله عليه وسلم يَوْمَ الاثْنَيْنِ، وَدُفِنَ يَوْمَ الثُّلاثَاءِ»[٦٢٨].

395. Abū Salamah b. 'Abd al-Raḥmān b. 'Awf narrated: "The Messenger of Allāh ﷺ passed away on a Monday and was buried on Tuesday."

قَالَ أَبُو عِيسَىٰ: هَذَا حَدِيثٌ غَرِيبٌ.

Abū 'Īsā said: "This is a *gharīb* (strange) ḥadīth."

---

626 *Sunan al-Bayhaqi* (6216)
627 *Sharḥ Ṣaḥīḥ al-Bukhārī*
628 *Muwaṭṭā Mālik* (539)

Ibn Ḥajar al-Haytamī said,

> To reconcile between this ḥadīth and the previous one, it can be said that the companions 🙏 started to prepare the body of the Prophet ﷺ at the end of Tuesday and only finished the preparation during the latter portion of the night of Wednesday.

Al-Bājūrī said,

> **"Abū ʿĪsā said: "This is a *gharīb* (strange) ḥadīth":** I.e. the *mash-hūr* (well-known) [wording] is what preceded in the previous narration, in that he was buried on the Wednesday. The reconciliation between the two narrations is mentioned above.

٣٩٦- حَدَّثَنَا نَصْرُ بْنُ عَلِيٍّ الْجَهْضَمِيُّ، قَالَ: حَدَّثَنَا عَبْدُ اللهِ بْنُ دَاوُدَ، قَالَ: حَدَّثَنَا سَلَمَةُ بْنُ نُبَيْطٍ، عَنْ نُعَيْمِ بْنِ أَبِي هِنْدَ، عَنْ نُبَيْطِ بْنِ شَرِيطٍ، عَنْ سَالِمِ بْنِ عُبَيْدٍ، وَكَانَتْ لَهُ صُحْبَةٌ، قَالَ: أُغْمِيَ عَلَىٰ رَسُولِ اللهِ صلىٰ الله عليه وسلم فِي مَرَضِهِ فَأَفَاقَ، فَقَالَ: حَضَرَتِ الصَّلَاةُ؟ فَقَالُوا: نَعَمْ، فَقَالَ: مُرُوا بِلَالًا فَلْيُؤَذِّنْ، وَمُرُوا أَبَا بَكْرٍ أَنْ يُصَلِّيَ لِلنَّاسِ – أَوْ قَالَ: بِالنَّاسِ – قَالَ: ثُمَّ أُغْمِيَ عَلَيْهِ، فَأَفَاقَ، فَقَالَ: حَضَرَتِ الصَّلَاةُ؟ فَقَالُوا: نَعَمْ، فَقَالَ: مُرُوا بِلَالًا فَلْيُؤَذِّنْ، وَمُرُوا أَبَا بَكْرٍ فَلْيُصَلِّ بِالنَّاسِ، فَقَالَتْ عَائِشَةُ: إِنَّ أَبِي رَجُلٌ أَسِيفٌ، إِذَا قَامَ ذَلِكَ الْمَقَامَ بَكَىٰ فَلَا يَسْتَطِيعُ، فَلَوْ أَمَرْتَ غَيْرَهُ، قَالَ: ثُمَّ أُغْمِيَ عَلَيْهِ فَأَفَاقَ، فَقَالَ: مُرُوا بِلَالًا فَلْيُؤَذِّنْ، وَمُرُوا أَبَا بَكْرٍ فَلْيُصَلِّ بِالنَّاسِ، فَإِنَّكُنَّ صَوَاحِبُ أَوْ صَوَاحِبَاتُ يُوسُفَ، قَالَ: فَأُمِرَ بِلَالٌ فَأَذَّنَ، وَأُمِرَ أَبُو بَكْرٍ فَصَلَّىٰ بِالنَّاسِ، ثُمَّ إِنَّ رَسُولَ اللهِ صلىٰ الله عليه وسلم وَجَدَ خِفَّةً، فَقَالَ: انْظُرُوا لِي مَنْ أَتَّكِئُ عَلَيْهِ، فَجَاءَتْ بَرِيرَةُ وَرَجُلٌ آخَرُ، فَاتَّكَأَ عَلَيْهِمَا فَلَمَّا رَآهُ أَبُو بَكْرٍ ذَهَبَ لِيَنْكِصَ، فَأَوْمَأَ إِلَيْهِ أَنْ يَثْبُتَ مَكَانَهُ، حَتَّىٰ قَضَىٰ أَبُو بَكْرٍ صَلَاتَهُ.

ثُمَّ إِنَّ رَسُولَ اللهِ صلىٰ الله عليه وسلم قُبِضَ، فَقَالَ عُمَرُ: وَاللهِ لَا أَسْمَعُ أَحَدًا يَذْكُرُ أَنَّ رَسُولَ اللهِ صلىٰ الله عليه وسلم قُبِضَ إِلَّا ضَرَبْتُهُ بِسَيْفِي هَذَا قَالَ: وَكَانَ النَّاسُ أُمِّيِّينَ لَمْ يَكُنْ فِيهِمْ نَبِيٌّ قَبْلَهُ، فَأَمْسَكَ النَّاسُ، فَقَالُوا: يَا سَالِمُ، انْطَلِقْ إِلَىٰ صَاحِبِ

رَسُولِ اللهِ صلىٰ الله عليه وسلم فَادْعُهُ، فَأَتَيْتُ أَبَا بَكْرٍ وَهُوَ فِي الْمَسْجِدِ فَأَتَيْتُهُ أَبْكِي دَهِشًا، فَلَمَّا رَآنِي قَالَ: أَقُبِضَ رَسُولُ اللهِ صلىٰ الله عليه وسلم؟ قُلْتُ: إِنَّ عُمَرَ يَقُولُ: لا أَسْمَعُ أَحَدًا يَذْكُرُ أَنَّ رَسُولَ اللهِ صلىٰ الله عليه وسلم قُبِضَ إِلَّا ضَرَبْتُهُ بِسَيْفِي هَذَا، فَقَالَ لِي: انْطَلِقْ، فَانْطَلَقْتُ مَعَهُ، فَجَاءَ هُوَ وَالنَّاسُ قَدْ دَخَلُوا عَلَىٰ رَسُولِ اللهِ صلىٰ الله عليه وسلم فَقَالَ: يَا أَيُّهَا النَّاسُ! أَفْرِجُوا لِي، فَأَفْرَجُوا لَهُ فَجَاءَ حَتَّىٰ أَكَبَّ عَلَيْهِ وَمَسَّهُ، فَقَالَ: ﴿إِنَّكَ مَيِّتٌ وَإِنَّهُم مَّيِّتُونَ ﴿٣٠﴾﴾ [الزُّمَر: ٣٠]، ثُمَّ قَالُوا: يَا صَاحِبَ رَسُولِ اللهِ صلىٰ الله عليه وسلم! أَقُبِضَ رَسُولُ اللهِ صلىٰ الله عليه وسلم؟ قَالَ: نَعَمْ، فَعَلِمُوا أَنْ قَدْ صَدَقَ، قَالُوا: يَا صَاحِبَ رَسُولِ اللهِ صلىٰ الله عليه وسلم! أَيُصَلَّىٰ عَلَىٰ رَسُولِ اللهِ؟ قَالَ: نَعَمْ، قَالُوا: وَكَيْفَ؟ قَالَ: يَدْخُلُ قَوْمٌ فَيُكَبِّرُونَ وَيُصَلُّونَ وَيَدْعُونَ، ثُمَّ يَخْرُجُونَ، ثُمَّ يَدْخُلُ قَوْمٌ فَيُكَبِّرُونَ وَيُصَلُّونَ وَيَدْعُونَ، ثُمَّ يَخْرُجُونَ، حَتَّىٰ يَدْخُلَ النَّاسُ، قَالُوا: يَا صَاحِبَ رَسُولِ اللهِ! أَيُدْفَنُ رَسُولُ اللهِ صلىٰ الله عليه وسلم؟ قَالَ : نَعَمْ، قَالُوا: أَيْنَ؟ قَالَ: فِي الْمَكَانِ الَّذِي قَبَضَ اللهُ فِيهِ رُوحَهُ، فَإِنَّ اللهَ لَمْ يَقْبِضْ رُوحَهُ إِلَّا فِي مَكَانٍ طَيِّبٍ، فَعَلِمُوا أَنْ قَدْ صَدَقَ، ثُمَّ أَمَرَهُمْ أَنْ يُغَسِّلَهُ بَنُو أَبِيهِ، وَاجْتَمَعَ الْمُهَاجِرُونَ يَتَشَاوَرُونَ، فَقَالُوا: انْطَلِقْ بِنَا إِلَىٰ إِخْوَانِنَا مِنَ الأَنْصَارِ نُدْخِلْهُمْ مَعَنَا فِي هَذَا الأَمْرِ، فَقَالَتِ الأَنْصَارُ: مِنَّا أَمِيرٌ وَمِنْكُمْ أَمِيرٌ، فَقَالَ عُمَرُ بْنُ الْخَطَّابِ: مَنْ لَهُ مِثْلُ هَذِهِ الثَّلاثِ: ﴿ثَانِيَ ٱثْنَيْنِ إِذْ هُمَا فِي ٱلْغَارِ إِذْ يَقُولُ لِصَٰحِبِهِۦ لَا تَحْزَنْ إِنَّ ٱللَّهَ مَعَنَا﴾ [التَّوْبَة: ٤٠] مَنْ هُمَا؟ قَالَ: ثُمَّ بَسَطَ يَدَهُ فَبَايَعَهُ وَبَايَعَهُ النَّاسُ بَيْعَةً حَسَنَةً جَمِيلَةً[629].

396. Sālim b. ʿUbayd رضي الله عنه narrated: "During his sickness, Allāh's Messenger ﷺ fell unconscious; when he later recovered consciousness he asked, 'Has the time of the prayer commenced?' They replied, 'Yes.' Then he said, 'Order Bilāl to call to the prayer, and order Abū Bakr to lead the people in prayer.' Then again, he lost consciousness; when he was revived, he said, 'Has the time of the prayer commenced?' They said, 'Yes.' He ﷺ said, 'Order Bilāl to call to the prayer, and order Abū Bakr to lead the people in prayer.'

ʿĀ'ishah said, 'My father is a man with a soft heart, prone to being

629 *Sunan Ibn Mājah* (1234)

moved. If he stands in that position, he will cry and he would not be able to control it. If you wish you can appoint someone else.' He again lost consciousness, and when he revived this time, he said, 'Order Bilāl to call to the prayer, and order Abū Bakr to lead the prayer, for indeed, you women are the companions of Yūsuf.' Thereupon, Bilāl was ordered to make the call to prayer and he did so, and Abū Bakr was ordered to lead the people in prayer, and he did so. Then the Messenger of Allāh ﷺ found some respite from his illness and so he ﷺ said, 'Find someone for me upon whom I may lean.' Barīrah and another man came and he ﷺ leaned upon them. When Abū Bakr ؓ saw him, he began to move back so that the Prophet ﷺ could take his place, but the Prophet ﷺ indicated to him that he should remain firm in his place, until Abū Bakr ؓ completed his prayer.

Then, the Messenger of Allāh ﷺ passed away, upon which 'Umar ؓ said, 'By Allāh, if anyone mentions that the Messenger of Allāh ﷺ has died, I will strike his neck with this sword of mine.' The Arabs were illiterate and never before Muḥammad ﷺ had there been a Prophet amongst them. The people desisted [from any action] and said, 'O Sālim, go to the Messenger of Allāh's companion and call him.' I came to Abū Bakr ؓ whilst he was in the *masjid*. I approached him whilst crying and in a state of shock. When he saw me, he said, 'Did the Messenger of Allah ﷺ pass?' I replied, 'Indeed, but 'Umar is saying, 'If I hear anyone mention that the Messenger of Allāh ﷺ has died, I will strike his neck with this sword of mine.''

Abū Bakr then said to me, 'Come,' and so I proceeded with him until we reached the people, who had entered the room of the Messenger of Allāh ﷺ. He ؓ said, 'O people! Make way for me.' They made way for him until he bent down to the Prophet ﷺ and touched him; he then said: "{Verily, you [O Muḥammad] will die and verily, they [too] will die.}"[630]

The people asked, 'O companion of the Messenger of Allāh ﷺ, has the Messenger of Allāh ﷺ died?' He answered, 'Yes.' They knew that he had spoken the truth.

They said, 'O companion of the Messenger of Allāh! Is the Messenger of Allāh ﷺ to be prayed upon?' He ؓ said, 'Yes.' To which they

630 Qur'ān 39:30

replied, 'And how?' He said, 'A group shall enter, say the *takbīr*, pray and then invoke Him. Then they shall leave, another group shall enter and do the same until everyone has prayed.'

The people asked, 'O companion of the Messenger of Allāh! Is the Messenger of Allah ﷺ to be buried?' He said, 'Yes.' They said, 'Where?' He answered, 'In the same place that Allāh took his soul, for indeed, Allah did not take his soul except in a good and pure place.' And they knew that he had spoken the truth. Then he ordered the offspring from the Prophet's father's side to wash him.

The Muhājirūn then assembled to decide the succession to the Prophet ﷺ. They said, 'Let us go to our brothers from amongst the Anṣār and include them in this matter.' The Anṣār said, 'Amongst us is a leader and amongst you is a leader.' 'Umar b. al-Khaṭṭāb ؓ said, 'Who is that person from your midst who possesses these three: {The second of two; when they two were in the cave, when he said unto his comrade: 'Grieve not. Indeed! Allah is with us.'}?' 'Umar then extended his hand to give the pledge of allegiance. Subsequently, all those present followed suit and wholeheartedly gave allegiance to Abū Bakr ؓ.

Ibn Ḥajar al-Haytamī said,

> This shows that Prophets can fall unconscious (al-Ghazālī stated that their unconsciousness can be short or long in duration and al-Subkī stated that in this state their hearts are still awake) since it is considered as a sickness that does not entail a defect or a flaw; contrary to madness and insanity which Prophets are protected from experiencing. The reason that Allāh allows His Prophets to fall sick is so that their reward can be increased and to consolidate the people (i.e. to strengthen them with the knowledge that even Prophets are subject to hardship and sickness) and to avert the possibility of any extreme glorification on the part of the people after they witness the miracles of the Prophet (i.e. to prevent people from worshipping Prophets after seeing their miracles).
>
> This ḥadīth shows that the person who should be asked to lead the prayer is the one with the best understanding of religion, who can recite the Qur'ān in the best manner and has the most sense of piety. The fact that the Prophet ﷺ ordered Abū Bakr ؓ to lead the prayer

more than once is a strong indication that he was the most deserving to be his successor.

The similarity between ʿĀʾishah 🙵 and the woman mentioned in the story of Yūsuf ﷺ is that both did not reveal the true purpose behind their requests and instead gave different justifications. Zulaykhah invited the women and showed them good hospitality whilst her real purpose was to let them see the beauty of Yūsuf so that they could relate to her for falling in love with him. Similarly, ʿĀʾishah 🙵 stated that she disliked her father leading the people in the prayer because his soft heart would cause him to cry when reading the Qurʾān. In reality, she made that request because she feared that the people would dislike him for taking the place of the Prophet ﷺ, as she clearly revealed in another ḥadīth documented by al-Bukhārī.

There are different ḥadīths, each of which states different people that the Prophet ﷺ leaned upon. In *Ṣaḥīḥ al-Bukhārī* and Muslim it states that they were two men: al-ʿAbbās and ʿAlī 🙵. In *Ṣaḥīḥ Muslim*, they were al-ʿAbbās and his son al-Faḍl 🙵, and in another ḥadīth, they were al-ʿAbbās and Usāmah b. Zayd 🙵. In *Sunan al-Dāraquṭnī* they were Usāmah and al-Faḍl, in *Ṣaḥīḥ Ibn Ḥibbān* they were Barīrah and Nūbah, and in the book of Ibn Saʿd they were al-Faḍl and Thawbān. The reconciliation between these ḥadīths, if all are proven authentic, is that he ﷺ went out of his house more than once and on each occasion he leaned upon different people.

The signal of the Prophet ﷺ to Abū Bakr 🙵 (to remain as the *imām* of the prayer) indicates that he prayed behind Abū Bakr. However, in *Ṣaḥīḥ al-Bukhārī* and Muslim it states that he ﷺ sat on the left side of Abū Bakr, thus Abū Bakr stood leading the prayer behind the Prophet ﷺ and the people followed the lead of Abū Bakr. This explains the basis of the view of al-Shāfiʿī that it is allowed for a person praying in congregation to leave following the *imām* [i.e. leave the congregation by intending to pray individually] and then follow another *imām*.

The reason ʿUmar 🙵 denied the death of the Prophet ﷺ and threatened anyone who dared to say that is because he thought that he was just unconscious. As for the meaning of the statement that Arabs were illiterate and that never before Muḥammad ﷺ was there a Prophet amongst them, it is that the Arabs never had the knowledge of how a Prophet would die, which can be attained either through witnessing that or through scripture, and Arabs never had either (i.e. they were not from the People of the Book. Therefore they did not have a scripture and no Prophet was sent to them before the Prophet Muḥammad ﷺ).

Referring to Abū Bakr as the companion of the Prophet ﷺ indicates that he was known amongst the people with that description as if they agreed that it is his description that Allāh has confirmed in the Qur'ān (i.e. the verse wherein it says in its meaning "he ﷺ says to his companion....").

Abū Bakr addressed the people after he verified the death of the Prophet ﷺ and said, "Whoever worships Muḥammad then know that Muḥammad has died, and whoever worships Allāh, then Allāh is Alive and does not die." Then he recited the verse **{"You will die and so they shall too..."}** Thereupon, the people began to cry. This shows the courage and knowledge of Abū Bakr as he quoted the Qur'ān to refute the claim that the Prophet did not die and stayed firm in the face of such a difficult calamity.

The response of the companions to the news differed, 'Umar could not believe the news and threatened anyone who claimed that the Prophet ﷺ had died, 'Abdullāh b. Unays could not get up and remained seated upon hearing the news and 'Uthmān could not speak. Abū Bakr was the firmest and he arrived whilst his eyes were full of tears.

Ibn Baṭṭāl said,

Al-Bukhārī documented in his *Ṣaḥīḥ* that 'Ā'ishah رضي الله عنها narrated: "Allāh's Messenger ﷺ died whilst Abū Bakr رضي الله عنه was at a place called al-Sunah (al-'Aliya). 'Umar stood up and said, 'By Allāh! Allāh's Messenger is not dead!' 'Umar [later on] said, 'By Allāh! Nothing occurred to my mind except that.' He said, 'Verily! Allāh will resurrect him and he will cut the hands and legs of some men.' Then Abū Bakr came and uncovered the face of Allāh's Messenger, kissed him and said, 'Let my mother and father be sacrificed for you, [O Allāh's Messenger], you are good in life and in death. By Allāh in Whose Hands my life is, Allāh will never make you taste death twice.' Then he went out and said, 'O oath-taker! Don't be hasty.' When Abū Bakr spoke, 'Umar sat down. Abū Bakr praised and glorified Allāh and then said, 'No doubt! Whoever worshipped Muḥammad, then Muḥammad is dead, but whoever worshipped Allāh, then Allāh is Alive and shall never die.' Then he recited Allah's Statement: **{[O Muḥammad] Verily you will die, and they also will die.}**[631] He also recited, **{Muḥammad is no more than an Apostle; and indeed many Apostles have passed away before him, If he dies or is killed, will you then turn back on your heels? And he who turns back on his heels, not the least harm will he do to Allāh and Allāh will give reward to those who are grateful.}**[632]

The statement of Abū Bakr ﵁ that the Prophet ﷺ will not taste death twice was in response to the statement of ʿUmar and others who said that the Prophet ﷺ died and will be resurrected again in this life. This is to state that he dies once in this life and will be resurrected on the Day of Judgment. This ḥadīth shows the virtue of Abū Bakr and that he was more knowledgeable than ʿUmar ﵁. This event showed his sensibility, firmness and his ability to understand events in the light of the Qurʾān and it also shows his high status amongst the Muslims.[633]

٣٩٧- حَدَّثَنَا نَصْرُ بْنُ عَلِيٍّ، قَالَ: حَدَّثَنَا عَبْدُ اللهِ بْنُ الزُّبَيْرِ، شَيْخٌ بَاهِلِيٌّ قَدِيمٌ بَصْرِيٌّ، قَالَ: حَدَّثَنَا ثَابِتٌ الْبُنَانِيُّ، عَنْ أَنَسِ بْنِ مَالِكٍ قَالَ: لَمَّا وَجَدَ رَسُولُ اللهِ صلى الله عليه وسلم مِنْ كُرَبِ الْمَوْتِ مَا وَجَدَ، قَالَتْ فَاطِمَةُ: وَاكَرْبَاهُ! فَقَالَ النَّبِيُّ صلى الله عليه وسلم: «لا كَرْبَ عَلَى أَبِيكِ بَعْدَ الْيَوْمِ إِنَّهُ قَدْ حَضَرَ مِنْ أَبِيكِ مَا لَيْسَ بِتَارِكٍ مِنْهُ أَحَدًا الْمُوافَاةُ يَوْمَ الْقِيَامَةِ»٦٣٤.

397. Anas b. Mālik ﵁ narrated: "When the Messenger of Allāh ﷺ was experiencing the agonies of death, Fāṭimah ﵂ said, 'What a calamity that has inflicted my father!' Thereupon, the Messenger of Allāh ﷺ said, 'No calamity will inflict your father after today. That which has befallen your father is inevitable and none will be saved from it until the Day of Reckoning.'"

Al-Bājūrī said,

631 Qurʾān 39:30
632 Qurʾān 3:144
633 *Sharḥ Ṣaḥīḥ al-Bukhārī*
634 *Sunan Ibn Mājah* (1629)

"Fāṭimah ﷺ said, 'What a calamity that has inflicted my father!": I.e. due to the agony she saw her father endure, she faced a similar amount of pain. Thus, the Prophet consoled her with his statement, **"No calamity will inflict your father after today."** This is because the agony was connected to the bodily form, and after that day, the sensory connection would be terminated. He was moving soon to a sanctified state and the agony was soon to dissipate. He was moving to the most beautiful of bliss, of which no eyes have seen, no ears have heard and the human heart cannot comprehend. Indeed, the trials of this life are temporary, whereas the yield of the hereafter is everlasting.

Al-Sindi said,

> The meaning of the statement of the Prophet ﷺ, "No calamity will inflict your father after today" is that the agony he felt would come to a halt through his death.[635]

٣٩٨- حَدَّثَنَا أَبُو الْخَطَّابِ زِيَادُ بْنُ يَحْيَىٰ الْبَصْرِيُّ، وَنَصْرُ بْنُ عَلِيٍّ، قَالا: حَدَّثَنَا عَبْدُ رَبِّهِ بْنُ بَارِقٍ الْحَنَفِيُّ قَالَ: سَمِعْتُ جَدِّي أَبَا أُمِّي سِمَاكَ بْنَ الْوَلِيدِ يُحَدِّثُ أَنَّهُ سَمِعَ ابْنَ عَبَّاسٍ يُحَدِّثُ أَنَّهُ سَمِعَ رَسُولَ اللهِ صلىٰ الله عليه وسلم يَقُولُ: «مَنْ كَانَ لَهُ فَرَطَانِ مِنْ أُمَّتِي أَدْخَلَهُ اللهُ تَعَالَىٰ بِهِمَا الْجَنَّةَ»، فَقَالَتْ عَائِشَةُ: فَمَنْ كَانَ لَهُ فَرَطٌ مِنْ أُمَّتِكَ؟ قَالَ: «وَمَنْ كَانَ لَهُ فَرَطٌ يَا مُوَفَّقَةُ!» قَالَتْ: فَمَنْ لَمْ يَكُنْ لَهُ فَرَطٌ مِنْ أُمَّتِكَ؟ قَالَ: «فَأَنَا فَرَطٌ لأُمَّتِي، لَنْ يُصَابُوا بِمِثْلِي»[٦٣٦].

398. 'Abdullāh b. 'Abbās ﷺ narrated: "I heard Allāh's Messenger ﷺ say, 'The person who experiences the loss of two young children [during his lifetime], Allāh shall admit him in Paradise by them!' 'Ā'ishah asked, 'What about the one from your nation who experiences the death of one young child [during his lifetime]?' He replied, 'O successful! The one who loses one child shall also enter Paradise.' 'Ā'ishah then inquired, 'What about those from among your nation who have not lost any children?' He replied, 'I am the *faraṭ* (one who precedes and takes care of affairs for those who follow) of my nation in the Hereafter, for no loss equals the loss of my death.'"

---

635 *Sharḥ Sunan Ibn Mājah*
636 *Sunan al-Tirmidhī* (1062)

Al-Bājūrī said,

"I am the *faraṭ* of my nation ": This refers to the *ummat al-ijābah* (the nation who accepted his call). *Faraṭ* means that he preceded [in death] and will take care of the affairs [in the hereafter] for those of his nation who will follow him.

Ibn al-Qayyim said,

From the ḥadīths that encourage us to have children is this ḥadīth.[637]

Al-Bayḍāwī said,

The meaning of this ḥadīth is that the deceased children precede their parents to Paradise and prepare for their parents places therein.[638]

ʿAlī al-Qārī said,

The praise of the Prophet ﷺ to ʿĀʾishah ؓ ("O successful") was due to her questioning. He mentioned this to indicate that she is guided to the good as her questions were an evidence of her concern for the Muslims.[639]

---

637 *Tuḥfat al-Mawlūd*
638 *Tuḥfat Abrār Sharḥ Maṣābīḥ al-Sunnah*
639 *Mirqāt al-Mafātīḥ*

باب ما جاء في ميراث رسول الله صلى الله عليه وسلم
[55] On Allāh's Messenger's ﷺ Inheritance

'Abd al-Razzāq al-Badr said,

> This chapter is dedicated to mentioning that which the Prophet ﷺ left behind after his death, and to clarify that the inheritance of Prophets is knowledge and anything else is left for charity.

٣٩٩- حَدَّثَنَا أَحْمَدُ بْنُ مَنِيعٍ، قَالَ: حَدَّثَنَا حُسَيْنُ بْنُ مُحَمَّدٍ، قَالَ: حَدَّثَنَا إِسْرَائِيلُ، عَنْ أَبِي إِسْحَاقَ، عَنْ عَمْرِو بْنِ الْحَارِثِ، أَخِي جُوَيْرِيَةَ – لَهُ صُحْبَةٌ – قَالَ: «مَا تَرَكَ رَسُولُ اللهِ صلى الله عليه وسلم إِلَّا سِلَاحَهُ، وَبَغْلَتَهُ، وَأَرْضًا جَعَلَهَا صَدَقَةً» ٦٤٠.

399. 'Amr b. al-Ḥārith ◈, the brother of Juwayriyah ◈ (who was a companion) said: "The Messenger of Allāh ﷺ did not leave behind anything except his weapons, his mule and a piece of land that he allocated for charity."

Al-Bājūrī said,

> Allāh enriched his heart with complete richness and expanded it to the utmost measure. And what richness is greater than that of one who was given the keys to the earth's treasures, yet he turned away from it; and wealth streamed to him, yet he gave it all away. He did not appropriate any of it, nor create for himself a landed estate. No sheep, camel, slave, bondmaiden, dīnār or dirham was left behind except that which has been reported.

Ibn Ḥajar al-'Asqalānī said,

> The Juwayriyah referred to in this ḥadīth is the mother of the believers, Juwayriyah bint al-Ḥārith.
>
> The slaves of the Prophet ﷺ who were mentioned in the ḥadīths were either freed or died during his lifetime [as stated in the ḥadīth in *Ṣaḥīḥ*

al-Bukhārī which reads, "When Allah's Apostle died, he did not leave any *dirham* or *dinār* (i.e. money), a slave or a slave woman, neither did he leave anything else besides his white mule, his arms and a piece of land which he had given in charity."][641]

Ibn Baṭṭāl said,

The king of Aylah sent the Prophet ﷺ a white mule as a gift.[642]

٤٠٠- حَدَّثَنَا مُحَمَّدُ بْنُ الْمُثَنَّىٰ، قَالَ: حَدَّثَنَا أَبُو الْوَلِيدِ، قَالَ: حَدَّثَنَا حَمَّادُ بْنُ سَلَمَةَ، عَنْ مُحَمَّدِ بْنِ عَمْرٍو، عَنْ أَبِي سَلَمَةَ، عَنْ أَبِي هُرَيْرَةَ، قَالَ: جَاءَتْ فَاطِمَةُ إِلَىٰ أَبِي بَكْرٍ، فَقَالَتْ: مَنْ يَرِثُكَ؟ فَقَالَ: أَهْلِي وَوَلَدِي، فَقَالَتْ: مَا لِي لا أَرِثُ أَبِي؟ فَقَالَ أَبُو بَكْرٍ: سَمِعْتُ رَسُولَ اللهِ صلىٰ الله عليه وسلم يَقُولُ: «لا نُورَثُ»، وَلَكِنِّي أَعُولُ مَنْ كَانَ رَسُولُ اللهِ صلىٰ الله عليه وسلم يَعُولُهُ، وَأُنْفِقُ عَلَىٰ مَنْ كَانَ رَسُولُ اللهِ صلىٰ الله عليه وسلم يُنْفِقُ عَلَيْهِ[٦٤٣].

400. Abu Hurayrah ؓ narrated: "Fāṭimah ؓ came to Abū Bakr and asked him, 'Who shall inherit from you?' He replied, 'My wife and my children.' She said, 'Then why is it so, that I cannot inherit from my father?' He replied, 'I heard the Messenger of Allāh ﷺ say, 'We (i.e. the Prophets) are not inherited from.' However, I will support those whom the Messenger of Allāh ﷺ used to support and I will spend upon those whom he spent upon.'"

'Abd al-Razzāq al-Badr said,

Fāṭimah ؓ came to Abū Bakr ؓ after he became the successor of the Prophet ﷺ to ask him for her share from that which her father ﷺ had left behind. It seems that she was not aware of his statement that no one inherits from him. This can be supported by the fact that she did not object to the statement of the Prophet ﷺ after she heard it and this is why Abū Bakr did not distribute that which the Prophet ﷺ had between his wives and daughters ؓ. Nonetheless, Abū Bakr ؓ explained that he was now responsible for the affairs of the Muslims. Therefore he would make sure to keep the arrangements of the Prophet ﷺ stay

641 *Fatḥ al-Bārī*
642 *Sharḥ Ṣaḥīḥ al-Bukhārī*
643 *Sunan al-Tirmidhī* (1608)

as they were and thus, he would continue to give her the support that she used to receive from the Prophet ﷺ and spend upon everyone that the Prophet ﷺ spent upon during his lifetime.

Ibn Ḥajar al-ʿAsqalānī said,

> The ḥadīths indicating that Fāṭimah رضي الله عنها refused to talk with Abū Bakr after he denied her what she thought to be her right in the Messenger's ﷺ properties do not mean that she boycotted him. Rather, she refused to talk with him regarding the matter and she did not boycott him, which is forbidden to do so as stated in the ḥadīth.
>
> Given the high level of piety and sensibility of Fāṭimah رضي الله عنها, it appears that she did not boycott Abū Bakr. This can be corroborated by the ḥadīth documented by al-Bayhaqī who reported from the way of al-Shaʿbī that Abū Bakr visited Fāṭimah and ʿAlī b. Abī Ṭālib said to her that Abū Bakr sought permission to visit her. She said, "Are you happy for me to allow him?" He replied, "Yes." So she allowed him to enter upon her.
>
> Some of our scholars said that the forbidden type of boycott between Muslims is that when two people ignore each other when they meet. It is evident that what she did was avoid meeting him, as it seems to be the case that she was too busy with her sadness and sickness.
>
> The reason she became upset though she heard the ḥadīth is because she understood the ḥadīth in a different manner to Abū Bakr. Her understanding led her to believe that she was not subject to this ḥadīth (meaning she was an exception to the general statement) whilst Abū Bakr understood the ḥadīth to be applicable to everyone, and the interpretation of both are possible.

٤٠١- حَدَّثَنَا مُحَمَّدُ بْنُ الْمُثَنَّىٰ، قَالَ: حَدَّثَنَا يَحْيَىٰ بْنُ كَثِيرٍ الْعَنْبَرِيُّ أَبُو غَسَّانَ، قَالَ: حَدَّثَنَا شُعْبَةُ، عَنْ عَمْرِو بْنِ مُرَّةَ، عَنْ أَبِي الْبَخْتَرِيِّ، أَنَّ الْعَبَّاسَ، وَعَلِيًّا، جَاءَا إِلَىٰ عُمَرَ يَخْتَصِمَانِ يَقُولُ كُلُّ وَاحِدٍ مِنْهُمَا لِصَاحِبِهِ: أَنْتَ كَذَا، أَنْتَ كَذَا، فَقَالَ عُمَرُ، لِطَلْحَةَ، وَالزُّبَيْرِ، وَعَبْدِ الرَّحْمَنِ بْنِ عَوْفٍ، وَسَعْدٍ: أَنْشُدُكُمْ بِاللهِ أَسَمِعْتُمْ رَسُولَ اللهِ صلىٰ الله عليه وسلم يَقُولُ: «كُلُّ مَالِ نَبِيٍّ صَدَقَةٌ، إِلَّا مَا أَطْعَمَهُ، إِنَّا لا

نُورَثُ؟﴾، وَفِي الْحَدِيثِ قِصَّةٌ.[644]

401. Abū al-Bakhtarī narrated: "Both al-ʿAbbās and ʿAlī b. Abī Ṭālib disputed [over the inheritance of the Prophet ﷺ] so they went to ʿUmar [during his reign as the Caliphate] whilst each of them accused the other. ʿUmar said to Ṭalḥah, al-Zubayr, ʿAbd al-Raḥmān b. ʿAwf and Saʿd b. Abī Waqqāṣ, 'Do you not bear witness that you heard the Messenger of Allāh ﷺ say, 'The wealth that a Prophet [leaves behind] is for charity, except that which he used to feed and clothe his family. Indeed, we are not inherited from." This ḥadīth also has a story [which is being shortened here]."

Al-Bājūrī said,

> **"Whilst each of them accused the other":** They disputed regarding the land of Banī Naḍīr which the Messenger left behind, and which ʿUmar placed under their control.

> They accused each other of things similar to not being fit to oversee such an estate, without cursing each other – as some falsely assumed, for that is not fit for those of their station.

Al-Ṣanʿānī said,

> The meaning of this ḥadīth is that all of the wealth that Allāh's Messenger ﷺ left behind was for his nation as charity. The money he used to feed his family was exempt from this ruling as Allāh allowed him to do so and it appears that even this was considered a charity for them (his family) during his lifetime.

> It was said that the wisdom for Prophets leaving nothing behind as inheritance was so that their heirs would not wish for their death. As for the inheritance mentioned in the *āyāt*: {**Sulaymān inherited Dāwūd**}[645] and {**Who will inherit me and inherit from the family of Yaʿqūb**}[646], both refer to knowledge.[647]

Al-Khaṭṭābī said,

> Mālik b. Aws said: "ʿUmar b. al-Khaṭṭāb ؓ sent a messenger to call

---

644 *Sunan Abī Dāwūd* (2963)

645 Qur'ān 27:16

646 Qur'ān 19:6

647 *Al-Tanwīr Sharḥ al-Jāmiʿ al-Ṣaghīr*

me to present myself before him. I went and found ʿUmar sitting on a bare bed, with no mattress. I greeted him and sat down, and he said, 'O Mālik, some families from your people have come to us and I have ordered that some shares be allocated to them. Take them and divide among them.' I said, 'O Commander of the Faithful! I would prefer that you appoint someone else to do this.' He said, 'Take them [and perform the task.]' Then his doorkeeper Yarfaʾ came to him and said, 'Will you give ʿUthmān, ʿAbd al-Raḥmān b. ʿAwf, al-Zubayr and Saʿd b. Abī Waqqāṣ ☙ permission to enter?' He responded, 'Yes.' So he let them in, they entered and sat down. Then after a while, Yarfaʾ came and said to ʿUmar, 'Do you allow ʿAlī and al-ʿAbbās ☙ to enter?' He replied, 'Yes.' So he let them in, and they entered. Al-ʿAbbās said, 'O Commander of the Faithful, judge between me and this one (ʿAlī).'

The group, ʿUthmān and his companions, said, 'O Commander of the Faithful! Judge between them and give them a break from one another.' ʿUmar said, 'I ask you by Allāh, by whose permission the heaven and earth exist, do you know that the Messenger of Allāh ﷺ said, 'We cannot be inherited from; what we leave behind is charity?'' The group replied, 'He did say that.' Then ʿUmar ☙ turned to ʿAlī and al-ʿAbbās ☙ and said, 'I ask you by Allāh, do you know that the Messenger of Allāh ﷺ said that?' They said, 'He did say so.'

ʿUmar said, 'Allāh allocated for the Messenger something exclusive for him when He said: {**And what Allāh gave as spoils (*fay*) to His Messenger (Muḥammad ﷺ) from them, for which you made no expedition with either cavalry or camels. But Allāh gives power to His Messengers over whomsoever He wills. And Allāh is Able to do all things.**}'[648] Then he said, 'And Allāh gave his Messenger the war spoils of Banī al-Naḍīr but by Allāh, he did not keep it for himself and withhold it from you, rather he gave it to you and distributed it amongst you, until only this wealth was left. The Messenger of Allāh ﷺ gave his family what they needed for the whole year from this wealth, then he took what was left and put it in the Bayt al-Māl.' Then he addressed the group, 'I ask you by Allāh, do you know this?' They replied, 'Yes.' Then he said to ʿAlī and al-ʿAbbās ☙, 'I ask you by Allāh, do you know this?' They replied, 'Yes.'

ʿUmar said, 'Then Allāh took the soul of His Prophet ﷺ, and Abū

---

648 Qurʾān 59:6

Bakr ؓ said, 'I am the successor of the Messenger of Allāh ﷺ.' By Allāh, Abū Bakr took it and used it in the same manner that the Messenger of Allāh ﷺ had done. Then you and him (al-'Abbās and 'Alī) went to Abū Bakr, you (al-'Abbās) demanding your share from the inheritance of your nephew (i.e. the Prophet ﷺ) and he ('Alī) demanding the share of his wife from the inheritance of her father (i.e. the Prophet ﷺ) and Abū Bakr said to you that he had heard the Messenger of Allāh ﷺ say, 'We cannot be inherited from. All of that which we leave behind is to be given for charity' and Allāh knows that he was honest and sincere, and sought the truth.

Then Allāh took the soul of Abū Bakr and I said, 'I am the successor of the Messenger of Allāh and the successor of Abū Bakr.' I took over and I used it as the Messenger of Allāh ﷺ and Abū Bakr ؓ had done. And you have come to me and spoken to me, when you were both in agreement. When I thought that I might give it to you, I said, 'If you wish, I will give it to you both, on condition that you make a promise to Allāh that you will use it as the Messenger of Allāh ﷺ did, as Abū Bakr ؓ did and as I have done since the beginning of my reign.' You replied, 'Give it to us on that basis.' Thus I gave it to you. I ask you by Allāh, did I not give it to them on that basis?' The group replied, 'Yes.' Then he turned to 'Alī and al-'Abbās and said, 'I ask you by Allāh, did I not give it to you on that basis?' They replied, 'Yes.' He said, 'And now you are seeking a different judgement from me? If you are not able to manage it properly, then give it to me and I will take care of it.'"

Abū Dāwūd said, "Al-'Abbās and 'Alī ؓ came the second time asking 'Umar to divide it in two halves between them so that each one could be responsible for his part but 'Umar refused to divide it." This is a very good explanation and is indicated from the context of the ḥadīth where it mentions that al-'Abbās and 'Alī were in agreement regarding the matter but they differed upon a new idea that came into their mind at that time which was to divide it. Also, it cannot be that they acknowledged the statement of the Prophet ﷺ and yet still came to demand inheritance. 'Umar refused to divide it due to his fear that the people coming after al-'Abbās and 'Alī may not possess their wisdom, insight, piety and knowledge and so they would claim its ownership.[649]

---

649 *Ma'ālim al-Sunan*

٤٠٢- حَدَّثَنَا مُحَمَّدُ بْنُ الْمُثَنَّى، قَالَ: حَدَّثَنَا صَفْوَانُ بْنُ عِيسَى، عَنِ أُسَامَةَ بْنِ زَيْدٍ، عَنِ الزُّهْرِيِّ، عَنْ عُرْوَةَ، عَنْ عَائِشَةَ، أَنَّ رَسُولَ اللهِ صلى الله عليه وسلم قَالَ: «لا نُورَثُ مَا تَرَكْنَا فَهُوَ صَدَقَةٌ»[٦٥٠].

402. ʿĀʾishah ﵂ narrated: "The Messenger of Allāh ﷺ said, 'We cannot be inherited from. All of that which we leave behind is for charity.'"

Al-Bājūrī said,

> It has been falsely stated that the two *shaykhs* were oppressive by denying ʿAlī and Fāṭimah to inherit from her father. The truth is that the Prophet's ﷺ estate was in the way of charity, as explicitly stated in this narration, thus his ownership lifted with his death and it became an endowment.

ʿAbd al-Razzāq al-Badr said,

> ʿĀʾishah said this despite the fact that she would have been a heir to the Prophet ﷺ if he did leave an inheritance. This is a proof of her fairness and charitableness.

٤٠٣- حَدَّثَنَا مُحَمَّدُ بْنُ بَشَّارٍ، قَالَ: حَدَّثَنَا عَبْدُ الرَّحْمَنِ بْنُ مَهْدِيٍّ، قَالَ: حَدَّثَنَا سُفْيَانُ، عَنْ أَبِي الزِّنَادِ، عَنِ الأَعْرَجِ، عَنْ أَبِي هُرَيْرَةَ، عَنِ النَّبِيِّ صلى الله عليه وسلم قَالَ: «لا يَقْسِمُ وَرَثَتِي دِينَارًا وَلا دِرْهَمًا، مَا تَرَكْتُ بَعْدَ نَفَقَةِ نِسَائِي، وَمُؤْنَةِ عَامِلِي فَهُوَ صَدَقَةٌ»[٦٥١].

403. Abu Hurayrah ﵁ narrated: "The Prophet ﷺ said, 'My inheritance is not to be distributed by *dinārs* and *dirhams*. Whatever is remaining, after setting aside the expenditure of my wives and workers, is for charity.'"

Ibn Baṭṭāl said,

> The statement of the Prophet ﷺ in this ḥadīth does not entail an order because he did not leave behind any money to be divided as he died whilst his armour was still pawned. Thus he ﷺ meant that his

650 *Ṣaḥīḥ al-Bukhārī* (4035) and *Ṣaḥīḥ Muslim* (1758)
651 *Ṣaḥīḥ al-Bukhārī* (2776) and *Ṣaḥīḥ Muslim* (1760)

heirs will not have any money from him after his death as he will not leave behind any.

He ﷺ excluded the expenditure of his wives after his death because they were his dependants and leaving them without support entails what Allāh said: **{And it is not [conceivable or lawful] for you to harm the Messenger of Allāh.}**[652]

The workers mentioned in this ḥadīth are his workers who worked in the land he possessed from Fadak, Banī al-Naḍīr and Khaybar (his war booty) as he used the income generated from these lands to spend upon his family and the rest he gave in charity to benefit the Muslims. This remained until the time of ʿUmar, who gave the wives of the Prophet ﷺ the choice either to continue receiving their share from these lands or to allocate for them some properties. ʿĀ'ishah and Ḥafṣah ﷺ chose to take the properties and so he excluded them from their share in the lands and gave them what they wanted. These were then left for their heirs after they died.

Al-Ṭabarī said, "This is evidence that it is allowed to allocate some income for those whose time is dedicated to managing acts that are considered as good deeds such as the *mu'adhdhin* (caller to prayer), teachers, judges, rulers, scholars etc."[653]

Al-Bājūrī said,

"And workers": [Another opinion concerning the meaning of this is that] it refers to the caliphs after him, such as Abū Bakr and ʿUmar, who subsisted on this money for the entirety of their caliphates. Likewise was the case for ʿUthmān, and when he was not in need of it due to his own wealth, he divvied it up between Marwān and other relatives. This wealth remained in their hands until ʿUmar b. ʿAbd al-ʿAzīz returned it to the state treasury.

٤٠٤ - حَدَّثَنَا الْحَسَنُ بْنُ عَلِيٍّ الْخَلَّالُ، قَالَ: حَدَّثَنَا بِشْرُ بْنُ عُمَرَ، قَالَ: سَمِعْتُ مَالِكَ بْنَ أَنَسٍ، عَنِ الزُّهْرِيِّ، عَنْ مَالِكِ بْنِ أَوْسِ بْنِ الْحَدَثَانِ، قَالَ: دَخَلْتُ عَلَى عُمَرَ فَدَخَلَ عَلَيْهِ عَبْدُ الرَّحْمَنِ بْنُ عَوْفٍ، وَطَلْحَةُ، وَسَعْدٌ، وَجَاءَ عَلِيٌّ، وَالْعَبَّاسُ،

---

652 Qur'ān 33:53
653 *Sharḥ Ṣaḥīḥ al-Bukhārī*

يَخْتَصِمَانِ، فَقَالَ لَهُمْ عُمَرُ: أَنْشُدُكُمْ بِالَّذِي بِإِذْنِهِ تَقُومُ السَّمَاءُ وَالأَرْضُ، أَتَعْلَمُونَ أَنَّ رَسُولَ اللهِ صلى الله عليه وسلم قَالَ: «لا نُورَثُ، مَا تَرَكْنَاهُ صَدَقَةٌ؟»، فَقَالُوا: اللَّهُمَّ نَعَمْ، وَفِي الْحَدِيثِ قِصَّةٌ طَوِيلَةٌ٦٥٤.

404. Mālik b. Aws b. al-Ḥadathān narrated: "I entered upon ʿUmar and ʿAbd al-Raḥmān b. ʿAwf, Ṭalḥah and Saʿd also came. At a later point, ʿAlī and ʿAbbās also entered whilst they were in the midst of an argument. ʿUmar asked them, 'Do you bear witness by the One whose permission allows the heavens and earth to exist that the Messenger of Allāh ﷺ said, 'We are not inherited from. Whatever is left behind is charity." They replied, 'O Allāh, yes.'" There is a long story behind this ḥadīth.

ʿAbd al-Razzāq al-Badr said,

> **"There is a long story behind this ḥadīth":** This has been mentioned in the two *Ṣaḥīḥs* (*Ṣāḥīḥ al-Bukhārī:* 3094 and *Ṣāḥīḥ Muslim:* 1757).

٤٠٥ - حَدَّثَنَا مُحَمَّدُ بْنُ بَشَّارٍ، قَالَ: حَدَّثَنَا عَبْدُ الرَّحْمَنِ بْنُ مَهْدِيٍّ، قَالَ: حَدَّثَنَا سُفْيَانُ، عَنْ عَاصِمِ ابْنِ بَهْدَلَةَ، عَنْ زِرِّ بْنِ حُبَيْشٍ، عَنْ عَائِشَةَ، قَالَتْ: مَا تَرَكَ رَسُولُ اللهِ صلى الله عليه وسلم دِينَارًا وَلا دِرْهَمًا وَلا شَاةً وَلا بَعِيرًا. ٦٥٥ قَالَ: وَأَشُكُّ فِي الْعَبْدِ وَالأَمَةِ.

405. ʿĀʾishah ﵂ narrated: "The Messenger of Allāh ﷺ left behind no *dinārs, dirhams*, sheep or camels." [The narrator of this ḥadīth] said: "I am in doubt regarding whether she also mentioned male and female slaves."

ʿAbd al-Razzāq al-Badr said,

> This displays that the worldly to the Prophet ﷺ was too worthless to gather or to leave as inheritance. Rather, his desire and task was to spread Allāh's religion and deliver His revelation. Thus, the inheritance he left was knowledge, and one who takes from it has gained an abundant share.

---

654 See ḥadīth 401
655 *Musnad Aḥmad* (25053)

From the most beautiful narrations concerning this is: Abū Huray-rah ☙ walked in the market of Madīnah. He stood and shouted, "O people of the market! How slack you are!" The people asked, "O Abu Hurayrah! Why do you say that?" He replied, "The inheritance of the Messenger of Allah ﷺ is distributed whilst you are still here and not collecting your share from it!" The people asked, "Where is it distributed?" He replied, "It is now being distributed in the masjid. Thereupon, the people rushed to the masjid and Abū Hurayrah waited in the market until their return. When they returned, he asked them about what happened so they said, "We went there but we saw nothing being distributed." He said, "Have you not seen anyone in the masjid?" They said, "Yes, we did! We saw some people praying, and some people reciting the Qur'ān, and some people studying that which is lawful and that which is forbidden." He said, "Woe to you! That is the inheritance of Muḥammad ﷺ."[656]

656 *Al-Muʿjam al-Kabīr* (402)

باب ما جاء في رؤية رسول الله صلى الله عليه وسلم في المنام
[56] On Seeing the Prophet ﷺ in Dreams

'Abd al-Razzāq al-Badr said,

The author concluded his book with this chapter to affirm the relationship between knowing the description of the Prophet ﷺ and the ability to verify seeing him in dreams. This is because a person who does not know the attributes and description of the Prophet ﷺ cannot verify if the one in his dream is the Prophet ﷺ or not.

This emphasises the importance of religious knowledge, and the importance of studying the Prophet's ﷺ virtues, his traits and his description. Thus, if a Muslim reads this blessed book – al-Shamā'il by al-Imām al-Tirmidhī – or any other dependable book, he will gain discernment on this subject matter, and be safe from Satanic deception, by the permission of Allāh. For indeed, many of the laity have been deceived into thinking they saw the Prophet in their dreams, and much innovation and misguidance spread from this.

٤٠٦ - حَدَّثَنَا مُحَمَّدُ بْنُ بَشَّارٍ، قَالَ: حَدَّثَنَا عَبْدُ الرَّحْمَنِ بْنُ مَهْدِيٍّ، قَالَ: حَدَّثَنَا سُفْيَانُ، عَنْ أَبِي إِسْحَاقَ، عَنْ أَبِي الْأَحْوَصِ، عَنْ عَبْدِ اللهِ بْنِ مَسْعُودٍ، عَنِ النَّبِيِّ صلى الله عليه وسلم قَالَ: «مَنْ رَآنِي فِي الْمَنَامِ فَقَدْ رَآنِي، فَإِنَّ الشَّيْطَانَ لَا يَتَمَثَّلُ بِي»٦٥٧.

406. 'Abdullāh b. Mas'ūd ؓ narrated: "The Prophet ﷺ said, 'The one that has seen me in a dream has indeed seen me, for Shaytān cannot impersonate me.'"

Ibn Ḥajar al-Asqalānī said,

The phrase **"... for Shaytān cannot"** indicates that although Allāh gave him the ability to appear in any form he wants, He does not allow him to appear in the form of the Prophet ﷺ. This was the opinion

---
657 *Sunan Ibn Mājah* (3900) and *Sunan al-Tirmidhī* (2276)

of a group who said concerning the ḥadīth, "What this refers to is when a person sees him as he really looked." Some of them restricted it even further and said, "He must see him as he looked when he died, so he must even take into consideration the number of his white hairs which were no more than twenty." The correct view is that he may be seen at any age or in any condition, so long as he appears as he really looked, whether as a youth, in the prime of manhood, in old age or any other time of his life.

Ayyūb said, "If a man told Muḥammad (meaning Ibn Sīrīn) that he had seen the Prophet ﷺ [in a dream], he would say, "Describe to me the one whom you saw." If he gave a description that he did not recognise, he would say, "You did not see him."

Al-Qurṭubī said, "There are different opinions about the explanation of this ḥadīth. Some people said that it means seeing his real actual person in the literal sense, meaning that whoever sees him in a dream sees him actually, and hence seeing him in a dream is the same as seeing him whilst awake. However, the corruption of this opinion can be noticed with basic intellect because it necessitates that anyone who sees him [in a dream] will see him in the form he died in and also that two persons should not be able to see him at two different places if they dream at the same time. This opinion also means that he ﷺ is alive, leaves his grave, walks about in the markets, speaks to people and they speak to him. It also entails that his grave does not contain his body, and hence his grave is empty and those visiting are just going to an empty grave and greeting someone who is not there, since (according to this claim) he can really be seen at any time of the day (in a dream), in places other than his grave. Anyone who has the least grip on his senses will not hold on to such ignorance.

Another group said whoever sees him in the physical form he is known of during his lifetime [in the authentic ḥadīth] has truly seen him in the dream and if his physical form was different then it is a false dream. However, it is known that he ﷺ can be seen in a dream in a state that befits him but different to his state during his lifetime, such as when a person sees in his dream that the body of the Prophet ﷺ has filled the dreamer's house, which is interpreted to mean that the house is full of blessings. Let alone, if the Shaytān could impersonate his physical form or anything that is attributed to him, then that would contradict the generality of the Prophet's ﷺ statement, 'Shaytān cannot impersonate me.' The correct understanding of this ḥadīth is that it is possible to see him in different ways and states, so either the dream means exactly what happens in it or it needs to be interpreted for witnessing him ﷺ in a dream can occur either to warn the person against evil, give him glad tidings or to remind him."[658]

Al-Bājūrī said,

"For Shaytān cannot impersonate me": I.e. he does not have the ability to do so. Allāh protected him from the devil inside and outside of sleep.

Ibn ʿAllān transmitted that the view of the majority of scholars was that the devil cannot impersonate Allāh, just as he cannot impersonate the Prophets.

٤٠٧ - حَدَّثَنَا مُحَمَّدُ بْنُ بَشَّارٍ، وَمُحَمَّدُ بْنُ الْمُثَنَّى، قَالَا: حَدَّثَنَا مُحَمَّدُ بْنُ جَعْفَرٍ، قَالَ: حَدَّثَنَا شُعْبَةُ، عَنْ أَبِي حُصَيْنٍ، عَنْ أَبِي صَالِحٍ، عَنْ أَبِي هُرَيْرَةَ، قَالَ: قَالَ رَسُولُ اللهِ صلى الله عليه وسلم: «مَنْ رَآنِي فِي الْمَنَامِ فَقَدْ رَآنِي، فَإِنَّ الشَّيْطَانَ لَا يَتَصَوَّرُ أَوْ قَالَ: لَا يَتَشَبَّهُ بِي»[٦٥٩].

407. Abū Hurayrah ؓ narrated: "The Messenger of Allāh ﷺ said, 'The one that has seen me in a dream has indeed seen me, for Shaytān cannot take my form.'"

ʿAbd al-Razzāq al-Badr said,

This has a similar meaning to the aforementioned report of Ibn ʿAbbās.

٤٠٨ - حَدَّثَنَا قُتَيْبَةُ، قَالَ: حَدَّثَنَا خَلَفُ بْنُ خَلِيفَةَ، عَنْ أَبِي مَالِكٍ الْأَشْجَعِيِّ، عَنْ أَبِيهِ قَالَ: قَالَ رَسُولُ اللهِ صلى الله عليه وسلم: «مَنْ رَآنِي فِي الْمَنَامِ فَقَدْ رَآنِي»[٦٦٠].

قَالَ أَبُو عِيسَى: وَأَبُو مَالِكٍ هَذَا هُوَ: سَعْدُ بْنُ طَارِقِ بْنِ أَشْيَمَ، وَطَارِقُ بْنُ أَشْيَمَ

---

658 *Fatḥ al-Bārī*
659 *Ṣaḥīḥ al-Bukhārī* (110) and *Ṣaḥīḥ Muslim* (6056)
660 *Musnad Aḥmad* (15880)

هُوَ مِنْ أَصْحَابِ النَّبِيِّ صلىٰ الله عليه وسلم، وَقَدْ رَوَىٰ عَنِ النَّبِيِّ صلىٰ الله عليه وسلم أَحَادِيثَ.

سَمِعْتُ عَلِيَّ بْنَ حُجْرٍ، يَقُولُ: قَالَ خَلَفُ بْنُ خَلِيفَةَ: رَأَيْتُ عَمْرَو بْنَ حُرَيْثٍ صَاحِبَ النَّبِيِّ صلىٰ الله عليه وسلم وَأَنَا غُلَامٌ صَغِيرٌ.

408. Ṭāriq b. Ashyam ﷺ narrated: "The Messenger of Allāh ﷺ said, 'The one that has seen me in a dream has indeed seen me.'"

Abū 'Īsā said: The Abū Mālik here is Sa'd b. Ṭāriq b. Ashyam. Ṭāriq b. Ashyam was a companion of the Prophet ﷺ and he reported ḥadīths from him.

I heard 'Alī b. Ḥujr say that Khalaf b. Khalīfah said, "I saw 'Amr b. Ḥurayth – the Prophet's ﷺ companion – while I was a young boy.

'Abd al-Razzāq al-Badr said,

> This has a similar meaning to the aforementioned reports of Ibn 'Abbās and Abū Hurayrah.

Al-Nawawī said,

> The meaning of this ḥadīth is that seeing the Prophet ﷺ in a dream is something true and not a false dream. However, it is not allowed to establish a ruling in religion that contradicts any of the established rulings based on a dream even in this case. This is because a dreamer does not fulfil any of the conditions of testimony. However, if a person sees the Prophet ﷺ in a dream wherein he orders the person to do something that is considered recommended in religion, or to avoid something that is considered disliked or forbidden in religion, or instructs the person to do something that has a benefit, then it is agreed upon that it is recommended to comply. This is because the ruling of the act that is instructed to be performed or avoided is already established in the religion before the dream.[661]

٤٠٩ – حَدَّثَنَا قُتَيْبَةُ هُوَ ابْنُ سَعِيدٍ، قَالَ: حَدَّثَنَا عَبْدُ الْوَاحِدِ بْنُ زِيَادٍ، عَنْ عَاصِمِ بْنِ كُلَيْبٍ، قَالَ: حَدَّثَنِي أَبِي، أَنَّهُ سَمِعَ أَبَا هُرَيْرَةَ، يَقُولُ: قَالَ رَسُولُ اللهِ صلىٰ الله

661 *Sharḥ Ṣaḥīḥ Muslim*

عليه وسلم: «مَنْ رَآنِي فِي الْمَنَامِ فَقَدْ رَآنِي، فَإِنَّ الشَّيْطَانَ لا يَتَمَثَّلُنِي»، قَالَ أَبِي: فَحَدَّثْتُ بِهِ ابْنَ عَبَّاسٍ، فَقُلْتُ: قَدْ رَأَيْتُهُ، فَذَكَرْتُ الْحَسَنَ بْنَ عَلِيٍّ، فَقُلْتُ: شَبَّهْتُهُ بِهِ، فَقَالَ ابْنُ عَبَّاسٍ: إِنَّهُ كَانَ يُشْبِهُهُ[٦٦٢].

409. Abū Hurayrah ﵁ narrated: "The Messenger of Allāh ﷺ said: 'Whoever sees me in a dream has indeed seen me, for the Shaytān cannot impersonate me.'"

Kulayb [the one narrating this report from Abū Hurayrah] said: "I mentioned this ḥadīth to Ibn ʿAbbās ﵁ and stated that I saw him ﷺ in a dream. I said to Ibn ʿAbbās that I found the image in my dream very similar to that of al-Ḥasan b. ʿAlī. Ibn ʿAbbās said, 'Truly, al-Ḥasan was very similar to the Prophet ﷺ in appearance.'"

Al-Bājūrī said,

> **"Ibn ʿAbbās said, 'Truly, al-Ḥasan was very similar to the Prophet ﷺ in appearance":** It has also been narrated that he resembled al-Ḥusayn. It is reported from ʿAlī ﵁ that al-Ḥasan resembled Allāh's Messenger ﷺ more from the head to the chest, and al-Ḥusayn resembled him ﷺ more in the body lower than that.

٤١٠- حَدَّثَنَا مُحَمَّدُ بْنُ بَشَّارٍ، قَالَ: حَدَّثَنَا ابْنُ أَبِي عَدِيٍّ، وَمُحَمَّدُ بْنُ جَعْفَرٍ، قَالا: حَدَّثَنَا عَوْفُ بْنُ أَبِي جَمِيلَةَ، عَنْ يَزِيدَ الْفَارِسِيِّ - وَكَانَ يَكْتُبُ الْمَصَاحِفَ - قَالَ: رَأَيْتُ النَّبِيَّ صلى الله عليه وسلم فِي الْمَنَامِ زَمَنَ ابْنِ عَبَّاسٍ، قَالَ: فَقُلْتُ لابْنِ عَبَّاسٍ: إِنِّي رَأَيْتُ رَسُولَ اللهِ صلى الله عليه وسلم فِي النَّوْمِ، فَقَالَ ابْنُ عَبَّاسٍ: إِنَّ رَسُولَ اللهِ كَانَ يَقُولُ: «إِنَّ الشَّيْطَانَ لا يَسْتَطِيعُ أَنْ يَتَشَبَّهَ بِي، فَمَنْ رَآنِي فِي النَّوْمِ فَقَدْ رَآنِي»، هَلْ تَسْتَطِيعُ أَنْ تَنْعَتَ هَذَا الرَّجُلَ الَّذِي رَأَيْتَهُ فِي النَّوْمِ؟ قَالَ: نَعَمْ، أَنْعَتُ لَكَ رَجُلًا بَيْنَ الرَّجُلَيْنِ، جِسْمُهُ وَلَحْمُهُ أَسْمَرُ إِلَى الْبَيَاضِ، أَكْحَلُ الْعَيْنَيْنِ، حَسَنُ الضَّحِكِ، جَمِيلُ دَوَائِرِ الْوَجْهِ، مَلأَتْ لِحْيَتُهُ مَا بَيْنَ هَذِهِ إِلَى هَذِهِ، قَدْ مَلأَتْ نَحْرَهُ، قَالَ عَوْفٌ: وَلا أَدْرِي مَا كَانَ مَعَ هَذَا النَّعْتِ - فَقَالَ ابْنُ عَبَّاسٍ: لَوْ رَأَيْتَهُ فِي الْيَقَظَةِ مَا اسْتَطَعْتَ أَنْ تَنْعَتَهُ فَوْقَ هَذَا[٦٦٣].

---

662. *Musnad Aḥmad* (7168)
663 *Musnad Aḥmad* (2410)

410. ʿAwf b. Abī Jamīlah narrated that Yazīd al-Fārisī, who was a scribe of the Qur'ān, said: "I saw the Prophet ﷺ in my sleep in the time of Ibn ʿAbbās ؓ. I informed Ibn ʿAbbās regarding my experience and he said, 'The Messenger of Allāh ﷺ used to say, 'Verily, the Shayṭān cannot imitate my form, therefore whoever sees me in his sleep has indeed seen me.' Can you describe for us the man whom you saw?' I said: 'Yes, I saw a man of a medium build; his skin was white with a hint of red. His eyes were [dark as if they had been applied] with kohl and he possessed a beautiful smile. He had a handsome, rounded face and his beard went from here to here, almost filling his upper chest.'"

ʿAwf (one of the narrators) said: "I do not recall any other features besides these that he described."

Ibn ʿAbbās said: "Had you seen him whilst awake you would not have been able to describe him better."

قَالَ أَبُو عِيسَىٰ: وَيَزِيدُ الفَارِسِيُّ هُوَ: يَزِيدُ بْنُ هُرْمُزَ، وَهُوَ أَقْدَمُ مِنْ يَزِيدَ الرَّقَاشِيِّ، وَرَوَىٰ يَزِيدُ الفَارِسِيُّ، عَنِ ابْنِ عَبَّاسٍ أَحَادِيثَ، وَيَزِيدُ الرَّقَاشِيُّ لَمْ يُدْرِكِ ابْنَ عَبَّاسٍ، وَهُوَ يَزِيدُ بن أَبَانَ الرَّقَاشِيُّ، وَهُوَ يَرْوِي عَنْ أَنَسِ بْنِ مَالِكٍ. وَيَزِيدُ الفَارِسِيُّ، وَيَزِيدُ الرَّقَاشِيُّ كِلَاهُمَا مِنْ أَهْلِ البَصْرَةِ، وَعَوْفُ بْنُ أَبِي جَمِيلَةَ هُوَ: عَوْفٌ الأَعْرَابِيُّ.

Abū ʿĪsā said: This Yazīd al-Fārisī is Yazīd b. Hurmuz, and he preceded Yazīd al-Raqāshī. Yazīd al-Fārisī narrated aḥādīth from Ibn ʿAbbās, whereas Yazīd al-Raqāshī did not get to meet Ibn ʿAbbās. Yazīd al-Raqāshī is Yazīd b. Abān al-Raqāshī, and he narrated from Anas b. Mālik. Both Yazīd al-Fārisī and Yazīd al-Raqāshī were Basran. ʿAwf b. Abī Jamīlah here is ʿAwf al-Aʿrābī.

Ibn Ḥajar al-Haytamī said,

> The reason ʿAwf mentioned Yazīd being a scribe of the Qur'ān was to indicate towards the blessedness of his occupation and his discernment, and due to this he saw this magnificent dream.

Al-Bājūrī said,

"And his beard went from here to here": I.e. from one ear to the other. He is indicating through this statement that his blessed beard was thick and wide.

"ʿAwf (one of the narrators) said: 'I do not recall any other features besides these that he described'": I.e. he did not remember the other descriptions mentioned. This indicates that there were further descriptions but he forgot them.

"Abū ʿĪsā said": The author mentioned these sentences here to clarify the difference between Yazīd al-Fārisī and Yazīd al-Raqāshī, as both were Basran. Some people have treated them as the same individual due to them having the same name and land, which is a mistake.

٤١١ - حَدَّثَنَا أَبُو دَاوُدَ سُلَيْمَانُ بْنُ سَلم البَلخِيُّ، قَالَ: حَدَّثَنَا النَّضْرُ بْنُ شُمَيْلٍ، قَالَ: قَالَ عَوْفٌ الأَعْرَابِيُّ: أَنَا أَكْبَرُ مِنْ قَتَادَةَ.

411. ʿAwf al-Aʿrābī narrated: "I am older than Qatādah."

ʿAbd al-Razzāq al-Badr said,

> This is cited here to explain who Abī Jamīlah al-Aʿrābī (the narrator from Yazīd al-Fārisī in the previous narration) was.

٤١٢ - حَدَّثَنَا عَبْدُ اللهِ بْنُ أَبِي زِيَادٍ، قَالَ: حَدَّثَنَا يَعْقُوبُ بْنُ إِبْرَاهِيمَ بْنِ سَعْدٍ، قَالَ: حَدَّثَنَا ابْنُ أَخِي ابْنِ شِهَابٍ الزُّهْرِيُّ، عَنْ عَمِّهِ، قَالَ: قَالَ أَبُو سَلَمَةَ: قَالَ أَبُو قَتَادَةَ: قَالَ رَسُولُ اللهِ صلى الله عليه وسلم: «مَنْ رَآنِي - يَعْنِي فِي النَّوْمِ - فَقَدْ رَأَى الْحَقَّ.»[٦٦٤]

412. Abu Qatādah ﵁ narrated: "The Messenger of Allāh ﷺ said, 'The one who sees me (meaning in a dream) has indeed seen a thing that is true.'"

ʿAbd al-Razzāq al-Badr said,

> This has the same meaning as the preceding narrations.

٤١٣ - حَدَّثَنَا عَبْدُ اللهِ بْنُ عَبْدِ الرَّحْمَنِ الدَّارِمِيُّ، قَالَ: حَدَّثَنَا مُعَلَّى بْنُ أَسَدٍ، قَالَ:

664 *Ṣaḥīḥ al-Bukhārī* (6996) and *Ṣaḥīḥ Muslim* (2267)

حَدَّثَنَا عَبْدُ الْعَزِيزِ بْنُ الْمُخْتَارِ، قَالَ: حَدَّثَنَا ثَابِتٌ، عَنْ أَنَسٍ: أَنَّ رَسُولَ اللهِ صلى

الله عليه وسلم قَالَ: «مَنْ رَآنِي فِي الْمَنَامِ فَقَدْ رَآنِي، فَإِنَّ الشَّيْطَانَ لَا يَتَخَيَّلُ بِي»،

وَقَالَ: «وَرُؤْيَا الْمُؤْمِنِ جُزْءٌ مِنْ سِتَّةٍ وَأَرْبَعِينَ جُزْءًا مِنَ النُّبُوَّةِ».٦٦٥

413. Anas b. Mālik ؓ narrated: "The Messenger of Allāh ﷺ said: 'Whoever sees me in a dream has indeed seen me, for the Shaytān cannot impersonate me.' He also said: 'The dream of a believer is one portion of the forty six portions of Prophethood.'"

Ibn al-ʿUthaymīn said,

> The meaning of the words of the Prophet ﷺ, "The dream of the believer is one portion of the forty six portions of Prophethood" is that the dreams of the believers come true, because they are like parables that the angels give to the one who sees them. They may tell of something that is happening or that is going to happen, so it happens in accordance with the dream. So these dreams are like the revelation of Prophethood in that they come true, yet they are different from it. Hence they are one of the forty six portions of Prophethood.[666]

Ibn Ḥajar al-Haytamī said,

> The reason why the dreams of the believers are likened to Prophethood is because both entail knowing some of the unseen; hence no one must interpret them without knowledge.

٤١٤ - حَدَّثَنَا مُحَمَّدُ بْنُ عَلِيٍّ، قَالَ: سَمِعْتُ أَبِي يَقُولُ: قَالَ عَبْدُ الله بْنُ الْمُبَارَكِ:

«إِذَا ابْتُلِيتَ بِالْقَضَاءِ فَعَلَيْكَ بِالْأَثَرِ».

414. ʿAbdullāh b. al-Mubārak said: "If you are trialled by becoming a judge, then resort to the narrations."

Ibn Ḥajar al-Haytamī said,

> ʿAbdullāh b. al-Mubārak considered taking the position of a judge a trial due to its great impact upon people.

Al-Bājūrī said,

---

665 *Ṣaḥīḥ al-Bukhārī* (6994)
666 *Majmūʿ Fatāwah al-Shaykh Ibn al-ʿUthaymīn*

"Then resort to the narrations": I.e. from the Prophet and the four rightly guided caliphs, in their rulings and judgements, and do not resort to your own opinion.

٤١٥ - حَدَّثَنَا مُحَمَّدُ بْنُ عَلِيٍّ، قَالَ: حَدَّثَنَا النَّضْرُ بْنُ شُمَيْلٍ، قَالَ: أَنْبَأَنَا ابْنُ عَوْفٍ، عَنِ ابْنِ سِيرِينَ، قَالَ: «هَذَا الحَدِيثُ دِينٌ، فَانْظُرُوا عَمَّنْ تَأْخُذُونَ دِينَكُمْ».

415. Ibn Sīrīn said: "These ḥadīths are the religion. Therefore, pay heed to whom you take your religion from."

Ibn Ḥajar al-Haytamī said,

> The reason why the author placed this ḥadīth and the one before it at the end of the book is to encourage people to learn the knowledge of the Sunnah and to refer to it, especially during the times of trials and tests. Hence, one should find pious knowledgeable people to take this knowledge from.

Al-Bājūrī said,

> This knowledge refers to the religious sciences, which entails *tafsīr*, *ḥadīth* and *fiqh*. There is no doubt that these three are the [basis of] religious knowledge, and those besides them are concomitant to them.

Ibn ʿAbd al-Barr said,

> Al-Mughīrah said, "We used to examine the conduct and prayers (piety) of the person before we would take knowledge from him."[667]

Shams al-Din al-Safīrī said,

> Al-Nawawī said, "We only learned the knowledge from those whose piety was manifested, knowledge was verified, competency was unquestionable and who were known for this."[668]

Ibn Mufliḥ said,

> Al-Imām Mālik said, "Knowledge must not be taken from four types of people and can be taken from anyone besides them. It is not taken from a person whose foolishness is shown in public, a person who has

667 *Al-Tamhīd*
668 *Sharḥ Ṣaḥīḥ al-Bukhārī*

> lied before, a person who follows his desires and calls people to follow that which suits his desires, and an old man who is known for worship and virtue but he does not understand that which he teaches.[669]

Al-Suyūṭī said,

> Some of the scholars said, "It is recommended to start listening to (i.e. learning) the knowledge of ḥadīth after the age of thirty. This was the view of the people of Shām. And it was said after the age of twenty, which was the view of the people of Kūfah. Sufyān al-Thawrī said, "If a man wanted to learn ḥadīth, he would worship for twenty years beforehand." Abū Abdullāh al-Zubayrī, who was a Shāfiʿī scholar, said, "It is recommended to learn ḥadīth in one's twenties, because it is when his mind reaches maturity. Before that, I prefer a person to occupy himself in memorising Qur'ān and studying *fiqh*.[670]

669 *Al-Ādāb al-Sharʿiyyah*
670 *Tadrīb al-Rāwī*